ALPINE
PLANTS
of the
NORTHWEST
Wyoming to Alaska

Jim Pojar & Andy MacKinnon
with
Rosamund Pojar, Curtis Björk and Hans Roemer

LONE
PINE

Lone Pine Publishing
2311 – 96 Street NW
Edmonton, Alberta, Canada T6N 1G3

Website: www.lonepinepublishing.com

Library and Archives Canada Cataloguing in Publication

Pojar, Jim, 1948–
    Alpine plants of the Northwest: Wyoming to Alaska / Jim Pojar and Andy MacKinnon.

Includes bibliographical references and index.
ISBN 978-1-55105-892-4

    1. Mountain plants—Canada, Northern. 2. Mountain plants—Canada, Western. 3. Mountain plants—Northwestern States. I. MacKinnon, A. (Andrew), 1956– II. Title.

QK115.P63 2013   581.7'5380971   C2012-906479-3

Editorial Director: Nancy Foulds
Project Editor: Nicholle Carrière
Editorial: Nicholle Carrière, Genevieve Boyer, Sheila Quinlan
Production Manager: Gene Longson
Layout & Production: Volker Bodegom, Alesha Braitenbach, Greg Brown, Janina Kuerschner
Photo Editor: Gary Whyte
Maps: Volker Bodegom
Cover Design: Gerry Dotto
Front Cover Image: © David Gluns
Back Cover Images (counterclockwise from top): old-man-of-the-mountains (*Hymenoxys grandiflora*), Jim Pojar; Lapland rosebay (*Rhododendron lapponicum*), Hans Roemer; yellow glacier-lily (*Erythronium grandiflorum*) and western springbeauty (*Claytonia lanceolata*), Jim Pojar; mountain monkshood (*Aconitum delphiniifolium*), Virginia Skilton

A complete list of illustration and photography credits appears on pages 511–13. Every effort has been made to accurately credit sources. If there are any errors, please contact the publisher.

Disclaimer: This guide is not meant to be a "how-to" reference for using plants. We do not recommend experimentation by readers, and we caution that many plants, including some traditional medicines, may be poisonous or otherwise harmful. Self-medication with herbs is unwise, and wild plant foods should be used with caution and only with expert advice.

We acknowledge the financial support of the Government of Canada through the Canada Book Fund (CBF) for our publishing activities.

 Canadian   Patrimoine
Heritage   canadien

PC: 16

CONTENTS

4

LIST OF KEYS AND CONSPECTUSES

ACKNOWLEDGEMENTS

We'd like to thank the many people who contributed to this book.

Jim initially wrote the bulk of the text (keys, species descriptions); it was reviewed by Andy, and then by Curtis Björk and Hans Roemer. Rosamund Pojar, Andy and Jim wrote the species Notes. Jim and Andy wrote the introductions and box essays. JoAnne Nelson wrote the "Bedrock Geology" section in the introduction. Photographs were collated and selected by Andy, Jim, Curtis and Hans. All written material was ultimately edited by Jim and Andy, who are responsible for any errors.

Andy drafted the maps, and Jim revised them as required. They were subsequently checked by our regional reviewers: David Murray and Mary Stensvold (Alaska); Bruce Bennett (Yukon); Curtis Björk ("Pacific Northwest"—Washington, Oregon, Idaho, Montana and southern BC); Joe Antos (Washington and Oregon); and Hans Roemer (Haida Gwaii, Vancouver Island, Olympic Peninsula and southern BC).

We especially thank the many talented photographers who contributed their images to this book. Photographers and photo references are listed on p. 511.

This field guide would not have been possible without the foundational work done over the past decades by the indefatigable taxonomists who wrote or contributed to the floras and other technical works listed on pp. 508–10.

Finally, we thank our friends at Lone Pine Publishing who put this book together: editors Nicholle Carrière, Gary Whyte, Genevieve Boyer and Sheila Quinlan; and on production/layout, Volker Bodegom, Alesha Braitenbach, Greg Brown and Janina Kuerschner.

–Jim Pojar and Andy MacKinnon

alpine meadow, Admiralty Island, Southeast Alaska

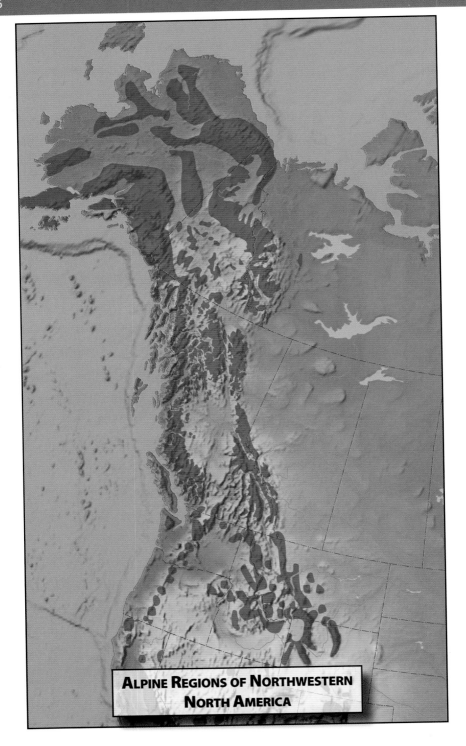

ALPINE REGIONS OF NORTHWESTERN NORTH AMERICA

INTRODUCTION

cliff paintbrush (*Castilleja rupicola*), Skyline Divide, North Cascades, WA

ABOUT THIS GUIDE

Alpine areas are absent from most of North America but are a common backdrop (the "purple mountain majesties" of the song "America the Beautiful") to western parts of the continent. Indeed in much of the northwest, it can be difficult to find a place where a mountain does not dominate the view. Harsh climates render mountaintops treeless—or at least reduce the tree species to prostrate shrubs. In the alpine, extreme environmental conditions produce spectacular tundra, grasslands, heathlands and wildflower meadows unlike anything at lower elevations other than in the far north, where alpine and arctic tundra merge. The high country is often physically demanding to access, but hardy adventurers are well rewarded with splendid vistas and floral displays. This book is designed to help you identify alpine plants.

The alpine zone is the mountainous area from treeline to the summits of the high peaks. This book is about (mostly) flowering plants of the alpine zone and also of the upper subalpine (parkland) zone, which is the elevational band from **timberline** (the upper limit of continuous cover of upright trees) to **treeline** (the upper limit of trees, here clumped and in stunted, **krummholz** form). It describes species with the bulk of their range in the alpine zone and includes some primarily subalpine species—and even a few montane species that push into high elevations—especially those of open habitats such as meadows, rocky slopes and cliffs. We also include many arctic-alpine species, plants of low-lying arctic tundra that have extended their ranges south along the great mountain chains of the northwest cordillera. Many of the cordilleran species treated have elevational spans that subside northward, typically stooping gradually from subalpine and alpine zones in the southern mountains to montane valley bottoms and slopes in Alaska and Yukon. Uptight suncress (*Boechera stricta*), field locoweed (*Oxytropis campestris*) and sticky goldenrod (*Solidago simplex*) are examples of this pattern. The circumpolar cloudberry (*Rubus chamaemorus*) does the opposite; infrequent and restricted to low-elevation bogs at the southern limit of its range, it becomes more frequent and widespread—from low to fairly high elevations—northward. And some species, such as purple mountain saxifrage (*Saxifraga*

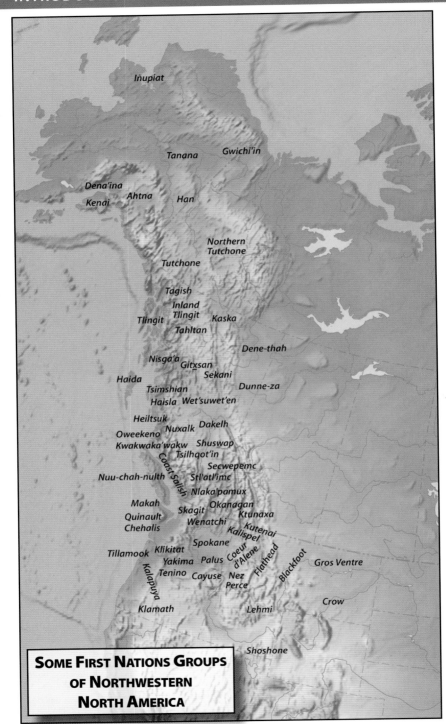

Iñupiat

Tanana Gwich'in

Dena'ina
Kenai Ahtna Han

Northern
Tutchone

Tutchone

Tagish

Inland
Tlingit Tlingit Kaska
Tahltan

Dene-thah

Nisga'a
Gitxsan Sekani
Haida
Tsimshian Dunne-za
Haisla Wet'suwet'en

Heiltsuk
Oweekeno Nuxalk Dakelh
Kwakwaka'wakw Shuswap
Tsilhqot'in
Secwepemc
Nuu-chah-nulth Stl'atl'imc
Coast Salish Nlaka'pamux

Makah Okanagan
Quinault Skagit Ktunaxa
Chehalis Wenatchi Kutenai
Kalispel
Spokane Coeur
Tillamook Klikitat d'Alene Flathead
Yakima Palus Blackfoot Gros Ventre
Kalapuya Tenino Cayuse Nez
Perce Crow

Klamath Lehmi

Shoshone

SOME FIRST NATIONS GROUPS
OF NORTHWESTERN
NORTH AMERICA

oppositifolia), moss campion (*Silene acaulis*) and snow draba (*Draba nivalis*), start out at high elevations in the south and stay high northward, but also descend to lower elevations at higher latitudes.

This guide describes most of the vascular plant species that you'll find in alpine habitats of northwestern North America, from central Oregon and northern Wyoming north to the Arctic Ocean, and from the Rocky Mountains to the Pacific Ocean. South of our region, the alpine plants change, as elements of the rich Sierra and southern Rocky Mountain floras appear. East of our region are the Great Plains and (in the north) boreal forest and taiga, and to the west and north are oceans. The book covers alpine plants for 6 states, 2 provinces and 2 territories in 2 countries.

We wrote this book for a variety of users: for the curious who have often wondered, "What is that gorgeous flower?"; for those who want an easy-to-use guide for a visit to the alpine; for naturalists keen to learn more about alpine ecosystems; for students working at high elevations; and for resource managers looking for an up-to-date reference work. When technical terms are unavoidable, they are defined in the glossary or explained in the text.

Not all species you'll encounter are in the guide. Some genera—sedges (*Carex*), for example—simply have too many species for comprehensive treatment in a field guide. In such cases, we include the frequently occurring species and provide references to more technical works to assist in identification of infrequent and rare species.

This book integrates information on human uses of plants with the plant descriptions. We have compiled information on traditional uses of plants derived from both published (see References, pp. 508–10) and unpublished studies spanning many decades. The information appears in the Notes section for individual species. A map showing the locations of most of the First Nations referred to in the text is on p. 8.

Note: We've provided information on many historical uses of plants, to give readers a better sense of the rich cultural and natural heritage of our high elevations. **This book is not meant to be a regional "how-to" guide to eating or otherwise using or experimenting with wild plants, many of which are poisonous.**

In preparing this guide, we used several technical references, listed on pp. 508–09. Other non-technical field guides are available for parts of our region; they are listed on p. 508.

arctic lupine (*Lupinus arcticus*), Pink Mountain, BC

HOW TO USE THIS GUIDE

The guide is organized so that species that resemble each other or are most likely to be confused with one another appear in the same section. The major sections of the book are Trees; Shrubs; Wildflowers; Graminoids; and Ferns & Allies. Within these broad sections, we have organized plants by large families or by groups of smaller families.

For most readers, the quickest way to identify an unfamiliar plant using this guide is to skim through the individual illustrated accounts to find those species or groups of species that the plant most closely resembles. Alternatively, if your plant has flowers, browse the flower colour layouts on pp. 93–107, then carefully compare the written plant descriptions to determine which species or group your plant belongs to. Sometimes, it may not be clear which features provide the most consistent distinctions between or among closely related species. To complicate matters further, the appearance of any individual plant varies with its age, the time of year, weather, location, soil types, disturbances or other factors that affect growing conditions. The existence of local variants can also add to the difficulty of identifying a species.

For the most perplexing groups, especially those with closely related species, a technical key is necessary for positive identification. We have provided keys, with specialized terms kept to a minimum, for most major plant groups and some of the larger genera in this guide. These are simple, two-branched keys that rely on vegetative and floral characteristics. Where flowers are necessary to distinguish among species or genera,

subalpine meadow, Trophy Mountain, Wells Gray Park, BC

Provinces, territories and states are abbreviated as follows:

CANADA

Alberta	AB
British Columbia	BC
Yukon	YT
Northwest Territories	NT

United States

Alaska	AK
Arizona	AZ
California	CA
Colorado	CO
Idaho	ID
Montana	MT
Nevada	NV
New Mexico	NM
Oregon	OR
Utah	UT
Washington	WA
Wyoming	WY

and all that remains on your plant is the fruit or withered flowers of the previous year, a bit of imagination and reconstruction can help determine the path to follow in the key. When confusion arises at a branch in the key, explore both options, then determine which appears more plausible for your plant.

The most common and widespread species are described in the greatest detail. Less common or localized species are discussed as "Similar Species," usually under their more common cousins. Some rare species, or those whose distribution is generally outside of our area or at lower elevations, are not included.

Species accounts typically describe the general characteristics of the plant; the leaves, flowers and fruits; where it's found; and mention similar species (if any) with which the plant could be confused. All measurements are metric; for users more familiar with Imperial measurements, approximate conversions are as follows:

1 centimetre (cm) = 0.4 inch
1 metre (m) = 1.1 yards or 3.25 feet
1 kilometre (km) = 0.6 miles
0° Celsius (°C) = 32° Fahrenheit (°F)

Characteristics most important for identification are **bolded**. Species accounts are illustrated with photos and sometimes with line drawings as well. Photo credits are on pp. 511; line drawing credits are on p. 512–13.

Distributions outside our region are sometimes described by technical terms that are defined in the Glossary (pp. 499–507). For example, **circumpolar** describes species distributed around the globe at high latitudes in the Northern Hemisphere (e.g., arctic willow, *Salix arctica*); **cordilleran** describes species distributed primarily in our western mountains (e.g., Sitka mountain-ash, *Sorbus sitchensis*); **amphiberingian** describes species distributed on both sides of the Bering Strait (e.g., cow-parsnip, *Heracleum maximum*); and **endemic** describes species that occur only in (a part of) our region and nowhere else (e.g., copperbush, *Elliottia pyroliflora*).

Species accounts are accompanied by range maps. In order to cover the entire north-south range of about 4500 km on a species distribution map only 4 cm high—a scale of 1:120 million—much simplification was necessary. These maps are based on the best information available at the time of publication. The database grows constantly, and known ranges of species change as we learn more about our flora.

PLANT NAMES

All plants in this book have both common and scientific names.

Scientific names (also called binomial or Latin names) are the names that scientists use to identify species. They consist of a genus (the plural is genera) name and a species name. For example, the plant nodding campion is called *Silene uralensis*, where *Silene* is the genus name and *uralensis* is the species name or specific epithet. Scientific names usually appear in italics because they are derived from another language, typically Latin or Greek. Think of these names as analogous to yours, with the genus name as your surname and the species name as your given name. If your name is, say, Barack Obama, then there are likely other Obamas around, and they're related to you, but you're the only Barack Obama. Similarly, if you're name is *Silene uralensis*, there are other *Silene*s around (for example, moss campion, *Silene acaulis*), and they're related to you, but you're the only *Silene uralensis*.

Scientific names in this book are generally from the megaproject-in-progress *Flora of North America North of Mexico* (Flora of North America Editorial Committee, 1993ff), abbreviated throughout the book as *FNA*. Fifteen volumes of the 30-volume series have been published so far, and are available in book form or online (floranorthamerica.org). In a few instances, we don't agree with the scientific names *FNA* uses, and these exceptions are noted. In cases where species have long or widely been known by other scientific names, we've also listed these synonyms.

Most people use common names when referring to different kinds of plants. While there is, in theory, only one correct scientific name for each plant species, there can be numerous common names for any particular species, and a single common name may refer to several species. We've listed what we believe to be the most-used common name for each plant—or sometimes we've devised names. Two or more common names are included for some species. For example, *Silene uralensis* is often referred to as nodding campion, but the plant is also called Japanese lanterns.

In past books, we've argued that scientific names are worth learning because they are generally more stable over time—common names come

spotted saxifrage (*Saxifraga bronchialis* ssp. *austromontana*)

and go, but scientific names endure. It's becoming more and more difficult to make that argument with a straight face. As taxonomists learn more about the flora, often employing new techniques such as genetic analysis, we botanists are reconsidering many traditional ideas about which plants are related to which other plants. As better information becomes available, new genera are erected (or sometimes resurrected), and plants are shifted from one genus to another. For example, we used to have many species in the genus *Aster* in our alpine flora. Now all that's left is the singular alpine aster (*Aster alpinus*), with its previous siblings dispersed among the genera *Eurybia*, *Eucephalus*, *Dieteria*, *Oreostemma* and *Symphyotrichum*. And it doesn't stop there: entire plant families are being "let go" (as they say in boardrooms), subsumed or deconstructed. For example, we've retained the figwort family (Scrophulariaceae) in this book for nostalgic and utilitarian purposes, but all of our alpine "scroph" genera have now been reallocated to other families.

mountain monkeyflower (*Mimulus tilingii*), pink monkeyflower (*M. lewisii*) and arctic sweet coltsfoot (*Petasites frigidus*), Vancouver Island, BC

If we can no longer argue for scientific names on the basis of stability, we can still make an argument for clarity. After all, even after scientific names change, there is still only one official scientific name—the new one. (Numerous common names usually remain.) You can also learn scientific names to impress people, around the barbeque or at other social gatherings. Inexplicably to some, Carla Bruni married former French president Nicolas Sarkozy. She explained that, after a courtship stroll in the Élysée Palace gardens, it struck her that "He knows all the Latin names, all these details about tulips and roses. I said to myself, 'My God, I must marry this man.'"

Nicolas Sarkozy and Carla Bruni

Where space allows, the origins of the common and scientific names are explained in the Notes.

OUR ALPINE ENVIRONMENT

Climate

Northwestern North America has lots of terrific topography, much of it at elevations sufficiently lofty to support alpine ecosystems. The term **alpine** can most simply refer to high-mountain environments that exclude the growth of trees and tall shrubs. By definition the alpine zone is treeless; more precisely, the **tree growth form** is absent, though tree species are frequent—in stunted or krummholz form—at lower alpine elevations.

Climate is the overriding factor determining the treeless or at least non-forested nature of the alpine. Temperatures in mid- and high-latitude alpine areas are cold for most of the year,

with much wind and snow. Temperatures remain low most of the time even during the growing season, which has an emphatically short frost-free period. Frost can occur at any time. Mean annual temperatures range from –4° to 0°C, and the average monthly temperature remains below 0°C from 7 to 11 months of the year. The alpine and the arctic are the only zones in the region where the average temperature for July (the warmest month) is less than 10°C. Generally, a great deal of precipitation falls in the alpine zone, mostly as snow, though some areas (e.g., parts of the U.S. Rocky Mountains) have summer-wet, winter-dry climates and relatively low snowpacks. The short, cold growing season, compounded by prolonged snow cover, ice, punishing wind, intense solar radiation and extreme winter conditions, is too much for the establishment and growth of erect trees or upright shrubs.

That sounds grim, but the alpine environment is not necessarily harsh or extreme for organisms (unlike most humans) that are well adapted to the conditions. Indeed the conditions can be ideal if the organism has appropriate traits—the "right stuff." The microclimate, the climate near the ground, is not nearly as forbidding as the first impressions of upright humans might indicate. True, the lapse rate of atmospheric temperature with increasing altitude means that the higher you go in the mountains the cooler it becomes, at least in the middle of the day and in the absence of a temperature inversion—cooler by about –0.5 to –0.8°C per 100 m of elevation gain, or by about –6°C per 1000 m of elevation gain during the growing season. But absorption of solar radiation by rocks, soil and vegetation heats up the air temperature

krummholz subalpine fir (*Abies lasiocarpa*), Grassy Mountain, BC

near the ground during the day. The alpine environment is much colder and windier at human height than at plant height. Air temperatures are much warmer in the boundary layer near the ground surface than they are 1 to 2 m above and often in the wind. At about 10 cm above the ground, moderate daily air temperatures often prevail. Growing season temperatures in the rooting zone of the soil can be higher beneath alpine tundra than under forest at timberline. Compared to upright trees, small, compact plants have the thermal advantage at and above treeline.

The air is thinner and often clearer high up in the mountains than down in the valleys, and solar radiation is correspondingly more intense across the visible spectrum and especially into the ultraviolet. Cloudiness also increases in frequency with altitude, which can dampen or counter the trend toward increasing radiation. The bright light is both a blessing and a bane. During the growing season, there is usually plenty of light—even on cloudy days—for plants to photosynthesize, grow and ultimately reproduce in the brief time available. But alpine plants must also devise ways to attenuate the fierce and potentially damaging ultraviolet radiation, as must humans who spend time at high elevations.

Wind is a major factor, though it is neither universally nor consistently windy in the alpine zone. Wind cools things down generally, at least during the day. More to the point, it affects the physiology of plants by reducing their retention of heat and water; it can both chill and desiccate alpine plants and thus affect their growth. Wind can also scour unprotected plant surfaces by blasting them with snow crystals or grit; hence, it influences the elevation of treeline, among other things.

Physically, wind moves snow around, modifying the distribution and depth of snow cover. Aside from macroclimate, snow cover is the primary environmental factor affecting the nature and distribution of alpine ecosystems, considering both winter snow cover (protection from winter weather and soil freezing) and growing season snow cover (truncation of growing season). Wind blows snow from peaks and ridges and deposits it on leeward slopes, apportioning it according to microtopography, setting up gradients of snow cover and growing-season patterns and mosaics of moisture and plant cover. Upper windward slopes (typically west- or southwest-facing in our region) have shallower snowpacks or sometimes are virtually snow-free (for which mountain sheep are grateful) and consequently come alive earlier in spring and experience drought or shut down (enter dormancy) earlier in summer. Plants in areas of high snow

windward and leeward alpine ridge, Blunt Range, BC

accumulation do not emerge until late summer, so have only a few weeks to do their business. Caribou and mountain goats are grateful in high summer for mountain snow patches, places to rest and cool off and to partly escape from biting insects.

Landscape and Geomorphic Processes

Alpine landscapes owe their character both to formative geological events and processes (discussed in the sections on Bedrock Geology and Physiography, pp. 23–29) and to more recent (usually) glaciations and erosion. All higher mountains in our region were glacially modified during the Pleistocene and Holocene, though in many cases by alpine, not continental, glaciers. Much ice remains, especially in the Pacific Mountains of British Columbia and Alaska. In less snowy areas, particularly in the southern interior of the region, only scattered glaciers remain, and they are rapidly wasting away.

High in the mountains, the terrain is often steep and rugged, with tall cliffs and snow-capped peaks. Rock, ice and snow prevail, but some areas have expanses of gentler rolling terrain, probably smoothed by glacial action.

cliffs and cirque, Wall Lake, Waterton Lakes National Park, AB

Glaciers also scoured out valleys and shaped steep cliffs and valley walls. When they melted, glaciers left a variety of surface features. Erosional alpine landforms include cliffs, avalanche tracks and steep-walled, armchair-shaped cirque basins, often occupied by tarns. Important depositional landforms include **moraines** (till deposited beneath and along the edges of glaciers), outwash terraces and rocky slopes where gravity has caused frost-shattered fragments of rock to slide or fall down the slope and accumulate beneath as **talus** (coarse debris) or **scree** (fine debris).

Alpine geomorphic processes that held sway after the glaciers retreated 10,000 to 12,000 years ago, and that continue to modify contemporary landscapes, include mass movement, nivation, solifluction and frost action. **Mass movement** refers to relatively rapid, gravity-induced movement of a large mass of land surface as a unit, as in a landslide. **Nivation** is the removal by meltwater of sediments around a snowfield or snowbank, resulting in a depression or shallow basin. Various types of **patterned ground** occur in most tundra areas. Stepped lobes of varying sizes across slopes result from **solifluction**, the slow creep downslope of saturated soils and rocks over permafrost or bedrock. Gravity creep on more gradual slopes results in stone stripes, garlands and nets. Freezing and thawing on flat terrain churn the soil (**cryoturbation**), forcing buried stones to the surface, where they can form frost boils and polygons. **Frost action** or frost wedging (also called **gelifraction**) is the weathering

process whereby rocks are split and wedged apart by recurring thaw-freeze cycles, giving rise to accumulations of talus or scree at the base of slopes, or to rockfields known as **felsenmeer** (German for "sea of rocks") on shallow or nearly level slopes. A **fellfield** is basically felsenmeer stabilized by patches of vegetation and sandy-gravelly deposits among the rocks or, put another way, a stony meadow—rocky habitat on exposed summits, plateaus and ridges with patchy (less than 50 percent) cover of low plants and abundant surface rocks.

Formation of **needle ice** is a frequent phenomenon at high elevations. It requires wet soil and temperatures that slowly drop below freezing. Thin ice first forms at the soil surface, and freezing proceeds slowly downward. Free water from deeper in the wet soil is sucked up through soil pores to freeze into ice needles perpendicular to the surface. The needles can continue growing for several days, and the growing volume of ice raises the soil surface, which breaks up, crumbles and dries out. The icy upheaval can break the roots and stems of pioneering plants, which are also exposed to wind desiccation. Plants have difficulty becoming established where needle ice formation is active.

Alpine plants are typically small, close to the ground and often widely separated by bare ground. Compared to a forest, alpine tundra does not modify or ameliorate the microclimate very much. The physical environment largely determines the vegetation. Whether the terrain is gentle or rugged, the smallest differences in the microenvironment are important. In the open and windy alpine, even a few centimetres difference in topography has a pronounced effect on factors that influence plants—soil temperature,

solifluction, Netalzul Mountain, BC

felsenmeer (boulder field), Mt. Albert Edward, Vancouver Island, BC

gelifraction (frost riving), Harvey Mountain, BC

depth of thaw, exposure to wind and snow cover. The result is a complex mosaic of vegetation and soil types. At the middle and lower elevations of the alpine zone, depending on the topography, there is a mix of patchy or patterned vegetation, along with limited areas of continuous plant cover. Soils are typically shallow and derived from glacial drift and weathered bedrock. Cold slows the processes of both weathering and soil formation, thus soil development is often absent or weak. Alpine soils are also subject to strong diurnal swings in surface temperatures and to frequent freeze-thaw cycles in the upper soil. Cold, often wet from snowmelt and shallow over bedrock, rocky till or permafrost, alpine soils are strongly affected by frost churning and other geomorphic processes that disrupt and dislocate horizons, displace and incorporate materials from other horizons, and mechanically sort soil particles. Permafrost, frequent at high elevations in the northern half of the region and sporadic in the southern half, also retards soil development through its effects on soil temperature, moisture and cryoturbation. Permafrost also forms a root-restricting layer, and when it melts can trigger mass movements.

Adaptations of Alpine Plants

Alpine plants must cope with a variety of environmental challenges: low winter temperatures; a short, unpredictable and mostly cold growing season; strong wind; high light intensity; low nitrogen supply; and (in some areas) low precipitation, moisture stress and even drought.

Winter temperatures can be shockingly cold, but if plants are dormant and protected by a blanket of snow, low temperatures are not a significant factor. All parts of terrestrial alpine plants must be able to "freeze with impunity" (Savile, 1972), but winter hardiness is not a distinctively alpine adaptation. Essentially, all the cells of winter-hardy alpine plants are frozen and contain little or no liquid water, so more or fewer degrees of freezing do not really matter. However, plants not sheltered by snow or with exposed parts must contend with snow abrasion and desiccation by wind. Desiccation is doubly important in winter because, if the ground is frozen, lost water cannot be replaced until the ground thaws.

Alpine treeline is probably generally a function of critically low soil temperatures and their effect on tree growth (Körner, 1999), but local patterns of treeline are strongly influenced by wind abrasion and desiccation. Typically, our conifers at treeline have a dense, shrub-like thicket of branches within 0.3 to 1 (or 2) m of the ground, where the lowest branches are protected by snow. Above that height we often see no growth or 1 to 2 m of essentially bare trunk. If the leader survives above the level where the wind

needle ice, Garibaldi Park, BC

carries lots of snow, then lateral branches can develop and persist, and the bare "pole" is then topped by a small crown or "flag" of foliage. The height of the basal thicket indicates the prevailing winter snow depth on the site. Other morphological adaptations include dwarfism in tundra shrubs, the deciduous habit (as in willows [*Salix*] and scrub birch [*Betula glandulosa*]), protection via old leaves that persist for several years (as in purple mountain saxifrage, three-toothed saxifrage [*Saxifraga tricuspidata*], moss campion, cinquefoils [*Potentilla*], drabas [*Draba*] and tussock-forming grasses) and "turtling" (avoidance by hunkering down in snowbeds; e.g., Tolmie's saxifrage [*Micranthes tolmiei*]).

Summer survival involves both physiological and morphological adaptations. Alpine plants must be substantially cold resistant all summer, yet also able to metabolize normally in the hardy state, and to avoid delay in resuming growth after a chilly or frosty night. At middle and more southerly latitudes, large daily temperature fluctuations are the rule—"summer every day and winter every night"—and plants must be able to "hit the ground running" as they warm up in the morning. But midsummer day length increases the farther north one goes, so from northern BC to the Beaufort Sea, high elevations are less prone to growing-season frost. Deciduous shrubs such as willows and scrub birch have a competitive advantage over most conifers in northern subalpine and alpine areas. Evidently, it makes more sense to crank it on during the short, but intense summers then drop non-hardy, broad leaves to escape the rigours of winter, rather than retaining tough, slow-growing, nutrient-conservative evergreen needles year-round.

Morphological adaptations to low growing-season temperatures include growth form, dwarfing, deep pigmentation, hairiness, dish-shaped flowers and leaf characteristics. Our high-elevation vascular plants have taken up 5 major growth forms:

1. Dwarf or low shrubs, as in krummholz conifers, mountain-heathers (*Cassiope, Phyllodoce*), mountain-avens (*Dryas*), scrub birch and many willows;

subalpine fir (*Abies lasiocarpa*) at treeline, with basal thicket, pole and flag, Babine Mountains, BC

yellow glacier-lilies (*Erythronium grandiflorum*) caught by an early summer frost, Marriott Basin, BC

2. Graminoids (grasses, sedges and rushes) often forming tufts or tussocks;
3. Perennial herbs with leaves mostly at the base, often in rosettes (many saxifrages);
4. Mats or cushions (moss campion is the prototypical cushion plant); and
5. Perennial, upright, dicotyledonous herbs with more or less broadly leafy stems (**forbs**—not graminoids or lily-type plants or mats/cushions); e.g., explorer's gentian (*Gentiana calycosa*) and arrow-leaved groundsel (*Senecio triangularis*).

Ferns, horsetails/scouring-rushes (*Equisetum*) and lycopods (*Lycopodium, Selaginella*) each have a distinctive but minority growth form.

Annual alpine plants are very rare in our region; species with bulbs or other fleshy underground structures (**geophytes**; e.g., glacier-lilies [*Erythronium*]) are uncommon; and true succulents (e.g., western roseroot [*Rhodiola integrifolia*] and fellfield springbeauty [*Clatytonia megarhiza*]) are also rare. Succulence is an effective adaptation for water retention, but at high altitudes, it must be accompanied by good frost tolerance, unlike in warm deserts. Note that strong wind is the common denominator for all places where alpine cushion plants naturally grow. Some ecologists interpret the cushion habit not as a primary adaptation to temperature, but rather in greatly enhanced capacity for moisture and nutrient storage. Indeed, retention of litter and nutrient recycling could be the most beneficial effect of the cushion.

moss campion (*Silene acaulis*), Spitsbergen Island, Norway

Phenotypic (i.e., nurture not nature) dwarfing in woody plants can result from snow abrasion during winter, but in herbs, it is an outcome of low summer temperatures. A dwarf can still produce viable seeds—even if only a few—and in a hurry. Another aspect of this is the delayed elongation of leafless flowering stems (as in poppies and drabas), which often hold tight while flowering and then fully extend in fruit. Genetic dwarfing has been programmed into many alpine species, including dwarf willows (e.g., *Salix cascadensis, S. rotundifolia*), cinquefoils (e.g., *Potentilla elegans, P. uniflora* group), buttercups (*Ranunculus eschscholtzii, R. pygmaeus*), alpine bittercress (*Cardamine bellidifolia*), dwarfprimroses (*Douglasia*) and mountain monkeyflower (*Mimulus tilingii*). Dwarfing usually involves the vegetative growth shoots and not the reproductive parts, so alpine flowers often seem disproportionately large. Mostly they aren't actually larger than the flowers of related species of lower elevations, but alpine species often do have larger flowers relative to the rest of the plant.

Deep pigmentation—often dark red or purple—is a thermal asset in warming up chilled, sluggish organs and trapped air when the sun comes out. As a type of sunscreen, it probably also protects sensitive or vulnerable tissue and stem cells during plant emergence in spring and senescence in autumn. These anthocyanin pigments are present in all green leaves, but most of the time they are masked by green chlorophyll. You can see such reddish purple spring and fall colours in Sitka valerian (*Valeriana sitchensis*), mountain-sorrel (*Oxyria digyna*), most woodrushes (*Luzula*), western roseroot, arctic sweet coltsfoot (*Petasites frigidus*), louseworts (e.g., *Pedicularis bracteosa*), leatherleaf saxifrage (*Leptarrhena pyrolifolia*) and some other saxifrages (e.g., rusty saxifrage [*Micranthes ferruginea*], three-toothed saxifrage).

three-toothed saxifrage (*Saxifraga tricuspidata*), Babine Mountains, BC

Hairs are a notable feature of many alpine plants. Dense hairiness (pubescence) reduces water loss caused by evapotranspiration, diffuses the intense alpine light, protects plants from abrasion, provides a measure of temperature control and can deter plant-eating animals—in particular herbivorous insects. Depending on their colour, hairs reflect more or less of the visible light rays but trap the heat rays, warming the surface of the plant in a greenhouse effect. Some essentially transparent hairs (as in the catkins of arctic willow) probably provide the most effective greenhouse, passing most incoming light but trapping outgoing infrared radiation. Dark hairs on flowerbuds, as on arctic poppy (*Papaver radicatum*), snow buttercup (*Ranunculus nivalis*),

hairy, young arctic lupine (*Lupinus arcticus*), Onion Mountain, BC
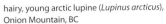

yellow glacier-lily (*Erythronium grandiflorum*) and western springbeauty (*Claytonia lanceolata*), Skwaha Mountain, BC

fall colours, western roseroot (*Rhodiola integrifolia*), Evelyn Mountain, BC

yellow mountain-avens (*Dryas drummondii*) and woolly hawkweed (*Hieracium triste*), absorb even more heat than white or grey hairs, warming the developing flowers. Some earliest flowering species are among the hairiest; for example, willows with woolly catkins (arctic willow, S. *richardsonii*), mop-top (*Anemone occidentalis*), skycresses (*Smelowskia*), woolly lousewort (*Pedicularis lanata*), arctic lousewort (*P. langsdorffii*) and mountain sapphire (*Eritrichium nanum*). Hairs and their ramifications are crucial to identifying species of pussytoes (*Antennaria*), drabas and several other mustard-family genera, willows, cinquefoils, daisies and fleabanes (*Erigeron*), and many grasses.

Flowers shaped like parabolic reflectors or satellite dishes focus light on the ovaries, which speeds up their maturation. Such flowers can also provide a warm basking area for insect visitors. Temperature in the dish of flowers such as poppies and mountain-avens can be elevated several degrees above the ambient temperature.

Because of the short, cold, unpredictable growing season, the key challenge for alpine plants is to complete flowering and fruiting quickly. The short growing season is reflected in rapid initiation of growth in spring, preformed flower buds and vegetative reproduction. Alpine plants can get going in a hurry after snowmelt by metabolizing carbohydrate reserves stored in fleshy roots or stems (e.g., alp-lily [*Lloydia serotina*], glacier-lilies, springbeauties, bistorts

[*Bistorta*], some louseworts [e.g., woolly lousewort] and horned dandelion [*Taraxacum ceratophorum*]). Evergreen leaves are also a shortcut to photosynthetic production, as in mountain-heathers, Lapland rosebay (*Rhododendron lapponicum*), Alaska pincusion plant (*Diapensia obovata*) and some saxifrages. Winter-green leaves are another option, in which the last leaves produced in summer remain green and function at least in the following early spring. This occurs in species such as alpine saxifrage (*Micranthes nivalis*), mountain-avens, many species in the pink (Caryophyllaceae) and mustard (Brassicaceae) families, and the basal leaves or parts of leaves in some monocots, including grasses, sedges, cotton-grasses (*Eriophorum*) and beargrass (*Xerophyllum tenax*).

Most alpine plants produce flower primordia (budlets) at least the year before, and sometimes 2 to 3 years before, actually flowering. Some alpine species such as yellow glacier-lily (*Erythronium grandiflorum*), mountain marsh-marigold (*Caltha leptosepala*) and western springbeauty (*Claytonia lanceolata*) start growing even under the snow and can flower within a few hours of snowmelt or indeed through the snow. Another reproductive (albeit asexual) tactic is vegetative reproduction. Many species have **rhizomes** (belowground sprouting stems) or **stolons** (aboveground runners) that can "spread the mustard" horizontally. Rhizomes persist from year to year, forming new buds and carrying successive clonal generations outward from the parent plant. A relatively few species, such as alpine bistort (*Bistorta vivipara*) and nodding saxifrage (*Saxifraga cernua*), produce bulbils or plantlets in lieu of flowers, but most plants are not absolutely celibate; they usually have a mix of rhizomes or stolons and flowers (e.g., spiderplant, *Saxifraga flagellaris*), or of bulbils and flowers (alpine bistort and nodding saxifrage). Vegetative reproduction also enables rapid colonization of bare ground.

REPRODUCTIVE DYNAMICS

Sexual reproduction in flowering plants involves a sequence of events: pollination of flowers, fertilization of egg cells in ovules within ovaries, development of embryos within ovules, production of viable seed, dispersal of seeds, successful germination of seeds and establishment of new plants. Alpine flowering plants must compromise between the yearly imperative to reproduce quickly and the long term, intergenerational need to maintain sufficient genetic diversity to respond and adapt to changing environments. There is a variety of ways to strike such a dynamic balance, several of which are very popular in our alplands.

Breeding System

Most of our alpine species are hermaphrodites; that is, their flowers are bisexual, with both female and male bits. The sexes are usually in close proximity and self-pollination often can occur (accidentally or by design), but over evolutionary time the majority trend has been strong selection for mechanisms that promote cross-pollination and reduce inbreeding. **Self-incompatibility** (self-infertility) ensures outcrossing (and presumably genetic diversity) but must be accompanied by reliable pollination—as by a reasonably faithful and constant insect pollinator attracted to showy, rewarding flowers—if the populations are to survive and persist. The louseworts include many showy-flowered species that are self-incompatible and have specialized pollinator relationships. Alpine milkvetch (*Astragalus alpinus*) is self-incompatible and is pollinated largely by bumblebees. Purple mountain saxifrage, yarrow (*Achillea millefolium*) and horned dandelion are all mostly self-incompatible but have less specialized pollinator relationships, their flowers being visited by a broader spectrum of insects.

Dioecious species (unisexual plants—sexes on separate plants, all flowers either male or female) also have guaranteed (enforced)

spider plant (*Saxifraga flagellaris*), Spitsbergen Island, Norway

outcrossing or no sexual reproduction at all. Willows are probably the most important group of dioecious alpine plants, but dioecism crops up fairly frequently in a few other genera, including pussytoes, bluegrasses (*Poa*), campions (*Silene*) and meadow-rues (*Thalictrum*). Most high-elevation willows are largely insect-pollinated; probably some casual wind pollination also occurs. Although willow catkins appear adapted for wind pollination, many of them produce abundant pollen and nectar that attract foraging insects.

Monoecious species, which have unisexual flowers but plants with both male and female flowers, like a corn plant, are represented mostly by many species of sedge, which are wind-pollinated but with male and female spikes usually separated a bit spatially and in flowering period. Scrub birch and Sitka alder (*Alnus viridis* ssp. *sinuata*) are also monoecious.

arctic willow (*Salix arctica*) and bumblebee, Cassiar Mountains, BC

Pollination

Plants worldwide rely on wind, water, flies, bees, butterflies, moths, hummingbirds, bats, marsupials and even mosquitoes to pollinate their flowers. You might expect wind pollination to dominate in open, windy, alpine environments. There are indeed many wind-pollinated species at high elevations, including the graminoids (grasses, sedges and relatives, rushes and wood-rushes), scrub birch, mountain-sorrel, docks (*Rumex*), meadow-rues and sages (*Artemisia*). Sometimes they even dominate alpine vegetation, but more often the plant cover consists primarily of species that are biotically pollinated—by insects, birds or the plants themselves.

Most animals can see colours and shapes, and flowering plants have contrived to attract animals to their flowers and to enlist them in transferring pollen from the anthers of one flower to the receptive parts (stigmas) of the female sex organs of another flower of the same species. In seeking the attentions of potential pollinators, flowering plants have evolved a variety of attractants and rewards— colours, shapes, scents and foods (nectar, pollen). Most species with showy, brightly coloured flowers are pollinated by insects, as are many species with smaller, duller flowers, including white-flowered sandworts (*Minuartia*) and saxifrages. Flowers pollinated by bees tend to be yellow, blue or purple, often with nectar guides (patterns of lines or spots or hairs), and are often structurally complex, requiring some learning to operate (e.g., the bilaterally symmmetric flowers of the pea family, or of louseworts and larkspurs [*Delphinium*]). Flowers pollinated by small, unspecialized flies tend themselves to be relatively small and unspecialized: white, yellow or greenish, radially symmetric bowls or saucers, with easily accessible pollen and/or nectar (e.g., sandworts, springbeauties, buttercups, anemones, cinquefoils and Indian

hellebore [*Veratrum viride*]). Some large alpine families—including aster, buttercup, mustard and pink families—seem ancestrally predisposed to yellow or white flowers. Insects, moreover, are pragmatic and efficient; bees, for example, favour blue flowers, but this doesn't stop them from visiting white flowers (or willow catkins, for that matter) if the nectar or pollen rewards are there. Flowers pollinated by butterflies are brightly coloured and do not require much strength from insect visitors, but produce nectar in tubes or slits that can be accessed by long tongues. They also provide landing platforms on which the butterflies can alight and probe for nectar. Typical butterfly flowers include phloxes, moss campion, dwarf-primroses, western mountain balm (*Monardella odoratissima*), many aster family species and Columbia lily (*Lilium columbianum*). Plants pollinated by nocturnal hawkmoths (Sphingidae) feature pale, night-blooming flowers, horizontally disposed (because hawkmoths hover), with dissected outlines and abundant nectar in long tubes. Parry's campion (*Silene parryi*) is the only species in our region to closely fit this syndrome, though blue columbine (*Aquilegia coerulea*) is visited by hawkmoths in addition to bumblebees and hummingbirds. Some insect-pollinated species are strongly self-incompatible, and many are self-compatible to lesser or greater degrees. Some other species—especially small, inconspicuous flowers with little or no nectar or fragrance such as some starworts (*Stellaria*) and pearlworts (*Sagina*)—are fully **self-compatible** and pollinate and fertilize themselves efficiently if rather prosaically, producing viable seeds quickly.

A handful of our species are adapted for pollination by hummingbirds. Hummingbird flowers include the reddish or scarlet paintbrushes (e.g., *Castilleja miniata*, *C. rupicola*), red columbine

fanleaf cinquefoil (*Potentilla flabellifolia*) and hoverfly

subalpine daisy (*Erigeron glacialis*) with owlet moth, Marriott Basin, BC

(*Aquilegia formosa*) and Columbia lily. But hungry hummingbirds will forage for nectar wherever they can find it, and they do not restrict their attention only to red flowers. We have even seen them on the ground sucking from the flowers of kinnikinnik (*Arctostaphylos uva-ursi*).

Polyploidy

Every plant cell contains a complement of genes arrayed along a set of chromosomes in the cell nucleus. Most cells making up a plant have a double set of chromosomes and are **diploid.** But the sex cells (the egg and the sperm nuclei in pollen) have half the number and are called **haploid;** the number of their different chromosomes is called the **base number.** Similarly, the human species has a base chromosome number of 23; there are 23 different chromosomes in an egg or sperm nucleus. Except for those sex cells, human bodies are diploid, consisting of cells with a double set of chromosomes (2n=46). In the flowering plant genus *Draba*, for example, the base number is 8 (i.e., 8 different chromosomes in the haploid state), and several of our drabas (e.g., *D. nivalis*, *D. fladnizensis* and *D. lonchocarpa*) are also diploids (2n=16). Many more species of *Draba* are **polyploids,** with 4 (tetraploid), 6 (hexaploid), 8 (octoploid) or even more sets of chromosomes.

Outcrossing among individuals and populations helps to maintain genetic diversity within species. Some plant species take outcrossing to extremes by hybridizing with other, usually closely related species. Hybridization is common in vascular plants, occurring in a wide range of groups from spruces to cinquefoils, with

dwarf alpine hawksbeard (*Crepis nana*), Denali National Park and Preserve, AK

estimates of 40 to 50 percent of flowering plants having a hybrid origin. Interspecific hybrids can have a life of their own and can sometimes persist in hybrid swarms by backcrossing with the parental species or by forming fertile, fully hybrid populations. But, more typically, interspecific hybrids are sterile, like mules, largely because of dysfunctional, mixed-up **meiosis**— the nuclear division that precedes cell division in the formation of sex cells. Individual chromosomes lack similar (**homologous**) partners to pair up with during the intracellular square dance that normally halves the number of chromosomes and results in haploid eggs and pollen nuclei. But sometimes the hybrids can leap into fertility by doubling their set of chromosomes and becoming polyploids. Occasionally in meiosis, the chromosomes of a cell divide but the cell wall does not form. This spontaneous "mistake" results in a cell with twice the normal chromosome number, including 2 copies of the diploid complement of each parent. If this cell carries on dividing to produce a piece of the plant on which the flowers are formed, each chromosome will have a compatible pairing partner, normal meiosis can occur, and these flowers can produce tetraploid seeds.

Polyploidy can produce physiological changes such as increased cell size and larger leaves and flowers. Some of these changes can be adaptive in different environments and could increase the ecological amplitude of the species. Nonetheless, there is little compelling evidence that polyploids do better under stressful or extreme conditions, or are more frequent or abundant at high rather than at low elevations. What polyploidy does very effectively is restore fertility to sterile diploid hybrids by doubling their chromosome number, resulting in 2 of each type of chromosome and providing homologous partners for meiosis. Thus, interspecific hybridization followed by polyploidy can lead to the rapid formation of new species, especially if the new hybrid becomes a tetraploid and is thus effectively reproductively isolated from its diploid ancestors (triploid progeny are sterile).

The other major way that infertile hybrids can propagate themselves is through **apomixis,** a general term for the various kinds of asexual, vegetative reproduction in plants. It includes reproduction via rhizomes, stolons, bulbils or plantlets, and the production of seeds without sex. Such seeds have embryos derived entirely from the tissues of the parent plant and are thus genetically identical to the parent. Most apomicts are not obligately so; occasional sexual reproduction and hybridization periodically produce new and variable combinations of genes, and the best new genotypes can then be carried forward by continued apomixis.

Polyploidy is very frequent in the mustard, pink, rose, grass and sedge families. Various combinations of hybridization, polyploidy and apomixis have been instrumental in the diversification of several of our most important alpine genera, including the willows, cinquefoils, pussytoes, suncresses, drabas, bluegrasses and sedges.

Dispersal

Cross-pollination and seed dispersal are the 2 major vehicles of gene flow available to flowering plants. The dispersal system has important ecological consequences, and there are interesting correlations between dispersal type and habitat. As with wind pollination, we would expect wind dispersal to be very effective in an open, windy environment like the alpine. Many high-elevation species have very small, light seeds that can be blown or tumbled great distances; mountain-heathers, rushes and orchids all have tiny, light seeds. Other species have winged or flanged seeds or fruits, for example, scrub birch, mountain-sorrel, many carrot family plants, Columbia lily, Indian hellebore, some of the suncresses and some gentians and louseworts. Plumed or long-hairy seeds or fruits occur in anemones, cotton-grasses, willows, willowherbs (*Epilobium*), mountain-avens and most aster family species (those with a plumose pappus). Paintbrushes and some larkspurs and penstemons have loose, often net-like seed coats, which could increase loft.

Some other species with unornamented seeds could be adapted for wind dispersal in a less obvious way. They have upright capsules on rigid stems that remain erect above the first encrusted snows of early winter. Strong winds vibrate the stems and shake out or jostle the seeds loose from their fruits, and then blow them along the surface before heavier snows set in. In the winter landscape, this "censer" or saltshaker mechanism is probably a very effective mode of dispersal for poppies, campions, saxifrages, grass-of-Parnassus (*Parnassia*), primroses (*Primula*), paintbrushes, louseworts and wood-rushes. It could conceivably account for movement along ridges even for such relatively heavy, unappendaged seeds such as those of yellow glacier-lily and arctic lupine.

Fleshy fruits are also a good way to get around, via the digestive tracts of birds and mammals on the move, yet plants with berries are uncommon at high elevations in our region. Most are in the shrubby genera *Vaccinium* (blueberries, huckleberries, lingonberry), *Empetrum* (crowberry), *Arctous* (alpine bearberries), *Arctostaphylos*

northern grass-of-Parnassus (*Parnassia palustris*), Canadian Rockies

(kinnikinnik), *Gaultheria* (teaberries), *Ribes* (currants, gooseberries) and *Sorbus* (mountain-ash).

The fruits of many alpine species can function as "sticktights." For example, the seeds of alpine mountain-trumpet (*Collomia debilis*), which are sticky when moistened; the bristly fruits of purple sweet-cicely (*Osmorhiza purpurea*), the beaked achenes of buttercups and the beaked perigynia of sedges; the awned spikelets of grasses; the plumose achenes of anemones and mountain-avens; and aster family achenes with pappus bristles—all can adhere to fur or feathers and be transported long distances. Many other plants of wet, muddy, high-elevation habitats probably are dispersed in mud that sticks to the feet and plumage of birds and the feet and fur of mammals. No particular morphological adaptations are required for such dispersal; the rather unremarkable seeds or fruits of saxifrages, alpine pearlwort (*Sagina saginoides*), buttercups, mountain marsh-marigold, Alaska wild-rhubarb (*Aconogonon alaskanum*), sedges and rushes no doubt often get carried away in the mud.

THE REGION

Bedrock Geology: Whence the Mountains

The story of the northwestern landscape is written in its names: Montana, the Rocky Mountains, the Valhallas, the Eaglenest Range. Or in more detail: Mt. Olympus, Cloudraker Peak, Cathedral, Temple, Wodan, Nimbus, Skypilot, Sharktooth, Tombstone and Denali, the highest point on the continent. They conjure a bold, jagged, ragged world of rock against sky. You would look in vain for names like these between eastern Alberta and St. John's, or from Inuvik to the Mississippi delta, though far to the east you can find places with such names as the White Mountains, the Blue Ridge Mountains and Old Smoky, and a great many grandly named hills—Mont Réal, Mont St. Hilaire. North America is asymmetric—the dramatic architecture of the west in contrast to the (mostly) gently ridged Appalachian country to the east, with the prairies and vast, flat lands in between. One senses that it has something to do with the coasts, with the edges of the continent.

As it does. The present edges of the North American continent are also the edges of the North American plate, one of the 12 major lithospheric plates that, along with a host of smaller ones, make up the mobile outer carapace of the earth. The plates are made up of crust, either continental or oceanic, with a thick, relatively rigid underpinning of mantle ultramafic rock. (The earth's mantle is rarely exposed at the surface. Ingall's Peak in the North Cascades is made of dark, crystalline mantle rock; Twin Sisters in the western Cascades of brown, weathering rock made of pure olivine.) Below the lithosphere, temperatures are sufficiently hot to make the mantle plastic enough to flow, which it does, westward, at the rate of a few centimetres per year—about the same speed as your fingernails grow.

Beginning about 400 million years ago, great slabs of ocean lithosphere in the Pacific region began to descend under the western margin of the North American continent. As the slabs partly melted, buoyant bubbles of magma rose to form new island arc chains. For the early part of its history, this active plate margin would have resembled the western Pacific today, with its festoons of island arc chains and small ocean basins like the Japan Sea separating them from the main continent. But not all materials are so local in origin. Some parts of our Cordillera have travelled vast distances to arrive on our shores—the oceanic rocks of the Cache Creek terrane contain Permian age (260 million years old) fusulinid and coral faunas that are endemic to China and Japan; they crossed the Pacific Ocean on a fast-moving oceanic plate. The terranes that make up the outer part of the Cordillera, including the Brooks Range and the St. Elias Mountains, contain early Paleozoic (480–420 million years old) sponges and corals that are endemic to the northern Urals of Siberia. It is thought that these Arctic-realm terranes travelled from the eastern Arctic region north of Svalbard into the Pacific region, seeding active volcanic island arcs of the Insular terrane

on the way, and finally ran up against the Cordilleran margin in the mid-Jurassic, about 175 million years ago.

Around that time, North America, a vast, thick, cold, rigid slab of lithosphere thousands of kilometres wide, began moving ponderously west, an inexorable snowplow made of rock. The thin crust and hot, mobile mantle at shallow depths beneath the island arcs and marginal ocean basins were caught between this juggernaut and the long-stable Pacific subduction zones to the west. They collided, they stacked, they crumpled, and finally they piled high into a wedge-shaped mass that eventually became the Rocky Mountains.

The fundamental structure of North America's western mountains is the result of the immense Jurassic-Cretaceous squeeze. The linear granitic mountain belts to the west—the Coast Mountains and the Sierra Nevada—mark the site of continuing arc magmatism caused by inexorable subduction of the Pacific lithosphere beneath the advancing continent. The Ominecas and the Rockies, the Cassiars, Selwyns and Mackenzies are all built on the great stackings of sedimentary strata—limestone, dolostone, sandstone and shale—of the ancient North American plate margin. In the Cassiars, the very top of the stack is seen to be rocks of the offshore peri-Laurentian ocean basins and arcs of earlier times.

Within this overall story, each range has its own character, its own individual tale. The very highest mountains on the continent, Denali and Logan, are being pushed up by collision with a lithospheric block, the Yakutat terrane, carried northward by the Pacific plate. The solitary Olympic Mountains are made of fairly young (30 to 50 million years old), offscraped deep-ocean sediments that were carried north to collide with the southern buttress of Vancouver Island. The Brooks Range of far northern Alaska is composed of lands that once lay on the far side of the Arctic Ocean near Svalbard and Severnaya Zemlya. The Cascade volcanic chain, which extends from Lassen Peak in northern California to Mt. Meagher in southwestern British Coumbia, includes some of the youngest mountains in the Cordillera, most less than one million years old. The Cascade Range is underpinned by mainly subalpine highlands of older Cenozoic volcanic rock, but its true heights are the isolated alpine islands of its lone volcanoes, such as Mt. Rainier at 4392 m.

The lofting of mountains continues, caused by thermal expansion driven by temperatures of 800°C a mere 35 km under our feet. Miocene basalts, erupted as flat flows 12 to 5 million years ago, are now tilted from the BC interior upward to project across the present height of the Coast

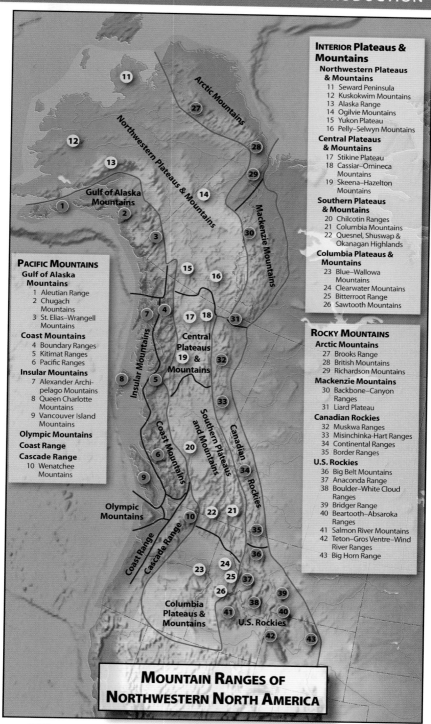

INTERIOR Plateaus & Mountains

Northwestern Plateaus & Mountains
- 11 Seward Peninsula
- 12 Kuskokwim Mountains
- 13 Alaska Range
- 14 Ogilvie Mountains
- 15 Yukon Plateau
- 16 Pelly–Selwyn Mountains

Central Plateaus & Mountains
- 17 Stikine Plateau
- 18 Cassiar–Omineca Mountains
- 19 Skeena–Hazelton Mountains

Southern Plateaus & Mountains
- 20 Chilcotin Ranges
- 21 Columbia Mountains
- 22 Quesnel, Shuswap & Okanagan Highlands

Columbia Plateaus & Mountains
- 23 Blue–Wallowa Mountains
- 24 Clearwater Mountains
- 25 Bitterroot Range
- 26 Sawtooth Mountains

ROCKY MOUNTAINS

Arctic Mountains
- 27 Brooks Range
- 28 British Mountains
- 29 Richardson Mountains

Mackenzie Mountains
- 30 Backbone–Canyon Ranges
- 31 Liard Plateau

Canadian Rockies
- 32 Muskwa Ranges
- 33 Misinchinka-Hart Ranges
- 34 Continental Ranges
- 35 Border Ranges

U.S. Rockies
- 36 Big Belt Mountains
- 37 Anaconda Range
- 38 Boulder–White Cloud Ranges
- 39 Bridger Range
- 40 Beartooth–Absaroka Ranges
- 41 Salmon River Mountains
- 42 Teton–Gros Ventre–Wind River Ranges
- 43 Big Horn Range

PACIFIC MOUNTAINS

Gulf of Alaska Mountains
- 1 Aleutian Range
- 2 Chugach Mountains
- 3 St. Elias–Wrangell Mountains

Coast Mountains
- 4 Boundary Ranges
- 5 Kitimat Ranges
- 6 Pacific Ranges

Insular Mountains
- 7 Alexander Archipelago Mountains
- 8 Queen Charlotte Mountains
- 9 Vancouver Island Mountains

Olympic Mountains

Coast Range

Cascade Range
- 10 Wenatchee Mountains

MOUNTAIN RANGES OF NORTHWESTERN NORTH AMERICA

Mountains. Thus the BC Coast Mountains of today are yet another stage of mountain building, a rejuvenation of the mountain landscape of the west. It is this constant change that gives wildness to the shape of the alpine. The land soars slowly upward, while ice and water empowered by height sculpt the land into rank upon rank of vast standing waves. The mountains that we see are the mirror of the great tumult that created them, hidden away in the deep earth below.

PHYSIOGRAPHY, OR THE LAY OF THE LAND

Our region can be divided up into three broad physiographic systems. These systems, roughly parallel and northwest-southeast in orientation, are the Pacific Mountains, the coastal rampart; the Rocky Mountains, the continental divide; and the Interior Plateaus and Mountains, which lie in between.

Pacific Mountains

The Pacific Mountains array parallels the Pacific Ocean from Alaska to southern Chile, in our region generally extending 200 to 300 km inland. On their windward (western) side, these mountains experience North America's rainiest—and snowiest—weather. Many of the peaks, especially in the north, feature glaciers, and in Alaska, some of these glaciers descend to tidewater. Along the coasts of British Columbia and southeastern Alaska, steep mountains drop precipitously to the sea in complex archipelago-fjord systems. The major mountain arcs include (from north to south) the Gulf of Alaska Mountains, Coast Mountains, Insular Mountains, Olympic Mountains, Coast Range and Cascade Range.

The Gulf of Alaska Mountains (including the Aleutian Range, Chugach Mountains and St. Elias-Wrangell Mountains) are the northernmost portion of the Pacific Mountains, covering southern Alaska, southwestern Yukon and northwestern BC. Some of North America's bulkiest and snowiest mountains are here, including Yukon's Mt. Logan (5959 m), and they feature extensive glaciers, the largest non-polar icefields on earth. Much of this area is protected within the international UNESCO World Heritage Site composed of Canada's Kluane National Park and Reserve and Tatshenshini-Alsek Provincial Park, and the United States' Wrangell–St. Elias National Park and Preserve and Glacier Bay National Park and Preserve.

The Coast Mountains cover approximately 1600 km from southwestern Yukon through transboundary southeastern Alaska and

Takakia Lake, Queen Charlotte Mountains, Haida Gwaii, BC

northwestern BC to BC's south coast (Fraser River). They have extensive icefields in the northern Boundary Ranges and in the southern Pacific Ranges. The highest mountain wholly within BC, Mt. Waddington (4019 m), is in the Coast Mountains. Bedrock is mostly intrusive igneous but is composed of materials from many different geographic origins and ages.

The Insular Mountains occur in Southeast Alaska (Alexander Archipelago Mountains) and on Haida Gwaii (Queen Charlotte Mountains) and Vancouver Island (Vancouver Island Mountains). These rugged ranges were formed approximately 100 million years ago, when the North American plate collided with a chain of volcanic islands in the Pacific. Folded and faulted volcanic and sedimentary bedrock predominates.

The Olympic Mountains occur on Washington's Olympic Peninsula. Bedrock is primarily sedimentary and volcanic. The Olympics aren't particularly high, topping out at Mt. Olympus (2427 m), but a lot of precipitation from the Pacific piles up on them and they support abundant snowfields and glaciers.

The Coast Range of Washington and Oregon extends approximately 320 km from Gray's Harbor to the Coquille River. Bedrock is primarily volcanic in origin, with sedimentary deposits largely derived from marine sediments. Mountain crests are not particularly lofty—Mary's Peak is highest at 1248 m—and there's not much alpine habitat.

The Cascade Range (including the Wenatchee Mountains as an eastern extension) extends 1100 km from southern BC (south and east of the Fraser River) to northern California. The range is composed primarily of volcanic rock, with some sedimentary and granitic rock in northern sections. The highest peaks, with Mt. Rainier (4392 m) the tallest, are all volcanoes that tower above the general, rather uniform, summit level of the chain. The volcanic cones and peaks have been built up by outpourings of Pleistocene and Recent lava and ash upon the older erosion surface. Some of the volcanoes are still considered active, including Mt. St. Helens, which last erupted in 1980.

Interior Plateaus and Mountains

The Interior Plateaus and Mountains system occupies the area between Pacific and Rocky Mountains, and consists of a series of plateaus—some at fairly high elevations and those farther north supporting alpine habitat—and mountain ranges that bulk above them. This interior or intermontane system contains the Northwestern, Central, Southern, and Columbia Plateaus and Mountains.

The **Northwestern Plateaus and Mountains** area (between the coastal Gulf of Alaska Mountains and the Mackenzie and Arctic Mountains to the east and north) includes many mighty mountain ranges (Kuskokwim Mountains, Alaska Range, Ogilvie Mountains, Pelly-Selwyn Mountains), as well as the Seward Peninsula and the Yukon Plateau. North America's highest peak, Denali (Mt. McKinley) at 6194 m, surmounts the Alaska Range.

The **Central Plateaus and Mountains** area covers much of northern interior BC and a bit of southern Yukon, between the Coast Mountains and the northern Canadian Rockies. It includes the Stikine Plateau and the Cassiar-Omineca and Skeena-Hazelton Mountains. In both the Northwestern and Central areas, the plateaus support extensive alplands, with the northerly latitudes

compensating for the moderate elevations. South of here, plateau surfaces support forests.

The **Southern Plateaus and Mountains** represents the area between the Coast Mountains and the northern Cascades to the west and the southern Canadian Rockies to the east. It includes various high-elevation plateaus (Quesnel, Shuswap and Okanagan Highlands), the snowy Columbia Mountains, which have 6 main ranges (the Cariboo, Monashee, Selkirk, Purcell, Cabinet and Salish mountains), as well as the rainshadow Chilcotin Ranges, which include the Chilcotin Mountains and the Camelsfoot, Clear and Marble ranges. The Columbia Mountains contain many high mountains with alpine habitat; Mt. Sir Sandford (3519 m) in the BC Selkirks is the highest peak. The geology is varied, with metamorphic, sedimentary and volcanic rocks often intruded by granitic stocks and batholiths, and includes areas of karst (porous, eroded limestone) terrain.

The **Columbia Plateaus and Mountains** is a broad basaltic floodplain studded with isolated mountain ranges formed partly of basalts and partly of a hodgepodge of other geological formations, with a nearly 2 km thickness of lava poured out over the landscape 15 to 20 million years ago. It covers portions of northeastern Oregon, southeastern Washington and central Idaho between the Cascade Range and the U.S. Rocky Mountains. The primary alpine habitat in the area is found in the Blue-Wallowa Mountains in the west, and the ranges of west-central Idaho in the east. The highest elevations are Thompson Peak (3277 m) in the Sawtooths, followed by Sacajawea Peak (2999 m) in the Wallowas.

remnant glacier, Stikine (Klastline) Plateau, BC

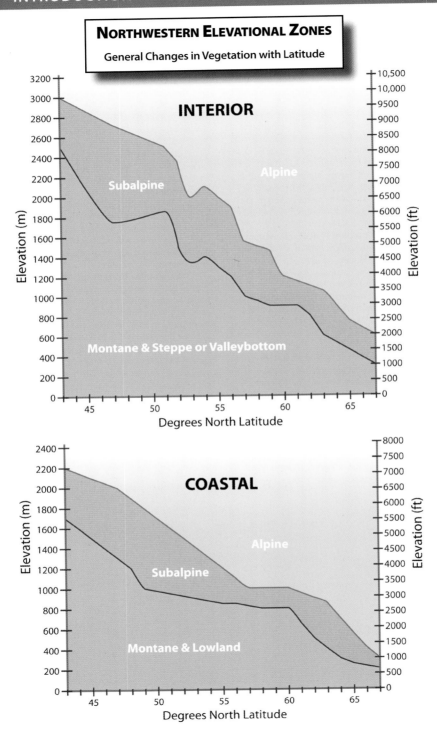

Northwestern Elevational Zones

General Changes in Vegetation with Latitude

INTERIOR

Alpine

Subalpine

Montane & Steppe or Valleybottom

Elevation (m) / Elevation (ft)

Degrees North Latitude

COASTAL

Alpine

Subalpine

Montane & Lowland

Elevation (m) / Elevation (ft)

Degrees North Latitude

Rocky Mountains

The Rocky Mountains system forms the eastern boundary of our region and straddles the Continental Divide; precipitation falling on the eastern flank of these mountains flows to the Gulf of Mexico or Hudson Bay, on the western flank to the Pacific Ocean, and in the north to the Arctic Ocean or Bering Sea. The bedrock includes sedimentary, igneous and metamorphic rocks, mostly heavily sculpted by glaciation. The Rocky Mountain array includes the Canadian and U.S. Rockies, as well as the Arctic and Mackenzie Mountains, whose inclusion in the Rockies system might surprise some people.

The Arctic Mountains (Alaska's Brooks Range, Yukon's British Mountains and Richardson Mountains) extend approximately 1100 km east-west across northern Alaska and Yukon. These mountains divide waters flowing into the North Pacific–Bering Sea from waters flowing into the Arctic Ocean, and generally mark the northerly extent of trees. The highest peak is Mt. Chamberlin (2749 m).

The Mackenzie Mountains (including the Backbone-Canyon Ranges and the Liard Plateau) separate Yukon and Northwest Territories for approximately 800 km between the Peel River and the Liard River. They are almost entirely composed of folded sedimentary rock. Keele Peak, at 2972 m, is the highest mountain. In the rainshadow of the Selwyn Mountains and often under the sway of arctic air masses, they have a cold, relatively dry climate and low treeline.

The Canadian Rockies extend from BC's Liard River south to northern Montana. They're bordered on the east by the Great Plains and on the west by the Rocky Mountain Trench. Included are BC's Muskwa and Misinchinka-Hart ranges, the Continental Ranges (BC-AB) and, dipping into Montana's Glacier National Park, the Border Ranges. They are composed primarily of layered sedimentary rock laid down up to 1.5 billion years ago under an ancient sea. The tallest peak in the Canadian Rockies is Mt. Robson (3954 m).

The U.S. Rockies in our region extend from eastern Idaho and adjacent Montana to northwestern Wyoming. The northern U.S. Rockies include the Big Belt Mountains and the Anaconda, Boulder, Bridger and White Cloud ranges. The origin of the U.S. Rockies is much the same as that of their Canadian counterparts—the uplift of strata of the old inland sea sediments, plus occasional granitic intrusions, ancient basement rocks and minor additional formations of mostly very old age. These mountains are often parallel chains of ranges between the Great Plains to the east and the Columbia Plateau to the west. The highest peaks are, for Idaho, Borah Peak (3859 m), and for Montana, Mount Haggin (3245 m).

Southwestern Montana and adjacent northern Wyoming fall within what some call the central Rockies, which in our region include the Beartooth Mountains and Absaroka Range, the Salmon River Mountains, the spectacularly pointy Teton, Gros Ventre and Wind River ranges, and the Big Horn Mountains. The bedrock is almost all sedimentary from the old inland sea, with scattered intrusive igneous rocks (as in the Tetons) and ancient basement rocks. The mountaintops are high, none more so than Gannett Peak in Wyoming at 4209 m.

CLIMATE

The mountain climate varies dramatically with changes in latitude, as temperatures decline from south to north. The effects of this change can be seen in the gradual lowering of treeline (the bottom edge of the alpine zone) from south to north. Treeline shifts by approximately 110 m with every degree of latitude. For example, treeline is generally between 3300 and 3600 m elevation in Colorado, whereas it's at 1000 m in the northern Canadian Rocky Mountains and lower still in Alaska and the Yukon. Climatic variation also occurs along the longitudinal gradient, most notably reflecting the distance from the Pacific Ocean, the location on wetter windward or drier leeward mountain slopes and the maritime (more equable) vs. continental (more seasonally variable) character of regional climates. In general, treeline is several hundred metres lower on the windward side of the Pacific Mountains than in the Rocky Mountains owing to heavy and prolonged snow cover at high coastal elevations. The numbers in the graphs on the opposite page should be taken as a very rough guide only; treeline and subalpine elevations vary considerably with aspect and local climatic and topographic factors. Beyond 67° to 69° N latitude is the northern treeline and the Arctic.

Differences in temperature have a wide range of effects on these mountain landscapes. Southern temperatures are warmer, and with higher temperatures come increased evaporation, drier soils, smaller rivers, fewer glaciers and longer growing seasons. Southern parts of the Rockies are also drier because of their location farther inland from the Pacific. Prevailing winds blow from west to east across our region, and as the air from the Pacific rises, it cools and drops much of its moisture as rain or snow on western slopes, leaving eastern slopes noticeably drier

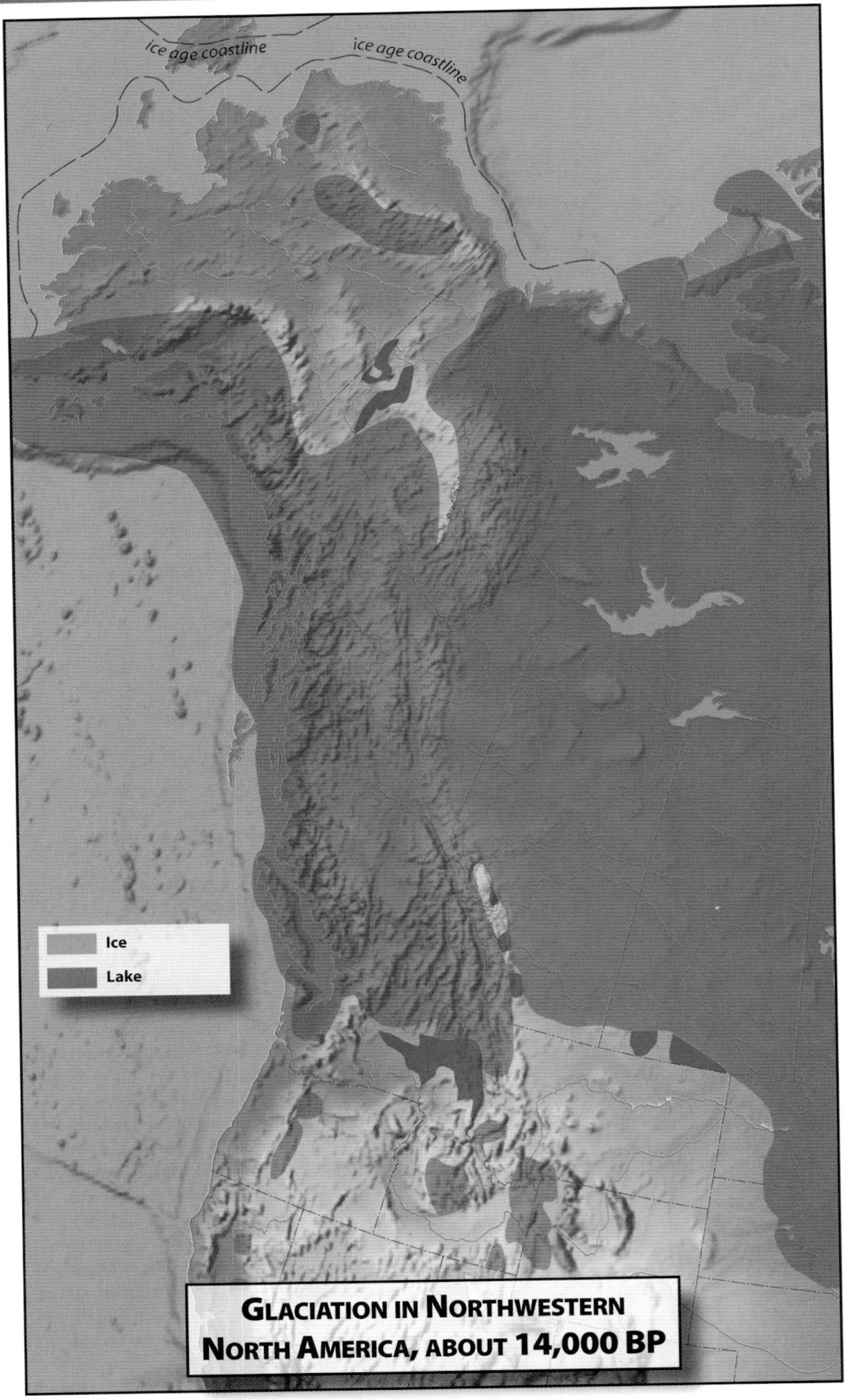

ice age coastline   ice age coastline

Ice

Lake

**GLACIATION IN NORTHWESTERN
NORTH AMERICA, ABOUT 14,000 BP**

and cooler. In the Pacific Mountains, the amounts of rain and snow that fall on western slopes are truly staggering: Mt. Olympus receives more than 600 cm average annual precipitation; both Mt. Rainier and Mt. Baker in the Washington Cascades have recorded 28 m of snowfall in one year. In the Rocky Mountains, the Canadian Rockies lie relatively closer to the Pacific coast than the U.S. Rockies, and they receive larger amounts of rain and snowfall as moisture-laden air rises to flow over their peaks. To the south, air masses pass over a vast expanse of dry basins and plateaus before they reach the eastern ranges of the cordillera, so prevailing winds in the U.S. Rockies are much drier than those to the north.

PREHISTORIC TIME

Northwestern North America has a complicated glacial history, but we can generalize that almost all areas currently in the alpine zone in our region were covered by ice during the most recent Pleistocene ice age, the Wisconsin (100,000–10,000 years ago). Most coverage was from the Cordilleran ice sheet; some eastern parts of the region were overridden by the continental Laurentide ice sheet. Contemporary alpine areas south (as in northern U.S. Rockies) or north (as in the Brooks Range) of the ice sheets would have been under the sway of alpine glaciers during the Wisconsin ice age.

The map on the opposite page depicts our region at a slice of ice age time, 14,000 years ago (BP = before present). The blue offshore line around northern and western Alaska represents ancient shoreline, as sea level was rising and widening the Bering Strait. At 18,000 years BP, the Bering land bridge existed, but the southern limit of ice in the Pacific Northwest had not yet attained its maximum extent, so we chose the later scenario.

Regionally, 2 large glacial refugia (ice-free areas) were available for northwestern plants, the Pacific Northwest and Beringia. Species could have retreated south, north or to both refugia during glacial advances. There is strong evidence for additional, smaller refugia. On the Pacific coast, refugia probably existed on parts of the Alexander Archipelago, Haida Gwaii, northwestern Vancouver Island (Brooks Peninsula) and at middle elevations in the Olympic Mountains. Inland "cryptic" refugia have been proposed along the east side of the Mackenzie Mountains and the Canadian Rockies (between the Cordilleran and Laurentide ice sheets), in northwestern BC and on "nunataks" (peaks protruding above the ice).

VEGETATION

Our region covers 400 million hectares—an area more than one-third that of Europe—over 55° of longitude and 25° of latitude, and includes North America's highest elevations (topped by Denali at 6194 metres) as well as its wettest and coldest climates. As you might expect in such a large and spectacular piece of the continent, vegetation varies considerably. We will generally discuss plant communities by elevation zone, but most plants grow in more than one type of plant community, and species from adjacent vegetation types and zones often intermix.

Lower Elevations

This field guide is about higher-elevation plants, so we won't describe lower-elevation vegetation here in any detail. Still, the lower elevations within our region are subject to similar, but generally warmer and drier, sorts of regional climatic processes as are upper elevations, and some of the patterns that we see in alpine vegetation are reflected down in the valleys.

Lower-elevation ecosystems on the Pacific coast—at least as far north as Prince William Sound—are primarily coastal temperate rainforests. Sodden conifer forests dominated by western hemlock (*Tsuga heterophylla*), western redcedar (*Thuja plicata*), Pacific silver fir (*Abies amabilis*), Sitka spruce (*Picea sitchensis*) and (in the south) coastal Douglas-fir (*Pseudotsuga menziesii* ssp. *menziesii*) tower over understoreys of heather family shrubs, ferns and bryophytes.

Immediately on the lee side of the Pacific Mountains, the climate is dramatically drier, and lower-elevation vegetation reflects this. In the Columbia Plateaus, much of the landscape is dominated by grasslands and shrub-steppe, with various bunchgrasses and sagebrush (*Artemisia* spp.) species. These ecosystems extend north as fingers and lobes of shrub-steppe in BC's southern interior, where they're gradually replaced by open montane forests with grass and shrub understoreys.

Farther north, the Central and Northwestern Plateaus are generally fairly elevated at their bases—for example, Prince George, BC, is at 676 m—so the lowest elevations over much of this area are already in the montane zone.

From eastern Washington and Idaho and western Montana to approximately 54° N latitude in southeastern BC, on the windward (west) sides of mountain ranges, we see valley forests similar in many respects to those of the coast, and fundamentally for the same reason. Weather systems from the west encounter mountain ranges and drop their precipitation on the windward hillslopes. These inland temperate rainforests are also dominated by western hemlock and western redcedar, but they contain many interior species as well.

Lower elevations around the Rocky Mountains—the foothills—vary from shrub-steppe in the U.S. Rockies (featuring a wide variety of shrubs, including sagebrushes and junipers [*Juniperus*]) to montane forests of lodgepole pine (*Pinus contorta* var. *latifolia*) and trembling aspen (*Populus tremuloides*) in the Canadian Rockies, to montane boreal spruce forest farther north.

Montane

Montane forests are in the zone between lowland and subalpine ecosystems. They are often very diverse, containing a mix of lower-elevation and higher-elevation species.

On the wet west side of the Pacific Mountains, montane forests contain a mix of lower-elevation species (such as western hemlock and western redcedar) and their subalpine counterparts mountain hemlock (*Tsuga mertensiana*) and yellow-cedar (*Xanthocyparis nootkatensis*), along with Pacific silver fir.

As at lower elevations, ecosystems east of the coastal ramparts are noticeably drier. From southern BC and adjacent Alberta south, montane landscapes are dominated by successional stands of conifers, including interior Douglas-fir (*Pseudotsuga menziesii* ssp. *glauca*), lodgepole pine, ponderosa pine (*Pinus ponderosa*) and western larch (*Larix occidentalis*), often mixed with trembling aspen and paper birch (*Betula papyrifera*). Northward, montane forests consist largely of lodgepole pine, hybrid white spruce (*Picea engelmannii* x *glauca*) and subalpine fir (*Abies lasiocarpa*). From northern BC north, montane landscapes are covered by boreal forest, with white spruce (*Picea glauca*) and black spruce (*Picea mariana*), lodgepole pine and trembling aspen (both of which drop out northward), paper birch and balsam poplar (*Populus balsamifera* ssp. *balsamifera*). Around 68° to 69° N, we reach the northern treeline, beyond which is arctic tundra on the North Slope (the area sweeping down from the Arctic Mountains to the Beaufort and Chukchi seas).

Subalpine

The subalpine zone extends from the upper edge of the montane zone to the upper limit of trees (usually conifers) in an upright form. It is sometimes said to end at **timberline** (the upper limit of continuous forests of fairly erect trees), but for the purposes of this guide, the subalpine zone tops out at the upper limit of trees as trees.

subalpine meadow, Hazelton Mountains, BC

Thus parkland and elfin forest are part of the subalpine zone.

Above the subalpine zone is the alpine zone, where trees occur only in **krummholz** (dwarfed, stunted, twisted) form. Subalpine forests are sometimes called "snow forests" because they grow at elevations with relatively abundant preciptation (both rain and snow), and their dense trees protect the thick snowpack from melting and evaporating in spring. Many delicate, moisture-loving wildflowers grow in this zone.

Subalpine forests in and west of the Pacific Mountains are said to be in the Mountain Hemlock zone. Lower elevations are characterized by continuous forest cover of mountain hemlock, Pacific silver fir and yellow-cedar, with other coniferous species in the mix depending on latitude and how wet the climate is. The understorey is often dominated by heather family shrubs such as white-flowered rhododendron (*Rhododendron albiflorum*), rusty false azalea (*Menziesia ferruginea*), copperbush (*Elliottia pyroliflora*) and blueberries and huckleberries (*Vaccinium*).

Subalpine forests on the leeward side of the Pacific Mountains and throughout the Plateaus and Mountains north to about 56° N latitude are dominated by Engelmann spruce, subalpine fir and lodgepole pine, with primarily montane species such as Douglas-fir, grand fir (*Abies grandis*) and western larch in the mix lower down. Climates vary considerably in these inland subalpine forests and so does understorey vegetation, from huckleberries, blueberries and common juniper (*Juniperus communis*) in drier climates to devil's-club (*Oplopanax horridus*) and ferns in wetter climates and on wetter sites.

At upper elevations, subalpine forests throughout our region south of about 56° N latitude become parkland, a mix of discontinuous forest interspersed with heathland, meadow and grassland. Tree species are similar to lower subalpine elevations, sometimes in the interior with whitebark pine (*Pinus albicaulis*), limber pine (*Pinus flexilis*) and alpine larch (*Larix lyallii*) toward treeline. The heathlands, meadows and grasslands have alpine analogues and will be described there.

North of approximately 56° N, the Engelmann spruce–subalpine fir forests are gradually replaced by forests of white spruce and subalpine fir. At higher subalpine elevations, the continuous forest gives way to scrub-parkland, and fairly tall (1–2.5 m) shrubs dominate, especially scrub birch and various willows.

Alpine

The alpine zone includes very short (less than 1 m tall) vegetation commonly called tundra, from treeline to ridgetop. In this cold, wind-swept environment, some areas may be free of snow early in spring (and even through most of winter), whereas others lie blanketed with drifts for most or all of summer. The alpine flower display on mountaintops usually peaks in July—a date influenced more by snow accumulation than by latitude.

Alpine vegetation occurs in a fine-grained mosaic, where minor changes in moisture, exposure and substrate can determine life and death for some plants. A bump a few centimetres high can change radiation levels, wind strength and snow accumulation levels to the point where small plants can begin to grow.

Alpine heath communities are widespread in our region, especially in wetter climates, on sites with considerable snow accumulation and stable substrates. These heathlands typically grow on acidic soils that are moist but well drained, where snowpack gives winter protection but melts by midsummer. In drier climates, they tend to be restricted to north and east slopes and to snow accumulation areas such as cirque basins and gullies. The ground cover is a springy carpet—often proliferating over and obscuring rocks, holes, wet sinks and dry pockets—of evergreen dwarf shrubs, especially heather family plants such as mountain-heathers and crowberry, often in combination with low blueberries. Other common heathland species include clubmosses (*Diphasiastrum, Huperzia, Lycopodium*), partridge-foot (*Luetkea pectinata*), sibbaldia (*Sibbaldia procumbens*), woolly hawkweed, arnicas (*Arnica*), woodrushes and purple hairgrass (*Vahlodea atropurpurea*). Hypermaritime heathland and tundra extend along the outer Pacific coast from northern Vancouver Island to Prince William Sound at progressively lower elevations until one reaches the Alaska Peninsula and the Aleutian Islands, where distinctive treeless vegetation covers all elevations but is beyond the scope of this book.

Alpine meadow communities occur on slopes and swales with well-developed soil and continuous winter snowpack that melts off in early summer. On sites with ample moisture and deep soils, lush, often waist-high meadows are dominated by forbs and large, sometimes tussocky sedges, often with gorgeously displayed Sitka valerian, Indian hellebore, arrow-leaved groundsel, subalpine daisy (*Erigeron glacialis*), mop-top, lupines, arnicas, mountain sagewort (*Artemisia norvegica*), cow-parsnip, bistorts, cinquefoils, louseworts, paintbrushes, glacier lilies and buttercups—plus showy sedge (*Carex spectabilis*) and its Rocky Mountain and northern counterparts. Oh boy!

On drier, often steeper slopes with shallower soils, the meadows are just as showy but have a more compact, tidier aspect and a different composition. Grasses such as bluegrasses, fescues (*Festuca*), alpine timothy (*Phleum alpinum*) and spike trisetum (*Trisetum spicatum*) are abundant, as are

colourful steep scree, Olympic Mountains, WA

alpine heath on ridges, meadows in swales, Hazelton Mountains, BC

relatively small, tufted sedges. There is a diversity of forbs including wild-buckwheats (*Eriogonum*), alpine bistort, sandworts (*Minuartia*, *Eremogone*), suncresses (*Boechera*), stonecrops (*Sedum*), larkspurs, anemones, phloxes, cinquefoils, lupines, locoweeds, penstemons, paintbrushes, groundsels (*Senecio*), arnicas and pussytoes (*Antennaria*).

Alpine grasslands are widespread in areas with cold, dry, windy climates—and consequently low snowpacks—and well-developed soils. Common species are fescues (*Festuca* spp.), bluegrasses (*Poa* spp.), spike trisetum, timber oatgrass (*Danthonia intermedia*) and alpine sweetgrass (*Anthoxanthum monticola* ssp. *alpinum*), as well as sedges.

Areas with late snowmelt and cold, wet soil are tough sites indeed, and plant species diversity is often low. Soil erosion during snowmelt and growing season cryoturbation (frost churning) add to the stresses. Snowbeds typically are occupied by dwarf sedges such as black alpine sedge (*Carex nigricans*), as well as Drummond's rush (*Juncus drummondii*), woodrushes, partridge-foot, Tolmie's saxifrage and buttercups. Wet meadows and fens often feature a soaking sod of sedges and cotton-grasses, with marsh-marigold, louseworts and bog orchids (*Platanthera* spp.). Along streams and shores, sedges occur together with willow thickets and a variety of forbs such as river beauty (*Epilobium latifolium*), marsh-marigold, buttercups, saxifrages, leatherleaf saxifrage, arctic sweet coltsfoot and groundsels (*Senecio*).

alpine grassy tundra and subalpine parkland, Grassy Mountain, BC

subalpine fen, Hazelton Mountains, BC

Dry, convex, exposed ridges and upper slopes, where strong winds allow little snow accumulation, support tundra consisting primarily of dwarf willows and other prostrate shrubs, cushion- and mat-forming herbs, grasses, sedges and lichens. On such mountaintop habitats, the mineral composition of the bedrock greatly influences the vegetation because the primary source of nutrients is the disintegrating rock. In interior mountain ranges with calcium-rich bedrock, mountain-avens (*Dryas octopetala*, *D. integrifolia*) typically characterizes such tundra, especially in drier climates and on drier sites. Compared to acidic, nutrient-deficient rock such as granite and sandstone, the nutrient-rich substrate supports more species, including a good selection of dwarf cinquefoils, saxifrages, sandworts, drabas, pussytoes, alpine daisies (*Erigeron*), arnicas, packeras (*Packera*), bluegrasses and mini-fescues, and sedges such as *Carex nardina* and *C. rupestris*. Understandably, most of these plants hug the ground in cushions, mats or rosettes and are often densely hairy with thickly cutinized leaves, the better to retain warmth, moisture, nutrients and to escape or withstand wind. Some species cannot tolerate prolonged snow cover. For example, mousetail alpine-sedge (*Kobresia myosuroides*) can dominate dry ridge tundra, but only where snowpack is light and ephemeral.

Fellfields are areas where freeze-thaw cycles result in characteristic patterns of frost-wedged rocks, usually on a level or gently sloping surface stabilized by vegetation mats. Common species in these unsettled ecosystems are cushion plants such as moss campion, saxifrages and cinquefoils. The same general idea on a larger scale is seen in felsenmeer, boulder fields where the primary vegetation is lichens and bryophytes.

alpine fellfield tundra, Boundary Ranges, YT

Scree and talus ecosystems are relatively steep, unstable areas, usually below cliffs or bluffs or ridgelines. Vascular plant cover is variable and often patchy, depending on how active the slope is, but mountain-sorrel, dwarf alpine hawksbeard, drabas, poppies, saxifrages, cinquefoils, lichens and bryophytes often do well here.

CLIMATE CHANGE

Over the past 100 years or so, global climate change has set the biosphere on a course toward ecological upheaval. We are already experiencing biome shifts; species losses, gains and reassembly in altered communities; changes to snowpack and to stream temperatures, flows and fish habitat; melting of permafrost; increased frequency of extreme events in general, with growing damage from storms, floods, erosion (including land-slides), droughts and wildfires; more frequent and extensive outbreaks of forest pests such as bark beetles and needle and leaf diseases; and increasing impacts from invasive species. As climate continues to change, northwestern North America can expect continuing transformations in biodiversity on land and in water and across all levels of biological organization (genes, species, ecosystems) and the interactions among them.

Our region has high levels of climate **variability** (seasonal, year-to-year and decadal variation related to the strength, interaction and frequency of atmospheric circulations such as the Aleutian Low, El Niño–Southern Oscillation, the Pacific Decadal Oscillation and the Arctic Oscillation) and **change** (long-term trends). In thinking about what could happen at high elevations during this century, we must consider both climate variability and climate change. For example, depending on where you live, you may think it's been unusually wet during summer for the past 10 to 20 years. However, the miserable weather could be part of a wet phase of the Pacific Decadal cycle as much as it may be a function of climate change.

Climate change scenarios are based on a set of global climate models and levels of greenhouse gas emissions, and they are applied over big areas. Scenarios represent a range of possible future climates, not narrow predictions. Moreover, projections of climate change and its impacts in the northwest are inherently fuzzy because the region has such complex topography and climatic processes, as well as pronounced ecological gradients. Nonetheless, scenarios based on currently available information suggest that we can expect the changes listed below. Keep in mind that projections of temperature changes have greater certainty than projections of precipitation changes.

Probable trends in the coming decades include the following:
- Increasing temperature, with mean annual temperatures warming by 3°C to 5°C by 2050. Temperature changes historically have been, and are projected to be, largest in the winter months.

silky phacelia (*Phacelia sericea*), North Cascades, WA

- Warmer, wetter winters generally; progressively warmer, drier summers in the southern half of the region; wetter but ultimately warmer summers in much of the north as this century progresses.
- Ultimately decreasing snowfall and snow-pack, except maybe in some northern parts of the region; dwindling glaciers.
- Changing snowpack; more thaw-freeze events, more icy layers and crusts.
- Earlier snowmelt; earlier ice-melt and later freeze-up of rivers and lakes.
- Increasing water temperatures of rivers and lakes, though systems with lots of glacial meltwater will stay cold as long as the glaciers last.
- Complex changes to the amount and timing of streamflows, depending on watershed type and location; more rain-on-snow events.
- Melting permafrost; earth slumps and rock-slides increasing in frequency.
- Increasing impacts from wildfires (fire severity increases, fire season lengthens) and outbreaks of forest pests.
- Shifting "climate envelopes" (the spatial extent of suitable climatic conditions) of ecological zones and of species.

Ecological Responses

Climate largely determines the nature and distribution of terrestrial ecosystems, and through its effects on the water cycle also plays a major role in the nature of rivers, lakes and other aquatic ecosystems. Climate change is already driving changes in ecosystem structure (vegetation, species composition), function (productivity, decomposition, water and nutrient cycling), processes (disturbance regimes, successional pathways, hydrological regimes) and distribution. Responses of northwestern cordilleran ecosystems are complex and difficult to predict because they reflect the cumulative effects of changing climate, land- and resource-use activities, and invasive species.

Please reflect upon 2 major points before considering projected ecosystem trends and impacts:

First, ecosystems do not migrate, species do. Ecosystems will not move *in toto* inland or northward or upward to newly suitable climate envelopes. Ecosystem change will result from changes at the population and species level. Existing ecosystems will lose some species, gain others and experience shifts in abundance and dominance of the species that persist. Species are responding "individualistically" to environmental change. Some species will stay put, and their populations will either wax or wane. Other species will move, if they can, to suitable habitats elsewhere, and will reassemble in most likely different combinations, including some novel ones. New arrivals will interact with persistent species, plus exotic immigrants, to create new ecosystems.

Second, most plant species cannot move fast enough to keep up with the projected changes. The potential geographic range, or potential niche, of many species will shift markedly or expand, but species that migrate slowly will need many decades and probably centuries to move accordingly or to realize their niche. Long-distance dispersal will play a key role, as it has in the past. Species with poor dispersal capabilities could be out of luck, at least locally. Species whose potential range shrinks could disappear quickly if reproductive individuals die off en masse and environmental conditions are no longer suitable for their progeny or younger generations.

Projections to the end of this century include:

- A general shift of bioclimates from south to north.
- Expansion of moist, temperate, coastal and interior conifer forests upslope and north at the expense of subalpine and boreal forests.
- Expansion of cool-temperate subalpine forests northward and upslope. Even so, large diebacks of trees are expected owing to warmer, drier conditions and drought-facilitated insect, disease and fire damage.
- Dwindling of cold, subalpine/subarctic woodlands in the north.
- Decreased snowpack and shrinking glaciers. Some glaciers will disappear and others will diminish greatly, leaving behind big areas of deglaciated terrain as fresh substrate for colonization and ecological succession.
- Species populations and genetic diversity will be affected, insofar as insularity increases (as treeline moves upward), as disjunctions increase (for example, by long-distance dispersal) or as currently continuous, widespread species distributions become fragmented.
- Shrinking alpine bioclimate throughout the region, though this trend will probably be geographically idiosyncratic, not monolithic. Alpine ecosystems will retreat and some alpine "sky islands" could disappear as upwardly mobile subalpine forests and shrublands lignify the neighbourhood. Some scenarios project subalpine conditions into much of the region's contemporary alpine zone. Many of our alplands are at risk—a sobering thought for us all.

Trees

alpine larch (*Larix lyallii*), Mt. Frosty, Manning Park, BC

TREES

Normally we—especially those of us who are foresters—would say that trees are woody, single-stemmed plants taller than 10 m at maturity. But at high elevations, we must give the trees some slack. Yes, this book is mostly *not* about trees, but they still grow at fairly high altitudes, and even when stunted, they have a disproportionately large impact on microenvironments and neighbouring or sheltering plants. Moreover, the altitudinal limit of tree growth marks a striking ecological threshold for plant life, a switch between very different life forms and a fundamental shift in environmental regimes.

Key to the Trees

1a. Trees with scale-like leaves, concealing the twigs . . . . *Xanthocyparis nootkatensis* (p. 47)

1b. Trees with needles. 2

  2a. Needles in clusters of 12 or more, on short, woody shoots; deciduous 3

    3a. Needles 3-angled, 1–2 cm long, in clusters of 12–25 . . . . *Larix laricina* (p. 43)

    3b. Needles 4-angled, 2–3.5 cm long, in clusters of 30–40 . . . . *Larix lyallii* (p. 43)

  2b. Needles single or in bundles of 2 or 5. 4

    4a. Needles borne singly, not in bundles. 5

      5a. Needles stalkless; seed cones upright at maturity. 6

        6a. Most branches appearing flattened with spreading foliage in "sprays"; needles with lines of tiny white dots (stomata) on lower surface only . . . . *Abies amabilis* (p. 39)

        6b. Branches without spray-like foliage, appearing half-rounded in cross-section by upswept needles; needles with white lines of stomata on both surfaces . . . . *Abies lasiocarpa* (p. 39)

      5b. Needles stalked; seed cones drooping at maturity 7

        7a. Needles 2-sided, flexible, blunt. 8

          8a. Seed cones 3–6 cm long; needles half-rounded to 4-angled in cross-section, crowded bottlebrush-fashion all around twigs, with white lines of stomata on both surfaces . . . . *Tsuga mertensiana* (p. 42)

          8b. Seed cones 1.5–3 cm long; needles flattened, mostly in 2 rows, in flat "sprays," with whitish lines of stomata on lower surface only . . . . *Tsuga heterophylla* (p. 42)

        7b. Needles 4-sided, stiff, sharp-pointed. 9

          9a. Seed cones persist on trees for many years, egg-shaped; trees with narrow shape and usually with bulbous "crowsnest" of dense branchlets at the top; boreal species, north of about 52° N . . . . *Picea mariana* (p. 41)

          9b. Seed cones falling off after maturity, ellipsoid-cylindric; trees comparatively broad, without bulbous top; more southerly, coastal or widespread species. 10

            10a. Needles somewhat flattened, with white lines of stomata on upper surface; cones 5–10 cm long; coastal . . . . *Picea sitchensis* (p. 41)

            10b. Needles 4-angled in cross-section, with white lines of stomata on all leaf surfaces; cones 2–7 cm long ; mostly interior 11

              11a. Young twigs usually hairless; needles mostly <2 cm long; cone scales fan-shaped, smooth and rounded at tip; boreal, with rare disjuncts south to eastern ID and southwestern MT . . . . *Picea glauca* (p. 41)

              11b. Young twigs usually minutely hairy; needles often 2–3 cm long; cone scales narrowly diamond-shaped or elliptic, jagged or irregularly wavy at tip; wide-spread cordilleran. . . . . *Picea engelmannii* (p. 40)

    4b. Needles in bundles of 2 or 5 12

      12a. Needles in bundles of 2 . . . . *Pinus contorta* (p. 46)

      12b. Needles in bundles of 5 13

        13a. Seed cones 4–8 cm long, remaining closed on tree and opened by animals or disintegrating . . . . *Pinus albicaulis* (p. 44)

        13b. Seed cones 7–15 cm long, opening while attached to tree. . . . . *Pinus flexilis* (p. 45)

Subalpine Fir • *Abies lasiocarpa*

General: Evergreen, coniferous, to 20–40 m tall at moderate elevations, typically stunted ("elfinwood") at timberline and twisted ("krummholz" or "shintangle") near treeline, fragrant; branches short, thick; **crown spire-like to conic.**

Bark: Grey, thin, smooth in young trees, with **resin blisters;** in older trees, furrowed, sometimes blocky or platy.

Leaves: Needles 2–3 cm long, flattened, thickest in the centre, **mostly blunt,** sometimes notched (shaded) or pointed (exposed) at tip, crowded, **tending to sweep upward,** bluish green, with **rows of tiny, white dots (stomata) on both surfaces.**

Cones: Pollen (male) cones about 1 cm long, bluish, hanging; **seed (female) cones cylindric to barrel-shaped,** 5–10 cm long, deep purple when young, lighter with age, **upright** on upper branches, **shedding scales with seeds,** leaving only the slender, candle-like core.

Where Found: Coniferous forests on mountain slopes and northern plateaus; montane to alpine zones; frequent and widespread in the southern ¾ of the region, southeastern AK, southern YT and southwestern NT through BC and south-western AB to CA, AZ and NM; cordilleran; outer coastal populations occur infrequently in southeastern AK, central Vancouver I. and the Olympic Peninsula, but not on Haida Gwaii.

Similar Species: Pacific silver fir or amabilis fir (**A. amabilis**) often occurs at timberline, especially in snowy coastal ranges. It has a rounded, rather puffy crown, **flattened, spray-like foliage** and needles with **rows of stomata on the lower surface only.** Pacific silver fir occurs mostly in and west of the coastal mountains, from southeastern AK and northern coastal BC (except Haida Gwaii) to northern CA, and extends inland along the Skeena and Nass drainages of west-central BC.

Notes: Subalpine fir is also known as *A. bifolia* and *A. balsamea* ssp. *lasiocarpa*. • *FNA* splits sub-alpine fir into 2 species: coastal *A. lasiocarpa* and interior *A. bifolia*. There are morphological and chemical differences between the 2 taxa, but intermediate forms prevail in our region. It seems pointless to distinguish the 2 here, so we will stick with *A. lasiocarpa*. • If you find intact cones on the ground, it is probably because squirrels cut them off and dropped them there.

Engelmann Spruce • *Picea engelmannii*

General: Evergreen, coniferous, to 25–50 m tall at moderate elevations, often stunted, shrub-like and twisted near treeline; branches spreading horizontally to somewhat drooping; **twigs usually minutely hairy, with small, peg-like stubs** left by fallen needles; crown narrow, conic.

Bark: Reddish brown to grey, thin, forming loose scales.

Leaves: Needles 2–3 cm long, **4-angled in cross-section, sharply pointy-tipped, rigid, tending to curve upward and toward branch tip,** bluish green, with **rows of tiny, white dots (stomata) on all 4 surfaces.**

Cones: Pollen (male) cones 1–1.5 cm long, dark purple to yellow; seed (female) cones cylindric, 3–7 cm long, reddish to purplish when young, light brown at maturity, **hanging down** on upper branches, with thin, flexible **scales 13–20 mm long, narrowly diamond-shaped to elliptic, tapering to irregularly wavy or jagged tips.**

Where Found: Coniferous forests on mountain slopes and southern plateaus; montane and subalpine zones; frequent and widespread mostly inland in the southern ⅓ of the region, central BC and south-western AB to northern CA and Mexico; cordilleran.

Similar Species: White spruce (p. 41) has **hairless twigs and fan-shaped cone scales, 10–15 mm long,** with **nearly smooth, rounded tips.**

Notes: Engelmann spruce is also known as *Picea glauca* ssp. *engelmannii*.
• Engelmann spruce and white spruce hybridize freely where their ranges over-lap, as in much of central interior British Columbia (about 52°–57° N), where most individual trees have intermediate characteristics and appear hybrid. One can make a strong case for a single species with 2 subspecies, but large portions of the ranges of these widespread trees do not overlap. We follow tradition and *FNA* in recognizing 2 species. Both Engelmann spruce and white spruce also hybridize with Sitka spruce, especially in the mountains and valleys of north-western British Columbia, where coastal and interior environments merge.
• The species is named for George Engelmann (1809–84), a St. Louis physician and botanist. • *Picea* is Latin for "pitchy pine," from *pix* or *picis* for "pitch"; "spruce" could be from the German *spross*, for "a sprout," because *sprossen-bier* (spruce beer) was made from young spruce shoots. Spruce beer helped prevent scurvy among early explorers. Alternatively, "spruce" could come from the Middle English name for Prussia ("Pruce"), whence trees were sold to the English by Hanseatic League merchants, hence "Pruce's tree" and "spruce," "sprws" or "spruce."

White Spruce • *Picea glauca*

General: Evergreen, coniferous, to 25–40 m tall at moderate elevations; branches spreading horizontally to slightly drooping; **twigs hairless,** with small, peg-like stubs left by fallen needles; crown broadly conic to spire-like.

Bark: Grey-brown, thin, forming loose, irregular scales.

Leaves: Needles **1–2 cm long,** 4-angled in cross-section, sharply **pointy-tipped,** rigid, **spreading from all sides of branches (bottlebrush-like),** bluish green, with rows of tiny, white dots (stomata) on all 4 surfaces.

Cones: Pollen (male) cones 1–1.5 cm long, pale red; seed (female) cones cylindric, 2–6 cm long, purplish when young, light brown at maturity, **hanging down** on upper branches, with thin, flexible **scales 10–15 mm long, fan-shaped,** broadest toward the **smooth, rounded tips.**

Where Found: Coniferous forests on mountain slopes and northern plateaus; montane and subalpine zones; frequent and widespread, mostly in the northern inland ¾ of the region, in AK, YT and NT south to MT and WY; transcontinental boreal; typically forms treeline in the far north, both in the mountains and on the arctic slope.

Similar Species: Engelmann spruce (p. 40) is most similar. • **Black spruce** (*P. mariana*) is a transcontinental, essentially boreal species that often occurs with white spruce in the north. It has **minutely rusty-hairy young twigs; small (1–3 cm long), egg-shaped, persistent cones; short (0.6–2 cm long) needles;** and a **bulbous, club-shaped crown.** It typically grows in bogs and muskegs, but north-ward, often occurring in upland boreal forest and forms treeline in the far north, especially on cold aspects and in wet terrain in AK, YT and NT south to central BC and AB. • **Sitka spruce** (*P. sitchensis*) is a coastal species that sometimes forms treeline on exposed, hypermaritime mountains on Haida Gwaii and in south coastal AK. It has 4-angled, **some-what flattened needles,** with conspicuous **white stomatal rows only on the upper surface, long (5–10 cm) cones** and long (15–22 mm) cone scales.

Notes: For First Nations of the taiga, white spruce and black spruce were the most impor-tant plants in everyday life. All parts of the trees were used for food, medicine, shelter, fuel and tools. Teas were made from the cones, twigs and hardened pitch, and were used to treat colds, sore throats and for general health. The inner bark and young branch tips (buds) were eaten for the same purposes. The sticky gum (pitch) and inner bark were applied externally in poultices for sores and wounds. Boughs were used for bedding, roots for making ropes and fishnets, and the wood for building everything from tools and utensils to snowshoes, sleds and shelters. Roofing and shingles were made from the bark, with pitch for waterproofing. Southern groups used white spruce in similar ways, though they had a greater choice of tree species for "apps."

black spruce   Sitka spruce

Mountain Hemlock
Tsuga mertensiana

General: Evergreen, coniferous, to 30–40 m tall, often stunted, shrub-like and twisted near treeline; branches arranged in "sprays," spreading horizontally or somewhat drooping but tending to have an upward sweep at tips, the leading shoot somewhat drooping; **twigs roughened by small, peg-like stubs** left by fallen needles; crown broadly and irregularly conic.

Bark: Reddish brown to grey, thick, ridged, fissured.

Leaves: Needles 1–3 cm long, **blunt, spreading in all directions from twigs (bottlebrush-like),** thus the sprays not flattened, bluish green, **both surfaces with inconspicuous rows of tiny, white dots (stomata).**

Cones: Pollen (male) cones bluish; seed (female) cones cylindric, 3–6 cm long, purplish when young, brown when mature, with **broadly fan-shaped scales** 8–15 mm long.

Where Found: Coniferous forests on mountain slopes; lowland (in bogs) to alpine zones; frequent and widespread in the coastal mountains from southern AK to CA, sporadic inland; Pacific maritime endemic.

Similar Species: Western hemlock (*T. heterophylla*) has **smaller (1.5–3 cm long), egg-shaped cones** and **needles in flattened sprays.** It does not usually grow at high elevations, but when it does, it can appear somewhat like mountain hemlock.

Notes: Western hemlock is the state tree of Washington. • *Tsuga* means "hemlock" and is the Japanese vernacular name for their native hemlocks. • *Mertensiana* honours K.H. Mertens (1796–1830), a German naturalist who accompanied Count F.P. Lütke's expedition on the corvette *Senjavin*; he discovered mountain hemlock at Sitka, Alaska, in 1827.

Alpine Larch, Subalpine Larch • *Larix lyallii*

General: Deciduous, coniferous, to 10–25 m tall, usually erect, occasionally stunted and shrub-like; trunk short, stout, usually straight; branches spreading horizontally, occasionally drooping; **young twigs densely woolly-hairy; crowns sparse, broad, irregular,** with gnarled, unevenly spaced branches.

Bark: Yellowish grey, thin and smooth when young; in age, dark reddish brown, fissured and scaly.

Leaves: Needles deciduous, 4-angled in cross-section, in **bunches of 30–40 on twig spurs (short shoots)** or singly on current year's twigs, 2–3.5 cm long, light green turning **golden yellow in autumn.**

Cones: Pollen (male) cones yellowish; **seed (female) cones ellipsoid to egg-shaped, upright,** purplish when young, brown at maturity, **2.5–5 cm long,** on curved stalks; **scales rounded, woolly-hairy on lower surface, subtended by awn-tipped bracts that protrude well beyond scales;** seeds small (body 3 mm long), yellow to purple, with wing 6 mm long.

Where Found: Rocky slopes and bedrock benches with thin, cold soils, gravelly ridges and talus, especially on north aspects where snow falls early and stays late; subalpine and lower alpine zones; frequent but patchily distributed primarily in the southeastern part of the region, south-central and south-eastern BC and southwestern AB to north-central WA, northern ID and western MT; cordilleran.

Similar Species: Tamarack (*L. laricina*) sometimes forms alpine treeline in the far north, especially on calcium-rich substrates. It has **shorter needles (1–2 cm long)** and **seed cones (1–2 cm long)** and hairless twigs, as well as a transcontinental, boreal distribution.

Notes: Larches are our only native conifers to shed their needles in autumn. In the case of alpine larch, which reaches higher eleva-tions than other timberline trees, the ecological interpretation is that the energetic cost of replacing the needles every year is outweighed by the benefits of avoiding the stress (mechanical, moisture) of keeping needles through the winter. Moreover, larch needles have a greater surface-to-mass ratio than evergreens, and more of each needle is exposed to light. Larches have a greater rate of photosynthesis, perhaps twice that of evergreen conifers in com-parable habitats, but they need lots of light and ample moisture—they lose more water through evapotrans-piration than do evergreens—otherwise they get outcompeted. • *Larix* is the classical name for larch; *lyallii* honours David Lyall (1817–95), a Scottish surgeon and naturalist who worked in North America. The name "larch" may be derived from the wood's use in building and carpentry, from the Latin *lar*, "a house," and the Old Norse and Russian *lar*, "a chest."

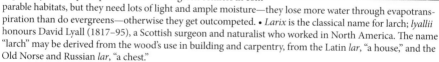

Whitebark Pine • *Pinus albicaulis*

General: Evergreen, coniferous, to 20 m but seldom more than 15 m tall, often stunted and shrub-like; trunk sometimes straight and erect but more often twisted and contorted, or with several twisted trunks; often branched from the base, the branches spreading to ascending; twigs stout, often glandular-hairy; crown rounded, irregularly spreading or sprawling.

Bark: Whitish to pale grey, thin and smooth when young; in age, grey-brown and platy with narrow fissures.

Leaves: Needles 5 per bundle, mostly ascending and upcurved, 3–7 cm long, stiff, yellow-green, clustered toward branch tips.

Cones: Pollen (male) cones reddish; **seed (female) cones remaining on tree and opened by animals or disintegrating when mature, rarely falling intact to the ground,** broadly egg-shaped, **4–8 cm long,** purplish becoming brown, often very pitchy, unstalked or nearly so; **scales thick, pointy-tipped, without prickles;** seeds large (7–11 mm long), brown, wingless.

Where Found: Exposed, windswept ridges and rock outcrops, rocky slopes with thin soils, talus, colluvial/fluvial fans and occasionally sandy-gravelly river terraces; montane (rarely) to alpine zones; frequent but typically scattered mostly inland in the southern ½ of the region; central BC and west-central AB, from about 56° N south in the Coast-Cascade (and Olympic) Mtns through WA and OR to CA; also to ID and NV and in the Rockies to MT and WY; cordilleran.

Similar Species: Limber pine (p. 45) has seed cones 7–15 cm long that open while still attached to the tree.

Notes: Whitebark pine is currently undergoing a worrying decline in our high-elevation forests, a sobering example of the ripple effect of environmental change. The species is not regenerating very successfully because of 1) the widespread mortality of young trees because of the introduced white pine blister rust (*Cronartium ribicola*); 2) the collateral mortality of mature, cone-bearing trees from bark beetle attack; 3) more frequent drought in some parts of its range; and 4) fewer fires that might provide suitable sites for seedlings. It could be that warmer winter temperatures at high elevations have enabled mountain pine beetle (*Dendroctonus ponderosae*) outbreaks in lodgepole pine stands to spread up into parts of the whitebark pine range where previously this had not occurred or attacks had not been so numerous. • Whitebark pine has coevolved with Clark's nutcracker (*Nucifraga columbiana*). The nutcrackers tear the cones apart in autumn, eat some of the seeds and store the excess in ground caches for winter use. Seeds cached in favourable sites and not retrieved may then germinate in spring. This is the chief mechanism of seed dispersal for whitebark pine, thus we have a mutualism between a conifer and a bird. • Some southern interior BC First Nations peoples harvested the cones in early autumn. They crushed the seeds and mixed them with saskatoon berries for eating or pounded them to make a type of flour. To open the scales and soften the seeds, they roasted the cones in a pit overnight or in the coals of a fire before extracting the seeds. The inner bark (cambium) was scraped off and eaten by some groups, and the fibrous roots were used to weave watertight containers and canoes. • *Albicaulis* means "white stem."

Limber Pine
Pinus flexilis

General: Evergreen, coniferous, to 25 m but usually to 9–15 m tall in our region, often stunted or deformed and shrub-like; trunk sometimes straight and erect but often twisted and contorted, usually short, stout and strongly tapered; branches large, plume-like, spreading to ascending; crown broadly rounded, often asymmetric.

Bark: Light grey, thin, and smooth when young; in age, dark brown and furrowed between scaly ridges and rectangular plates.

Leaves: Needles 5 per bundle, spreading to ascending, slightly upcurved, 3–7 cm long, stiff, dark green, crowded toward ends of branchlets.

Cones: Seed (female) cones opening unaided and shedding seeds while attached to the tree, cylindric-oval, 7–15 cm long, straw-coloured, short-stalked, blunt; scales thick, blunt; seeds large (10–15 mm long), reddish brown, wingless.

Where Found: Rocky slopes, outcrops and ridges, and coniferous forests; montane to alpine zones; frequent but typically scattered in the southeastern corner of the region, mostly in the Rockies, in southwestern AB and adjacent BC through MT, WY and ID to CA, AZ and NM; southern cordilleran.

Similar Species: Whitebark pine (p. 44) has similar form, foliage and nut-like, wingless seeds, but its **seed cones are 2–3 times shorter** than those of limber pine and **are usually opened on the tree by animals.**

Notes: The large seeds are eaten by First Nations peoples as well as by other mammals and Clark's nutcrackers.
• Limber pine is so called because it is "limber" or flexible, hence also *flexilis*. The pliant branches and boughs can bend without breaking, the better to endure heavy wind and snow.

Lodgepole Pine • *Pinus contorta* var. *latifolia*

General: Evergreen, coniferous, to 30–40 m tall; trunk usually straight with even taper, but often stunted, deformed and shrub-like near treeline; upper branches mostly spreading, lower branches often descending; twigs slender, red-brown; crown short, open, pyramidal, rounded.

Bark: Cinnamon brown to grey, thin, usually separating into small, loose, scales, sometimes persistent and fissured.

Leaves: Needles 2 per bundle, 4–8 cm long, yellow-green.

Cones: Pollen (male) cones orange-red, 0.5–1.5 cm long; **seed (female) cones maturing in 2 years, then shedding seeds or remaining closed, hanging on tree for several years,** broadly oval to nearly spheric when open, often lopsided, 2–6 cm long, tawny to red-brown; scales prickle-tipped; seeds with body about 5 mm long and large wing 10–14 mm long.

Where Found: Common and widespread in coniferous and mixedwood forests, on a wide variety of sites from rock outcrops and gravelly terraces to deep, rich soils and peat bogs; montane (primarily) and subalpine zones; throughout the southern ¾ of the region in and east of the Coast-Cascade Mtns, southern YT and southwestern NT plus a little bit of northern Southeast AK (around Skagway and Haines), through BC and AB to OR, UT and CO; cordilleran.

 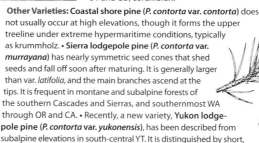

Other Varieties: Coastal shore pine (*P. contorta* var. *contorta*) does not usually occur at high elevations, though it forms the upper treeline under extreme hypermaritime conditions, typically as krummholz. • Sierra lodgepole pine (*P. contorta* var. *murrayana*) has nearly symmetric seed cones that shed seeds and fall off soon after maturing. It is generally larger than var. *latifolia*, and the main branches ascend at the tips. It is frequent in montane and subalpine forests of the southern Cascades and Sierras, and southernmost WA through OR and CA. • Recently, a new variety, **Yukon lodge-pole pine** (*P. contorta* var. *yukonensis*), has been described from subalpine elevations in south-central YT. It is distinguished by short,

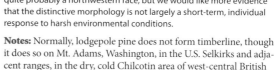

squat stature; double stems that are forked above; large, long lower branches; frequent 3-needled bundles; and furrowed, platy bark, among other features, including some chemical and genetic evidence. There is quite probably a northwestern race, but we would like more evidence that the distinctive morphology is not largely a short-term, individual response to harsh environmental conditions.

Notes: Normally, lodgepole pine does not form timberline, though it does so on Mt. Adams, Washington, in the U.S. Selkirks and adjacent ranges, in the dry, cold Chilcotin area of west-central British Columbia and in the northern Canadian Rockies (e.g., Stone Mountain Provincial Park in northeastern British Columbia). • Many lodgepole pine populations have cones sealed by resin that must be melted by fire or heat before the seeds can be released. The cones that persist for years on trees or on the ground can build up a bank of seeds until a disturbance (usually a wildfire) provides suitable conditions for seed release and germination in sufficient numbers that dense monocultures ("doghair" stands) often develop. • Lodgepole pine is susceptible to damage from many diseases and insects, most notably the mountain pine beetle (*Dendroctonus ponderosae*). Extensive, mature, even-aged pine stands are especially prone to attack by bark beetles and to big wildfires, stand-replacing disturbances that renew the cycle of this early successional, shade-intolerant species.

Yellow-cedar, Yellow-cypress, Alaska Cedar
Xanthocyparis nootkatensis

General: Evergreen, coniferous, usually 20–40 m tall at moderate elevations, occurring in dwarf form in boggy or high-elevation elfinwood, and as krummholz (twisted, much-branched and shrub-like) in open bogs and near treeline; **branches long, slender, drooping, the branchlets small and strongly drooping;** crown conic.

Bark: Greyish brown, irregularly ridged and fissured, in vertical strips.

Leaves: Scale-like in 4 rows, opposite, somewhat overlapping, 1.5–3 mm long, **bluish green,** with sharp-pointed, spreading tips.

Cones: Pollen (male) cones about 4 mm long; **immature seed (female) cones round, bumpy, light green "berries"** about 1 cm across, covered with a white, waxy powder, **ripening to brown cones** with 4–6 woody, mushroom-shaped scales; seeds winged.

Where Found: Moist to wet coniferous forests on mountain slopes and rocky ridges, gullies, avalanche tracks, bog-forests and coastal muskeg; lowland to subalpine zones; frequent in and west of the coastal mountains, from southeastern AK to northern CA; rare and disjunct inland in southeastern BC and northeastern OR; Pacific maritime endemic.

Similar Species: Take care to distinguish yellow-cedar from rare high-elevation, even krummholz individuals of western redcedar, which has flattened (rather than rounded) leaf-bearing twigs and football-shaped (not spheric or cubic) cones.

Notes: Yellow-cedar is also known as *Chamaecyparis nootkatensis* and *Callitropsis nootkatensis.* • This species is aromatic but very differently so than its better-known cousin western redcedar (*Thuja plicata*). When crushed, the foliage has a peculiar mildewy smell, and the inner bark and wood smell like raw potatoes. • Very long-lived, rot-resistant and a tough survivor in harsh environments, yellow-cedar is nevertheless vulnerable to frost. Its widespread dieback in southeastern Alaska and on British Columbia's northern coast appears to be attributable to a type of freezing injury to tree roots. Susceptibility of the roots to freezing damage is related to reduced protective snowpack and premature "dehardening" in spring. This could be an example of a general phenomenon—paradoxically, climate warming may actually increase the risk of frost damage to plants. Mild winters and warm, early springs can induce premature plant development, resulting in the exposure of tender parts to subsequent late-season frosts. • Yellow-cedar was formerly called *Chamaecyparis,* Greek for "false cedar." The rationale for the new name is that this species' closest relationship is not with *Chamaecyparis,* but with a relictual species, *Xanthocyparis* (*Callitropsis*) *vietnamensis,* endemic to the mountains of northern Vietnam. This is thought to be one of several conifer lineages that long ago spanned the northern Pacific Rim and subsequently retreated to mere echoes of their former greater ranges. The literal translation of the former full name is "Nootka false-cypress," so called because the cones resemble a smaller version of those of true cypresses (*Cupressus* spp.). "Cedar" is from the Greek *kedros,* meaning either "a cedar" or "a juniper"; the common name refers to the yellow colour of the wood.

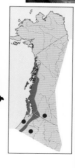

DRAWING THE LINE

The **alpine zone** is the mountainous area from (and including) **treeline** to the summits of the high peaks. The term **treeline** designates the upper limit of the occurrence of tree species, regardless of their stature, whereas **timberline** refers to the upper limit of forest, of continuous cover of upright trees 3 m or more in height. In some places, the boundary between trees (usually conifers) at lower elevations and low, shrubby or herbaceous vegetation higher up is sharp and distinct. But often, the boundary is indistinct or fragmented because the transition from forest to tundra is broad and gradual. With increasing elevation, tree cover gradually shortens, and the forest thins out into parkland, with trees in isolated clumps and irregular, small patches (**tree islands**). The tree clumps form a mosaic with subalpine heath, meadow, shrubland, grassland and wetland vegetation. Some call the dwarfed forests or clumps of stunted trees **elfinwood**. Yet higher, trees become increasingly stunted, twisted, deformed and shrub-like. Such clumps, belts or, ultimately, cushions are called **krummholz** (German for "crooked wood") or, colloquially, **shintangle**. According to Ben Gadd in *Handbook of the Canadian Rockies*, krummholz refers to genetic, not environmental, dwarfing, as in the Siberian dwarf pine (*Pinus pumila*). The correct word for our stunted, shrubby, twisted trees at treeline is apparently "kruppelholtz," but it hasn't caught on.

Lake O'Hara, Canadian Rockies, BC

subalpine parkland, Skeena Mountains, BC

The **montane zone** in northwestern North America includes all mid-elevation lands, mostly continuously forested. The **subalpine zone** occurs above the montane zone and below the upper limit of upright trees, mostly conifers in our region, though trembling aspen (*Populus tremuloides*) and even black cottonwood (*Populus trichocarpa*) occasionally form treeline here and there. The subalpine zone includes continuous forest in its lower portions and parkland in its upper ecotonal portion. Above the subalpine zone is the **alpine zone**, by definition treeless, though tree species are common in lower parts of the zone, in stunted or krummholz form. We consider krummholz to be alpine vegetation, and krummholz formations to mark the beginning of the alpine zone.

stunted limber pine (*Pinus flexilis*), Beartooth Plateau, WY

Another kind of treeline occurs at the boundary between montane forest and dry grassland or shrubland at low elevations in the semiarid, southern interior part of our region. Similarly, in some high, wide, northern valleys subject to cold-air ponding, a mosaic of subalpine grasslands, shrublands and wetlands occupies the valley bottoms, a skirt of forest covers lower slopes and treeless vegetation occurs at upper elevations. Thus, in both landscapes, a "double treeline" can develop.

The **arctic timberline**, also known as the "forest-tundra zone," forms a broad, low-elevation transition between the boreal forest and arctic tundra. Northward in our region, it becomes increasingly difficult to distinguish between "arctic" and "alpine," especially in far northern Alaska and Yukon. Yet even at relatively low elevations on the North Slope, there is usually sufficient relief, complex terrain and abundant microhabitats that the vegetation has more in common with the alpine zone than the arctic tundra.

krummholz subalpine fir (*Abies lasiocarpa*), French Peak, BC

arctic-alpine treeline, Richardson Mountains, YT (below)

krummholz whitebark pine (*Pinus albicaulis*), Cathedral Lakes Park, BC

Shrubs

alpine-azalea (*Kalmia procumbens*), Cariboo Mountains, BC

SHRUBS (Including Dwarf Woody Plants)

We will, for the purposes of this field guide, define shrubs as woody, usually multi-stemmed plants less than 3 m tall when mature. Dwarf shrubs, which are woody or mostly woody plants less than 20–30 cm tall and which sometimes do not look much like shrubs (e.g., mountain-avens, crowberry), are also included here.

The shrubs of northwestern high elevations represent several plant families and genera; we have organized them by major plant families and by similar species within families. After starting with common juniper (*Juniperus communis*), a conifer, we treat the catkin bearers: Sitka alder (*Alnus viridis* ssp. *sinuata*), low birches (*Betula*) and the willows (*Salix*). There are many willows, some of which are difficult to tell apart, but do not be alarmed. It helps to partition them into dwarf vs. erect shrubs, then into those with hairy vs. hairless ovaries and capsules, and finally to examine the leaves. Following the willows is the rose family, a diverse assemblage of mostly very distinctive genera and species. Next, a handful of gooseberries and currants, tasty and not. Finally, we describe shrubs of the heather family, as well as the somewhat similar diapensia. Note that most of our shrubby species occur in 3 families: willow (difficult to sort out), rose (distinctive genera) and heather (easy to sort out).

The dominant shrubs of our alplands are mostly willows and heather-family species. The willows and their frequent consort, scrub birch (*Betula glandulosa*), have deciduous leaves, whereas the shrubs in the heather family are a mix of evergreens, such as the mountain-heathers (*Cassiope*, *Harrimanella* and *Phyllodoce*) and crowberry (*Empetrum nigrum*), and deciduous plants, such as white-flowered rhododendron (*Rhododendron albiflorum*) and several blueberry and huckleberry (*Vaccinium*) species, and alpine bearberry (*Arctous*). Generally speaking, it is not a good idea to be an evergreen in the alpine unless you stay very close to the ground or can be assured of snow cover. Yes, evergreen leaves conserve nutrients because you don't have to replace all your leaves every year in a very short growing season. But stick your head up, and the ever-present wind will abrade you with snow in winter and can quickly reduce core temperature and induce moisture stress, especially if you've broken dormancy.

The reproductive strategies of high-elevation shrubs reflect both the available vectors of flower pollination and seed dispersal and the evolutionary heritage of the plants. Wind is capricious and indiscriminate, but the alpine is reliably windy. Wind pollination and dispersal are effective strategies in such open, non-forested environments. Common juniper, the catkin-bearing shrubs and shrubby species of sagewort (*Artemisia* spp.) are well adapted for both mechanisms. The rest of our alpine shrubs are pollinated by animals, mostly insects, except for the wind-pollinated crowberry. Note that some willows such as arctic willow (*Salix arctica*) can have it both ways—the catkins are pre-adapted for wind pollination, but the plant also produces flowers that, en masse, are very showy and produce lots of pollen and nectar, thereby attracting numerous insect visitors.

In contrast, there is more of a mix between wind and animal dispersal of seeds in subalpine and alpine shrubs. The majority exhibit adaptations such as small, light, winged, hairy or plumed seeds for wind dispersal, but there is also a sizeable minority of species that have fleshy fruits (mostly berries) adapted for dispersal by birds and mammals. This seems, however, to be the case only for shrubs and is perhaps a legacy of the forest origins of most of the fleshy-fruited genera (*Vaccinium*, *Gaultheria*, *Ribes* and *Sorbus*) that have shouldered their way up into high elevations.

Key to the Shrubs

1a. Erect shrubs, usually >40 cm tall 2

    2a. Leaves evergreen or persistent for several years 3

        3a. Leaves stiff, needle-like or awl-shaped, sharp-tipped; producing solitary, bluish or greenish, berry-like female cones . . . . ***Juniperus communis* (p. 53)**

        3b. Leaves leathery, lance-elliptic, with rolled margins; producing a few capsules with numerous tiny seeds . . . . ***Rhododendron lapponicum* (p. 88, taller lower-elevation form)**

    2b. Leaves deciduous, neither needle-like nor grey-hairy and wedge-shaped 4

        4a. Flowers and fruits in catkins 5

            5a. Fruit a capsule containing numerous seeds, each bearing a cottony tuft of hairs; winter buds covered by 1 scale . . . . ***Salix* (pp. 56–65)**

            5b. Fruit a samara (single-seeded, somewhat winged, hairless nutlet); winter buds with 2 or more scales 6

                6a. Female catkins cone-like, becoming woody, persistent long after seeds released; leaves oval to elliptic, finely sawtoothed; twigs sticky when young but not densely glandular . . . ***Alnus viridis* (p. 55)**

                6b. Female catkins not cone-like, disintegrating when mature; leaves oval to round or kidney-shaped, coarsely blunt- or round-toothed; twigs often densely glandular . . ***Betula glandulosa*, *B. nana* (p. 54)**

4b. Flowers and fruits not in catkins **7**

  7a. Leaves pinnately compound, with 5 or more leaflets **8**

    8a. Leaves large, divided into 7–13 well-spaced leaflets; flowers white, small, numerous in clusters at branch ends; fruit berry-like, orange to red . . . . *Sorbus* (p. 67)

    8b. Leaves smaller, divided into 3–7 closely clustered leaflets; flowers yellow, large, solitary or few in clusters near branch tips; fruit a cluster of dry achenes . . . . *Dasiphora fruticosa* (p. 71)

  7b. Leaves simple, not compound **9**

    9a. Fruits dry achenes in small heads

    . . . .*Artemisia, Ericameria* (see aster family in Wildflowers section, **pp. 348–354**)

    9b. Fruits berries, generally not persistent through winter **10**

      10a. Leaves palmately lobed, maple-leaf-like; flowers saucer-shaped . . . . *Ribes* (p. 72)

      10b. Leaves unlobed, oval; flowers urn-shaped . . . . *Vaccinium* (pp. 81–83)

    9c. Fruits dry capsules or pod-like follicles, persistent **11**

      11a. Flowers small, numerous in dense clusters at branch ends, ovaries 5 per flower; fruits pod-like follicles **12**

        12a. Flowers pink; follicles hairless; from southern BC south . . . . . *Spiraea densiflora* (p. 68)

        12b. Flowers white; follicles hairy; from northern BC north . . . . *Spiraea stevenii* (p. 68)

      11b. Flowers solitary at branch ends or few to several in clusters below topmost leaves; ovary 1 per flower; fruits capsules **13**

        13a. Flowers copper- or salmon-coloured to greenish orange **14**

          14a. Flowers few to several in clusters below uppermost leaves, small (4–5 mm across), urn-shaped, the petals 4, united most of their length; twigs forking at tip like spokes of an umbrella, skunky when crushed; leaves glandular-hairy; coastal and interior . . . . *Menziesia ferruginea* (p. 87)

          14b. Flowers solitary at branch ends, large (to 3 cm across), wheel-shaped, the petals 5, not united, wide-spreading; leaves hairless, shiny; coastal . . . . . *Elliottia pyroliflora* (p. 87)

        13b. Flowers white, large, 1.5–2.5 cm across, in axillary clusters of 1–4 below topknot of leaves; leaves sparsely rusty-hairy . . . . *Rhododendron albiflorum* (p. 88)

1b. Low, depressed or dwarf shrubs, usually <20–30 cm tall **15**

  15a. Leaves evergreen or persistent for several years **16**

    16a. Leaves deeply twice dissected in 3s into linear, pointed segments, mostly in thick tufts at the base . . . . *Luetkea pectinata* (p. 69)

    16b. Leaves not deeply divided into lobes or segments but margins may be toothed **17**

      17a. Leaves linear, often needle-like **18**

        18a. Leaves opposite or in whorls **19**

          19a. Leaves in whorls of 3, stiff, sharp-pointed; fruits bluish to greenish, berry-like cones . . . . *Juniperus communis* (p. 53)

          19b. Leaves in irregular whorls of 4, rather soft, blunt; fruits black "berries" . . . . *Empetrum nigrum* (p. 75)

        18b. Leaves alternate **20**

          20a. Leaves linear to lance-elliptic, mostly >10 mm long . . . .*Rhododendron tomentosum, R. columbianum* (p. 89)

          20b. Leaves linear to needle-like, mostly <12 mm long **21**

            21a. Leaves grooved beneath **22**

              22a. Leaves 3–7 mm long; flowers inconspicuous, reddish purple; fruits berry-like . . . . *Empetrum nigrum* (p. 75)

              22b. Leaves 4–15 mm long; flowers showy, bell- or flask-shaped, pink, yellowish, or bluish to purple; fruits capsules . . . . *Phyllodoce* (p. 76)

            21b. Leaves rounded beneath, to 5 mm long; flowers broadly bell-shaped, white to pinkish . . . . *Harrimanella stelleriana* (p. 77)

17b. Leaves broader, not needle-like **23**

  23a. Cushion-like shrublets; leaves alternate but crowded, overlapping or tufted; petals not fused; southern **24**

    24a. Leaves overlapping along crowded branches, often hardened and crusted; flowers single at branch ends, pink or purplish. ***Kelseya uniflora*** **(p. 69)**

    24b. Leaves in basal tufts; flowers white, in spike-like clusters atop long stalks . . . . ***Petrophytum*** **(p. 69)**

  23b. Plants not cushion-like shrublets or if so, northern species; petals fused at least toward base. **25**

    25a. Leaves opposite **26**

      26a. Leaves toothed; flowers bilaterally symmetric . . . . ***Penstemon*** (see figwort family in Wildflowers section, **pp. 283–287**)

      26b. Leaves not toothed; flowers radially symmetric **27**

        27a. Leaves scale-like, <6 mm long, overlapping, usually in 4 ranks on stem . . . . ***Cassiope*** **(p. 77)**

        27b. Leaves not scale-like, mostly >5 mm long, not 4-ranked **28**

          28a. Leaves narrowly oblong to elliptic; flowers pink, stamens 5 or 10, attached to base of ovary. **29**

            29a. Leaves mostly 10–20 mm long; stamens 10; low, spreading to erect shrub . . . . ***Kalmia microphylla*** var. ***microphylla*** **(p. 78)**

            29b. Leaves 3–8 mm long; stamens 5; prostrate, mat-forming shrub . . . . ***Kalmia procumbens*** **(p. 78)**

          28b. Leaves oval to spoon-shaped; flowers usually whitish, stamens 5; forming low cushions or mats. ***Diapensia obovata*** **(p. 73)**

    25b. Leaves alternate **30**

      30a. Leaves elliptic-oblong, glandular above, brownish-scaly below; flowers bright purple; fruits dry capsules . . . . ***Rhododendron lapponicum*** **(p. 88)**

      30b. Leaves not glandular or brownish-scaly; flowers white to pinkish; fruits berries or berry-like **31**

        31a. Leaves shiny and green above, paler and brown-dotted (short, whiskery, glandular hairs) below; corolla 4-lobed . . . . . . ***Vaccinium vitis-idaea*** **(p. 81)**

        31b. Leaves not brown-dotted below; corolla 5-lobed. **32**

          32a. Leaves oval to elliptic, somewhat pointy-tipped; flowers bell-shaped . . . . ***Gaultheria*** **(p. 79)**

          32b. Leaves narrowly egg- to spoon-shaped, rounded to blunt at tip; flowers urn-shaped . . . . ***Arctostaphylos uva-ursi*** **(p. 80)**

15b. Leaves deciduous or at least dying at the end of one growing season **33**

  33a. Flowers numerous in heads; low, compact shrubs with greyish-hairy stems and leaves **34**

    34a. Leaves deeply divided or dissected, with sagebrush odour . . . . ***Artemisia alaskana, A. frigida*** (see aster family in Wildflowers section, **pp. 353, 351**)

    34b. Leaves sometimes wavy-margined but not divided or dissected, lacking sagebrush odour . . . . ***Ericameria*** (see aster family in Wildflowers section, **p. 354**)

  33b. Flowers not in heads; plants otherwise **35**

    35a. Flowers and fruits numerous in catkins; winter buds covered by 1 scale. . . . . . . ***Salix*** **(pp. 56–65)**

    35b. Flowers solitary or a few in clusters; winter buds covered by more than 1 scale. **36**

      36a. Fruits berry-like. **37**

        37a. Leaf margins smooth or sawtoothed; ovary inferior, forming a berry crowned by the sepals or calyx teeth . . . . ***Vaccinium*** **(pp. 81–83)**

        37b. Leaf margins scalloped with rounded teeth; ovary superior, forming a berry cupped by the sepals . . . . ***Arctous*** **(p. 79)**

      36b. Fruits dry. **38**

        38a. Leaves without teeth; flowers purple; fruit a capsule . . . . ***Therorhodion*** **(p. 88)**

        38b. Leaves blunt-toothed or toothless; flowers white or yellow; fruit a cluster of achenes with long, feathery styles. . . . . ***Dryas*** **(pp. 70–71)**

Common Juniper • *Juniperus communis*

General: Prostrate to sprawling or ascending, multi-stemmed, 0.5–3 m long, usually less than 1 m tall; bark very thin, reddish brown, older bark shredding and scaly.

Leaves: Stiff, sharp, awl-shaped needles, evergreen, jointed to the stem, mostly in whorls of 3, 0.5–1.5 cm long, grooved and glaucous on upper surface, dark green on lower surface.

Cones: Seed (female) cones fleshy, berry-like, egg-shaped to globular, 0.5–1 cm long, green in first year, ripening in second year to bluish black; seed and pollen cones on separate plants.

Where Found: Dry rocky, gravelly or sandy open slopes, bluffs, open forests, wet maritime peatlands, heathlands and tundra; lowland to alpine zones; common and widespread throughout region; circumpolar.

Varieties: Highly variable in both growth form and habitat. *FNA* delineated vars. *montana* and *depressa* in our region. A more recent revision based on morphology and DNA proposes that there are 3 varieties in the northwest: the coastal peatland **var. *charlottensis*** and the more widespread **vars.**

depressa and **sibirica** (var. *montana*). Our high-elevation plants are most likely not var. *charlottensis* and are more likely the mat-forming var. *sibirica* than the sometimes spreading-ascending var. *depressa*, but this morphological distinction is not compelling.

Notes: The Dena'ina and Gwich'in liked to burn branches of this shrub on the fire; the incense-like aroma was said to be good for colds. A tea made from boiled branches and berries was also drunk for colds, sore throats and respiratory ailments. The Inupiat of northwestern Alaska suck on one berry per day or boil the berries to make tea and drink some every day to help avoid or cure colds or indigestion and to treat urinary infections. Some Alaskan peoples and the Haida used the tea to treat urinary problems, but it was taken with caution because it could cause miscarriages. Some Gwich'in say that juniper can be used as a laxative and for bathing. • *Juniperus* is the classical name for this plant; *communis* means "common." • Juniper is an attractive garden ornamental. The berries are used to flavour gin and sauerkraut.

Scrub Birch, Dwarf Birch, Glandular Birch • *Betula glandulosa*

General: Upright, **ascending or spreading** (dwarfed at high elevations and far-northern latitudes), 0.3–2 m tall, with one or several main stems; young twigs densely **glandular-warty** (the crystalline glands look like octopus suckers) and short-hairy; bark grey or reddish brown.

Leaves: Alternate, deciduous, **oval to circular,** round at tip, **wedge-shaped to rounded at the base,** 1–3 cm long, rather thick and leathery, often gland dotted; margins coarsely **blunt-toothed;** upper surface dark green and hairless, lower surface paler and often sparsely hairy.

Flowers: Tiny, unisexual, lacking sepals and petals, numerous in **upright, cylindric catkins** that flower before or as leaves emerge; male and female catkins on the same plant, 1–2.5 cm long; ovary 1; stamens 2.

Fruits: Nutlets small, 1-seeded, with narrow wings; catkins disintegrating at maturity.

Where Found: Peatlands, streambanks, moist to dry open forests, gravelly terraces, rocky slopes, timberline thickets, heathlands and tundra; lowland (arctic coast) to alpine zones; common and widespread in the north, infrequent southward; widespread in boreal-subarctic North America.

Similar Species: Arctic dwarf birch (*B. nana*) is shorter (to 1 m), **often sprawling,** with smaller (0.5–1.5 cm long), circular to kidney-shaped leaves, **often broader than long, squared-off to heart-shaped at the base,** and sticky but sparsely glandular-warty, with sparsely hairy twigs. Ours is **ssp. *exilis*,** an amphiberingian plant mostly of arctic and subarctic tundra. Some taxonomists consider *B. glandulosa* and *B. nana* to be different forms of the same species. Intermediates are common where their ranges overlap, as in northern AK, YT and NT.

Notes: The leaves turn yellow or orange to coppery red in autumn, enflaming entire mountainsides in the North. • The Dena'ina placed the branches beneath food on the ground to prevent it from getting dirty or on their backs when carrying meat to prevent their clothes from being stained. The Gwich'in report using the branches as flooring inside their tents. The Inupiat of northwestern Alaska picked the buds just as they opened in early spring and soaked them in oil, grease or, more recently, alcohol to make a tincture for salves for skin burns, cuts, diaper rash, toothaches, sore throats and nasal congestion. • *Betula* means "pitch." The tree was so-called by Pliny the Elder because bitumen was distilled from the bark. People in Roman Britain used this bitumen to glue their broken clay pots back together. Birchbark tar was also used as a chewing gum for cleaning teeth. *Glandulosa* means "full of glands" or "glandular." • In northern parts of its range, scrub birch reproduces almost entirely vegetatively, by layering, and produces fewer male and female catkins, fewer flowers and less pollen than it does farther south, where it reproduces largely by sexual means.

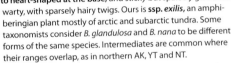

Sitka Alder, Slide Alder
Alnus viridis ssp. *sinuata*

General: Ascending (prostrate at high elevations), **coarse**, 1–5 m tall, usually with several stems; twigs sticky when young; bark yellowish brown or grey, mostly smooth.

Leaves: Alternate, deciduous, oval to elliptic, 2–10 cm long, pointed at tip, **paper-thin; margins shallowly lobed (sinuate) and finely sawtoothed;** upper surface hairless, usually shiny, lower surface hairy in the angles between veins, shiny and slightly sticky at least when young; **leaf buds pointed, unstalked** or nearly so.

Flowers: Tiny, unisexual, lacking sepals and petals, numerous in catkins that flower as leaves emerge; **male and female catkins on same plant; female catkins cone-like,** stalked, persistent, in clusters of 3–8; male catkins unstalked, drooping, in clusters of 2–4; ovary 1 with 2 linear stigmas; stamens 3–5.

Fruits: Samaras small, 1-seeded, **broadly winged;** seed cones 1–2 cm long, egg-shaped.

Where Found: Moist mountain slopes, streambanks, avalanche tracks, timberline thickets, open boreal forests, peatlands, heathlands and tundra; lowland to alpine zones; common and widespread (though most occurrences are not alpine) in the northwestern part of the region; frequent but more localized southward; cordilleran.

Subspecies: The taxonomy of this complex of shrubby alders has flip-flopped several times over the past several decades, and we are not much wiser for it. **Ssp. *sinuata*** has light or yellowish green leaves with doubly sawtoothed margins and tends toward a more coastal distribution, becoming general south of 55° N. According to *FNA*, the amphiberingian **ssp. *fruticosa* (Siberian alder)** also occurs in our region but not at high elevations, and has thicker, darker green, mostly singly sawtoothed leaves. Beyond the region, **ssp. *crispa* (green alder)** extends from the Rockies across boreal eastern North America.

Notes: Sitka alder is also known as *A. crispa* var. *sinuata* and *A. sinuata*. • The Dene made a medicinal tea from the green catkins to treat venereal disease in men and used a root decoction to ease menstrual cramps. The Cree reportedly boiled the stems to prepare an emetic for an upset stomach. The Gwich'in made medicinal preparations from boiled bark for treating skin sores, eczema, insect bites, sunburns and rashes. The liquid would be applied externally to soothe aching joints or drunk to ease a stomach ache. Many First Nations groups made dyes by boiling bark and stem pieces, wove baskets from the bark and burned the wood for fuel and to smoke salmon and meat. For the Dena'ina, this species was particularly important for making shelters where there was not much other wood around. They would stick one stem in the ground and make a circle of other stems around it, then bend them and tie them to the centre stem to provide a framework for their skin tents. They also used alder stems to

make snares, fish traps, digging and bark-peeling sticks, and even snowshoes. • *Alnus* is the classical Latin name for alder; *viridis* means "green," and *sinuata* means "with a wavy margin," referring to the leaves. • The name "alder" comes from the Anglo-Saxon *alor* or *aler*, which is from the same root as the Old High German *elo* or *elawer*, meaning "reddish yellow," the colour of the freshly cut wood. The letter *d* was added to the name later.

WILLOW FAMILY (Salicaceae)

The willow family has but 2 genera, *Populus* (aspens, poplars and cotton-woods) and *Salix* (willows). *Salix* is by far the larger genus, with up to 450 mostly shrubby species worldwide, largely in temperate and cold regions of the Northern Hemisphere. With more than 25 species, it is also one of the largest genera in the alpine flora of our region and certainly one of the most important in terms of ecosystem function (colonization, stabilization, cover, sheltered microhabitat, and food for herbivores and pollinating insects).

Willows are deciduous, woody plants that have alternate, often rather narrow leaves with stipules that usually do not hang on very long. The winter buds are covered by a single scale; willows are the only shrubs in our region that have single bud scales. Willows are unisexual; individual plants are either female or male. The tiny flowers consist of either a pistil (ovary, style and stigma) or a set of stamens (filament and anther), with 1 or 2 nectaries and a subtending, scale-like bract at the base. Several to many individual flowers are crowded into spike-like, female or male catkins (sometimes called "pussy willows"). The flowers are pollinated both by wind and by insects attracted to the nectar and pollen. In fruit, the fertilized ovaries form capsules with numerous tiny seeds, each surrounded by long, soft, white hairs.

mature stems of Alaska willow

Early on, there may appear to be little ornamental difference between male and female catkins. As the males mature, however, the anthers atop the filaments of the stamens become fully exposed and flush from orange-red or purple through shades of gold and yellow, depending on the species. It is a spectacular though fleeting display (for examples, see arctic willow, p. 60, and Richardson's willow, below) and is confined to the male of the species.

Willows were used by First Nations peoples in many ways, though it is often difficult to determine which species and for what purpose. Generically, however, willows were involved in everything from weaving baskets and making snowshoes to starting fires, smoking meat and fish, and as medicines. String was made from the bark in the spring when the sap was running. The string was twisted and braided, then made into fishnets or used for binding and tying. Bark was also woven into baskets, capes and hats. Long stems served as lashing, fish hangers or were used in basket rims, temporary snowshoes, lean-tos, animal snares, fish weirs and barbeque sticks. Stems were also burned to smoke meat and fish, as flooring in food caches and to make a type of screen to protect babies' faces from mosquitoes. In addition, willows were fashioned into beaver pelt stretchers, tent poles, fish-drying racks, cutlery and floor mats. The Dena'ina reportedly carried bunches of willow stems with them that they waved above their heads, usually while walking or running through the taiga. The stem bunches made a high-pitched sound that was said to scare away wolves. A menstruating woman being followed by a bear would twist a willow stem into a circle, spit on it and then throw it in the direction that she wanted the bear to go. Children played on whistles made from the stems and with dolls made from strips of bark. The fresh leaves were chewed to heal mouth sores. Even today, the flowers (pussy willows) are used to decorate homes and churches.

Salix is an ancient Latin name for willows and may be derived from the Latin *salire*, "to leap," because they grow so quickly. An old saying reflects this rapid growth: "The willow will buy a horse before the oak will pay for a saddle." Alternatively, *Salix* could come from the Celtic *sal*, "near," and *lis*, "water." "Willow" is from the Old English *welig*, *wylig* or *willage*, meaning "wicker basket," because of the pliancy or "willingness" of the branches. *Salix* is also called "osier" and "sallow." "Osier" is French from the Medieval Latin *oseria*, which in turn is derived from *oseretum*, meaning "whithy-bed," where a withe is a flexible stem or branch, especially useful for basket making. "Sallow" is the Old English *seahl* from the Latin *salix*.

anther

filament

STAMENS

bract

stigma

capsule

nectary

bract

male catkin

female catkin

Willow Catkins

male catkins of Richardson's willow

Key to *Salix*

1a. Dwarf or prostrate, often mat-forming or trailing shrubs, usually <20 cm tall. **2**

  2a. Leaves dark green and embossed above, glaucous (with a whitish bloom like a ripe plum) and net-veined below **3**

    3a. Leaves 1.5–6.5 cm long, silky beneath at least when young; catkins with 20–40 or more flowers; capsules 4.5–5 mm long. . . . . *S. reticulata* (p. 59)

    3b. Leaves 0.5–2.5 cm long, hairless beneath; catkins with 4–20 flowers; capsules 3–4 mm long . . . *S. nivalis* (p. 59)

  2b. Leaves not embossed above or net-veined below. **4**

    4a. Ovaries hairy, sometimes only toward tip **5**

      5a. Leaves green, not glaucous beneath **6**

        6a. Branches with dried, skeletonized leaves; leaf margins usually fringed with hairs . . . . *S. phlebophylla* (p. 60)

        6b. Dried leaves on branches not skeletonized; leaf margins not fringed with hairs . . . . . *S. polaris* (p. 60)

      5b. Leaves glaucous beneath. **7**

        7a. Leaf margins finely sawtoothed . . . . *S. chamissonis* (p. 60)

        7b. Leaf margins untoothed **8**

          8a. Styles usually <0.5 mm long; both leaf surfaces very hairy . . . . *S. niphoclada* (p. 62)

          8b. Styles usually >0.5 mm long; upper surface of leaves sparsely hairy to hairless **9**

            9a. Ovaries short-silky (rarely hairless); leaves persistent more than 1 year, veins sweeping along margin to tip; catkins small (1–2.5 cm), female catkins with 10–35 flowers; plants 3–7 cm tall, mat-forming by rhizomes. . . . . *S. cascadensis* (p. 61)

            9b. Ovaries long-hairy (rarely hairless); leaves not persistent, veins not sweeping along margin to tip; catkins larger (1.5–15 cm), female catkins with 30–50 or more flowers; plants 3–30 cm tall, mat-forming by layering or ascending branches . . . . *S. arctica, S. petrophila* (p. 60)

    4b. Ovaries not hairy. **10**

      10a. Leaves green on both surfaces, not glaucous beneath, margins hairless; ovaries hairless . . . . *S. rotundifolia* (p. 61)

      10b. Leaves glaucous beneath, margins fringed with short hairs; ovaries hairless or hairy in patches or streaks near tip. . . . . *S. stolonifera* (p. 61)

1b. Erect shrubs >20 cm tall **11**

  11a. Lower surface of mature leaves green, not glaucous or obscured by dense hairiness **12**

    12a. Catkins develop with leaves, female catkins on short, leafy shoots. **13**

      13a. Ovaries hairless. . . . . *S. commutata* (p. 65)

      13b. Ovaries silky-hairy . . . . *S. eastwoodiae* (p. 65)

    12b. Catkins develop before the leaves, female catkins unstalked, borne directly on branches . . . . *S. tweedyi* (p. 64)

  11b. Lower surface of mature leaves glaucous or obscured by dense hairiness. **14**

    14a. Lower surface of mature leaves obscured by dense hairiness **15**

      15a. Leaves densely white-woolly beneath, bright green above . . . . *S. alaxensis* (p. 64)

      15b. Leaves silky or long-woolly beneath, not bright green above. **16**

        16a. Catkins unstalked; ovaries and capsules white-woolly . . . . *S. barrattiana* (p. 63)

        16b. Catkins on short, leafy shoots; ovaries and capsules hairless or sparsely hairy . . . *S. wolfii* (p. 63)

    14b. Lower surface of mature leaves glaucous, variably hairy or hairless **17**

      17a. Leaf margins toothed **18**

        18a. Mature leaves hairless beneath. **19**

          19a. Ovaries and capsules hairless. **20**

            20a. Stipules persistent for several years; leaf margins blunt-toothed . . . . *S. richardsonii* (p. 65)

            20b. Stipules not persistent more than 1 year; leaf margins sawtoothed . . . . *S. barclayi* (p. 64)

          19b. Ovaries and capsules hairy . . . . *S. pulchra* (p. 63)

18b. Mature leaves hairy beneath **21**

21a. Leaves sawtoothed . . . . *S. tweedyi* (p. 64)

21b. Leaves blunt-toothed **22**

22a. Female catkins on leafy shoots, flowering as leaves emerge; leaves embossed above, with deep, impressed veins . . . . *S. vestita* (p. 63)

22b. Female catkins not on distinct leafy stalks, flowering before leaves emerge; leaves not embossed on upper surface **23**

23a. Ovaries and capsules hairless; mature leaves soft-hairy above; persistent stipules egg- to lance-shaped . . . . *S. richardsonii* (p. 65)

23b. Ovaries and capsules silky; mature leaves mostly hairless above; persistent stipules linear . . . . *S. pulchra* (p. 63)

17b. Leaf margins untoothed **24**

24a. Ovaries and capsules hairless **25**

25a. Juvenile leaves hairless or sparsely hairy; stipules usually absent or rudimentary . . . . *S. farriae* (p. 65)

25b. Juvenile leaves densely hairy; stipules large, leaf-like . . . . *S. richardsonii* (p. 65)

24b. Ovaries and capsules hairy **26**

26a. Stipules absent **27**

27a. Female catkins globe- or barrel-shaped; leaves densely greyish-white-hairy on both surfaces . . . . *S. brachycarpa* (p. 62)

27b. Female catkins narrowly cylindric; leaves yellow-green, rather sparsely hairy on upper surface . . . . *S. niphoclada* (p. 62)

26b. Stipules present, at least on later leaves **28**

28a. Female catkins borne directly on stems, flowering before leaves emerge . . . . *S. pulchra* (p. 63)

28b. Female catkins borne on distinct, leafy shoots, flowering as leaves emerge **29**

29a. Leaf stalks 3–25 mm long, yellowish; leaves 3–8 cm long; capsule stalks 0.3–2.8 mm long . . . . *S. glauca* (p. 62)

29b. Leaf stalks 1–5 mm long, often reddish; leaves 1–4 cm long; capsule stalks 0–0.5 mm long **30**

30a. Female catkins globe- or barrel-shaped; leaves densely greyish-white-hairy on both surfaces . . . . *S. brachycarpa* (p. 62)

30b. Female catkins narrowly cylindric; leaves yellow-green, rather sparsely hairy on upper surface . . . . *S. niphoclada* (p. 62)

Barratt's willow (male catkins)

skeleton-leaf willow (female catkins)

arctic willow (fall colours)

DWARF SHRUBS WITH HAIRY OVARIES AND CAPSULES

Net-veined Willow, Net-leaf Willow
Salix reticulata

General: Dwarf, **prostrate**, 3–10 cm tall, from rhizomes and creeping, often buried branches; twigs greenish to yellow to red-brown, hairless.

Leaves: Alternate, elliptic-circular to broadly oblong, **1.5–6.5 cm long, rounded at tip;** margins mostly toothless and rolled under; **upper surface dark green, glossy, embossed with deep veins, lower surface glaucous, net-veined,** silky-hairy to hairless.

Flowers: Tiny, unisexual, lacking sepals and petals, **20–40 or more,** in catkins that flower as leaves emerge; catkins small, stout, on leafy twigs, most twigs with typical foliage terminate in a catkin; floral bracts pale greenish yellow to tawny, hairless; ovary 1, **densely silky (usually)** or hairless; stamens 2.

Fruits: Capsules red, silky or hairless, **4.5–5 mm long,** stalkless or on short stalks to 0.8 mm long.

Where Found: Meadows, heathlands, mossy seepage areas, fellfields and turfy tundra; subalpine and alpine zones; common throughout the **northern** ⅔ of the region, reportedly disjunct in CO; arctic-alpine, circumpolar.

Subspecies: *S. reticulata* ssp. *glabellicarpa* has **hairless or patchily hairy ovaries and capsules.** It is rare on cliffs and ledges, and is endemic to Haida Gwaii and southeastern AK.

Similar Species: Without flowers or fruits net-veined willow could be confused with alpine bearberry (p. 79). They have similar leaves but those of alpine bearberry are thinner and green, not glaucous on the lower surface; bearberry also lacks the single bud scales of a willow.

S. r. ssp. *glabellicarpa*

Notes: Net-veined willow is an important "tundra green" food for the Inuit of Baffin I., Northwest Territories.

Dwarf Snow Willow • *Salix nivalis*

General: Very similar to net-veined willow (above) but more mat-forming (1–5 cm tall). **Leaves: 0.5–2.5 cm long, hairless beneath. Flowers:** Female catkins with **4–20 flowers. Fruits:** Capsules 3–4 mm long. **Where Found:** Moist meadows, fellfields and rocky slopes; alpine zone; more frequent in the **southern** ½ of the region; cordilleran.

Notes: Dwarf snow willow is also known as *Salix reticulata* ssp. *nivalis* and *S. reticulata* var. *saximontana*. • *S. nivalis* has been treated as a subspecies of *S. reticulata*, but *FNA* maintains that the area of overlap in central British Columbia is relatively small and the evidence of intergradation is weak.

Arctic Willow • *Salix arctica*

General: Dwarf to suberect, usually **prostrate or trailing but sometimes ascending,** to 30–40 cm tall; twigs thick, yellow-green to brown. **Leaves:** Narrowly to broadly elliptic to oval, 1–8 cm long; **margins toothless;** hairless and shiny above, **sparsely white-hairy and glaucous beneath;** usually at least some leaves have long, white hairs on lower surface and margins, **forming a beard at the tip. Flowers:** Catkins long, stout, on prominent, leafy shoots, female catkins often longer than 10 cm; **ovaries hairy; floral bracts dark,** long-hairy; styles and anthers reddish to reddish purple. **Fruits:** **Capsules hairy. Where Found:** Mesic to dry meadows, thickets, heath, tundra, fellfields, rocky slopes and ridges; montane to alpine zones; frequent in most of the northern ¾ of the region but absent from Haida Gwaii and rare on Vancouver I; arctic-alpine, circumpolar.

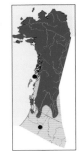

Similar Species: This is a widespread and extremely variable species; several subspecies are recognized by some taxonomists. • One of these races, **Rocky Mountain willow (*S. petrophila*;** *S. arctica* vars. *petraea* and *petrophila*), is now a separate species and is a smaller (2–10 cm tall) plant with **tawny floral bracts** and **leaves that are nearly hairless beneath.** It occurs from southern BC and southwestern AB to CA, NV and NM. • Arctic willow can be difficult to distinguish from **creeping willow (p. 61), which has hairless ovaries,** especially where the 2 species grow together. It is reported to hybridize with *S. barclayi, S. stolonifera* and *S. polaris,* among others.

Notes: Arctic willow is also known as *Salix arctica* ssp. *crassijulis, S. arctica* ssp. *torulosa.*

Polar Willow, Snowbed Willow • *Salix polaris*

General: Mat-forming, dwarf, 1–9 cm tall; stems partly buried; twigs brownish, hairless, usually glaucous. **Leaves:** Elliptic to egg-shaped or nearly circular, 0.5–3 cm long; margins smooth; **lower surface green, glossy, mostly hairless. Flowers: Ovaries hairy;** styles long (0.7–1.2 mm); floral bracts dark, hairless or hairy. **Fruits: Capsules reddish, glossy, sparsely hairy. Where Found:** Moist snowbed and seepage areas, tundra, fellfields and scree slopes; upper subalpine and alpine zones; frequent in the northern part of the region; arctic-alpine, incompletely circumpolar.

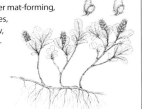

Similar Species: Skeleton-leaf willow (*S. phlebophylla*) is another mat-forming, dwarf shrub. It has small (to 1 cm long), rather leathery, oval leaves, with green, glossy undersurfaces similar to those of polar willow, but the **margins are fringed** with hairs. The leaves persist for several years, **disintegrating** on branches except for a **skeleton of veins.** Skeleton-leaf willow grows on dry, gravelly, windswept ridges, on arctic and alpine tundra, and is an arctic-alpine, amphiberingian species, locally frequent in central and northern AK and YT to northwestern NT.

Notes: Both of these species have disproportionately large capsules.

Chamisso's Willow • *Salix chamissonis*

General: Prostrate, dwarf; branches red-brown, trailing; twigs yellow-green. **Leaves:** Elliptic to egg-shaped, 3–5 cm long, hairless, blunt to rounded at the tip; margins finely glandular-**sawtoothed;** upper surface deep green and lustrous, **lower surface glaucous. Flowers:** Catkins cylindric and many-flowered, female catkins 3–7 cm long; **ovaries usually crinkly-grey-hairy;** floral bracts dark, hairy. **Fruits: Capsules usually crinkly-grey-hairy. Where Found:** Wet to dry meadows, streambanks, shores, snowbeds, fellfields and tundra; montane to alpine zones; scattered and locally frequent in the **far north;** arctic-alpine, amphiberingian.

Notes: This species is named for Adelbert Ludwig von Chamisso (1781–1838), a German poet and naturalist. He was the botanist on the Russian ship *Rurik,* which visited Alaska in 1816 and 1817.

Cascade Willow • *Salix cascadensis*

General: Mat-forming, dwarf, 3–7 cm tall. **Leaves:** Narrowly elliptic to lance-shaped, 1–2.5 cm long, pointy-tipped; margins smooth; lower surface whitish and long-hairy when

young, becoming hairless. **Flowers:** Catkins small, female catkins 1–2.5 cm long with 10–35 flowers; ovaries usually grey-hairy, sometimes hairless; floral bracts dark, sparsely hairy. **Fruits:** Capsules usually grey-hairy, sometimes hairless. **Where Found:** Mesic to dry, rocky slopes, ridges, meadows, fellfields and tundra; upper subalpine and alpine zones; locally frequent in the **southern** ⅓ of the region.

Variety: Var. *thompsonii* is a phase of *S. cascadensis* with hairless ovaries.

Dwarf Shrubs with Hairless Ovaries and Capsules

Least Willow, Round-leaf Willow • *Salix rotundifolia*

General: Tiny, dwarf, 0.5–5 cm tall, **stems embedded in turf or mat-forming** on rocky surfaces; twigs yellow-brown or reddish brown, hairless. **Leaves: Nearly circular to elliptic, 0.3–1.5 cm long,** blunt to rounded at tip, with 3 distinct veins; both surfaces hairless and green, upper surface very glossy.

Flowers: Catkins small, few-flowered (2–12); **ovaries hairless;** floral bracts brown, sparsely hairy. **Fruits: Capsules glossy, reddish brown. Where Found:** Dry, exposed ridges, mesic to moist turfy tundra, scree, talus and fellfields; lowland (arctic coast) to alpine zones; frequent in the north, disjunct (as var. *dodgeana*) in the Rockies of northwestern WY and adjacent MT; arctic-alpine, amphiberingian-cordilleran.

Varieties: Var. *rotundifolia* is 1–5 cm tall, with **roundish leaves** 0.5–1.5 cm long and female catkins with **4–12 flowers.** • Var. *dodgeana* (Dodge's willow) is **very small,** 0.5–2 cm tall, with **oval leaves** about 0.5 cm long and female catkins usually with only **2–4 flowers.** It occurs more consistently at higher elevations.

Notes: Least willow is also known as *Salix dodgeana, S. leiocarpa* and *S. polaris* var. *leiocarpa*.

Creeping Willow • *Salix stolonifera*

General: Dwarf, **mat-forming,** 2–10 cm tall, stems trailing or partly buried; branches thick, sometimes ascending; twigs greenish brown, hairless, rather glossy. **Leaves: Elliptic to nearly circular, 1.5–4 cm**

long, rounded at tip; margins toothless or glandular-toothed on the lower half, fringed with short hairs; upper surface hairless, green and glossy, **lower surface glaucous and sparsely hairy. Flowers:** Catkins short (1.5–5 cm), stout, on prominent, leafy shoots; **ovaries hairless** or with a few hairs near the tip; floral bracts dark, long-hairy. **Fruits: Capsules hairless** or with a few hairs near the tip. **Where Found:** Moist to mesic meadows, heathlands, tundra, rocky slopes, ridges and fellfields; montane to alpine zones; frequent in the northwestern part of the region, especially in the coastal mountains; disjunct in western AB.

Notes: This species is reported to hybridize with *S. arctica* and *S. barclayi*.

ERECT SHRUBS (>20 CM TALL) WITH HAIRY OVARIES AND CAPSULES

Grey-leaf Willow, Blue-green Willow • *Salix glauca*

General: Erect or spreading, 0.3–2 m tall; branches reddish brown to greyish, usually hairy; twigs densely to sparsely hairy.

Leaves: Alternate, elliptic to lance-shaped, 3–8 cm long, on yellowish stalks to 2.5 cm long, pointed to somewhat rounded at the tip; **margins untoothed;** upper surface slightly glossy to dull green, moderately to sparsely **soft-hairy, lower surface glaucous and variably white-hairy.**

Flowers: Tiny, unisexual, lacking sepals and petals, numerous, in catkins that flower as the leaves emerge; catkins stout, on leafy twigs, **female catkins 2–8 cm long, cylindric;** floral bracts light brown, with wavy hairs; **ovary 1, densely hairy;** stigmas 4, long and dark.

Fruits: Capsules sparsely grey-hairy, 4.5–9 mm long, on short stalks; styles 0.5–1.5 mm long.

Where Found: Mesic to wet thickets (in the north often forms treeline thickets with other willows and scrub birch), open boreal forests, peatlands, streambanks, fellfields and tundra; lowland (arctic coast) to alpine zones; common in the northern ½ of the region, frequent but more localized southward; circumpolar.

Similar Species: It can be difficult to distinguish this species from short-fruit willow (below), but grey-leaf willow has broader leaves that are usually more pointed at the tip, longer catkins and longer stalks on its leaves **(stalks usually 4–15 mm)** and capsules **(stalks 0.3–2.8 mm).**

Notes: Grey-leaf willow is extremely variable, probably because of frequent hybridization and high polyploidy (multiple sets of chromosomes) combined with broad distribution and ecological amplitude. *FNA* recognizes 4 varieties, 3 of which occur in our region. • First- and second-year twigs and winter buds are fuzzy-hairy. The dried leaves and spent female catkins often stay on the plant through the winter.

Short-fruit Willow • *Salix brachycarpa*

General: Low, upright, 0.3–1.3 m tall; twigs reddish brown, densely hairy. **Leaves:** Oblong to narrowly egg-shaped, 1–4 cm long, **short-stalked (1–3 mm long);** margins untoothed; hairy on both sides (especially glaucous lower surface) with **densely matted, greyish white hairs. Flowers:** Catkins short **(female catkins 0.5–2 cm long), globe- or barrel-shaped,** on short, leafy shoots; **ovaries densely white-woolly;** styles 0.5–1.5 mm long; floral bracts pale, hairy. **Fruits: Capsules densely white-woolly,**

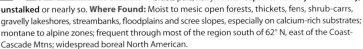

unstalked or nearly so. **Where Found:** Moist to mesic open forests, thickets, fens, shrub-carrs, gravelly lakeshores, streambanks, floodplains and scree slopes, especially on calcium-rich substrates; montane to alpine zones; frequent through most of the region south of 62° N, east of the Coast-Cascade Mtns; widespread boreal North American.

Similar Species: Short-fruit willow resembles both grey-leaf willow (above) and barren-ground willow (below) but has **cuter, roly-poly catkins.**

Barren-ground Willow, Snow Willow
Salix niphoclada

General: Similar to short-fruit willow (above); assumes a low, mat-like form in some exposed alpine situations. **Leaves:** Yellow-green, **upper surface rather sparsely hairy. Flowers:** Female catkins longer **(2–6 cm) than those of short-fruit willow,** cylindric, more loosely flowered; styles shorter (0.2–0.8 mm). **Where found:** Dry to moist meadows, thickets, streambanks and terraces, tundra, limestone talus

and stony slopes; lowland (arctic coast) to alpine zones; frequent in the northern ½ of the region, southward less frequently in BC to about 52° N (Chilcotin District); cordilleran.

Notes: Barren-ground willow is also known as *Salix brachycarpa* ssp. *niphoclada*.

Diamond-leaf Willow • *Salix pulchra*

General: Low to medium, upright or spreading, 0.2–2 m tall; twigs brownish, glossy, smooth or densely hairy in patches.
Leaves: Lance-elliptic to compressed diamond-shaped, 2–7 cm long, short-stalked, pointy-tipped at both ends, **mostly hairless;** margins untoothed, sawtoothed or blunt-toothed; **shiny green above, glaucous below; stipules linear, long (3–15 mm or more), persistent** 2–4 years. **Flowers:** Catkins appear before leaves emerge, **stalkless,** female catkins 1–6 cm long; **ovaries silky-hairy;** floral bracts dark, hairy.
Fruits: Capsules silky-hairy. Where Found: Moist to wet thickets, open forest, shorelines, wetlands and tundra, often forming large thickets above timberline; lowland (arctic coast) to alpine zones; frequent throughout the northern ⅓ of the region; arctic-alpine, amphiberingian.

Other Species: Rock willow (*S. vestita*) has leathery, broadly egg-shaped to elliptic leaves, the upper surface glossy, green, **embossed, with deep veins** (like those of net-veined willow, p. 59), the **lower surface glaucous and long-hairy. The catkins are on leafy shoots and develop with the leaves; the ovaries and capsules are hairy.** Rock willow occurs in moist to dry, open forests and along rocky streambanks and timberline ridges in upper montane to lower alpine zones. Rock willow is a cordilleran, interruptedly trans–North American species, locally frequent in the southeastern part of the region.

rock willow

Notes: Diamond-leaf willow is also known as *Salix planifolia* ssp. *pulchra* and *S. pulchra* var. *yukonensis.* • This species is differentiated from our other medium-sized willows by the combination of hairless leaves that are green above and glaucous beneath, persistent linear stipules, catkins that emerge before the leaves and hairy ovaries. • The Alaskan Inuit eat the inner portion of the young, tender shoots raw. Later, the young leaves—best when they are 3–4 cm long—are eaten raw mixed with seal oil. They are said to taste bitter at first but have a sweet aftertaste. Quantities are collected, mixed with seal oil and put in storage containers in cold places for the winter. • Ptarmigan (*Lagopus* spp.) feed heavily on diamond-leaf willow.

Barratt's Willow • *Salix barrattiana*

General: Low to medium, upright to depressed, 0.3–1.5 m tall; branches gnarled, dark brown, twigs straggly-hairy; **buds and stipules oily. Leaves:** Narrowly to broadly elliptic to lance-shaped, mostly erect, 3–9 cm long; margins untoothed; **both surfaces grey-hairy, becoming less so** with age, lower surface not glaucous; **stipules leaf-like, glandular, yellow-oily. Flowers: Catkins unstalked, upright,** appearing just before leaves emerge, female catkins 4–10 cm long; **ovaries densely silky-hairy;** floral bracts dark, long-hairy. **Fruits:** Capsules sparsely hairy. **Where Found:** Moist to wet gravel bars, outwash fans and terraces, streambanks, shrub fens, wet meadows and tundra, on calcium-rich substrates, often forming pure thickets; montane to alpine zones; frequent in the northern ½ of the region, sporadically frequent southward; northern cordilleran.

Similar Species: Idaho willow (*S. wolfii*) has **shorter (1–4 cm long), fatter catkins on short, leafy shoots** and **hairless or sparsely hairy ovaries and capsules.** It occurs in wet meadows and thickets, fens, streambanks, springs, shores and on the margins of snow-beds, in subalpine and alpine zones. Idaho willow is locally frequent in the southeastern part of the region, from southwestern MT and ID to northeastern OR, south to NV, UT and CO.

Notes: Barratt's willow is recognizable in the field, even from a distance, by the characteristic blue-green colour of the leaves. It is our only willow that can be identified without opening the herbarium folder because the oily buds leave stains that soak through to the outside of the paper. • The oily substance on the buds and stipules has a balsamic fragrance similar to that of balsam poplar. • Joseph Barratt (1796–1882) was a geologist in Connecticut and Pennsylvania.

Felt-leaf Willow, Alaska Willow • *Salix alaxensis*

General: Shrub or small tree, usually erect, sometimes gnarled and sprawling, 1–8 m tall; branches and **young twigs densely woolly or sparsely hairy and with a white-waxy bloom. Leaves:** Narrowly elliptic to broadly egg-shaped, 4–10 cm long; margins untoothed, rolled under; **lower surface densely white-felty,** strongly contrasting with **green, sparsely hairy upper surface;** stipules long (to 2 cm), narrow, leaf-like. **Flowers:** Catkins upright, **unstalked or nearly so,** flowering well before leaves emerge, female catkins 5–12 cm long; ovaries sparsely to densely hairy; styles 1.3–3 mm long. **Fruits:** Capsules sparsely to densely hairy. **Where Found:** Moist to wet gravel bars, outwash fans, terraces and banks of fast-flowing streams, lakeshores, forest openings, raw morainal deposits, talus slopes, meadows and tundra; montane to alpine zones; frequent throughout the northern ½ of the region, sporadically frequent southward; amphiberingian.

Varieties: Var. *alaxensis* has branchlets that are **densely yellowish and white woolly-hairy.** • Var. *longistylis* has branchlets that are **without woolly hairs but strongly glaucous.**

Notes: The Alaskan Inuit report eating the leaves, which some did not like because of the felty surface, and also the young stems or shoots. The velvety layer of the latter was peeled off, and the tender shoots eaten raw or dipped in seal oil. They are said to be cool, sweet and juicy, tasting like cucumber. In the Arctic, the inner bark was peeled off as a winter tidbit and tastes best at thaw time eaten raw or with seal oil and sugar. • This species is one of the "diamond willows," so-called because of the diamond-shaped depressions and associated scarring on their stems. Infection by a fungus (*Valsa sordida*) appears to result in the lesions and sharply contrasting colouration in the heartwood. The wood can be fashioned into decorative canes, lamps, rustic furniture and, most importantly, bolo ties. • Felt-leaf willow, especially var. *alaxensis*, can reach considerable height, even tree size, in alpine gullies and arctic valleys. Moose browse this species heavily, pulling down and breaking sizeable branches and trunks. If the shrubs keep growing, they can eventually "escape" above the browsing level, becoming small trees too thick for moose to break. • This willow is reportedly a timber-producing species in Iceland.

ERECT SHRUBS (>20 CM TALL) WITH HAIRLESS OVARIES AND CAPSULES

Barclay's Willow • *Salix barclayi*

General: Low to medium, 1–3 m tall; branches mostly erect, twigs yellow-green to red-brown, glossy, hairy or hairless. **Leaves:** Elliptic to lance-egg-shaped, 3–8 cm long, tips pointed to tapered; **margins usually finely sawtoothed;** upper surface shiny, green, sparsely hairy to nearly hairless, **lower surface glaucous, mature leaves hairless or nearly so,** drying blackish; stipules broad, leaf-like, not persisting over winter. **Flowers:** Catkins on short, leafy branchlets, appearing with leaves, female catkins 3–8 cm long; ovaries hairless; **styles 0.5–2.5 mm long;** floral bracts dark, hairy. **Fruits:** Capsules hairless. **Where Found:** Moist to mesic thickets, fens, shores, gullies, raw morainal deposits, often forming large thickets; montane to alpine zones; frequent through much of the region from about 64° N southward, mostly east of the coastal mountains; northern cordilleran.

Similar Species: Plants without catkins can be distinguished from Richardson's willow (p. 65) by the lack of old, dry stipules. • Tweedy's willow (*S. tweedyi*; *S. barrattiana* var. *tweedyi*) ranges from south-central BC to WA, ID and WY, on streamsides, shores, talus slopes and tundra, sometimes reaching the alpine zone in the Rocky Mtns of MT, ID and WY. It has sawtoothed leaf margins similar to Barclay's willow, but the elliptic **leaves are hairy at maturity,** and the **catkins are borne directly on the twigs,** not on leafy branchlets. • Farr's willow (p. 65) has leaves that do not dry black and often have reddish hairs on the upper surface midrib, reddish leaf stalks and ovaries, and **shorter styles (0.4–1 mm long).**

Notes: *S. barclayi* is reported to hybridize with *S. arctica*, *S. commutata*, *S. richardsonii* and *S. stolonifera*.

Richardson's Willow • *Salix richardsonii*

General: Low to medium, 0.3–4 m tall (to 1.5 m in the alpine); twigs brownish, **white-hairy. Leaves:** Elliptic to egg-shaped, 3–8 cm long; margins untoothed or toothed; **upper surface green and usually moderately hairy, lower surface glaucous, hairy or hairless;** stipules

large (to 3 cm long), leaf-like, **persistent for several years. Flowers:** Catkins unstalked or nearly so, appearing before leaves emerge; ovaries hairless. **Fruits:** Capsules hairless. **Where Found:** Moist thickets, fens, meadows, streambanks, gravelly shores and tundra; montane to alpine zones; frequent in the northern ⅓ of the region; amphiberingian.

Similar Species: Farr's willow (**S. farriae;** S. hastata var. farriae) is typically shorter (less than 1 m tall in the alpine) with **stipules lacking or much smaller,** and the hairs on young leaves often persisting on the upper surface midrib of the mostly hairless mature leaves, which can be untoothed or shallowly sawtoothed. The **catkins are on short, leafy shoots** and **develop with the leaves.** This species occurs in wet to moist meadows, streambanks and tundra, in montane to lower alpine zones. It is scattered but locally frequent from OR, ID and WY to central BC, and disjunct in northwestern BC, southern YT and western NT.

Notes: Richardson's willow is also known as *Salix lanata* ssp. *richardsonii*. • The persistent dried stipules give Richardson's willow a distinctive scraggly appearance, the better to distinguish it from Barclay's and other willows with which it forms large timberline thickets. • John Richardson (1787–1865) was a Scottish naturalist attached to John Franklin's expedition to arctic America.

Under-green Willow • *Salix commutata*

General: Low to medium, 0.5–2 m tall; branches mostly erect, twigs yellow-green to red-brown, hairy. **Leaves:** Elliptic to broadly oblong, 3–10 cm long; margins finely sawtoothed to untoothed; **both surfaces green with long, white hairs;** stipules broad, leaf-like. **Flowers:** Catkins appearing with leaves, **on leafy branchlets; ovaries usually hairless, often reddish. Fruits: Capsules usually hairless,** often reddish. **Where Found:** Wet to moist thickets, peatlands, stream-banks, gullies, raw morainal deposits and tundra, often forming large thickets; low-land to alpine zones; frequent in the southern ¾ of the region; cordilleran.

Similar Species: Sierra willow (*S. eastwoodiae*) has smaller, narrower leaves and usually **hairy ovaries.** It is found in meadows and on streambanks, shores and talus slopes, in subalpine and alpine zones, from WA, ID and MT to CA, NV and WY.

Notes: Under-green willow is one of our latest-flowering willows.

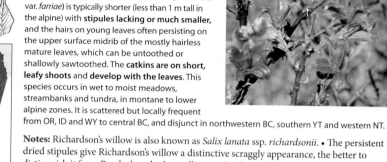

ROSE FAMILY (Rosaceae)

Members of the rose family worldwide are trees, shrubs (often thorny) or herbs. They have alternate, simple or pinnately compound leaves usually with **stipules** (appendages at the base of the leaf stalk). The flowers are radially symmetric, typically with 5 sepals united at the base (collectively called the **calyx**), 5 free petals arising from a cup- or saucer-like structure (called the **hypanthium,** formed by the fused bases of the sepals) atop the flower stalk, numerous stamens in several whorls and a single compound or several simple ovaries. The fruits of the rose family are very diverse and can be dry (achenes, follicles) or fleshy (apple-like pomes, cherry-like drupes or raspberry-like aggregations of drupelets). Strawberries are false fleshy fruits, dry achenes embedded in the tasty hypanthium. The family is characterized by the presence of stipules and the hypanthium, and the generally 5-part form of the flower (except for *Dryas* species).

Rosaceae is a large family with nearly 3400 species worldwide and is of considerable economic importance. Most of the important bush and tree fruits of temperate regions belong to the rose family, including apple (*Malus*); pear (*Pyrus*); cherry, plum, prune, peach, nectarine, apricot and almond, all species of *Prunus*; blackberry, raspberry and loganberry, all species of *Rubus*; and strawberry (*Fragaria*). Notable ornamental trees and shrubs occur within the family, for example, spiraea (*Spiraea*), ninebark (*Physocarpus*), cotoneaster (*Cotoneaster*), hawthorn (*Crataegus*), flowering quince (*Chaenomeles*), mountain-ash (*Sorbus*), Japanese cherry (*Prunus*), rose (*Rosa*) and shrubby cinquefoil (*Dasiphora fruticosa*).

Many alpine species in this family are herbs; please see Rosaceae in the Wildflowers section (pp. 164–183).

shrubby cinquefoil

Key to Shrubby Rosaceae

1a. Fruits fleshy; erect shrub with pinnately compound leaves, the leaves with 7–13 leaflets . . . . ***Sorbus* (p. 67)**
1b. Fruits dry 2
    2a. Erect to ascending shrub 3
        3a. Leaves simple, merely toothed; fruits follicles . . . . ***Spiraea* (p. 68)**
        3b. Leaves pinnately compound with usually 5 leaflets; fruits achenes . . . . ***Dasiphora fruticosa* (p. 71)**
    2b. Dwarf, spreading, sprawling or mat-forming shrub 4
        4a. Leaves dissected into linear segments; flowers numerous in elongated clusters; fruits follicles (looks much like a herb but considered a semi-shrub) . . . . ***Luetkea pectinata* (p. 69)**
        4b. Leaves not dissected, at most toothed 5
            5a. Flowers numerous in cylindric clusters . . . . ***Petrophytum* (p. 69)**
            5b. Flowers solitary 6
                6a. Leaves with margins scalloped or toothless, often rolled under, white-woolly on the lower surface; flowers long stalked, petals 8–10, white or yellow; fruits achenes with feathery-hairy styles . . . . ***Dryas* (pp. 70–71)**
                6b. Leaves with smooth, flattened margins, not white-woolly beneath; flowers nearly stalkless, petals 5, pink; fruits follicles . . . . ***Kelseya uniflora* (p. 69)**

Luetka
pectinata

Dasiphora
fruticosa

Kelseya
uniflora

Petrophytum

Dryas
octopetala

Spiraea
splendens

Sorbus sitchensis

Sorbus scopulina

Sitka Mountain-ash • *Sorbus sitchensis*

General: **Erect to spreading**, with several stems, 1–3 m tall; winter buds and young growth with rusty hairs, not sticky.

Leaves: Alternate, deciduous, **pinnately compound**, the **7–11 bluish green leaflets** oblong to oblong-egg-shaped, 2–7 cm long, **rounded to blunt at the tips; margins saw-toothed for not more than ¾ of their length.**

Flowers: Small, saucer-shaped, numerous (15–80), in branched, half-rounded clusters atop stems; petals 5, white to cream, oval, 4–6 mm long; sepals mostly hairless; stamens 15–20.

Fruits: **Berry-like** (technically miniature apples), nearly globe-shaped to ellipsoid, 8–10 mm long, **red with a whitish bloom;** edible but tart and bitter, much favoured by some birds such as waxwings, robins and varied thrushes.

Where Found: Mesic to moist open forests, glades, edges of tree clumps, stream-banks, rockslides, thickets and meadows; montane to alpine zones; frequent through most of the region south of 61° N; cordilleran.

Subspecies: South of the limit of Pleistocene glaciation, *S. sitchensis* ssp. *grayi* predominates. It is distinguished by leaflets that are toothed only above midleaf.

Similar Species: **Western mountain-ash (*S. scopulina*)** occasionally reaches sub-alpine elevations, occupying similar habitats over a similar but slightly larger and more inland range. It has generally **pointier leaflets that are more finely toothed nearly their full length,** with somewhat sticky winter buds and grey- or brown-hairy new growth, **flatter-topped flower clusters,** white-hairy sepals and **glossy, reddish orange fruits** without a bloom.

Notes: The berries of Sitka mountain-ash are not very palatable, but the Haida ate them sometimes and the Gitxsan used them as a strong physic. The Stl'atl'imc of southern British Columbia picked small shoots in the spring and ate them raw. Ethnobotanist Nancy Turner reports that Nlaka'pamux elder Annie York added a cluster of berries to the top of a jar of blueberries when canning them. The berries were occasionally made into a tart jelly that was served with game. • The Nuxalk rubbed the berries into their scalps to combat lice and dandruff. The Nuxalk, Tlingit and Kenai used the bark in medicinal mixtures for coughs and fever; other Alaskan groups such as the Dena'ina used the bark to treat sore throats and tonsillitis. Some report that the bark, leaves and dried berries can be used to treat ulcers, hemorrhoids, sores, tuberculosis and "difficult" urination. The juice of boiled bark was drunk for constipation. A gargle for sore throats could be made from the astringent berries. • The Gitxsan used the wood to make axe handles and sometimes side sticks for snowshoes. The Dena'ina preferred this plant for making switches for steam baths, not only because of its fragrance, but also because the leaves stayed on even when they were dry. The astringent bark was also used to tan hides. • *Sorbus* is an ancient name for the service tree (*S. domestica*); conversely, the name "service" is from the Old English *syrfe*, "to serve," a corruption of *sorbus*. It was named "mountain-ash" presumably because the pinnately compound leaves of *Sorbus* somewhat resemble those of true ashes (*Fraxinus*).

western mountain-ash (both photos)

Subalpine Spiraea • *Spiraea densiflora*

General: Low shrub from strong, creeping rhizomes; erect to spreading, with several stems and many **thin, wiry branches,** 30–70 cm tall; hairless.

Leaves: Alternate, deciduous, short-stalked, **oval to oblong-elliptic,** 1.5–4 cm long; **margins blunt-toothed mostly above the middle;** bright green above, paler and prominently veined below, hairless on both surfaces or fine-hairy beneath.

Flowers: Small, numerous in showy, branched, nearly flat-topped clusters atop the stems; petals 5, **rose pink,** narrowly oval, 1.5–2 mm long; **sepals mostly hairless;** stamens numerous.

Fruits: Follicles pod-like, small, somewhat leathery, shiny, **hairless,** 3–4 mm long, in clusters of 4–5.

Where Found: Moist forest openings and edges, thickets, meadows, streambanks and open rocky slopes; montane and subalpine zones; frequent in the southern ⅓ of the region; cordilleran.

Notes: Subalpine spiraea is also known as *S. splendens.* • *Spiraea* is from Greek *speiraia,* meaning "a plant used for garlands or wreaths"; some garden species are called "bridal-wreath."

Alaska Spiraea, Steven's Spiraea
Spiraea stevenii

Leaves: Toothed nearly to the base. Flowers: White; sepals hairy. Fruits: Hairy follicles. Where Found: Moist to wet meadows, thickets, streambanks, edges of peatlands and peaty tundra; montane to alpine zones; locally frequent in the northern ⅓ of the region; amphiberingian.

Notes: Alaska spiraea is also known as *S. beauverdiana.* • The species is named for Christian von Steven (1781–1863), a Russian state councillor and a student of Crimean flora.

Partridge-foot, Mountain Spiraea • *Luetkea pectinata*

General: Dwarf, mat-forming semi-shrub from rhizomes and branching runners; flowering stems erect to ascending, 5–20 cm tall, hairless or sparsely hairy in grooves along the stem.

Leaves: Evergreen, hairless, numerous, 7–20 mm long, mostly **crowded in thick tufts** at the base and along the runners, the narrowly wing-margined stalk about as long as the **fan-shaped blade**, which is **dissected in 3s**, the ultimate segments linear, pointy-tipped; stem leaves alternate, similar but smaller.

Flowers: Small, numerous, **saucer-shaped**, in **spike-like clusters** atop the stems; petals 5, white, oval to spoon-shaped, 3–4 mm long; sepals 5, triangular, hairless; stamens about 20, slightly shorter than petals.

Fruits: Follicles pod-like, short-stalked, somewhat leathery, 4–5 mm long.

Where Found: Mesic to wet forest openings, edges of tree clumps, meadows, heathlands, open rocky slopes, mossy seepage areas and snowbed tundra; subalpine and alpine zones; frequent throughout the southern ¾ of the region; cordilleran.

Notes: Partridge-foot is also known as *Spiraea pectinata*. • *Luetkea* commemorates Count F.P. Luetke (1797–1882), a Russian sea captain, commander and arctic explorer whose expedition circumnavigated the world; *pectinata* comes from "pectinate," meaning "like the teeth of a comb," and refers to the linear leaf segments. • "Partridge-foot" refers to the divided leaves, thought to resemble the feet of partridge (grouse or ptarmigan) or their tracks.

Tufted Rockmat • *Petrophytum caespitosum*

General: Similar to partridge-foot; **prostrate, mat-forming. Leaves:** Persistent, mostly basal, tufted, **undivided, spoon-shaped, grey-green, 1-veined beneath. Flowers:** Small, white, **bell-shaped**, in **spike-like clusters**; sepals hairy; **stamens about 20,** nearly twice as long as petals, giving a bottle-brush effect. **Where Found:** Dry rock crevices and over shelving rock surfaces, usually on limestone or granite; montane to alpine zones; locally frequent in the southeastern part of the region; cordilleran–Great Plains.

Similar Species: Olympic Mountain rockmat (*P. hendersonii*) is endemic to the Olympic Mtns on cliffs and talus slopes. Its **leaves are 3-veined beneath,** and the flowers have **35–40 stamens.**

Notes: *Petrophytum* is from the Greek *petros*, "rock," and *phyton*, "plant"; *caespitosum* means "tufted."

Kelseya • *Kelseya uniflora*

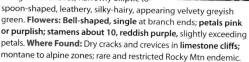

General: Dwarf shrub, densely tufted, cushion-forming, 3–8 cm thick, to 80 cm across, **intricately branched. Leaves:** Persistent, alternate but crowded and overlapping along the branches, narrowly elliptic to spoon-shaped, leathery, silky-hairy, appearing velvety greyish green. **Flowers: Bell-shaped, single** at branch ends; **petals pink or purplish; stamens about 10, reddish purple,** slightly exceeding petals. **Where Found:** Dry cracks and crevices in **limestone cliffs;** montane to alpine zones; rare and restricted Rocky Mtn endemic.

Notes: This species is presumably named for its discoverer, Rev. F.D. Kelsey (1849–1905). It is the floral emblem of the Montana Native Plant Society, whose newsletter is called *Kelseya*. • *Petrophytum* and *Kelseya* used to be lumped with *Luetkea*, and all 3 genera were once considered part of *Spiraea*.

White Mountain-avens
Dryas octopetala

General: **Prostrate, mat-forming;** stems trailing, freely branching and rooting; flowering stalks erect, 5–20 cm tall.

Leaves: Alternate, leathery, tardily deciduous, oblong to lance-egg-shaped, **broadest near the middle,** 0.8–4 cm long; **margins coarsely blunt-toothed,** rolled under; **upper surface strongly wrinkled, green, mostly hairless** but often warty-glandular, **usually densely white-woolly beneath,** sometimes nearly hairless, the midvein below with **gland-tipped brown hairs and/or brown scales** with long, branched, white hairs.

Flowers: Showy, 2–3 cm across, saucer- or wheel-shaped, **single** atop leafless, hairy stalks; **petals 8–10, white to cream** (rarely yellowish), oblong to elliptic, 8–17 mm long; sepals 8–10, **narrowly lance-shaped,** white-woolly; stamens numerous.

Fruits: Achenes numerous, about 3 mm long, with long (to 3–4 cm), feathery styles.

Where Found: Dry to mesic gravelly slopes and ridge crests, fellfields, rocky tundra and heath, typically on calcium-rich soils; subalpine and alpine zones; frequent in the northern ½ of the region, infrequent southward, circumpolar.

Similar Species: Entire-leaved mountain-avens (*D. integrifolia*) has smaller leaves **broadest below the middle, the upper surface not much wrinkled,** the midvein of the lower surface **without glands and the margins smooth or weakly toothed.** It occurs in habitats similar to those of white mountain-avens and over a similar range in our region. *D. octopetala* is generally more abundant in YT, southern BC and the Rockies; *D. integrifolia* more so in northwestern BC and AK.

Notes: Both white and entire-leaved mountain-avens clearly prefer limey substrates. They are among the most characteristic and dominant plants and among the most important constituents of biomass in large areas of alpine tundra, especially in mountain ranges with calcium-rich bedrock, a relatively dry local climate, and low snowpack. • The 2 white mountain-avens appear to hybridize sometimes where they grow together. Both species have several forms, some of which (*D. octopetala* ssps. *alaskensis*, *hookeriana* and *incisa*; and *D. integrifolia* ssp. *sylvatica*) have been recognized as distinct subspecies or even species. Distinguishing these is a complicated business based on leaf shape and the type of hairs and/or glands on the underside midvein of the leaves and is beyond the scope of this field guide. • The flowers of white mountain-avens function as parabolic reflectors and track the movement of the sun, concentrating sunlight on the ovaries and warming them by approximately 3°C above the ambient air temperature. This enables the development of larger seeds in the brief alpine growing season.

entire-leaved mountain-avens

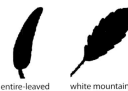

entire-leaved mountain-avens   white mountain-avens

Yellow Mountain-avens • *Dryas drummondii*

Leaves: Similar to those of white mountain-avens (p. 70). **Flowers:** 2 cm long, **pale yellow, nodding** atop stalks 10–25 cm tall; **petals never fully opening; sepals broadly oval,** dark-glandular-hairy. **Fruits:** Achenes bearing silky, golden yellow, feathery plumes; plumes entwined when young, later spreading to a fluffy white head; each 1-seeded achene eventually carried off on the wind. **Where Found:** Moist to mesic, calcium-rich river bars, raw glacial moraines, scree slopes, ridge crests and gravelly roadsides; lowland to alpine zones; frequent in most of the northern ½ of the region, infrequent southward; rare on Vancouver I. and in the Olympic Mtns; North American but primarily northwestern cordilleran.

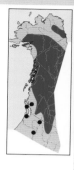

Notes: Classic studies in Glacier Bay, Alaska, demonstrated that yellow mountain-avens is important in the development of vegetation communities following glacial retreat. This species is one of the earliest dominant colonizers during primary succession and remains so for 20 to 40 years. It probably performs well because of the presence of nitrogen-fixing bacteria that live in its root nodules, and it usually forms ectomycorrhizal associations with fungi, enabling it to grow vigorously on bare mineral soil and enriching the successional environment with nitrogen, phosphorus and organic matter. • *Dryas* refers to the Dryades, mythical Greek wood nymphs or "oak nymphs"; the Greek *drys* also means "oak." The name "mountain-avens" was given presumably because the flowers somewhat resemble those of *Geum* (avens) species. "Avens" may come from the Old French word *avence*, which is from the Medieval Latin *avencia* or *avancia*, meaning "antidote," because some avens species were said to ward off "the devil and evil spirits, venomous serpents and wild beasts" (Watts, 2000).

Shrubby Cinquefoil • *Dasiphora fruticosa*

General: Erect to spreading, mounded or even somewhat matted, **much branched,** 0.3–1.3 m tall; young branches silky-hairy, bark on older branches reddish brown, shredding.

Leaves: Alternate but clustered at nodes, deciduous, numerous, short-stalked, **pinnately compound, the leaflets usually 5,** oblong to narrowly elliptic, 0.5–2 cm long, greyish green, sparsely silky-hairy; margins untoothed, often rolled under.

Flowers: Showy, **2–3 cm across,** saucer-shaped, single in leaf axils or in small clusters at branch tips; **petals 5, yellow,** nearly circular, 7–14 mm long; sepals 5, soft-hairy; stamens 25–30.

Fruits: Achenes numerous, clustered, egg-shaped, 1.5–2 mm long, coarsely white-hairy.

Where Found: Dry to wet meadows, thickets, peatlands, rocky slopes and ridges, gravelly flats, talus, fellfields and tundra, usually on calcium-rich substrates; montane to alpine zones; frequent throughout the region, except mostly absent from the Pacific coast and rare on Vancouver I. and in central BC; species complex circumboreal with large gaps.

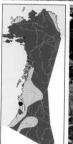

Notes: Shrubby cinquefoil is also known as *Potentilla fruticosa* ssp. *floribunda* and *Pentaphylloides floribunda*. • This species is our only truly shrubby *Potentilla*, though it is currently placed in a separate genus. • The Blackfoot of Alberta used the dry, flaky bark as tinder for making friction fires. The Chugach Inuit report boiling the plant and drinking the tea as a medicine for tuberculosis. Other Alaskans say that the old people would wipe their faces with the leaves before the flowers grew. • This species is a popular garden ornamental with many cultivars. • *Dasiphora* is from the Greek *dasys*, meaning "shaggy, rough or hairy," and aptly describes the appearance of the stems. "Cinquefoil" comes from the French *cinq* and *feuilles* or the Latin *cinque foliola*, both meaning "5 leaves."

Mountain Gooseberry • *Ribes montigenum*

General: Spreading, freely branched, 0.2–1 m tall; stems bristly-hairy and glandular, the nodes usually with **3–5 slender spines,** 4–6 mm long.

Leaves: Alternate, deciduous, 1–4 cm wide, 5-lobed for more than ½ their length; margins deeply toothed; **both surfaces hairy and/or stalked-glandular.**

Flowers: Small, **greenish white to yellowish or pinkish,** saucer-shaped, 3–8 in drooping clusters from leaf axils, stalks 1–4 mm long, jointed below flowers; petals 5, red to pinkish or purplish, 1–1.5 mm long, narrowed to stalk-like base; sepals 5, greenish white to yellowish or pinkish, egg-shaped, 3–4 mm long; hypanthium pink to orangey, hairy, bristly-glandular; stamens 5, purplish red.

Fruits: Berries nearly globe-shaped, **bright red,** 4–10 mm long, **coarsely bristly with stalked-glandular hairs** (lollipop-like); somewhat palatable.

Where Found: Mesic to dry, open forests, talus slopes, rocky ridges and ledges; sub-alpine and alpine zones; frequent south of about 49° N; cordilleran.

Similar Species: Black gooseberry (*R. lacustre*) occasionally reaches lower alpine eleva-tions, at least in southern parts of the region. It has **hairless or sparsely hairy leaves, maroon flowers** and **blackish, bristly-glandular berries.** Black gooseberry grows on streambanks and in avalanche tracks and moist places around rocks and at the edges of tree clumps throughout the southern ¾ of the region. • Two varieties of **northern gooseberry** or Canadian gooseberry (*R. oxyacanthoides* **var. *hendersonii*** and **var. *setosum*)** can occur at high elevations in MT, ID and WY on rocky slopes, cliffs and talus. They have **finely hairy and glandular leaves** but **greenish white flowers** and reddish to purplish black, palatable, **hairless berries.**

northern gooseberry

Notes: *Ribes* is said to be from the Arabic *ribas*, meaning "acid-tasting." "Gooseberry" is thought to be a garbling of either the French *groseille* (red currant) or of the Latinization of *groseille* by 16th-century botanists as *grossula*—in either case assimilated to "goose."

Maple-leaved Currant • *Ribes acerifolium*

General: Erect to spreading, much-branched, 0.5–1 m tall; stems often glandular but **without bristles or spines. Leaves:** Maple-leaf-shaped, 3–8 cm wide, **cleft halfway to midrib into 5 lobes,** finely hairy, sprinkled with glands. **Flowers:** Pinkish, saucer-shaped, 7–15 in drooping clusters from leaf axils, stalks jointed below flowers; petals red, 1–1.5 mm long; sepals pinkish or pinkish white, 2–3 mm long; hypanthium greenish white, sparsely glandular-hairy.

Fruits: Berries blue-black with a whitish bloom, slightly hairy, sparsely glandular; unpalatable. **Where Found:** Moist meadows, streambanks and rocky ridges, often around tree clumps; frequent; montane to alpine zones; Pacific Northwest endemic.

Similar Species: Sticky currant (*R. viscosissimum*) is very aromatic and has leaves and flowers covered with **soft, sticky hairs,** the **leaves shallowly 3–5-lobed,** the **flowers greenish white to cream** and bell-shaped. It grows in moist to dry, open forests and glades, and at the edges of tree clumps in subalpine parkland. Sticky currant ranges from montane to subalpine zones and is frequent inland from southern BC and adjacent AB to CA, AZ and CO.

Notes: Maple-leaved currant is also known as *Ribes howellii*. • This and other *Ribes* species are alternate hosts for white pine blister rust (*Cronartium ribicola*), the fungus that kills whitebark pine (p. 44), limber pine (p. 45) and other 5-needled pines. The rust, introduced to western North America less than a century ago, has long been believed to require currants or gooseberries to complete its life cycle (but see small-flowered paintbrush, p. 267). • "Currant" is a name originally applied to a dried small grape from Corinth called *Uva corinthiaca*. Readers of a certain age may remember a TV commercial for the Chrysler Cordoba motorcar, in which a suave Ricardo Montalban extolled the virtues of "Corinthian leather" interior appointments.

Diapensia, Alaska Pincushion Plant
Diapensia obovata

General: Dwarf, **sprawling**, much-branched shrub from a taproot; stems 5–10 cm long, prostrate, forming **small, tight mats or cushions;** branches ascending to 5 cm tall.

Leaves: Evergreen, thick, lustrous, yellow-green, mostly opposite, crowded and overlapping, **egg- to spoon-shaped,** 3–10 mm long, hairless, rounded at the tip; margins rolled under; lower surface pale.

Flowers: Solitary atop reddish stalks 0.5–5 cm tall, **cup-shaped,** subtended by 3 bracts; **corolla white to cream, sometimes pinkish,** 5-lobed, 7–9 mm long; sepals 5, yellowish green, 4–7 mm long, persistent and enclosing the fruit at maturity; **stamens 5,** alternate with petals.

Fruits: Capsules egg-shaped, 3-chambered, 3–6 mm long; seeds numerous.

Where Found: Dry to moist, acidic meadows, heathlands, rocky or gravelly slopes, fellfields and tundra; subalpine and alpine zones; locally frequent in the northern ¼ of the region; arctic-alpine, amphiberingian.

Notes: Diapensia is also known as *D. lapponica* ssp. *obovata*. • *Obovata* means "inverted ovate" (egg-shaped with the broadest end uppermost), which describes the leaf shape. "Pincushion plant" describes the growth form. Its Norwegian name is *fjellpyrd*, meaning "mountain decoration."

EVERGREEN HABIT

Many alpine plants are evergreens, most prominently the treeline conifers (with the notable exception of larch, p. 43) and dwarf shrubs such as mountain-avens (*Dryas*), Lapland rosebay (*Rhododendron lapponicum*), lingonberry (*Vaccinium vitis-idaea*), the mountain-heathers (*Cassiope, Phyllodoce, Harimanella*) and several other heather-family genera (*Empetrum, Kalmia, Arctostaphylos*). A very few alpine herbs are evergreen, for example, leatherleaf saxifrage (*Leptarrhena pyrolifolia*), arctic wintergreen (*Pyrola grandiflora*); and also some lycopods (the clubmosses, *Lycopodium*, and spikemosses, *Selaginella*). Evergreen-leaved species dominate alpine vegetation in the high-snowfall parts of the region and in certain habitats (often snow accumulation sites) elsewhere in less snowy, inland or far northern parts of the region.

What are the advantages of the evergreen habit? Evergreens—especially coniferous trees—can gather sunlight and grow much of the year, whenever it is warm enough. But this advantage is curtailed at high elevations, where the growing season and mild temperatures are brief. Perhaps evergreens are hardier, better able to survive the harsh alpine environment. Yes they often have tough-textured, needle-like or rolled leaves with a thick epidermis and cuticle, which resist tattering by wind and reduce water loss through evapotranspiration. But they are vulnerable to other effects of wind: scouring and abrasion by dust and snow (especially in winter if the leaves are not protected by the snowpack); reduction in tissue temperature; and moisture stress during winter (especially if the ground is frozen and roots can't take up water).

Conifers and other northern or high-elevation evergreens are, however, more efficient at growing at low temperatures and on nutrient-poor soils. The key is probably a frugal, nutrient-conservative lifestyle. Evergreen plants have lower rates of photosynthesis and respiration than comparable deciduous plants, thus require less energy and nutrients to survive. They do not have to grow a new set of leaves every spring, so they expend considerably less energy annually on leaves. The downside is that evergreens must maintain and protect those long-lived leaves, which grow slowly, typically have a reduced surface area and increased armour, and are "out there" year-round. And evergreens cannot capitalize on brief periods of optimal growing conditions as quickly and efficiently as their deciduous counterparts. Deciduous shrubs with broad leaves, such as willows and dwarf birch, have a competitive advantage in our short but intense summers—especially at northern latitudes with long days and short, frost-free nights. They can then drop their leaves to "escape" winter.

Nonetheless, some of our evergreens have met the high-elevation challenge very successfully. Timberline trees may look hard done by, but they are remarkably tenacious once they get a foothold, and in many parts of the region tree species are infiltrating and ultimately occupying heathlands and meadows. The mountain-heathers and partridgefoot (*Luetkea pectinata*) dominate large areas of snowy northwestern alplands. Alpine-azalea (*Kalmia procumbens*), Lapland rosebay, northern Labrador tea (*Rhododendron tomentosum*), crowberry (*Empetrum nigrum*) and lingonberry are widespread, and all are locally abundant where their particular habitat needs are met. And mountain-avens are nitrogen-fixing, keystone species, colonizing and dominating calcium-rich, windswept tundra, fellfields and well-drained gravelly deposits.

HEATHER FAMILY (Ericaceae)

The heather family in our region consists mostly of shrubs, but also includes herbs in the Indian-pipe (*Monotropa*) subfamily, which includes the wintergreens (e.g., arctic wintergreen, p. 298). Most Ericaceae species are evergreen shrubs; some are deciduous, especially in *Vaccinium*, *Rhododendron* and related genera. Our shrubs range from dwarf, mat-forming or creeping to medium-sized or erect. The leaves are usually alternate along the stem, sometimes opposite, or in basal rosettes (*Monotropa* subfamily), **simple** (not compound or divided), lacking **stipules** (appendages at the base of leaf stalks); the margins are entire or toothed. The flowers are radially symmetric, occasionally somewhat bilaterally symmetric as in *Rhododendron* or *Elliot-*

four-angled mountain-heather

tia, mostly with 4 or 5 sepals that are distinct or united at the base (collectively forming the **calyx**); 4 or 5 petals that are distinct or more typically fused (collectively forming the **corolla**) and urn-, globe-, bell-, bowl- or star-shaped; stamens mostly twice as many as corolla lobes, the anthers often with awns, opening by pores or slits; a 4–5-chambered ovary; and 1 style . The fruits are dry capsules, fleshy berries or berry-like drupes. The seeds are few and bony, or numerous and small or tiny and dust-like.

With about 4100 species worldwide, Ericaceae is a large family, especially in its present expanded form. In the past and on the basis of differences in habit, flower structure and pollen, many botanists treated *Monotropa* and related mycotrophic genera (such as *Hemitomes* and *Pterospora*), *Pyrola* and related genera (*Chimaphila, Moneses, Orthilia*) and *Empetrum* in their own families: Monotropaceae, Pyrolaceae and Empetraceae, respectively. There has, however, been a long history of support for a more inclusive, blended heather family. Recent studies, which since about 1990 have included DNA and other molecular analyses, indicate that accommodating these genera in a roomier Ericaceae makes the best evolutionary sense.

Vaccinium species are important producers of edible berries, both wild and commercial, including blueberries, huckleberries and cranberries. *Rhododendron* (including many deciduous species known as azaleas) and *Kalmia* are notable genera for ornamental shrubs, whereas others such as *Arbutus* and *Menziesia* are favoured by some. *Arctostaphylos uva-ursi, Kalmia procumbens* and *Rhododendron lapponicum* find a place in many rock gardens.

The leaves of some genera, including *Rhododendron* and *Kalmia*, contain andromedotoxins and are poisonous to humans, domestic pets and livestock.

mixed mountain-heathers

Crowberry, Mossberry • *Empetrum nigrum*

General: Low, spreading or creeping, freely branching, heath-like; stems 10–70 cm long, prostrate, mat-forming; branches ascending to 20 cm tall, sparsely white-hairy.

Leaves: Roughly whorled or alternate and spirally arranged, evergreen, leathery, linear, 3–7 mm long, minutely glandular-hairy or hairless, spreading, numerous and crowded; margins rolled under; **lower surface grooved.**

Flowers: Small, **inconspicuous, purplish crimson,** solitary (but often with 1–2 neighbours along the branches) and **unstalked in leaf axils,** subtended by 3 scale-like bracts smaller than the sepals, bisexual or sometimes unisexual (males and females on separate plants); petals 3, 2–3 mm long, soon dropping off; sepals 3, greenish pink becoming **reddish purple,** shorter than petals, persistent on fruit; stamens 2–4 (usually 3 in male flowers), longer than petals, persistent on fruit; ovary with a lobed stigma.

Fruits: Berry-like drupes, black, globe-shaped, 4–10 mm across; seeds 6–9, pale, stone-like.

Where Found: Wet to moist acidic sites, including bogs, open forests, meadows, heathlands, rocky slopes and outcrops, fell-fields and tundra; lowland to alpine zones; frequent throughout the northern ¾ of the region, infrequent southward; widespread circumpolar.

Similar Species: Crowberry resembles some mountain-heathers (species of *Phyllodoce* and *Harrimanella*) but has black berries and inconspicuous flowers. It was sometimes considered distinctive enough to merit its own family but *FNA* now includes it within Ericaceae.

Notes: Crowberry flowers typically have 9 scale-like segments: 3 bracts, then 6 inner segments that have been interpreted either as 3 petals plus 3 sepals or else as all sepals. Plants with bisexual flowers have been designated by some as *Empetrum hermaphroditum* or as *E. nigrum* ssp. or var. *hermaphroditum.* • The flowers bloom very early in the growing season and are primarily wind  pollinated. • Crowberry is eaten by northern First Nations groups—Dene-thah, Wet'suwet'en, Dena'ina, Gwich'in and Alaskan Inuit, among others—and is often mixed with other more flavourful berries and bear grease. The berries are stored mixed with lard or as dried berry cakes. They reportedly make good pies and jelly, though they are rather acidic and insipid tasting. • Crowberry contains 13 different anthocyanins and has among the highest antioxidant activity of any of our native berries. Beer and sparkling wines can also be made from the berries, which are a favourite food of bears. • The Dena'ina and Gwich'in used the strained liquid from stems and leaves that had been boiled or soaked in hot water as medicine for diarrhea, stomach problems and bad colds. The berry juice was said to be good for kidney troubles. Boiled, strained and cooled root tea (sometimes with a little sugar added) was applied as a wash for sore eyes and snow blindness. • *Empetrum* is from the Greek *en petros,* meaning "in or on rock" and alluding to the typical rocky habitat; *nigrum* means "black." The name "crowberry" was given presumably because the fruit is flat black like a crow's plumage, though often berries and other plants were named after animals because they were considered to be inferior, in this case, fit only for crows. It is also called "mossberry" in the North, perhaps because it grows down in the moss layer or has a mossy look.

Pink Mountain-heather • *Phyllodoce empetriformis*

General: **Low,** freely branching, **matted;** stems ascending, 5–50 cm tall, finely hairy and glandular when young, becoming hairless.

Leaves: Alternate, evergreen, leathery, **linear, 4–15 mm long,** hairless, spreading-ascending, numerous, crowded; margins with tiny, glandular teeth or smooth, rolled under; **lower surface grooved.**

Flowers: Solitary to many in clusters atop flowering stems, on minutely glandular-hairy stalks to 2.5 cm long, fragrant, **bell-shaped,** erect to nodding; **corolla pink to deep rose,** 4–8 mm long, **hairless,** the 5 lobes curled back; sepals 5, reddish, oval, 2–3 mm long, minutely fringed; stamens 10, shorter than corolla, filaments hairless; style 1, protruding beyond corolla.

Fruits: Capsules rather woody, nearly globe-shaped, 3–4 mm across, glandular-hairy; seeds tiny, numerous, narrowly winged.

Where Found: Dry to moist, acidic, open forests, rocky glades, meadows, heathlands and tundra; upper montane to alpine zones; frequent in most of the southern ¾ of the region, absent from Haida Gwaii; cordilleran.

Notes: The hybrid between pink and yellow mountain-heathers is called *P.* × *intermedia* and is common where the 2 species occur together. The hybrids have pale pink, cylindric to oval flowers. • *Phyllodoce* comes from the name of a Greek sea nymph (the allusion is obscure); *empetriformis* means "like *Empetrum*," which it is.

Yellow Mountain-heather
Phyllodoce glanduliflora

General: Low, freely branching, **matted;** stems ascending to erect, 10–40 cm tall, finely glandular-hairy when young, hairless with age. **Leaves:** Similar to those of pink mountain-heather (above) but 4–12 mm long, **finely glandular-hairy.**
Flowers: Clustered atop flowering stems, on **densely glandular-hairy stalks** 1–3.5 cm long, **flask-shaped,** nodding to erect; **corolla yellowish to greenish white,** 5–9 mm long, **glandular-hairy** on the outside, the 5 lobes spreading; sepals greenish, lance-shaped, 3–4 mm long, **glandular-hairy;** stamens with **hairy filaments;** style not protruding from corolla. **Fruits:** Capsules rather woody, nearly globe-shaped, 3–5 mm in diameter, glandular-hairy. **Where Found:** Dry to moist, open forests, meadows, heathlands and tundra; upper montane to alpine zones; frequent throughout the southern ¾ of the region; cordilleran.

Similar Species: This species hybridizes with and is sometimes designated as a subspecies of **Aleutian mountain-heather (*P. aleutica*),** which has flowers with **hairless, non-glandular corollas** and **stamens with hairless filaments.** Aleutian mountain-heather grows in meadows, heathlands and alpine tundra, mostly in the Aleutian Islands but extending to the Prince William Sound area and the Talkeetna Mtns of interior AK. • **Purple mountain-heather (*P. caerulea*)** has **lavender to dark purple flowers.** It is a circumpolar species of North American tundra and snowbeds and occurs from far western AK interruptedly east to the Atlantic.

Notes: Yellow mountain-heather is also known as *Phyllodoce aleutica* ssp. *glanduliflora*. • The species name *glanduliflora* refers to the glandular hairs on the flowers and their stalks.

Alaska Mountain-heather, Alaska Moss-heather
Harrimanella stelleriana

General: Dwarf, branching, forming **dense, soft mats; stems thread-like,** prostrate; branches spreading, ascending at tips, 5–15 cm tall, hairless to minutely hairy.

Leaves: **Alternate,** evergreen, leathery, **spreading,** more or less 4-ranked, linear-oblong, 3–5 mm long, hairless; upper surface flat, lower surface convex and somewhat keeled.

Flowers: Solitary at branch ends, on stout, fine-hairy stalks barely exceeding the leaves, **broadly bell-shaped, often nodding; corolla white or tinged pink,** 5–7 mm long, hairless, the 5 lobes longer than the tube; sepals 5, reddish; stamens 10, filaments swollen at base.

Fruits: Capsules erect, 5-chambered, nearly globe-shaped, about 5 mm across.

Where Found: Moist meadows, sheltered rocky slopes, heathlands, late-melt snowbeds and tundra; subalpine and alpine zones; frequent in the Pacific coastal mountains, more so on the north coast, infrequent inland; amphiberingian.

Similar Species: Resembles crowberry (p. 75) and pink and yellow mountain-heathers (p. 76) but has white flowers and leaves that are rounded beneath.

Notes: Alaska mountain-heather is also known as *Cassiope stelleriana*. • The genus is named for American railway tycoon and financier E.H. Harriman (1848–1909), a patron of science and the organizer of the 1900 Harriman expedition to Alaska. The name is perhaps also an eponymous nod to the sasquatch ("hairy man"), who might sleep on mats of this species in subalpine parkland. The species name honours Georg Wilhelm Steller (1709–46), the first European naturalist to study the plants and animals of Alaska, and who also notably described the now-extinct Steller's sea cow and a perhaps-still-extant sea monkey.

White Mountain-heather, Mertens' Moss-heather • *Cassiope mertensiana*

General: Dwarf, branching, **mat-forming; stems stiff, with leaves appearing 4-angled** and about 4 mm wide; branches ascending, 5–30 cm long/tall, hairless or finely hairy.

Leaves: Opposite, in 4 rows, evergreen, leathery, pressed to stem, overlapping, canoe-shaped, 3–5 mm long, **rounded on outer face,** not papery-margined, without curly hairs at tips.

Flowers: Solitary from leaf axils, usually in small groups near branch tips, nodding on reddish stalks 5–30 mm long, **bell-shaped; corolla white,** 5–8 mm long, the 5 lobes egg-shaped, **about ⅓ as long as the tube;** sepals 5, reddish; stamens 10, not swollen at base.

Fruits: Capsules erect, 5-chambered, nearly globe-shaped, 2–4 mm across.

Where Found: Open forests, meadows, rocky slopes, heathlands and tundra; upper montane to alpine zones; frequent in the southern ¾ of the region but uncommon on Haida Gwaii; cordilleran.

Subspecies: *C. mertensiana* has 4 subspecies: **ssp. *mertensiana*** (hairy stems; widespread) and **ssp. *gracilis*** (hairless stems; OR, MT, ID) occur in our region, whereas the other 2 occur in CA.

Similar Species: Four-angled mountain-heather or arctic white mountain-heather (**C. tetragona**) has leaves that are **deeply grooved on the back.** An arctic-alpine circumpolar species, it is frequent in the northern ¾ of the region, inland of the coastal mountains, in AK, YT and NT (replacing white mountain-heather) south through BC and southwestern AB to WA and MT. It occupies wind-swept habitats in moister, snowy climates and sheltered snow-accumulation sites in drier climates.
• **Club-moss mountain-heather** (**C. lycopodioides**) differs in its slim stems (about **2 mm thick** including appressed leaves) and **papery-margined leaves** not in 4 distinct rows and with a few **curly hairs at the tips,** at least when young. It occurs on montane to alpine, rocky slopes, meadows and heathlands, and is an amphiberingian species, infrequent in coastal southern AK and northern coastal BC (frequent on Haida Gwaii) south to northern Vancouver I. and northern WA.

Notes: The Inuit traditionally use four-angled mountain-heather to make fires. • A golden brown dye can be extracted from *Cassiope* branches.

Alpine-Azalea • *Kalmia procumbens*

General: Dwarf, much-branched, **prostrate to sprawling, mat-forming;** stems 5–30 cm long, 2–10 cm tall, hairless or minutely hairy.

Leaves: Opposite, evergreen, leathery, lance-oblong to elliptic, **3–8 mm long;** margins rolled under; upper surface usually hairless, grooved and dark green, lower surface finely short-hairy and whitish.

Flowers: Few in clusters or sometimes solitary at branch tips, **cup-shaped,** on reddish purple stalks 0.5–2 cm long; **corolla pink,** sometimes whitish, **3–5 mm long,** the 5 lobes spreading, **cleft for** ½ their length; sepals 5, reddish, about 1.5 mm long, persistent; **stamens 5.**

Fruits: Capsules somewhat woody, **2–3-chambered,** egg-shaped, 3–4 mm long; seeds numerous, winged.

Where Found: Coastal bogs, dry to mesic, acidic heath-lands, stony slopes and tundra; lowland to alpine zones; frequent in the northern ½ of the region, infrequent southward; arctic-alpine, circumpolar with large gaps.

Notes: Alpine-azalea is also known as *Loiseleuria procumbens*. • "Azalea" is Latin for "of dry habitats." Linnaeus originally named the plant *Azalea procumbens* because in Lapland, it grew hugging the ground (procumbent) in dry habitats.

Alpine Bog-laurel • *Kalmia microphylla* var. *microphylla*

General: Low, branched, **spreading to erect;** stems 5–20 cm tall, finely hairy when young, becoming hairless.

Leaves: Opposite, evergreen, leathery, lance-oblong to elliptic, **1.5–2 cm long;** margins rolled under; upper surface shiny and dark green, lower surface greyish white with dense, short hairs.

Flowers: Solitary or in few-flowered clusters at branch tips, **bowl-shaped,** on slender, reddish stalks 1–3 cm long; **corolla deep pink to rose,** about 1 cm across, **7–9 mm long, shallowly 5-lobed,** the bowl with 10 pouches in which the anthers are tucked in bud; sepals about 3 mm long; **stamens 10,** flattened filaments hairy toward the base.

Fruits: Capsules 5-chambered, nearly globe-shaped, about 4 mm across.

Where Found: Bogs, wet meadows, turfy seepage areas, snowbeds, streambanks and lakeshores; subalpine and lower alpine zones; infrequent in the southern ¾ of the region; cordilleran.

Varieties: Taller plants with larger leaves and flowers and growing at lower elevations belong to **western bog-laurel (K. microphylla var. occidentalis;** *K. polifolia* in part).

Notes: As a flower opens, the anther of each stamen is tucked into a tiny petal pouch, and the filament is held under tension like a bow. When an insect visitor touches the filament, the anthers snap out and dust the insect with pollen. • The leaves contain andromedotoxin, which is poisonous to livestock and humans. Take care not to collect *Kalmia* when harvesting Labrador tea (p. 89); the leaves have similar shapes. • *Kalmia* honours Peter Kalm (1715–79), a Swedish botanist and a student of Linnaeus; he collected specimens in eastern North America. The name "laurel" was presumably given because someone thought the leaves looked and smelled like bay (laurel) leaves.

Alpine-wintergreen, Teaberry
Gaultheria humifusa

General: Dwarf, branched, **creeping**, often **forming small mats** to 5 cm tall; stems prostrate to ascending, 10–30 cm long, usually finely hairy.

Leaves: Alternate, evergreen, leathery, broadly egg-shaped to elliptic, **1–2.5 cm long**, hairless; margins thickened, smooth to finely sawtoothed, the teeth sometimes bristle tipped.

Flowers: Solitary on short stalks in leaf axils, **bell-shaped; corolla reddish to pink**, 3–4 mm long, 5-lobed; sepals 5, slightly shorter than corolla, hairless; stamens 10, filaments swollen toward the base.

Fruits: Berry-like, the **fleshy, reddish calyx** surrounding a many-seeded, globed-shaped capsule, 5–7 mm across.

Where Found: Moist to wet, open coniferous forests, streambanks, meadows, bogs and rocky slopes; subalpine and lower alpine zones; infrequent in the southern ⅓ of the region; cordilleran.

Similar Species: Western teaberry (*G. ovatifolia*) is spreading but **not mat-forming**, with **larger leaves (2–4 cm long)** and **white to pale pink flowers** with **hairy sepals.** It is found in open forests, heathlands and rocky slopes; its distribution is much the same as alpine-wintergreen but in montane to subalpine (not alpine) zones.

Notes: "Wintergreen" likely refers to the leaves, which stay green year-round; also, the leaves and fruits of some *Gaultheria* species taste and smell like wintergreen. • The berries are edible, but care should be taken because they contain methyl salicylate (oil of wintergreen), which is related to aspirin and can be toxic in large doses. Children should avoid eating them. • It is also known as "teaberry" because the leaves were used to make a tea to treat asthma and diarrhea, restore strength and promote menstruation or the production of breast milk.

Black Alpine Bearberry, Torpedo-berry • *Arctous alpina*

General: Dwarf, **much-branched, mat-forming;** stems prostrate, branches erect, short, to 15 cm tall, hairless, with shreddy bark.

Leaves: Alternate but in rosette-like clusters, **withering** and persistent below leaves of the current year, turning deep red in autumn, broadly egg- to lance-shaped, **1–2.5 cm long**, rounded at tip; **margins blunt-toothed**, fringed toward the base and along the leaf stalk; **embossed above**, conspicuously **net-veined below.**

Flowers: In clusters of 2–3 at branch tips, appearing before leaves unfold, **urn-shaped;** corolla yellowish green when young, becoming **white to cream**, 4–5 mm long, 5-lobed; stamens 10, filaments flattened, widened and usually hairy toward the base.

Fruits: Drupes berry-like, juicy, globe-shaped, **purplish black,** lustrous, 5–10 mm across.

Where Found: Dry to mesic heathlands, gravelly or rocky ridges, fellfields and stony tundra; lowland (arctic coast) to alpine zones; frequent in the northern ½ of the region, infrequent southward; arctic-alpine, circumpolar.

Similar Species: Red alpine bearberry (*A. rubra*; *Arctostaphylos rubra, Arctostaphylos alpina* var. *rubra*) has **scarlet berries** and **larger leaves** (mostly 2–5 cm long) with hairless margins and stalks. It grows in moist to mesic, open forests, swamps, peaty thickets, heathlands and tundra, in montane (usually) to lower alpine zones, with much the same distribution in our region except a disjunction in WY. • When not in flower or fruit, both of these alpine bearberries could be confused with net-veined willow (p. 59).

Notes: Black alpine bearberry is also known as *Arctostaphylos alpina*. • The genus *Arctous* (which means "northern," or, more fundamentally, "the land of bears") is distinguished from *Arctostaphylos* in having leaves with winged stalks and blunt-toothed margins, anthers without horns or awns, juicy rather than mealy berries, and 5 (not 10) nutlets per berry. • Both black alpine bearberry and kinnikinnik (p. 80) form distinctive associations called "arbutoid mycorrhizae" between their roots and soil fungi. The roots have fungi growing both on and in them; the fine filaments of these fungi help the plant to obtain water and some minerals, and the plant in exchange delivers sugars to the fungi. • Black alpine bearberries were eaten fresh by the Dene but were not a favourite because they are rather insipid. The Gwich'in called the berries "bird's eyes" and would add them to pemmican.

Kinnikinnik, Bearberry
Arctostaphylos uva-ursi

General: Dwarf, branched, **trailing, often forming mats** by rooting along the stems; stems prostrate and creeping, ascending at tip, 5–15 cm tall, minutely hairy; twigs with brownish red, shredding bark.

Leaves: Alternate, **evergreen**, leathery, narrowly egg- to spoon-shaped, 1–3 cm long, rounded at tip; **margins not toothed;** green above, paler below, hairless or minutely hairy on margins and midrib.

Flowers: Solitary to several in clusters at branch tips, short-stalked, **urn-shaped;** corolla pinkish white, 4–6 mm long, 5-lobed; sepals 5, much shorter than corolla.

Fruits: Drupes berry-like, like a miniature cherry, **mealy** (not juicy), **bright red**, globe-shaped, 5–12 mm across.

Where Found: Dry, open forests, sandy gravelly flats, open rocky slopes and exposed ridges; lowland to lower alpine zones; common throughout most of the region but mostly at lower elevations; widespread circumboreal.

Similar Species: Kinnikinnik could be confused with lingonberry (p. 81), which typically holds its leaves **at right angles (90°) to the stem** and has distinctive whisker-glands on the underside of the leaves; kinnikinnik holds its leaves **mostly obliquely (at roughly 45°) to the stem.**

Notes: The Gwich'in called this plant "stoneberry" because the fruits are dry and mealy with large, hard seeds. However, they mashed the berries up with pounded, dried fish, loche (burbot) liver or fish eggs to make a type of pemmican. The Dena'ina found the berries more palatable when mixed with oil or lard. Bearberries were also stored in oil or lard and often taken when travelling and camping. They were important as a survival food in the early days and kept well in caches. The longer they were stored, the sweeter they became, and storage softened the hard seeds to make them easier to eat. The berries were also cooked in soups and stews by several groups. • The dried leaves were used in smoking mixtures by southern First Nations groups, but not by the Wet'suwet'en until after contact with Europeans. • Fungi and the roots of most terrestrial plants form mutually beneficial associations called mycorrhizae ("fungus-roots"). In alpine and arctic areas, plants form different sorts of mycorrhizae with different kinds of fungi. The mycorrhizal fungi of tundra plants are generally dark septate endophytes, some of which have been identified in culture as *Phialocephala fortinii*. This fungal species is the common Rocky Mountain associate of kinnikinnik, white mountain-heather (p. 77), false azalea (p. 87), partridge-foot (p. 69) and probably other species. • *Arctostaphylos* is from the Greek *arktos*, "bear," and *staphyle*, "bunch of grapes"; the specific epithet translates from Latin as "berry bear" (*uva* for "berry," and *ursus* for "bear"). "Kinnikinnik" is from an eastern Native name (possibly Algonquin) meaning "that which is mixed," and was applied to any smoking mixture.

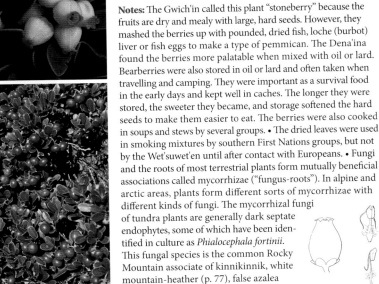

Lingonberry, Mountain-cranberry
Vaccinium vitis-idaea

General: **Dwarf,** branched, **mat-forming;** stems trailing to ascending, 5–25 cm long/tall, minutely hairy.

Leaves: Alternate, **evergreen,** leathery, narrowly elliptic to egg-shaped, 0.5–1 cm long, rounded to shallowly notched at tip; **margins not toothed,** somewhat rolled under; shiny, green above, paler and spotted with **short brown (whiskery) glandular hairs below.**

Flowers: Solitary to several in compact clusters at branch tips, short-stalked, **bell-shaped,** nodding; **corolla pinkish white,** 3–5 mm long, **4-lobed** to near the middle; **sepals 4,** much shorter than corolla; stamens 8, **filaments hairy.**

Fruits: Berries bright red, tart, **globe-shaped,** 6–10 mm across.

Where Found: Wet to dry, boreal forests, bogs, thickets, open rocky slopes and exposed ridges, heathlands, stony barrens and tundra; lowland to alpine zones; common in the northern ⅔ of the region, infrequent southward; subarctic-arctic, circumpolar.

Similar Species: See kinnikinnik (p. 80).

Notes: Edible but initially hard and tart, the berries are best after the first autumn frost. They remain on the plant through winter, and children in the North often collect handfuls of them as the snow disappears. The berries were eaten fresh or mixed with lard or oil for storage or added to pemmican. The Nisga'a would whip lingonberries with snow for a dessert. Today, they usually mix the berries with sugar and lard to make this treat. They are also excellent for making jam, jelly and cranberry sauce. • The Cree and Dene would boil the stems and roots and drink the decoction for bladder problems. The raw berries were good for treating fever and "cleaning out" the stomach. The Gwich'in consider lingonberry juice to be good for kidney problems, colds, coughs and improving the appetite. The juice is also used to dye porcupine quills. • Lingonberry is akin to the Old Norse and Middle English *lyng,* meaning "heather" or "heath." *Vitis-idaea* literally means "vine of Mt. Ida," a mountain in Crete where this plant grew.

Grouseberry, Grouse Whortleberry, Bilberry • *Vaccinium scoparium*

General: **Low,** somewhat matted, **colonial** via rhizomes; stems 10–25 cm tall, closely branched; **twigs whisk-broom-like,** numerous, slender, **strongly angled, greenish,** hairless.

Leaves: Alternate, **deciduous,** nearly stalkless, narrowly egg-shaped, **broadest at midleaf, 0.5–1 cm long,** pointy-tipped, margins finely sawtoothed; hairless, shiny and green above, dull and conspicuously veined below.

Flowers: **Solitary** in leaf axils, urn-shaped; corolla pearly pink, about 4 mm long and wide, with 5 short lobes; sepals 5, indistinct; stamens 10.

Fruits: Berries bright red (rarely purplish), globe-shaped, 3–6 mm across.

Where Found: Dry to mesic forests, glades and edges, meadows, heathlands and open, rocky slopes, extending up to and above treeline; montane to lower alpine zones; frequent in the southern ½ of the region; cordilleran.

Similar Species: Whortleberry or low bilberry (*V. myrtillus*) occupies similar habitats but has **larger leaves (2–3 cm long) and flowers,** minutely hairy, **less broom-like twigs** and darker, **blue-black** to dark red berries. It is a circumboreal species locally frequent in the southeastern part of the region, southeastern BC and southwestern AB to OR, AZ and NM.

Notes: Grouseberry often forms a dense ground cover in open coniferous forests. It is probably the most drought tolerant of our *Vaccinum* species. • "Grouseberry" is apt because grouse eat all aboveground parts of the plant. "Whortleberry" comes via myrtleberry (*V. myrtillus*), which was apparently first called "hurtleberry" but evolved into "whortle" or "myrtle." *Wyrtil* is an old word for "shrub." "Bilberry" is from the Danish *bollebar,* meaning "dark berry."

Cascade Blueberry, Blue-leaved Huckleberry
Vaccinium deliciosum

General: Low, often matted, clumped or colonial; stems 15–30 cm tall, densely branched; twigs slender, rarely angled, greenish brown.

Leaves: Alternate, **deciduous,** narrowly egg-shaped, 2–4 cm long, usually blunt or rounded at tip; margins often distantly toothed along upper half; upper surface hairless and dull green, pale green with **whitish bloom beneath.**

Flowers: Solitary in leaf axils, nodding, **globe- to broadly urn-shaped;** corolla pinkish, 4–6 mm long and nearly as wide, with 5 short lobes; sepals fused into a saucer-like calyx, the 5 lobes indistinct; stamens 10.

Fruits: Berries usually deep blue with a pale grey bloom, nearly globe-shaped, 6–9 mm across.

Where Found: Mesic to moist forests, glades and edges, meadows and heathlands; montane to lower alpine zones; locally frequent in the southwestern part of the region; Pacific Northwest endemic.

Similar Species: Dwarf blueberry (*V. caespitosum*) has **narrowly urn-shaped to nearly cylindric flowers** about twice as long as wide and more **distinctly toothed leaves,** widest above the middle, **green on both sides** and **prominently net-veined beneath.** It occurs in forests, bogs, meadows and tundra, in lowland to alpine zones. A boreal North American species, it is frequent through all but the far north.

dwarf blueberry

Notes: Cascade blueberry often forms the dominant ground cover at high elevations in the Cascade, Olympic and Vancouver I. mountains, colouring entire slopes and plateau parklands when its leaves turn red in autumn, "slathering the open slopes like coals from an open forge" (Pyle, 1995).

Bog Blueberry, Bog Bilberry
Vaccinium uliginosum

General: Low, spreading to erect, often forming mats or extensive colonies; stems 10–50 cm tall; twigs round in cross-section, **not angled,** pale green when young, greyish red when older.

Leaves: Alternate, **deciduous,** narrowly to broadly egg-shaped or elliptic, widest above the middle, 0.8–1.5 cm long, blunt or rounded at tip, hairless or hairy; **margins not toothed,** somewhat rolled under; green or greyish green above, pale green or with a slight bloom and often strongly **net-veined beneath.**

Flowers: Clusters of 2–4 (sometimes 1) in leaf axils, urn-shaped; corolla pink, often with broad, white stripes, 4–6 mm long, with **4 (usually)** or 5 short lobes; sepals 4–5; **stamens usually 8.**

Fruits: Berries blue with a strong bloom, globe-shaped, 5–8 mm across.

Where Found: Bogs, boggy forests, dry to wet thickets, heathlands and tundra; lowland to alpine zones; frequent throughout the northern ½ of the region, infrequent southward; circumpolar.

Notes: Bog blueberry is also known as *Vaccinium occidentale.* • Alberta Métis are reported to have used blueberries (the fruits and/or stems and leaves) to treat acne and vomiting, and to prevent pregnancy or miscarriage. The berries were also used to bring blood after childbirth and to bring on menstruation. The Saskatchewan Cree used them to slow excessive menstruation and to make a person sweat. Other groups used the berries to facilitate the expulsion of afterbirth. The Dene boiled the root to make a decoction for headaches.

Black Huckleberry
Vaccinium membranaceum

General: Medium-sized, clump-forming; stems erect to spreading, 0.2–1.5 m tall, much-branched; young twigs slightly angled, yellowish green, greyish and shredding when older.

Leaves: Alternate, **deciduous**, elliptic-oblong to egg-shaped, 2–6 cm long, gradually narrowing to pointed tip; **margins finely sawtoothed** nearly full length; bright green above, paler and sparsely glandular beneath, turning red or purplish in autumn.

Flowers: Solitary in leaf axils, **appearing as or after the leaves expand**, urn-shaped; corolla creamy pink to bronze, 3–6 mm long, with 5 short lobes; calyx shallowly 5-lobed; stamens 10.

Fruits: Berries usually dark purplish red to black, without bloom, globe-shaped, 8–13 mm across.

Where Found: Dry to moist forests and glades, old burns and clearcuts, rocky slopes, timberline thickets and heathlands; montane and upper subalpine zones; frequent in much of the southern ¾ of the region, infrequent northward; cordilleran.

Similar Species: Oval-leaved blueberry (**V. ovalifolium**) and **Alaska blueberry (V. alaskaense)** are typically understorey shrubs of lowland and montane coniferous forests, but both reach subalpine elevations and occasionally occur at treeline, along the coast from southern AK to OR and frequently (oval-leaved blueberry) or rarely (Alaska blueberry) inland to the Canadian Rockies. Both differ from black huckleberry in their leaf margins, which are **untoothed to lightly toothed on the lower half.** The flowers of oval-leaved blueberry appear before the leaves, the blue berries have a strong whitish bloom, and the flower and fruit stalks are curved and not enlarged below the ovary. The flowers of Alaska blueberry appear with or after the leaves, the purplish black berries have little or no bloom, and the flower/fruit stalks are straight and enlarged immediately below the ovary. *FNA* considers oval-leaved blueberry and Alaska blueberry to be the same species, but we disagree.

Notes: Black huckleberry is the best high-elevation berry for eating, superior to all others in our opinion. • Traditionally, First Nations peoples harvested the berries of all *Vaccinium* species and ate them both raw and cooked. Most BC groups would cook the berries and make dry cakes or fruit leathers for winter storage.

The Gwich'in and Dena'ina would mix them (especially lingonberries, bilberries and blueberries) with pounded, dried fish or fish eggs, and then add oil or lard (e.g., from moose or bear) to make a dessert, which when frozen resembled ice cream. The Nisga'a, Wet'suwet'en, Dene-thah, Cree and Dene would just mix the berries with lard or oil for storage, and some groups added them to pemmican. *Vaccinium* berries are still collected and made into jams, jellies, syrups, pies, muffins and breads. Northern peoples would store the berries in a variety of ways—either in oil or water, then placed in animal stomachs or intestines, or in birchbark or wooden boxes where available. These would then be frozen or stored under the muskeg and would keep for a very long time.

Conspectus of *Vaccinium*

SPECIES	HABIT	TWIGS	LEAVES
vitis-idaea (p. 81)	dwarf, mat-forming; stems trailing to ascending, 5–25 cm long/tall	round to slightly angled in cross-section, minutely hairy	evergreen, leathery, narrowly elliptic to egg-shaped, 0.5–1 cm long; shiny and green above, paler and with dark whiskers beneath; margins not toothed, somewhat rolled under
scoparium (p. 81)	low, somewhat matted, colonial via rhizomes; stems 10–25 cm tall, closely branched	numerous, whisk-broom-like, slender, strongly angled, greenish, hairless	deciduous, narrowly egg-shaped, broadest at middle, 0.5–1 cm long, pointy-tipped; hairless and shiny green on upper surface, dull and veined beneath; margins finely sawtoothed
myrtillus (p. 81)	low, ascending, to 40 cm tall	less broom-like, strongly angled, greenish, short-hairy along grooves	deciduous, egg- to lance-shaped, 2–3 cm long; light green and veined beneath; margins finely sawtoothed
deliciosum (p. 82)	low, often matted, clumped or colonial; stems 15–30 cm tall, densely branched	slender, rarely angled, greenish brown, usually hairless, rarely minutely hairy	deciduous, narrowly egg-shaped, 2–4 cm long, usually blunt or rounded at tip; hairless and pale green with whitish bloom beneath; margins often distantly toothed along upper half ; autumn colour red to bronzy russet
caespitosum (p. 82)	dwarf or low, mat-forming, clumped to colonial; stems 5–30 cm tall, densely branched	round, yellow-green to reddish, usually finely hairy	deciduous, narrowly egg- to spoon-shaped, 1–3 cm long, widest above middle; green on both sides, net-veined beneath; margins distinctly toothed from tip to midpoint or below; autumn colour red and orange
uliginosum (p. 82)	low, spreading to erect, often forming mats or colonies; stems 10–50 cm tall	round in cross-section, not angled, pale green when young, greyish red when older, hairless or minutely hairy	deciduous, egg-shaped or elliptic, widest above middle, 0.8–1.5 cm long, blunt or rounded at tip, hairless or hairy; green or greyish green above, paler or with a slight bloom and often strongly net-veined beneath; margins not toothed, somewhat rolled under; autumn colour pale purplish pink
membranaceum (p. 83)	medium-sized, clump-forming, erect to spreading; stems 0.2–1.5 m tall, much branched	slightly angled and yellowish green when young, greyish and shredding when older, hairless or hairy in lines	deciduous, elliptic-oblong to egg-shaped, 2–6 cm long, gradually narrowing to pointed tip; bright green on upper surface, paler and sparsely glandular beneath; margins finely sawtoothed nearly entire length; autumn colour flaming red or purplish
ovalifolium (p. 83)	medium, erect to ascending; stems 0.4–1.5 m tall	strongly angled, brown, reddish or yellow when young, grey when older, hairless	deciduous, oval, 2–4 cm long; lower surface glaucous and without hairs on midvein; margins smooth or with a few fine teeth; autumn colour yellow
alaskaense (p. 83)	medium, erect; stems 0.5–1.5 m tall	somewhat angled, yellowish green when young, grey when older	deciduous, elliptic, 2.5–6 cm long; lower surface glaucous with scattered hairs on midvein; margins smooth or somewhat wavy or with a few fine teeth

FLOWERS	BERRIES	HABITAT
solitary to several in compact clusters at branch tips; corolla bell-shaped, nodding, pinkish white, 3–5 mm long, 4-lobed; sepals 4, much shorter than corolla; stamens 8, filaments hairy	bright red, tart, globe-shaped, 6–10 mm across	wet to dry coniferous forests, bogs, open rocky slopes and exposed ridges, heathlands, stony barrens and tundra; lowland to alpine zones
single in leaf axils; corolla urn-shaped, pearly pink, 3–4 mm long and wide, with 5 short lobes; sepals 5, indistinct; stamens 10	bright red (reportedly occasionally purplish), globe-shaped, 3–6 mm across	dry to mesic forests, glades and edges, meadows, heathlands and open rocky slopes; extending up to and above treeline
single in leaf axils; corolla urn- to globe-shaped, pinkish, 3–5 mm long, 5–7 mm wide	blue-black to dark red, without whitish bloom, 7–9 mm across	open coniferous forests and heathlands; medium to high elevations
single in leaf axils; corolla globe-shaped to broadly urn-shaped, pinkish, 4–6 mm long and nearly as wide, with 5 short lobes; sepals fused into saucer-like calyx, the 5 lobes indistinct; stamens 10	usually deep blue with pale grey bloom, nearly globe-shaped, 6–9 mm across	mesic to moist forests, glades and edges, meadows and heathlands; montane to lower alpine zones
single in leaf axils; corolla white to pink, narrowly urn-shaped to nearly cylindric, 4–7 mm long, to twice as long as wide	blue with whitish bloom, 5–8 mm across	forests, bogs, meadows and tundra; lowland to alpine zones
clusters of 2–4 (sometimes 1) in leaf axils; corolla urn-shaped, pink, often with white stripes, 4–6 mm long, with 4 (usually) or 5 short lobes; sepals 4 or 5; stamens usually 8, filaments hairless	blue with strong bloom, globe-shaped, 5–8 mm across	bogs, boggy forests, dry to wet thickets, heathlands and tundra; lowland to alpine zones
single in leaf axils, appearing as or after leaves expand; corolla urn-shaped, creamy-pink to bronze, 3–6 mm long, with 5 short lobes; calyx shallowly 5-lobed; stamens 10	dark purplish red to black, glossy, without bloom, globe-shaped, 8–13 mm across	dry to moist forests and glades, old burns and clear-cuts, rocky slopes, timberline thickets and heathlands; montane and upper subalpine zones
single in leaf axils, appearing before or just as leaves start to develop; corolla urn-shaped, pinkish, 5–7 mm long, longer than wide	blue to blue-black, usually with bloom, 6–9 mm across; stalks curved, not enlarged just below berry	moist coniferous forests and openings, bogs and heathlands; lowland to subalpine zones
single in leaf axils, appearing after leaves more than half developed; corolla globe-shaped, bronze to pinkish green, 5–7 mm long, wider than long	blue-black to purplish black, usually without bloom, 7–10 mm across; stalks straight, enlarged just below berry	moist coniferous forests; lowland to subalpine zones

Some Berries of the *Vaccinium*s

lingonberry, p. 81

grouseberry, p. 81

Cascade blueberry, p. 82

dwarf blueberry, p. 82

bog blueberry, p. 82

black huckleberry, p. 83

black huckleberry, p. 83

oval-leaved blueberry, p. 83

Alaska blueberry, p. 83

Copperbush • *Elliottia pyroliflora*

General: Medium-sized, 0.5–2 m tall; **stems erect to spreading,** with loose, shredding copper-coloured bark on older branches; twigs green, hairless or sparsely short-hairy in lines.

Leaves: Alternate but some appearing whorled, especially at branch tips, somewhat leathery but **deciduous,** lance-shaped to narrowly elliptic, broadest toward the rounded but abruptly pointed tip, 2–5 cm long, **hairless** at least when mature; **margins not toothed;** shiny, **green above, glaucous beneath.**

Flowers: Mostly **solitary** (sometimes 2–3 together) at branch ends, showy; **corolla wheel-shaped, salmon pink or copper-coloured,** the 5 petals nearly distinct, oblong-elliptic, spreading, 10–15 mm long; sepals 5, 6–10 mm long; stamens 8–10, filaments flattened; **styles upcurved,** about 1 cm long.

Fruits: Capsules 5–6-chambered, nearly spheric, 5–9 mm across.

Where Found: Moist to wet forests and glades, commonly with mountain hemlock (p. 42), streambanks, bog edges, rocky ridges and heathlands at timberline, often in subalpine thickets with false azalea and white-flowered rhododendron; montane and subalpine zones; windward coastal mountains, locally frequent along the Pacific coast; Pacific maritime endemic.

Similar Species: Copperbush, false azalea (below) and white-flowered rhododendron (p. 88) are all medium-sized, leggy, subalpine, heath-family shrubs that could be confused when not in flower. Copperbush has hairless, shiny, green leaves that are glaucous beneath; false azalea has glandular-hairy leaves that are often bluish green; and white-flowered rhododendron has shiny leaves with rusty hairs on the upper surface.

Notes: Copperbush is also known as *Cladothamnus pyroliflorus.* • The genus is named for Stephen Elliott (1771–1830), an American botanist and banker. • *Pyroliflora* refers to the flower that, with its curved protruding style, looks like a giant *Pyrola.* The name "copperbush" is a nod to the unique colour of the flowers, but could also refer to the coppery, shedding (exfoliating) bark. • With its many sprouting branches, copperbush rivals white-flowered rhododendron, also known as mountain misery, in nuisance value to bushwhackers in coastal subalpine forests.

False Azalea • *Menziesia ferruginea*

General: Medium-sized, 0.5–2 m tall, **skunky when bruised; stems erect to spreading;** young twigs fine-hairy, the hairs somewhat glandular and rust-coloured, older branches often hairless, with shredding bark.

Leaves: Alternate, clustered at branch tips, thin, **deciduous,** elliptic to egg-shaped, 3–6 cm long, light green to blue-green, pointy-tipped or rounded and abruptly bristle-tipped (**midvein protrudes beyond leaf tip**); margins finely toothed and fringed; **glandular-hairy on both surfaces, especially the lower, glaucous beneath.**

Flowers: In clusters of 2–10 at the ends of previous year's shoots, on glandular-hairy **stalks 1–3 cm long, curving down in flower, ascending-erect in fruit;**
corolla urn-shaped, salmon or bronze to greenish orange, 4-lobed, 6–10 mm long; calyx saucer-shaped, indistinctly 4-lobed; stamens usually 8, filaments hairy near the base.

Fruits: Capsules 4-chambered, egg-shaped, 5–8 mm long, hairless or nearly so.

Where Found: Forests and glades, edges of tree clumps, streambanks, gullies, timberline thickets and heathlands; lowland to subalpine zones; frequent in the southern ⅔ of the region; cordilleran.

Notes: The leaves turn bright yellow and crimson-orange in autumn, and some forms have strikingly bluish green summer foliage. This shrub can be a nice ornamental in acidic soils. • Both false azalea and white-flowered rhododendron can reproduce vegetatively by sprouting from root crowns, which can become very large and very old—70 to 80 years old in some cases. • The genus is named for Archibald Menzies (1754–1842), a physician and naturalist with Captain George Vancouver on the *Discovery*; *ferruginea* means "rusty," referring to the rusty fuzz on the twigs.

White-flowered Rhododendron, Mountain Misery
Rhododendron albiflorum

General: Medium-sized, 0.5–2 m tall; **stems erect to spreading,** with shredding bark; young twigs coarsely reddish-hairy.

Leaves: Alternate but in clusters along the branches and often appearing whorled, especially at branch tips, **deciduous,** narrowly elliptic to lance-shaped, 4–8 cm long, pointed at both ends; entire or wavy-margined to minutely sawtoothed; **upper surface yellowish green,** shiny, with fine, **rusty hairs.**

Flowers: In **groups of 1–4** along previous year's shoots and below current year's leaves, showy, fragrant, somewhat nodding, on stalks to 1.5 cm long; **corolla nearly radially symmetric, bowl-shaped, white to cream,** to 2.5 cm across, the 5 spreading lobes fused near the base; calyx divided to near the base, the 5 sepals 8–15 mm long; stamens usually 10, filaments hairy.

Fruits: Capsules 5-chambered, thick-walled, egg-shaped, 6–8 mm long.

Where Found: Forests and glades, meadows around tree clumps, stream-banks, timberline thickets and heathlands; montane and subalpine zones; frequent in the southern ½ of the region; cordilleran.

Notes: The leaves turn beautiful shades of bronze, crimson and orange in autumn. • White-flowered rhododendron produces complex chemical compounds that reduce the diversity and abundance of other plant species beneath or around these shrubs. These hostile "allelopathic" compounds seem to be concentrated in senescent leaves. • *Rhododendron* is from the Greek *rhodos*, "rose," and *dendron*, "tree"; the name was originally given to a rose-flowered oleander and then transferred to these plants. The specific epithet *albiflorum* refers to the creamy white flowers, as does the common name. This plant is also known as "mountain misery" because it grows thickly on mountainsides and tends to sprawl downslope, bedevilling bushwhackers trying to move uphill through it.

Lapland Rosebay • *Rhododendron lapponicum*

General: Dwarf, **mat-forming;** stems prostrate to ascending, 5–30 cm long, sometimes (in subalpine woodlands, taiga and arctic tundra) an erect shrub 50–70 cm tall; twigs scaly and hairy.

Leaves: Alternate, **evergreen** or tardily deciduous, leathery, elliptic-oblong, 0.5–2 cm long, usually blunt-tipped; margins not toothed, somewhat rolled under; **scaly-glandular** on both surfaces, dark green above, brownish below.

Flowers: In clusters of 2–6 at branch ends, showy, fragrant, on stalks to 1.5 cm long; **corolla bilaterally symmetric, broadly funnel-shaped, deep purple to rose purple,** 7–14 mm long, 5-lobed; calyx with 5 small, triangular lobes, fringed, hairy and scaly on the outer surface; stamens 5–10, filaments purple.

Fruits: Capsules 5-chambered, thick-walled, scaly-glandular, egg-shaped, 5–8 mm long.

Where Found: Dry to mesic fellfields, stony slopes and tundra, sometimes also in open forests, typically on calcium-rich substrates; subalpine and alpine zones; locally frequent in the northern ½ of the region, south in the Rockies to about 52° N; arctic-alpine, circumpolar.

Similar Species: Glandular Kamchatka rhododendron (*Therorhodion glandulosum*; *R. camtschaticum* ssp. *glandulosum*) is a low (to 10 cm tall), sprawling shrub with **deciduous,** spoon-shaped, **glandular-hairy leaves** 1–4 cm long and **purplish flowers 1.5-2.5 cm long.** It is an amphiberingian species found from around treeline up into alpine meadows, heathlands and tundra, on the Seward Peninsula and in the lower Yukon R. valley, AK. • **Kamchatka rhododendron** (*T. camtschaticum*; *R. camtschaticum*) has leaves that are **hairy but not glandular** or are sparsely glandular-hairy. It occurs in heathlands, meadows, woodlands and tundra, on the coast and islands of southern AK.

Notes: Lapland rosebay's fondness for lime is very unusual in its acid-loving family and genus.

Northern Labrador Tea
Rhododendron tomentosum

General: Low, branched, **sprawling to erect; stems** 10–50 cm long/tall, branchlets rusty soft-hairy.

Leaves: Alternate, evergreen, leathery, fragrant when crushed, **linear to narrowly oblong,** mostly 1–3.5 cm long; margins strongly rolled under; dark green above, **rusty-woolly below.**

Flowers: Numerous in umbrella-shaped clusters at branch tips, on glandular, **rusty-hairy stalks hooked near the top;** corolla star-shaped, **white to cream,** about 1 cm across, to 8 mm long, the 5 petals nearly distinct; sepals 5, about 1 mm long, hairy, margins glandular-hairy; stamens usually 10.

Fruits: Capsules 5-chambered, oval, 3–5 mm long, on hooked stalks, splitting open from the base.

Where Found: Bogs, moist heathlands, dry rocky and wet peaty tundra; lowland to alpine zones; frequent in the northern ⅓ of the region; arctic-alpine, the species complex circumpolar.

Similar Species: This plant could be confused with **Labrador tea (*R. groenlandicum*;** *Ledum groenlandicum*), which is **taller,** with **larger (2–5 cm long), lance-egg-shaped leaves** and **white-hairy, curved flower stalks.** Labrador tea is more typical of lower-elevation peatlands, though the 2 species can occur together in the North. • **Trapper's tea (*R. columbianum*;** *L. glandulosum*) has similar flowers but is an **erect shrub 1–2 m tall,** with glandular-scaly twigs, **thinner, wider, oval to elliptic leaves to 6 cm long** that are scaly, glandular and sometimes thinly hairy but **not woolly beneath,** the margins slightly rolled under. It grows in moist forests, along streambanks and in bogs, fens and swamps, in montane to subalpine zones. Trapper's tea is frequent in the southern, inland ½ of the region, in BC from about 54° N and from southwestern AB to CA, NV, UT and CO.

trapper's tea

Notes: Northern Labrador tea is also know as *Ledum decumbens*, *L. palustre* and *L. palustre* ssp. *decumbens*. • In the past, some taxonomists lumped the 2 types of Labrador tea as subspecies in *L. palustre*. More recently and remarkably, DNA and other evidence have come down on the side of submerging *Ledum* in *Rhododendron*. • Northern Labrador tea was used by northern First Nations as a tea and to treat colds, "weak" blood, tuberculosis, arthritis, dizziness, stomach problems and heartburn. It was also used as a laxative and a wash for sores, as well as to relieve nervous tension and to treat burns, eczema, hair loss, eye infections, sore nipples and baby skin rashes. Meat, especially strong-tasting meat such as fishy bear flesh, was soaked in a decoction of boiled leaves and branches to improve the taste. • **Caution:** This plant contains ledol, which can cause paralysis and cramps, so it should be taken in moderation (i.e., infrequently and in diluted preparations). Nonetheless, it has been used in the North for a very long time.

Wildflowers

alpine mountain-trumpet (*Collomia debilis*), Olympic Mountains, WA

Wildflowers

This section covers the non-woody (herbaceous or mostly so) flowering plants, except for the rushes, sedges and grasses. It includes what most people think of as wildflowers and is the largest and showiest section of the book.

There are hundreds of species of high-elevation wildflowers in our region, distributed unequally among 35 or so families. We have organized the treatments by family, in a sequence of our own devising, reflecting a combination of presumed evolutionary trends and selected morphological similarities. Within a family, we attempt to place similar genera and species close together. Below are thumbnail sketches of some of the bigger families, intended as a general guide to the larger groups and to some features to look for when confronting an unknown wildflower. The characterizations are for these families as represented in our region, not for their worldwide appearance.

But a book is an imperfect search engine. Colour is a powerful cue for most humans, so we also provide an omnibus colour key to the wildflowers in this guide. With practice, you could come to appreciate the time-saving, family-first approach, but just flipping though pages of colour photos can be effective, especially if you don't have a clue where else to start.

Bering chickweed

Pink Family (Caryophyllaceae): Leaves opposite, small, "simple" (with a single blade, not compound with leaflets); flowers radially symmetric, usually white or pink; petals 5, distinct; sepals 5, distinct or sometimes united into a tube; fruits capsules, usually splitting open at the tip by teeth or larger segments.

Saxifrage Family (Saxifragaceae): Leaves simple, usually alternate or all at the base; flowers radially symmetric; petals 5, distinct; sepals 5, distinct or fused toward the base with the ovary; stamens 5–10; styles usually 2; fruits capsules or follicles, often 2-beaked.

purple mountain saxifrage

one-flowered cinquefoil

Rose Family (Rosaceae): Leaves alternate, simple or compound, usually with "stipules" (a pair of small scales or flanges at the base of the leaf stalk); flowers radially symmetric; petals usually 5, distinct, often showy; sepals 5, united at the base into a cup (hypanthium) around the ovary, usually alternating with 5 smaller bractlets; stamens numerous; fruits dry achenes or follicles, or fleshy.

Buttercup Family (Ranunculaceae): Leaves alternate, simple or compound, lacking stipules; flowers diverse in form—radially symmetric with simple petals (anemones, buttercups) or spurred petals (columbines) or bilaterally symmetric (delphiniums, monkshood)—and colour (white, yellow, red, blue, purple); petals mostly 5–10 (sometimes 2 or 4 or lacking), distinct; stamens numerous; fruits mostly follicles or achenes.

mountain marsh-marigold

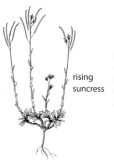

rising suncress

Mustard Family (Brassicaceae): Leaves alternate or mostly at the base; flowers radially symmetric; petals and sepals 4, distinct, in a cross-like arrangement, attached at the base of the ovary; stamens 6; fruits 2-chambered, pod-like siliques or shorter silicles.

Evening-primrose Family (Onagraceae, *Epilobium* spp.): Leaves mostly opposite, simple; flowers radially symmetric; petals and sepals 4, distinct, attached to the top of the ovary; capsules linear, 4-chambered, opening by 4 segments, the seeds numerous, with a tuft of hairs at one end.

river beauty

alpine lupine

Pea Family (Fabaceae): Leaves alternate, usually compound, with stipules; flowers similar to sweet peas, bilaterally symmetric with 5 dissimilar petals, the uppermost largest (the "banner"), 2 lateral "wings," and a partially fused pair (the "keel") that enclose the 10 stamens and 1-chambered ovary; fruits legumes.

Figwort Family (Scrophulariaceae): Leaves opposite or alternate, simple or compound; flowers usually bilaterally symmetric, sometimes radially symmetric; petals fused into a tubular "corolla" (collective term for all the petals), 4–5-lobed with 2 lips, sometimes wheel-shaped, rarely lacking; sepals 4–5, distinct or united; stamens 2, 4 or 5; fruits capsules.

small-flowered penstemon

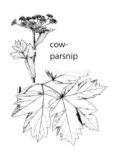

cow-parsnip

Carrot Family (Apiaceae): Leaves alternate or basal, usually compound, often finely divided and fern-like; flowers small, numerous in umbrella-shaped clusters; petals, sepals and stamens 5; fruits dry, seed-like, often ribbed.

Primrose Family (Primulaceae): Leaves simple, mostly untoothed, in basal rosettes; flowers radially symmetric; petals and sepals 5, fused and tubular in the lower part, lobed above; stamens 5; ovary 1-chambered; style 1; stigma head-like; fruits capsules, opening by 5 teeth or larger segments.

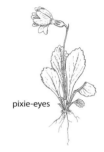

pixie-eyes

spreading phlox

Phlox Family (Polemoniaceae): Leaves alternate or opposite, simple or variously divided; flowers radially symmetric; petals 5, fused and tubular below, flaring to 5 lobes above; sepals 5, fused below; stamens 5; ovary 3-chambered; style 1; stigmas 3; fruits capsules.

Gentian Family (Gentianaceae): Leaves simple, untoothed, opposite or whorled; flowers radially symmetric, usually blue or greenish; petals 4–5, fused and tubular or bell-shaped below, lobed above, or wheel-shaped; sepals 4–5; stamens 4–5; ovary 1-chambered; fruits capsules, opening by 2 segments.

explorer's gentian

mountain forget-me-not

Borage Family (Boraginaceae): Leaves alternate, simple, rough-hairy; flowers radially symmetric, usually in coiled clusters; petals 5, fused and tubular below, flaring to 5 lobes above, often with 5 bulges in the throat; sepals 5, fused below; stamens 5; ovary 4-lobed; style 1, arising from the base of the ovary between the 4 lobes; fruits usually 1-seeded nutlets.

Aster Family (Asteraceae): Flowers in dense heads that look like individual flowers (e.g., daisies and dandelions); petals 5, fused, strap-shaped (ray florets) or tubular (disc florets); fruits dry, seed-like achenes, often with a tuft of fine bristles.

subalpine daisy

white glacier-lily

Lily Family (Liliaceae): Leaf veins parallel; flowers radially symmetric; petals and sepals 3, often similar (tepals); stamens 6; ovary 3-chambered; style 1; stigmas 3; fruits capsules (ours).

White Flowers

Iceland koenigia
p. 108

alpine bistort
p. 109

western bistort
p. 110

Alaska
wild-rhubarb
p. 111

cushion wild-
buckwheat
p. 117

contented alpine
wild-buckwheat
p. 117

White Flowers

Bostock's montia
p. 119

western
springbeauty
p. 120

Beringian
springbeauty
p. 120

Columbia lewisia
p. 123

Bering chickweed
p. 126

long-stalked
starwort
p. 127

White Flowers

alpine pearlwort
p. 128

Kaiser's sandwort
p. 129

longstem
sandwort
p. 129

fescue sandwort
p. 130

ballhead sandwort
p. 130

Yukon sandwort
p. 131

White Flowers

large-fruited
sandwort
p. 132

arctic sandwort
p. 132

boreal sandwort
p. 133

northern
sandwort
p. 133

Drummond's
catchfly
p. 136

Parry's campion
p. 137

White Flowers

tufted saxifrage
p. 143

Tolmie's saxifrage
p. 143

spotted saxifrage
p. 144

Taylor's saxifrage
p. 144

three-toothed
saxifrage
p. 144

pygmy saxifrage
p. 147

White Flowers

nodding saxifrage
p. 147

starstruck saxifrage
p. 148

rusty saxifrage
p. 148

western saxifrage
p. 149

rusty-haired saxifrage
p. 149

alpine saxifrage
p. 150

White Flowers

red-stemmed saxifrage
p. 150

brook saxifrage
p. 151

Nelson's saxifrage
p. 151

leatherleaf saxifrage
p. 153

smooth alumroot
p. 154

bear flower
p. 155

White Flowers

creamy coralbells
p. 156

fringed grass-of-Parnassus
p. 158

cloudberry
p. 164

Sitka burnet
p. 166

white globeflower
p. 184

mountain marsh-marigold
p. 185

White Flowers

mop-top
p. 187

northern anemone
p. 188

alpine anemone
p. 188

narcissus anemone
p. 189

Haida false rue-anemone
p. 195

Edwards' mock-wallflower
p. 203

White Flowers

uptight suncress
p. 205

Rocky Mountain rockcress
p. 206

Kamchatka rockcress
p. 207

alpine bittercress
p. 208

heart-leaved bittercress
p. 209

umbel bittercress
p. 210

White Flowers

alpine skycress
p. 211

smooth
northern-rockcress
p. 213

inscrutable
northern-rockcress
p. 213

Aleutian cress
p. 214

mountain
candytuft
p. 214

tall draba
p. 222

White Flowers

snow draba
p. 223

milky draba
p. 224

Austrian draba
p. 224

pointy-leaf draba
p. 224

smooth draba
p. 227

northern draba
p. 228

White Flowers

grey-leaf draba
p. 228

balloon milkvetch
p. 251

subarctic
milkvetch
p. 252

silky locoweed
p. 254

arctic eyebright
p. 280

bog bunchberry
p. 288

White Flowers

cow-parsnip
p. 292

Rose's angelica
p. 292

Gray's
mountain-lovage
p. 293

Macoun's
woodroot
p. 293

snowbank
spring-parsley
p. 294

arctic wintergreen
p. 298

White Flowers

arctic starflower
p. 299

rock-jasmine
p. 302

northern
fairy-candelabra
p. 302

Alaska
dwarf-primrose
p. 304

spike
fairy-trumpet
p. 315

Nuttall's flaxflower
p. 316

White Flowers

whitish gentian
p. 319

deer-cabbage
p. 324

Sitka mist-maiden
p. 327

silverleaf phacelia
p. 329

alpine cryptantha
p. 332

northern bedstraw
p. 336

White Flowers

edible valerian
p. 337

Sitka valerian
p. 338

mountaintop
thistle
p. 346

pygmy pussytoes
p. 356

racemose
pussytoes
p. 357

umber pussytoes
p. 357

White Flowers

woolly pussytoes
p. 357

tidy pussytoes
p. 358

alpine pussytoes
p. 358

Rocky Mountain
pussytoes
p. 358

yarrow
p. 361

common Easter
daisy
p. 363

White Flowers

entire-leaved
daisy
p. 364

arctic sweet
coltsfoot
p. 365

Olympic Mountain
aster
p. 367

snowbed bitter
fleabane
p. 372

cut-leaf daisy
p. 373

Alberta fleabane
p. 373

White Flowers

Salish fleabane
p. 373

fanleaf fleabane
p. 373

tufted fleabane
p. 374

Evermann's
fleabane
p. 375

arctic-alpine
fleabane
p. 376

one-flower
fleabane
p. 376

White Flowers

Olympic Mountain fleabane p. 378    woolly fleabane p. 378    pale fleabane p. 378    Denali fleabane p. 379    white glacier-lily p. 405    subalpine mariposa lily p. 406

White Flowers

Yellow

Brandegee's onion p. 409    alp-lily p. 410    mountain death-camas p. 411    bear-grass p. 412 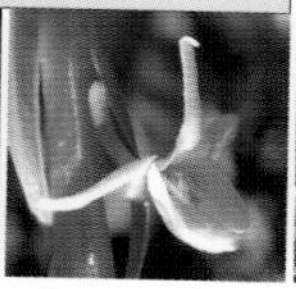   fragrant white bog orchid p. 413   subalpine wild-buckwheat p. 115

Yellow Flowers

parsnip-flower wild-buckwheat p. 115    golden alpine wild-buckwheat p. 116    marum-leaf wild-buckwheat p. 116    spreading stonecrop p. 124    lance-leaved stonecrop p. 124    cushion saxifrage p. 142

Yellow Flowers

spiderplant p. 145    thyme-leaved saxifrage p. 145    yellow mountain saxifrage p. 146    yellow marsh saxifrage p. 146    western St. John's wort p. 159    Macoun's poppy p. 160

Yellow Flowers

arctic poppy p. 161    Gordon's ivesia p. 166    sibbaldia p. 167    caltha-leaved avens p. 167    alpine avens p. 168    fan-leaved cinquefoil p. 172

WILDFLOWERS • COLOUR KEY

WILDFLOWERS · COLOUR KEY

Yellow Flowers

arctic cinquefoil p. 172	elegant cinquefoil p. 172	two-flowered cinquefoil p. 173	short and curly cinquefoil p. 173	one-flowered cinquefoil p. 174	snow cinquefoil p. 174

Yellow Flowers

bluff cinquefoil p. 175	blue-leaved cinquefoil p. 175	early cinquefoil p. 176	Drummond's cinquefoil p. 176	sheep cinquefoil p. 177	shortleaf cinquefoil p. 177

Yellow Flowers

cliff wood-beauty p. 177	yellow anemone p. 189	Cooley's buttercup p. 191	subalpine buttercup p. 192	snow buttercup p. 193	pygmy buttercup p. 193

Yellow Flowers

Rocky Mountain snow buttercup p. 194	water-plantain buttercup p. 194	yellow columbine p. 197	Cascade wallflower p. 202	alpine yellow-cress p. 212	sticky tansy-mustard p. 212

Yellow Flowers

Cascade twinpod p. 216	common twinpod p. 216	arctic bladderpod p. 216	Wallowa bladderpod p. 217	spoonleaf bladderpod p. 217	thickleaf draba p. 222

Yellow Flowers

slender draba
p. 222

Macoun's draba
p. 225

denseleaf draba
p. 225

Yellowstone draba
p. 226

few-seeded draba
p. 226

leeward draba
p. 227

Yellow Flowers

Wind River draba
p. 227

Ogilvie
Mountains draba
p. 229

tubby draba
p. 229

golden draba
p. 229

yellow willowherb
p. 240

tundra milkvetch
p. 250

Yellow Flowers

field locoweed
p. 254

Maydell's
locoweed
p. 255

twinflower violet
p. 260

round-leaved
violet
p. 260

sulphur
paintbrush
p. 268

western
paintbrush
p. 269

Yellow Flowers

Unalaska
paintbrush
p. 269

northern
paintbrush
p. 269

capitate
lousewort
p. 276

Oeder's
lousewort
p. 276

Lapland
lousewort
p. 277

coiled-beak
lousewort
p. 277

Yellow Flowers

Labrador
lousewort
p. 277

towering
lousewort
p. 278

mountain
monkeyflower
p. 281

yellow
penstemon
p. 287

American
thorough-wax
p. 291

Martindale's
biscuit-root
p. 296

WILDFLOWERS • COLOUR KEY

Yellow Flowers

Idaho
desert-parsley
p. 296

cous biscuit-root
p. 297

Sandberg's
desert-parsley
p. 297

Brandegee's
desert-parsley
p. 298

dwarf alpine
hawksbeard
p. 340

woolly hawkweed
p. 341

Yellow Flowers

short-beaked
mountain-
dandelion
p. 342

horned dandelion
p. 343

alpine dandelion
p. 343

alpine false
dandelion
p. 344

silver sagebrush
p. 350

Rocky Mountain
sage
p. 351

Yellow Flowers

salon sagewort
p. 351

caribou weed
p. 352

mountain
sagewort
p. 352

boreal sage
p. 353

Alaskan sagebrush
p. 353

three-forked
mugwort
p. 353

Yellow Flowers

whitestem
goldenbush
p. 354

singlehead
goldenbush
p. 354

rainiera
p. 360

silverback luina
p. 360

golden fleabane
p. 379

stemless
goldenweed
p. 381

Yellow Flowers

Lyall's
serpentweed
p. 381

northern
goldenrod
p. 382

woolly sunflower
p. 382

Pacific alpinegold
p. 383

old-man-of-the-
mountains
p. 383

Parry's arnica
p. 385

Yellow Flowers

narrowleaf arnica
p. 386

broadleaf arnica
p. 386

smallhead arnica
p. 387

Rydberg's arnica
p. 387

sticky-leaf arnica
p. 387

nodding arnica
p. 385

Yellow Flowers

snow arnica
p. 385

hairy arnica
p. 388

clasping arnica
p. 388

dwarf mountain
groundsel
p. 390

arrow-leaved
groundsel
p. 390

tall groundsel
p. 390

Yellow Flowers

clasping
groundsel
p. 391

Olympic Mountain
groundsel
p. 391

large-headed
groundsel
p. 391

western groundsel
p. 392

black-tipped
groundsel
p. 392

Elmer's
groundsel
p. 392

Yellow Flowers

dwarf arctic
packera
p. 394

Ogotoruk packera
p. 395

high-alpine
packera
p. 395

cleftleaf
packera
p. 395

splitleaf
packera
p. 396

Rocky Mountain
packera
p. 396

Yellow Flowers

woolly packera
p. 397

brown-haired
arctic-groundsel
p. 398

purple-haired
arctic-groundsel
p. 398

Yukon
arctic-groundsel
p. 399

Haida-groundsel
p. 400

yellow glacier-lily
p. 405

Orange Flowers

orange mountain-dandelion
p. 342

rayless alpine packera
p. 397

orange arctic-groundsel
p. 399

tiger lily
p. 406

Red & Pink Flowers

pink plumes
p. 110

mountain-sorrel
p. 112

arctic dock
p. 113

Lapland mountain sorrel
p. 113

umbellate pussypaws
p. 118

fellfield springbeauty
p. 121

Red & Pink Flowers

creeping springbeauty
p. 121

alpine lewisia
p. 122

western roseroot
p. 125

moss campion
p. 135

nodding campion
p. 136

pink campion
p. 137

Red & Pink Flowers

hawkweed-leaved saxifrage
p. 149

cliff-saxifrage
p. 154

pale poppy
p. 162

nagoonberry
p. 165

smooth-stem parrya
p. 203

skewed suncress
p. 206

Red & Pink Flowers

river beauty
p. 239

rock willowherb
p. 240

alpine willowherb
p. 241

smooth willowherb
p. 242

slim-pod willowherb
p. 242

longstalk clover
p. 245

Red & Pink Flowers

dwarf clover
p. 245

whip-root clover
p. 246

Parry's clover
p. 246

northern
sweetvetch
p. 247

alpine sweetvetch
p. 248

western
sweetvetch
p. 248

Red & Pink Flowers

sickle milkvetch
p. 252

mountain
owl-clover
p. 265

small-flowered
paintbrush
p. 267

elegant
paintbrush
p. 267

showy paintbrush
p. 268

scarlet paintbrush
p. 270

Red & Pink Flowers

alpine paintbrush
p. 270

Elmer's paintbrush
p. 271

cliff paintbrush
p. 271

arctic lousewort
p. 273

woolly lousewort
p. 274

Sudeten
lousewort
p. 274

Red & Pink Flowers

whorled
lousewort
p. 274

pink
monkeyflower
p. 280

Mackenzie River
dwarf-primrose
p. 304

Yukon
dwarf-primrose
p. 304

cliff
dwarf-primrose
p. 305

snow
dwarf-primrose
p. 305

Red & Pink Flowers

Rocky Mountain
dwarf-primrose
p. 305

pixie-eyes
p. 306

Parry's primrose
p. 307

arctic primrose
p. 307

Alaska phlox
p. 313

spreading phlox
p. 313

WILDFLOWERS • COLOUR KEY

Red & Pink Flowers

white-edged phlox
p. 314

western mountain balm
p. 335

edible thistle
p. 346

rosy pussytoes
p. 359

alpine dustymaidens
p. 359

buff fleabane
p. 375

Red & Pink Flowers

Olympic onion
p. 408

short-styled onion
p. 409

wild chives
p. 409

northern false asphodel
p. 411

Blue & Purple Flowers

purple mountain saxifrage
p. 142

violet suksdorfia
p. 156

northern geranium
p. 163

blue columbine
p. 196

mountain monkshood
p. 197

tall larkspur
p. 198

Blue & Purple Flowers

rockslide larkspur
p. 198

blue corydalis
p. 199

Pallas' wallflower
p. 202

rising suncress
p. 205

purple bittercress
p. 209

purple-flowered skycress
p. 211

Blue & Purple Flowers

alpine lupine
p. 243

arctic lupine
p. 244

prickly milkvetch
p. 250

alpine milkvetch
p. 251

sticky locoweed
p. 255

blackish locoweed
p. 256

Blue & Purple Flowers

Huddelson's locoweed
p. 256

stalked-pod locoweed
p. 256

Scamman's locoweed
p. 257

arctic locoweed
p. 257

early blue violet
p. 259

Alaska violet
p. 259

Blue & Purple Flowers

Olympic violet
p. 260

common butterwort
p. 261

northern kittentails
p. 263

cutleaf kittentails
p. 263

fringepetal kittentails
p. 264

Wyoming kittentails
p. 264

Blue & Purple Flowers

weasel snout
p. 264

bird's-beak lousewort
p. 275

elephant's-head lousewort
p. 275

alpine speedwell
p. 279

Cusick's speedwell
p. 279

Tweedy's snowlover
p. 281

Blue & Purple Flowers

shrubby penstemon
p. 283

Davidson's penstemon
p. 283

oval-leaved penstemon
p. 284

mountain penstemon
p. 284

Alberta penstemon
p. 284

thinstem penstemon
p. 285

Blue & Purple Flowers

dusky penstemon
p. 285

small-flowered penstemon
p. 286

globe penstemon
p. 286

lovely penstemon
p. 287

purple sweet-cicely
p. 291

northern shootingstar
p. 301

Blue & Purple Flowers

pretty shootingstar
p. 301

Cusick's primrose
p. 307

sky pilot
p. 310

elegant sky pilot
p. 310

showy Jacob's-ladder
p. 311

tall Jacob's-ladder
p. 311

Blue & Purple Flowers

cushion phlox
p. 314

alpine mountain-trumpet
p. 315

pygmy gentian
p. 319

inky-blue gentian
p. 320

explorer's gentian
p. 320

broad-petalled gentian
p. 321

Blue & Purple Flowers

Rocky Mountain fringed gentian
p. 321

four-parted gentian
p. 322

delicate gentian
p. 322

star gentian
p. 323

mountain harebell
p. 325

arctic harebell
p. 326

Blue & Purple Flowers

Parry's harebell
p. 326

Yukon harebell
p. 326

ballhead waterleaf
p. 328

silky phacelia
p. 329

mountain sapphire
p. 331

showy mountain sapphire
p. 331

Blue & Purple Flowers

mountain forget-me-not
p. 332

tall bluebells
p. 333

greenleaf bluebells
p. 334

alpine bluebells
p. 334

American saw-wort
p. 347

dwarf saw-wort
p. 347

Blue & Purple Flowers

narrow-leaved saw-wort p. 348   Bering sagewort p. 350   Parry's Easter daisy p. 362   cushion Easter daisy p. 363   mountain Easter daisy p. 363   alpine aster p. 366

Blue & Purple Flowers

arctic aster p. 366   Cascade mountaincrown p. 367   leafybract aster p. 368   subalpine daisy p. 372   Leiberg's fleabane p. 374   rockslide fleabane p. 374

Blue & Purple Flowers

Rydberg's fleabane p. 375   tundra fleabane p. 377   large-flower fleabane p. 377

Green to Bronze or Maroon Flowers

leafy dwarf knotweed p. 109   Ms. Davis' knotweed p. 111   blunt-sepalled starwort p. 127   Chamisso's starwort p. 128   Wright's golden-saxifrage p. 153   five-stamen mitrewort p. 155

Green to Bronze or Maroon Flowers

alpine meadow-rue p. 195   monument plant p. 323   mountain mare's-tail p. 401   Indian hellebore p. 407   western mountain-bells p. 410

BUCKWHEAT FAMILY (Polygonaceae)

The buckwheats are a medium-sized family (about 1200 species worldwide) mostly of north temperate regions, though *Polygonum* occurs on all continents. Aside from an herbaceous annual or 2 and a few woody-based *Eriogonum* species, the high-elevation Polygonaceae of our region are perennial herbs, the stems often with swollen nodes. Except in *Eriogonum*, the alternate leaves have membranous sheathing stipules at the base of the leaf stalks. The small, usually bisexual, sometimes unisexual, flowers are typically numerous in open or tight clusters atop stems or in leaf axils. The flowers are radially symmetric with 6 (sometimes only 3, 4 or 5) distinct, scale-like sepals/petals (**tepals**), typically in 2 whorls of 3 each. The inner series of tepals are sometimes enlarged or modified with wings or bumps, and the tepals may be persistent, enlarged and membranous in fruit. There are usually 6–9 stamens, a single, 1-chambered, superior ovary and typically 3 styles. The fruit is a flattened, angled or winged, nut-like achene with 1 seed.

Key to the Genera of Polygonaceae

1a. Leaves without sheathing stipules; flowers stalked in a toothed cup of fused bracts; stamens 9
.... ***Eriogonum*** (pp. 114–117)

1b. Leaves with sheathing stipules; flowers not cupped by fused bracts; stamens 3–6 or 8 2

  2a. Plants tiny annuals; tepals mostly 3; stamens 3 (rarely 4) .... ***Koenigia*** (below)

  2b. Plants mostly perennials; tepals 4–6; stamens 6 or 8 3

    3a. Tepals 4; stamens 6; leaves kidney-shaped, mostly at the base; achenes lens-shaped, winged
.... ***Oxyria*** (p. 112)

    3b. Tepals 5 or 6; stamens 6 or 8; leaves not kidney-shaped; achenes 3-angled, not winged 4

      4a. Tepals 6; stamens 6; inner 3 tepals usually enlarging in fruit .... ***Rumex*** (p. 113)

      4b. Tepals 5; stamens mostly 8; inner tepals not enlarging in fruit 5

        5a. Leaves mostly at the base, a few on the stem; flower clusters spike-like atop stem; stem unbranched
.... ***Bistorta*** (pp. 109–110)

        5b. Leaves mostly along the stem; at least some flower clusters in leaf axils; stems usually branched, rarely unbranched 6

          6a. Annuals (ours); leaves 0.5–2.5 cm long; sheathing stipules membranous, silvery-translucent, often disintegrating into fibres; few-flowered clusters mostly in leaf axils .... ***Polygonum*** (p. 109)

          6b. Perennials; leaves 2–20 cm long, mostly >5 cm long; sheathing stipules papery, reddish brown, not shredding; many-flowered clusters atop stems and in leaf axils .... ***Aconogonon*** (p. 111)

Iceland Koenigia • *Koenigia islandica*

General: Tiny, **annual herb** from a slender taproot; **stems reclining to ascending, 1–10 cm long/tall,** simple or branched, hairless, often reddish.

Leaves: Leaves few, mostly along stem, alternate or nearly opposite, somewhat fleshy; **blades elliptic to egg-shaped,** hairless, 1–6.5 mm long, short-stalked to nearly unstalked; sheathing stipules funnel-shaped, wax-papery, brownish.

Flowers: Tiny, inconspicuous, few to several in leafy-bracted, umbel-like clusters atop the stem or in leaf axils; **tepals 3 (sometimes 4),** egg-shaped to elliptic, greenish, whitish or reddish, 1–1.8 mm long; **stamens mostly 3.**

Fruits: Achenes 2- or rarely 3-angled, **unwinged,** hairless, enclosed by tepals.

Where Found: Moist to wet, gravelly seepage sites, bare soil around snow patches, streambanks, shores and patterned ground; lowland (arctic coast) to alpine zones; infrequent to rare (probably overlooked) in the inland part of the region; arctic-alpine, circumpolar and disjunct in southern South America.

Notes: This species is the only truly arctic-alpine annual in our region with the exception of annual forms of icegrass (p. 460); some small *Polygonum* species (p. 109) and Polemoniaceae are annual and occasionally alpine. • The genus is named after Johann Gerhard König (1728–85), a pupil of Linnaeus.

Leafy Dwarf Knotweed • *Polygonum minimum*

General: **Annual herb** from a slender taproot; **stems spreading to ascending,** 3–20 cm tall, simple or branched from the base, **often zig-zagged, wiry, reddish brown.**

Leaves: Alternate, **elliptic to nearly round,** regularly spaced below, scarcely reduced upward; blades 5–25 mm long, short-stalked; sheathing stipules cylindric, silvery-translucent, 1–4 mm long, ragged-edged.

Flowers: 1–3 on **erect to spreading stalks** in leaf axils, sometimes crowded near branch tips; flowers 1.5–2.5 mm long, lobed about ⅔ the distance to the base; **tepals 5,** green with white or pinkish margins, oblong, **rounded at tip; stamens 8;** styles 3.

Fruits: Achenes 3-angled, greenish black, smooth, shiny, about 2 mm long.

Where Found: Dry to vernally moist sites, forest openings, meadows, bare soil, rocky slopes; upper montane to alpine zones; infrequent in the southern ½ of the region; cordilleran.

Similar Species: Douglas' knotweed (*P. douglasii*) is **taller (10–50 cm),** with **erect, green stems, narrower (linear to lance-shaped) leaves** reduced in size upward and **flowers on bent-down stalks** in long, narrow, loose clusters in leaf axils and atop the stem. It is found on dry, rocky slopes, in montane to lower alpine zones, and is frequent in the southern ½ of the region, infrequent north to about 58° N in BC and rare in YT. • Kellogg's knotweed (*P. polygaloides* ssp. *kelloggii*, *P. kelloggii*) can also occur at high elevations in dry to vernally moist meadows, seeps and thickets, from southern coastal BC to CA, AZ and NM. It has **linear leaves,** flowers crowded in a narrow, long-bracted, **spike-like cluster atop the stem, pointy-tipped tepals** and yellowish to greenish brown achenes.

Notes: *Polygonum* is from the Greek *poly,* "many," and *gony,* "knee joint," or *gone,* "seed," of which there are many. • Knotweeds (some also called knotgrasses) get their name from the swollen nodes on the stems. In Shakespeare's *A Midsummer Night's Dream,* Lysander taunts Hermia about her height and refers to her as being made of "hindering knotgrass," probably because it was believed that knotgrass would slow the growth of children.

Alpine Bistort • *Bistorta vivipara*

General: Perennial from a **short, thick, often contorted rhizome,** with acrid, vinegary juice; stems erect, 1–2, unbranched, **8–30 cm tall,** hairless.

Leaves: Mostly basal, lance-shaped to oblong; blades 3–10 cm long, green and lustrous above, glaucous below, **blunt to somewhat pointy-tipped,** some stalks longer than blades, margins usually rolled under; stem leaves 2–4, alternate, nearly linear, reduced and becoming unstalked upward; sheathing stipules membranous, brown, cylindric.

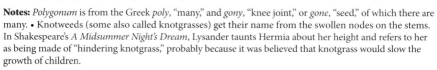

Flowers: Numerous in a **narrowly cylindric** (2–9 cm long, 0.5–1.0 cm wide), spike-like cluster atop the stem; upper flowers mostly sterile; lower flowers replaced by small pink to purple, green or brownish bulblets; **flowers white or pale pink,** lobed ⅔ or more of the distance to the base; tepals 5, **2–4 mm long;** stamens 5–8.

Fruits: Achenes rarely produced, 3-angled, dark brown, 2–3 mm long.

Where Found: Moist forest openings, meadows, thickets, streambanks, rocky slopes and barrens, heathlands and tundra; lowland (arctic coast) to alpine zones; frequent throughout all but the southwestern part of the region; arctic-alpine, circumpolar.

Notes: Alpine bistort is also known as *Polygonum viviparum.* • The pecan-sized, starchy rhizomes are eaten raw or roasted by indigenous northern peoples, who preserve them in seal oil or by freezing. They are said to taste like almonds, not pecans, and are also eaten by ptarmigan and lemmings. The slightly peppery leaves are used as a potherb or for seasoning. A decoction of the leaves was considered a good remedy for diarrhea and a treatment for gum problems and inflammation of the mouth. • *Vivipara* means "producing living young," in this case, budding baby plants still attached to the single parent. Aborted stamens and the rarity of fruits suggest that sexual reproduction is rare; the bulblets are probably the primary means of (asexual) reproduction.

Western Bistort, American Bistort
Bistorta bistortoides

General: Mostly 20–70 cm tall. **Leaves:** Basal, pointy-tipped. **Flowers:** In a **short-cylindric,** thumb-shaped, bottlebrush-like cluster (2–5 cm long, 1–2.5 cm wide); **flowers white or pale pink; anthers yellow; tepals 4–5 mm long; bulb-lets absent;** flowers fertile. **Where Found:** Moist to mesic meadows and streambanks; subalpine and alpine zones; frequent in the **southern** ⅓ of the region; cordilleran.

Notes: Western bistort is also known as *Polygonum bistortoides.* • The starchy rhizomes were roasted or stewed by the Cheyenne, Blackfoot and Cherokee, and are also eaten by bears and rodents. • *Bistorta* and *bistortoides* both come from the Latin *bis,* "twice," and *torta,* "twisted," to mean "twice twisted," in reference to the stems and twisted ("writhing") rhizomes. "Bistort" became the medieval common name.

Pink Plumes, Meadow Bistort
Bistorta plumosa

General: Resembles western bistort (above) but is 10–40 cm tall. **Flowers:** In short, cylindric clusters; **flowers deep pink; anthers purple. Where Found:** Moist to wet meadows, streambanks, heathlands and peaty tundra; montane to alpine zones; frequent in the **northern** ⅓ of the region; amphiberingian.

Notes: Pink plumes is also known as *Polygonum plumosum* and *P. bistorta* ssp. *plumosum.* • As with the other bistorts, pink plumes has edible rhizomes and leaves. • Inland Dena'ina call the plant "crescent-root" for the crescent shape of its rhizomes, which they chewed after eating fish eggs to help clean their teeth.

Alaska Wild-rhubarb • *Aconogonon alaskanum*

General: Perennial from a thick, woody root; stems erect, 30–150 cm tall, hollow, simple or branched.

Leaves: All on the stem, alternate, **lance-shaped to lance-oval,** long-tapering to pointy tip; blades 5–20 cm long, dark green above, paler beneath, margins crisped, stalks short or nearly lacking; **sheathing stipules wax-papery, reddish brown,** not shredding.

Flowers: Small, numerous, in bundles of 2–4 aggregated in **open clusters mostly atop the stem;** flowers 2–4 mm long, lobed to near the base; **tepals 5,** white, cream or greenish, egg-shaped; stamens 8; styles 3.

Fruits: Achenes 3-angled, **tan to greyish brown,** shiny, **2.5–3.5 mm long.**

Where Found: Moist cutbanks, roadsides, permafrost slumps, open forests, meadows, sandy shores, streambanks, talus slopes, heathlands and tundra; montane to alpine zones; frequent in the northern ¼ of the region; subarctic-alpine, amphiberingian.

Varieties: *FNA* makes a distinction between the hairy **var. *alaskanum*** and the hairless **var. *glabrescens*.**

Similar Species: Poke knotweed (*A. phytolaccifolium*, *Polygonum phytolaccifolium*) has **longer (4–7 mm), yellowish brown achenes,** flower clusters usually both in leaf axils and atop the stem and a southern distribution. It occurs in subalpine and alpine meadows, and on talus slopes and streambanks from WA, ID, MT and OR to CA and NV.

Notes: Alaska wild-rhubarb is also known as *Polygonum alpinum* vars. *alaskanum* and *lapathifolium*, and *P. alaskanum*. • Alaskan indigenous peoples collected the young stems in early summer before the plants flowered, then peeled and cut them into small pieces to use as others use domesticated rhubarb. Young leaves were mixed with other greens and boiled. Some Gwich'in in the upper Yukon River drainage mixed young leaves in a thick pudding of flour, sugar and water, and would also add whitefish or cony fish pipes (part of the fish stomach) and fish eggs. • *Aconogonon* is from the Greek *acon*, "whetstone," and *gone*, "seed," perhaps alluding to the edged seeds.

Ms. Davis' Knotweed, Newberry's Fleeceflower • *Aconogonon davisiae*

General: Usually several, ascending to erect stems **12–40 cm tall. Leaves:** Numerous, **egg-shaped to elliptic, somewhat leathery, often glaucous, blunt. Flowers:** Small (2–4.5 mm long), greenish to pinkish white, **in small clusters in axils of (and partially concealed by) upper leaves. Where Found:** Moist, rocky slopes and volcanic fellfields, often on talus or pumice, sometimes on serpentine; subalpine and alpine zones; locally frequent in the southern ¼ of the region; Pacific Northwest endemic.

Notes: Ms. Davis' knotweed is also known as *Polygonum newberryi*. • Nancy Jane Davis (1833–1921), an educator from Pennsylvania, collected plants in California and sent them to Harvard botanist Asa Gray. California botanist Willis Jepson called her a "plant lover, noble in mind and generous in purpose." • John Strong Newberry (1822–92), a surgeon and naturalist, was primarily a paleontologist on the 1858 Pacific Railroad Survey in California and on several other expeditions.

Mountain-sorrel • *Oxyria digyna*

General: Perennial from a long, stout, fleshy taproot; branched crown; acrid, vinegary juice; stems 1 to several, erect, 5–40 cm tall, hairless, often **reddish tinged.**

Leaves: Somewhat fleshy, **mostly basal, round to kidney-shaped,** hairless, blades 1–6 cm wide, shorter than the long stalks, margins slightly wavy; stem leaves similar, lacking or 1–2; stipules loose-sheathing, membranous, translucent, brownish or reddish.

Flowers: Very small, numerous, in whorls of 3–7 in a dense, narrow, 2–20 cm long cluster atop the stem; **tepals 4, greenish or reddish,** elliptic or egg-shaped to nearly circular, 1.2–2.5 mm long, outer 2 narrower than inner 2; stamens 6, dangly; ovary 1-chambered; styles 2, stigmas frilly, reddish; anthers and stigmas protruding well out from tepals.

Fruits: Achenes lens-shaped, **broadly winged,** 3–5 mm wide.

Where Found: Moist rock outcrops, ledges, gullies, talus and scree slopes, streambanks, snowbed sites and rocky places in tundra; frequent throughout the region; lowland (arctic coast) and upper montane to alpine (elsewhere) zones; arctic-alpine, circumpolar.

Notes: The tart, lemony young leaves can be eaten as a salad green. The leaves may also be used to soothe warts and skin irritations. The Inuit cooked the leaves and stems or ate them raw or mixed with seal blubber. The leaves were fermented as a type of sauerkraut. The juice was sweetened and thickened with flour. The stems and leaves are also an important food for muskoxen, caribou and geese. The fleshy rhizomes are eaten by arctic hares and lemmings. • **Caution:** Mountain-sorrel contains oxalic acid and can be dangerous if consumed in large quantities. • *Oxyria* means "acid-tasting," from the Greek *oxys*, "sour," and *aria*, "possession"; *digyna* means "2 gynoecia," or ovaries. "Sorrel" is from the French *surelle*, the diminutive of the Low German *suur*, meaning "sour."

GLACIAL REFUGIA AND DNA

The present-day arctic flora—perhaps 1500 species globally—was largely established by 3 million years ago. During the Pleistocene (about 2.5 million to 12,000 years ago), at least 11 major glaciations covered much of the circumpolar North, and arctic plants retreated to unglaciated areas (glacial refugia). This sometimes separated populations of a species long enough that they diverged into separate lineages, an evolutionary process reflected in the DNA of purple mountain saxifrage (p. 142) and some other circumpolar species, including mountain-sorrel (above).

As you might expect from such a wide-ranging species, mountain-sorrel exhibits differences in morphology and physiology between arctic and alpine ecotypes. But even within the morphologically uniform alpine populations of western North America, it has a lot of cryptic genetic diversity that can be revealed by DNA analysis. Plants of mountain-sorrel from northwestern BC—an area generally believed to have been entirely covered by ice in the late Pleistocene—show unexpectedly high levels of genetic diversity in their chloroplasts, a condition usually associated with unglaciated areas. The DNA data suggest that parts of the area escaped at least the last major glacial advance in the late Pleistocene, and may have also escaped earlier widespread glaciations. Beringia was clearly the largest and most significant refugium in the northern part of our region, but some other areas—including the eastern front of the Mackenzie Mountains and perhaps northwestern BC—may also have provided refugia for mountain-sorrel and other plants and animals during the last ice age. Notably, recent phylogeographic studies of mountain goats and thinhorn mountain sheep have found parallel genetic evidence for these "cryptic refugia" in the northern cordillera.

Arctic Dock • *Rumex arcticus*

General: Perennial from a taproot or short, fleshy rhizome; stems erect, solitary, 10–70 cm tall, hairless, **often tinged reddish purple.**

Leaves: Mostly basal, long-stalked, blades narrowly **lance-shaped to oblong,** 5–20 cm long, dark green, rather fleshy, hairless, blunt to pointy-tipped, margins somewhat wavy; stem leaves alternate, much reduced in size upward, nearly unstalked; sheathing stipules membranous, shed or partially persistent at maturity.

Flowers: Small, numerous, on **indistinctly jointed stalks** in a narrow cluster; **flowers bisexual (male and female parts in each flower), reddish,** 2–3 mm long; tepals 6, the **inner 3 egg-shaped, enlarging to 4–8 mm long** at maturity; stamens 6; styles 3, stigmas frilly.

Fruits: Achenes 3-angled, reddish brown, shiny, 3–4 mm long, enclosed by the enlarged inner tepals, which have smooth margins and **lack tubercles** (grain-like swellings).

Where Found: Moist to wet meadows, sandy-gravelly shores, streambanks, snowbeds, peaty heathlands and tundra; lowland (arctic coast) to alpine zones; frequent in the northern ⅓ of the region; arctic-alpine, amphiberingian.

Notes: Arctic dock and Alaska wild-rhubarb (p. 111) are considered by northern groups (Inuit, Dena'ina) to be "partners"—both are referred to as wild-rhubarb and are used in the same manner. The stems and leaves are eaten as a green vegetable and are also combined in a flour and sugar mixture. In the old days, the leaves were stored in an animal stomach or intestine container and placed in cool lake water or a pit cache. The seeds can be eaten as a snack or ground to make a flour. Both the leaves and roots were used medicinally. Roots, dug in late summer, were boiled or soaked in hot water and the decoction drunk by the Dena'ina for stomach and bladder problems; some say it is also effective against tuberculosis, constipation, and even hangovers. If a person had a serious illness, the root decoction would be ingested to induce vomiting and cleanse the system. The leaves can be used to make a poultice for blisters, burns and scalds. • **Caution:** *Rumex* species contain oxalic acid and can be dangerous if consumed in large quantities. • Today, "dock" is any kind of sorrel-type plant. The name was formerly given to burdock (*Arctium minus*) and later transferred to other broad-leaved plants. "Dock" is derived from the German *docke* or Norwegian *docca*, meaning "bundles of flax or hemp" and is synonymous with "bur" in reference to the tangle that results when the long fibres mess with *Arctium* burs (the inspiration for Velcro).

Lapland Mountain Sorrel • *Rumex lapponicus*

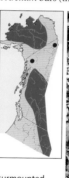 

Leaves: Mostly **egg-shaped,** at least the lower ones **arrowhead-shaped** with basal lobes pointing downward. **Flowers:** Unisexual, with male and female flowers on separate plants, on **distinctly jointed stalks,** numerous in long, interrupted clusters; flowers reddish, the outer 3 tepals becoming sharply bent back, the **inner 3 tepals erect, heart-shaped, 3–4.5 mm long. Fruits:** Achenes brown, 2–2.5 mm long, loosely enclosed by inner tepals, which have a **small tubercle near the base. Where Found:** Moist to mesic meadows, streambanks, river terraces, thickets and forest openings; montane to alpine zones; scattered and locally frequent in the northern ¾ of region, infrequent southward; amphiberingian.

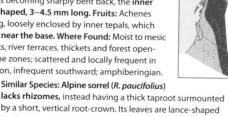

Similar Species: Alpine sorrel (*R. paucifolius*) lacks rhizomes, instead having a thick taproot surmounted by a short, vertical root-crown. Its leaves are lance-shaped to elliptic (**not arrowhead-shaped**), **tapering to rounded or wedge-shaped bases.** The flowers are also unisexual and on separate plants, on jointed stalks, reddish, the inner tepals heart-shaped, 3–4 mm long and **lacking tubercles.** It occurs in moist meadows and on grassy slopes and streambanks, in montane to alpine zones. A cordilleran species, it is frequent in the southern ⅓ of the region, east of the Cascades crest, southern BC and southwestern AB to CA, NV, UT and CO.

alpine sorrel

Notes: Lapland mountain sorrel is also known as *Rumex alpestris* and *R. acetosa* ssp. *alpestris*. • Species of *Rumex*, which have reddish, enlarged inner tepals, as well as *Oxyria digyna*, which has reddish, winged achenes, are much showier in fruit than in flower. Arrays of small, inconspicuous flowers, small scale-like tepals and dangly anthers and frilly stigmas protruding well beyond the tepals are all features characteristic of wind-pollinated plants.

THE GENUS *ERIOGONUM* (Wild-buckwheat)

Our high-elevation *Eriogonum* species are mostly perennial herbs, sometimes woody at the base, from taproots surmounted by a stem-base. The flowering stems are prostrate or reclining to erect. The leaves are mostly at the base, alternate to whorled, lance-shaped to nearly circular, lacking stipules, the margins untoothed. The flowers are stalked, in bell- to top-shaped cups of fused involucral bracts, these involucres 5–10-toothed and with 2 to several flowers, aggregated in simple or compound umbels or in head-like clusters atop the stems. The flowers are small, white to red or variously yellow, of 6 tepals fused toward the base, with 9 stamens, a single-chambered ovary and 3 styles. The fruits are brown or blackish achenes, 3-angled and not winged.

Eriogonum is a huge genus with about 250 species, all North American. One of the largest genera on the continent, it is exceeded only by *Carex* (with about 480 North American species), *Astragalus* (350 species), and *Penstemon* (280 species). Both *Eriogonum* and *Astragalus* have evolved rapidly in the arid basin and range regions of western North America.

Eriogonum is from the Greek *erion*, "wool," and *gony*, "knee," and refers to the hairy nodes (joints) of the species first described, *E. tomentosum* (dogtongue wild-buckwheat).

Several Aboriginal groups made medicines from the powdered roots of various species of this genus. The Blackfoot used tea made from boiled leaves for colds and stomach aches, and to halt lengthy menses. Leaf poultices were applied to treat rheumatism, sores, burns and venereal disease, and the leaves were also used as a disinfectant and emetic. Many *Eriogonum* species provide excellent fodder (nectar and pollen) for bees. All of our high-elevation species can be cultivated in rock gardens and are highly prized by alpine gardeners.

Key to *Eriogonum*

1a. Bracts at base of inflorescence obvious, leafy 2

    2a. Involucral lobes at least ½ as long as tubes, usually bent back or spreading 3

        3a. Lacking whorl of leaf-like bracts at midstem; leaves spoon-shaped to elliptic
. . . . ***E. umbellatum*** (p. 115)

        3b. Whorl of leaf-like bracts at midstem; leaves narrowly lance-shaped
. . . . ***E. heracleoides*** var. ***heracleoides*** (p. 115)

    2b. Involucral lobes <½ as long as tubes, erect. 4

        4a. Umbels subtended by 2 linear bracts; flowers white to cream or rose
. . . . ***E. pyrolifolium*** (p. 117)

        4b. Umbels subtended by 4–10 bracts; flowers yellow 5

            5a. Flowers hairless on the outside . . . . ***E. marifolium*** (p. 116)

            5b. Flowers hairy on the outside. 6

                6a. Leaves 1–2 cm long; flowers woolly on the outside toward the base
. . . . ***E. androsaceum*** (p. 116)

                6b. Leaves 2–7 cm long; flowers soft-hairy all over on the outside
. . . . ***E. flavum*** var. ***piperi*** (p. 116)

1b. Bracts at base of inflorescence small, scale-like 7

    7a. Flowering stems woody and leafy above the base to at least ⅓ their length
. . . . ***E. microthecum*** (p. 115)

    7b. Flowering stems neither woody nor leafy above the base 8

        8a. Flowers yellow; tepals all about the same size . . . . ***E. crosbyae*** (p. 116)

        8b. Flowers white or cream to rose or reddish; outer tepals twice as wide as inner ones
. . . . ***E. ovalifolium*** (p. 117)

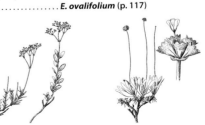

E. androsaceum   *E. microthecum*   *E. crosbyae*

Subalpine Wild-buckwheat
Eriogonum umbellatum var. *majus*

General: Stems prostrate to spreading, forming compact mats 10–50 cm wide; flowering stems erect, 15–30 cm tall, usually white-woolly, **lacking midstem whorl of bracts. Leaves:** In loose basal rosettes; **blades spoon-shaped to elliptic,** 5–30 mm long, narrowed gradually to stalks, **green and hairless on upper surface, woolly-hairy on lower;** stem leaves lacking. **Flowers: Numerous in umbels** subtended by a whorl of leaf-like bracts; involucres woolly-hairy, 3–6 mm long; **flowers cream-coloured,** sometimes greenish- or reddish-tinged, 3–7 mm long, tepals egg- to spoon-shaped. **Where found:** Dry rocky slopes, meadows, forest openings, talus and scree slopes, and tundra; montane to alpine zones; frequent in the southern interior ⅓ of the region; cordilleran.

Varieties: *E. umbellatum* is a widespread and extremely variable species complex of western North America, with an astounding 41 varieties currently recognized, several of which occur at high elevations. • **Haussknecht's sulphur flower (var. *haussknechtii*)** has **bright yellow flowers.** It is found in the Cascade Mtns of WA and OR, and is frequent on Mt. Hood and Mt. Adams. • **Desert sulphur flower (var. *desereticum*)** has leaves that are **hairless on both surfaces** and **pale yellow to cream flowers.** It sometimes attains high elevations in subalpine conifer parklands and has a scattered distribution in southern ID, southwestern MT and southwestern WY to northern NV and northern UT.

Similar Species: Subalpine wild-buckwheat could be confused with **parsnip-flower wild-buckwheat (below),** which has **narrower leaves** and flowering stems with a **whorl of leaf-like bracts at about midlength.**

Notes: Subalpine wild-buckwheat is also known as *Eriogonum subalpinum* and *E. umbellatum* ssp. *subalpinum.* • True buckwheat is *Fagopyrum esculentum,* widely cultivated for fodder and as a pseudo-cereal. • *E. umbellatum* is called wild-buckwheat because the flowers are in umbrella-like clusters that look vaguely similar to those of *Fagopyrum.* "Buckwheat" could be from the 15th-century Low German *bukweten,* meaning "goat-wheat," for a grain inferior to true wheat.

Parsnip-flower Wild-buckwheat
Eriogonum heracleoides var. *heracleoides*

General: Spreading mats with erect, white-woolly flowering stems 5–40 cm tall, with a whorl of leaf-like bracts near midstem. **Leaves: Narrowly lance-shaped,** 2–5 cm long, white-woolly below, green and nearly hairless above. **Flowers:** In umbels subtended by **3–10 leaf-like bracts; tepals white to cream or yellowish white,** 4–8 mm long. **Where found:** Dry meadows, sandy-gravelly flats, slopes and ridges, shrub-steppe and woodlands; montane to lower alpine zones; frequent inland in the southern ⅓ of the region; cordilleran.

Similar Species: Slenderbush wild-buckwheat (*E. microthecum*) is **shrubby,** at least toward the base, does not form mats, has **leafy stems** and white to pink (occasionally yellowish) **flowers in open, branched clusters.** It occurs on rocky slopes and in shrublands and open forests, in montane to alpine zones, and is frequent in the southeastern part of the region, from north-central WA, ID and MT to CA, AZ and NM.

Notes: The Okanagan made a tea from the roots to cure diarrhea. They boiled the roots and stems to treat infected cuts, colds, blood poisoning, tuberculosis, cancer and other sicknesses, and made leaf poultices for cuts and sores. This plant was also used in steam baths for aching joints and muscles, and in sweat lodges for purification. Strong decoctions were used by the Nlaka'pamux to treat syphilis.

Golden Alpine Wild-buckwheat
Eriogonum flavum var. *piperi*

General: Forms loose to compact mats, to 60 cm wide; flowering stems erect to ascending, white-woolly, 5–25 cm tall. **Leaves: Narrowly lance-shaped to oblong, blades 2–7 cm long,** usually densely white-woolly beneath, greenish and less hairy above. **Flowers:** Numerous in umbels or somewhat head-like clusters, subtended by **4–6 leaf-like bracts; flowers pale to bright sulphur yellow, densely hairy on the outside,** 4–7 mm long; tepals 6, all about the same size. **Fruits:** Achenes with **sparsely hairy beaks. Where Found:** Dry grasslands, stony meadows, shrublands, open forests, exposed ridges, rock outcrops and scree slopes; montane to alpine zones; frequent inland in the southern ⅓ of the region; southern cordilleran. **Similar Species:** Rock-jasmine wild-buckwheat (*E. androsaceum*) occurs in the high Rockies of southwestern AB, northwestern MT and adja-

cent BC, on dry, sandy or gravelly ridge crests, talus slopes and meadows. It is **shorter** (3–10 cm) than golden-alpine wild-buckwheat, with **smaller (1–2 cm long) elliptic leaves,** pale yellow flowers and **hairless achenes**.

Marum-leaf Wild-buckwheat
Eriogonum marifolium

General: Forms compact mats; **flowering stems erect,** 5–40 cm tall. **Leaves:** Egg-shaped, 3–30 mm long, **woolly beneath, greenish and nearly hairless above. Flowers:** Unisexual, males and females on separate plants; in head-like clusters subtended by **5–10 leaf-like bracts; tepals yellow;** male flowers dull yellow, 1.5–3 mm long; female flowers bright yellow, often turning reddish with age, 4–7 mm long. **Where Found:** Dry meadows, sandy often volcanic flats and slopes, shrublands, grasslands and open coniferous forests; montane to alpine zones; scattered and locally frequent in the southwestern corner of the region.

Similar Species: Crosby's wild-buckwheat (*E. crosbyae*) is shorter (to 20 cm), with spoon-shaped leaves that are **white-woolly on both surfaces,** bisexual, mostly **bright yellow flowers** and tepals that are hairless on the outside, **sometimes glandular or minutely blistered toward the base.** It is found in rock outcrops, sandy flats, slopes and ridges, shrublands, woodlands and tundra, in montane to alpine zones, and is scattered in central and southwestern ID, western MT, southeastern OR and northwestern NV.

Notes: "Marum-leaf" and *marifolium* both acknowledge a resemblance to Mediterranean germander (*Teucrium marum*), a garden plant in the mint family.

Cushion Wild-buckwheat
Eriogonum ovalifolium var. *nivale*

General: Forms compact mats; **flowering stems erect,** white-woolly, 1–12 cm tall. **Leaves:** Roundish, 5–10 mm across, **densely white-woolly to silvery hairy** on both surfaces. **Flowers:** Numerous in head-like clusters, subtended by **3 scale-like bracts;** involucres bell-shaped with 5 short teeth; **tepals white or cream to rose or reddish,** 4–5 mm long, the **outer wider than the inner. Where Found:** Dry meadows, sandy to gravelly

often granitic ridges, talus and scree slopes and fellfields; montane to alpine zones; locally frequent in the southern ¼ of the region east of the coastal mountains; cordilleran. **Varieties:** Dwarf cushion wild-buckwheat (***E. ovalifolium* var. *depressum*)** is scattered in the Rockies of southwestern AB, ID, MT and WY, and also in eastern OR and northeastern NV. It has **elliptic leaves** that are **greenish and thinly woolly-hairy** on the upper surface and **spreading (not erect) flowering stems.**

Notes: A decoction of roots was used in Nevada for colds, and the Gosiute of southwestern Utah prepared a poultice or wash to treat venereal disease.

Contented Alpine Wild-buckwheat
Eriogonum pyrolifolium

General: Flowering stems prostrate to ascending, 4–15 cm long/tall. **Leaves:** In loose rosettes; blades elliptic to egg-shaped or roundish, **1–4 cm long,** woolly (var. *coryphaeum*) or sometimes hairless (var. *pyrolifolium*) beneath, **green and hairless above. Flowers:** In head-like clusters or tight umbels subtended by **2 linear bracts,** white or greenish white (but not yellow) aging to rose or reddish, **soft-hairy on the outside,** 4–6 mm long; anthers purple; **tepals all about same size. Where Found:** Dry meadows, shrublands, sandy-gravelly or pumice slopes and ridges, open forests and scree slopes; montane to alpine zones; locally frequent inland in the southern ¼ of the region; southern cordilleran.

Similar Species: Contented alpine wild-buckwheat resembles several other high-elevation *Eriogonum* species, especially golden alpine wild-buckwheat (p. 116), marum-leaf wild-buckwheat (p. 116) and dwarf cushion wild-buckwheat (above). However, contented alpine wild-buckwheat has a distinctive combination of somewhat oval, **floppy leaves** longer than 1 cm, green and hairless on the upper surface and not in tight mats, plus white to pinkish (not yellow) flowers.

Notes: Some say the flowers have an unpleasant smell; nonetheless, these are handsome plants well suited to rock gardens.

PURSLANE FAMILY (Portulacaceae)

Our Portulacaceae are annual to perennial, more or less fleshy herbs, with simple, entire (not toothed or lobed), alternate or opposite leaves. The flowers are radially symmetric, wheel- or bowl-shaped, the petals usually 5 (more in *Lewisia*, 4 in *Cistanthe*), the sepals usually 2 and persistent, the stamens 3–5, sometimes more, and the ovary 1-chambered. The fruits are capsules with dark, lustrous seeds.

Key to the Genera of Portulacaceae

1a. Petals 4; stamens 3; flowers in dense, umbel-like clusters. . . . . *Cistanthe umbellata* (below)

1b. Petals and stamens 5 or more; flowers solitary or in open clusters 2

    2a. Capsules opening around their circumference, like a Russian doll; petals usually 6–8; stigmas often >3
    . . . . *Lewisia* (pp. 122–123)

    2b. Capsules splitting open from the top by segments; petals 5; stigmas 3. 3

        3a. Stem leaves usually 2, distinct or joined at the base . . . . *Claytonia* (pp. 119–121)

        3b. Stem leaves >2, distinct . . . . *Montia* (p. 119)

     Cistanthe   *Lewisia*   *Claytonia*   *Montia*

Umbellate Pussypaws
Cistanthe umbellata

General: Perennial from a taproot and branching stem-base, spreading, forming mats to 25 cm across; flowering stems 1 from each rosette of leaves, reclining to erect, to 15 cm long/tall.

Leaves: Clustered in 2 to many basal rosettes, somewhat fleshy, **spoon-shaped,** on thick stalks, hairless, 1–7 cm long; stem leaves usually lacking.

Flowers: Numerous in **dense, head-shaped, umbel-like clusters** 1–2 cm in diameter; **petals 4, white to pinkish,** oblong, 3–8 mm long; sepals 2, papery, white- to pinkish-margined, circular, slightly longer and considerably wider than petals; **stamens 3,** anthers red or yellow; ovary 1-chambered; stigmas 2.

Fruits: Capsules globe-shaped, 2–3 mm, opening by 2 segments; seeds 1–8, black, shiny.

Where Found: Dry sandy or gravelly slopes, ridges, open woodlands and scree; montane to alpine zones; locally frequent in southern ¼ of the region; southern cordilleran.

Similar Species: Umbellate pussypaws superficially resembles a wild-buckwheat (*Eriogonum* spp.) but is fleshy, with larger sepals and fruits that are capsules not achenes.

Notes: Umbellate pussypaws is also known as *Spraguea umbellata* and *Calyptridium umbellatum.*
• *Cistanthe* is from *Cistus* (rockrose genus) and the Greek *anthos*, meaning "flower," presumably because the flowers of the 2 genera are similar.

Bostock's Montia
Montia bostockii

General: Perennial from slender **rhizomes and stolons (runners),** rooting at nodes; stems solitary, erect, 5–15 cm tall.

Leaves: Alternate, **not in basal rosette,** mostly along stem, disposed to one side, **linear to narrowly lance-shaped,** somewhat fleshy, hairless, 1–4 cm long.

Flowers: In round-topped clusters of 2–12 flowers on stalks 5–25 mm long, nodding in bud but erect in bloom, the cluster subtended by a **single bract;** petals 5, white (rarely pinkish) with yellow blotches at the base and often with pink veins, 1–1.5 cm long; stamens 5; stigmas 3.

Fruits: Capsules opening by 3 segments; seeds 1–3, black, minutely pebbly.

Where Found: Moist to wet meadows, turfy seepage, scree and tundra; subalpine and alpine zones; locally frequent in the northern ⅓ of the region; endemic.

Notes: Bostock's montia is also known as *Claytonia bostockii.* • Hugh S. Bostock (1901–94) was one of the Geological Survey of Canada's most dedicated and respected scientists. Between 1924 and 1954, he explored Yukon by foot, canoe and packhorse, surveying and mapping the physiography and geology of the territory. He also collected plants and was particularly taken by alpine flowers.

THE GENUS *CLAYTONIA* (Springbeauty)

The high-elevation species of springbeauty in our region are all somewhat fleshy, hairless perennials, with mostly ascending stems from tubers or rhizomes or woody stem-bases. The leaves are 1 to several at the base—or lacking or withered by flowering time—with an opposite pair or rarely 3 on the stem. Usually there are several flowers in a bracted cluster at the stem tips. The showy, wheel- or saucer-shaped flowers have 5 usually white or pink petals, 2 leaf-like, unequal sepals, 5 stamens and 3 stigmas. The fruits are capsules that open from the top by 3 segments. The usually 3–6 seeds are black, shiny and smooth to granular-pebbly. Springbeauties have beautiful spring flowers that are among the earliest delights for high-country wanderers.

Key to *Claytonia*

Western Springbeauty
Claytonia lanceolata

General: From spheric **tubers** 1–2 cm in diameter; 1 to several stems, ascending to erect, their aboveground portions to 12 cm tall. **Leaves:** 1 or a few basal leaves, often absent at flowering; **stem leaves 2**, unstalked, **lance- to egg-shaped**, 1–6 cm long. **Flowers:** In loose clusters of 3–15 or so on stalks 1–5 cm long; **bract 1, subtending the lowest flower;** flowers 1–2 cm across, petals white to pink, magenta, yellow or orange, 5–15 mm long. **Where Found:** Moist shrublands, grasslands, meadows and snowbed sites; steppe to alpine zones; frequent primarily in the inland southern ½ of the region, south of about 53° N; cordilleran.

Similar Species: Western springbeauty has a broad ecological range and a wide range of flower colour. Some taxonomists recognize a separate amphiberingian species, **Rydberg's springbeauty** (*C. multiscapa; C. lanceolata* vars. *flava, multiscapa* and *pacifica; C. czukczorum, C. tuberosa* var. *czukczorum*), that has **several bracts subtending the flower cluster** and white to deep yellow or yellow-orange petals. It replaces *C. lanceolata* (in the strict sense) on Vancouver I., also occurs in the Olympic Mtns and is reported from ID, MT, WY, southeastern BC and northern AK and YT.

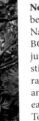

Notes: Western springbeauty is also called "Indian potato" because the underground corms were used by many First Nations peoples as a source of starch. The Potato Range in BC's Chilcotin District is named after this plant. In June, just after flowering, the corms are harvested with digging sticks and eaten raw or cooked. The corms would be stored raw in underground caches or pits (Secwepemc) or cooked and then and dried for winter use. The leaves can also be eaten when young as a salad green or cooked as a vegetable. To ensure future harvests, people were careful to take only the largest corms, replanting the small ones.

Rydberg's springbeauty

Beringian Springbeauty • *Claytonia tuberosa*

General: From spheric **tubers** sometimes with thin rhizomes; usually 1 brittle, flowering stem per tuber. **Leaves:** Basal leaves lacking or few; stem leaves 2, **linear to lance-shaped. Flowers:** In clusters with 1 to several bracts, the few flowers 1–2 cm across; **petals white with yellow blotch at the base. Where Found:** Moist, stony tundra; montane to alpine zones; locally frequent in the northern ⅓ of the region; amphiberingian.

Similar Species: Ogilvie springbeauty (*C. ogilviensis*) has turnip- to globe-shaped tubers and **egg-shaped stem leaves abruptly contracted to the stalks.** The umbel-like flower clusters have several bracts, 2–6 flowers, each 1–1.5 cm across, with bright to dark **purple petals.** Found on stony slopes and talus in the alpine zone, it is rare in west-central YT and endemic to the Ogilvie Mtns.

Notes: The tubers were collected by Alaskan Inuit and roasted or cooked in stews. The leaves were eaten raw or cooked.

Ogilvie springbeauty

Fellfield Springbeauty
Claytonia megarhiza

General: From a thick, **fleshy taproot** surmounted by a somewhat woody, branching stem-base; flowering stems 1 to several, short, 2–10 cm long. **Leaves:** Basal leaves 2–10 cm long (about same length as flowering stems), numerous in a shiny rosette, **spoon-shaped, blunt-tipped,** with winged stalks; stem leaves 2, lance-shaped. **Flowers:** In clusters of 2–6 with several bracts; flowers 1–2 cm across, **petals white to rosy pink,** 5–15 mm long. **Where Found:** Scree, talus, gravelly ridges, rock crevices, fellfields and

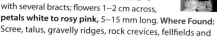

snowbeds; subalpine and alpine zones; infrequent in the inland southern ⅓ of the region, disjunct in west-central NT; cordilleran.

Similar Species: Siberian narrow-leaved springbeauty (*C. acutifolia; C. acutifolia* ssp. *graminifolia, C. eschscholtzii*) also has a long, thick taproot and woody stem-base, but its basal leaves are narrower, **linear to lance-shaped,** stiff and **pointy-tipped.** The petals are white to pinkish with **yellow blotches** at the base or wholly white, 10–14 mm long. This amphiberingian species is found in moist to wet shrublands, heathlands, stony slopes and tundra, in lowland (arctic coast) to alpine zones, and is infrequent in western coastal AK.

Creeping Springbeauty, Alaska Springbeauty • *Claytonia sarmentosa*

General: Loosely matted, from slender **rhizomes and runners;** flowering stems 1 to several, erect, 5–20 cm tall. **Leaves: Basal leaves elliptic to spoon-shaped,** blades 2–8 cm long, 1–2 cm wide, tapering to long stalks; stem leaves 2, egg-shaped. **Flowers:** In clusters of 3–8, without bracts; flowers 1.5–2 cm across, **petals pink,** with darker veins and yellow blotch at the base. **Where Found:** Moist to wet stream-banks, rocky slopes, tundra, mossy seepage and snowbed sites; montane to alpine zones; frequent in the northern ⅓ of the region; amphiberingian.

Similar Species: Scamman's springbeauty (*C. scammaniana; Montia scammaniana*) also grows from rhizomes but has **narrower basal leaves,** usually **less than 1 cm wide.** The flowers are 1–2 cm across, the petals bright pink to purplish with darker veins. This amphiberingian species is found on scree, talus and tundra, in subalpine and alpine zones. It is infrequent in central and northern AK and YT.

Notes: Creeping springbeauty is also known as *Montia sarmentosa.*

THE GENUS *LEWISIA*

Plants in this genus are low, fleshy, perennial herbs from taproots or **corms** (bulb-like underground stems), the leaves mostly at the base. The flowering stems are often shorter than or equal to the leaves, bearing 1 to several, pink or white flowers with 3–16 petals, 2–8 sepals and 3–8 stigmas. The fruits are globe- to egg-shaped capsules, opening around their circumference like a Russian doll, and have numerous dark, shiny seeds. *Lewisia* was named after Captain Meriwether Lewis (1774–1809) of the Lewis and Clark expedition.

Key to *Lewisia*

1a. Plants with globe- or egg-shaped corms; stem leaves 2–3 (occasionally 4–5), semi-whorled.... **L. triphylla (below)**

1b. Plants with large, fleshy taproots; stem leaves reduced, bract-like 2

   2a. Sepals apparently 4 (2 sepal-like bracts subtend the 2 sepals); restricted to ID..... **L. sacajaweana (p. 123)**

   2b. Sepals 2, bracts well below them 3

      3a. Flowering stems 10–30 cm tall, with bracts alternate or lacking; flowers 2 to several per stalk
      .... **L. columbiana (p. 123)**

      3b. Flowering stems usually <10 cm tall, with a pair of opposite bracts; flowers mostly 1 per flowering stem.... 4

         4a. Petals pink to white; sepals mostly rounded or blunt at tip, margins usually glandular-toothed;
         leaves linear, 3–9 cm long .... **L. pygmaea (below)**

         4b. Petals mostly white; sepals pointy-tipped, margins mostly not toothed, not glandular; leaves
         narrowly lance-shaped, 4–15 cm long .... **L. nevadensis (below)**

Alpine Lewisia • *Lewisia pygmaea*

General: From a thick taproot and stem-base; stems 1 to several, ascending to sprawling, often shorter than leaves. **Leaves:** Clustered at the base, few to many, withering at or soon after flowering time, fleshy, linear to narrowly lance-shaped, hairless, 3–9 cm long; stem leaves lacking. **Flowers:** Ours with mostly solitary (rarely 2 or more) flowers atop several **stalks 1–8 cm tall;** flowers 1.5–2 cm across; **petals 5–9, pink or magenta to whitish,** elliptic to oblong, 5–10 mm long; **sepals 2,** about ½ as long as petals, **blunt, margins usually glandular-toothed;** stamens 4–8; stigmas 3–6. **Where Found:** Dry to vernally moist, rocky slopes, outcrops, sandy-gravelly meadows, ridges and fellfields; montane to alpine zones; infrequent in the southern ⅓ of the region, disjunct and rare in southwestern YT and (reportedly) south-central AK.

sepal

Similar Species: Nevada lewisia (L. nevadensis; *L. pygmaea* var. *nevadensis*) has usually **white petals, pointy-tipped sepals with untoothed margins** and tends to be more robust (with leaves to 15 cm long) than alpine lewisia. It occurs on moist gravelly flats, grassy slopes and in meadows, in montane to alpine zones, and is infrequent from WA and ID to CA, AZ and NM.
• **Three-leaved lewisia (L. triphylla)** occasionally occurs in the alpine, typically in sandy meadows near melting snow, over a range similar to that of alpine lewisia. It has a roundish **corm,** basal leaves withering before flowering time, and **2–3 (to 5) linear, paired or whorled stem leaves.** The white or pinkish flowers are similar to those of the preceding 2 species but smaller, with petals 4–7 mm long.

three-leaved lewisia

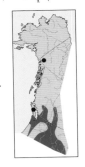

Notes: These species often bloom immediately after snowmelt. • The Nlaka'pamux people believed that eating the roots of alpine lewisia would drive them insane. The Blackfoot of Alberta and possibly other southern interior BC peoples ate the roots, which were considered inferior to bitterroot (*L. rediviva*).

Columbia Lewisia • *Lewisia columbiana*

General: From a thick, fleshy taproot; **stems 10–30 cm tall,** erect, branching, with alternate bracts. **Leaves:** Clustered at the base, **narrow, fleshy, evergreen. Flowers: Numerous in open clusters,** similar to those of alpine lewisia (opposite); **petals white with pink veins to rose or magenta,** oblong to egg-shaped, 5–13 mm long. **Where Found:** Dry to mesic, rocky or gravelly slopes, rock ledges, crevices and outcrops; montane to alpine zones; scattered but locally frequent in the southern ⅓ of the region; Pacific Northwest endemic.

Varieties: We have 3 varieties: **var. *columbiana*,** with leaves 2–10 cm long and petals 7–11 mm long; **var. *rupicola*,** with leaves 2–3 cm long and petals 10–13 mm long; **var. *wallowensis*,** with leaves 2–4 cm long and petals 5–10 mm long. See *FNA* for details.

Similar Species: Sacajawea's bitterroot (***L. sacajaweana***) has a rosette of flattened, **spoon-shaped leaves** and **white flowers 1–2 cm long,** on very short stems. It is found only on high peaks in central ID and was originally considered part of Kellogg's bitterroot (*L. kelloggii*), found in the Sierra Nevada of CA. Recent research indicates that the ID plants are morphologically and genetically distinct from the Sierra plants. Sacajawea's bitterroot was named in honour of the Shoshone woman who shepherded the Lewis and Clark expedition from North Dakota to the Pacific.

STONECROP FAMILY (Crassulaceae)

Our stonecrops are succulent, hairless, perennial herbs from rhizomes, with simple, alternate or opposite leaves, usually with numerous flowers in bracted, compact clusters at stem tips. The flowers are radially symmetric, showy and star-shaped, with 4–5 petals and sepals that can be distinct or somewhat united at base, 8 or 10 stamens and 5 ovaries, distinct or basally united, each with a nectar gland at the base. The fruits are a clutch of many-seeded, pod-like follicles.

Key to the Genera of Crassulaceae

1a. Leaves (of species in our region) plump, basal and along the stem, the largest mostly on the lower ½ of flowering stems or on low, sterile stems; flowers yellow . . . . *Sedum* (p. 124)

1b. Leaves strongly flattened, mostly along the stem, the largest toward the top of the stems; flowers (of species in our region) pink or reddish purple . . . . *Rhodiola* (p. 125)

Key to *Sedum* (Stonecrop)

1a. Stem leaves mostly opposite, oval to spoon-shaped 2

    2a. Mature fruits (follicles) spreading; petals distinct to the base . . . . *S. divergens* (p. 124)

    2b. Mature follicles erect, only styles spreading; petals fused for about 1 mm at the base . . . . . *S. debile* (p. 124)

1b. Stem leaves alternate, narrowly lance-shaped to elliptic 3

    3a. Leaves keeled below, linear or linear-lance-shaped, long-tapering to pointed tips; plantlets usually present in upper leaf axils . . . . *S. stenopetalum* (p. 124)

    3b. Leaves not keeled, the tips blunt to sharp; plantlets lacking from flowering stems 4

        4a. Basal leaves egg-shaped to elliptic, stem leaves elliptic-oblong to lance-shaped; follicles spreading . . . . *S. borschii* (p. 124)

        4b. Basal leaves lance-shaped to elliptic-egg-shaped, stem leaves lance-shaped; follicles erect . . . . *S. lanceolatum* (p. 124)

Spreading Stonecrop • *Sedum divergens*

General: Mat-forming with numerous spreading, leafy shoots; flowering stems reclining to ascending-erect, 5–15 cm tall. **Leaves: Opposite,** green to bright red, 4–9 mm long, **oval to nearly spheric with wrinkles or dimples, crammed together on sterile shoots,** more sausage-like on flowering stems. **Flowers:** In compact clusters of 5–25 with leafy bracts; petals 5, **distinct,** yellow, pointy-tipped, about 6 mm long. **Fruits:** Follicles basally fused for about 2 mm, then **strongly spreading. Where Found:** Dry rocky or gravelly slopes, cliffs, outcrops and talus; lowland (northern coast) to alpine zones, mostly high elevations in the southern part of the range; frequent in the central ½ of the region, infrequent south to WA (Olympic and Cascade Mtns) and OR (Mt. Hood).

Similar Species: Weak-stem stonecrop (*S. debile*) has **erect follicles,** with only the styles spreading, and **petals fused at base** for about 1 mm. It occurs on dry, rocky slopes and ledges, gravel bars, ridges, scree and talus, in montane to alpine zones, and is scattered and locally frequent in the southeastern corner of the region, central ID, southwestern MT, southeastern OR and western WY to NV and UT.

Notes: The small, roundish, fleshy leaves were treated as berries and eaten raw or with oolichan grease. The Nisga'a, Haida, Gitxsan and Stl'atl'imc collected them in the autumn, especially after a frost, or in the spring before the plants flowered. The Nisga'a call them "lava berries" because the plant grows abundantly on lava beds in the Nass Valley. • Several species of stonecrop, including spreading stonecrop, are recommended for use in "green roofs," where plants are grown on roofs for the attendant environmental benefits.

Lance-leaved Stonecrop
Sedum lanceolatum

General: Mat-forming with numerous short, leafy shoots; flowering stems ascending to erect, curved at the base, 5–25 cm tall. **Leaves:** Lower leaves crowded on basal, sterile shoots, occasionally with plantlets in leaf axils; **stem leaves alternate, lance-shaped,** often sausage-like, not keeled, green to reddish green, turning golden in autumn, 5–20 mm long. **Flowers:** Petals yellow, lance-shaped, 6–9 mm long in high-elevation plants; stamens shorter than petals. **Fruits: Follicles erect. Where Found:** Dry, rocky slopes, cliffs, bluffs, outcrops and talus; lowland to subalpine, occasionally alpine zones; frequent in the southern inland ⅔ of the region; cordilleran.

Similar Species: Stiff stonecrop (*S. stenopetalum*) has **linear leaves** that are **strongly keeled below with a firm midrib** and long-tapering to **pointy tips, spreading follicles** and usually **plantlets (detachable leaf clusters) in upper leaf axils.** It is found on dry rocky slopes, grasslands, shrublands, cliffs, talus and scree, in steppe to subalpine (rarely lower alpine) zones. This species is frequent in southern BC and southwestern AB, south to CA, ID and WY. • **Soupy stonecrop (*S. borschii*)** has **elliptic-oblong to lance-shaped, blunt stem leaves** and **spreading follicles.** Restricted to ID and MT, it occurs on dry rocky slopes, cliffs and bluffs, in montane to lower alpine zones.

Notes: The leaves of all *Sedum* species are edible but should be eaten in moderation because they are known to have emetic and cathartic properties and can cause headaches. • *Sedum* is a classical name for several succulents and comes from the Latin *sedeo,* "to sit," in reference to the tendency of these plants to perch on rock walls and stones. "Stonecrop" is from the Old English *stancrop,* meaning "that which is gathered, cropped or cut off stone." • Lance-leaved stonecrop is the preferred host plant for the Rocky Mountain Apollo butterfly (*Parnassius smintheus*).

Western Roseroot, King's Crown, Midsummer Men • *Rhodiola integrifolia* ssp. *integrifolia*

General: From short, thick, branching, scaly rhizomes, forming rubbery clumps or mats; flowering stems numerous, erect to spreading, 5–35 cm tall/long, dying back in winter to the top of the rhizome.

Leaves: Alternate, crowded along the stem, reduced and scale-like below, larger farther up the stem, **egg-shaped to elliptic-oblong, 5–40 mm long, 1.5 cm wide, flattened,** green to pinkish, turning red in autumn, often glaucous; margins smooth to toothed.

Flowers: Numerous in large, dense, **umbrella-shaped clusters** atop the stems, mostly **unisexual;** petals 4–5, mostly **dark red,** elliptic-oblong, 1.5–5 mm long; sepals shorter than petals, persistent; stamens 8 or 10, protruding from flowers.

Fruits: Follicles erect with spreading tips, plump, reddish; seeds numerous, pear-shaped or ellipsoid, winged.

Where Found: Dry to moist, rocky slopes, cliffs, talus, scree, meadows and tundra; lowland to alpine zones; frequent in most of the region, from rocky seashores to alplands; ssp. *integrifolia* is amphiberingian.

Similar Species: Rose crown (**R. rhodantha;** *Sedum rhodanthum*) has **narrower (lance-shaped to linear-oblong) leaves and bisexual flowers in a spike- or head-like cluster,** the petals larger, **6–13 mm long, pale pink to rose or greenish.** It grows on streambanks, in seepage areas and moist to wet meadows, in montane to alpine zones. Endemic to the Rockies, it is frequent in the southeastern part of the region, from south-central MT to AZ and NM. • Some taxonomists have treated *R. integrifolia* as part of **roseroot (R. rosea),** which has yellow or yellowish green flowers and according to *FNA* occurs in our region only in AK.

Notes: Western roseroot is also known as *Rhodiola alaskana, R. rosea* ssp. *integrifolium, Sedum integrifolium.* • The Inuit used the succulent stems and leaves as a green vegetable, usually gathered in early summer. The Inupiat of northwestern Alaska ate the roots raw, dipped in oil, in spring. Some eastern groups fermented and ate the plants and juice together with blubber. The Dena'ina of Alaska made a medicinal tea for colds, sore throats and mouth sores, for washing cuts and even for facilitating childbirth. It was also used as an eyewash and for bathing sore feet. • *Rhodiola* is the diminutive of the Greek *rhodon,* "rose"; *integrifolium* means "entire leaf," in reference to the lack of lobes. "Roseroot" refers to the smell of the cut rhizome of *R. rosea.* The name "king's crown" refers to the dense, crown-like cluster of flowers or maybe to the regal array of spreading, flower-topped stems. • On Midsummer's Eve, a girl could pick 2 pieces of the plant, one representing herself and the other her lover, and set them on a slate or trencher. The length of time the male piece lived and whether or not it curled in toward hers indicated the strength and length of the lover's fidelity.

PINK FAMILY (Caryophyllaceae)

The pinks are a fairly large family with about 3000 species worldwide, primarily found in northern temperate regions, and well represented in mountainous areas and around the Mediterranean. Our Caryophyllaceae are perennial herbs with the following characteristics: stems with swollen nodes; opposite, small, mostly narrow, **simple leaves;** radially symmetric, usually white or pink flowers with 4–5 sepals (in *Silene* fused into a tube), 4–5 distinct petals, 5–10 stamens and a single **superior ovary.** The fruits are usually 1-chambered capsules opening at the top by scale-like segments, teeth or lids; the seeds are usually numerous.

Key to the Genera of Caryophyllaceae

1a. Sepals united into a tube; ovaries stalked. . . . . *Silene* **(pp. 134–137)**

1b. Sepals distinct, not united below; ovaries not stalked 2

  2a. Petals 2-cleft or notched at the tip, or lacking 3

    3a. Styles usually 3; capsules egg-shaped or ellipsoid . . . . *Stellaria* **(pp. 127–128)**

    3b. Styles usually 5; capsules cylindric . . . . *Cerastium* **(below)**

      4

  2b. Petals entire, not notched or cleft at the tip, or lacking 5

    4a. Leaves lance-elliptic to egg-shaped. . . . .

      5a. Capsules inflated, 3-chambered, opening by 3 segments . . . . *Wilhelmsia physodes* **(p. 129)**

      5b. Capsules not inflated, 1-chambered, opening by 6 teeth. 6

        6a. Leaves 10–70 mm long . . . . *Moehringia macrophylla* **(p. 129)**

        6b. Leaves 2–7 mm long. . . . . *Arenaria longipedunculata* **(p. 129)**

        7

    4b. Leaves linear, awl-like or narrowly lance-shaped. . . . .

      7a. Styles 4–5 . . . . *Sagina* **(p. 128)**

      7b. Styles usually 3 8

        8a. Capsules opening by 3 teeth . . . . *Minuartia* **(pp. 131–133)**

        8b. Capsules opening by 6 teeth . . . . *Eremogone* **(p. 130)**

Bering Chickweed
Cerastium beeringianum

General: From a taproot and short, prostrate sterile stems, forming loose to dense mats or clumps 5–40 cm across; flowering stems leafy, ascending, 5–25 cm tall, usually with a mix of simple and glandular hairs; **lacking small tufts of leaves in axils** of primary leaves.

Leaves: Basal leaves lacking; **stem leaves lance- to spoon-shaped,** 5–20 mm long, **pointy-tipped or blunt,** hairy on both surfaces.

Flowers: Usually 3–6 in an open cluster, erect on glandular-hairy stalks; petals 5, white, 6–12 mm long, deeply 2-cleft; sepals 5, often purplish, densely glandular-hairy, about ½ as long as petals; stamens 10; **styles 5.**

Fruits: Capsules cylindric, curved, 8–10 mm long, with 10 teeth.

Where Found: Mesic to moist tundra (alpine and arctic), felsenmeer, gravelly ridges, scree and talus slopes, cliffs, ledges, heathlands, gravelly or sandy meadows, river terraces and open forests; lowland (arctic coast) to alpine zones; frequent in most of the region, mostly inland of the coastal mountains; arctic-alpine, broadly amphiberingian extending east to NL.

Similar Species: Field chickweed (*C. arvense* ssp. *strictum*) has a more greyish green look, **narrower (narrowly lance- to awl-shaped), more sharply tipped leaves** and **small, sterile leafy shoots in some leaf axils.** It is a very variable and widespread circumpolar species of mesic to dry rocky slopes, bluffs, grassy meadows, forest openings and gravelly tundra, in lowland to alpine zones but typically at lower elevations than Bering chickweed. It is frequent in our region, mostly south of 64° N. In alpine habitats, the 2 can be confused—compare the bracts of the flower cluster; all are papery-margined in field chickweed, the lower wholly green in Bering chickweed.

field chickweed

Long-stalked Starwort
Stellaria longipes

General: Low clumps or mats from rhizomes, stems single or clustered, erect or straggling, 4-angled, hairless to slightly soft-hairy, 3–30 cm tall/long.

Leaves: Mostly along stem, unstalked, 4–25 mm long, narrowly lance- to egg-shaped, **stiff, shiny, yellowish green or bluish green,** sharp-pointed, mostly hairless.

Flowers: Solitary or few to several, on **bracted stalks 5–30 mm long** in an open cluster atop the stem, star-shaped, **5–10 mm across; petals 5,** white, deeply 2-cleft, 3–8 mm long, 1–1.5 times as long as the 3-veined, papery-margined, lance-shaped sepals; stamens 5 or 10; styles 3.

Fruits: Capsules egg-shaped, 4–6 mm long, longer than sepals, blackish purple, opening by 6 segments.

Where Found: Mesic to moist, rocky slopes, grassy meadows, shores, disturbed sandy-gravelly sites, scree slopes, fellfields and tundra; lowland to alpine zones; frequent throughout the region except for the outer coast; circumpolar.

Similar Species: This variable species complex includes a **bluish green form** (pictured), with more **egg-shaped leaves** and mostly solitary flowers, which occurs mostly at **high elevations** and is called by some (including us) *S. monantha.* FNA doesn't recognize it, but you will when you see it. • **Alaska starwort** (*S. alaskana*) has softer leaves and **larger flowers** (1–2 cm across) with petals shorter than the **long (7–10 mm), narrow sepals.** It is a rare species of rock outcrops, scree, talus and alpine tundra, endemic to southern coastal AK and southwestern YT. • **Umbellate starwort** (*S. umbellata*) has lance-oblong to elliptic, somewhat succulent leaves and **very small (2 mm across) flowers without petals,** in somewhat **umbel-like clusters,** the **stalks bent** or curving down with age. This amphiberingian species is infrequent in AK, YT and western NT, southern BC and southwestern AB to CA, AZ and NM, in moist meadows and on streambanks, seepages and rocky slopes, in montane to alpine zones. • **Thick-leaved starwort** (*S. crassifolia*) forms **tangled mats** of delicate stems and somewhat fleshy leaves, and has **flowers single in leaf axils or a few in leafy-bracted clusters,** the **petals equalling or slightly longer than the sepals.** It occurs in wet meadows, fens, streambanks and snowbeds, in lowland (arctic coast) to alpine zones, but at high elevations only in the southernmost part of its range. It is infrequent in AK, YT and NT through inland BC and AB, disjunct in WY, UT and CO. • **American starwort** (*S. americana*) has glandular-hairy stems with numerous large (1–3 cm long), egg-shaped leaves. It has distinctive twisted fruit stalks that push the opening capsule—with its few large seeds—into the ground. Restricted to south-western AB to south-central MT, it occurs on rocky slopes and talus, in subalpine and alpine zones.

Notes: Long-stalked starwort includes *Stellaria edwardsii, S. laeta, S. monantha, S. stricta* and *S. subvestita.* • Except for long-stalked, Alaska and American starworts, these species aren't really true alpines. They are most frequent at low to moderate elevations but can get high especially in the southern part of the region. • To test whether arctic foxes might disperse the seed of various Greenlandic plant species, scientists fed the seeds of 22 plant species to foxes and subsequently collected the fox scat and tested it for seed germination. The seeds of long-stalked starwort showed enhanced germination compared to the controls after passing through the digestive system of the foxes.

Blunt-sepalled Starwort, Rocky Mountain Starwort • *Stellaria obtusa*

General: Creeping, mat-forming; stems prostrate, branched, 3–20 cm long. **Leaves:** Egg-shaped, hairless or fringed at the base. **Flowers:** Single on thin stalks in leaf axils, very small (1.5–2 mm across); **petals lacking; sepals 4–5, obscurely veined, blunt. Where Found:** Moist glades, meadows, streambanks, thickets and talus slopes; montane to alpine zones; infrequent in the southern part of the region.

Chamisso's Starwort • *Stellaria dicranoides*

General: Forming dense cushions to 10 cm across, stems 1–4 cm tall, branched; branches covered with persistent withered leaves. **Leaves:** Green, somewhat fleshy, 3–5 mm long, lance-shaped to elliptic, hairless, overlapping. **Flowers: Single on short stalks in axils of upper leaves, unisexual,** small (3–4 mm across); **petals lacking; sepals 5, pointy-tipped,** 2–4 mm long; stamens 10, in male flowers the filaments dilated at the base and alternating with brownish, stubby nectaries to form a ring. **Fruits:** Capsules egg-shaped, straw-coloured, with 1 large, brown seed. **Where Found:** Dry scree, fell-fields, rock outcrops and gravelly tundra; subalpine and alpine zones; infrequent in AK and YT; arctic-alpine, amphiberingian.

Notes: Chamisso's starwort is also known as *Arenaria chamissonis* and *A. dicranoides.* • *Stellaria* means "star-like," from the Latin *stella*, "star," because of the flower shape. • *S. dicranoides* was collected by Berthold Seemann (1825–71), a German naturalist on the 26-gun frigate HMS *Herald* in Alaska in the mid-1800s. Seeman's botanical explorations are described in his 1852 classic *The Botany of the Voyage of H.M.S. Herald.*

Alpine Pearlwort • *Sagina saginoides*

General: Small, yellowish green, hairless perennial from a taproot, forming mats or sometimes tufts 5–15 cm across; stems several, sprawling to ascending, simple to few-branched, 3–12 cm long, the flowering stems to 7 cm high.

Leaves: Basal leaves in rosettes, linear, abruptly sharp-pointed, 5–20 mm long; stem leaves 2–6 pairs, **linear, 4–20 mm long.**

Flowers: Solitary, small, erect, at stem tips and from leaf axils; petals white, 1–2 mm long, elliptic, **entire; sepals usually 5 (rarely 4),** greenish with **white (rarely purple) margins,** elliptic, slightly longer than petals; stamens 10 (occasionally 5); **styles mostly 5.**

Fruits: Capsules egg-shaped, 2.5–3.5 mm long, opening by mostly 5 segments; fruiting stalks at first bent down, later erect.

Where Found: Moist to wet, open, gravelly areas, mudflats, shores, streambanks, seepages, ledges and snowbeds; montane to alpine zones; frequent in the southern ⅓ of the region, infrequent northward to about 64° N; circumpolar.

Similar Species: Snow pearlwort (**S. nivalis;** S. intermedia) forms low, dark green cushions and has **awl-like to linear stem leaves, 4 (sometimes 5) greenish sepals with purple margins** and fruiting stalks that are straight throughout maturation. It occurs on moist sandy or gravelly shores, raw moraines, snowbeds and wet tundra, in lowland to alpine zones. This circumpolar, arctic-alpine species is infrequent in the northern ½ of the region, from AK, YT and NT to coastal BC, southwestern AB and MT.

Notes: *Sagina* is medieval Latin for spurry (*Spergula arvensis*, formerly included in *Sagina*), meaning "nourishing" or "fattening," alluding to spurry's early use as fodder. It is called "pearlwort" perhaps because this plant was reportedly used to treat an eye disease known as pearl, or it could be descriptive of the small, unopened fruit capsule or flower bud.

Kaiser's Sandwort, Merckia
Wilhelmsia physodes

General: Forming small mats from spreading rhizomes; stems slender, freely branching and rooting, 2–10 (to 20) cm long, with purplish gland-tipped hairs.

Leaves: Elliptic to egg-shaped, pointy-tipped; **blades 5–15 mm long,** slightly fleshy, fringed.

Flowers: Single on hairy stalks 5–25 mm long; petals 5, white, **5–6 mm long,** narrowly lance-shaped, pinched-off toward the base; sepals 5, green (often purple-tinged), egg-shaped, slightly shorter than petals; stamens 10; styles 3.

Fruits: Capsules nearly spheric, swollen, hairless, becoming shiny and somewhat leathery, 7–10 mm across, 6-lobed but **opening by 3 segments;** seeds 8–16.

Where Found: Moist to wet, muddy or sandy streamsides, gravel bars and lakeshores; lowland (arctic coast) to lower alpine zones; frequent in the northern ⅓ of the region; amphiberingian.

Notes: Kaiser's sandwort is also known as *Arenaria physodes* and *Merckia physodes*. • This is a taxonomically isolated, monospecific genus; according to recent molecular evidence, it is closely related to seaside sandwort (*Honckenya peploides*). • *FNA* suggests that *Wilhelmsia* may acknowledge Christian Wilhelms (1819–37), a plant collector in the Caucasus. We reckon that the swollen, buttocks-like capsules reminded someone of Kaiser Wilhelm. *Physodes* means "inflated" or "puffed-out," referring to the rotund capsules.

Longstem Sandwort
Arenaria longipedunculata

General: From a taproot and branching stem-base, forming tufts or mats to 10 cm across; flowering stems numerous, erect to ascending, 2–4 cm tall, minutely glandular-hairy.

Leaves: Lance-elliptic to egg-shaped, pointy-tipped, 2–7 mm long; margins thickened; stem leaves 1–4 pairs.

Flowers: Single, small, erect at stem tips, on glandular-hairy **stalks 1–2 cm long;** petals 5, white, **2.5–4 mm long,** elliptic, rounded at tip; sepals 5, egg-shaped, slightly shorter than petals; stamens 10; **styles 3.**

Fruits: Capsules tightly grasped by sepals, ellipsoid, 4–5 mm long, slightly longer than sepals, **opening by 6 teeth.**

Where Found: Moist, open gravelly areas; montane to alpine zones; infrequent in the northern ⅓ of the region, disjunct in southeastern BC and adjacent AB; amphiberingian.

Similar Species: Bigleaf sandwort (*Moehringia macrophylla*; *Arenaria macrophylla*) has elliptic to lance-shaped **leaves 1–7 cm long** and petals 2–6 mm long. It occurs in open forests, meadows and rocky slopes, in lowland to subalpine zones, and is frequent in the southern part of the region, occasionally to timberline, in southern BC to CA, UT, MT, CO and NM. • *A. longipedunculata* was long included in *A. humifusa*, a smaller, eastern arctic, amphi-Atlantic species.

Notes: *Arenaria* used to be—in North America, anyway—a large, broadly circumscribed genus that included several groups now recognized in *FNA* as distinct genera. Based on morphological and molecular evidence, we now have *Minuartia* and *Eremogone*, as well as *Wilhelmsia*, *Moehringia* and a shrunken *Arenaria*. • *Arenaria* is from the Latin *arena*, "sand," as sandy habitats are common for this genus. The suffix "wort" is from *wyrt*, the Old English word for "plant," usually a plant with food or medicinal value.

Fescue Sandwort, Thread-leaved Sandwort
Eremogone capillaris var. *americana*

General: Forming tufts or loose mats from a branched, somewhat woody stem-base; flowering stems numerous, erect to ascending, 5–20 cm tall, usually glaucous (bluish green), **glandular-hairy** on upper part of stems and in flower clusters.

Leaves: Basal leaves numerous, persistent, linear, grass-like, **2–8 cm long, rather soft**, pointy-tipped; stem leaves in 1–4 pairs, also grass-like, the lowest to 4 cm long, reduced upward; leaves often glaucous.

Flowers: One to several in small, **open clusters,** on glandular-hairy stalks; petals 5, white, egg- to spoon-shaped, 6–10 mm long, **broadly rounded, sometimes slightly notched** at tip; sepals 5, egg-shaped, sharp-tipped, about ½ as long as petals, glandular-hairy, margins membranous and often purplish-tinged; stamens 10; styles 3.

Fruits: Capsules egg-shaped, 5–8 mm long, opening by 6 segments.

Where Found: Dry to mesic meadows, shrublands, forest openings and rocky slopes; montane to alpine zones; frequent in the southern ⅓ of the region, mostly east of the coastal mountains.

Similar Species: Prickly sandwort (*E. aculeata*) has shorter (usually less than 3 cm long), rigid, prickly, glaucous basal leaves. It occupies a range of habitats similar to that of fescue sandwort, from MT to eastern WA and OR, south to CA, NV and UT.

Notes: Fescue sandwort is also known as *Arenaria capillaris* ssp. *americana*. • In the *Arenaria* alliance, *Eremogone* is distinctive in its tufted or matted, woody-based habit combined with its hair- or needle-like leaves and erect flowering stems.

Ballhead Sandwort
Eremogone congesta

General: Similar to fescue sandwort (above), but plants **usually hairless throughout. Leaves:** Green, not glaucous (not bluish green). **Flowers:** Several to numerous in **dense, head-like or sometimes looser clusters. Where Found:** Dry to mesic meadows, open sandy or gravelly sites, rocky slopes, outcrops, ridges and fellfields; steppe to alpine zones; frequent in the southern ¼ of the region, mostly inland.

Notes: Ballhead sandwort is also known as *Arenaria congesta*. • This is a highly variable species; *FNA* recognizes 9 varieties. Vars. *congesta* and *lithophila* probably are the 2 that reach high elevations in our region.

THE GENUS *MINUARTIA* (Sandwort)

Our high-elevation *Minuartia* species often form mats or cushions, with prostrate to ascending stems from a taproot. The small, linear to awl- or lance-shaped leaves tend to occur along the stems as well as at the base. The flowers are single atop the stems or sometimes in leaf axils, or in few-flowered clusters at stem tips, on erect to curved-spreading stalks. The star-shaped flowers have 5 mostly white, sometimes pink or lilac, mostly entire petals, 5 mostly green sepals, 10 stamens and 3 styles. The fruits are egg-shaped to ellipsoid capsules, opening by 3 segments.

Key to *Minuartia*

1a. Sepals blunt or rounded at tip **2**

  2a. Leaves similar to larch (p. 43) needles, very narrow, 7–8 times as long as wide, with long, sharp-pointed tips; flowers usually >3 per cluster . . . . **M. yukonensis (below)**

  2b. Leaves broader, 4–5 times as long as wide, with rounded or squared-off tips; flowers 1–5 per cluster **3**

    3a. Capsules 10–18 mm long, more than twice as long as sepals; flowers 1, on stalks 4–10 mm long . . . . **M. macrocarpa (p. 132)**

    3b. Capsules 3–10 mm long, equalling or slightly longer than sepals; flowers 1–5, on stalks 3–30 mm long **4**

      4a. Leaves flat; flowers 3–5; petals white or often lilac; capsules 5–6 mm long . . . . **M. biflora (p. 132)**

      4b. Leaves 3-angled or submarine-shaped in cross-section; flowers mostly 1, occasionally 2–3 . . . . **5**

        5a. Clusters of secondary leaves absent in axils of primary leaves; flowers 1, relatively large, to 6–7 mm across and 11 mm long, petals white, often pink- or purple-tinged; capsules 9–10 mm long . . . . **M. arctica (p. 132)**

        5b. Clusters of secondary leaves present in axils of primary leaves; flowers smaller, typically about 5 mm across and 5–6 mm long, petals white; capsules 3.5–6 mm long . . . . **M. obtusiloba (p. 132)**

1b. Sepals sharp-pointed at tip **6**

  6a. Flower stalks glandular-hairy **7**

    7a. Taproot thickened, woody; rhizomes or runners present; leaves 1-veined; sepals 3–7 mm long . . . . **M. nuttallii (p. 133)**

    7b. Taproot slender, not woody; rhizomes and runners absent; leaves 3-veined (most easily seen on old, dried leaves); sepals 2.5–3 mm long . . . . **M. rubella (p. 133)**

  6b. Flower stalks hairless **8**

    8a. Flowers 1; sepals 1.5–2.5 mm long, 1-veined; petals slightly longer than sepals; leaves 1–4 mm long . . . . **M. rossii (p. 133)**

    8b. Flowers 1 or several; sepals 2–4 mm long, mostly 3-veined; petals shorter than sepals; leaves 3–10 mm long **9**

      9a. Stems 1-flowered **10**

        10a. Sepals linear to lance-shaped; petals lacking or vestigial . . . . **M. austromontana (p. 133)**

        10b. Sepals lance- to egg-shaped; petals 0.8–1 times as long as sepals . . . . **M. elegans (p. 133)**

      9b. At least some stems with 2–3 (sometimes up to 5) flowers; sepals broadly elliptic to egg-shaped; petals 0.6–1 times as long as sepals, or absent . . . . **M. stricta (p. 133)**

Yukon Sandwort, Larch-leaved Sandwort
Minuartia yukonensis

General: Tufted to mat-forming, with slender, glandular-hairy stems, trailing to ascending, and leafy shoots 5–30 cm long. **Leaves: Needle-like,** sharp-tipped, **7–18 mm long,** densely clustered on branches. **Flowers: 3–13** in an open cluster; petals white, 6–11 mm long, longer than sepals; **sepals blunt, stalked-glandular,** green with papery, sometimes purplish margins. **Where Found:** Dry, rocky slopes, scree and meadows; montane to alpine zones; infrequent in the northern ⅓ of the region; amphiberingian.

Notes: Yukon sandwort is also known as *Arenaria laricifolia*. • *Minuartia* honours Juan Minuart (1693–1768), a Spanish apothecary and botanist.

Large-fruited Sandwort, Long-pod Stitchwort
Minuartia macrocarpa

General: Forming loose tufts or mats with hairless or sometimes glandular-hairy stems, the trailing leafy shoots to 40 cm long. **Leaves: Flat,** linear to lance-shaped, 3-veined, margins fringed. **Flowers: Single** on glandular-hairy stalks; petals white, rarely tinged pink or purple, 8–14 mm long, much longer than sepals; **sepals blunt,** stalked-glandular, often purplish. **Fruits: Capsules narrowly ellipsoid, 1–1.8 cm long,** more than twice as long as sepals. **Where Found:** Rocky or sandy slopes, shores, gravelly ridges, stony tundra and heathlands; lowland (arctic coast) to alpine zones; frequent in the northern ⅓ of the region; amphiberingian.

Notes: Large-fruited sandwort is also known as *Arenaria macrocarpa*. • This species has by far the largest capsules of any North American *Minuartia*. • "Stitchwort" was a plant that could alleviate a stitch in the side.

Arctic Sandwort • *Minuartia arctica*

General: Forming mats with trailing, leafy shoots; flowering stems 3–10 cm tall, hairy or glandular-hairy. **Leaves:** Oblong to linear, **rounded 3-angled (submarine-shaped) in cross-section, 1-veined,** blunt, 0.5–2 cm long. **Flowers: Single** atop glandular-hairy stalks 5–30 mm long; petals white, often tinged pink or purple, **8–12 mm long, 1.5–2 times as long as sepals; sepals blunt,** green tinged with purple, stalked-glandular; **Fruits: Capsules 9–10 mm long. Where Found:** Rocky slopes, meadows, scree, tundra, heathlands, snowbeds and tundra; lowland (arctic coast) to alpine zones; frequent in the northern ¼ of the region; amphiberingian.

Similar Species: Arctic sandwort is very variable and not always easy to distinguish from the following 2 species. • **Mountain sandwort (*M. biflora*)** has **flat leaves** and **3–5 flowers** on stalks 5–10 mm long, the petals white or often lilac, **4–7 mm long, slightly (to 1.5 times) longer than the sepals, the capsules 5–6 mm long.** It grows on dry to mesic, calcium-rich, rocky slopes, fellfields, snowbeds, heathlands and tundra, in montane to alpine zones. A low arctic–alpine, circumpolar species, it is scattered in the northern ⅓ of the region, from AK, YT, northwestern NT to BC and southwestern AB. • **Alpine sandwort (*M. obtusiloba*; *Arenaria obtusiloba*)** is very glandular, with linear, 3-angled, **3-veined, spruce-needle-like leaves** and **clusters of secondary leaves in the axils of the primary leaves. The flowers are mostly solitary** (occasionally 2–3) and smaller than those of arctic sandwort, on stalks 3–15 mm long, the **petals mostly white, the capsules 3.5–6 mm long.** It occurs on rocky slopes, fellfields, tundra and snowbeds, in montane to alpine zones. This amphiberingian, arctic-alpine species is frequent throughout the region inland of the Pacific coastal mountains.

Notes: Arctic sandwort is also known as *Arenaria arctica*. • Plants from western North America previously identified as *Arenaria sajanensis* and referred to as *M. biflora* are likely to be *M. obtusiloba* according to *FNA*. • Plant macrofossils of arctic sandwort and other arctic species from 60,000 to 7500 years ago occur together with fossils of aquatic, littoral and steppe plants in the eastern Siberian arctic. This suggests the presence of productive meadow and steppe vegetation in the late Pleistocene, potentially important grazing areas for large herbivores. This is additional evidence for the "mammoth steppe" of unglaciated Beringia, when both sides of the Bering Strait were connected by a land bridge and a spectacular megafauna roamed the cold, arid grasslands, including the woolly mammoth, American mastodon, steppe bison, horse, saiga antelope, short-faced bear, scimitar-toothed tiger and lion, as well as persistent species such as the Dall's sheep, caribou, wolf and grizzly bear. What a biome that was!

alpine sandwort

Boreal Sandwort, Reddish Sandwort
Minuartia rubella

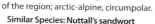

General: From a **slender taproot,** forming small cushions or mats 4–20 cm across; **trailing shoots and rhizomes lacking,** the slender ascending stems stalked-glandular, 2–15 cm tall. **Leaves:** Awl-shaped, tending to cluster toward the base, 2–10 mm long, stiff, **3-veined,** often stalked-glandular; stem leaves in 2–6 pairs, sometimes with clustered secondary leaves in their axils. **Flowers: 2–7** in an open array or rarely 1, **on glandular-hairy stalks;** petals white or sometimes reddish, roughly the same length **(2.5–3 mm)** as sepals; **sepals pointy-tipped, glandular-hairy,** often purplish green. **Where Found:** Dry, sandy-gravelly flats and slopes, scree, rocky meadows, tundra and fellfields; lowland (arctic slope) to alpine zones; frequent in most of the region; arctic-alpine, circumpolar.

Similar Species: Nuttall's sandwort (**M. nuttallii**; *Arenaria nuttallii*) is also glandular-hairy throughout, but from a **thickened, woody taproot** and more matted (to 60 cm across), with rhizomes and brittle, trailing shoots. The numerous stem leaves are **broadly lance-shaped to linear** and **1-veined,** often with secondary leaf clusters in axils; the sepals are pointy-tipped and 3–7 mm long. It is found on dry, sandy or rocky slopes and ridges, shrublands, forest openings, talus and fellfields, in montane to alpine zones, frequent in the southeastern part of the region, from southeastern BC and southwestern AB to CA, UT and CO.

Notes: Boreal sandwort is also known as *Arenaria rubella*. • It seems to prefer calcium-rich sites. • Another common name for boreal sandwort is "beautiful sandwort," though we think it is surpassed in beauty by arctic sandwort (p. 132).

Northern Sandwort, Elegant Sandwort
Minuartia elegans

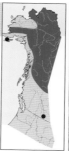

General: Loosely tufted, forming small cushions or mats to 30 cm across; stems erect, often greenish purple, hairless, 3–8 cm tall. **Leaves:** Linear to awl-shaped, crowded toward the base, **3–10 mm long,** green to purplish green, **1-veined,** hairless, rounded at tip; stem leaves often with clustered secondary leaves in their axils. **Flowers: Single** on long (1–4 cm) stalks; petals white, mostly a little shorter than sepals; sepals 2–4 mm long, purplish, **lance-egg-shaped, pointy-tipped,** hairless, 3-veined. **Where Found:** Dry, rocky slopes, gravelly ridges, rocky meadows, moist tundra and fellfields; montane to alpine zones; frequent in the northern ½ of the region; arctic-alpine, amphiberingian.

Similar Species: Ross' sandwort (**M. rossii**; *Arenaria rossii*), the northernmost species of this complex, is cushion-forming, with generally **shorter (1–4 mm) leaves** and **oblong-egg-shaped, 1-veined,** pointy-tipped to blunt **sepals 1.5–2.5 mm long.** It occurs in moist to dry, turfy, gravelly or sandy calcium-rich barrens, heathlands and tundra, in lowland to alpine zones. A high arctic–alpine, largely North American species, it is infrequent in the **far north** of the region, northern AK, YT and NT. • **Rocky Mountain sandwort** (**M. austromontana**) is the central Rocky Mountain member of the *M. rossii* complex. It has **linear-lance-shaped, 3-veined, pointy-tipped sepals** 2–3 mm long, the **petals usually absent;** if present, they are much shorter than the sepals. It is found on dry, rocky, calcium-rich slopes, scree and fellfields in the alpine zone, and is frequent from southeastern BC and southwestern AB to northeastern OR, UT and WY. • **Rock sandwort** (**M. stricta**) differs from the other 3 species in this group in having at least some stems with **2 to several flowers** and **broadly elliptic to egg-shaped sepals** about 3 mm long, the petals 0.6–1 times as long as the sepals, or absent. It occurs on moist, typically granitic, gravelly floodplains, rocky slopes, wet meadows, heathlands and tundra, in montane to alpine zones. A low arctic–alpine species, it is circumpolar with large and frequent gaps and is infrequent in the northern ¼ of the region, AK, YT and NT, and disjunct in CA and CO.

Notes: Northern sandwort is also known as *Arenaria elegans, A. rossii* var. *columbiana* and *A. rossii* ssp. *elegans*. • Some plants—especially in extreme habitats—have few if any flowers, presumably reproducing asexually via the small bundles of secondary leaves or plantlets in the leaf axils.

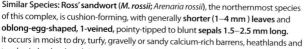

THE GENUS *SILENE* (Campion, Catchfly)

The genus *Silene* (campion or catchfly) as now treated in *Flora of North America* includes *Lychnis* and *Melandrium*. In the past, 2 or all 3 have often been recognized as distinct genera. Considerable confusion in taxonomy and names has resulted; compare, for example, the northern treatments by Hultén (1968), Welsh (1974) and Cody (2000). Our high-elevation species are all perennial herbs, usually with upright, clustered stems from a taproot, cushion-forming in one instance. The linear to lance- or spoon-shaped leaves tend to be concentrated toward the stem-base. The flowers are several to few or solitary atop the stems or sometimes in leaf axils, and are often glandular-hairy and sticky-slimy. The flowers are distinguished by 5 sepals (collectively the **calyx**) united into a cylindric to urn-shaped, often striped tube. The 5 petals are white, pink or purplish with **blades** (the upper, expanded part, variously lobed or toothed at the tip) and stalk-like bases; there are 10 stamens and 3 or 5 styles. The fruits are egg- to globe-shaped, short-stalked capsules, opening by 3–5 segments and frequently splitting into 6–10 teeth.

moss campion

Except for the common and widespread moss campion (p. 135) and the often locally abundant Parry's campion (p. 137), these high-elevation *Silene* generally are rather infrequent and tend to have small populations.

Key to *Silene*

1a. Plants forming dense cushions usually <15 cm tall; calyx tube (united sepals) hairless. . . . . **S. acaulis** (p. 135)

1b. Plants not cushion-forming; calyx tube hairy 2

  2a. Styles 5; flowers mostly 1–3 3

    3a. Flowers usually >1; seeds not winged 4

      4a. Flowers 1–4 (sometimes up to 8); calyx broadly cylindric to narrowly ellipsoid, 13–18 mm long in fruit; southeastern, south of 49° N in our region. **S. drummondii** ssp. **striata** (p. 136)

      4b. Flowers usually 3; calyx ellipsoid or sometimes bell-shaped, 10–12 mm long in fruit; north of 58° N . . . . **S. ostenfeldii** (p. 136)

    3b. Flowers usually 1, sometimes 2–3 (or more in some uncommon forms of *S. uralensis*); seeds winged 5

      5a. Flowers often nodding when in bud or young; petals dusky purplish red, included within or protruding slightly beyond sepals; calyx inflated . . . . **S. uralensis** (p. 136)

      5b. Flowers erect; petals white or pinkish, protruding well beyond sepals; calyx not inflated 6

        6a. Stems 2–10 cm tall; flowers usually 1, occasionally 2–3; south of 51° N. . . . **S. hitchguirei** (p. 136)

        6b. Stems 10–45 cm tall; flowers 1–3; north of 57° N. . . . . **S. involucrata** (p. 136)

  2b. Styles 3; flowers 3 or more 7

    7a. Calyx purple, purplish-tinged or purple-veined, club-shaped in fruit; petals usually rose pink, sometimes whitish . . . . **S. repens** (p. 137)

    7b. Calyx green, with greenish or purple veins, barrel-shaped in fruit; petals mostly whitish, tinged with pink, lavender or dark purple 8

      8a. Stems 3–20 cm tall 9

        9a. Hairs on flower stalk and calyx glandular, with colourless crosswalls . . . . **S. sargentii** (p. 137)

        9b. Hairs on flower stalk and calyx not glandular, with purple crosswalls. . . . . . . **S. suksdorfii** (p. 137)

      8b. Stems to 30 cm or taller. 10

        10a. Petals with prominent lateral teeth on each of the 2 lobes; flower stalk and calyx glandular-hairy . . . . **S. parryi** (p. 137)

        10b. Petals lacking prominent lateral teeth on the lobes; flower stalk and calyx with greyish white hairs and few or no glands. . . . . **S. douglasii** var. **douglasii** (p. 137)

Moss Campion • *Silene acaulis*

General: Perennial from a stout taproot and branched, somewhat woody stem-base, forming **dense tufts or cushions** to 40 cm across; flowering stems numerous, erect, 3–6 (sometimes to 15) cm tall, unbranched, hairless, **old leaves persistent at the base.**

Leaves: Mostly basal, **crowded and overlapping,** so dense as to obscure stems, unstalked, **linear to narrowly lance-shaped,** 5–15 mm long, pointy-tipped; margins leathery, often fringed toward the base.

Flowers: Single atop stems (**but often profuse on cushions**), on very short to rather long stalks, bisexual or unisexual, **about 1 cm across;** petals 5, **bright pink,** rarely white, 8–12 mm long, flaring egg-shaped above, rounded to shallowly notched at tip; sepals 5, green, often purple-margined, united into cylindric to bell-shaped calyx; stamens 10; styles 3.

Fruits: Capsules cylindric, 1–2 times as long as calyx, opening by 6 bent-back teeth.

Where Found: Moist to dry rocky or gravelly ridges, outcrops, scree, fellfields and tundra; lowland (arctic coast) to alpine (mostly) zones; frequent throughout the region, especially inland; arctic-alpine, circumpolar.

Subspecies: *S. acaulis* is a variable species, often separated into the predominantly arctic **ssp.** *acaulis* (with short, flat leaves and short-stalked flowers) and the cordilleran **ssp.** *subacaulescens* (a larger, less-compact plant with longer, narrower leaves and larger, longer-stalked flowers). However, the distinctions are not always clear, intermediates are frequent and there seems little purpose in maintaining the 2 subspecies.

Notes: Moss campion is fairly easy to grow in rock gardens at low elevations, but it is a challenge to recreate the "wild type" of hemispheric cushions covered with flowers. • Numerous studies at lower elevations have demonstrated the importance of competition in structuring plant communities. Indeed, rugged individualism and cutthroat competition have been an article of faith among most ecologists, at least in post–World War II North America. At higher elevations, however, cooperation gains importance. A Swedish (are you surprised?) study found that above 1280 m, more species were found in and around moss campion cushions than in similar-sized areas without moss campion. This species seems to act as a "nurse plant," moderating harsh environmental conditions around it.

GROWTH FORMS

Plants come in all shapes and sizes, but alpine plants have pursued only a few lines of adaptation along the spectrum of life-history traits. Some options seem to have been forsworn (e.g., no trees, nothing tall at all, few broad leaves), presumably because they have been tried and found wanting in the challenging alpine environment. The cushion growth form has been successful at high elevations, especially in dry, cold habitats, and gives ridge crest tundra and fellfields a distinctive look. Moss campion 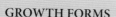 (above) is the protypical alpine cushion plant.

Strong wind is the common denominator for all places where alpine cushion plants naturally grow. Air flows over the streamlined cushion much as over an airplane wing, and the form provides the maximum photosynthetic surface with the minimum exposure to physical damage. Moreover, it's warmer within; temperatures can be several degrees Celsius warmer inside than outside the cushion. Some ecologists, however, interpret the cushion habit not as a primary adaptation to temperature, but rather in terms of greatly enhanced capacity for moisture and nutrient storage. Indeed, retention of litter and nutrient recycling could be the most beneficial effect of the cushion form.

Nodding Campion, Japanese Lanterns
Silene uralensis

General: Flowering stems usually several, erect to ascending, 5–30 (to 40) cm tall, simple or branched, purplish, usually hairy becoming glandular-hairy upward.

Leaves: Mostly basal, in tufts, narrowly lance-shaped, 1–10 cm long, margins fringed; stem leaves 1–5 pairs.

Flowers: 1–3 (sometimes more), erect or **often nodding,** all erect in fruit; petals 5, **dull purple, red or pink,** egg-shaped, short (1–4 mm); sepals 5, united into an **egg-shaped, inflated, papery calyx** 1–1.8 cm long, glandular-hairy, with **10 prominent purple or brown veins.**

Fruits: Capsules equal to or slightly longer than calyx, opening by 10 bent-back teeth; **seeds broadly winged.**

Where Found: Mesic to dry meadows, rocky slopes, gravel bars, talus, fellfields and tundra; lowland (arctic coast) to alpine zones; frequent in the northern ½ of the region, sporadic southward in the Rockies; arctic-alpine, circumpolar.

Similar Species: Rocky Mountain campion (*S. hitchguirei*; *Lychnis montana, L. apetala* var. *montana, S. uralensis* ssp. *montana*), an alpine tundra species of the **southeast** (southwestern AB, MT, WY, CO and UT), has **usually single, consistently erect flowers** with white or pink petals, an **elliptic, purple-veined, uninflated calyx** and **narrowly winged seeds.**
• **Arctic campion (*S. involucrata*;** *Lychnis apetala* vars. *involucrata* and *elatior, L. furcata, L. tayloriae, Melandrium affine, M. tayloriae, S. furcata*) is typically **taller (10–45 cm),** with **1–3 erect flowers** per stalk, a **bell- to egg-shaped, uninflated, purple-veined calyx,** white petals and larger, broadly winged seeds. A **northern circumpolar** species found in AK, YT, NT and northern BC, it is infrequent on sandy-gravelly

terraces, rocky slopes and ledges, and in grassy meadows and gravelly tundra, in lowland (arctic coast) to alpine zones. • **Beringian campion (*S. ostenfeldii*;** *Melandrium ostenfeldii, M. dawsonii, Lychnis dawsonii, L. taimyrense, L. triflora* var. *dawsonii*) is similar to arctic campion but has **seeds without wings** and typically **3 flowers** with a **green- or purple-veined, mostly ellipsoid calyx.** It is an amphiberingian species that occurs in northern habitats similar to those of arctic campion.

Notes: Nodding campion is also known as *Lychnis apetala* and *Melandrium apetalum.*
• Nodding campion was one of the plants collected during failed mid-19th-century expeditions to rescue Sir John Franklin and crew and was later identified by the great British botanist and explorer Sir Joseph Dalton Hooker (1817–1911).

Drummond's Catchfly • *Silene drummondii* ssp. *striata*

Flowers: 1–4 (sometimes up to 8) per stem, erect; petals dull reddish purple, sometimes cream-coloured (as in photos), clearly protruding beyond sepals; calyx 1.3–1.8 cm long in fruit, broadly cylindric to narrowly ellipsoid, about 2 times as long as broad, with 10 greenish or purplish veins. **Fruits:** Seeds not winged. **Where Found:** Mesic to dry, open forests, rocky or grassy slopes and meadows; montane to alpine zones; infrequent in the southeastern part of the region; primarily a Rocky Mtn species.

Notes: Drummond's catchfly is also known as *Lychnis striata, L. drummondii* var. *striata* and *Silene drummondii* var. *striata.* • *Silene* is from the Latin *sialon,* "saliva," or from the Greek *seilenos,* a type of woodland satyr or deity. Silenus, the foster father of Bacchus, was quite a drinker and was often covered in beery foam, hence the name was applied to members of this genus that have "viscous secretions" or slimy-glandular hairs on the stem. • "Catchfly" refers to the sticky-glandular stems that act like flypaper. In contrast, the scientific names of these plants don't seem to stick, but they do leave a disquieting residue of synonyms.

Pink Campion • *Silene repens*

General: Stems erect to straggling, leafy (2–5 pairs), 7–35 cm tall/long. **Leaves:** Linear to lance-shaped or narrowly oblong. **Flowers:** 5–20 per stem, ascending, in a branched, often compact cluster; **petals rose-pink (rarely white)**, 1.5–2 cm long, flaring and **2-lobed** above; calyx 1–1.5 cm long, cylindric or narrowly bell-shaped in flower, club-shaped in fruit, usually **purple, purple-tinged or obscurely 10-purplish-veined. Fruits:** Seeds not winged. **Where Found:** Dry to moist, grassy slopes and shores, open forest, shrublands, rock outcrops, talus and scree; montane to alpine zones; frequent in the northern ⅓ of the region, disjunct and infrequent in WA, ID, MT and WY; broadly amphiberingian.

Notes: Pink campion is also known as *Silene purpurata*, *S. repens* ssp. *australis* and *S. repens* ssp. *purpurata*. • "Campion," from the Latin *campus* and the French *campion*, meaning "sports field" or "plain," was attached to *Lychnis coronaria* (rose campion) because its red flowers were once used to create chaplets or crowns for the champions of public games. However, it could also be because rose campion grows in grassy fields.

Parry's Campion, Parry's Catchfly • *Silene parryi*

General: Stems erect, unbranched, **10–50 cm tall**, soft-hairy, sticky-glandular. **Leaves:** Lance- to spoon-shaped, mostly in basal tufts, with 2–4 pairs along the stem. **Flowers:** 3–7 on ascending, **glandular-hairy stalks** in rather short, narrow clusters; petals white, often tinged green or purple, stalk-like at the base, spreading to blades 3–5 mm long and **deeply 2-lobed, each lobe with 2 prominent, lateral teeth** (sometimes petals appear 4-lobed), a pair of flap-like appendages arising from each petal near the centre; **calyx sticky-glandular-hairy**, bell-shaped, inflated, 1–1.5 cm long, with 10 purplish or greenish veins. **Fruits:** Capsules included in calyx tubes, opening by 3 segments, each tardily splitting into 2 teeth; **seeds not winged. Where Found:** Dry to mesic forest glades, rocky and grassy slopes, gravelly ridges and meadows; montane to alpine zones, mostly below treeline; frequent in the southern mostly inland ⅓ of the region; cordilleran.

Similar Species: Douglas' campion (*S. douglasii* var. *douglasii*) is usually **not sticky-glandular** but rather short-grey-hairy, with the same flap-like petal appendages as Parry's campion, but **no prominent lateral teeth.** It grows in similar habitats and has a similar range. On Vancouver I., it replaces Parry's campion, but both species occur in the Olympic Mtns. • **Suksdorf's campion** or Suksdorf's catchfly (*S. suksdorfii*) appears to be related to Parry's campion but is **smaller (less than 15 cm tall)** and more densely tufted, with **broadly winged seeds and calyx hairs with purple crosswalls.** It occurs on rocky slopes, gravelly ridges and talus, in subalpine and alpine zones, and is infrequent in WA, OR and CA, typically on the Cascade volcanoes. • **Sargent's campion** or Sargent's catchfly (*S. sargentii*; *Lychnis californica*, *S. lacustris*) is distinguished from Suksdorf's campion by **colourless crosswalls** on the calyx hairs and narrower **stem leaves (linear** vs. lance-shaped). It is found in forest openings and shrublands, and on grassy, gravelly or rocky slopes and ridges, in montane to alpine zones. It is infrequent in WA, ID, NV and CA.

Notes: Parry's campion is pollinated primarily by hawkmoths, thus it is mostly a nocturnal bloomer. On a sunny day, the flowers can appear shrivelled and spent, but they open up at dusk.

Douglas' campion

SAXIFRAGE FAMILY (Saxifragaceae)

Saxifragaceae is a widespread, medium-sized family of about 600 species, primarily of north temperate and arctic-alpine regions, and often found in rocky habitats. Ours are perennial herbs with alternate or basal, **simple leaves** (with a single blade, not compound with leaflets) with or without **stipules** (a pair of small scales or flanges at the base of the leaf stalk) and small flowers in clusters at the stem tips. The leaves, though distinctive, can look frustratingly similar, especially among *Mitella, Heuchera, Elmera, Conimitella* and *Telesonix*, and within *Micranthes*. The flowers often provide the best clues to identification. They are mostly radially symmetric, with 4–5 sepals that are separate or partly so, 4–5 separate petals that are entire, lobed or dissected, sometimes smaller than the sepals or absent. There are usually 5 or 10 stamens. The fruits are capsules, ours mostly with 1–2 chambers.

Key to the Genera of Saxifragaceae

1a. Petals absent; sepals 4; stamens 8 . . . . *Chrysosplenium wrightii* (p. 153)

1b. Petals usually present; sepals 5; stamens 5 or 10 2

  2a. Stamens 5 3

    3a. Petals dissected into 4–10 linear segments . . . . *Mitella* (p. 155)

    3b. Petals not dissected, entire or merely lobed 4

      4a. Petals with 4–7 lobes . . . . *Elmera racemosa* (p. 156)

      4b. Petals entire or 2-lobed 5

        5a. Ovary 2-chambered 6

          6a. Large plants, 10–60 cm tall, without bulblets; basal leaves 5–10 cm wide; far northern species . . . . *Boykinia richardsonii* (p. 155)

          6b. Smaller plants, 10–30 cm tall, with bulblets at stem-bases; basal leaves 1–4 cm wide; southern species . . . . *Suksdorfia* (p. 156)

        5b. Ovary 1-chambered 7

          7a. Fused sepals (calyx) joined to ovary for ⅓–½ their length . . . . *Conimitella williamsii* (p. 156)

          7b. Fused sepals (calyx) joined to ovary for >½ their length . . . . *Heuchera* (p. 154)

  2b. Stamens 10 8

    8a. Two halves of ovary almost separate, united only toward the base; basal leaves 3–10 cm long, glossy, green, leathery, narrowly egg-shaped to elliptic . . . . *Leptarrhena pyrolifolia* (p. 153)

    8b. Two halves of ovary united to much above the base; leaves various but not as above 9

      9a. Styles partially united; petals pink to red; leaves alternate, stalked . . . *Telesonix heucheriformis* (p. 154)

      9b. Styles free above fertile part of ovary; petals either white or yellow, except pinkish purple in *S. oppositifolia*, which has opposite, unstalked leaves . . . . *Saxifraga* (pp. 142–147) and *Micranthes* (pp. 143, 148–151)

Chrysosplenium wrightii   Mitella   Elmera racemosa   Boykinia richardsonii   Suksdorfia   Conimitella williamsii

Heuchera   Leptarrhena pyrolifolia   Telesonix heucheriformis   Saxifraga   Micranthes

THE GENERA *SAXIFRAGA* AND *MICRANTHES* (Saxifrage)

Saxifraga used to consist of nearly 500 mostly herbaceous species worldwide. As now revised, it is still by far the largest genus in the family, with nearly 400 species. In the traditional broad sense, *Saxifraga* is also one of the largest genera in our alpine flora, with more than 30 species. Based largely on recent molecular studies, but also on long-recognized morphological differences, the species described here—traditionally all considered species of *Saxifraga*—are divided into 2 genera, *Saxifraga* and *Micranthes*. They are perennial herbs from fibrous roots, rhizomes or stolons, with leaves in basal rosettes, sometimes also on the stem, mostly alternate and often somewhat fleshy. The flowers are single or in clusters, with 5 sepals, 5 petals and 10 stamens. As a general rule, species with basal and stem leaves are in *Saxifraga* and those with basal leaves only are in *Micranthes* (a notable exception is *M. tolmiei*, which has leaves crowded on the lower part of the stems). Also, the seeds of *Saxifraga* species are smooth or warty, whereas those of *Micranthes* are longitudinally ridged.

Saxifraga is from Latin *saxum*, "rock," and *frangere*, "break," meaning "rock-breaker" or "breakstone." It was thought that saxifrages were capable of breaking the rocks upon which they grew, hence some species were ground up and fed to patients with gallstones as a supposed cure. *Micranthes* means "small-flowered."

Key to *Saxifraga* and *Micranthes*

1a. Leaves opposite and tightly overlapping; flowers purple . . . . **Saxifraga oppositifolia** (p. 142)
1b. Leaves alternate; flowers not purple. 2

    2a. Leaves mostly not toothed or lobed; flowers yellow or yellowish white drying yellow, or white 3
        3a. Leaves conspicuously fringed with stiff, bristle-like hairs. 4
            4a. Flowering stems lacking or very short, scarcely exceeding the stubby shoots; plants forming dense, rounded cushions or mats with trailing branches
            . . . . **S. eschscholtzii** (p. 142)
            4b. Flowering stems 3–15 cm tall 5
                5a. Plants with conspicuous stolons (runners); flowers yellow . . **S. flagellaris** (p. 145)

                5b. Plants without stolons; flowers white to cream or yellowish white 6
                    6a. Leaves with 3 tooth-like lobes at the tip. . . . . **S. taylorii** (p. 144)
                    6b. Leaves not toothed or lobed . . . . **S. bronchialis, S. cherlerioides** (p. 144)
        3b. Leaves not bristle-fringed or only sparsely so 7
            7a. Plants loosely tufted; leaves 1–4 cm long, not fleshy . . . . **S. hirculus** (p. 146)
            7b. Plants mat- or cushion-forming; leaves 0.3–2 cm long, fleshy. 8
                8a. Flowers white. . . . . **Micranthes tolmiei** (p. 143)
                8b. Flowers yellow. 9

                  9a. Flowers barely rising above the tight cushion; petals greenish yellow, 2–3 mm long . . . . **S. aleutica** (p. 142)
                  9b. Flowers on distinct stalks or stems; petals yellow, 4 mm or longer. 10
                      10a. Leaves 5–20 mm long, linear to narrowly oblong; flowers usually 2–15 on long, leafy stems . . . . **S. aizoides** (p. 146)
                      10b. Leaves 3–10 mm long, lance-oblong to spoon-shaped; flowers usually single on short, bracted stalks 11
                        11a. Sepals erect to spreading in flower, at most sparsely fringed; petals pale yellow . . . . **S. serpyllifolia** (p. 145)

                      11b. Sepals strongly bent back, usually glandular-fringed; petals bright yellow . . . . **S. chrysantha** (p. 145)
    2b. Leaves toothed or lobed; flowers white, greenish, or pinkish 12
        12a. Flowering stems with at least 1 and usually several leaves 13
            13a. Basal leaf blades round to kidney-shaped, about as wide as long, distinctly stalked; plants often with bulblets. 14
                14a. Flowers partly or mostly replaced by bulblets 15
                  15a. Flowers usually 1–2 atop stem; bulblets in axils of basal leaves and upper stem leaves; basal leaves 1–2 cm wide. . . . . **S. cernua** (p. 147)

15b. Flowers several to many in a diffuse cluster, the branches often arching and each usually with a flower at the tip; basal leaves 2–10 cm wide .... ***S. mertensiana*** (p. 147)

14b. Flowers normal; any bulblets are in axils of leaves at the base of flowering stems.. 16

16a. Petals about 9–15 mm long; white bulblets usually present; north of 60° N .... ***S. radiata*** (p. 147)

16b. Petals mostly <5 mm long; bulblets often present.................. 17

17a. Stem leaves 3–5; sepals 0.7–1 mm wide; south of 49° N .... ***S. debilis*** (p. 147)

17b. Stem leaves 1–3; sepals 1.5–2 mm wide; throughout the region .... ***S. hyperborea*** (p. 147)

13b. Basal leaf blades broadly egg-shaped to oblong-elliptic to spoon- or wedge-shaped, longer than wide, tapering at base, 3-lobed or 3-toothed at tip; bulblets absent.. 18

18a. Leaves fringed with stiff, bristle-like hairs .... ***S. taylorii*** (p. 144)

18b. Leaves not bristle-fringed 19

19a. Basal leaves stiff, topped by 3 spiny teeth, leaf margins glandular-hairy .... ***S. tricuspidata*** (p. 144)

19b. Basal leaves not stiff, not topped by 3 spiny teeth, leaf margins not glandular-hairy 20

20a. Plants forming cushions or mats; leaves 3–5-lobed, the bases mostly 1–1.5 mm wide .... ***S. cespitosa*** (p. 143)

20b. Plants solitary or tufted, not matted, stems arising from basal rosette of leaves; leaves at most shallowly 3-lobed, the bases >1.5 mm wide .... ***S. adscendens*** (p. 143)

12b. Flowering stems leafless or with bracts only, mainly in flower cluster 21

21a. Leaf blades lance- to wedge-shaped, tapering to a broad, indistinct stalk; plants often with bulblets.. 22

22a. Leaves coarsely 7–12-toothed; flower clusters with long, ascending branches; flowers several to many, sometimes some replaced by bulblets .... ***Micranthes ferruginea*** (p. 148)

22b. Leaves untoothed or 3–5-toothed toward tip; flower clusters with short branches; flowers few (usually 1–3), the others replaced by bulblets 23

23a. Flower stalks erect to ascending; plants mostly north of 60° N .... ***M. foliolosa*** (p. 148)

23b. Flower stalks bent down; plants south of 45° N... ***M. bryophora*** (p. 148)

21b. Leaf blades round, kidney-shaped, elliptic or lance-, egg-, spoon- or fan-shaped, distinctly stalked; plants without bulblets 24

24a. Leaves with stalks 1–3 times the length of the blades; blades round to kidney-shaped, heart-shaped to squared-off at the base, distinctly toothed all around 25

25a. Flower cluster spike-like............................ ***M. spicata*** (p. 151)

25b. Flower cluster open or compact and conic to somewhat head-like... 26

26a. Petals oblong to elliptic, mostly unspotted, rarely with orange spots; flower cluster open or compact/congested, conic or head-like, 3–20 cm long .... ***M. nelsoniana*** (p. 151)

26b. Petals broadly elliptic to nearly round, with 2 yellow spots at the base; flower cluster open, loose, flat-topped, 20–60 cm long .... ***M. odontoloma*** (p. 151)

24b. Leaves with stalks about as long as blades; blades merely narrowing at the base, toothed only toward the tip.. 27

27a. Leaves spoon- or fan-shaped to narrowly wedge-shaped, toothed only toward tip.. 28

28a. Filaments club-shaped .... ***M. lyallii*** (p. 150)

28b. Filaments linear **29**

  29a. Leaves lance-shaped to narrowly spoon- or wedge-shaped; branches of flower cluster hairless . . . . . . ***M. razshivinii*** (p. 150)

  29b. Leaves fan-shaped; branches of flower cluster hairy . . . . ***M. calycina*** (p. 150)

27b. Leaves lance-, egg- or diamond-shaped or elliptic, mostly toothed much of their length, sometimes vaguely so **30**

  30a. Flower clusters cylindric, (interruptedly) spike-like **31**

    31a. Plants 10–50 cm tall; leaves 2–8 cm long; petals reddish purple, equalling sepals; north of 59° N . . . . . . ***M. hieraciifolia*** (p. 149)

    31b. Plants 20–75 cm tall; leaves 3–15 cm long; petals lacking or sometimes 1 to few petals present, pink to purplish, shorter than sepals; south of 49° N . . . . ***M. subapetala*** (p. 149)

  30b. Flower clusters tightly globe-shaped or pyramidal to open, wide-spreading, flat-topped **32**

    32a. Fused sepals (calyx) joined to ovary for more than ½ their length; flower clusters congested, even in fruit **33**

      33a. Leaves lance- to egg-shaped or deltoid; south of 49° N **34**

        34a. Leaves egg-shaped to deltoid or broadly diamond-shaped; petals 1.5 times or more as long as sepals; flower cluster usually yellowish to cream, stalked-glandular; ID and MT to AZ and NM . . . . ***M. rhomboidea*** (p. 149)

        34b. Leaves lance- to egg-shaped; petals shorter than sepals; flower cluster hairless or sparsely purplish-stalked-glandular; restricted to southwestern MT . . . . ***M. tempestiva*** (p. 149)

      33b. Leaves mostly egg-shaped to roundish; north of 53° N . . . **35**

        35a. Lower surfaces of leaves reddish-brown-hairy; petals mostly white; flowers mostly 10–40 per cluster . . . . ***M. nivalis*** (p. 150)

        35b. Lower surfaces of leaves hairless or nearly so; petals white (usually tinged pink or purple) with purple margins; flowers mostly 2–10 per cluster . . . . ***M. tenuis*** (p. 150)

    32b. Fused sepals (calyx) joined to ovary for much less than ½ their length; flower clusters usually more open **36**

      36a. Plants north of 59° N; sepals strongly bent back; petals with 2 yellow spots at the base . . . . ***M. reflexa*** (p. 150)

      36b. Plants south of 60° N; sepals not strongly bent back; petals unspotted **37**

        37a. Flower array an open to compact (but branched) pyramid of clusters; sepals hairless; leaves irregularly toothed . . . . ***M. occidentalis*** (p. 149)

        37b. Flower cluster open, flat-topped; sepals brown-hairy; leaves with regular teeth (resembling cogs on a gear wheel) **38**

          38a. Petals greenish, often purple-margined . . . ***M. tischii*** (p. 149)

          38b. Petals white . . . . ***M. rufidula*** (p. 149)

Nelson's saxifrage

Purple Mountain Saxifrage
Saxifraga oppositifolia

General: Loose to dense **mats or thick cushions** to 20 cm across and 2–7 cm tall, with condensed, crowded or trailing **branches that appear 4-angled;** flowering stems erect, with 1 to few pairs of leaves, **very short, 2–50 mm tall.**

Leaves: Mostly on branches, **very small, scale-like,** 2–5 mm long, somewhat leathery, persistent, **fringed with bristly hairs, opposite,** overlapping, in 4 rows.

Flowers: Showy, 1–2 cm across, urn- to bell-shaped, **single** at branch tips; **petals pink-purple** (rarely white), mostly 5–12 mm long, 2–3 times as long as the green to purplish, coarsely fringed sepals; anthers dark violet with bright orange pollen.

Fruits: Capsules with slender, spreading tips, 6–9 mm long.

Where Found: Tundra, felsenmeer, gravelly ridges, rocky slopes, cliffs and ledges; most abundant on moist but well-drained, **calcium-rich substrates;** lowland (arctic coast) to alpine zones; frequent throughout almost the entire region; widespread arctic-alpine, circumpolar.

Notes: Some leaves stay green all winter, turning red and dying at the end of their second growing season, and some leaves have specialized pores (**hydathodes**) at the tip, used when the plant cannot store all of its waste products in vacuoles (micro garbage bags) in the cell sap. The plant disposes of the excess waste, which is wet but full of calcium, through the hydathodes, and it appears as a white ring on the leaf when the water evaporates. • Rock ptarmigan and reindeer feed together in winter on the snowy plains of the Svalbard Archipelago in Norway. The reindeer dig through the snow to expose their winter food—polar willow (p. 60) and purple mountain saxifrage are among the most important—and the ptarmigan use the excavated craters to access the same food plants. • A generalization about plants of severe, unpredictable, arctic or alpine environments (in comparison to plants of temperate environments) predicts that self-compatibility, apomixis, vegetative reproduction and polyploidy should increase, all pushing populations toward genetic uniformity. Purple mountain saxifrage, however, remains self-incompatible, insect-pollinated, largely outcrossing and genetically diverse even *in extremis*.

Cushion Saxifrage, Barnacle Saxifrage
Saxifraga eschscholtzii

General: Forms **small mats** with trailing branches or **rounded cushions** 1–3 cm tall, with leafless, **very short (0–1 cm) flowering stems. Leaves:** Very small (1–3 mm long), in spheric basal clusters, **stiffly bristle-fringed,** greyish, similar to those of purple mountain saxifrage (above) but **alternate. Flowers:** Small, inconspicuous, single at branch tips, mostly **unisexual,** male and female flowers on separate plants; **petals yellow** to pinkish white or cream, narrow, 1–2 mm long, about as long as the greenish to reddish purple, coarsely fringed sepals. **Fruits:** Capsules purplish, on thread-like stalks 1 cm long. **Where Found:** Rocky outcrops, shale or gravelly slopes and shores, cliffs, ledges and lichen tundra; most abundant on moist but well-drained, calcium-rich substrates; lowland to alpine zones; infrequent in the far north of the region; arctic-alpine, amphiberingian.

Similar Species: Aleut saxifrage (*S. aleutica*), endemic to the western Aleutian Is., has **greenish to greenish yellow petals** and **leaves without fringed margins.**

Tufted Saxifrage
Saxifraga cespitosa

General: Tufted or mat-forming from a taproot and stem-base, which is clothed in old, withered leaves; flowering stems with 1 to several small leaves, 3–15 cm tall, stalked-glandular.

Leaves: Mostly basal, 5–20 mm long, wedge- to spoon-shaped, **with 3–5 finger-like lobes at the tip,** gradually narrowing to flattened stalks, margins glandular-fringed.

Flowers: About 1 cm across, broadly bell-shaped, 1–5 in a loose cluster; petals creamy white, mostly 3–7 mm long, egg-shaped, to twice as long as the purplish, stalked-glandular sepals.

Fruits: Capsules 5–10 mm long.

Where Found: Moist to dry, open, gravelly areas, cliffs, ledges, rocky slopes, fellfields and tundra; lowland to alpine zones; frequent in most of the region; circumpolar.

Similar Species: Wedge-leaf saxifrage (*S. adscendens*; *S. adscendens* ssp. *oregonensis*) is **biennial,** forms **tiny tufts** (not mats) often shorter (2–10 cm tall) than tufted saxifrage, and has wedge-shaped leaves with **3 shallow lobes at the tip.** It occurs on moist cliffs, ledges, scree slopes and fellfields, in subalpine and alpine zones, and is frequent south of 65° N, mostly in and east of the coastal mountains, in AK, YT and NT south to OR, NV, UT and CO.

Notes: *S. cespitosa* is a widespread, highly variable species complex, but the extreme diversity of form has thwarted taxonomic attempts at reliable subdivision. The plants range from good-sized cushions with large, showy flowers (e.g., in the Olympic Mtns), to just a few clumped stems with rather inconspicuous flowers in most areas farther north.

wedge-leaf saxifrage

Tolmie's Saxifrage
Micranthes tolmiei

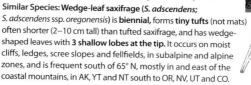

General: From slender stem-bases, forming low mats with numerous trailing, leafy, sterile branches; flowering stems 3–10 cm tall, leafless or with 1–3 leaves, often with pink- to purple-tipped, stalked glands.

Leaves: Mostly on branches, 5–15 mm long, lance- to spoon-shaped, **fleshy, round-tipped,** persistent for several years, margins smooth or fringed at the base.

Flowers: About 1 cm across, saucer-shaped, 1–5 (to 10) at branch tips; petals white, well-separated, 3–5 mm long, lance-shaped, about twice as long as the oval sepals; stamens 10, **filaments shaped like bowling pins.**

Fruits: Capsules 7–12 mm long, often purplish-mottled.

Where Found: Moist scree, felsenmeer, rocky slopes and crevices, streambanks and snowbeds; typically watered by melting snow; upper subalpine and alpine zones; frequent in the coastal mountains south of about 58° N, infrequent inland; arctic-alpine, cordilleran.

Notes: Tolmie's saxifrage is also known as *Saxifraga tolmiei*. • **Sausage-like, fleshy leaves** give Tolmie's saxifrage the look of a *Sedum* (stonecrop). This saxifrage can survive with a very short growing season. It is often found—and can be the most common species—in snow-patch areas that do not melt out until late summer.

PRICKLY OR BRISTLY SAXIFRAGES

These 5 saxifrages share a matted or cushion growth habit; stiff or leathery leaves that are variously spine-toothed or bristle-fringed; white to cream-coloured petals (yellow in spiderplant) that are often spotted; and an affinity for open, exposed, rocky, gravelly or sandy habitats that are usually dry, though Taylor's saxifrage occurs on moist, often shady, rocky sites. These perennials have densely leafy branches, including old, persistent leaves. The flowering stems are glandular-hairy (except for the smooth-stemmed Taylor's saxifrage), have several small, alternate leaves and are 5–15 (to 25) cm tall. The star-saucer-shaped flowers are 1–2 cm across, with few to several in rounded to flat-topped clusters at the stem tips.

Spotted Saxifrage
Saxifraga bronchialis ssp. *austromontana*

Leaves: Not toothed but spine-tipped and fringed with stiff, bristle-like hairs; lance-shaped to narrowly elliptic. **Flowers: Petals white to cream** (drying cream or pale yellow), inner surface yellow-spotted on the lower half, **upper half purple- or red-spotted, not narrowed to a stalk-like base. Where Found:** Rock outcrops, gravelly ridges and scree; subalpine and alpine zones; frequent in the southern ⅔ of the region; cordilleran.

Subspecies: Funston's saxifrage (*S. b.* ssp. *funstonii*) has petals that are **yellow-spotted on the inner surface** and **narrowed to a stalk-like base.** This amphiberingian subspecies is found in tundra and rock fields, in subalpine and alpine zones, and is frequent north of 57° N.

Similar Species: Yellow-dot saxifrage (*S. cherlerioides*; *S.b.* ssp. *cherlerioides*) has tightly packed, **glandular-fringed basal leaves** and short (1–6 cm tall) flowering stems, the **yellow-spotted petals not narrowed to a stalk-like base.** An amphiberingian species, it is found on scree slopes and gravelly flats in the Aleutian Is. and southern AK.

Taylor's Saxifrage • *Saxifraga taylorii*

Leaves: Crowded near the base, **3-lobed at the tip, fringed with stiff, bristly, non-glandular hairs,** wedge-shaped, nearly as wide as long. **Flowers:** Petals creamy white, **unspotted. Where Found:** Moist cliffs, rock outcrops, gullies and talus slopes; subalpine to alpine zones; mountains of Haida Gwaii (frequent) and northwestern Vancouver I. (rare); **BC coast endemic.**

Notes: This species is named for Roy L. Taylor (1932–), former director of the UBC Botanical Garden and a student of Saxifragaceae and the flora of Haida Gwaii.

Three-toothed Saxifrage, Prickly Saxifrage • *Saxifraga tricuspidata*

Leaves: Prickly 3-toothed at the tip, **fringed with soft, glandular hairs,** broadest at the tip, wedge-shaped at the base; often reddish-tinged. **Flowers:** Petals creamy white, usually yellow- or orange-spotted.

Where Found: Dry, open, sandy, gravelly or rocky sites; lowland to alpine zones; common and widespread inland and north of 52° N; boreal-arctic-alpine, North American.

Notes: Germination of three-toothed saxifrage seeds is inhibited by short day lengths and favoured by longer day lengths, ensuring that plants germinate in appropriate seasons.

Spiderplant, Stoloniferous Saxifrage
Saxifraga flagellaris

General: Solitary plants with several long, leafless, **thread-like, red or brownish runners** (stolons) to 10 cm long, **ending in buds or rooting plantlets;** flowering stems erect, leafy, stalked-glandular, 3–15 cm tall. **Leaves:** Mostly in a basal rosette, oblong to spoon-shaped, **not toothed** but pointy-tipped and **fringed with coarse, spiny hairs and stalked glands.**

Flowers: Showy, 1.5–2.5 cm across, cup- to bell-shaped, 1–3 atop stems; **petals bright golden yellow,** veined on inner surface, 4–10 mm long, much longer than the glandular-hairy sepals. **Where Found:** Tundra (alpine and arctic), gravelly ridges and scree slopes;

lowland (arctic coast) to alpine zones; frequent in the northern ⅓ of the region, scattered and locally frequent southward; circumpolar.

Notes: The strawberry-like runners help spiderplants survive on active substrates such as frost boils, stone polygons and scree slopes in much the same way as a domestic cat, legs splayed, remains atop her humans in bed, despite their squirming. • Different saxifrage species have different reproductive strategies in the high arctic. Spiderplant, as well as starstruck saxifrage (p. 148) and nodding saxifrage (p. 147), allocates most of its photosynthetic carbon to vegetative tissues and reproduces primarily vegetatively. In contrast, alpine saxifrage (p. 150), tufted saxifrage (p. 143) and slight saxifrage (p. 150) invest most of their carbon in flowering tissues and reproduce primarily by seed.

YELLOW-FLOWERED SAXIFRAGES WITHOUT PRICKLY OR BRISTLY LEAVES

These yellow-flowered saxifrages are all tufted from slender-branched stem-bases, often with sterile, leafy shoots. Thyme-leaved saxifrage and golden saxifrage (below) occur in mesic to dry tundra and rock fields. Evidently closely related, both have mostly basal, spoon-shaped, somewhat fleshy, shiny, hairless leaves in dense rosettes; short (2–8 cm), often glandular-hairy stems with few leaves; and petals narrowed to a short, stalk-like base.

Yellow mountain saxifrage (p. 146) and yellow marsh saxifrage (p. 146) are generally taller (to 15–20 cm or more) and have more numerous, longer stem leaves, petals lacking a stalk-like base and generally favour moist to wet habitats.

Thyme-leaved Saxifrage
Saxifraga serpyllifolia

General: Mat-forming with densely leafy, trailing shoots; stems erect, stalked-glandular. **Leaves:** Basal leaves 3–8 mm long; stem leaves 1–4 or lacking. **Flowers:** Mostly solitary

atop stems; petals rather pale yellow, 4–8 mm long, veined on inside surface; sepals green to purplish, **sparsely if at all fringed, erect to spreading in flower, bent back in fruit.**

golden saxifrage

Where Found: Mesic to dry tundra, gravelly ridges, scree slopes and felsenmeer; mostly alpine; locally frequent in the **northwestern part of the region;** arctic-alpine, amphiberingian.

Similar Species: Golden saxifrage or goldbloom saxifrage (**S. chrysantha**; S. serpyllifolia ssp. chrysantha) has **bright yellow petals** and **densely fringed, strongly bent-back sepals.** It is infrequent in the alplands of the **U.S. Rocky Mtns,** from MT to NM.

Yellow Mountain Saxifrage, Evergreen Saxifrage • *Saxifraga aizoides*

General: Mat-forming with leafy, mostly prostrate vegetative stems; flowering stems numerous, erect or ascending, 5–15 cm tall, glandular-hairy at least toward the top. **Leaves:** Along the stem, several to numerous, **5–20 mm long,** narrowly oblong to linear, **fleshy,** smooth or somewhat whisker-fringed, **stalkless. Flowers: Few to several** (2–15, rarely 1) in clusters atop stems, 5–10 mm across; petals yellow, sometimes orange-spotted on upper surface, elliptic, **3–7 mm long;** sepals greenish, triangular, hairless, **not fringed, spreading. Where Found:** Moist, typically calcium-rich streambanks, silty river flats, gravel bars, rocky seepage areas and talus slopes; montane to alpine zones; frequent in the northeastern part of the region; arctic-montane/alpine, amphi-Atlantic.

Notes: The leaves can remain green all winter. They also have lime-secreting hydathodes—specialized pores that get rid of excess waste water—toward the tip. • Reproduction can be difficult and uncertain in harsh alpine environments, so many alpine species, including yellow mountain saxifrage, retain the option of mating with someone they truly love—themselves. This "selfing" produces slightly fewer seeds per pod than open-pollinated flowers and the "selfed" seeds have lower rates of germination, so such inbreeding can have genetically undesirable long-term consequences. Still, it is likely better than not reproducing at all, and such behaviour can be beneficial, as when genomes are purged of deleterious alleles, resulting in "clean genes." Surveys suggest that perhaps half of all flowering plants self-fertilize more often than they outcross. The best reproductive strategy depends on the genetic history of populations (how much deleterious genetic load they carry) and the degree to which the plants are resource-limited for reproduction.

Yellow Marsh Saxifrage • *Saxifraga hirculus*

General: Stems loosely tufted, erect, 5–30 cm tall, often brownish-hairy. **Leaves:** Basal and 3–7 along the stem, **1–4 cm long,** lance- to spoon-shaped, smooth or nearly so, **not fleshy, basal leaves stalked. Flowers:** 1–2 (to 4) atop stem, 1–2 cm across; petals bright yellow, often with orange spots near the flower centre, egg-shaped, **6–18 mm long,** veined; sepals greenish to reddish, **fringed, ascending-spreading. Where Found:** Wet meadows, mossy seepage areas and tundra, bogs and fens; lowland (arctic coast) to alpine zones; frequent in the northern ⅓ of the region, disjunct in the U.S. Rockies (MT, UT, CO and NM); arctic-alpine, circumpolar.

Notes: The younger leaves stay green on the plant over winter. • This saxifrage is sometimes so plentiful in wet sites that the mass of flowers tints the tundra yellow.

SAXIFRAGES WITH WHITE-FLOWERS, LEAFY FLOWERING STEMS, ROUND TO KIDNEY-SHAPED, STALKED BASAL LEAVES AND USUALLY WITH BULBLETS

The first 3 species of this group are very small plants with pale **bulblets often atop the stem-base,** in the axils of the roundish, palmately lobed basal leaves. The last 2 (nodding saxifrage and Mertens' saxifrage) are larger plants with **bulblets atop the stem-base and in the flower cluster.**

Pygmy Saxifrage • *Saxifraga hyperborea*

General: Dwarf, often purplish; stems solitary or in small tangled tufts, without rhizomes or stolons, often weak, spreading to erect, 2–5 cm tall, usually soft-hairy and stalked-glandular. **Leaves:** Basal leaves round to kidney-shaped, palmately mostly 3–5-lobed, hairless, stalked, **often with bulblets in axils;** stem leaves 1–3, smaller and fewer-lobed. **Flowers:** 1–3 (to 5) atop stems, not replaced by bulblets; petals white to pink or purple, 2–5 mm long. **Where Found:** Moist to wet, gravelly slopes, talus, scree, streambanks, shores, shaded ledges and cliff crevices, snowbeds and wet tundra; subalpine to alpine zones; locally frequent in most of the region; arctic-alpine, circumpolar.

Similar Species: Rocky Mountain pygmy saxifrage (*S. debilis*; *S. cernua* var. *debilis*, *S. hyperborea* ssp. *debilis*, *S. rivularis* var. *debilis*) has larger, **5–7-lobed basal leaves and 3–5 stem leaves similar to the basal ones.** It occurs in meadows, snowbed and seepage areas, lakeshores, shady talus, ravines and cliffs, in sub-alpine and alpine zones, and is found in the **U.S. Rockies** in MT, WY, UT, CO and NM. • **Snowbed saxifrage** (*S. radiata*; *S. exilis*) almost always has bulblets in the axils of the basal leaves and has much larger flowers, the **petals 9–15 mm long,** white with purple veins. This amphi-beringian species grows on moist to wet tundra, snowbeds and streambanks, in montane to alpine zones, and is frequent north of 62° N in AK, YT and NT.

snowbed saxifrage

Notes: Pygmy saxifrage is also known as *Saxifraga rivularis* in part.

Nodding Saxifrage • *Saxifraga cernua*

General: Stems 1 to few, slender, erect, 5–30 cm tall, stalked-glandular. **Leaves:** Basal leaves round to kidney-shaped, **1–2 cm wide,** 3–7-lobed, long-stalked, shrivel-ling in summer, with **bulblets in axils;** stem leaves reduced upward, at least upper ones usually with reddish purple bulblets. **Flowers:** 1–2 (to 5) atop stem or lacking, nodding in bud; petals white, unspotted, 5–12 mm long; **usually some flowers replaced by bulblets. Where Found:** Moist ledges, cliff crevices, scree slopes, stream-banks and shores; lowland (arctic coast) to alpine zones; frequent in most of the region except the Pacific coast; arctic-alpine, circumpolar.

Similar Species: Mertens' saxifrage or wood saxifrage (*S. mertensiana*) has round to kidney-shaped, shallowly **lobed and toothed basal leaves 2–10 cm wide** and **open, arching-branched arrays of several to many (30+) flowers,** some of which are replaced by pinkish bulblets. It is found on wet mossy cliffs, rocky slopes and in waterfall spray zones, in lowland to subalpine zones (rarely alpine). It is frequent in the southern ½ of the region, southern coastal AK and adjacent BC to CA, ID and MT.

Notes: Nodding saxifrage reproduces primarily by vegetative means—bulblets—and its insect-pollinated flowers rarely set seed. Still, several studies have demonstrated unexpectedly high genetic variation within and among populations of this species, suggesting that the occa-sional sexual event can work wonders in helping maintain this diversity.

White Flowers and Lance- to Wedge-shaped, Indistinctly Stalked Basal Leaves; Often with Bulblets

Starstruck Saxifrage • *Micranthes foliolosa*

General: Stems mostly single, slender, erect, 5–20 cm tall, often sparsely stalked-glandular. **Leaves:** All basal, often with bulblets, lance-wedge-shaped to spoon-shaped, **5–20 mm long, 3–5 small teeth toward the tip. Flowers:** Few, 1 atop stem or 2–5 (or more) singly at the end of each flowering branch, **others replaced by bulblets,** flower clusters with **short, stiff ascending branches;** petals white, **yellow-spotted at the base,** 3–8 mm long. **Where Found:** Wet tundra, streambanks and snowbeds; low to high elevations; scattered along the arctic coast and in the northern mountains, disjunct in CO; high arctic–alpine, circumpolar.

Similar Species: Bud saxifrage (*M. bryophora*; *S. bryophora*) has nearly entire leaves and bent-down flower stalks. It occurs in wet meadows and on cliffs and ledges, in subalpine and alpine zones in CA and is disjunct in ID.

Notes: Starstruck saxifrage is also known as *Saxifraga foliolosa* and *S. stellaris* var. *comosa*. • Both species are apparently closely related to rusty saxifrage (below).

Rusty Saxifrage • *Micranthes ferruginea*

General: Stems 1 to several, 10–40 cm tall, purplish-stalked-glandular. **Leaves: 2–10 cm long,** somewhat fleshy, **with 7–13 small teeth. Flowers: Several to many** (10–20 or more) in open clusters with **long, ascending branches,** lower flowers often replaced by bulblets; petals white, 3–6 mm long, the upper 3 larger and with 2 yellow spots, the **lower 2 unspotted. Where Found:** Moist rock outcrops and ledges, gravelly slopes, roadsides and streambanks; lowland to alpine zones; frequent in the southern ⅔ of the region, mostly coastal in southern AK; cordilleran.

Notes: Rusty saxifrage is also known as *Saxifraga ferruginea*. • This is a widespread and very variable species. According to *FNA*: "Plants with bulbils replacing flowers are more common in the southern part (southern Alberta and British Columbia southwards) of the range …" Are southerners losing their mojo?

WHITE FLOWERS AND ELLIPTIC, LANCE-, EGG- OR DIAMOND-SHAPED LEAVES

These are tufted perennials from short, thick rhizomes, the flowering stems single or a few together, leafless and stalked-glandular. The leaves are usually shallowly toothed through most of their length, sometimes indistinctly so. The flowers are several to many, the petals usually white, sometimes pink to purplish or greenish, and mostly 2–3 mm long.

Hawkweed-leaved Saxifrage
Micranthes hieraciifolia

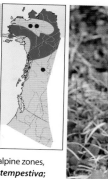

General: Stems 10–50 cm tall. **Leaves:** Elliptic, 2–8 cm long, remotely several-toothed, somewhat fleshy, often hairy. **Flowers:** Numerous in a showy, cylindric, interrupted spike-like cluster; **petals reddish purple, 1.5–3 mm long, equalling sepals. Where Found:** Moist meadows, turfy heathlands, tundra and solifluction slopes, mostly on calcium-rich soils; lowland (arctic coast) to alpine zones; frequent in the northern ⅓ of the region; arctic-alpine, circumpolar.

Similar Species: Yellowstone saxifrage (*M. subpetala*; *S. oregana* var. *subpetala*) is **larger,** with stems 20–75 cm tall and leaves 3–15 cm long. The

purplish flowers lack petals or, when present, the **petals are 1–2 mm long, shorter than the sepals.** It grows in wet meadows and on streambanks and wet ledges, in subalpine and alpine zones, and is locally frequent in MT, ID and WY. • **Storm saxifrage** (*M. tempestiva*; *S. tempestiva*) is **smaller,** with stems 3–15 cm tall and leaves 5–30 mm long. The flowers have **creamy white petals** to 1.5 mm long, **shorter than the sepals.** It occurs on moist ledges, rocky slopes and snowbeds, in subalpine and alpine zones, and is known only from MT, in the Bitterroot Mtns and Anaconda Range.

Notes: Hawkweed-leaved saxifrage is also known as *Saxifraga hieraciifolia.*

Western Saxifrage • *Micranthes occidentalis*

General: Stems 10–30 cm tall, with purple-tipped, stalked glands especially toward flowers. **Leaves:** Egg-shaped to elliptic, 1.5–4 cm long, coarsely toothed, reddish-brown-hairy on the undersurface especially when young; leaf stalks flattened, only slightly winged. **Flowers:** In an **open to compact (but definitely branched) pyramid of clusters;** petals white, usually unspotted; **sepals hairless. Where Found:** Moist to dry meadows, ledges and gravelly slopes; montane to alpine zones; frequent in the southern ½ of the region, infrequent northward, cordilleran.

Similar Species: Snowball saxifrage or diamond-leaf saxifrage (*M. rhomboidea*; *S. rhomboidea*) has stems with yellow- or cream-tipped, stalked glands; indistinctly to coarsely toothed leaves with **winged stalks;** and flowers in a **single, dense, head-like cluster,** the petals creamy white. It occurs in moist meadows, fellfields and on rocky slopes, in montane to alpine zones, and is frequent in the U.S. Rockies, from MT and ID to AZ and NM.

Notes: Western saxifrage is also known as *Saxifraga occidentalis.*

Rusty-haired Saxifrage • *Micranthes rufidula*

General: Smaller (5–20 cm tall) than western saxifrage (above). **Leaves: Very regularly toothed** (like cogs on a gear wheel), usually **densely rusty-woolly on the underside. Flowers:** In open, branched, flat-topped clusters; sepals often brown-hairy. **Where Found:** Vernally moist rock outcrops and ledges; lowland to alpine zones; frequent in the southwestern part of the region.

Similar Species: Olympic saxifrage (*M. tischii*), a dwarf (2–7 cm tall) alpine form with **greenish petals,** often with purple margins, has been recognized as a distinct species. It grows on wet, shaded ledges and in crevices, and is rare on central Vancouver I. and in the Olympic Mtns.

Notes: Rusty-haired saxifrage is also known as *Saxifraga rufidula* and *S. occidentalis* var. *rufidula.* • Rusty-haired saxifrage largely replaces western saxifrage on Vancouver I. and the Olympic Peninsula.

Alpine Saxifrage, Snow Saxifrage
Micranthes nivalis

General: Stems 5–20 cm tall. **Leaves:** Egg-shaped to round-ish, **1–4.5 cm long**, toothed, green and hairless above, often purplish and **reddish-brown-hairy below**, thick, somewhat leathery. **Flowers:** More than 5, usually 10–40, in dense, somewhat head-like clusters; petals white or pink-tinged; sepals erect, spreading in fruit. **Where Found:** Tundra, rocky slopes and ledges, mostly on acidic rocks; montane to alpine zones; frequent in the northern mostly inland ½ of the region, scattered southward in BC and AB; arctic-alpine, circumpolar.

Similar Species: Yukon saxifrage (*M. reflexa*; *S. reflexa*) has elliptic to egg-shaped leaves that are reddish-brown-hairy on both surfaces and 12–20 flowers in an **open cluster, white petals with 2 yellow spots at the base,** the **sepals strongly bent back,** and **club-shaped stamens** that are often some-

what petal-like. This arctic-alpine, northern cordilleran species is found on dry to mesic tundra, heathlands, gravelly slopes, ledges and fellfields, in montane to alpine zones. It is frequent in the northern ⅓ of the region, mostly AK, YT, western NT and northern BC. • **Slight saxifrage (*M. tenuis*; *S. nivalis* var. *tenuis*) is **smaller** (2–10 cm tall) with **mostly hairless leaves** 5–15 mm long and **fewer (2–10) flowers in a head-like cluster**, the **petals white, tinged pink or purple**, not spotted, and the sepals erect. An arctic-alpine, circumpolar species, it grows on tundra, rocky slopes, gravelly ridges and shaded ledges, in lowland (arctic coast) to alpine zones. It is frequent in the northern ⅓ of the region, AK, YT, NT and northern BC.

Yukon saxifrage

Notes: Alpine saxifrage is also known as *Saxifraga nivalis*. • Some taxonomists have distinguished plants with crinkly, rust-coloured hairs on the underside of their leaves and pink to reddish purple petals as a separate taxon, *M. rufopilosa* or *M. nivalis* var. *rufopilosa*, perhaps derived from hybrids between *M. nivalis* and *M. tenuis*.

WHITE FLOWERS AND SPOON-, EGG- OR FAN-SHAPED TO NARROWLY WEDGE-SHAPED LEAVES TAPERED AT THE BASE, TOOTHED ONLY TOWARD THE TIP

Red-stemmed Saxifrage, Lyall's Saxifrage
Micranthes lyallii

General: Stems 5–30 cm tall, usually reddish. **Leaves:** 1–8 cm long, **spoon- or fan- to egg-shaped, wedge-shaped at the base,** tapering to long stalk about equalling blade, **coarsely toothed toward the tip. Flowers:** 8–15 in an open cluster; petals white, often with 2 yellowish green spots near the base; **stamens club-shaped. Fruits:** Capsules green to yellow, purplish toward the tip. **Where Found:** Streambanks, seepage sites, moist to wet meadows and gravelly slopes; montane to alpine zones; frequent in the central ¾ of the region.

Similar Species: Alaska saxifrage (*Micranthes razshivinii*; *S. razshivinii*, *S. davurica* misapplied) is smaller (3–15 cm tall), with **lance- to narrowly spoon-shaped leaves, also coarsely toothed near the tip. The white to cream petals are often purple-tinged and **unspotted**, the **stamens have linear filaments**, and the capsules are purplish black. It is found on moist tundra, streambanks, solifluction and scree slopes, in subalpine and alpine zones, and is frequent in the northern ⅓ of the region (north of 59° N), in AK, YT, western NT and northwesternmost BC. • **Fanleaf saxifrage (*M. calycina*; *S. calycina*, *S. davurica* ssp. *grandipetala*) is a segregate of Alaska saxifrage but has broader, fan-shaped leaves and **hairy branches** in the flower cluster. An amphiberingian species, it grows on streambanks, snowbeds, scree slopes and tundra, in montane to alpine zones, and is infrequent in western AK.

Alaska saxifrage

Notes: Red-stemmed saxifrage is also known as *Saxifraga lyallii*.

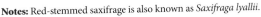

WHITE FLOWERS, ROUND TO KIDNEY- OR HEART-SHAPED LEAVES DISTINCTLY TOOTHED ALL AROUND, SQUARED OFF AT THE BASE; NO BULBLETS

Brook Saxifrage • *Micranthes odontoloma*

General: Bigger (**20–70 cm tall**) than red-stemmed saxifrage (p. 150), with which it often hybridizes. **Leaves: Round to kidney-shaped, coarsely toothed all around;** distinct stalks substantially longer than leaf blades, which are **heart-shaped to squared-off at the base. Flowers:** 10–30 or more in an **open cluster; petals white, with 2 yellow spots at the base.**
Where Found: Wet meadows, moist glades and streambanks; montane to subalpine, occasionally alpine zones; frequent in the southern ⅓ of the region; cordilleran.

Notes: Brook saxifrage is also known as *Saxifraga odontoloma* and *S. arguta* (of some authors).
• Researchers suggest that north-eastern disjunct populations of brook saxifrage are the remnants of a more continuous distribution during the warmer, drier Hypsithermal Interval (9000–6000 years ago), when what is today boreal forest was grassland.

Nelson's Saxifrage
Micranthes nelsoniana

General: Stems 5–35 cm tall.
Leaves: 2–9 cm wide and ½ to nearly as long, **kidney-shaped to round, coarsely toothed all around**, stalks distinct and longer than blades. **Flowers:** 10 to many in a compact to somewhat open, **conic or head-like cluster; petals white to pinkish, mostly unspotted** (rarely orange-spotted), egg-shaped to oblong; sepals green to purplish, bent back. **Where Found:** Moist, shady cliffs, scree and talus slopes, felsenmeer, snowbeds, streambanks and seepage sites; lowland to alpine zones; frequent almost throughout the region; amphiberingian.

Similar Species: When on Haida Gwaii, be careful not to confuse Nelson's saxifrage with Haida-groundsel (p. 400), an endemic species with similar leaves. • **Spike saxifrage** (**M. spicata;** *S. spicata*) has spike-like flower clusters and cream to yellowish petals. It grows on moist to wet tundra, heathlands, rocky slopes and streambanks, in lowland to alpine zones. An endemic species, it is infrequent in western and central AK and adjacent YT.

Notes: Nelson's saxifrage is also known as *Saxifraga nelsoniana* and *S. punctata.*

LEAF SILHOUETTES OF OTHER GENERA IN THE SAXIFRAGE FAMILY
(pp. 153–156)

leatherleaf saxifrage
(*Leptarrhena pyrolifolia*)

Wright's golden-saxifrage
(*Chrysosplenium wrightii*)

smooth alumroot
(*Heuchera glabra*)

crevice alumroot
(*Heuchera micrantha*)

round-leaved alumroot
(*Heuchera cylindrica*)

littleleaf alumroot
(*Heuchera parvifolia*)

cliff-saxifrage
(*Telsonix heucheriformis*)

five-stamen mitrewort
(*Mitella pentandra*)

Brewer's mitrewort
(*Mitella breweri*)

bear flower
(*Boykinia richardsonii*)

creamy coralbells
(*Elmera racemosa*)

conehead mitrewort
(*Conimitella williamsii*)

violet suksdorfia
(*Suksdorfia violacea*)

buttercup-leaved suksdorfia
(*Suksdorfia ranunculifolia*)

Leatherleaf Saxifrage • *Leptarrhena pyrolifolia*

General: From robust rhizomes, often forming mats; flowering stems erect, unbranched, 10–40 cm tall, purplish red, short-hairy and stalked-glandular especially toward the top.

Leaves: Mostly basal, oval to oblong-elliptic, 3–10 cm long, hairless, **leathery, glossy, green,** rough and deeply veined on the upper surface, pale green below, margins round-toothed; flowering stems with 1–4 smaller, alternate leaves.

Flowers: Many (20–100) small, bell-shaped to deeply saucer-shaped flowers in several clusters forming a branched group atop stem, compact at first, expanding in fruit; **petals white** or pink-tinged, narrowly spoon-shaped, a bit longer than the sepals; sepals green, 1–1.5 mm long; **stamens 10,** pink, filaments linear.

Fruits: Capsules 2, follicle-like, the **halves almost separate, united only toward the base,** 6–9 mm long, usually **bright purplish red.**

Where Found: Streambanks, flushes, seepage areas, wet thickets and meadows; montane to alpine zones; frequent in the southern ¾ of the region, more abundant in snowier mountain ranges; cordilleran.

Notes: Bright red stems and fruiting clusters set against lustrous, green, leathery leaves make a striking display. This saxifrage is a great plant for rock gardens. • The Aleuts used an infusion of leaves to treat influenza. The Nlaka'pamux people applied a poultice of chewed leaves to wounds. • *Leptarrhena* is from the Greek *leptos*, "fine" or "slender," and *arrhen*, "male," referring to the slender filaments of the stamens; *pyrolifolia* means "leaves like *Pyrola*" (i.e., leathery and evergreen), hence the common name.

Wright's Golden-saxifrage, Wright's Golden-carpet • *Chrysosplenium wrightii*

General: Small tufts or clumps from pale stolons (runners); stems succulent, leafy, erect to spreading, usually branched, 2–12 cm tall/long, usually with long, reddish brown hairs.

Leaves: Basal leaves **round to kidney-shaped,** 4–18 mm long, **fleshy,** hairless or with thick, white or brownish hairs, margins with **5–9 broad, rounded teeth,** slender-stalked, the stalks with reddish brown, crinkly hairs; stem leaves lacking or 1–2, similar, alternate.

Flowers: 3–15 or more, rather inconspicuous in a cluster atop stem; **petals lacking; sepals 4,** broadly rounded, **greenish yellow, purple or red-orange** mottled with purple; **stamens 8.**

Fruits: Capsules, **cup-like** after splitting open, the 2 free parts 2-lobed, spreading.

Where Found: Seepage areas, streambanks, moist solifluction and scree slopes; lowland (arctic coast) to alpine zones; infrequent in the northern ⅓ of the region; arctic-alpine, amphiberingian.

Notes: The ripe capsules split open into a shallow, cup-like configuration, well suited to splash-cup dispersal. In other *Chrysosplenium* species, the small, smooth seeds can be ejected 40 cm or more by a direct hit with a fat water drop. • The lower part of this plant is often covered with mud. • Looking for Mr. Wright? Charles Wright (1811–85) was a member of the North Pacific Exploring and Surveying Expedition (1853–56) under Cadwalader Ringgold and John Rodgers. • The generic name combines the Greek *chrysos*, "gold," and *splenos*, "spleen," because of the flower colour of some species and an ancient belief that the plant had medicinal value for treating the spleen.

Smooth Alumroot, Alpine Alumroot • *Heuchera glabra*

General: From strong horizontal to ascending rhizomes; stems 1 to several, erect, 15–60 cm tall, often stalked-glandular-hairy toward the top.

Leaves: Basal leaves rounded, heart-shaped, 3–10 cm across, **wider than long**, sparsely glandular-hairy to nearly hairless, **palmately 5-lobed**, the lobes themselves shallowly lobed and coarsely sharp-toothed, **stalks long, mostly hairless; stipules fringed with short hairs,** fused to leaf stalks.

Flowers: Numerous in an open cluster atop stem, branches and flower stalks thread-like, flowers vase-shaped; **petals 5, white, narrowly elliptic, at least twice as long as sepals; sepals 5, greenish,** united below and joined to the ovary almost to its top, resulting in a whitish, stalked-glandular, **bell-shaped hypanthium 2–3.5 mm long; stamens 5,** longer than and opposite sepals.

Fruits: Capsules egg-shaped, 4–6 mm long; seeds finely spiny.

Where Found: Moist rock crevices, ledges and cliffs, streambanks, talus slopes and rocky meadows; montane to alpine zones; frequent in the southern ⅔ of the region, primarily the coastal mountains; Pacific maritime.

Similar Species: Crevice alumroot or small-flowered alumroot (*H. micrantha*) has **5–7-lobed leaves mostly longer than wide,** often long-hairy leaf stalks and **stipules fringed with long, eyelash-like hairs.** It grows in forests, on moist to dry streambanks and talus slopes and in rock crevices, in lowland to lower alpine zones, mostly in the southwestern part of the region, southwestern BC to CA and ID. • **Round-leaved alumroot** or poker alumroot (*H. cylindrica*) has **round-toothed leaves** and **narrow, spike-like flower clusters.** The petals are **mostly linear, fewer than 5** (sometimes lacking), the **petals and stamens shorter than the sepals,** with a yellowish green to cream hypanthium 6–9 mm long. It grows in dry, rocky, sunny habitats from low to high elevations in the inland southern ⅓ of the region. • **Littleleaf alumroot** or common alumroot (*H. parvifolia*) has flowers with a **saucer-shaped (not bell-shaped) hypanthium, 2.5–5 mm long,** the **elliptic petals 1.5–2 times as long as the sepals.** It occurs in rock crevices and on rocky slopes, on sedimentary rock (especially limestone), in montane to lower alpine zones, in southwestern AB, ID, MT and WY to CA, AZ and NM.

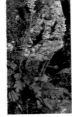

round-leaved alumroot

Notes: The pounded, dried roots of several *Heuchera* species are very astringent (like alum) and reportedly were applied by First Nations and herbalists as a poultice for cuts and sores, to stop bleeding and promote healing. The Tlingit used smooth alumroot to treat inflammation of the testicles from syphilis. The Skagit pounded crevice alumroot and rubbed it into young girls' hair to make it grow thicker. • *Heuchera* is named in honour of Johann Heinrich von Heucher (1677–1747), an Austrian-born professor of medicine in Wittenberg and Dresden and a botanist. Hence, *Heuchera* should be pronounced *hoy-kher-a*, which could get you some funny looks.

stipule

seed

flower

Cliff-saxifrage • *Telesonix heucheriformis*

General: Mat-forming from thick rhizomes and scaly stem-base; stems erect, 5–23 cm tall, leafy, stalked-glandular, hairy.

Leaves: Mostly basal, kidney-shaped, **2–7 cm wide,** somewhat fleshy, doubly scalloped, long-stalked, stalked-glandular.

Flowers: 5–25 in an often one-sided, bracted cluster atop stem, narrowly bell-shaped; **petals 5, pink to violet-purple, 3–7 mm long,** egg- to spoon-shaped; **sepals 5, maroon,** narrowly egg-shaped, about as long as petals; **stamens 10.**

Fruits: Capsules egg-shaped; seeds oblong, brown, shiny.

Where Found: Moist nooks and crannies on cliffs, talus slopes and rocky ridges, usually on limestone, often on north aspects; montane to alpine zones; infrequent in the southeastern corner of the region.

Notes: Cliff-saxifrage is also known as *Boykinia heucheriformis*, *Saxifraga heucheriformis* and *Telesonix jamesii* var. *heucheriformis*. • *Telesonix* is from the Greek *teleos*, "complete," and *onyx*, "claw," perhaps alluding to the entire, unlobed petals. • Cliff-saxifrage can be a stunning rock garden plant.

Five-stamen Mitrewort
Mitella pentandra

General: From slender rhizomes, occasionally with creeping shoots; stems erect, 10–50 cm tall, generally leafless, finely glandular-hairy to nearly hairless.

Leaves: Basal leaves oval with heart-shaped base, 3–8 cm long, nearly hairless to sparsely stalked-glandular on both surfaces, shallowly 5–9-lobed, doubly sharp-toothed, stalks long and sparsely hairy.

Flowers: Several to many (6–25) in a narrow cluster atop stem, flowers saucer-shaped; **petals 5, greenish yellow, 2–3 mm long, dissected into 2–5 pairs of thread-like lateral segments** (much like a TV antenna), much longer than the 5 triangular sepals; **stamens 5, opposite the petals.**

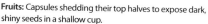

Fruits: Capsules shedding their top halves to expose dark, shiny seeds in a shallow cup.

Where Found: Moist to wet forests and glades, streambanks, meadows, avalanche tracks and talus slopes; montane to alpine zones (most abundant at subalpine elevations); frequent in the southern ⅔ of the region; cordilleran.

Similar Species: Brewer's mitrewort (*M. breweri*) occupies similar habitats but has **roundish leaves** and **stamens alternating with petals.** It is frequent in the southern ⅓ of the region.

Notes: Seed dispersal is at least partly by a "splash cup" mechanism, whereby raindrops scoring direct hits eject the small, smooth seeds from the shallow fruit cup. • In the 20 years following the 1980 eruption of Mount St. Helens, five-stamen mitrewort was one of the plants most successful in poking through the tephra, flowering and producing fast-growing seedlings. • *Mitella* is the diminutive of the Latin *mitra*, "a turban-like hat," alluding to the shape of the young fruit; *pentandra* means "5 men," referring to the 5 stamens.

Bear Flower, Alaska Boykinia • *Boykinia richardsonii*

General: Clumped from rhizomes and a thick stem-base covered with persistent brownish leaf bases and stipules; stems erect, unbranched, **10–60 cm tall,** leafy, covered with brown, stalked glands.

Leaves: Mostly basal, kidney-shaped, **5–11 cm wide,** coarsely toothed to shallowly lobed, long-stalked, with stalked glands; stem leaves smaller, shorter-stalked to stalkless.

Flowers: In 3-flowered, glandular branches in a bracted, **spike-like, cylindric cluster** atop stem, flowers showy, saucer- to bell-shaped; **petals 5, white to pink** with purplish veins, **8–15 mm long,** elliptic to egg-shaped, pointy-tipped; sepals 5, maroon, glandular; **stamens 5.**

Fruits: Capsules egg- to top-shaped, 9–12 mm long; seeds numerous, brown, smooth.

Where Found: Moist meadows, tundra, willow thickets, streambanks and gullies; lowland to alpine zones; frequent in the far north of the region; arctic-alpine; a showy Beringian endemic, "almost certainly a relict from the late Tertiary" (Hultén, 1968).

Notes: Bear flower is not just a catchy name—it and common horsetail (p. 494) are the most important summertime foods for grizzlies in northern Yukon. • This species is named for Samuel Boykin (1786–1848), an early American physician and naturalist, and John Richardson (1787–1865), a Scottish naturalist with John Franklin's arctic expedition.

Creamy Coralbells • *Elmera racemosa*

General: Stems leafy, erect, 10–35 cm tall, stalked-glandular toward the top; entire plant hairy or stalked-glandular.

Leaves: Basal leaves kidney-shaped, 2–5 cm wide, **wider than long**, long-stalked, shallowly palmately 5–9-lobed, margins with a single or double set of rounded teeth; stem leaves similar, usually 2–3, shorter-stalked; stipules large, membranous, brownish.

Flowers: 10–25 in a long, narrow cluster atop stem, **bell-shaped**, 5–12 mm long; petals 5, **white or cream, with 4–7 lobes**; sepals 5, greenish yellow, united much of their length, **joined to ovary only at the base;** stamens 5.

Fruits: Capsules egg-shaped, 4–5 mm long; seeds numerous, minutely granular surfaced.

Where Found: Mesic rock crevices, cliffs, ridges, talus slopes, close to long-lasting snow; subalpine and alpine zones; infrequent in the southwestern part of the region; endemic.

Similar Species: If not in flower, this species is difficult to distinguish from a *Heuchera*. If with flowers, *Elmera* has lobed petals and the **fused sepals (calyx) are joined to the basal ¼ of the ovary;** *Heuchera* petals are unlobed with the **calyx joined to at least the basal ½ of the ovary. • Conehead mitrewort (*Conimitella williamsii*)** has **basal leaves only, unlobed white petals** and a cone-shaped hy, anthium joined at the base to the ovary for ⅓–½ **its length.** A Rocky Mountain endemic, it grows on cliffs, moist ledges, crevices and rocky slopes, often on limestone, in montane to alpine zones, and is infrequent in the southeastern part of the region, southwestern AB, MT, ID, WY and CO.

Notes: Both *Elmera* and *Conimitella* are monotypic genera endemic to western North America. • Adolf D. E. Elmer (1870–1942) was an American botanist who collected in California and Washington, as well as in the Philippines.

Violet Suksdorfia • *Suksdorfia violacea*

General: Clumped from scaleless **stem-bases with many bulblets;** stems erect, 10–20 cm tall, leafy, more or less stalked-glandular.

Leaves: Basal leaves 1–3, often withered by flowering time, kidney-shaped, **1.5–3 cm wide, nearly hairless,** coarsely lobed or toothed, stalks long and slender; stem leaves similar to basal leaves, 3–5, stalks shorter; stipules of upper stem leaves enlarged.

Flowers: 2–20 in a somewhat flat-topped cluster atop stem, **hypanthium narrowly bell-shaped; petals 5, usually violet or pink,** 6–9 mm long, spoon-shaped to elliptic, slightly unequal, erect; sepals 5, 2–3 mm long; **stamens 5.**

Fruits: Capsules egg-shaped, 5–7 mm long.

Where Found: Moist (at least in spring), mossy, rocky ledges, crevices and shaded cliffs; montane to subalpine zones; infrequent in the southeastern part of the region.

Similar Species: Buttercup-leaved suksdorfia (*S. ranunculifolia*) has a **broadly bell-shaped hypanthium** and spreading **white petals 3–5 mm long.** It grows on moist, mossy, rock outcrops and ledges, in montane to subalpine zones, and is infrequent south of about 54° N, in southern BC and southwestern AB to WA, OR, CA, ID and MT.

Notes: *Suksdorfia* is named for Wilhelm Nikolaus Suksdorf (1850–1932), a German-born botanist who lived in Bingen, Washington; he was one of the foremost plant collectors in the Pacific Northwest.

buttercup-leaved suksdorfia

PRETTY IN PINK (AND PURPLE)

Most of the representatives of the pink family (Caryophyllaceae) in our high-elevation flora have white flowers, sometimes tinged with pink or purple. Similarly, most of our saxifrage family (Saxifragaceae) species have white, cream, yellow or greenish flowers. Yet the flagship arctic-alpine species in each family has brilliant pink (moss campion) or pink-purple (purple mountain saxifrage) blooms. Why?

We think it has to do with reproduction. Pale-flowered, alpine members of the pink and saxifrage families tend to have relatively small flowers that are self-pollinated or pollinated by flies and other small, short-tongued, unspecialized insects. The mostly out-breeding, showier flowers (individually and *en masse*) of moss campion are pollinated mostly by bees and butterflies, and of purple saxifrage mostly by bumble-bees. Both species bloom relatively early and often occur in austere habitats in which both flowers and pollinators are naturally scarce. On arctic-alpine fell-fields, ridges and stony tundra, it could be that the most efficient and mutually beneficial arrangement for low-density flowers and their relatively sparse pollinators is a common floral signal and flexible (serial fidelity) pollinator behaviour. In this case, the signal for oases of abundant, easily obtained resources is a mass of pink-purple flowers, displayed not only by moss campion and purple mountain saxifrage, but also by several other early flowering, bee-pollinated, spaced-out species, including woolly lousewort, arctic lousewort, Lapland rosebay, several locoweeds, alpine clovers and dwarf-primroses.

moss campion
purple mountain saxifrage

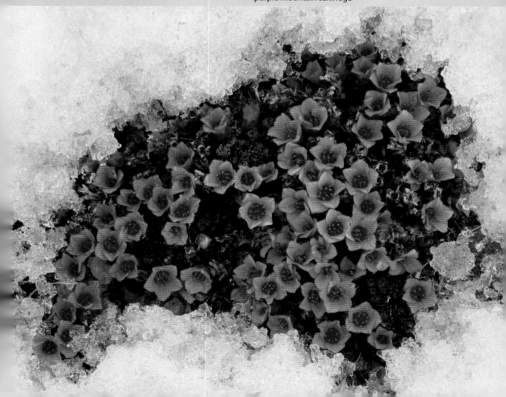

Grass-of-Parnassus Family (Parnassiaceae)

Parnassia was often included in Saxifragaceae, but it always was a poor fit. Some recent treatments—supported by chemical data—assigned the genus its own family, based in part on the distinctive flowers with 1-chambered ovaries and glandular, often elaborate, sterile stamens. But the molecular phylogenists have been busy, proposing in draft *FNA* treatment to place *Parnassia* in Celastraceae, the family that includes the familiar northwestern shrub falsebox (*Paxistima myrsinites*). They have some explaining to do, as Ricky Ricardo might have said to Lucy.

Fringed Grass-of-Parnassus • *Parnassia fimbriata*

General: Hairless perennial from a short, stout rhizome and fibrous roots; stems 1 to several, ascending to erect, 15–35 cm tall.

Leaves: Mostly basal, **kidney-shaped,** 2–6 cm wide, wider than long, glossy, green, heart-shaped at base, rounded at tip, on stalks 3–10 cm long, **margins untoothed; stem leaf solitary,** clasping, about **halfway or more up the stem.**

Flowers: **Single,** erect atop stems, bowl-shaped; petals 5, **white** with 5–7 greenish or yellowish veins, **fringed on lower half with hairs in comb-like arrangement,** 8–14 mm long, at least twice as long as the 5 **toothed or fringed sepals;** fertile stamens (the 5 with anthers) alternating with broad, succulent, **yellow, gland-tipped sterile stamens divided into 5–9 or more finger-like lobes without enlarged tips.**

Fruits: Capsules egg-shaped, about 1 cm long; seeds numerous, angled, with loose, inflated seed coats.

Where Found: Moist to wet meadows, forest glades, streambanks, wetlands and open seepage sites; rocky, drier habitats when on limestone; montane to alpine zones; frequent in the southern ¾ of the region; cordilleran.

Similar Species: Northern grass-of-Parnassus (*P. palustris*) has its **stem leaf attached usually below midstem, egg-shaped to nearly circular leaves and 7–13-veined petals without a marginal fringe.** It occurs in habitats similar (but typically richer in calcium) to those of fringed grass-of-Parnassus, in montane to subalpine zones. *P. palustris* is a circumpolar species, frequent and tending to replace *P. fimbriata* in the northern ½ of the region, south sporadically through interior BC to CA, AZ and NM. • **Mini grass-of-Parnassus (*P. kotzebuei*)** is **smaller (5–20 cm tall),** with egg-shaped leaves 1–3-veined at the base, **no stem leaf** and small, top-shaped flowers with **fringe-less petals 3–7 mm long,** about as long as the sepals. It grows in wet to moist meadows and on streambanks and sandy shores, in montane to alpine zones, and is frequent in the northern ½ of the region, inland of the Pacific coastal mountains and north of 54° N, scattered south to WA, NV and WY. An amphiberingian species, its range extends east across North America. • **Cascade grass-of-Parnassus (*P. cirrata* var. *intermedia*)** also has fringed petals, but its **sepals usually have entire margins** and its **sterile stamens are divided into 5–12 or more filaments with enlarged tips.** It is found in wet meadows, marshes and on streambanks, in montane to alpine zones, in WA, OR, CA, NV and ID.

mini grass-of-Parnassus

Notes: Inspired by the beauty of the flowers, Flemish botanist Mathias de l'Obel called *P. palustris* plants *gramen Parnassi*, meaning "grass (a general term for herbaceous plants with entire leaves) of Mt. Parnassus," the holy mountain of Apollo and the Muses in Greece.

northern grass-of-Parnassus

Western St. John's Wort
Hypericum scouleri ssp. *nortoniae*

General: Perennial from rhizomes and long runners; stems slender, erect, 5–20 cm tall, few-branched in the flower cluster, hairless.

Leaves: Opposite along stem, oblong-elliptic to egg-shaped, 1–2 cm long, hairless, **black, glandular dots near margin,** tip blunt to rounded.

Flowers: Solitary in leaf axils or a few in clusters atop stems, reddish in bud, wheel-shaped, 1–2 cm across; **petals 5, golden yellow, sometimes red-tinged,** with **marginal black glands,** wide-spreading, 7–14 mm long, at least twice the length of the 5 sepals; **stamens 50–100;** styles 3.

Fruits: Capsules membranous, lance-shaped, 6–10 mm long; seeds finely net-veined.

Where Found: Moist to wet meadows, lakeshores, streambanks and scree slopes; subalpine to lower alpine zones; infrequent in southern BC and southwestern AB to CA, AZ and CO; cordilleran.

Subspecies: The small, high-elevation form described above has been called *H. scouleri* ssp. *nortoniae* or *H. formosum* var. *nortoniae*. FNA declares that recent taxonomic work has revealed a range of intermediate forms between subspecies *nortoniae* and *scouleri*, thus there is no reason to maintain the 2 subspecies. Nonetheless, high-elevation plants look distinctive, and we continue to refer them as ssp. *nortoniae*.

Notes: The dark red compounds hypericin and pseudohypericin are responsible for the colour of the gland-dots in this genus. They are photosensitizing chemicals that cause blistering on the muzzles of grazing animals. *Hypericum perforatum*, which is introduced in North America, is the chief trouble-maker. The species is also increasingly used as an antidepressant, though we still don't know what the active ingredients are. • *Hypericum* could be from the Greek *hyper*, "above, over, on," and *ereike*, "of the heath," because European St. John's wort grows on heathlands or waste land with poor drainage and peaty or coarse soils. Alternatively, it might be from the Greek *hyper*, "above," and *eikon*, "image," alluding to the ancient custom of decorating religious figures with *Hypericum* species to ward off evil spirits. It was believed that St. John's wort (probably *H. perforatum*) gathered on St. John's Day (June 24) and hung in the window would protect the house against thunder and evil spirits, for which the devil punctured holes in the leaves with a needle in retaliation.

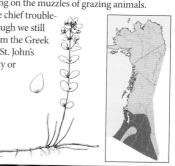

Poppy Family (Papaveraceae)

The poppy family in our region is small but spectacular, featuring several species in the genus *Papaver*. Poppies are loosely tufted perennials with coloured sap; the stems are erect to sprawling, 5–30 cm tall, leafless and hairy. The pinnately lobed or divided leaves are all at the base of the stem and are usually hairy. The solitary flowers sit atop the stems, nodding in bud, erect to spreading in bloom, showy and saucer- to bowl-shaped. There are usually 4 yellow to pale pink or white petals, 2 sepals (soon deciduous) and numerous stamens. The stigmas are flattened lobes or rays on a disc atop the 1-chambered ovary, radiating like spokes on a wagon wheel. The fruits are barrel- to egg- or top-shaped capsules, often with dark or pale, coarse hairs, opening by small pores at the top, like a saltshaker. The seeds are small and numerous (i.e., poppy seeds).

Key to *Papaver*

1a. Leaves 3-lobed, mostly hairless; flowers white or pale yellow . . . . *P. walpolei* (p. 162)

1b. Leaves 5- to many-lobed, mostly hairy; flowers mostly yellow (whitish to pinkish in some) 2

    2a. Capsules >4 times longer than wide . . . . *P. macounii* ssp. *discolor* (below)

    2b. Capsules 1–2.5 times as long as wide 3

        3a. Capsule bristle-hairs ivory-coloured; flowers yellow or white to pinkish 4

            4a. Plants usually >20 cm tall; flowers yellow to whitish, to 6 cm across; plants of central AK and central YT
            . . . . *P. nudicaule* ssp. *americanum* (below)

            4b. Plants usually <15 cm tall; flowers rose to salmon pink or whitish to orange-yellow, to 2.5 cm across 5

                5a. Leaves bristly-hairy; flowers rose to salmon pink or whitish; plants of the northwest (south-
                central AK, southwestern YT, northwestern BC) . . . . *P. alboroseum* (p. 162)

                5b. Leaves hairless or sparsely hairy; flowers yellow to orange-pink; plants of the southeast (south-
                western AB, southeastern BC, northwestern MT) . . . . *P. pygmaeum* (p. 162)

        3b. Capsule bristle hairs brownish to black; flowers yellow 6

            6a. Leaves with 5–7 primary lobes; lobes mostly undivided; capsules egg- to rugby-ball-shaped
            . . . . *P. radicatum* (p. 161)

            6b. Leaves with >5 primary lobes; lobes mostly divided again 7

                7a. Flowering stems straight, erect, mostly >20 cm tall; capsules oblong-ellipsoid
                . . . . *P. lapponicum* (p. 161)

                7b. Flowering stems curved, ascending or reclining, <15 cm tall/long; capsules barrel- to top-
                shaped (like an upside-down traffic cone) . . . . *P. mcconnellii* (p. 161)

Macoun's Poppy • *Papaver macounii* ssp. *discolor*

General: In loose tufts, nearly hairless to hairy; flowering stems 1 to few, to 35 cm tall.

Leaves: Long-stalked, to 12 cm long, brown-hairy to nearly hairless; blades oblong to lance-shaped, divided into **2–3 pairs of main lateral lobes,** upper surface dark green, lower surface pale green.

Flowers: To 5 cm across, **yellow;** stigmatic disc conic, rays 4–6, converging to a small but prominent point.

Fruits: Capsules 1–2.5 cm long, club-shaped, **more than 4 times longer than broad,** with stiff, appressed, **brownish hairs.**

Where Found: Mesic tundra and fellfields; lowland (arctic coast) to alpine zones; frequent in the northern ⅓ of the region; arctic-alpine, amphiberingian.

Similar Species: Boreal poppy (*P. nudicaule* ssp. *americanum*) also is relatively tall (to 40 cm) and has large, yellow or whitish flowers, but differs in its grey-green leaf undersurfaces and its **nearly globe- to football-shaped capsules,** to 1.5 cm long, **to 2.5 times longer than broad,** with stiff, appressed, **ivory-coloured hairs.** It grows on dry, gravelly banks, rocky slopes, outcrops and ridges, in montane to lower alpine zones. This endemic subspecies is rare or infrequent in central AK and central YT.

Notes: Macoun's poppy is also known as *Papaver keelei* and *P. scammanianum.*

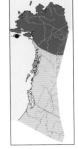

Arctic Poppy • *Papaver radicatum*

General: Flowering stems curved, erect or ascending, **mostly less than 15 cm tall,** with light-coloured, coarse hairs.

Leaves: Green, not glaucous on both surfaces, hairy, usually **with 5–7 primary lobes, the lobes themselves usually undivided.**

Flowers: Showy, 2–6 cm across, **yellow;** stigmatic disc convex, with 4–7 rays.

Fruits: Capsules egg- to rugby-ball-shaped (sometimes top-shaped), 1–1.5 cm long, **1–2.5 times as long as broad,** brown-hairy.

Where Found: Rocky slopes and ridges, gravelly shores, fellfields, scree, talus and tundra; lowland (arctic coast) to alpine zones; frequent in the northern ⅓ of the region, infrequent southward, especially in the Rockies; arctic-alpine, circumpolar.

Subspecies: Ssp. *radicatum* (*P. lapponicum* ssps. *labradoricum, occidentale* and *porsildii, P. nigroflavum, P. nudicaule* var. *labradoricum, P. radicatum* var. *labradoricum, P. radicatum* ssps. *occidentale* and *porsildii*) is the northern circumpolar subspecies. • **Ssp.** *kluanensis* (*P. kluanensis*) is the more southerly, cordilleran subspecies. Where their ranges overlap in southern AK and YT, they can be distinguished by flower size: ssp. *kluanensis* has flowers 2 cm or less across, whereas ssp. *radicatum* has flowers more than 2 cm across.

Similar Species: McConnell's poppy (*P. mcconnellii; P. denalii*) also has **short, curved, often reclining stems less than15 cm tall/long.** But it has **glaucous, grey- or blue-green leaves with usually 7 primary lobes, the lobes themselves mostly divided; large, yellow flowers** to 6 cm across; and **barrel- to top-shaped capsules** to 1.5 cm long, 1–2.5 times as long as wide and brown-hairy. It grows on calcium-rich rock outcrops, ridges, shaly scree and talus slopes, in

subalpine and alpine zones. An endemic arctic-alpine species, it is locally frequent in central and northern AK, YT and northwestern NT. • **Lapland poppy** (*P. lapponicum; P. hultenii, P. radicatum* ssp. *lapponicum*) has **taller (20–35 cm), straight, erect stems** with grey-green to green leaves that are white-hairy on both surfaces; **flowers to 3.5 cm across** with **yellow petals,** sometimes with pink tips, and **oblong-ellipsoid capsules** to 2 cm long, 1–2.5 times as long as broad and brown-hairy. It grows on steep, rocky slopes, gravel bars, shores and tundra, in lowland (arctic coast) to alpine zones. A nearly circumpolar arctic-alpine species, it is frequent in the northern ⅓ of the region, in northern AK, YT and NT, and rare in northern BC.

Notes: Judging from the many synonyms, this and some other northern poppies have had a rocky taxonomy. In our opinion, *FNA's* treatment is still provisional. Even if you are uncertain about species identification, you can always revel in arctic-alpine poppies, in their bright flowers and the brave face they present to the highest elevations and the most extreme habitats.

Lapland poppy (both photos)   McConnell's poppy

Pale Poppy • *Papaver alboroseum*

General: In small, hairy tufts; flowering stems curved, reclining to erect, 5–15 cm long/tall. **Leaves:** Grey-green on both surfaces, white- to brown-hairy, **1–2 pairs of primary lateral lobes. Flowers:** To 2.5 cm across, rose to salmon pink or whitish with yellow blotch at the base; stigmatic disc convex, with 5–7 rays. **Fruits:** Capsules roundish to rugby-ball-shaped, 1–1.3 cm long, 1–2 times as long as broad, **ivory-hairy. Where Found:** Shaly scree, ash and cinder slopes, gravelly ridges, rocky

tundra, sandy-gravelly outwash and riverbars; lowland (glacier forelands) to alpine zones; infrequent in the northwestern and central parts of the region; amphiberingian.

Similar Species: Walpole's poppy (*P. walpolei*) is also small with pale (white or pale yellow) flowers but has **hairless, dark green leaves** mostly with **3 primary lobes** and **top-shaped, dark-hairy capsules.** It is infrequent but locally abundant on rocky ridges, talus and scree slopes, fellfields, tundra and gravel bars, especially in limestone terrain, in subalpine and alpine zones. An amphiberingian arctic-alpine species, it is found in western and northern AK, and north-central YT. • **Pygmy poppy** (*P. pygmaeum;*

P. radicatum var. *pygmaeum*) is most similar to pale poppy but has **hairless or sparsely hairy leaves, yellow to**

salmon or orange-pink flowers and is a southern plant. It grows on rocky ridges and talus and scree slopes in the alpine zone. Pygmy poppy is endemic and infrequent in the high Rockies of southeastern BC, southwestern AB and northwestern MT.

Notes: Pale poppy is also known as Portage poppy because it is frequent and well-known on gravelly outwash at the toe of Portage Glacier near Anchorage, Alaska.

Walpole's poppy   pygmy poppy (both photos)

POPPY FLOWERS AS PARABOLIC HEATERS

The flowers of arctic poppy are shaped like satellite dishes and they track the sun daily—indeed, for 24 hours each day where there is midnight sun—with the petals reflecting the sun's light and heat toward the ovary. The petals have special epidermal cells designed to focus light inward toward the centre of the flower. In studies, flowers with their petals removed did not track the sun, and their ovaries were as much as 6°C cooler than flowers with petals. The petal-less flowers also produced fewer, smaller seeds. Insect pollinators of arctic poppy sometimes stop to warm themselves by basking inside the flowers. Several other alpines such as cinquefoils, mountain-avens, buttercups and anemones have similarly shaped flowers that probably also function as parabolic reflectors.

Northern Geranium
Geranium erianthum

General: Hairy perennial from a thick rhizome and stout stem-base; stems erect to ascending, 20–80 cm tall.

Leaves: Basal leaves few, **deeply palmately divided** into 3–7 irregularly toothed segments, 2–10 cm long, wider than long, long-stalked, appressed-hairy; stem leaves similar, opposite, unstalked.

Flowers: Cluster of 2–5 atop the stem, **saucer-shaped, 4–6 cm across; petals 5, blue to pinkish purple** (rarely white), with darker veins, 1.5–2 cm long, fringed and hairy on inner surface toward base; sepals 5, about ½ as long as petals, bristle-tipped; stamens 10, filaments long-hairy; ovary deeply 5-lobed, 5-chambered; styles 5.

Fruits: Capsules 5-parted, **elastic, splitting at maturity;** styles fused to form a central column that, when dry, splits into 5 single-seeded segments, each suddenly recoiling and carrying with it part of the capsule, simultaneously flinging out the seed (somewhat like a catapult).

Where Found: Moist, open forests, meadows, roadsides, clearings, streambanks and avalanche tracks; montane to alpine zones; frequent in the northwestern part of the region mostly in the coastal mountains, infrequent inland; amphiberingian.

northern geranium

tall larkspur

mountain monkshood

Similar Species: The leaves of northern geranium could be confused with those of **tall larkspur** (p. 198) and **mountain monkshood** (p. 197), which can occur in the same meadows, but the leaves of the larkspur and the monkshood are sparsely hairy or hairless (see also leaf silhouettes, left). • The white-flowered **Richardson's geranium** (*G. richardsonii*) and the pink-flowered **sticky geranium** (*G. viscosissimum*) both can occur in subalpine meadows in the southeastern part of the region, but both species are typically found at low to moderate elevations.

Notes: The Dena'ina would boil or soak the roots in hot water and drink or gargle with the liquid to treat sore throats, mouth sores, ulcers, diarrhea and heart problems and to increase urine flow. This tea was also given to new mothers and their children to cleanse their systems. Other groups boiled the leaves and drank the tea for stomach trouble and tuberculosis. When cooled, the tea could be applied to sore eyes. • *Geranium* comes from the Greek *geranion*, which in turn comes from *geranos*, meaning "a crane", in reference to the fruit's long beak (like a crane's bill). *Erianthum* means "woolly flower" and refers to the hairy blossoms.

Rose Family (Rosaceae)

Members of the rose family worldwide are trees, shrubs (often thorny) or herbs. They have alternate, simple or pinnately compound leaves usually with **stipules** (appendages at the base of the leaf stalk). The flowers are radially symmetric, typically with 5 sepals united at the base (collectively called the **calyx**), 5 free petals arising from a cup- or saucer-like structure (called the **hypanthium**, formed by the fused bases of the sepals) atop the flower stalk, numerous stamens in several whorls and 1 compound or several simple ovaries. The fruits of our rose family herbs include dry achenes and follicles or raspberry-like aggregations of drupelets.

Key to the Genera of Rosaceae

1a. Plants with woody stems . . . . including *Dryas, Kelseya, Luetkea* (see Shrubs, pp. 66–71)

1b. Plants perennial herbs; some slightly woody at the base 2

   2a. Petals lacking; flowers in a spike atop stem . . . . *Sanguisorba stipulata* (p. 166)

   2b. Petals present; flowers not in terminal spikes 3

      3a. Stamens 5; ovaries 2–15 4

         4a. Leaves palmately compound with 3 leaflets toothed at tip . . . . *Sibbaldia procumbens* (p. 167)

         4b. Leaves pinnately compound with 20 or more divided leaflets . . . . *Ivesia* (p. 166)

      3b. Stamens and ovaries numerous 5

         5a. Fruits fleshy . . . . *Rubus* (below, p. 165)

         5b. Fruits dry 6

            6a. Styles persistent, elongate and often feathery-hairy in fruit. . . . . *Geum* (pp. 167–168)

            6b. Styles deciduous or short and inconspicuous in fruit, not feathery-hairy . . . *Potentilla* (pp. 169–177)

Cloudberry, Bakeapple
Rubus chamaemorus

General: Somewhat similar to nagoonberry (opposite); dwarf herb from a slender, long-creeping rhizome; flowering shoots 10–30 cm tall. **Leaves: 1–3, round-kidney-shaped, shallowly 5–7-lobed, somewhat leathery, margins finely sawtoothed. Flowers:** Solitary, unisexual, male and female flowers on separate plants; **petals white, 7–18 mm long. Fruits:** Raspberry-like; reddish at first, **amber to yellow when ripe,** 1.2–1.5 cm wide. **Where Found:** Bogs and wet peaty tundra, usually with sphagnum moss; lowland (arctic coast) and mostly montane but extending into subalpine and alpine zones in the north; frequent in the northern ½ of the region, infrequent southward; low-arctic, circumpolar.

Notes: Cloudberries are collected in large amounts by all northern peoples in the fall and stored frozen in the tundra for winter use. The Gwich'in stored the fruits in birchbark baskets under tundra moss to prevent them from freezing too hard. Highly prized by northerners, the berries were eaten raw with seal oil or, more recently, with sugar. The berries have a baked-apple taste, hence the alternative common name "bakeapple." They are a rich source of vitamin C, which is retained if the berries are frozen shortly after harvest. • Nectar is secreted by the male but not the female flowers. The most frequent insect visitors are flies. • "Cloudberry" is from the Old English *clud*, meaning "rock" or "hill," and presumably alludes to the plant's rocky northern or mountainous habitat in Europe.

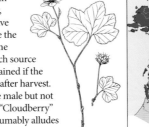

Nagoonberry • *Rubus arcticus*

General: Dwarf herb (rarely somewhat woody at base) from a slender rhizome; annual flowering shoots erect, 5–15 cm tall, several, tufted, finely **soft-hairy.**

Leaves: Alternate, deciduous, 2–5 per flowering shoot, long-stalked, **palmately compound or shallowly lobed; leaflets or lobes 3,** usually rounded at tip, **coarsely sawtoothed,** greenish on both surfaces, smooth to hairy above, paler and usually hairy beneath especially on the veins.

Flowers: Showy, star- to bowl-shaped, usually 1–3, on stalks atop the shoots; **petals usually 5, pink to reddish pink,** narrowly egg- to spoon-shaped, 1–1.5 (<2) cm long, erect to spreading; sepals (calyx lobes) narrowly triangular to lance-shaped, 5–13 mm long, bent back; stamens 30–40.

Fruits: Druplets **raspberry-like,** fleshy, coherent in a **red to purplish cluster,** about 1 cm across.

Where Found: Peatlands, wet thickets, meadows, open forests and peaty tundra; montane to alpine zones; frequent north of 49° N and mostly in and east of the coastal mountains, infrequent southward; the species complex circumpolar.

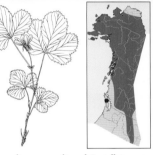

Subspecies: Ssp. *arcticus* (amphiberingian-Eurasian) has **1–3 flowers usually standing above the leaves,** the triangular **sepals hairy and glandular. •** Ssp. *acaulis* (also known as dwarf raspberry; widespread in North America) has usually **1 flower not overtopping the leaves,** the **sepals mostly hairless, not glandular,** long and narrow but expanded toward the tip. • Ssp. *stellatus* (amphiberingian) has **3-lobed leaves rather than 3 leaflets** and solitary, **larger flowers,** the petals to 2 cm long.

Notes: The latter 2 subspecies of nagoonberry are also known as *Rubus acaulis* ssp. *acaulis* and *R. stellatus* ssp. *stellatus*, respectively. • The berries are collected and eaten fresh; they are highly prized for their superior taste by northern peoples but are generally not stored because they are difficult to harvest in large amounts. • "Nagoon" is from the Tlingit word *neigoon*. *Rubus* is the ancient Latin name for bramble, based on *ruber*, "red."

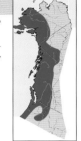

Sitka Burnet • *Sanguisorba stipulata*

General: Hairless herb from stout rhizomes; stems erect to ascending, 20–100 cm tall.

Leaves: Mostly basal, blades 5–35 cm long, **pinnately compound,** divided into **9–21 egg-shaped to oblong, coarsely sawtoothed leaflets,** long-stalked with membranous stipules; stem leaves 1–3, alternate, much smaller.

Flowers: Numerous (15–300 or more), small, saucer-shaped, in a **dense, cylindric spike (sometimes tapering at the top),** 5–12 cm long, atop stem; **petals absent;** calyx with **4 whitish lobes,** oval, 2.5–3 mm long; **stamens 4,** white, filaments somewhat dilated upward, **much longer (at least 3 times) than calyx lobes.**

Fruits: Achenes enclosed in the **4-angled, slightly winged calyx base.**

Where Found: Fens, swamps, streambanks, meadows, glades, thickets and seepage areas; lowland to lower alpine zones; frequent in much of the region south of 63° N; amphiberingian.

Notes: Sitka burnet is also known as *Sanguisorba canadensis* ssp. *latifolia* and *S. sitchensis.* • *Sanguisorba* is from the Latin *sanguis,* "blood," and *sorbeo,* "to soak up," probably alluding to its traditional Eurasian use to stanch bleeding, intimated by the dark red flowers of some species and the medieval Doctrine of Signatures. Herbalists recommend that the leaves be made into a tea and that root decoctions can be used for internal and external bleeding, dysentery or genital discharges. • "Burnet" is Middle English meaning "dark brown" (from the French *brunette*) and refers to the rich, reddish brown colour of the flowers of some species of *Sanguisorba.*

Gordon's Ivesia • *Ivesia gordonii*

General: Tufted herb from a stout taproot and stem-base covered with blackish leaf bases; **flowering stems erect or ascending,** 5–20 cm tall, with 1 leaf or leafless.

Leaves: Mostly basal, numerous, bright green, glandular-hairy, **pinnately compound (fern-like)** with 20 or more crowded, **overlapping leaflets,** each deeply divided into several oblong lobes 3–10 mm long.

Flowers: Small, **top- to bell-shaped,** several to many in **ball-like heads** atop stems; petals 5, **yellow fading to whitish,** spoon-shaped, 1.5–3 mm long, **shorter than or equal to sepals;** sepals yellowish, erect, triangular, alternating with linear mini-bracts; stamens 5.

Fruits: Achenes 2–4 (to 6), flattened, egg-shaped, smooth, brownish, about 2 mm long.

Where Found: Gravelly river benches and banks, rocky, exposed ridges, talus slopes, dry meadows and fellfields; montane to alpine zones; locally frequent in the Rocky Mtn states, Cascades and Sierras, from WA to MT south to CO, UT and CA; cordilleran.

Similar Species: Tweedy's ivesia (*I. tweedyi*) has shallowly **bowl-shaped flowers** with **petals equal to or slightly longer than the sepals.** It occupies similar habitats (often on serpentine rock) in central WA, northern ID and adjacent MT.

Notes: *Ivesia* commemorates Dr. Eli Ives (1779–1861), an American physician and botanist; *gordonii* acknowledges Alexander Gordon (ca 1795–?), an English horticulturist and collector of North American plants.

Sibbaldia • *Sibbaldia procumbens*

General: **Dwarf herb** from a branched stem-base and spreading, woody rhizomes; stems many, **spreading-ascending to prostrate, tufted or mat-forming,** 2–15 cm long, whiskery-hairy.

Leaves: Basal and alternate along stems, long-stalked, **palmately compound; leaflets 3, wedge-shaped, 5–30 mm long, squared-off and 3- to 5-toothed at the tip,** often purplish beneath, sparsely appressed-hairy on both surfaces.

Flowers: Small, star- to saucer-shaped, 3–12 in stalked, leafy-bracted clusters in leaf axils and atop stems, flowering shoots often shorter than leaves; **petals 5, pale yellow, lance-shaped, 1–2 mm long,** set in a considerably **larger, green calyx;** sepals triangular, 2.5–5 mm long, stiff-hairy, alternating with lance-shaped mini-bracts; **stamens 5,** alternate with petals.

Fruits: Achenes 5–15, egg- to pear-shaped, smooth, brown, about 1.5 mm long.

Where Found: Dry to moist, gravelly meadows, rock outcrops and ridges, snowbeds, fellfields, tundra and disturbed soils; montane to alpine zones; frequent throughout, except rare north of 65° N; subarctic-alpine, circumpolar with large gaps.

Notes: Is it sibbaldia or is it one of those alpine cinquefoils? Check the flower—sibbaldia has 5 stamens and tiny petals (less than 3 mm long); cinquefoils have more than 10 stamens and usually conspicuous flowers (petals more than 5 mm long). • Sibbaldia has been called a "snowbed specialist," a species that does well in areas with later snowmelt. This species and Rocky Mountain snow buttercup (p. 194) have leaf expansion schedules that are synchronized with snowmelt, likely giving them a competitive advantage under most climate-change scenarios. • *Sibbaldia* is named after Sir Robert Sibbald (1641–1722), a Scottish naturalist and physician, and the first professor of medicine at the University of Edinburgh.

Caltha-leaved Avens
Geum calthifolium

General: Hairy herb 10–35 cm tall. **Leaves:** Mostly basal, long-stalked, with **1 big, rounded leaflet at the top and 1–3 (to 7) tiny leaflets below. Flowers:** Large, saucer-shaped, 1–2 (to 4) atop leafless or few-leaved stems; petals yellow, 9–13 mm long. **Fruits:** Achenes numerous, bristly-hairy, beaked with **long (1–1.5 cm), straight, hairy styles. Where Found:** Bogs, wet, rocky slopes, heathlands and meadows; lowland to (mostly) subalpine and alpine zones; infrequent but locally abundant on Pacific coastal islands and adjacent mainland; amphiberingian.

Similar Species: If you are scrambling on the highest peaks of Haida Gwaii and you find an avens with leaves that have a **big, 3-lobed terminal leaflet and 6–14 smaller lateral leaflets,** it should be **Queen Charlotte avens (*G. schofieldii*),** one of the species originally known only from these misty isles but subsequently found on the Brooks Peninsula on northwestern Vancouver I. It is one of the most attractive but rarest and least-seen species of avens in North America. Found on wet cliffs and in rock crevices and runnels, it is named after legendary BC bryologist Wilf Schofield (1927–2008).

Queen Charlotte avens

Alpine Avens, Ross' Avens
Geum rossii

General: Tufted, from thick, scaly rhizomes and stout stem-bases covered with remains of old leaves; flowering stems erect, 5–30 cm tall, low at first, elongating in fruit, with short (to 1 mm), spreading hairs on the upper part.

Leaves: Numerous and crowded at the base, short-stalked, short-hairy to nearly hairless, erect to spreading, **interruptedly pinnately divided**, 3–13 cm long, the blades elliptic-oblong, with **7 or more pairs of entire to coarsely toothed main leaflets** (which do not lie flat), the **top leaflet similar to the lateral ones**; stem leaves several, alternate, much smaller.

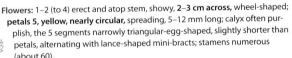

Flowers: 1–2 (to 4) erect and atop stem, showy, **2–3 cm across**, wheel-shaped; **petals 5, yellow, nearly circular**, spreading, 5–12 mm long; calyx often purplish, the 5 segments narrowly triangular-egg-shaped, slightly shorter than petals, alternating with lance-shaped mini-bracts; stamens numerous (about 60).

Fruits: Achenes narrowly spindle-shaped, stiffly coarse-hairy, the styles persistent, **2–5 mm long,** straight, smooth; several to many in a hemispheric head.

Where Found: Stony tundra, meadows, snowbeds and fellfields, often in calcium-rich soils; montane to alpine zones; frequent in the north (mostly unglaciated AK, YT and NT) and again in the Rocky Mtn states, disjunct in the Wenatchee and Wallowa Mtns; arctic-alpine, amphiberingian.

Similar Species: Glacier avens (*G. glaciale*) is **hairier**, with **long (2–5 mm), soft, yellowish hairs** on the stems and the undersurface of leaves. It has **larger flowers (3–4.5 cm across)**, with **5–9 (most often 7) petals** (other *Geum* species nearly always have 5 petals). It grows on dry, stony tundra and heathlands, mostly north of 64° N in AK and YT. The showy flowers bloom very soon after snowmelt. • **Old man's whiskers** or prairie smoke (*G. triflorum*) occasionally extends into meadows above treeline. It has distinctive **nodding, bell-shaped flowers** with **pink, cream or reddish purple petals** and achenes with **very long, feathery-hairy styles**. Ranging from southern YT and NT to CA and NM, it reaches high elevations mostly in the Rockies.

glacier avens (both photos)   old man's whiskers (both photos)

Notes: The leaves of alpine avens turn red or bronze in autumn and can put on quite a display where it dominates tundra slopes. • Alpine avens engages in "extreme pre-formation." In other words, it initiates leaves and flowers at least 2 years prior to their full maturity; in Colorado, leaf and flower clusters develop over a period of 3 years. • The fine roots of alpine avens reduce the growth of tufted hairgrass (p. 465), sometimes a tundra co-dominant with the avens, in at least 2 ways: phenolic exudates directly inhibit growth, and the carbon in the cellulose indirectly inhibits growth, perhaps by stimulating the growth of soil microbes and so reducing the soil nitrogen available for the hairgrass. This could be an important mechanism in structuring alpine plant communities. • James Clark Ross (1800–62) was an arctic and antarctic explorer.

The Genus *Potentilla* (Cinquefoil)

Potentilla is one of the largest genera in the rose family, with about 400 mostly herbaceous species worldwide, nearly 100 of which occur in North America, mostly in temperate and cold climates. The alpine flora of our region includes more than 20 cinquefoil species, excluding the polysyllabic shrub formerly known as *Potentilla fruticosa* or *Pentaphylloides floribunda*, now *Dasiphora fruticosa* (p. 71).

Alpine cinquefoils are all perennial herbs, typically from a taproot or rhizome surmounted by a scaly stem-base, and with mostly basal, palmately or pinnately compound leaves, the leaflets with sawtoothed or dissected margins. The flowers consist of 3 whorls—mini-bracts, sepals and petals—that are fused at the base into a disc- or cup-shaped

structure called the **hypanthium.** Five mini-bracts form the outermost whorl. The middle whorl is composed of 5 sepals, usually larger than the mini-bracts. The innermost whorl consists of **5 usually yellow petals.** The stamens usually number about 20 and are attached to the rim of the hypanthium. Numerous ovaries are attached to a central knob, the receptacle. A nectar-secreting disc usually lines the inside of the hypanthium. The fruit is a cluster of achenes attached to the dry receptacle.

Potentilla comes from the Latin *potens*, "powerful," and *illus*, "little," in reference to the slight medicinal properties of common silverweed (*P. anserina*). Alternatively, in Europe of the Middle Ages, common silverweed was known as "little powerful one," a medicinal herb deployed against witches and in a love divination, as well as a remedy for all ills. "Cinquefoil" comes from the French *cinq* and *feuilles* or the Latin *cinque foliola*, both meaning "five leaves."

dwarf cinquefoil

Potentilla is another taxonomically challenging genus. Key factors include the usual suspects: a broad geographic distribution and ecological amplitude in topographically complex environments, combined with frequent hybridization and backcrossing, asexual reproduction ("apomixis"—the production of seeds without fertilization) and polyploidy. The genus was one of those studied in detail in the classic reciprocal transplant studies of Jens Clausen, David Keck and William Hiesey (1940), whose decades of research explored the nature of variation and the biological complexity in widespread perennial plants such as *Potentilla glandulosa* and *Achillea millefolium*. But cinquefoil taxonomy was never going to be straightforward, depending as it does on the species concept of the investigator and relying so much on notoriously variable characteristics such as leaf shape and hairiness. Floral morphology is rather uniform in *Potentilla*—the flower features are of limited taxonomic use, with the exception of calyx mini-bracts and

arctic cinquefoil

petal colour or size. Leaf characteristics such as the number and arrangement of leaflets, leaflet teeth and hairiness are much more important. Although some of them aren't bald, *Potentilla* taxonomists place great stock in hairs, as do specialists in *Salix* and *Draba*.

The 2008 draft *FNA* treatment of *Potentilla* serves up many changes to the circumscription and names of North American *Potentilla* species. Some represent major and perhaps unrecognizable departures from long-standing treatments in most existing western regional manuals. Do not be unduly alarmed, but brace yourself for some disorientation and recalibration. Especially at high elevations, where multi-species clusters—often partitioned by microhabitat—can occur in habitats such as alpine fellfields and tundra. Given the taxonomic flux, we regard the revised *FNA* treatment as provisional. Unravelling the evolutionary ganglion of our closely related arctic-alpine *Potentilla* could take a while; moreover, there are few taxonomists and many other tempting puzzles and problems.

"The western cordillera, from arctic Alaska to the mountains of Mexico, contains a rich trove of diversity in need of further investigation, with isolated mountain ranges and complex geology providing a prime setting for island biogeography and accompanying radiation in *Potentilla*" (*FNA* draft).

Key to *Potentilla*

1a. Leaves palmately compound, mostly with 3 leaflets. 2

    2a. Leaves not woolly on either side. 3

        3a. Leaflets toothed to no more than halfway to midvein, not deeply cleft or divided 4

            4a. Flowering stems 10–30 cm tall, erect; leaflets broadly wedge- to fan-shaped, at most sparsely hairy; mostly south of 51° N . . . . *P. flabellifolia* (p. 172)

            4b. Flowering stems usually <10 cm tall, sprawling to erect; leaflets broadly egg-shaped, soft-hairy especially on lower surface; mostly north of 51° N (outlier population of *P. hyparctica* in southwestern MT and northwestern WY) . . . *P. nana, P. hyparctica* (p. 172)

        3b. Leaflets divided usually halfway or more to midvein. 5

            5a. Leaflets small, 3–7 mm long, usually divided about halfway to the midvein into narrowly oblong lobes; petals 3–4 mm long . . . . *P. elegans* (p. 172)

            5b. Leaflets large, 1–6 cm long, divided to the base into linear lobes; petals 5–10 mm long . . . . *P. biflora* (p. 173)

    2b. Leaves white-, grey- or yellowish-woolly (felt-like) on the lower surface. 6

        6a. Leaf stalks and lower stem cobwebby white-woolly (with short, felted hairs) 7

            7a. Leaf stalks with long, straight, silky hairs and short, felted hairs . . . . *P. "subgorodkovii"* (see *P. uniflora* group, p. 174)

            7b. Leaf stalks and lower stem lacking long, silky hairs. 8

               8a. Calyx mini-bracts elliptic or lanceolate, nearly as broad as sepals; leaflets not over-lapping, central leaflet with 2–5 teeth per side, upper surface greenish, not densely hairy. . . . . *P. nivea* (p. 174)

               8b. Calyx mini-bracts linear, much narrower than sepals; leaflets overlapping, central leaflet with mostly 4–8 teeth per side, upper surface greyish, mostly densely hairy . . . . *P. crebridens* ssp. *hemicryophila* (p. 174)

        6b. Leaf stalks and lower stem with long, silky hairs but not short-woolly or felted 9

            9a. Long hairs of leaf stalks sparse; central leaflets mostly distinctly stalked; flowers usually few to many (3–15). . . . . *P. arenosa* (p. 175)

            9b. Long hairs of leaf stalks dense; central leaflets not distinctly stalked; flowers 1 to several (3–7). 10

               10a. Calyx mini-bracts broad (2–5 mm), egg-shaped; flowers mostly 3–7; leaflets with 3–7 teeth per side, the teeth rounded with bent-down margins . . *P. villosa* (p. 173)

               10b. Calyx mini-bracts narrower (1–3 mm), oblong or broadly lance-shaped to elliptic; flowers mostly 1–3; leaflets with 2–3 teeth per side, the teeth pointy-tipped with scarcely bent-down margins 11

                  11a. Leaflets densely silky-hairy on upper surface; calyx mini-bracts narrowly elliptic, 2–3.5 mm wide; flowers mostly 2–3 . . . . *P. villosula* (p. 173)

                  11b. Leaflets sparsely hairy on upper surface; calyx mini-bracts lance-shaped, 0.8–2 mm wide; flowers mostly 1 12

                      12a. Stem-base branches densely columnar, covered with stipules and persistent whole leaves . . . . *P. subvahliana* (p. 173)

                      12b. Stem-base branches not densely columnar, covered with stipules and sometimes also leaf stalks, but not whole leaves . . . . *P. "vulcanicola"* (see *P. uniflora* group, p. 174)

1b. Leaves palmately or pinnately compound, usually with 5 or more leaflets 13

    13a. Basal leaves palmately compound 14

        14a. Stems ascending-erect, often >20 cm tall; leaves greenish to white-woolly on lower surface. 15

            15a. Plants 10–40 cm tall; leaflets 5–7, mostly 1–3 cm long, usually green, bluish green, or sparsely greyish-silky on both surfaces. . . . . *P. glaucophylla* (p. 175)

            15b. Plants 30–80 cm tall; leaflets 7–9, 3–9 cm long, either white-woolly or greenish on lower surface. . . . . *P. gracilis* (p. 175)

villous cinquefoil

Principal Leaves Mostly with 3 Leaflets

Hairs, or lack of them, are key to this circle of cinquefoils. The 5 species in the first group (pp. 172–173) aren't strongly hairy and their leaves are greenish on both surfaces. The second, difficult group (pp. 173–175) is very hairy, with at least the undersurface of the leaves grey- to white-woolly (felt-like) and the leaf stalks and lower flowering stems variously hairy as well.

Fan-leaved Cinquefoil
Potentilla flabellifolia

General: Stems 10–30 cm tall. Leaves: Long-stalked (leaf stalks 2–3 times as long as blades), green on both surfaces, not white-woolly beneath; **leaflets broadly wedge- to fan-shaped,** unevenly and deeply blunt-toothed except at the base, **at most sparsely hairy. Flowers: 1–5;** petals heart-shaped, **6–12 mm long,** notched at tip. **Where Found:** Moist to wet meadows, glades, heathlands, streambanks, shores and scree slopes; montane to lower alpine zones; frequent in the southern ¼ of the region; cordilleran.

Arctic Cinquefoil • *Potentilla hyparctica*

General: Stems 2–20 cm but usually less than 10 cm tall. Leaves: Long-stalked (stalks to 2 times as long as blades), green on both surfaces, not woolly beneath; **leaflets egg-shaped,** coarsely but **evenly toothed** ⅓–½ **the distance to the midrib, sparsely to moderately hairy,** often also glandular. **Flowers:** 1–3 (to 5); petals pale to bright yellow, heart-shaped, **4–9 mm long;** filaments to 1.1 mm long; styles 0.6–0.9 mm long. **Where Found:** Rock outcrops, heathlands, meadows, fellfields, scree and talus slopes, solifluction lobes and tundra, mainly on acidic bedrock; lowland (arctic coast) to alpine zones; frequent in the north-ern inland ¾ of the region, disjunct in the Beartooth Mtns of MT and WY; arctic-alpine, circumpolar.

Subspecies: The high arctic **ssp. *hyparctica*** is 2–12 cm tall and very hairy, with calyx mini-bracts 1.5–2 mm wide; the low arctic–cordilleran **ssp. *elatior*** is 4–20 cm tall and sparsely hairy, with calyx mini-bracts 2–5 mm wide.

Similar Species: Dwarf cinquefoil (*P. nana*; *P. emarginata* ssp. *nana*, *P. hyparctica* in part) has **slightly longer styles (over 1 mm) and filaments (longer than 1.2 mm),** and a largely coastal range. It is found on heathlands, gravelly slopes, ridge crests, fellfields, scree and talus, in lowland to alpine zones, in coastal BC and AK.

Notes: Arctic cinquefoil was one of the species retrieved from the stomach of a large, male woolly mammoth that died about 20,000 years ago in northern Yakutia, Russia.

Elegant Cinquefoil • *Potentilla elegans*

General: Tiny, only 1–5 cm tall. **Leaves:** Long-stalked, green on both surfaces, not woolly beneath; leaflets triangular to fan-shaped, **3–7 mm long, deeply and unevenly cleft** ⅓–⅔ **the dis-tance to the midrib into oblong segments,** sparsely short-hairy and glandular to nearly hairless. **Flowers:** 1; petals pale yellow, heart-shaped, **3–4 mm long. Where Found:** Dry, rocky slopes, outcrops and fellfields; subalpine and alpine zones; rare in the northern ⅓ of the region; amphiberingian.

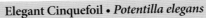

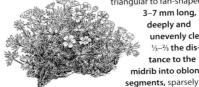

Two-flowered Cinquefoil
Potentilla biflora

General: Stems woody at base, 4–15 cm tall. **Leaves:** Long-stalked, green on upper surface, pale green and sparsely hairy but not white-woolly beneath, apparently palmately divided but actually with 3 divided leaflets; **leaflets 1–6 cm long, deeply divided to the base into linear segments,** margins rolled under. **Flowers:** 1–2; petals yellow, heart-shaped, 5–10 mm long. **Where Found:** Rocky or gravelly slopes, fellfields, heathlands and tundra, usually on calcium-rich substrates; lowland (arctic coast) to alpine zones; scattered but locally frequent in the northern ⅓ of the region; amphiberingian.

Short and Curly Cinquefoil
Potentilla villosula

General: Plants from stout, branched stem-bases; stems 2–15 (to 20) cm tall, densely covered with short, curly hairs mixed with long, straight hairs. **Leaves:** Short-stalked, greyish green, silky-hairy on upper surface, **densely white- to yellowish-white-woolly on lower surface,** stalks also densely long-hairy but not short-woolly; **leaflets with 2–3 coarse, triangular to egg-shaped teeth on each side. Flowers:** 2–3 (sometimes 1 or 4), often more than 2 cm across; petals pale yellow, heart-shaped, 8–10 mm long; **calyx mini-bracts narrowly elliptic, 2–3.5 mm wide. Where Found:** Rock outcrops, heathlands, scree and talus, gravel outwash and tundra, mainly on acidic bedrock, reportedly also on coastal bluffs and old sand dunes; lowland to alpine zones; frequent in the northwestern part of the region, disjunct in southwestern AB; amphiberingian. • The map depicts the combined ranges of short and curly and villous cinquefoils because their individual distributions are incompletely documented.

Similar Species: Villous cinquefoil (*P. villosa*; *P. nivea* var. *villosa*) has mostly **3–7 flowers** with petals 7–15 mm long, the **calyx mini-bracts egg-shaped and 2–5 mm wide,** and **leaflets with 3–7 teeth on each side.** It grows on sea cliffs, coastal bluffs and rocky and shingle beaches, occasionally inland at high elevations on rocky slopes, pumice barrens, scree and tundra, in lowland to alpine zones. An amphiberingian species, it is frequent along the coast from western and southern AK and BC to northwestern WA, and in the Cascades and Blue Mtns in OR. • **Tundra cinquefoil** (*P. subvahliana*; *P. vahliana* in part) has leaflets that are **sparsely hairy on the upper surface,** usually a **single flower**

and calyx mini-bracts that are **lance-shaped, 0.8–2 mm wide.** It is found on heathlands, stony slopes, rock outcrops and crevices, scree and talus (often on calcium-rich bedrock) and dry tundra, plus coastal bluffs and stabilized sand dunes, in lowland (arctic coast) to alpine zones. An arctic-alpine, amphiberingian species, it is scattered and locally frequent in the far north of AK, YT, NT and maybe (according to the *FNA* draft) also in northern BC and southwestern AB.

tundra cinquefoil

One-flowered Cinquefoil
Potentilla uniflora group

General: Stems 2–10 (occasionally to 25) cm tall.
Leaves: Short-stalked, greenish and silky to nearly hairless on upper surface, **greyish- or white-woolly beneath** with overlying long, silky hairs; **stalks with long, straight hairs, sometimes patchily short-woolly but not minutely curly-hairy;** leaflets deeply sharp-toothed. Flowers: 1 (occasionally 2–3); petals **5–10 mm long,** shallowly notched at tip; **calyx mini-bracts linear-oblong to lance-shaped, 1–3 mm wide.**
Where Found: Dry to mesic rocky slopes, crevices and outcrops, gravelly ridge crests, scree, fellfields, heathlands and tundra; lowland (arctic coast)

to alpine zones; primarily at high elevations; frequent throughout except absent from the Pacific coast and WA and OR; arctic-alpine, amphiberingian.

Similar Species: One-flowered cinquefoil can be confused with both **villous cinquefoil** (p. 173), which has wider calyx mini-bracts and generally larger flowers, and **short and curly cinquefoil** (p. 173), which has leaflets that are densely hairy on the upper surface; as well as with both **snow cinquefoil** (below), which has white-woolly but not long-hairy leaf stalks, and **bluff cinquefoil** (p. 175), which has long, silky and short, curly hairs on the leaf stalks and usually more flowers.

Other Species: The draft *FNA* treatment splits what has long been known as *P. uniflora* into 3 species: the northern **P. vulcanicola** (leaf stalks and lower stem with long, silky hairs but not woolly); the more cordilleran **P. subgorodkovii** (leaf stalks and lower stem white-woolly); and **P. uniflora** of the Russian Far East, which probably doesn't occur in North America. For now, we won't go that far, but you should be aware of these proposed changes.

Notes: One-flowered cinquefoil is also known as *Potentilla ledebouriana*.

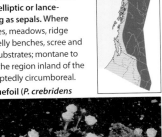

Snow Cinquefoil • *Potentilla nivea*

General: Similar to one-flowered cinquefoil (above) but **often taller (5–40 cm),** with **white-woolly leaf stalks lacking long, straight hairs. Leaves:** Leaflets not overlapping, central leaflet with 2–5 teeth per side, upper surface green, not densely hairy. **Flowers:** 1–3; petals 5–9 mm long; **calyx mini-bracts elliptic or lance-shaped, nearly as broad and long as sepals. Where Found:** Well-drained, grassy slopes, meadows, ridge crests, rock outcrops, sandy-gravelly benches, scree and tundra, typically on calcium-rich substrates; montane to alpine zones; frequent in most of the region inland of the Pacific coastal mountains; interruptedly circumboreal.

Similar Species: Beringian cinquefoil (*P. crebridens* **ssp. hemicryophila;** *P. nivea* in part) has similar leaf stalks, but the leaflets overlap, the **central leaflet has usually 4–8 teeth per side and the upper surface is greyish and mostly densely hairy.** Also, the **calyx mini-bracts are linear, narrower and shorter than the sepals.** It grows on dry, well-drained ridges, rocky slopes, outcrops and in meadows, on calcium-rich substrates, in montane to alpine zones. This amphiberingian species is locally frequent in northern AK and northern YT.

Beringian cinquefoil

Bluff Cinquefoil
Potentilla arenosa ssp. *arenosa*

General: Similar to the 3 species featured on p. 174, but **leaf stalks with long, straight and short, curly hairs, not white-woolly;** plants 5–30 cm tall. **Flowers:** 1–7 (to 15); petals 4–6 mm long. **Where Found:** Well-drained, rocky slopes, outcrops, ridge crests, gravel bars, cutbanks and tundra, typically on calcium-rich substrates; montane to alpine zones; infrequent in the northern ⅔ of the region, inland of the Pacific coastal mountains, southward in the Rockies; arctic-alpine, amphiberingian.

Notes: Bluff cinquefoil is also known as *Potentilla hookeriana* (misapplied), *P. nivea* var. *arenosa* and *P. n.* ssp. *hookeriana*.
• The species epithet *arenosa* means "full of sand" or "sandy."

PRINCIPAL LEAVES MOSTLY WITH 5 OR MORE LEAFLETS

Blue-leaved Cinquefoil, Vari-leaved Cinquefoil
Potentilla glaucophylla

General: Stems ascending to erect, **10–40 cm tall. Leaves:** Long-stalked, **green or bluish green, nearly hairless on upper surface, often sparsely appressed-hairy beneath** (occasionally sparsely greyish-silky on both surfaces), palmately or pinnately compound; **leaflets 5–7, 1–3 (to 5) cm long, strongly toothed mostly above the middle. Flowers:** 2–10 (to 20); petals heart-shaped, mostly 5–10 mm long. **Where Found:** Dry to mesic meadows, rocky and grassy slopes, fellfields and tundra; montane to alpine zones; frequent south of 63° N, except rare on much of the coast; cordilleran.

Varieties: Blue-leaved cinquefoil is a highly variable species, especially in leaf characteristics, as the alternative name suggests. The widespread **var. *glaucophylla*** has broadly lance-shaped leaflet teeth about halfway to the midvein; and the primarily Rocky Mountain (southwestern AB and southeastern BC to WY) **var. *perdissecta*** has linear-oblong leaflet teeth almost to the midvein.

Similar Species: Graceful cinquefoil (*P. gracilis*) is typically a species of low to moderate elevations but reaches the lower alpine zone in the southern ¼ of the region, especially in the Rocky Mountain states. It resembles blue-leaved cinquefoil but is larger (**typically 30–80 cm tall**), with **longer (3–9 cm) leaflets** that are **often white-woolly beneath or much paler on the lower surface** than on the upper.

Notes: Blue-leaved cinquefoil is also known as *Potentilla diversifolia*.

Early Cinquefoil • *Potentilla concinna*

General: Shorter (2–10, sometimes to 15 cm tall) **and hairier** than blue-leaved cinquefoil (p. 175). **Leaves:** White-woolly on lower surface at least, with 5–7 leaflets. **Flowers:** 2–6 (to 12); petals 4–9 mm long; **calyx mini-bracts elliptic to egg-shaped, 1–1.5 mm wide, blunt. Where Found:** Sandy grasslands, meadows, glades, open forests and foothill shrublands to rocky slopes, ridges, fellfields and tundra; montane to alpine zones; scattered but locally frequent in the southeastern ⅕ of the region; Great Plains–cordilleran.

Similar Species: The draft *FNA* treatment splits what has long been known as *P. hookeriana* (or as an inclusive *P. rubricaulis*) into 3 species: the more widespread cordilleran *P. rubricaulis* (strict sense; petals 5–7 mm long), the northern *P. furcata* (petals 3–5 mm long, pale yellow; flower stalks mostly more than 5 mm long) and the U.S. intermontane (ID, MT, WY, UT and CO) *P. modesta* (petals 3–5 mm long, yellow, flower stalks mostly less than 5 mm long). As with the one-flowered cinquefoil group (p. 174), we describe a **redstem cinquefoil group** (*P. rubricaulis* group) that includes all 3 of these species and represents greyish green, hairy, densely tufted perennials with **ascending stems 5–35 cm tall, leaves grey or white-woolly on the lower surface** and 3–20 flowers with petals 3–7 mm long. The redstem cinquefoil group has mostly 5 (sometimes 3–4) leaflets per leaf and the **calyx mini-bracts are narrower (linear to narrowly lance-shaped and less than 1.2 mm wide).** This species—or species complex—grows on sandy shores, in open forests, dry meadows and grasslands, and on rocky slopes and ridges, scree, fellfields and dry tundra, usually on calcium-rich substrates, in montane to alpine zones. An arctic-alpine group restricted to North America, it is widespread but scattered and locally frequent in most of the region inland of the Pacific coastal mountains, AK, YT and NT through BC and southwestern AB to UT and CO.

Drummond's Cinquefoil • *Potentilla drummondii*

General: Greenish plants 15–45 cm tall. **Leaves: Pinnately compound with 5–9 leaflets;** leaflets crowded, relatively large, 1–5 cm long, **cleft halfway to the midvein into linear or lance-shaped teeth,** greenish on both surfaces, nearly hairless or sparsely appressed-hairy. **Flowers:** 3–15; **petals 6–12 mm long. Where Found:** Meadows, glades, open, rocky slopes, ridges and tundra; montane to alpine zones; infrequent in the southern ½ of the region; cordilleran.

Similar Species: Though similar to blue-leaved cinquefoil (p. 175), Drummond's cinquefoil has consistently pinnate leaves that are not glaucous. • **Woolly cinquefoil** (*P. hippiana*; *P. argyrea*, *P. leucophylla*) is **white- to grey-woolly and/or silvery-silky all over,** with 7–13 leaflets lance-toothed up to halfway to the midvein, the **lower surface white-woolly,** the upper surface white-silky to rarely nearly hairless and greenish. The 10–30 flowers have petals 4–8 mm long. It occurs in dry grasslands, shrublands, open forests, meadows, rocky slopes and tundra, in steppe to alpine zones. A cordilleran–Great Plains species, woolly cinquefoil is locally frequent inland in the southern ½ of the region, northeastern and south-central BC and southern AB to ID, MT, WY, NV, UT, CO and NM.

woolly cinquefoil

Notes: In Washington and Oregon, Drummond's cinquefoil appears to be an important nectar plant for the endangered Mardon skipper butterfly (*Polites mardon*). • Thomas Drummond (1780–1853) was a noted Scottish botanical collector; *hippiana* honours Charles F. Hipp, a friend of the German botanist who described the species.

Sheep Cinquefoil • *Potentilla ovina*

General: Greyish to greenish, tufted, prostrate to ascending, 5–30 cm tall. **Leaves:** Pinnately compound, short-stalked, with **7–21 crowded leaflets,** each 5–20 mm long and **divided nearly to the base into 3–5 (to 7) linear to oblong segments,** greyish green and usually silky-hairy on both surfaces. **Flowers:** Few to several (1–11, to 20), rather small; **petals 4–8 mm long. Where Found:** Meadows, open, rocky slopes, talus, ridges and fellfields; montane to alpine zones; scattered to frequent inland in the southern ⅓ of the region.

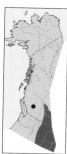

Notes: Sheep cinquefoil is also known as *Potentilla diversifolia* var. *pinnatisecta* and *P. pinnatisecta.*

Shortleaf Cinquefoil • *Potentilla brevifolia*

General: Yellowish green, finely **glandular-hairy,** 5–20 cm tall, sometimes mat-forming. **Leaves:** Long-stalked, pinnately compound with **usually 5 (sometimes 3–7) crowded and overlapping leaflets,** each 5–15 mm long, cleft 1–2 times, round-toothed, glandular hairy on both surfaces. **Flowers:** Mostly 3–10, rather small; petals bright yellow, broadly egg-shaped, 3–7 mm long. **Where Found:** Moist, rocky slopes, talus, scree, fellfields, grassy ridges and conifer parkland; subalpine and alpine zones; infrequent in the southeastern part of the region.

Cliff Wood-beauty, Sticky Cinquefoil
Drymocallis pseudorupestris var. *saxicola*

General: High-elevation plants are rather short (5–25 cm), matted and **sticky-glandular** to the touch on both stems and leaves. **Leaves: Pinnately compound with usually 7 uncrowded leaflets,** sawtoothed but not deeply cleft or incised. **Flowers: Petals pale yellow to cream or whitish,** 4–9 mm long. **Where Found:** This variety of cliff wood-beauty is the form most likely to reach the alpine zone in rocky habitats—cliffs, outcrops, ledges, talus and lava beds—especially in Rocky Mtn states; locally frequent in the southern ⅓ of the region.

Notes: Cliff wood-beauty is also known as *Potentilla glandulosa* var. *pseudorupestris.* • Often included in *Potentilla* but long regarded as a poor fit, this and several similar species have been assigned their own genus in the draft *FNA* treatment. There are substantive morphological and molecular reasons to do so, and in an ironic twist, the genus *Drymocallis* has been resurrected for the purpose. It was originally coined by Swedish-born American botanist Per Axel Rydberg (1860–1931), an energetic field botanist who became an authority on the flora (including *Potentilla*) of the Rocky Mountains. He was also a notorious taxonomic splitter whose meticulous but eye-glazing monographs entered a century of cold storage (at least in North America), only to be reanimated in this brave new millennium.

Conspectus of Alpine *Potentilla*

SPECIES	GENERAL	LEAVES

PERENNIAL SHRUB

| *Dasiphora* (*Potentilla*) *fruticosa* (p. 71) | to 1.3 m tall; stems spreading to erect; branches numerous, hairy when young, becoming hairless in age with brown, shreddy bark | clustered at nodes, numerous, short-stalked, pinnately compound; leaflets usually 5, oblong to narrowly elliptic, 0.5–2 cm long, greyish green, sparsely silky-hairy, margins untoothed, often rolled under |

PERENNIAL HERBS: PRINCIPAL LEAVES WITH 3 LEAFLETS

Leaves greenish on both surfaces, hairless to variously hairy (but not white- or grey-woolly on either surface)

flabellifolia (p. 172)	stems ascending to erect, 10–30 cm tall, sparsely long-hairy to hairless	long-stalked (leaf stalks 2–3× as long as blades), green on both surfaces, not white- or grey-woolly beneath; leaflets broadly wedge- to fan-shaped, unevenly and deeply 7–15-blunt-toothed except at base, at most sparsely hairy
hyparctica (p. 172)	stems ascending to erect, 2–20 cm but usually <10 cm tall, hairy, glandular	long-stalked (stalks to 2× as long as blades), green on both surfaces, not white- or grey-woolly beneath; leaflets egg-shaped, evenly 7–11-coarse-toothed halfway to midvein, sparsely to moderately hairy, often glandular
nana (p. 172)	stems ascending to erect, 1–7 cm tall, hairy	green on both surfaces, not white- or grey-woolly beneath; leaflets egg-shaped, evenly cut halfway to midvein into 7–9 (to 13) coarse teeth, moderately hairy, somewhat glandular
elegans (p. 172)	tiny, loose tufts; stems 1–5 cm tall, short-hairy	long-stalked, green on both surfaces, not white- or grey-woolly beneath; leaflets triangular to fan-shaped, 3–7 mm long, unevenly cleft ⅓–⅔ of the way to midrib into oblong lobes, sparsely short-hairy, glandular to nearly hairless
biflora (p. 173)	densely tufted; stems woody at base, 4–15 cm tall, sparsely hairy	long-stalked (stalks to 2× as long as blades), green on upper surface, pale green and sparsely hairy but not white- or grey-woolly beneath, apparently palmately divided but actually with 3 divided leaflets; leaflets 1–6 cm long, deeply divided to the base into linear segments, margins rolled under

Leaves generally very hairy, white- or grey-woolly, occasionally yellowish-woolly (felt-like) on lower surface; leaf stalks and lower stem with long, silky hairs but not short-woolly

| *villosula* (p. 173) | densely tufted, greyish green to yellowish green; stems 2–15 (to 20) cm tall, densely covered with short, curly hairs mixed with long, straight hairs | short-stalked (stalks shorter than to about as long as blades), greyish green silky-hairy on upper surface, densely white- or yellowish-white-woolly on lower surface, the stalks also densely long-hairy (not short-woolly); leaflets 0.8–2.5 cm long, with 2–3 coarse, triangular to egg-shaped teeth on each side |

	FLOWERS		
number	petals	calyx mini-bracts	filament length (mm)
1–7, in leaf axils	yellow, nearly circular, 7–15 mm long	narrowly lance-shaped, 4–10 mm long, as long or slightly longer than sepals	
1–5	bright yellow, heart-shaped, 6–12 mm long, notched at tip	elliptic to oval, 3.5–7 mm long, ¾ to nearly as long as sepals, rounded to blunt	1.5–3
1–3 (to 5)	pale to bright yellow, heart-shaped, 4–9 mm long, notched at tip	oblong to egg-shaped, 3.5–7 mm long, nearly as long as sepals	to 1.1; styles 0.6–0.9 mm
1–2	pale yellow, 4–8 mm long	oblong or egg-shaped, 2.5–5 mm long, roughly as long as sepals, blunt to rounded	1.2–1.6; styles 0.8–1.2
1	pale yellow, heart-shaped, 3–4 mm long, notched at tip	linear, elliptic or egg-shaped, about 2 mm long, nearly as long as sepals, rounded or blunt at tip	1–1.5
1–2	pale yellow to yellow, heart-shaped, 5–10 mm long, notched at tip, not overlapping	oblong or lance-egg-shaped, 2.5–4 mm long, ¾ to nearly as long as sepals, blunt or pointy-tipped	2.8–4
2–3 (occasionally 1 or 4)	pale yellow, heart-shaped, 8–10 mm long, shallowly notched at tip, strongly overlapping	narrowly elliptic, 2–3.5 mm wide, somewhat pointy-tipped, about as long as sepals	1.1–1.4

SPECIES	GENERAL	LEAVES
villosa (p. 173)	tufted, silvery greyish green; stems ascending, 5–25 cm tall, densely covered with mix of long and short hairs	short-stalked, greyish green silky-hairy on upper surface, densely yellowish-white-woolly on lower surface, the stalks also densely long-hairy (not short-woolly); leaflets 1.5–3 cm long, with 3–7 triangular to narrowly oblong teeth on each side
subvahliana (p. 173)	very densely tufted, greyish green to yellowish green; stems erect, 2–6 (to 11) cm tall, densely short-curly-hairy	short-stalked, upper surface dark greyish green, nearly hairless to moderately hairy, lower surface densely grey- or white-woolly, the stalks also densely long-hairy (not short-woolly); leaflets 0.8–2.5 cm long, with 2–3 triangular teeth on each side

Leaves white- or grey-hairy, occasionally yellowish-woolly (felt-like) on lower surface; leaf stalks and lower stem cobwebby, white-woolly (short, felted hairs)

uniflora group (p. 174)	densely tufted to cushion-forming, greyish green; stems ascending-erect, 2–10 (to 25) cm tall, spreading long-hairy, usually also woolly	greenish and silky to nearly hairless on upper surface, greyish- or white-woolly beneath and with overlying long silky hairs, the stalks with long, straight hairs and patchily short-woolly (not minutely curly-hairy); leaflets deeply 2–4-sharp-toothed about halfway to midvein
nivea (p. 174)	loosely tufted, greyish green; stems ascending-erect, 5–40 cm tall, cobwebby-woolly	upper surface green and nearly hairless or long-hairy, greyish- or white-woolly beneath, the stalks white-woolly but lacking long, straight hairs; leaflets not overlapping, central leaflet with 2–5 teeth per side
crebridens ssp. *hemicryophila* (p. 174)	loosely tufted, greyish green; stems ascending-erect, 8–20 cm tall, cobwebby-woolly	greyish and mostly densely long-hairy above, greyish- to white-woolly beneath, the stalks white-woolly but lacking long, straight hairs; leaflets overlapping, central leaflet with 2–8 teeth per side
arenosa (p. 175)	loosely tufted, greyish green; stems ascending-erect, 5–30 cm tall, short- and long-hairy (not cobwebby-woolly)	dark green and hairless or sparsely hairy above, greyish- or white-woolly beneath, the stalks with long, straight and short, curly hairs (not white-woolly); central leaflet with 3–4 teeth per side

PERENNIAL HERBS: PRINCIPAL LEAVES MOSTLY WITH 5 OR MORE LEAFLETS

glaucophylla (p. 175)	tufted, blue-green to green; stems spreading to ascending-erect, 10–40 cm tall, hairless or sparsely hairy	long-stalked, palmately or pinnately compound, green or bluish green and nearly hairless on upper surface, often sparsely appressed-hairy beneath, occasionally sparsely greyish-silky on both surfaces; leaflets 5–7, 1–3 (to 5) cm long, strongly toothed or lobed mostly above midleaf, central leaflet with 1–3 (to 5) teeth per side
gracilis (p. 175)	tufted; stems ascending to erect, 20–80 cm tall, appressed- or spreading-hairy	long-stalked, palmately compound, green and sparsely hairy above, paler and hairier (often white-woolly) beneath; leaflets 5–9, 3–9 cm long, coarsely 6–12-toothed or deeply lobed
concinna (p. 176)	tufted, low, greyish green or whitish green; stems spreading-ascending, 2–10 (to 15) cm long/tall, hairy	palmately to nearly pinnately compound, upper surface greenish and hairy to white-woolly, lower surface white- or grey-woolly; leaflets 5–7, mostly 1–3 cm long, central leaflet with mostly 2–5 teeth per side

FLOWERS

number	petals	calyx mini-bracts	filament length (mm)
mostly 3–7	pale yellow, broadly heart-shaped, 7–15 mm long, notched at tip, strongly over-lapping	egg-shaped, 2–5 mm wide, some-what pointy-tipped, about same length as sepals	1.8–2.1
1 (occasion-ally to 2)	pale yellow, triangular, 7–9 mm long, notched at tip, overlapping	lance-shaped, 0.8–2 mm wide, distinctly shorter than sepals	0.8–1
1 (occasion-ally 2–3)	yellow, heart-shaped, 5–10 mm long, shallowly notched at tip, overlapping	narrowly oblong to lance-shaped, 1–3 mm wide, distinctly shorter than sepals	0.8–1.3
1–3	pale yellow, heart-shaped, 5–9 mm long, notched at tip, not overlapping	elliptic or lance-shaped, 0.5–0.7 mm wide, nearly as broad and long as sepals	0.9–1.2
1–6	pale yellow, heart-shaped, 5–7 mm long, notched at tip, not overlapping	linear, 0.5–0.6 mm wide, shorter than sepals	1
1–7 (occasion-ally to 15)	pale yellow, triangular to heart-shaped, 4–6 mm long, notched at tip, weakly over-lapping	lance-shaped, 0.8–1.1 mm wide, slightly shorter than sepals	0.8–1
2–10 (occasion-ally to 20)	yellow, heart-shaped, 5–12 mm long, rounded to notched at tip	lance-shaped to elliptic, 2–5 mm long, shorter than sepals	1.5–3
4–50	yellow, heart-shaped, 4–11 mm long, notched at tip	narrowly lance-shaped to narrowly elliptic, 2–6 mm long, shorter than sepals	1–3.5
2–6 (occasion-ally to 12)	yellow, heart-shaped, 4–9 mm long, shallowly notched	narrowly elliptic to egg- to lance-shaped, 1–1.5 mm wide, blunt, slightly shorter than sepals	1–3.1

SPECIES	GENERAL	LEAVES
rubricaulis group (p. 176)	densely tufted, greyish green; stems ascending, 5–35 cm tall, hairy	palmately compound, upper surface greyish green and moderately to densely short- and long-hairy, lower surface white- or grey-woolly; leaflets mostly 5 (sometimes 3–4), 1–4 cm long, central leaflet with 3–8 teeth per side
drummondii (p. 176)	tufted, greenish; stems ascending-erect, 15–45 cm tall, nearly hairless to moderately hairy	pinnately compound, greenish on both surfaces, nearly hairless or sparsely appressed-hairy; leaflets 5–9, 1–5 cm long, central leaflet cleft halfway to midvein into 3–7 linear or lance-shaped teeth per side
hippiana (p. 176)	tufted, white- or grey-woolly and/or silvery silky-hairy all over; stems spreading to erect, 10–40 cm tall	pinnately compound, upper surface grey- or white-silky to rarely nearly hairless and greenish, lower surface white-woolly; leaflets 7–13, 1–5 cm long, lance-toothed up to halfway to midvein into mostly 7–12 teeth per side
ovina (p. 177)	tufted, greyish to greenish; stems spreading to ascending, 5–30 cm tall, silky-long-hairy	pinnately compound, greyish green and usually silky-hairy on both surfaces; leaflets 7–21, crowded, 0.5–2 cm long, divided nearly to base into 3–7 linear to oblong segments
brevifolia (p. 177)	mat-forming from stem-base with trailing rhizome-like branches, yellowish green; stems numerous, erect, 5–20 cm tall, finely glandular-hairy	pinnately compound, finely glandular-hairy on both surfaces, otherwise hairless or nearly so; leaflets 3–7 (mostly 5), crowded, 0.5–1.5 cm long, largest leaflets divided halfway to nearly to midvein into several lobes, each lobe with 2–3 primary rounded teeth
Drymocallis pseudorupestris var. *saxicola* (p. 177)	tufted to mat-forming from stem-base with long branches, sticky-glandular generally; stems erect, 5–25 cm tall	pinnately compound, abundantly glandular and also hairy on both surfaces; leaflets usually 7, uncrowded, sawtoothed but not deeply cleft or incised, uppermost leaflets clearly largest, 1–4 cm long

fan-leaved cinquefoil

FLOWERS			
number	**petals**	**calyx mini-bracts**	**filament length (mm)**
3–20	yellow to pale yellow, heart-shaped, 3–7 mm long, notched or rounded, sometimes overlapping	linear to narrowly lance-elliptic, <1.2 mm wide, pointy-tipped, mostly shorter than sepals	0.5–2
3–15	yellow, heart-shaped, 6–12 mm long, rounded or notched	narrowly lance-shaped to narrowly elliptic, 0.8–2 mm wide, shorter than sepals	2–3.5
10–30	yellow, egg/heart-shaped, 4–8 mm long, rounded or notched	linear to lance-shaped, 2–5 mm long, slightly shorter than sepals	0.5–2.5
1–11 (occasionally to 20)	yellow, heart-shaped, 4–8 mm long, notched	linear-lance-shaped to narrowly elliptic, 2–3.5 mm long, shorter than sepals	1–2.5
3–10	bright yellow, heart-shaped, 3.5–6.5 mm long, notched	lance-shaped, 2–4 mm long, shorter than sepals	1–2.5
2–12 (occasionally to 20)	cream to whitish or pale yellow, egg-shaped, 4–9 mm long, rounded, somewhat overlapping	linear-lance-shaped to broadly elliptic, 2–5 mm long, slightly shorter than sepals	1–2.5

one-flowered cinquefoil

Buttercup Family (Ranunculaceae)

Ranunculaceae is a fairly large family with about 2500 species, cosmopolitan but chiefly of cooler northern temperate regions. Ours are perennial herbs, with leaves at the base and mostly alternate along the stem (opposite in some *Ranunculus*), often compound or deeply divided (the exceptions are *Caltha* and some *Ranunculus*) and lacking stipules (in contrast to Rosaceae). The flowers are radially symmetric, except in *Aconitum* and *Delphinium*, and include both sepals and petals or have undifferentiated, usually showy segments that are distinct and variable in number. The usually many stamens are spirally arranged; the several to many ovaries are distinct, spirally arranged and **superior**. The fruits are typically 1-chambered follicles (dry fruits opening on the front suture, each the product of a single ovary) or achenes (*Anemone*, *Ranunculus* and *Thalictrum*). The follicles contain several to many seeds, whereas the achenes are single-seeded.

Key to the Genera of Ranunculaceae

1a. Flowers bilaterally symmetric 2

2a. Upper sepal hooded but not spurred; petals 2, concealed inside hood . . . . ***Aconitum*** (p. 197)

2b. Upper sepal spurred but not hooded; petals 4, not hidden by sepals . . . . ***Delphinium*** (p. 198)

1b. Flowers radially symmetric. 3

3a. Petals prominently spurred; fruit of several follicles . . . . ***Aquilegia*** (pp. 196–197)

3b. Petals not spurred 4

4a. Fruits several-seeded follicles; flowers white. 5

5a. Leaves simple or palmately compound. 6

6a. Leaves simple, margins coarsely toothed or scalloped to nearly toothless
. . . . ***Caltha leptosepala*** (p. 185)

6b. Leaves deeply 5-lobed to nearly compound, margins coarsely sharp-toothed
. . . . ***Trollius albiflorus*** (below)

5b. Leaves pinnately compound, 2 times divided into 3s . . . . ***Enemion savilei*** (p. 195)

4b. Fruits 1-seeded achenes; flowers yellow, green, purplish, blue, pink or white 7

7a. Flowers usually yellow, with both sepals and petals. . . . . ***Ranunculus*** (pp. 190–194)

7b. Flowers mostly not yellow, with sepals but lacking petals 8

8a. Stem leaves (if any) alternate; sepals greenish or greyish green, purple-tinged, less showy than stamens. . . . . ***Thalictrum*** (p. 195)

8b. Stem leaves usually in a whorl of 3; sepals white, yellow or pink to blue, petal-like, showy, much showier than stamens . . . . ***Anemone*** (pp. 186–189)

White Globeflower • *Trollius albiflorus*

General: Hairless, from a short stem-base with fibrous roots; flowering stems 1 to several, erect, 10–50 cm tall.

Leaves: Basal leaves several, stalked, **blades deeply palmately divided into 5–7 coarsely toothed segments; stem leaves 1–3 (to 5),** alternate, with wide, clasping, membranous sheaths.

Flowers: Usually 1 atop stem, saucer-shaped, 2.5–6 cm across; petals 15–25, yellow, oblong-tubular, concealed beneath stamens; **sepals 5–9, white in bloom,** pale yellow to greenish white before flowers open, egg-shaped to nearly circular, 1–2 cm long; stamens numerous.

Fruits: Follicles pod-like, 10–14, oblong, veined, 8–16 mm long including beak; **fruiting head cone-shaped.**

Where Found: Wet to moist meadows, streambanks and snowbeds; montane to alpine zones; frequent in much of the southern ⅓ of the region; cordilleran.

Similar Species: This plant could be mistaken for an *Anemone*, but it is hairless, and its fruits are follicles, not achenes.

Notes: White globeflower is also known as *Trollius laxus* var. *albiflorus*. • *Trollius* is derived from the Swiss-German name *trollblume*, from the Latin *trulleus* for "basin," whence *trul* (*trol*) in Old German for "something round," alluding to the flower shape. "Globeflower" refers to the shape of the flower in the European *T. europaeus*.

Mountain Marsh-marigold
Caltha leptosepala

General: Hairless, somewhat fleshy perennial from a short, thick stem-base with fibrous roots; flowering stems solitary, erect, 5–40 cm tall.

Leaves: Mostly basal, rarely 1 on stem, thick, waxy, long-stalked; blades oblong-egg-shaped to circular or kidney-shaped, 2–12 cm long, **margins coarsely blunt-toothed or scalloped to nearly toothless.**

Flowers: Solitary or 2 (to 4) atop stem, saucer-shaped, 2–4 cm across; petals absent; **sepals 6–12, white to cream** or greenish (sometimes yellow) **tinged bluish on the underside, oblong;** stamens 50 or more.

Fruits: Follicles pod-like, 4–15, narrowly oblong, 1–2 cm long; seeds longitudinally wrinkled or grooved.

Where Found: Wet to moist meadows, bogs, fens, pool margins, streambanks, snowbeds and seepage sites; lowland to alpine zones; frequent throughout the southern ¾ of the region; cordilleran.

Varieties: We have 2 varieties, which are recognized as separate species by some taxonomists; both occur on Vancouver I. and in the Olympic and Cascade Mtns. • **Elkslip mountain marsh-marigold (*C. leptosepala* var. *leptosepala*)** has **leaves that are longer than wide,** the margins more sharply toothed, the basal lobes small and not overlapping, with **usually solitary flowers** and **unstalked follicles.** It is a subalpine and alpine plant found mostly east of the coastal mountains. • **Twin-flowered mountain marsh-marigold** or broadleaf mountain marsh-marigold (*C. leptosepala* var. *biflora*) has **leaves that are nearly as wide as long,** the margins broadly round-toothed to nearly toothless, the basal lobes large and overlapping, with **mostly 2 flowers per stem** and **stalked follicles.** It is a lowland to subalpine plant found in and west of the Coast-Cascade mountains.

twin-flowered mountain marsh-marigold

Notes: "Developmental preformation," the initiation of leaves and/or flowers one or more growing seasons before they mature, is said to be nearly ubiquitous in alpine species. Mountain marsh-marigold is an archetypal preformer; the leaves and flowers are initiated at least one year before they mature. What's more, the seeds contain a rudimentary embryo (occupying less than 10% of the seed at dispersal) that must develop further prior to germination. This embryo development, which requires 4–7 months, appears to take place under the winter snowpack, allowing seeds to germinate as soon as the snow disappears. • *Caltha* is from the Greek *kalathos*, "goblet," in reference to the flower shape of the European species; *leptosepala* means "slender-sepalled." "Marigold," the name given to the European species with yellow flowers, seems to be derived from "Mary's gold," a name for a yellow daisy sacred to the Virgin Mary. "Elkslip"

is an alternative name given because elk feed on the plants or because they occur where elk feed. Also, some observers suggest that the leaf is the shape of an elk's lip, but you'd have to get close to the animal to judge for yourself. • White globeflower (p. 184) and mountain marsh-marigold belong to the cohort of early flowering alpines, both blooming as or immediately after the snow melts. Here a hard mid-summer frost has iced-up mountain marsh-marigold's precocious blooms.

The Genus *Anemone*

Anemones are perennial herbs, mostly hairy throughout, usually with highly divided leaves and 1 to several flowers atop the stem. Most leaves are at the stem-base, but typically there is a whorl of 3 stalkless leaves (interpreted as involucral bracts) on the stem below the flower. The flowers are showy, bowl- or saucer-shaped, without petals but with 5–6 (to 9) coloured sepals that look like petals. The fruits are clusters of numerous, hairy or hairless, seed-like achenes. In some species, as the achenes mature, their hairs lengthen dramatically.

Key to *Anemone*

1a. Fruiting achenes with feathery tips, 2–5 cm long; fruit clusters shaggy **2**

   2a. Flowers white or purple-tinged; basal leaves 3–4 times dissected, the ultimate segments relatively short, 1–3 mm wide . . . . ***A. occidentalis*** (p. 187)

   2b. Flowers purple to blue; basal leaves 2–3 times dissected, the ultimate segments relatively long, 2–4 mm wide . . . . ***A. patens*** (p. 187)

1b. Fruiting achene tips not feathery, <1.5 cm long; fruit clusters hairless or hairy but not shaggy **3**

   3a. Flowers yellow, solitary. . . . . ***A. richardsonii*** (p. 189)

   3b. Flowers cream to white, solitary to several **4**

      4a. Achenes hairless . . . . ***A. narcissiflora*** (p. 189)

      4b. Achenes densely woolly or long-hairy **5**

         5a. Leaves deeply divided into 3 broadly wedge-shaped main segments (leaflets); plants with rhizomes . . . . ***A. parviflora*** (p. 188)

         5b. Leaves deeply divided into linear or oblong segments; plants tufted, without rhizomes **6**

            6a. Plants 20–60 cm tall; flowers 1–7, cream to pale yellowish, sometimes pink or with a bluish tinge . . . . ***A. multifida*** (p. 188)

            6b. Plants 10–25 cm tall; flowers solitary, often bluish **7**

               7a. Flowers white, often bluish on outside surface; stamens whitish; style white . . . . ***A. drummondii*** (p. 188)

               7b. Flowers uniformly pale to dark blue or purple; stamens purple; style red . . . ***A. multiceps*** (p. 188)

WIND DISPERSAL

    Many high-elevation species have very small, light seeds that can be blown or tumbled great distances. Many heather family dwarf shrubs and all rushes and orchids have tiny, light seeds. Several species have winged seeds or fruits, including Engelmann spruce, dwarf birch, slide alder, mountain-sorrel, arctic dock; many carrot family plants, including cow parsnip and biscuit-roots; Columbia lily and Indian hellebore; and some of the suncresses, as well as Sitka burnet, fescue sandwort, Cusick's speedwell and towering lousewort. Plumed or long-hairy seeds or fruits occur in mop-top and other anemones, cotton-grasses, willows, willowherbs, avens, mountain-avens and Sitka valerian, plus most Asteraceae (those with a plumose pappus). Paintbrushes, false asphodel, some larkspurs and penstemons have loose, often net-like seed coats, which could increase loft.

    Some other species with not particularly small, unornamented seeds could be adapted for wind dispersal in a less-obvious way. They have upright capsules on rigid stems that remain erect above the first encrusted snows of early winter. Strong winds must often vibrate the stems and shake out ("censer" or salt-shaker mechanism) or jostle the seeds loose from their fruits and blow them for fairly long distances before heavier snows set in. In the winter landscape, this is probably a very effective mode of dispersal for poppies, campions, saxifrages, grass-of-Parnassus, primroses, paintbrushes, louseworts, harebells, sedges and woodrushes. It could conceivably account for movement along ridges even for such relatively heavy, unappendaged seeds as those of yellow glacier-lily, springbeauties and arctic lupine.

northern grass-of-Parnassus   yellow mountain-avens   dwarf alpine hawksbeard

Mop-top, Western Pasqueflower, Tow-headed Baby • *Anemone occidentalis*

General: Densely long-soft-hairy perennial from a tap-rooted, woody stem-base; flowering stems 1 to several, erect, 10–60 cm tall.

Leaves: Basal leaves several, long-stalked, **3–4 times pinnately dissected** into narrow, **linear ultimate segments 1–3 mm wide;** stem leaves usually 3, whorled, short-stalked, roughly similar in shape to basal leaves.

Flowers: Solitary atop the stem, saucer-shaped, 3–7 cm across; petals lacking; sepals 5–7, **creamy white,** sometimes tinged purple especially on the outside near the base, egg-shaped; stamens very numerous (150+).

Fruits: Achenes ellipsoid, soft-hairy, numerous in a long-stalked head, the **tips (styles) elongated** (2–5 cm long), curved, **silky-feathery.**

Where Found: Open, rocky slopes, mesic to moist meadows and glades; montane to alpine zones; frequent in much of the southern ⅓ of the region; cordilleran.

Similar Species: Pasqueflower or prairie crocus (**A. patens var. multifida;** *Pulsatilla patens* ssp. *multifida*) has **purple to blue flowers** and **basal leaves 2–3 times dissected** with ultimate segments 2–4 mm wide. It grows in grasslands, dry meadows and on rocky slopes and sandy-gravelly sites, in steppe to subalpine zones. It is frequent in eastern AK, YT and western NT and northernmost BC south in the Rockies through eastern BC, AB, MT, ID and WY to NM, and disjunct in the Wenatchee Mtns, WA. The species is circumboreal, but var. *multifida* is amphiberingian.

Notes: Mop-top is also known as *Pulsatilla occidentalis.*
• These 2 anemones have often been placed in the genus *Pulsatilla* on the basis of the long, feathery achene tips. Most other evidence supports their inclusion in *Anemone.* Both are very early bloomers.
• Small amounts of mashed anemone leaves have been used as counter-irritants for treating bruises and sore muscles. The Nlaka'pamux and Okanagan used root decoctions for stomach and bowel problems.
• **Caution:** Many members of this family and genus contain protoanemonin and are poisonous.

pasqueflower

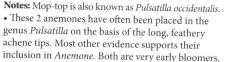

Northern Anemone • *Anemone parviflora*

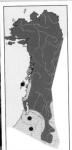

General: From a woody stem-base on **slender rhizomes;** stems 1 to several, erect, 5–30 cm tall, nearly hairless to densely soft-hairy.

Leaves: Basal leaves several, on stalks 2–10 cm long, compound, the blades divided into **3 main, wedge-shaped leaflets,** glossy, dark green, nearly hairless to soft-hairy, margins broadly toothed or lobed toward the tip; stem leaves (interpreted as involucral bracts) 2–3, stalkless.

Flowers: Solitary on a hairy stalk atop stem, saucer-shaped, 2–5 cm across; sepals 4–7, **frosty white, often tinged blue especially on the outside,** broadly elliptic to egg-shaped; stamens numerous (70–80).

Fruits: Achenes egg-shaped, 2–2.5 mm long, **densely woolly,** numerous in a long-stalked head, the tips (styles) short, 1–2.5 mm long, straight, hairless.

Where Found: Meadows, heathlands, seepage sites, thickets, streambanks, snowbeds, scree and tundra; montane to alpine zones; frequent throughout the northern ¾ of the region; mostly boreal North American, a bit eastern Asian.

Alpine Anemone, Drummond's Anemone • *Anemone drummondii*

General: Tufted from a branched, sometimes woody stem-base; stems ascending to erect, **10–25 cm tall,** stiff-hairy. **Leaves:** Basal leaves several, 2 times divided into 3s; leaflets irregularly incised, the **ultimate segments linear, 1–2.5 mm wide,** long-hairy to nearly hairless. **Flowers:** 1 (rarely 2) atop stem, 2–5 cm across; sepals 5–9, **white often tinged with blue on the outside,** hairy on the outside; stamens numerous, whitish; styles white. **Fruits:** Achenes egg-shaped, 2–4 mm long, **woolly,** numerous in a head, the tips (styles) straight, 2–4 mm long, hairless. **Where Found:** Steep rocky slopes, gravelly ridges, outcrops, scree and rocky meadows; subalpine and alpine zones; widespread but scattered and locally frequent in much of the region.

Varieties: Var. *drummondii* has ultimate leaf segments 1–1.5 mm wide and long-hairy. It ranges from southwestern BC to northern CA, disjunct in central ID. • Var. *lithophila* has broader (1.5–2.5 mm), hairless or hairy leaf segments, and is more widespread, ranging from AK, YT and NT south mostly in the Rockies to ID, MT and WY.

Similar Species: Purple anemone (A. multiceps; *Pulsatilla multiceps*) used to be included in *A. drummondii*. It has **flowers with blue to purple sepals,** purple stamens and red styles. Endemic to far northern AK and YT, it is locally frequent on rocky slopes, ridges, limestone and shale scree and tundra, in montane to alpine zones. • **Cut-leaved anemone (A. multifida)** is typically a **larger plant (20–60 cm tall)** of low to moderate elevations, though it does extend into the subalpine zone. Its leaves have **lance-shaped ultimate divisions 2–3.5 mm wide,** and the **2–7 flowers** (sometimes 1) vary in colour from **cream to yellowish tinged with blue, purple or red, especially on the outside, and are sometimes wholly pink.** It grows in grasslands, shrublands, open forests, rocky slopes, gravelly shores and meadows, and is frequent in almost the entire region, widespread in North America and disjunct in South America.

Notes: Anemones are propagated by seed or, for rhizomatous species, by dividing the rhizomes. Many of these species grow well in rock gardens, requiring little attention.

purple anemone

Narcissus Anemone
Anemone narcissiflora

General: Tufted from a sometimes woody stem-base; stems
erect, 7–**60 cm tall**, commonly
hairy. **Leaves:** Basal leaves several, palmately divided into
3 main sections, themselves
incised and lobed, the **ultimate
segments 3–10 mm wide,**
nearly hairless to silky-hairy. **Flowers:** 1 or 2–8 in an umbel
atop the stem, 2–5 cm across; sepals 5–9, **white to cream
or yellowish, often tinged with blue on the outside. Fruits:**
Achenes egg-shaped, **6–9 mm long, winged, hairless,** the
tips (styles) curved or hooked, 1–1.5 mm long, hairless.
Where Found: Meadows, shrublands, forest openings, heathlands, rocky slopes and tundra; lowland (arctic coast)

to alpine zones; frequent in the northern ½ of the region; arctic-alpine,
our varieties amphiberingian.

Varieties: The species complex has lots of variation; ours are mostly
var. *monantha* (*A. n.* ssps. *alaskana*, *interior* and *sibirica*), with **var.
*villosissima*** in westernmost AK.

Notes: Aleutian and Siberian peoples ate the early spring growth
on the upper end of the root. It has a mealy, waxy texture and
taste. The leaves were eaten like cress, and "Inuit ice cream" was
made by beating the green parts with oil to a creamy consistency.
Anemone roots were considered by Aboriginal northerners to be
powerful medicine and were used for treating wounds and by the Aleuts
as an antihemorrhagic. • **Caution:** This species could be poisonous.

Yellow Anemone
Anemone richardsonii

General: Stems single or a few together from **slender
rhizomes,** erect, **5–30 cm tall,** upper part hairy. **Leaves:**
Basal leaf 1, **simple,** kidney-shaped to nearly circular,
palmately 3-lobed, the 3 main lobes also lobed or
toothed, hairless or sparsely soft-hairy, the **ultimate
segments 4–10 (to 15) mm wide. Flowers:** 1 atop the
stem, 2–4 cm across; sepals 4–8, **yellow. Fruits:** Achenes
egg-shaped to oblong, 3–4 mm long, **not winged,
hairless,** several to many in a head, the tips (styles)
curved or hooked, 4–6 mm long, hairless.
Where Found: Moist to wet streambanks, seepage
sites, open forests, thickets, swamps, meadows and
peaty tundra; lowland (arctic coast) to alpine zones; frequent in the northern ⅔ of the region; amphiberingian.

Notes: A commonly held view
is that *Anemone* is from the
Greek *anemos*, "wind," hence
the generic common name
"windflower." It is said that
Anemos (the wind) uses these
small flowers to herald his
coming in early spring. Others
suggest that the name is a corruption of *Naaman*, the Semitic name for Adonis. According to a legend from the Far East, the crimson anemone (*A. coronaria*) sprang from the
blood of the slain Adonis. • The species is named for John Richardson (1787–1865),
a Scottish naturalist associated with John Franklin's expedition to arctic America.

The Genus *Ranunculus* (Buttercup)

Ranunculus is the largest genus in the buttercup family, with about 300 species worldwide, 77 of which occur in North America, mostly in temperate and cold climates. The alpine flora of our region includes a dozen or so buttercup species.

Alpine buttercups are all perennial herbs, typically from fibrous roots and/or rhizomes surmounted by a stem-base. Leaf shape is very diverse, the mostly basal leaves simple and entire or toothed, or variously lobed or compound, the lobes/leaflets often with toothed or lobed margins; the stem leaves are alternate. The saucer-shaped flowers are solitary or few to several, with usually 5 sepals, 5–15 distinct, yellow petals, each with a nectar gland at the base, 10 to numerous stamens and 5 to many ovaries. The fruit is an egg- or globe-shaped to cylindric cluster of 1-seeded achenes, which are flattened, smooth to veined or hairy, with a straight to hooked, persistent style (beak).

Key to *Ranunculus*

1a. Leaves simple, not lobed or dissected and at most minutely toothed; plants south of 48° N . . . **2**

  2a. Basal leaves lance- or egg- to heart-shaped, slightly less than twice as long as wide **3**

    3a. Leaf blades egg- to heart-shaped, squared-off to heart-shaped at the base
. . . . **R. populago** (p. 194)

    3b. Leaf blades lance- to egg-shaped or elliptic; pointed at the base
. . . . **R. alismifolius** in part (p. 194)

  2b. Basal leaves linear to lance-shaped or elliptic, more than twice as long as wide **4**

    4a. Leaf blades lance-shaped, mostly at least 1 cm wide; roots hairless
. . . . **R. alismifolius** in part (p. 194)

    4b. Leaf blades linear to narrowly elliptic, <1 cm wide; roots finely hairy . . . **R. oresterus** (p. 194)

1b. Leaves all distinctly toothed to deeply lobed to compound or dissected; plants mostly northern or more widespread **5**

  5a. Achenes strongly veined; petals 11–15 . . . . **R. cooleyae** (p. 191)

  5b. Achenes not strongly veined; petals usually 5 . . . . **6**

    6a. Sepals dark-brown-hairy on the outer surface **7**

      7a. Receptacles hairless; achenes 40–50 . . . . **R. nivalis** (p. 193)

      7b. Receptacles brown-hairy; achenes 50–90 . . . . **R. sulphureus** (p. 193)

    6b. Sepals hairless, whitish- or yellowish-soft-hairy on the outer surface **8**

      8a. Basal leaves simple, toothed, mostly unlobed **9**

        9a. Leaf bases squared-off to rounded; petals 5; sepals 3–5 mm long, hairless or thinly hairy . . . . **R. inamoenus** (p. 194)

        9b. Leaf bases heart-shaped; petals 5–10; sepals 5–8 mm long, soft-hairy
. . . . **R. cardiophyllus** (p. 194)

      8b. Basal leaves lobed, cleft or incised **10**

        10a. Achenes finely to sparsely hairy; basal leaves 5–9-lobed at least ½ their length
. . . . **R. pedatifidus** (p. 192)

        10b. Achenes hairless; basal leaves otherwise lobed or dissected **11**

          11a. Basal leaves dissected into linear segments . . . . **R. adoneus** (p. 194)

          11b. Basal leaves lobed or incised but not finely dissected **12**

12a. Petals about as long as sepals; stems often <5 cm tall **13**

13a. Flowering stems 1–4 cm tall; basal leaf blades <1 cm long; petals 1–3.5 mm long; achene beaks often straight, sometimes curved .... ***R. pygmaeus*** (p. 193)

13b. Flowering stems 3–10 cm tall/long; basal leaf blades mostly 1–2 cm long; petals 3–6 mm long; achene beaks curved or hooked. .... ***R. gelidus*** (p. 193)

12b. Petals longer than sepals; stems usually >5 cm tall **14**

14a. Leaf surfaces hairless .... ***R. eschscholtzii*** (p. 192)

14b. Leaf surfaces hairy .... ***R. occidentalis*** (p. 192)

Cooley's Buttercup
Ranunculus cooleyae

General: Hairless, from a fibrous-rooted stem-base; stems 1, erect, 2–14 cm tall in flower, to 23 cm in fruit.

Leaves: All or mostly basal, 1–4 cm long, 1.5–7 cm wide, on stalks to 10 cm long, **circular to kidney-shaped, deeply palmately 3–5-lobed,** the lobes again divided, **glossy, green,** margins round-toothed; stem leaf 0–1, scale-like.

Flowers: Solitary atop stem; **petals 11–15,** yellow, **lance- to spoon-shaped, 8–12 mm long;** sepals 5, persistent, greenish yellow; stamens and ovaries numerous.

Fruits: Achenes ellipsoid, 2–4 mm long, **strongly veined** lengthwise, the tips (beaks) thread-like, 1–2 mm long, hooked; numerous in a spheric or hemispheric head.

Where Found: Wet to moist snowbeds, streambanks, meadows, heathlands, rocky gullies, ledges and scree; subalpine and alpine zones; frequent in the Pacific coastal mountains from southern AK to west-central BC, sporadic inland and southward; Pacific maritime endemic.

Notes: Children sometimes hold buttercup flowers under their chins to see if their skin glows yellow, indicating they like butter. How glow? The distinctive sheen of the petals is a result of their outer epidermal layer, which contains the yellow pigment and is made up of exceptionally flat cells. Light bounces off these cells straight back in the direction it came from. The petals do not scatter the light, but act like flat mirrors, imparting a buttery glow to the directionally reflected light. Ultraviolet light, which bees use to navigate, is similarly reflected. Buttercup flowers probably gleam like neon signs to their pollinators. • *Ranunculus* is from the Latin diminutive of *rana*, "frog," because frogs abound in the many damp and wet places that species of this genus grow; *cooleyae* honours Grace Emily Cooley (1857–1916), a botany instructor at Wellesley College and a botanical explorer in Alaska, where she discovered "her" buttercup. • "Buttercup" comes from "buttoncop," in turn from the French *bouton d'or*, "golden button," and the Old English *cop*, "head," whence "buttonhead" or a rounded, cup- or globe-shaped flower.

Subalpine Buttercup
Ranunculus eschscholtzii

General: Mostly hairless, from a fibrous-rooted stem-base; stems 1 to several, erect to spreading, 5–25 cm tall.

Leaves: Mostly basal, on stalks 1–8 cm long; blades 5–40 mm long, **kidney- or heart-shaped, 3-cleft, segments again lobed;** stem leaves usually absent, sometimes 1–2, transitional to a 3-lobed bract; leaves usually hairless except fringed on margins.

Flowers: 1–3 atop stem on **hairless stalks;** petals 5–8, yellow, broadly **egg-shaped, 6–16 mm long;** sepals 5, early deciduous, **yellow wavy-hairy or hairless** on the outside.

Fruits: Achenes egg-shaped, 1–2 mm long, hairless or nearly so, the tips (beaks) slender, straight or somewhat curved when young; numerous in a cylindric to egg-shaped head.

Where Found: Moist meadows, rocky slopes, heathlands, streambanks, shores, scree and talus; montane to alpine zones; virtually throughout, common in the southern ⅔ of the region, less frequent northward; amphiberingian.

Similar Species: Western buttercup (*R. occidentalis*) has **distinctly hairy stems (usually) and leaves.** It is a widespread species of open forests, clearings, shores, grassy slopes and meadows, in lowland to lower alpine zones. It is frequent along the coast and in the coastal mountains, east to the Rockies in the northern ½ of BC; also southern AK and southwestern YT through BC to southwestern AB, CA and NV. Western buttercup occupies many habitat types spanning a wide range of elevations, and it exhibits a lot of variation. The variety usually encountered in our region **at high elevations is var. brevistylis,** in southern AK and southwestern YT to central BC and southwestern AB. • **Bird's-foot buttercup** (*R. pedatifidus*) is about the same size as subalpine buttercup and is generally soft-hairy, but has basal leaves cleft into 5–9 (usually 7) segments, a tendency toward smaller flowers **(petals 7–10 mm long), hairy flower stalks** and **finely hairy achenes.** Birdsfoot buttercup is a boreal/arctic-alpine and circumpolar species, widespread but infrequent in meadows, rocky slopes, fellfields, gravelly shores and open forests, in lowland (arctic coast) to alpine zones. It has a peculiar, spotty distribution in our region (perhaps corresponding to the distribution of a combination of calcium-rich soils and winter-dry/summer-wet climates) and is found on the North Slope of AK, YT and NT, central AK, central and southwestern YT, scattered in interior BC and southwestern AB, and rare in MT and WY to UT, CO and AZ.

western buttercup

bird's-foot buttercup

Snow Buttercup • *Ranunculus nivalis*

General: Stems 1 to several, stout, rather fleshy, erect, **10–25 cm tall**, hairless or sparsely hairy. **Leaves:** Basal leaves kidney-shaped, 3-lobed, the 2 lateral lobes also cleft or toothed, **hairless except for fringed margins.** **Flowers:** 1 atop stem; **petals 5 (rarely 6)**, yellow, **8–12 mm long; sepals densely brown-hairy on the outside. Fruits:** Achenes, the beaks straight; numerous in a cylindric to egg-shaped head, the **receptacle knob-like, hairless.** **Where Found:** Moist to wet streambanks, seepage sites, thickets, meadows, scree slopes and peaty tundra;

lowland (arctic coast) to alpine zones; frequent in the northern ½ of the region; arctic-alpine, circumpolar.

Similar Species: Sulphur buttercup (*R. sulphureus*) has **basal leaves that are merely shallowly lobed or toothed,** stiff, **brown hairs on the receptacle** and **more than 50 achenes** in a cluster (snow buttercup has less than 50). It occurs on moist tundra, wet meadows, snowbeds and mossy seepage sites, in lowland (arctic coast) to alpine zones. This arctic-alpine, circumpolar species is scattered but locally frequent in the northern ⅓ of the region, AK, YT and western NT, rare in northern BC.

Notes: Until just before dispersal, snow buttercup has green, photosynthetic achenes.

Pygmy Buttercup
Ranunculus pygmaeus

General: Dwarf, from a short stem-base with slender, fibrous roots; stems 1 to several, erect or ascending, **6–35 mm tall** (elongating in fruit), hairless or short- hairy above. **Leaves:** Basal leaf blades 5–10 mm long, **deeply 3-lobed or 3-cleft,** the lateral segments again lobed, bases squared-off or nearly heart-shaped. **Flowers:** 1 (some-times 2) atop stem; **petals 5,** yellow, **1–3.5 mm long. Fruits:** Achenes, the beaks awl-shaped, straight or curved; several to many in a globe-shaped to cylindric head. **Where Found:** Moist to wet seepage sites, snowbeds, turfy meadows, shady ledges and scree slopes; lowland (arctic coast) to alpine zones; widespread but scattered in most of the region except the southwestern corner, frequent in the north, infrequent in the south; arctic-alpine, circumpolar.

Similar Species: Arctic-alpine buttercup (*R. gelidus*; *R. grayi, R. gelidus* ssp. *grayi, R. verecundus*) is also dwarf but **bigger (3–10 cm tall/long)** than

pygmy buttercup, with **larger (5–20 mm long), more deeply divided, grey-green leaves** and **1–5 larger flowers with petals 3–6 mm long.** It grows in moist meadows and on gravelly seepage, scree and talus slopes, in montane to alpine zones. An arctic-alpine, amphiberingian species, it is infrequent and scattered from AK, YT and western NT south sporadically through interior BC and southwestern AB to WA, northeastern OR, MT, ID, WY, UT and CO.

arctic-alpine buttercup

Notes: The leaf stalks of pygmy buttercup can elongate when submerged. Young stalks accomplish this by cell division and elongation, mature stalks by elongation alone. This is valuable versatility in the intermittently seepy areas where pygmy buttercup often grows.

Rocky Mountain Snow Buttercup
Ranunculus adoneus

General: Hairless, from a stout stem-base with slender, fibrous roots; stems 1 to several, erect, **10–25 cm tall.** **Leaves:** Basal, **2–3 times palmately dissected into linear segments. Flowers:** 1–3 atop stem; **petals 5–10,** yellow, **8–15 mm long;** sepals green, sometimes purple-tinged. **Fruits:** Achenes, the beaks awl-shaped, straight; numerous in an egg-shaped head. **Where Found:** Moist to wet meadows, streambanks and snowbeds; subalpine and alpine zones; frequent in the southeastern corner of the region; endemic.

Notes: Typically found around melting snowbanks, this buttercup blooms as soon as the snow melts or even through melting snow. In Colorado snow bowls, snow buttercups on the margins emerge and flower 3–4 weeks earlier than those at the bottom of the bowls, and plants in early melting sites have larger achenes with better survival rates. • Alpine buttercups are beautiful but difficult to grow in the home garden, generally requiring good drainage, spring moisture, rich soil and summer dormancy.

Water-plantain Buttercup
Ranunculus alismifolius

General: From fibrous or slightly tuberous roots; stems 1 to several, erect to ascending, 10–40 cm tall, hairless or soft-hairy. **Leaves: Basal and stem leaves simple,** lance- to egg-shaped or elliptic; blades 2–10 cm long, **parallel-veined, margins smooth or slightly toothed. Flowers:** Few to several in a branched cluster; **petals 5–12,** yellow, 5–12 mm long. **Fruits:** Achenes plump, the beaks lance- to awl-shaped; in an **egg- to globe-shaped head. Where Found:** Moist to wet meadows, fens and streambanks; lowland to alpine zones; frequent in the southern ⅓ of the region; cordilleran.

Varieties: *FNA* distinguishes 6, of which 5 occur in our region. **Plantain-leaved buttercup (*R. a.* var. *montanus*),** with leaves resembling those of common plantain (*Plantago major*) not water-plantain (*Alisma*) and **7–12 (typically 10) narrow petals,** is the most striking and perhaps the most typically high-elevation variety. It occurs in ID, WY, NV, UT and CO. The other varieties usually have 5 petals.

Similar Species: Unlovely buttercup (*R. inamoenus* var. *inamoenus*) has long-stalked, **roundish to egg-shaped, simple, mostly round-toothed leaves,** and 3–7 flowers with **5 petals,** 4–9 mm long, and **sepals 3–5 mm long.** It grows in moist meadows and on rocky slopes, in montane to alpine zones, and is sporadic through interior BC and southwestern AB to more frequently WA, ID, MT and WY to UT, CO, AZ and NM. • **Heart-leaved buttercup (*R. cardiophyllus*;** *R. pedatifidus* var. *cardiophyllus*) is similar to unlovely buttercup but is generally hairier, with **heart-shaped basal leaves,** somewhat larger flowers, the

Cascade buttercup

5–10 petals 6–13 mm long, and **sepals 5–8 mm long.** It is found in grasslands, forest openings and meadows, in steppe to subalpine zones, and is infrequent from eastern BC and western AB sporadically (northeastern WA, southern MT, UT, WY and CO) to AZ and NM. • **Cascade buttercup (*R. populago*)** also has **egg- to heart-shaped basal leaves** with entire or minutely round-toothed margins, but is **mostly hairless,** with thickened roots, 5–6 petals, 4–9 mm long, and **achenes in a hemispheric head.** It occurs in wet meadows, fens, bogs and along streambanks and shores, in montane to subalpine zones, and is locally frequent in southeastern WA, OR, ID, western MT and northern CA. • **Blue Mountain buttercup (*R. oresterus*)** has **narrowly elliptic to linear basal leaves,** mostly less than 1 cm wide, **fine-hairy roots** and 5 petals, 4–6 mm long. It grows in moist meadows, in montane and subalpine zones, and is restricted to northeastern OR and central ID.

Haida False Rue-anemone • *Enemion savilei*

General: Hairless perennial; stems several, erect, 10–35 cm tall.

Leaves: Basal and alternate on the stem, **long-stalked, compound, twice divided into 3s, the leaflets irregularly lobed.**

Flowers: 1 **(occasionally 2),** saucer-shaped, 3–5 cm across; petals lacking; **sepals 5 (to 9), white, 10–17 mm long,** sometimes tinged pink at tips, broadly elliptic to egg-shaped; stamens numerous, filaments thread-like to club-shaped.

Fruits: Follicles unstalked, pod-like, oblong, upright to spreading, tipped with persistent styles (beaks).

Where Found: Moist, shady cliffs, rocky meadows, gullies and talus slopes; montane to alpine zones; scattered in BC insular ranges, locally frequent on Haida Gwaii, rare on nearby Porcher I. and also Brooks Peninsula on northern Vancouver I.; coastal BC endemic.

Notes: Haida false rue-anemone is also known as *Isopyrum savilei*. • Discovered in 1957 on Haida Gwaii (Queen Charlotte Islands), this species was thought to be endemic there, but it was subsequently found in a few other places. • The name *savilei* honours D.B.O. Savile (1909–2000), a research botanist in Ottawa and a botanical explorer of Haida Gwaii.

Alpine Meadow-rue • *Thalictrum alpinum*

General: Hairless dwarf from slender rhizomes; stems single, erect, **5–25 cm tall.**

Leaves: Usually all basal, pale green, leathery, 2–10 cm long, twice pinnately compound, the leaflets wedge-egg-shaped to circular, 3–5-lobed toward the tip.

Flowers: Few to several in an **elongate, narrow cluster, bisexual;** petals lacking; sepals 4 (sometimes 5), soon falling off, greyish green, purplish-tinged, egg-shaped, 1–2.5 mm long; stamens 8–15, conspicuous, the anthers yellow, nodding on thread-like, purple filaments; stigmas purple.

Fruits: Achenes 2–6, lance-egg-shaped, slightly curved, **prominently ribbed,** 2–3.5 mm long, the fruit stalks curved downward.

Where Found: Moist to wet, often calcium-rich meadows, seepage sites, thickets, fens, rocky ledges and turfy shores; montane to alpine zones; frequent in the northern ½ of the region, infrequent and sporadic southward; arctic-alpine, interruptedly circumpolar.

Related Species: Western meadow-rue (*T. occidentale***)** is much taller **(30–120 cm),** with **large, mostly stem leaves** and **unisexual flowers,** the males with greenish to whitish sepals 3.5–4.5 mm long and **purplish, drooping stamens 5–15 mm long,** the females producing 6–9 achenes. It occurs in open forests, thickets and meadows, in lowland to upper subalpine zones. This cordilleran species is frequent in the southern ¾ of the region, from southeastern AK and southern YT through BC (except the central coast) and western AB to CA, NV, UT and CO.

Notes: *Thalictrum* is presumably called meadow-rue because, with its much-divided leaves, it resembles common rue (*Ruta graveolens*). • The Flathead of Montana dried the achenes, chewed them until they were pulverized, and then rubbed the mash on their hair and body as a perfume.

western meadow-rue

Blue Columbine, Colorado Columbine
Aquilegia coerulea

General: Stems erect, **15–80 cm tall. Leaves:** Mostly basal, twice divided into 3s, the leaflets not crowded, hairless or occasionally soft-hairy. **Flowers:** Several, large, showy, erect, **5–10 cm across;** petals 5, white or cream, the **spurs blue, white** or sometimes pink, 3–7 cm long; **sepals ice blue or sometimes lavender. Fruits:** Follicles 2–3 cm long, erect, hairy. **Where Found:** Rocky slopes, open forests, meadows and talus; montane to alpine zones; frequent in the southeastern corner of the region, primarily in the U.S. Rockies.

Varieties: 2 occur in our region: **var. *ochroleuca*,** with white to pale blue or lavender sepals and petal spurs 3.5–5.5 cm long, occurs in ID, MT, NV, UT and WY; **var. *alpina*,** with pale blue sepals and petal spurs 3–3.5 cm long, is found only in WY.

Similar Species: Jones' columbine or limestone columbine (***A. jonesii***) is much smaller (less than 12 cm tall) but is a real stunner. The leaves are all basal and have **crowded, ruffled, roundish leaflets** that are **finely hairy and smoky blue-green.** The single flowers are large (4–6 cm across), showy, erect, **intensely blue to purple,** the **spurs shorter (8–15 mm long)** and the follicles hairless. It is found on rock outcrops and talus slopes, and is restricted to limestone, in subalpine and alpine zones. Jones' columbine is infrequent in the southeastern part of the region, in the Rockies of southwestern AB, MT and northwestern WY.

Notes: *Adaptive radiation* is the term used to characterize the rapid evolution of new species, morphologies and ecological roles in response to different factors. The spectacular adaptive radiation of columbines in western North America about 3 million years ago was a response to a broadened suite of pollinators, with hummingbirds and, most recently, hawkmoths added to bees and bumblebees. • Blue columbine is pollinated by day mostly by bumblebees looking for pollen, and by night by hawkmoths searching for nectar. Bumblebee pollination seems to be more effective in outcrossing—moving genes among individuals and populations—but the 2 types of pollinators seem to be equally effective in helping produce viable seed. • For alpine gardeners, Jones' columbine is near the apex of desire, but after mountain sapphire (p. 331), it is the most difficult to cultivate. • Blue columbine is the state flower of Colorado. • **Caution:** This plant could be poisonous.

Jones' columbine

Yellow Columbine • *Aquilegia flavescens*

General: Perennial from a taprooted, woody stem-base; stems erect, 20–70 cm tall.

Leaves: Mostly basal, long-stalked, **pinnately compound, twice divided into 3s,** hairless or soft-hairy, the leaflets 2–3-lobed; stem leaves few, alternate, short-stalked.

Flowers: Several, **nodding,** in a cluster atop stem, 2.5–5 cm across; **petals 5, cream-coloured with yellow spurs 1–2 cm long** that turn inward with a hook at the end; **sepals 5, petal-like, yellow or tinged with pink,** spreading; stamens numerous, protruding beyond the mouths of the spurs.

Fruits: Follicles pod-like, usually 5, erect, 1.8–2.7 cm long, hairy or glandular hairy, long-beaked; seeds black, wrinkled, pebbled.

Where Found: Moist meadows, glades and rocky slopes; subalpine and alpine zones; frequent in the southeastern part of the region; cordilleran.

Similar Species: Red columbine or Sitka columbine (*A. formosa*) is a wide-ranging northwestern species that often makes it into subalpine meadows but is typically a plant of low to moderate elevations. It has red flowers with yellow centres. Red columbine sometimes hybridizes with yellow columbine, resulting in pinkish red flowers.

Notes: *Aquilegia* is thought to be from the Latin *aquila*, "eagle," because the petals were thought to resemble eagle talons. It could also be from *aqua*, "water," and *lego*, "to collect," because the spurred flowers with their nectaries at the tips looked like ancient water jars. "Columbine" is from the Latin *columba*, "dove," because of a fancied resemblance of the flower to the 5 little heads of pigeons (doves) feeding together around a bowl. • In a survey of Montana consumer preferences of native plants for residential gardens, yellow columbine was the highest-rated perennial herb.

Mountain Monkshood • *Aconitum delphiniifolium*

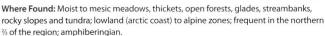

General: Stems single from a tuberous taproot, slender, erect, unbranched, 10–120 cm tall.

Leaves: Mostly alternate along the stem, stalked, **palmately divided to the base into 3–5 segments, themselves cleft into linear-oblong lobes,** hairless.

Flowers: Solitary or 3–15 in an open cluster; **flowers bilaterally symmetric,** on slender stalks, **usually dark blue-purple,** occasionally tinged with green, yellow or white, 2–4 cm long; **petals 2, concealed in a hood, spurred at the top; sepals 5, showy upper sepal (the hood) somewhat helmet-shaped;** stamens many.

Fruits: Follicles 3–5, **pod-like,** 1.5–2.5 cm long, **hairless to sparsely hairy;** seeds longitudinally winged, with many transverse, membranous baffles.

Where Found: Moist to mesic meadows, thickets, open forests, glades, streambanks, rocky slopes and tundra; lowland (arctic coast) to alpine zones; frequent in the northern ⅔ of the region; amphiberingian.

Notes: This plant's stature varies widely. Alpine plants are often dwarfed and have but one or a few flowers, in contrast to robust, valley-bottom individuals that exceed 1 m in height and have more than 10 flowers. • The general leaf shape is similar to that of *Delphinium*, some species of *Ranunculus* and *Anemone*, and *Geranium* species—compare their leaf silhouettes (p. 163). • One source says that *Aconitum* is an ancient Latin name for a "poisonous plant," from the Greek *akoniton*, which can also mean "wolfsbane" or "leopard's-bane," or it perhaps derives from *akon*, "a dart," because arrows were once dipped in monkshood juice. • All parts of the plant but especially the root tubers are **highly poisonous,** particularly for cattle. *Aconitum* and *Delphinium* both produce powerful diterpenoid alkaloids. • This could be the plant that, as recorded by David Nelson (on Captain Cook's third voyage), the Aleuts used the roots of to produce a deadly arrow poison.

Tall Larkspur, Mountain Larkspur • *Delphinium glaucum*

General: Perennial from a thick, tough rhizome; stems usually several, **hollow, erect, 40–200 cm tall, hairless,** glaucous, the **base usually green.**

Leaves: Numerous, alternate along stem, **absent toward the base at flowering time;** leaf blades palmately divided into usually **5 main segments, themselves 2–3 times sharply lobed;** hairless.

Flowers: **10–100 or more** in a long, narrow cluster atop stem; **flowers bilaterally symmetric with prominent, straight spur,** usually dark blue to deep purple (pale blue within), 1.5–2 cm long; **petals 4,** partly within but not concealed by upper sepal; **sepals 5, darker than petals, upper sepal spurred;** stamens many.

Fruits: Follicles pod-like, 1–2 cm long, **hairless to minutely hairy** (especially when young); seeds with winged margins.

Where Found: Moist, open forests, forest edges and glades, thickets, streambanks, meadows, rocky slopes and tundra; montane to alpine zones; frequent in the northern ⅔ of the region, less frequent southward; cordilleran.

Similar Species: Arctic larkspur (*D. brachycentrum*; *D. chamissonis*) is typically a **smaller plant** (10–50 cm tall), with **hairy stems leafier toward the often reddish base** and **hairy follicles.** It grows on rocky slopes, heathlands and tundra, in lowland (arctic coast) to alpine zones. This amphiberingian species is infrequent in northern AK and northern YT, and rare in south-central AK, southwestern YT and northern BC.

Notes: Tall larkspur displays a wide range in stature, depending on elevation and exposure. • Poisoning by larkspur is the most important cause of cattle loss in the mountain rangelands of western North America. More than 40 norditerpenoid alkaloids have been isolated from various *Delphinium* species; the culprit in livestock poisonings is likely the highly toxic methyllycaconitine, which is present in many larkspurs, including this species. • Some Alaskan peoples used tall larkspur to make a wash for lice, fleas and other similar pests. Some also drank a very small amount of the liquid from boiled larkspur root to treat tuberculosis. **Caution:** This species is **poisonous;** symptoms include abdominal pain, nausea, depressed respiration and finally asphyxiation.

Rockslide Larkspur, Olympic Mountain Larkspur *Delphinium glareosum*

General: Roots in a branched, dry, braided cluster; stems erect, **20–40 cm tall,** hairless, **bases sometimes reddish. Leaves:** On the stem and more numerous at the base, **rather fleshy. Flowers:** 5–12 in an open, branched cluster; petals bluish purple to bright blue, 1.5–2.5 cm long. **Fruits:** Follicles 1–1.7 cm long, hairless. **Where Found:** Steep, rocky slopes and ridges, talus and scree; infrequent in the southwestern portion of the region.

Similar Species: Two-lobe larkspur or upland larkspur (*D. nuttallianum*) has a small bundle of **somewhat  fleshy roots,** several **non-fleshy leaves,** and **bluish purple flowers, often with a whitish or yellowish centre.** It grows in meadows, open forests and shrublands, in steppe to subalpine zones, and is frequent in the inland southern ⅓ of the region, southern BC, WA, ID and MT to CA, AZ and NM.

Notes: In Colorado, two-lobe larkspur is pollinated primarily by queen bumblebees, solitary bees and hummingbirds. Pollinators will fly several hundred metres among different populations, thus in terms of pollen dispersal, isolated populations of the larkspur belong to a "metapopulation."

two-lobe larkspur

Blue Corydalis, Few-flowered Corydalis
Corydalis pauciflora

General: Hairless perennial from fleshy taproots with fibrous rootlets; stems usually 1, sometimes 2–3, erect, **5–18 cm tall.**

Leaves: 2–5, clustered near base of stem, alternate, **divided into 3 main segments, the segments deeply lobed, dark green, glaucous.**

Flowers: 2–5, crowded atop a stout stalk, **bilaterally symmetric, 1.5–2 cm long, sky blue to blue-purple** (occasionally lilac); **petals 4, outer 2 petals dissimilar, 1 of them spurred; sepals 2,** bract-like, shed early; stamens 6; style 1, stigma 4-lobed.

Fruits: Capsules ellipsoid, 1–1.5 cm long, bent down; seeds black, smooth, shiny.

Where Found: Wet to moist seepage sites, meadows, streambanks, snowbeds, heathlands and turfy tundra; montane to alpine zones; frequent but scattered in the northern ⅓ of the region, infrequent southward; arctic-alpine, amphiberingian.

Related Species: Steer's-head (*Dicentra uniflora*) has a **single flower** nodding on a short stalk barely exceeding to shorter than the **fern-like, smoky green leaves.** The flowers are 1–2 cm long, **white to peach or pink** tinged with light brown, **heart-shaped at the base, the outer 2 petals similar, swollen and pouched at the base,** spreading and **curved back upward to form "horns."** It is found in gravelly meadows and on rocky slopes, blooming very early, often near melting snowbanks, in montane to lower alpine zones. A cordilleran species, it is infrequent in the southern ⅓ of the region in and east of the Cascades, from southern BC through WA, OR, ID and MT to CA, UT and WY.

Notes: Blue corydalis is also known as *Corydalis arctica.* • Eversmann's Parnassian or Apollo (*Parnassius eversmanni*) is a butterfly that uses *Corydalis* species as host plants; in our region, most likely blue corydalis. • *Corydalis* is either from the Greek *korys,* "helmet," or *korydallis,* "crested lark." We prefer the latter explanation, which likens the petal spurs to a feathered crest, or the tails or claws of larks. Others argue that the flower is shaped like a helmet with crests (spurs).

steer's-head

Mustard Family (Brassicaceae)

The mustards are a large family of about 3800 species distributed primarily in temperate regions of the Northern Hemisphere. In our region, the family consists of mainly perennial (at high elevations) herbs with watery, often pungent sap, often with forked or star-shaped hairs, and with alternate, mostly **simple**, sometimes compound leaves. The flowers are radially symmetric, typically in clusters that elongate with age, and have 4 sepals, 4 petals, 6 stamens and 1 **superior**, 2-chambered ovary. The fruits are usually pod-like with 2 chambers separated by a **septum** (a membranous partition) and opening by 2 segments; if long and narrow, the fruits are called **siliques**, and if short and broad, **silicles**. The seeds are in 1 or 2 rows, the siliques sometimes **torulose** (constricted between the seeds, sort of like a python that has swallowed a series of croquet balls).

The family has considerable economic importance because of its food crops, weeds and ornamentals. Important food crops include cabbage, cauliflower, broccoli, rutabaga, kohlrabi, Brussels sprouts (all from *Brassica oleracea*), turnips (*B. rapa*), vegetable oil (*B. napus*), radish (*Raphanus*) and watercress (*Nasturtium officinale*). The family also produces condiments, including mustard (*Brassica, Sinapsis*), horseradish (*Armoracia*) and wasabi (*Eutrema japonicum*). Troublesome weeds that are widespread in at least the southern half of our region—though usually not at high elevations—include the hoary-cresses and pepper-grasses (*Lepidium* spp.), tumble-mustard (*Sisymbrium altissimum*), field pennycress (*Thlaspi arvense*), flixweed (*Descurainia sophia*), blue mustard (*Chorispora tenella*), alyssums (*Alyssum* spp.) and dyer's woad (*Isatis tinctoria*). The relatively innocuous shepherd's purse (*Capsella bursa-pastoris*), mustards (*Brassica* spp.) and wintercress (*Barbarea vulgaris*) are also widespread weeds. Ornamentals include wallflowers (*Cheiranthus, Erysimum*), wallcress (*Aubrieta*, also known as *Aubretia*), silver dollar plant or honesty (*Lunaria*), stocks (*Matthiola*), rocket (*Hesperis*), candytuft (*Iberis*), sweet alyssum (*Lobularia*) and rockcress (*Arabis*).

Key to the Genera of Brassicaceae

1a. Mature fruit (silicle) 1–3 times as long as wide, lance- or egg-shaped to elliptic, heart-shaped or circular 2
  2a. Silicles rounded in cross-section, nearly spheric to football-, egg- or heart-shaped 3
    3a. Petals white or pink-purple, without yellow tones; plants long-lived, growing from a strong, thick, woody root crown; leaves prominently lobed . . . . **Smelowskia** (pp. 210–211)
    3b. Petals yellow or yellowish with a purplish blush; plants short-lived, from a taproot or thin rhizomes, or from a delicate, weak root crown; if somewhat long-lived, then leaves not prominently lobed 4
      4a. Basal leaves entire or wavy-margined to toothed, unlobed . . . . **Physaria** (pp. 215–217)
      4b. Basal leaves pinnately lobed, with 2 rows of lobes on either side of midrib 5
        5a. Leaf rosettes indistinct or withering by flowering time; stems branched; fruits hairless . . . . **Rorippa alpina** (p. 212)
        5b. Leaf rosettes well developed and persistent; stems simple; fruits hairy . . **Physaria** (pp. 215–217)
  2b. Silicles distinctly flattened 6
    6a. Silicles broadest at middle or below, flattened parallel to relatively broad septum; stem leaves not clasping at base . . . . **Draba** (pp. 218–229)
    6b. Silicles broadest at or near tip, flattened at right angles to narrow septum; stem leaves clasping at base . . . . **Noccaea** (p. 214)
1b. Mature fruit (silique) more than 3 times as long as wide, narrowly elliptic or oblong to linear 7
  7a. Leaves mostly pinnately divided, with 2 rows of lobes on either side of midrib; occasionally (*Cardamine*) palmately lobed 8
    8a. Plants hairless or with simple hairs only . . . . **Cardamine** (pp. 208–210)
    8b. Plants hairy, with simple and branched hairs 9
      9a. Perennials with prominent basal leaves; petals white or pink to purple . **Smelowskia** (pp. 210–211)
      9b. Annuals or biennials with inconspicuous basal leaves; petals yellowish . . . . **Descurainia** (p. 212)
  7b. Leaves unlobed to coarsely toothed, occasionally vaguely lobed or "lyrate" (lyre-shaped, pinnately lobed with topmost lobe large and rounded, the lower lobes small) 10
    10a. Petals cream, yellow or orange 11
      11a. Plants usually hairless, sprawling, of wet habitats; seeds in 2 rows . . . . **Rorippa alpina** (p. 212)
      11b. Plants usually hairy, erect to prostrate or cushion-forming, of dry to moist habitats; seeds in 1 or 2 rows 12
        12a. Flowering stems conspicuously leafy, stems unbranched; seeds in 1 row; plants with appressed, 2–3-pronged hairs . . . . **Erysimum** (p. 202)

12b. Flowering stems leafless or with few leaves, or if leaves numerous then stems mostly branched; seeds in 2 rows; plants usually with variously branched hairs, also with or without simple hairs. . . . . ***Draba*** (pp. 218–229)

10b. Petals white to pink or purple **13**

13a. Plants with at least some branched hairs. **14**

14a. Siliques rounded or slightly 4-angled in cross-section, slightly if at all compressed . . . . ***Braya*** (p. 213)

14b. Siliques moderately to strongly flattened **15**

15a. Siliques <8 times as long as wide . . . . ***Draba*** (pp. 218–229)

15b. Siliques usually at least 8 times as long as wide. **16**

16a. Petals purple or lilac; seeds wingless; mostly north of 60° N . . . . ***Erysimum pallasii*** (p. 202)

16b. Petals white or cream; seeds winged or wingless; south of 60° N (ours) . . . . ***Arabis*** (p. 206)

13b. Plants hairless or hairy with simple hairs only **17**

17a. Stems leafless or few-leaved. **18**

18a. Plants glandular-hairy, rarely hairless; siliques 4–7 mm wide . . . . . ***Parrya nudicaulis*** (p. 203)

18b. Plants not glandular-hairy; siliques <4 mm wide **19**

19a. Leaves usually compound (pinnate, digitate or trifoliate), sometimes simple; plants mostly hairless; seeds in 1 row . . . . ***Cardamine*** (pp. 208–210)

19b. Leaves simple, margins entire or wavy-toothed to pinnately cut; plants hairy to nearly hairless; seeds in 1 (*B. humilis*) or 2 rows . . . . ***Braya*** (p. 213)

17b. Stems leafy **20**

20a. Stem leaves with earlobe-like, clasping bases . . . . ***Boechera*** (pp. 204–206)

20b. Stem leaves without earlobe-like, clasping bases (except *Arabis pycnocarpa*) **21**

21a. Stem leaves crowded at base of flower cluster; siliques 5–15 mm long; plants hairless or sparsely hairy . . . . ***Aphragmus eschscholtzianus*** (p. 214)

21b. Stem leaves not crowded at base of flower cluster; siliques 1–4 cm long. **22**

22a. Leaves egg-shaped to broadly diamond-shaped; stem leaves absent or 1–2 . . . . ***Cardamine bellidifolia*** (p. 208)

22b. Leaves lance-shaped to narrowly egg-shaped **23**

23a. Siliques round or slightly 4-angled in cross-section; leaves entire, basal leaves long-stalked; plants hairless. . . . . ***Eutrema edwardsii*** (p. 203)

23b. Siliques flattened; lower leaves often toothed, basal leaves stalked or stalk-less; plants hairy or hairless **24**

24a. Leaves entire or sometimes toothed; plants often hairy; flowering stems growing vertically. . . . . ***Arabis*** (p. 206)

24b. At least some leaves pinnately cleft (lyrate); plants mostly hairless; flowering stems growing at various angles, often not vertically . . . . ***Arabidopsis*** (p. 207)

star-flowered draba

Pallas' Wallflower, Arctic Wallflower
Erysimum pallasii

General: Perennial from a thick taproot and stem-base; stems 1 or several, erect or ascending, 3–35 cm tall, the base covered with old leaves; plants with **2-pronged hairs.**

Leaves: Mostly in a basal rosette, linear-lance-shaped, 3–5 cm long, tapering to narrow stalks, margins smooth to shallowly toothed; stem leaves few to several, reduced upward.

Flowers: Large, **showy, fragrant,** numerous on ascending to erect stalks in a cluster atop stem; **petals purple or lilac, 1–2 cm long,** the blade 3–5 mm wide, narrowing to a slender, stalk-like base.

Fruits: Siliques ascending to erect, **3–11 cm long, 2–4 mm wide, often dark purple, linear, often curved,** flattened parallel to partition, hairy;

style forming a beak 1–3 mm long; seeds about 2 mm long, **not winged.**

Where Found: Cliffs, talus and scree, sandy or gravelly cutbanks, tundra and heathlands; montane to alpine zones; frequent across the far north (north of 68° N), scattered southward, disjunct and rare in the Rocky Mtns of southwestern AB; high arctic–alpine, circumpolar.

Notes: At first, the flower cluster is so short and compact that the flowers appear as if they have developed at the base and are hiding among the leaves, but the axis elongates as the flowers mature and especially as the fruits form. Pallas' wallflower flowers and fruits only once in its life and then dies, but what a way to go! • This species is named in honour of Peter Simon Pallas (1741–1811), a German zoologist and a student of Siberian flora.

Cascade Wallflower, Sand-dwelling Wallflower • *Erysimum arenicola*

General: Stems few to several (sometimes single) from a branched stem-base, erect, 5–30 cm tall. **Leaves:** Basal leaves numerous, lance-shaped, 2–7 cm long, entire or wavy-toothed, with appressed, 2–3-pronged hairs, tapering to long stalks; stem leaves several, much like basal leaves. **Flowers:** Showy, several to many in compact clusters elongating with age; **petals bright lemon yellow,** 1.5–2.5 cm long. **Fruits:** Mature siliques linear, **flattened at intervals,** 3–12 cm long, 1.5–2.5 mm wide, ascending to erect, usually hairy. **Where Found:** Rocky, gravelly or sandy slopes, ridges, talus and scree; montane to alpine zones; scattered but locally frequent in the southwestern part of the region.

Similar Species: Ballhead wallflower (*E. capitatum*; *E. asperum* in part) has siliques that are **4-angled in cross-section** (vs. flattened in Cascade wallflower) and often orange-yellow petals. It is frequent and widespread in the southern ⅓ of the region, occasionally reaching alpine meadows and ridges, especially in the Cascades and Rockies (where it is often known as *E. nivale*).

Notes: Alpine populations of ballhead wallflower have higher rates of survival in all life stages than lower-elevation populations. Perhaps that's why lower-elevation individuals of this species generally manage to reproduce sexually only once in their lifetime, whereas alpine individuals commonly reproduce many times. (To impress an inattentive audience, you can refer to the former strategy as semelparity or monocarpy, and the latter as iteroparity or polycarpy, so long as you pronounce the terms correctly.) • *Erysimum* could mean "blistercress," from the Greek *erysimon*, derived from *eryo*, "to draw," because some species were used medicinally to induce blistering. But *FNA* says it is from *eryso*, "to ward off or cure," alluding to the reputed medicinal properties of some *Erysimum* species.

Smooth-stem Parrya, Parry's Wallflower
Parrya nudicaulis

General: Tufted or loosely clumped from a long, stout taproot and usually branched stem-base, the branches covered in old leaf bases; flowering stems single, erect or ascending, 5–30 cm tall.

Leaves: In a **basal tuft,** long-stalked, spoon- or lance-shaped to elliptic, 2–7 cm long, margins smooth to wavy or coarsely and irregularly toothed, hairless or with glandular hairs.

Flowers: Large, **showy, fragrant,** 3–20 on ascending stalks in an open cluster atop stem; **petals pink to rose purple or lavender,** occasionally white, **1.5–2 cm long,** with a broad blade and slender, stalk-like base; sepals greenish purple.

Fruits: Siliques erect, **2–5 cm long, 4–7 mm wide, oblong,** flattened parallel to the partition, constricted between seeds, hairless or glandular-hairy; style forming a distinct beak 1–3 mm long; seeds large, about 5 mm long, with loose, net-like seed coats that form wide wings.

Where Found: Moist to mesic meadows, heathlands, tundra, talus, snowbeds and fellfields; montane to alpine zones; frequent in the north; arctic-alpine, amphiberingian.

Notes: Some reference works suggest that sexual reproduction is less important in harsh arctic environments and that, when it occurs, pollination is primarily by wind. However, insects are important pollinators of many arctic-alpine plants, including smooth-stem parrya. Without pollinators, seed set is low; with pollen augmentation, seed set increases. Lighter-coloured flowers, more common in areas with increased growing-season temperatures, attract more pollinators but are apparently subject to greater herbivory. • The roots were collected by the Inuit and others and added to fish and meat stews. Some northern peoples ate the leaves in early spring and after the first frost in autumn. They also stored the leaves in seal oil for winter use. • *Parrya* is named in honour of William E. Parry (1790–1855), an arctic navigator and explorer.

Edwards' Mock-wallflower, Hole-in-the-wallflower
Eutrema edwardsii

General: Tufted, **hairless** perennial from a rather fleshy taproot and stem-base; stems 1 to several, spreading-ascending to erect, 8–35 cm tall.

Leaves: Basal leaves clumped, **narrowly egg-shaped to elliptic,** long-stalked, the somewhat fleshy blades 5–25 mm long, soon withering, **margins toothless; stem leaves 3–7,** lance-oblong, becoming unstalked and progressively smaller upward.

Flowers: Rather small, 3–20 in a cluster—at first head-like, later elongating to cylinder 5–15 cm long—atop stem; **petals white or cream,** 3–5 mm long, spoon-shaped; sepals purplish.

Fruits: Siliques **narrowly oblong to linear,** tapering at both ends, **rounded or slightly 4-angled in cross-section,** 1–2 cm long, ascending to erect, purplish, the **partition perforated.**

Where Found: Mesic to moist tundra, peaty ridges, turfy seepage, heathlands, talus and scree, often on calcium-rich or nitrogen-enriched sites; lowland (arctic coast) to alpine zones; frequent across the northern part of the region, disjunct in CO; arctic-alpine, circumpolar.

Notes: Plants from Alaska, Greenland and northern Canada grow at altitudes of sea level to 1800 m, whereas those of Colorado (formerly known by some as *E. penlandii*) grow above 3500 m. • The fleshy rhizomes of eastern Asian *Eutrema japonicum* are the main source of true wasabi. • *Eutrema* is from the Greek *eu*, "well," and *trema*, "hole," referring to perforations in the fruit partition. • The species is named for John Edwards, ship's surgeon on the *Hecla* on William E. Parry's arctic voyages and on the *Isabel* on John Ross' first voyage in 1818.

The Genus *Boechera* (Suncress)

Our high-elevation suncresses are perennial, mostly tufted, hairless or densely hairy herbs from a well-developed, often branching stem-base, with few to many stems, and with a cluster of basal leaves that are mostly entire to weakly toothed; the few to several, similar but progressively smaller, alternate stem leaves often have earlobe-like, somewhat clasping bases. The flowers are several to many atop the stem in clusters that are at first compact, but often greatly elongating in fruit; the petals are white, pink or purple and longer than the sepals. The fruits are typically linear siliques, straight or curved, variously oriented and flattened, with winged, margined or wingless seeds in 1 or 2 rows in each chamber of the silique.

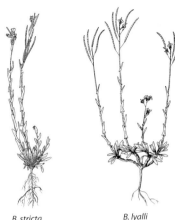

Boechera has often been regarded as a synonym of *Arabis*, but there is morphological and molecular evidence that the 2 genera are not closely related. *Boechera* researchers noted in 2006 that continuing molecular analyses would lead to a better understanding of the evolution of species in the genus, "and profound changes, with respect to species definition and circumscription, are to be expected in the near future." The near future began with the 2010 *FNA* treatment. No doubt more changes are in the offing.

As either *Arabis* or *Boechera*, the genus has always been taxonomically difficult. Many of the species have arisen as a result of hybridization (between distinct sexual species) followed by "polyploidy" (doubling—or more—of the set of chromosomes) and "apomixis" (asexual or vegetative reproduction). This evolutionary strategy is not unusual in arctic-alpine plants. For example, *Draba, Potentilla, Antennaria* and *Salix* have been up to similar tricks, and all of these genera are notoriously challenging. In some modern treatments, the difficulty of identification is compounded by reliance, in identification keys, on microscopic characteristics

B. stricta   *B. lyalli*

such as pollen morphology and the branching patterns of hairs. This field guide cannot engage in hair-splitting, but *FNA*'s *Boechera* treatment does provide a road map to ultimate identification for those with fortitude and good magnification.

Boechera is named after Tyge W. Böcher (1909–83), a Danish cytogeneticist and a student of subarctic and especially Greenland plants.

Key to *Boechera*

1a. Mature siliques mostly erect or ascending 2

    2a. Biennials or short-lived perennials, not woody at the base; mature siliques tightly appressed to axis of fruiting cluster; petals mostly white, sometimes pinkish . . . . **B. stricta (p. 205)**

    2b. Relatively long-lived perennials, woody at base; mature siliques ascending-erect, held close to axis of fruiting cluster, occasionally somewhat divergent or spreading away from it; petals mostly pink-purple, sometimes whitish 3

        3a. Mature siliques 3–5.5 mm wide; seeds broadly (1–2.5 mm) winged, petals cream to purplish . . . . **B. platysperma (p. 205)**

        3b. Mature siliques 1.3–2.5 mm wide; seeds narrowly (<1 mm) winged; petals dark purple to lilac or pinkish . . . 4

            4a. Basal leaf surfaces hairless or nearly so . . . . **B. lyallii (p. 205)**

            4b. Basal leaf surfaces hairy 5

                5a. Plants 3–15 cm tall; basal leaf surfaces densely hairy; siliques 1.3–3.5 mm wide . . . . **B. paupercula (p. 205)**

                5b. Plants 10–30 cm tall; basal leaf surfaces sparsely hairy; siliques 1.8–4 mm wide . . . . **B. calderi (p. 205)**

1b. Mature siliques arching, spreading or drooping 6

    6a. Siliques drooping, 3–6 mm wide . . . . **B. suffrutescens (p. 205)**

    6b. Siliques spreading more or less horizontally and to 1 side, 1.5–3.5 mm wide 7

        7a. Siliques 1.5–2.3 mm wide, on stalks 2–6 mm long; petals 4–6 mm long . . . . **B. lemmonii (p. 206)**

        7b. Siliques 2–3.5 mm wide, on stalks 4–8 mm long; petals 6–8 mm long . . . . **B. drepanoloba (p. 206)**

Rising Suncress, Jewelled Suncress • *Boechera lyallii*

General: Tufted perennial from a taproot and branched, somewhat woody stem-base; stems 1 to several, unbranched, erect, 5–20 cm tall, **glaucous, hairless.**

Leaves: Basal leaves numerous, lance-shaped, 1.5–3 cm long, **bright green, somewhat fleshy, usually hairless,** margins toothless, tapering to slender stalks; stem leaves several, oblong, unstalked, **with earlobe-like, clasping bases.**

Flowers: 2–15 in a short cluster elongating in fruit; **petals rose to purple, 6–9 mm long;** sepals greenish or purplish.

Fruits: Siliques linear, flattened, 3–6 cm long, **1.5–2.5 mm wide, erect-ascending** but not tightly appressed, rather somewhat spreading from axis of flower cluster, hairless; seeds in 2 rows, **1.5–2 mm long, narrowly (0.3–0.5 mm) winged.**

Where Found: Dry to mesic meadows, rock outcrops and crevices, scree and talus slopes, gravelly ridges and fellfields; subalpine and alpine zones; frequent in the southern ½ of the region, infrequent northward; cordilleran.

Similar Species: Small suncress (*B. paupercula*; *Arabis lyallii* var. *nubigena*, *A. nubigena*), of similar high-elevation habitats in WA, OR, ID, WY and CA, can be recognized by its **densely branched-hairy leaves. • Setting suncress (*B. suffrutescens*; *A. suffrutescens*)** has purple- or pink-tipped, whitish petals, is **strongly woody at the base** and has **drooping siliques 3–6 mm wide** with winged (1–1.5 mm) seeds. It is found on rock slides and dry, gravelly ridges, in montane to alpine zones, inland in WA, OR, ID, CA and NV. • **Flatseed suncress (*B. platysperma*; *A. platysperma*)** has **ascending-erect siliques 3–5.5 mm wide** with **broadly winged (1–2.5 mm) seeds.** It occurs in open forests and on rock outcrops and dry, gravelly ridges, in montane to lower alpine zones, from Mt. Hood, OR, south in the Cascades to CA.

Notes: Rising suncress is also known as *Arabis lyallii*. • This species is named for David Lyall (1817–95), a Scottish botanist who worked in America.

Uptight Suncress, Straight-up Suncress • *Boechera stricta*

General: Tufted biennial or short-lived perennial, stems few to several, usually 1–4 per branch of stem-base, erect, **15–80 cm tall. Leaves:** Basal leaves numerous in a rosette, lance-shaped, tapering to slender stalks, usually entire, **usually hairy with 2-rayed hairs;** stem leaves several to many, unstalked, with earlobe-like, clasping bases. **Flowers:** 8–40 or more in narrow clusters; **petals white,** often pinkish with age, 7–11 mm long. **Fruits:** Siliques linear, straight, 4–10 cm long, 1.5–3.5 mm wide, **erect, pressed tight to axis of flower cluster;** seeds in 2 rows, narrowly winged (0.3–0.8 mm). **Where Found:** Open, rocky or grassy slopes, gravel bars, roadsides, meadows and forest edges; montane (mostly) to lower alpine zones; frequent in much of the southern ⅔ of the region; widespread in North America.

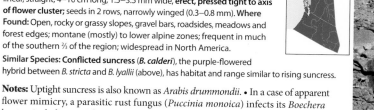

Similar Species: Conflicted suncress (*B. calderi*), the purple-flowered hybrid between *B. stricta* and *B. lyallii* (above), has habitat and range similar to rising suncress.

Notes: Uptight suncress is also known as *Arabis drummondii*. • In a case of apparent flower mimicry, a parasitic rust fungus (*Puccinia monoica*) infects its *Boechera* hosts—including uptight suncress—and subverts normal development. Instead of forming basal leaf rosettes, rusted plants develop long stems topped by flower-like clusters of yellow, infected leaves. The pseudo-flowers somewhat resemble buttercups and appear to fool flies, which are attracted into attempted pollination by the colour and a sugary, sweet-smelling exudate of the fungus. The exudate also contains fungal "spermatia," thus rust gametes are carried from one counterfeit flower to another and probably also to other uninfected host plants, enabling both outcrossing and dispersal of the fungus. • Thale cress (*Arabidopsis thaliana*) has long been used as a model organism to understand at a genetic level the molecular biology of many traits such as flowering. It was the first plant genome to be sequenced. Researchers have recently also sequenced the genome of uptight suncress and are investigating the molecular basis for such things as the timing of flowering and the production of compounds (glucosinolates) that deter insect herbivores.

Skewed Suncress, Windblown Suncress
Boechera lemmonii

General: Tufted perennial from a taproot and branched stem-base, stems 1 to few, erect, **5–25 cm tall. Leaves:** Basal leaves numerous, lance-spoon-shaped, 1–2.5 cm long, tapering to slender stalks, **branched-hairy (often densely grey-hairy);** stem leaves few to several, lance-shaped to oblong, with short or no clasping lobes at the base. **Flowers:** Usually 3–12 in rather loose clusters **becoming 1-sided** and elongating with age; **petals pink to purple, 4–6 mm long,** about twice as long as sepals. **Fruits:** Siliques linear, flattened, 2–5 cm long, 1.5–2.3 mm wide, **spreading to one side somewhat horizontally;** seeds in 1 row, slightly winged. **Where Found:** Scree, talus, meadows and fellfields; subalpine and alpine zones; infrequent in the southern ½ of the region, scattered northward; cordilleran.

Similar Species: Sicklepod suncress (*B. drepanoloba*, *Arabis lemmonii* var. *drepanoloba*), has wider siliques (more than 2 mm wide) and longer petals (6–8 mm) than skewed suncress. It's an apomictic hybrid (from *B. lemonii* and *B. stricta*, p. 205), with habitat preferences and a range similar to those of skewed suncress.

Notes: Skewed suncress is also known as *Arabis lemmonii*. • The species is named in honour of John G. Lemmon (1832–1908), a pioneer California botanist and a student of conifers.

Rocky Mountain Rockcress, Nuttall's Rockcress
Arabis nuttallii

General: Perennial from a taproot and simple or few-branched stem-base; stems 1 or few to numerous, unbranched, ascending to erect, 10–30 cm tall.

Leaves: Basal leaves numerous in a rosette, blades lance- to spoon-shaped, 5–30 mm long, **toothless,** tapering to slender stalks, **hairy or hairless;** stem leaves few to several, lance-oblong, **without earlobe-like, clasping bases,** 5–20 mm long, usually hairless.

Flowers: 5–25 in a short, dense cluster that later elongates; **petals white, 5–8 mm long;** sepals greenish, ½ as long as petals, the outer 2 bulging on 1 side at the base.

Fruits: Siliques linear, flattened, 1–2.5 cm long, 0.8–1.5 mm wide, ascending-erect, hairless; **seeds wingless.**

Where Found: Mesic to moist meadows, rocky or grassy slopes, willow thickets, streambanks, rock outcrops, talus slopes, open forests and roadsides; lowland to lower alpine zones; frequent in the southeastern part of the region, disjunct in YT at lower elevations; cordilleran.

Similar Species: Cascade rockcress or fork-haired rockcress (*A. furcata*; *A. suksdorfii*) has **longer (7–11 mm) petals, longer, wider siliques** (2–4 cm long, 1.7–2.2 mm wide) and **winged (0.2–0.8 mm) seeds.** It is found on rocky slopes, cliffs, ridges and meadows, in montane to alpine zones, and is infrequent in the Cascades from WA to central OR. • **Olympic rockcress** (*A. olympica*; *A. furcata* var. *olympica*) has **smaller petals (3–4 mm long)** and appressed-erect siliques. It is known from only 2 Olympic Mtns collections.

Notes: Rocky Mountain rockcress is also known as *Arabis bridgeri* and *A. macella*. • It is extremely variable in density and type of hairs, plant height, fruit width, leaf shape, flowering and fruiting time, and elevation. • Both scientific and common names honour Thomas Nuttall (1786–1859), the Philadelphia botanical collector, author and noted ornithologist.

Kamchatka Rockcress
Arabidopsis lyrata ssp. *kamchatica*

General: Tufted annual, biennial or perennial from a taproot surmounted by a stem-base, **hairless throughout or stem sparsely short-hairy toward base;** stems 1 to several, erect-ascending to spreading, 10–35 cm tall.

Leaves: Mostly in a basal rosette, broadly lance-shaped, **at least some lyrate** (pinnately cleft with large, rounded topmost lobe, lower lobes small) **with a distinctly larger terminal lobe,** the others entire or toothed, **hairless or nearly so,** 1.5–6 cm long, tapering to long, slender stalks; stem leaves 3–7, lance-shaped, becoming unstalked (but **without earlobe-like, clasping bases**), smaller upward.

Flowers: 3–20 in a cluster—at first compact, later rather lax and elongating—atop stem; **petals white,** sometimes purple-tinged, **about 5 mm long;** sepals greenish or pinkish, 2–3 mm long, the outer 2 slightly bulging at base.

Fruits: Siliques linear, flattened, usually constricted between seeds, **2–4 cm long,** ascending to erect but not appressed to axis of fruiting cluster; **seeds wingless.**

Where Found: Mesic to moist gravel bars, moraines, scree and talus slopes, open forests and disturbed areas; lowland to alpine zones; frequent in the northern ¾ of the region; amphiberingian.

Similar Species: Hairy rockcress (*Arabis pycnocarpa* **var.** *pycnocarpa*; *A. hirsuta* var. *pycnocarpa*) has **flowering stems growing straight up** (not spreading at various angles as in Kamchatka rockcress), **hairy, often purplish stems, leaves often toothed** but not lyrate, the **stem leaves clasping and often with earlobe-like bases,** and **siliques 4–6 cm long.** It grows in meadows, open forests and on gravel bars, rocky slopes, cliffs and ledges, in lowland to (occasionally) lower alpine zones. Hairy rockcress is frequent in most of the region except the far north, from southern AK, YT and NT to CA, AZ and NM; our variety is broadly amphiberingian.

Notes: Kamchatka rockcress is also known as *Arabis lyrata* ssp. *kamchatica* and *A. kamchatica*. • Populations of Kamchatka rockcress from serpentine soils have genotypes enhanced for heavy-metal detoxification and calcium and magnesium transport, the better to deal with the characteristic high heavy-metal content and low calcium-to-magnesium ratios of ultrabasic soils. • In one study, insect pollinators chose Kamchatka rockcress plants with many flowers, large petals, late start of flowering and early end of flowering, affecting the evolution of floral display and flowering time. • Rosettes of young spring leaves can be eaten raw in salads or cooked as a green vegetable. They have a radish flavour. • "Cress" is an ancient name and has been applied to several plant genera. The word could be derived from the Old English *caerse*, *cerse* or *cresse*, originally from an Indo-European base meaning "nibble" or "eat" and referring to salad plants.

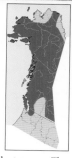

The Genus *Cardamine* (Bittercress)

Our high-elevation bittercresses are perennial, mostly hairless herbs from a taproot or rhizome, with leaves that are mostly basal or basal plus alternate on the stem, and mostly pinnately compound (1 of our species has palmately compound leaves; 2 species have simple leaves). The flowers are few to several, often in compact clusters atop the stem; the petals are white to pink or purple. The fruits are linear siliques, rounded in cross-section or somewhat flattened, with seeds in 1 row.

Cardamine is from the Greek *kardamon*, the ancient name for "cress." In turn, *kardamon* is from 2 Greek words: *kardia*, "heart," and *damao*, "subdue" or "sedate." Some claim it means "heart-healing" and that Linnaeus gave the name to a species of *Cardamine* because it was formerly used as a heart sedative. Some *Cardamine* are said to taste like the spice cardamom. The leaves of some species are edible and have a peppery taste (hence the name "bittercress"), and entire plants were eaten as a salad green.

Key to *Cardamine*

1a. Lower leaves mostly simple (not divided or lobed) **2**
    2a. Plants 2−10 cm tall, lacking rhizomes; leaves all or mostly basal in a rosette; petals 3−6 mm long
    . . . . **C. bellidifolia** (below)
    2b. Plants 20−60 cm tall, with rhizomes; leaves mostly along stem; petals 7−12 mm long . . . . **C. cordifolia** (p. 209)
1b. Lower leaves mostly compound **3**
    3a. Lower leaves palmately compound, rather fleshy; petals white, 8−13 mm long; plants of northwestern MT
    . . . . **C. rupicola** (p. 209)
    3b. Lower leaves pinnately compound; petals white to pink or purplish; mostly northern plants. **4**
        4a. Petals 2−5 mm long . . . . **C. umbellata** (p. 210)
        4b. Petals 5−10 mm long. **5**
            5a. Plants hairy, at least on upper part of stem; petals usually pink-purple. . . . . **C. purpurea** (p. 209)
            5b. Plants hairless or sparsely hairy; petals usually white. **6**
                6a. Terminal leaflet of stem leaves narrowly lance-shaped to linear, 1−4 cm long. . . . **C. digitata** (p. 209)
                6b. Terminal leaflet of stem leaves egg-shaped to elliptic, 0.6−1.3 cm long. . . . **C. microphylla** (p. 209)

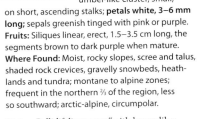

Alpine Bittercress
Cardamine bellidifolia

General: Dwarf, tufted, hairless, from a taproot and sometimes a branched stem-base; flowering stems 1 to many, ascending to erect, **2−10 cm tall. Leaves: Mostly in a basal rosette, simple (unlobed)**, blades 5−20 mm long, **oval**, narrowed to long, slender stalks, **margins smooth or rarely vaguely toothed;** stem leaves absent or 1−2. **Flowers:** Few in an umbel-like cluster, small, on short, ascending stalks; **petals white, 3−6 mm long;** sepals greenish tinged with pink or purple. **Fruits:** Siliques linear, erect, 1.5−3.5 cm long, the segments brown to dark purple when mature. **Where Found:** Moist, rocky slopes, scree and talus, shaded rock crevices, gravelly snowbeds, heathlands and tundra; montane to alpine zones; frequent in the northern ⅔ of the region, less so southward; arctic-alpine, circumpolar.

Notes: *Bellidifolia* means "with leaves like *Bellis*," *Bellis* being English daisy.

Heart-leaved Bittercress, Brook-cress
Cardamine cordifolia

General: From **extensive rhizomes;** flowering stems erect, 20–60 cm tall. **Leaves:** Mostly along stem, rather fleshy, hairless, **simple (unlobed), nearly round to heart- or kidney-shaped or deltoid, blades 2–9 cm wide,** on long, slender stalks, progressively smaller and shorter-stalked upward, **margins wavy, round-toothed. Flowers:** Several in compact clusters; **petals white, 7–12 mm long. Fruits:** Siliques linear, ascending to erect, 2–4 cm long. **Where Found:** Moist to wet, mossy streambanks, shores, springs, shaded gullies and meadows; montane to alpine zones; frequent in the southern ¼ of the region; cordilleran.

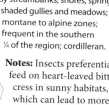
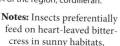

Notes: Insects preferentially feed on heart-leaved bittercress in sunny habitats, which can lead to more of this species growing in shady spots. Leaf toughness and thickness are greater in sunnier habitats, which would presumably be turnoffs for plant-eating insects. However, plants in sunny spots have lower levels of insect-repelling glucosinolates and greater water stress, which may make them a more attractive or at least more vulnerable snack.

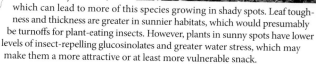

Purple Bittercress • *Cardamine purpurea*

General: Tufted, from a branching rhizome; flowering stems ascending to erect, 5–15 cm tall, **thinly spreading-hairy** in the upper part. **Leaves:** Mostly basal, usually hairless, lyrate-pinnately compound, with 1–3 pairs of **oval lateral leaflets** and at the tip a larger leaflet, broader than long, kidney-shaped to roundish and often wavy-margined; stem leaves mostly similar but smaller. **Flowers:** Several in a compact cluster, on ascending stalks; **petals purple to pink-purple** (rarely white), **5–8 mm long;** sepals about ⅓ as long as petals. **Fruits:** Siliques linear, erect, 1.5–2.5 cm long. **Where Found:** Moist to wet meadows, scree slopes, thickets, heathlands and tundra; lowland (along the Bering Strait) to alpine zones; frequent in the north; arctic-alpine, amphiberingian.

Similar Species: Bering bittercress (*C. microphylla*) is **hairless** and has **white or rarely lavender petals.** It is found on streambanks, gravel bars, moist tundra and heathlands, in lowland (Bering and Arctic coasts) to alpine zones. It is an arctic-alpine, amphiberingian species, frequent in the far north, in west-central and northern AK, northern YT and adjacent NT.
• **Narrowleaf bittercress (*C. digitata*;** *C. hyperborea, C. richardsonii*) is a third northern species. It has 5–7 **linear to narrowly lance-shaped leaflets** (including the topmost leaflet) and milky white, sometimes pinkish petals. It occurs on turfy streambanks, moist tundra and heathlands, often on the peaty sides of tundra hummocks, in lowland (Bering and Arctic coasts) to alpine zones. An arctic-alpine, amphiberingian species, it is frequent in west-central and northern AK through northern YT and NT, east to Hudson Bay. • **Cliff bittercress (*C. rupicola*;** *C. californica* var. *rupicola*) is restricted to **northwestern MT,** on calcium-rich talus, scree and cliffs. It has **palmately compound leaves** with mostly 5 **oval to lance-shaped leaflets** and white petals.

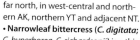

Umbel Bittercress • *Cardamine umbellata*

General: Short-lived perennial from slender rhizomes; flowering stems ascending to erect, 2–20 cm tall, mostly hairless. **Leaves:** Basal leaves in a rosette, **pinnately compound,** with 1–3 pairs of oval lateral leaflets and a larger, kidney-shaped, 3-lobed leaflet at the tip; stem leaves similar but smaller. **Flowers:** 2–12 in a small, crowded, **somewhat umbel-like cluster,** on ascending stalks; **petals white, 2–5 mm long;** sepals greenish or purplish, about ½ as long as petals. **Fruits:** Siliques linear, erect, 1.5–3 cm long. **Where Found:** Moist to wet, gravelly slopes, scree, meadows, river flats, streambanks, shores, heathlands and tundra; lowland (in north) to alpine (more so in south) zones; frequent in the Pacific coastal portion of the region, sporadically inland to the Rockies; amphiberingian.

Notes: Umbel bittercress is also known as *Cardamine oligosperma* var. *kamtschatica.*

The Genus *Smelowskia* (Skycress)

The North American *Smelowskia* are all high-elevation plants, and all 7 of the continent's species occur in our region. They are perennial, tufted or matted, densely hairy herbs from a well-developed, often branching stem-base, with few to many stems, and with a rosette of basal leaves mostly pinnately—sometimes palmately—lobed (rarely entire), plus similar but progressively smaller, alternate stem leaves. The flowers are few to several atop the stem in clusters that are at first compact but often greatly elongating in fruit; the white, pink or purple petals are longer than the sepals. The fruits are siliques or silicles, which are linear, oblong, ellipsoid, egg-, spindle- or pear-shaped, rounded or 4-angled in cross-section or somewhat flattened. The seeds are generally in 1 row.

We share this genus with central and eastern Asia. Imagine seeing other skycresses while mountaineering in Mongolia! The genus is named after Timotheus Smielowski (1769–1815), a Russian botanist and professor of pharmacology in St. Petersburg.

Key to *Smelowskia*

Alpine Skycress, Alpine False Candytuft
Smelowskia americana

General: Tufted, matted or cushion-forming, white-hairy (a mixture of fine, branched and unbranched hairs), from a strong taproot and long, branched stem-base covered with old leaf stalks; stems several to many, 5–25 cm tall. **Leaves:** Basal leaves on long, fringed stalks, blades 4–50 mm long, egg- to spoon-shaped, once or twice pinnately lobed or cleft, the segments linear to egg-shaped. **Flowers:** Several to many in head-like clusters; petals creamy white (rarely pinkish or lavender), 4–7 mm long; sepals dropping off early. **Fruits:** Siliques ellipsoid or oblong to linear, 5–13 mm long, **4-angled in cross-section, appressed** to axis of flower cluster, the **stalks nearly erect to ascending. Where Found:** Dry to mesic scree and talus slopes, rocky outcrops and ridges, fellfields; subalpine and (mostly) alpine zones; locally frequent in the southern ⅓ of the region; cordilleran.

Similar Species: Northern white skycress (*S. media*; *S. calycina* var. *media*) and **Beringian skycress (*S. porsildii*;** *S. calycina* vars. *porsildii* and *integrifolia*) are northern counterparts of alpine skycress. Northern white skycress has leaves similar to those of alpine skycress, but has **spreading fruit stalks**

and **non-appressed siliques.** It occurs on rocky, often calcium-rich substrates, scree and talus slopes, rock outcrops and ridges, gravelly shores and fellfields, in montane to alpine zones. This arctic-alpine species is locally frequent in the northern ¼ of the region, in northern and western AK and YT and northwestern NT. **Beringian skycress** has **densely grey-woolly, mostly unlobed leaves.** An arctic-alpine, amphiberingian species, it occupies similar habitats as northern white skycress in northern and western AK. • **Cascade skycress (*S. ovalis*)** is also similar to alpine skycress but has smaller petals (3.5–4.5 mm long), **smaller (2–6 mm), egg-shaped to roughly cylindric silicles** and **persistent sepals.** It grows on rocky slopes, talus, crevices and fellfields, in subalpine and alpine zones. A Cascades endemic, it is frequent from south-central BC to OR and northern CA, and is reported to be the high-elevation champ on Mt. Rainier.

Notes: Alpine skycress is also known as *Smelowskia calycina* var. *americana*.

Purple-flowered Skycress • *Smelowskia borealis*

General: Tufted or matted, grey-hairy, from a long taproot and stout stem-base; flowering stems several, ascending to sprawling, 5–30 cm tall/long. **Leaves:** Mostly in a basal rosette, wedge- to spoon-shaped, the blades 1–2.5 cm long, **palmately 3–7-lobed toward the tip,** densely hairy. **Flowers:** Numerous in clusters at first compact and head-like, **greatly elongating in fruit;** petals pink-purple to purple, 4–5 mm long; **sepals usually persistent. Fruits:** Siliques lance- to spoon-shaped, ascending to spreading, **curved to 1 side, flattened,** sometimes twisted, 1–2.5 cm long. **Where Found:** Calcium-rich sedimentary and metamorphic rock rubble, talus and scree slopes, rock slides and ridge crest fellfields; subalpine and alpine zones; locally frequent in the northern ¼ of the region; arctic-alpine, endemic.

Similar Species: Pear-fruited skycress (*S. pyriformis*) has **pinnately cleft leaves,** purple, lavender or white petals 2.5–4 mm long, **sepals that drop off early** and **pear-shaped, rounded fruits.** It is a rare endemic of high-elevation rock slides, scree and ridge crests in the Alaska Range. • **Bering Strait skycress (*S. johnsonii*)** has **densely silvery-hairy leaves** that are **usually unlobed** and sometimes 3-toothed at the tip, lavender to purplish petals and **ellipsoid fruits 5–6 mm long.** It is rare, restricted to the Bering Strait area of AK, and grows on steep, unstable, rocky or rubbly slopes.

Notes: Purple-flowered skycress is variable in hairiness, duration of sepals and overall look and habit, at least in part because of its unstable habitat and morphological changes as the plants mature. • All skycresses flower early, soon after the often-scanty snow melts.

Alpine Yellow-cress • *Rorippa alpina*

General: Usually hairless perennial from a stem-base; **stems usually sprawling to prostrate,** much-branched, 5–25 cm long.

Leaves: Basal and along stem; blades 5–40 mm long, egg- to lance-shaped, **margins coarsely toothed or wavy; stem leaves without earlobe-like, clasping bases.**

Flowers: Several to many in **elongate clusters from leaf axils and atop stem; petals yellow, 1.5–2 mm long;** sepals slightly shorter, dropping off early.

Fruits: Siliques/silicles oblong to lance- or egg-shaped, rounded in cross-section, 3–8 mm long, straight to slightly curved, **ascending to spreading horizontally; seeds in 2 rows.**

Where Found: Shores, streambanks, wet meadows and seepage areas; montane to alpine zones; frequent in the southeastern part of the region; cordilleran.

Notes: Alpine yellow-cress is also known as *Rorippa curvipes* var. *alpina* and *R. obtusa* var. *alpina*.

Sticky Tansy-mustard
Descurainia incisa ssp. *incisa*

General: Taprooted **annual or biennial, often stalked-glandular** but not hairy; **stems erect,** branched above, 12–50 cm tall.

Leaves: Basal and (mostly) along stem; blades 2–10 cm long, broadly lance- to egg-shaped, **pinnately lobed, the lobes lance-shaped to oblong,** margins toothed; **stem leaves without clasping bases.**

Flowers: Numerous in **clusters**—at first dense and compact, later elongate—**from leaf axils and atop stem; petals yellow, small, 1.5–3 mm long;** sepals nearly equalling petals, yellowish.

Fruits: Siliques linear, rounded in cross-section, 1–2 cm long, torulose, **ascending to spreading; seeds in 1 row.**

Where Found: Rocky and grassy slopes, sand and gravel bars, roadsides, streambanks, meadows, shrublands, forest openings, scree and talus slopes; montane to alpine zones; scattered and locally frequent in much of the southern interior ⅔ of the region, but at high elevations only in the southeast; cordilleran.

Similar Species: Mountain tansy-mustard or grey tansy-mustard (**D. incana;** *D. richardsonii*), is usually **fine-hairy (not glandular),** with **siliques appressed to the axis** of the flower cluster. It occurs in a wide range of habitats (like sticky tansy-mustard), in lowland to alpine zones but at high elevations only in the southeast, and is frequent in the inland part of the region except the far north, from southern AK, YT and NT to CA, UT and NM.

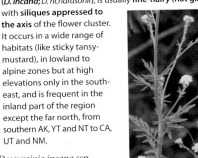

mountain tansy-mustard

Notes: Sticky tansy-mustard is also known as *Descurainia incana* ssp. *viscosa*. • The genus is named for François Descurain (1658–1740), a French apothecary and botanist.

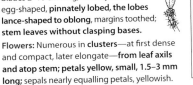

Smooth Northern-rockcress • *Braya glabella*

General: Tufted, hairy perennial from a taproot and branching stem-base; flowering stems few to several, ascending to erect, 3–20 cm tall, greenish or purple-tinged, **leafless or rarely with 1 stem leaf.**

Leaves: Basal leaves linear to oblong or spoon-shaped, 0.5–7 cm long, **usually entire,** sometimes weakly few-toothed, **often rather fleshy,** often purplish, sparsely hairy, often with a tuft of hairs at the blunt tip.

Flowers: Several to many in head-like clusters that often elongate in fruit; **petals white or tinged with purple or pink, 2–4.5 mm long;** sepals slightly shorter than petals.

Fruits: Silicles oval-elliptic or oblong to lance-oblong, 5–15 mm long, plump, ascending-erect to somewhat spreading; **seeds in 2 rows.**

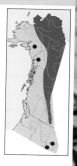

Where Found: Dry to mesic, often calcium-rich gravel bars, shores, scree, talus, rocky tundra, solifluction slopes and fellfields; lowland (arctic coast) to alpine zones; infrequent and scattered across the north, south in the Rockies to CO; arctic-alpine, the species complex circumpolar.

Subspecies: Ssp. *glabella* has oblong or lance-oblong fruits and loosely elongated fruiting clusters. • **Ssp.** *purpurascens* (*B. purpurascens*) has more or less elliptic fruits, compact fruiting clusters and often fleshy leaves.

Notes: Smooth northern-rockcress is also known as *Braya alpina* var. *americana, B. americana, B. arctica, B. bartlettiana* and *B. henryae.* • This species is notoriously variable and incompletely understood, partly because it isn't often collected. All the synonyms listed above have been recognized by some taxonomists as separate species or subspecies. • The genus is named after Franz Gabriel de Bray (1765–1832), a French ambassador to Bavaria and the head of the Regensberg Botanical Society.

Inscrutable Northern-rockcress • *Braya humilis*

General: Tufted, **usually hairy perennial or biennial** from a taproot; flowering stems 1 to several, simple or branched, erect to ascending, 5–30 cm tall, with forked hairs. **Leaves:** Basal leaves often in a rosette, lance-, egg- or spoon-shaped to oblong, 5–35 mm long, **margins smooth to wavy or shallowly toothed or pinnately cleft; stem leaves 3 or more,** similar to basal ones but smaller. **Flowers:** Numerous in clusters at first compact and head-like, later greatly elongating; **petals white or lilac, 3–5 mm long;** sepals about ½ as long as petals. **Fruits:** Siliques narrowly cylindric, straight, 1–3 cm long, ascending to erect, usually somewhat torulose, minutely hairy; **seeds in 1 row. Where Found:** Moist to dry, calcium-rich scree slopes, gravelly ridges, shores and river bars; lowland to alpine zones; scattered but locally frequent in the north and southward in the Rockies; widespread boreal-subarctic/arctic-alpine, North American and eastern and central Asian.

Notes: Inscrutable northern-rockcress is also known as *Braya richardsonii, B. humilis* ssps. *arctica, maccallae, porsildii* and *richardsonii,* and *Neotorularia humilis.* • This species is extremely variable, but "attempting to segregate most morphological forms of *B. humilis* into logical infraspecific taxa is an exercise in futility" (*FNA*). Because it differs in several key respects from *B. glabella* and other *Braya* species, *B. humilis* has been given its own genus—most recently *Neotorularia*—by some taxonomists.

Aleutian Cress, Eschscholtz's Little Nightmare
Aphragmus eschscholtzianus

General: Dwarf, tufted perennial from a short rhizome and thick stem-base covered with persistent old leaf stalks, **hairless or with sparse, short, unbranched hairs;** flowering stems few, ascending, **2–6 cm tall,** branched above.

Leaves: Basal leaves narrowly spoon- to egg-shaped, blades 5–12 mm long, somewhat fleshy, not toothed, tapering to long (5–30 mm), slender **stalks widened at the base;** stem leaves unstalked, **crowded atop stem immediately below flower cluster.**

Flowers: Few to several in compact clusters; petals white or purple with darker veins, 2–3 mm long, slightly longer than the often-purplish sepals.

Fruits: Silicles oblong-ellipsoid, flattened, disproportionately **large (5–15 mm long).**

Where Found: Moist to wet tundra and heathlands, banks of rivulets, solifluction lobes and scree slopes; montane to alpine zones; rare in the northwestern part of the region; amphiberingian.

Notes: "Little nightmare" alludes to the frisson of anxiety that results when attempting to spell *eschscholtzianus* correctly. There are 11 species in *Aphragmus*, but only this one in North America; the rest are Asian, found mostly in the Himalaya. • Johann F. Eschscholtz (1793–1891) was an Estonian zoologist and surgeon-naturalist on ships under Kotzebue, and reached California in 1816 and 1824. Although he was in North America a mere few weeks, many plants were named after him.

Mountain Candytuft • *Noccaea fendleri*

General: Hairless, often glaucous perennial from a taproot and stem-base; stems 1 to several, erect or ascending, 5–35 cm tall.

Leaves: Basal leaves numerous, often in a rosette, blades linear-oblong or lance- to egg- or spoon-shaped, 5–30 mm long, **margins smooth or wavy to few-toothed;** stem leaves several, lance-shaped to oblong, stalkless, with **earlobe-like, often clasping bases.**

Flowers: Several to many in rather lax clusters, elongating in fruit; **petals white (occasionally pinkish purple),** 3.5–8 mm long, twice as long as the sepals.

Fruits: Silicles arrowhead-, heart- or egg-shaped, 3–15 mm long, somewhat **flattened** at right angles to the narrow partition, on **spreading to descending stalks,** the margins keeled and **usually slightly winged, often notched at the tip.**

Where Found: Grassy and rocky slopes, gravelly terraces and fans, ridges, scree, talus, meadows and fellfields; montane to alpine zones; widespread and locally frequent in the southern ¼ of the region; cordilleran.

Subspecies: Ours are mostly ssp. *glauca*, and we also have ssp. *idahoensis*, endemic to central ID.

Similar Species: Arctic candytuft (*N. arctica*; *Thlaspi arcticum*) has white petals 3–5 mm long, fruits without wings and occurs in the **far north.** It grows on dry, turfy tundra, in lowland to alpine zones, and is rare on the arctic slope of AK and YT, and in the mountains of southwestern YT and adjacent AK.

Notes: Mountain candytuft is also known as *Thlaspi alpestre*, *T. fendleri*, *T. idahoense* and *T. montanum*. • It can hyperaccumulate nickel, which could be useful in a metal-based (toxic rock) defence system against herbivores, pathogens and Manuel Noriega. • *Noccaea* is named for Domenico Nocca (1758–1841), an Italian clergyman and the director of the botanical garden at Pavia.

The Genus *Physaria* (Bladderpod, Twinpod)

Our *Physaria* are perennials from stem-bases atop taproots, silvery to grey-green with dense, branched, usually star-shaped hairs and usually several spreading to erect stems. The leaves are mostly basal and in a rosette, stalked, with usually entire but sometimes wavy or lobed margins; the stem leaves are not clasping at the base. The few to several flowers have petals that are usually yellow and longer than the sepals. The fruits are globe-shaped or rounded to egg-shaped or ellipsoid silicles, inflated or not, partially flattened or not, usually hairy and often notched at the top or at both ends, with seeds in 2 rows. Note that *Physaria* now includes most of *Lesquerella*, which traditionally was a separate genus with smaller, firmer, not much inflated silicles. *Physaria* is from the Greek *physa*, "bladder" or "bellows," in reference to the inflated fruits of some species.

Key to *Physaria*

1a. Silicles papery, inflated, looking like 2 balloons pressed or glued together, usually notched at the base, the segments retaining seeds after separating 2

    2a. Silicles with only shallow notches at both ends, flattened at right angles to the septum (membranous partition); septum 7–10 mm long, pointy-tipped . . . . *P. alpestris* (p. 216)

    2b. Silicles deeply notched at the tip or at both ends, not flattened; septum 3–6 mm long, blunt-tipped 3

        3a. Silicles not notched at the base; seeds 4 (to 8) per chamber; petals 7–9 mm long . . . . *P. saximontana* (p. 216)

        3b. Silicles notched at the base; petals 8–12 mm long 4

            4a. Leaves usually toothed, rarely entire; silicles with ascending hairs, appearing fuzzy; seeds 4–8 per chamber; petals 10–12 mm long . . . . *P. didymocarpa* (p. 216)

            4b. Leaves entire; silicles with appressed hairs, not appearing fuzzy; seeds 8 per chamber; petals 8–10 mm long . . . . *P. integrifolia* (p. 216)

1b. Silicles firm, not or only slightly inflated, not notched at the base, the segments not retaining seeds after separating 5

    5a. Silicles hairless. 6

        6a. Petals spoon-shaped, 5–7 mm long; silicles not flattened . . . . *P. arctica* (p. 216)

        6b. Petals egg-shaped, 6–10 mm long; silicles mostly flattened. . . . . *P. calderi* (p. 216)

    5b. Silicles hairy 7

        7a. Silicles flattened 8

            8a. Silicles strongly flattened (apically and along margins) parallel to septum, the margins not keeled and without a nerve running up the face. . . . . *P. occidentalis* (p. 217)

            8b. Silicles flattened perpendicular to septum, with keeled margins or with a prominent mid-nerve . . . . *P. carinata* (p. 217)

        7b. Silicles not flattened or only slightly flattened along margins or near tip 9

            9a. Silicles lance-shaped to circular; fruiting stalks 10–20 mm long. . . . . *P. spatulata* (p. 217)

            9b. Silicles nearly spheric to broadly egg-shaped or ellipsoid; fruiting stalks 5–10 (to 15) mm long . . . 10

                10a. Basal leaves wavy-margined or lobed; silicles with appressed hairs, not appearing fuzzy ; OR . . . . *P. kingii* ssp. *diversifolia* (p. 217)

                10b. Basal leaves entire; silicles with ascending or spreading hairs, appearing fuzzy; MT 11

                     11a. Stems erect to spreading; silicles longer than broad. . . . . *P. klausii* (p. 217)

                     11b. Stems prostrate; silicles broader than long . . . . *P. humilis* (p. 217)

Cascade twinpod

Cascade Twinpod
Physaria alpestris

General: Stems sprawling to ascending, 5–15 cm long/tall. **Leaves:** Basal leaves egg-shaped, blades 3–5 cm long, **margins smooth. Flowers:** Petals yellow, spoon-shaped, 12–14 mm long. **Fruits: Silicles inflated, flattened toward midriff, shallowly notched at both ends, 14–18 mm long,** the septum lance-shaped, 7–10 mm long, pointy-tipped. **Where Found:** Open timberline forests, rocky ridges, scree and talus slopes, sandy-gravelly ridges (often volcanic or serpentine); montane to alpine zones; locally frequent on the eastern side of the Cascades of WA.

Common Twinpod • *Physaria didymocarpa*

General: Stems sprawling, to 10 cm long, rather leafy. **Leaves:** Basal leaves egg-shaped, blades mostly 1.5–4 cm long, **margins usually wavy or coarsely toothed. Flowers:** Petals yellow, spoon-shaped, 10–12 mm long. **Fruits: Silicles inflated, notched at both ends, slightly heart-shaped at base but deeply 2-lobed at tip,** 10–20 mm long, with **4–8 seeds in each chamber. Where Found:** Mostly at lower and medium elevations, occasionally reaching lower alpine elevations on rocky, exposed slopes and outcrops; locally frequent in the southeastern part of the region.

Similar Species: Snake River bladderpod (*P. integrifolia*) has narrower (linear to narrowly lance-shaped) leaves with smooth margins, smaller petals (8–10 mm long) and inflated **silicles with 8 seeds per chamber.** It grows on rocky, calcium-rich slopes, cliffs and clay banks, in subalpine and alpine zones, and is locally frequent in ID, MT and WY. • **Rocky Mountain twinpod (*P. saximontana*)** has round to egg- or spoon-shaped leaves with smooth or toothed margins and inflated silicles deeply notched at the top but **not notched at the base, with 4–8 seeds per chamber.** It occurs on dry, stony, calcium-rich slopes, talus and rocky ridges near or above treeline, in subalpine and lower alpine zones, and is infrequent east of the Continental Divide in the Rockies of MT and WY.

Arctic Bladderpod • *Physaria arctica*

General: Stems several, spreading to erect, 5–25 cm long/tall. **Leaves:** Basal leaves numerous in a rosette, **lance- to spoon-shaped,** blades 1–7 cm long, tapering to a stalked base, margins not toothed. **Flowers:** 2–15 in rather loose clusters; **petals yellow, spoon-shaped, 5–7 mm long. Fruits: Silicles nearly spheric to ellipsoid, 4–6 mm long, not flattened, hairless or nearly so,** on long, ascending to erect stalks. **Where Found:**

Gravel bars, rocky, calcium-rich slopes and ridges, scree, talus and fellfields; montane to alpine zones; frequent in the northern ⅓ of the region, disjunct in southwestern AB; arctic-alpine, broadly amphiberingian.

Similar Species: Calder's bladderpod (*P. calderi*; *Lesquerella arctica* ssp. *calderi*) has **broader, longer (7–10 mm), egg-shaped petals** and **slightly larger (to 8 mm), flattened silicles.** It is endemic to the Ogilvie and Richardson Mtns of YT and adjacent NT and AK.

Notes: Arctic bladderpod is also known as *Lesquerella arctica*.

Calder's bladderpod

Wallowa Bladderpod
Physaria kingii ssp. *diversifolia*

General: Stems prostrate or sprawling, 5–20 cm long/tall.
Leaves: Basal leaves with **wavy or lobed margins. Flowers:**
Petals yellow, 6–12 mm long. **Fruits:** Silicles nearly spheric,
slightly wider than long, slightly flattened, 3–5 mm long, **hairy,**
on S-shaped stalks. **Where Found:** Calcium-rich cliffs, crevices,
gravel bars and talus slopes; Elkhorn and Wallowa Mtns, northeastern OR.

Notes: Wallowa bladderpod is also known as *Lesquerella
diversifolia* and *L. kingii* ssp. *diversifolia*.

Spoonleaf Bladderpod
Physaria spatulata

General: Stems few to several, prostrate at high
elevations, 3–12 cm long. **Leaves:** Basal leaves
in rosettes, **lance- to spoon-shaped,** blades
1–4 cm long, **not toothed. Flowers:** Few to several in clusters, compact at first but elongating
somewhat in fruit; **petals yellow, 6–9 mm long.**
Fruits: Silicles lance-shaped to round, 3–6 mm
long, slightly flattened toward tip, on **S-shaped
stalks at least twice as long as silicles. Where
Found:** Dry ridges, grassy slopes, shrublands,
scree, talus and fellfields; montane to alpine
zones; frequent in the Rockies in the southeastern part of the region; Great Plains–cordilleran.

Similar Species: Western bladderpod
(*P. occidentalis*; *Lesquerella occidentalis*) has
**broader, egg-shaped to nearly circular
leaves** that are sometimes greenish above
and **longer petals (7–14 mm).** It occurs on dry, rocky slopes,
gravelly ridges and scree, in montane to alpine zones, and is
frequent from eastern WA/OR to ID, CA, UT and NV. • **Payson's
bladderpod** (*P. carinata* ssp. *paysonii*; *L. paysonii*) has **egg-
shaped to somewhat diamond-shaped basal leaves** and
silicles flattened at right angles to the partition. It grows
on talus and rocky ridges and in limber pine woodlands,
and is endemic to western WY and southeastern ID. • **Idaho
bladderpod** (*P. carinata* ssp. *carinata*; *L. carinata* ssp. *carinata*)
has similarly flattened silicles that are **keeled or nerved on
1 side.** It occurs on grassy and rocky slopes and in shrublands, usually on limestone, in ID, MT and WY. • **Bitterroot
bladderpod** (*P. humilis*; *L. humilis*) has **prostrate stems,
small, squat, nearly spheric silicles 3–4 mm long (broader
than long)** and egg-shaped leaves with

Idaho bladderpod

smooth margins. It occurs in rocky
rubble and is endemic to the Bitterroot
Mtns, MT. • **Divide bladderpod** (*P. klausii*;
L. klausii) has **upright to spreading
stems** and small (2–4 mm), egg-shaped
silicles that are **longer than broad**
and fuzzy-hairy. It grows on gravelly
slopes and shaly rubble in MT.

Notes: Spoonleaf bladderpod is
also known as *Lesquerella alpina* var.
spatulata and *Physaria reediana*
var. *spatulata*.

western bladderpod

The Genus *Draba*

Draba is the largest genus in the mustard family, with about 380 herbaceous species worldwide, mostly in boreal to arctic and high-elevation areas. The 4 centres of highest diversity are western North America, the subarctic region, the Himalayas and the high Andes of South America. The alpine flora of our region includes 45 or so draba species.

Our alpine *Draba* are small, mostly perennial herbs, typically from a taproot surmounted by a stem-base. A few are annuals, biennials or short-lived perennials. The plants are often matted or tufted, sometimes cushion-forming, with prostrate to erect, leafless or leafy stems. The leaves are simple, with entire or toothed margins; basal leaves are most commonly in a rosette. The flowers have the typical mustard family structure of 4 sepals, 4 petals (mostly white or yellow in ours), 6 stamens and 2 styles. The fruits are pod-like silicles or siliques (for convenience, we call all *Draba* fruits **silicles**) that are lance- to egg-shaped, elliptic, oblong or nearly circular, usually flattened in cross-section, plane or sometimes twisted, with 2 rows of seeds. The leaves, stems and fruits are often hairy, the hairs simple, forked, cross-like, star-like or branched like a shrub or comb, stalked or stalkless, with often more than 1 kind of hair present.

The Greek word *drabe*, "acrid," was used by Dioscorides to describe the taste of the leaves of a certain mustard family plant, thought by some to have been hoary cress (*Lepidium draba*).

Ominously for a field guide, *Draba* has a high rate of speciation and polyploidy (multiple copies of chromosome sets) compared to many other herbaceous plants, and the greatest species diversity and polyploidy occur in arctic and alpine regions of the globe. High rates of speciation are likely the result of Pleistocene glaciation and the resultant changes in habitats and species ranges, combined with proclivities within the genus toward hybridization, self-fertilization and polyploidy.

Draba is indeed a difficult genus to deal with, not least because most contemporary keys rely heavily on details of microscopic hairs. These hairs often cannot be discerned in the field and can be difficult to see even back in the lab with a dissecting microscope. There are more user-friendly aids to identification, but *Draba* will always be troublesome, because you need both flowers and fruits to figure most of them out. If you don't find them at just the right time while exploring the mountains, you could be out of luck. Many species bloom very early, on the highest, most exposed ridges. You must get up there pretty early in the season to see some of them, or search later on north aspects or shaded cliffs and scree for others. But what a treat when, panting and overheated, with wind chilling your damp back, you drop to your knees before tufts of tiny leaves topped with small, brightly coloured flowers—micro-explosions of colour!

The Radical Honesty self-improvement movement, spearheaded by psychotherapist Dr. Brad Blanton, advocates telling the truth, always—even if you are asked by someone for whom you care deeply, "Does this kilt make me look fat?" Such frankness can be disarming, charming or alarming, but is said by proponents and converts to result in better communication, improved work environments and stronger, more loving relationships! In the case of *Draba* and your whispered question, "Does it really matter what species of *Draba* this is?" No, it doesn't, not to the plant and not to you, unless the species is rare and endangered, you are trying to save it, and correct identification is crucial. Now, of course, it can be fun and gratifying to work your way through the maze, but sometimes it is more satisfying merely to acknowledge the beauty and complexity of these alpine gems.

Key to *Draba*

1a. Flowering stems leafless or sometimes with 1 leaf 2

    2a. Flowers white to cream 3

        3a. Leaves hairless except for margins 4

            4a. Leaf margins fringed with simple hairs; fruit stalks shorter than silicles; southern species
. . . . **D. globosa** (p. 224)

            4b. Leaf margins fringed with simple and forked hairs; lowest fruit stalks to about as long as silicles; northern circumpolar species. . . . . **D. lactea** (p. 224)

        3b. Leaves hairy on 1 or both surfaces 5

            5a. Lower surfaces of leaves mainly with simple and some forked hairs . . . . **D. fladnizensis** (p. 224)

            5b. Lower surfaces of leaves mainly with star-like hairs 6

                6a. Flowering stems and fruit stalks greyish with tiny, star-like hairs 7

                    7a. Silicles elliptic to oblong-elliptic, twisted or plane, 4–9 mm long; both leaf surfaces greyish with tiny, star-like hairs. . . . . **D. nivalis** (p. 223)

                    7b. Silicles linear to narrowly lance-oblong, 6–15 (to 18) mm long; upper leaf surfaces star-like-hairy or hairless or with simple and branched hairs . . . . **D. lonchocarpa** (p. 223)

6b. Flowering stems hairless or star-like-hairy only toward the base **8**
  8a. Lowest fruit stalks mostly shorter than silicles **9**
    9a. Silicles egg-shaped to oblong, 4–7.5 mm long; both leaf surfaces with star-like hairs . . . . **D. porsildii** (p. 223)
    9b. Silicles linear to narrowly lance-oblong, 6–15 (to 18) mm long; upper leaf surfaces hairless or with simple and branched hairs . . . . **D. lonchocarpa** (p. 223)
  8b. Lowest fruit stalks equal to or slightly longer than silicles **10**
    10a. Both leaf surfaces hairless or with star-like hairs, often concentrated toward the apex; flowers cream to white . . . . **D. lactea** (p. 224)
    10b. Both leaf surfaces greyish with tiny, star-like hairs; flowers cream or pale yellow . . . . **D. palanderiana** (p. 223)
2b. Flowers yellow. **11**
  11a. Lower leaf surfaces with mainly simple to forked hairs, or hairless **12**
    12a. Leaves hairless or nearly so except for fringe of hairs along margins. **13**
      13a. Leaves not fleshy. . . . . **D. densifolia** (p. 225)
      13b. Leaves somewhat fleshy **14**
        14a. Annual or short-lived, tufted perennial; leaves lance-shaped, hairless or with a few simple to branched hairs, margins often fringed with unbranched hairs; petals 1.5–3 mm long; styles very short, to 0.1 mm long; widespread though scattered in region . . . . **D. crassifolia** (p. 222)
        14b. Perennial forming dense cushions; leaves oblong to lance-shaped, hairless except for marginal fringe; petals 3.5–4 mm long; styles 0.1–0.5 mm long; restricted to MT . . . . **D. daviesiae** (p. 225)
    12b. Leaves hairy **15**
      15a. Petals linear, narrower than sepals . . . . **D. stenopetala** (p. 225)
      15b. Petals broader, wider than sepals **16**
        16a. Flowering stems very short; flowers not exceeding leaves; westernmost AK . . . . **D. aleutica** (p. 225)
        16b. Flowering stems much exceeding leaves. **17**
          17a. Silicles densely hairy . . . . **D. corymbosa** (p. 225)
          17b. Silicles hairless or with a few hairs **18**
            18a. Stems 4–17 cm tall; lower leaf surfaces with mostly simple hairs; silicles not inflated . . . . **D. pilosa** (p. 225)
            18b. Stems 1–6 cm tall; lower leaf surfaces with 2–5-rayed hairs; silicles inflated at least toward base . . . . **D. macounii** (p. 225)
  11b. Lower leaf surfaces with predominantly star-like or comb-like hairs. **19**
    19a. Lower leaf surfaces with mainly short-stalked or stalkless, star-like or comb-like hairs. **20**
      20a. Both leaf surfaces with comb-like hairs **21**
        21a. Silicles 5–10 mm long, flattened, about as long as their stalks; petals 4–6 mm long; leaf midvein usually obscure . . . . **D. incerta** (p. 226)
        21b. Silicles 3–6 mm long, inflated, to ½ as long as stalks; petals 2.5–4 mm long; leaf midvein prominent . . . . **D. oligosperma** (p. 226)
      20b. Both leaf surfaces with star-like hairs **22**
        22a. Petals white, cream or pale yellow; leaf stalks fringed at base . . . . **D. palanderiana** (p. 223)
        22b. Petals yellow. **23**
          23a. Tufted; leaf margins (stalks and blades) fringed with long, simple hairs; restricted to southern YT . . . . **D. scotteri** (p. 226)
          23b. Loosely tufted, mat-forming; restricted to ID **24**
            24a. Silicles 5–11 mm long, on hairless stalks; styles 1–2 mm long . . **D. argyrea** (p. 226)
            24b. Silicles 2–6 mm long, on hairy stalks; styles 0.2–1 mm long . . . . **D. sphaerocarpa** (p. 226)

19b. Lower leaf surfaces with mainly long-stalked, star-like hairs **25**

    25a. Upper leaf surfaces with mainly long-stalked, star-like hairs; leaf margins not fringed
. . . . *D. ventosa* (p. 227)

    25b. Upper leaf surfaces with simple, forked or few-branched hairs; leaf margins fringed **26**

      26a. Leaves >2 mm wide; stems and fruit stalks with simple and a few forked hairs; fruits flattened. . . . . *D. ruaxes* (p. 227)

      26b. Leaves <2 mm wide; stems and fruit stalks with mixture of star-like, forked and a few simple hairs; fruits inflated at least toward base **27**

        27a. Petals bright yellow, 2–4 mm long; silicles 3–5 mm long . . . . . . *D. novolympica* (p. 227)

        27b. Petals pale yellow, 5–6 mm long; silicles 6–9 mm long . . . . *D. paysonii* (p. 227)

1b. Flowering stems with 1–2 to several leaves. **28**

 28a. Flowers white to cream **29**

  29a. Silicles hairless or nearly so. **30**

   30a. Lowest fruit stalks to twice the length of silicles; stem leaves 0–3; lower leaf surfaces with mainly cross-like hairs. . . . . *D. juvenilis* (p. 227)

   30b. Lowest fruit stalks shorter than to about equal to silicles; stem leaves 2–20; lower leaf surfaces with star-like and/or comb-like hairs **31**

    31a. Plants usually >10 cm tall; stem leaves 2–20; leaf margins toothed to nearly entire, the stalks fringed with simple hairs; petals 4–5.5 mm long; silicles egg-shaped to oblong or lance-shaped . . . . *D. glabella* (p. 227)

    31b. Plants 4–12 cm tall; stem leaves 2–7; leaf margins often minutely toothed, the stalks mostly not fringed; petals 2–4 mm long; silicles linear to narrowly lance-shaped . . *D. chamissonis* (p. 223)

  29b. Silicles hairy **32**

   32a. Plants loosely tufted, 10–35 cm tall; stem leaves typically 3–8 . . . . **33**

    33a. Petals 4–6 mm long; silicles lance-shaped to elliptic, sparsely hairy with simple and 2–4-rayed hairs; styles 0.2–0.8 mm long. . . . . *D. borealis* (p. 228)

    33b. Petals 2.5–4 mm long; silicles narrowly lance-shaped to linear-oblong. **34**

     34a. Silicles usually densely covered with 3–7-rayed hairs; styles 0.1–0.6 mm long
. . . . *D. cana* (p. 228)

     34b. Silicles short-hairy with simple and 2–4-rayed hairs; styles nearly lacking
. . . . *D. praealta* (p. 222)

   32b. Plants densely tufted, 3–15 cm tall; stem leaves 1–2 (to 4) **35**

    35a. Petals 3.5–4.5 mm long; silicles oblong to elliptic, plane, 5–8 mm long; leaf margins entire or with 1 tooth on each side. . . . . *D. cinerea* (p. 228)

    35b. Petals 2–3.5 mm long; silicles narrowly lance-shaped, somewhat twisted, mostly 6–15 mm long; leaf margins entire . . . . *D. lonchocarpa* (p. 223)

 28b. Flowers yellow **36**

  36a. Plants with leafy runners . . . . *D. ogilviensis* (p. 229)

  36b. Plants tufted, lacking runners **37**

   37a. Perennials with fleshy leaves; leaves hairless except for fringed stalks or margins . . . *D. crassa* (p. 229)

   37b. Leaves not fleshy; both leaf surfaces variously hairy. **38**

    38a. Annuals, biennials or short-lived perennials; silicles hairless or nearly so, the lowest about as long as their stalks; styles nearly lacking **39**

     39a. Silicles 5–12 mm long; stems with mostly simple and sometimes fewer 2-rayed hairs, especially near base; upper leaf surfaces with simple and 2-rayed hairs
. . . . *D. albertina* (p. 222)

     39b. Silicles 10–17 mm long; stems with forked and cross-like hairs; upper leaf surfaces with mostly 2–4-rayed and some simple hairs . . . . *D. stenoloba* (p. 222)

    38b. Perennials; silicles hairy, the lowest longer than their stalks; styles 0.5–1.5 mm long. **40**

     40a. Plants 10–35 cm tall; leaves densely star-like-hairy on both surfaces; stem leaves 10–20 along length of stem; silicles 2–3.5 mm broad, twisted or plane . . . . . . *D. aurea* (p. 229)

     40b. Plants 3–15 cm tall; leaves with simple and 2–5-rayed hairs on both surfaces; stem leaves numerous, closely crowded on lower portion of stem; silicles 3–5 mm broad, plane
. . . . *D. aureola* (p. 229)

Short-lived Plants with Very Short Styles (<0.15 mm)	No Hairs (except on leaf margins)	Fleshy Leaves	Ashy Grey Leaves (very dense hairs)	Leafy Runners
D. albertina D. crassifolia D. praealta D. stenoloba	crassa crassifolia daviesiae densifolia (in part) globosa lactea (in part) ogilviensis	crassa crassifolia (somewhat) daviesiae	argyrea cinerea chamissonis nivalis palanderiana sphaerocarpa	ogilviensis

SCANNING ELECTRON MICROSCOPE PHOTOS OF DRABA HAIRS

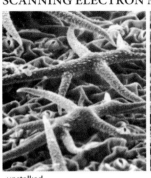
unstalked

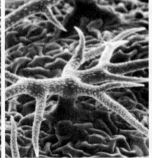
short-stalked

long-stalked

simple

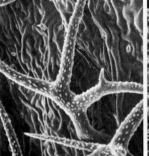
forked, 2-rayed

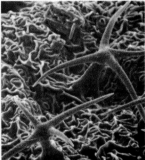
cross-like, 4-rayed

star-like or star-shaped

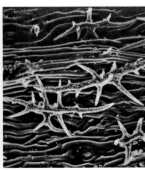
comb-like

ANNUALS, BIENNIALS AND SHORT-LIVED PERENNIALS

Our alpine flora includes 4 or 5 *Draba* species that sometimes are annuals, but as often as not are biennials to short-lived perennials, and only thickleaf draba is what we would call a true alpine plant. The others are montane-subalpine species whose range sometimes extends above treeline. They all have very short styles, less than 0.15 mm long.

Thickleaf Draba, Snowbed Draba
Draba crassifolia

General: Plants mostly hairless; stems 2–12 cm tall. Leaves: Basal leaves lance- to egg-shaped, somewhat fleshy, occasionally hairy-fringed; **stem leaves usually lacking. Flowers: Petals yellow,** often fading to white, 1.5–3 mm long. **Fruits:** Silicles narrowly elliptic to lance-shaped, 5–10 mm long, hairless. **Where Found:** Rocky ridges and talus, subalpine meadows, tundra and bare snowmelt areas; subalpine and alpine zones; infrequent in most of the region east of the Coast-Cascade Mtns; subarctic-alpine, North American, including Greenland, northwestern European.

Slender Draba • *Draba albertina*

General: Stems 5–25 cm tall. Leaves: Stem leaves usually 1–3; lower stems and upper surface of leaves with **simple hairs sometimes mixed with 2-branched hairs. Flowers: Petals yellow,** 2–3 mm long. **Fruits: Silicles linear-oblong to lance-shaped, 5–12 mm long, hairless.** **Where Found:** Open forests, meadows, rocky knolls and slopes, and streambanks, often on disturbed sites; montane to lower alpine zones; locally frequent in the southern ¾ of the region, mostly east of the Coast-Cascade Mtns; cordilleran.

Similar Species: Alaska draba (*D. stenoloba*) has **2–4-rayed (vs. mostly simple) hairs** on the lower stems and **longer silicles (10–17 mm).** It occurs in similar habitats as thickleaf draba, and is frequent but scattered from southern AK and YT through mostly inland BC and western AB to WA and OR.

Notes: Slender draba is also known as *D. crassifolia* var. *albertina* and *D. stenoloba* vars. *nana, ramosa.*

Tall Draba • *Draba praealta*

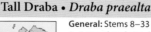

General: Stems 8–33 cm tall, with 2–5-rayed and simple hairs. Leaves: Stem leaves 1–9, upper surfaces with 3–5-rayed and some simple hairs. **Flowers: Petals white to cream,** 3–4 mm long. **Fruits: Silicles narrowly lance-shaped, 7–14 mm long, soft-hairy** with simple and 2–4-rayed hairs. **Where Found:** Rocky slopes, meadows, grassy ridges, woodlands, talus, cliffs and rocky ledges; montane to lower alpine zones; frequent but scattered in the southern ¾ of the region east of the Coast-Cascade Mtns; amphiberingian.

MOSTLY LEAFLESS STEMS AND WHITE FLOWERS

This group of perennial, tufted drabas has flowering stems with no leaves or sometimes 1 leaf, and white to cream flowers.

Snow Draba • *Draba nivalis*

General: Stems 2–10 cm tall, greyish with tiny, star-like hairs. **Leaves: Both surfaces greyish-hairy** with tiny, short-stalked, overlapping, **star-like hairs;** margins not fringed. **Flowers: Petals white, 2–4 mm** long. **Fruits: Silicles elliptic to oblong-elliptic, twisted or plane, 4–9 mm long, mostly hairless but on hairy stalks.** Where Found: Rock outcrops, fellfields, meadows, tundra, gravelly banks and shores; lowland (arctic coast) to alpine zones; frequent but scattered in the northern ¾ of the region; arctic-alpine, circumpolar.

Similar Species: **Lance-fruited draba** (**D. lonchocarpa;** D. lonchocarpa vars. *exigua, denudata, thompsonii;* D. nivalis ssp. *lonchocarpa;* D. nivalis vars. *denudata, elongata, exigua, thompsonii*) is distinguished by the **fringed bases of the leaf stalks.** The **upper leaf surfaces are usually hairless or with simple and branched hairs, the stems and fruit stalks hairless or nearly so, sometimes hairy throughout.** The **silicles are linear to lance-oblong,** plane or slightly twisted, **mostly 6–15 mm long.** It occurs on rock outcrops and ridges, talus, scree and tundra, in montane to alpine zones, and is an amphiberingian species frequent throughout the region south of about 62° N. • **Porsild's draba (D. porsildii;** D. nivalis var. *brevicula*), like snow draba, has **star-like hairs on both leaf surfaces** but has **fringed bases of leaf stalks and mostly hairless stems.** It is found on rock (often limestone) outcrops, gravelly slopes and ridges, talus, scree and meadows, in subalpine and alpine zones. A cordilleran species, it is infrequent to rare in the inland southern ¾ of the region, from southern AK and southern YT south in the Rockies of eastern BC and southwestern AB to MT and WY. Tetraploid D. porsildii perhaps originated from a diploid ancestor such as D. lonchocarpa. • **Palander's draba (D. palanderiana;** D. caesia of some authors) is kind of a far northern analogue of the previous 3 species. Both leaf surfaces are greyish with tiny, short-stalked, star-like hairs, the bases of leaf stalks are fringed, the stems are star-like-hairy toward the base, and the silicles are oblong to elliptic or egg-shaped, 4–8 mm long. It is distinguished by relatively **large (4–5.5 mm long), white, cream or pale yellow petals,** often drying yellowish. It grows on rock outcrops, talus, fellfields and tundra, in lowland (arctic coast) to alpine zones, and is an amphiberingian species frequent in much of AK, central and northern YT and western NT, rare in northern BC. • **Cape Thompson**

Porsild's draba

draba (D. chamissonis; D. kamtschatica, D. lonchocarpa ssp. *kamtschatica,* D. nivalis var. *kamtschatica*) strongly resembles snow draba but has several stem leaves. It is an amphiberingian species of wet cliffs and crevices, headlands, bluffs and tundra, in lowland to alpine zones, and is rare in southern AK, Haida Gwaii and northern Vancouver I.

Notes: Snow draba is also known as *Draba caesia.* • New species can arise when populations that could previously interbreed lose that ability and become reproductively isolated. In genera such as *Draba* in which "selfing" (mating with yourself) is common, some of the species we recognize contain populations that can no longer interbreed and produce viable seed. For example, in one study, snow draba from Norway and Alaska were crossed. Seed and pollen fertility in offspring were greatly reduced because of genetic sterility barriers. Perhaps many more cryptic species are lurking within *Draba.* Indeed, recent studies have revealed numerous stealth species within some supposedly well-known, circumpolar, taxonomic species of *Draba,* including snow draba and Austrian draba (p. 224). • Many arctic-alpine plants retain the ability to self-fertilize when insect pollinators are sparse. Not Palander's draba, though; its large, scented flowers are designed for outcrossing, and attempts to self-pollinate the species end with aborted fruits and non-viable seed.

lance-fruited draba

Milky Draba • *Draba lactea*

General: Stems 2–11 cm tall, **mostly hairless.** Leaves: Both surfaces hairless or with star-like hairs, often concentrated toward the tip; leaf stalks fringed near base with simple and forked hairs, the blades usually not. **Flowers: Petals cream to white,** 3–5 mm long. **Fruits:** Silicles oblong to lance-elliptic or egg-shaped, 4–8 mm long, **dark green, hairless.** Where Found: Rock outcrops, talus, rocky slopes and ridges, open, gravelly flats, seepage and snowbed swales, turfy tundra and meadows; lowland (arctic coast) to alpine zones; infrequent in the northern ½ of the region; arctic-alpine, circumpolar.

Notes: Milky draba is also known as *Draba allenii*, *D. fladnizensis* var. *heterotricha* and *D. pseudopilosa*. • Speciation in *Draba* is driven in large part by hybridization and polyploidy (multiple copies of chromosome sets). By way of explanation, the human species has a base chromosome number of 23; there are 23 different chromosomes in an egg or sperm nucleus. Except for those sex cells, human bodies are "diploid," consisting of cells with a double set of chromosomes (2n=46). In *Draba*, the base number is 8 (i.e., 8 different chromosomes), and several of our species (e.g., *D. nivalis*, *D. fladnizensis* and *D. lonchocarpa*) are also diploids (2n=16). For milky draba, however, it's a bit more complicated; about 90% of plants are hexaploid (2n=48) and the rest tetraploid (2n=32). Genetic detectives suggest that hexaploid milky draba likely auto-arose from tetraploid milky draba, which itself diverged from diploid Palander's draba (p. 223). Researchers reckon that milky draba arose several times in the Beringian area and migrated to reach its contemporary circumpolar distribution.

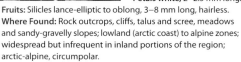

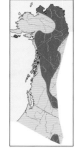

Austrian Draba
Draba fladnizensis

General: Stems 2–10 cm tall, **hairless.** Leaves: **Lower surface usually with both simple and some forked hairs,** upper surface often hairless; stalk margins fringed. **Flowers: Petals white,** 2–2.5 mm long. **Fruits:** Silicles lance-elliptic to oblong, 3–8 mm long, hairless. **Where Found:** Rock outcrops, cliffs, talus and scree, meadows and sandy-gravelly slopes; lowland (arctic coast) to alpine zones; widespread but infrequent in inland portions of the region; arctic-alpine, circumpolar.

Notes: Austrian draba is also known as *Draba fladnizensis* var. *pattersonii* and *D. pattersonii*. • Fladnitz is a village in Austria.

Pointy-leaf Draba • *Draba globosa*

General: Plants tufted or cushion-forming, **hairless except for fringed leaf margins;** stems 1–5 cm tall. Leaves: Narrowly lance-shaped, **pointy-tipped, not fleshy.** **Flowers: Petals white to pale yellow,** 2.5–4 mm long. **Fruits: Silicles egg-shaped, flattened, 4–8 mm long, prominently veined,** the stalks 2–6 mm long. **Where Found:** Rocky ridges, talus, tundra and meadows; alpine zone; infrequent in ID, MT, UT and WY; Rocky Mtn endemic.

Notes: Pointy-leaf draba is also known as *D. apiculata* and *D. densifolia* vars. *apiculata*, *decipiens* and *globosa*.

MOSTLY LEAFLESS STEMS, YELLOW FLOWERS, LOWER LEAF SURFACES WITH MAINLY SIMPLE OR FORKED TO FEW-BRANCHED HAIRS, OR HAIRLESS

Macoun's Draba • *Draba macounii*

General: Stems 1–6 cm tall, **usually hairy. Leaves: Lower surface with short-stalked, 2–5-rayed hairs;** upper surface hairless or with tangled, simple and forked hairs; leaf stalks fringed. **Flowers:** Petals yellow to pale yellow, drying whitish, **3–4 mm long. Fruits:** Silicles somewhat globe- to egg-shaped or ellipsoid, **inflated at least toward base,** 4–8 mm long, **hairless,** dark green. **Where found:** Rock outcrops, talus, snowbeds and tundra; montane to alpine zones; frequent but scattered in the northern ¾ of the region; cordilleran.

Similar Species: Reinforced draba (*D. pilosa*; *D. alpina* var. *pilosa*) is taller (stems 4–17 cm), with larger flowers **(petals 3.5–6 mm long)** and elliptic to lance-shaped silicles 5–11 mm long, **not inflated and hairless or sparsely hairy.** The leaves have a thickened midrib, thickened and fringed stalk and blade margins, and **surfaces with mostly simple hairs.** It grows on dry, gravelly slopes, sandy banks, meadows, snowbeds and wet tundra, in lowland (arctic coast) to alpine zones. Reinforced draba is an arctic-alpine, amphiberingian species and is infrequent in the northern ⅓ of the region, in AK, YT and NT. • **Baffin Bay draba (*D. corymbosa*;** *D. alpina* vars. *bellii* and *corymbosa*, *D. bellii*, *D. macrocarpa*) is distinguished by large (6–12 mm long), **hairy silicles,** stems that are hairy throughout and leaves with both surfaces hairy. It occurs in moist meadows and on rocky, often calcium-rich slopes, gravelly shores, silt and clay terraces and tundra, in lowland (arctic coast) to alpine zones. An arctic-alpine, interruptedly circumpolar species, it is infrequent in AK, YT and NT and rare in northwestern BC.

Notes: *D. macounii* is often confused with *D. alpina*, which according to *FNA* probably doesn't occur in our region.

Denseleaf Draba • *Draba densifolia*

General: Tufted, **often cushion-forming;** stems 2–15 cm tall, **usually hairless. Leaves:** Linear-oblong to narrowly lance-shaped, surfaces mostly hairless, the lower sometimes with short-stalked, 2–4-rayed hairs; **margins strongly fringed. Flowers:** Petals yellow, lance- to egg-shaped, 2–5 mm long. **Fruits:** Silicles egg-shaped to lance-elliptic, 3–7 mm long, **short-hairy. Where Found:** Rocky slopes and talus, rock outcrops, ridges and meadows; montane to alpine zones; frequent in the southern inland ⅓ of the region, rare northward; cordilleran.

Similar Species: Star-flowered draba (*D. stenopetala*) has distinctive **linear, yellow, sometimes purplish petals,** hairier leaves and stems, and **egg- to globe-shaped silicles inflated toward the base.** It grows on rock outcrops and ridges, cliffs, talus, scree and tundra, in subalpine and alpine zones. It is an amphiberingian species rare in central AK, central and southwestern YT and northwestern BC. • **Aleutian draba (*D. aleutica*)** is a densely matted perennial with very short (0.5–4 cm tall), hairy flowering stems, the yellowish green to pale yellow flowers not exceeding the leaves. It is found on snowbeds and fellfields, and is rare in westernmost AK.

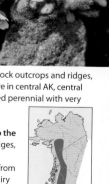

• **Davies' draba (*D. daviesiae*)** has **fleshy leaves** and is **endemic to the Bitterroot Mtns, MT.** It is found on cliffs, crevices, ledges, rocky ridges, talus slopes and meadows in the alpine zone. • Denseleaf draba could also be confused with **Payson's draba** (p. 227), but differs from the latter by having **hairless upper leaf surfaces,** only sparsely hairy lower leaf surfaces and often hairless fruit stalks.

Notes: Denseleaf draba is also known as *Draba caeruleomontana*, *D. nelsonii*, *D. pectinata* and *D. sphaerula*. • Denseleaf draba is one of the most variable North American *Draba*, occupying broad geographic and altitudinal ranges.

star-flowered draba

MOSTLY LEAFLESS STEMS, YELLOW FLOWERS, LOWER LEAF SURFACES WITH
SHORT-STALKED OR STALKLESS, MOSTLY COMB-LIKE OR STAR-LIKE HAIRS

Yellowstone Draba • *Draba incerta*

General: Tufted or cushion-forming, stem-base often obscured by old leaves; stems 5–15 cm tall, hairy. **Leaves:** Usually only basal, blades linear to lance-shaped, to 2 cm long, **both leaf surfaces with short-stalked, comb-like (and a few star-like) hairs,** margins fringed. **Flowers:** In 3–20-flowered clusters, **petals pale yellow, 4–6 mm long, fading to white. Fruits:** Silicles 5–10 mm long, hairless to slightly hairy. **Where Found:** Rock outcrops, talus and scree, fellfields, gravelly meadows and tundra, in montane to alpine zones; frequent in the southern ¾ of the region; cordilleran.

Similar Species: Three other similar drabas have **star-like (rather than comb-like) hairs on both leaf surfaces.** • Scotter's draba (*D. scotteri*), a tufted northern species, has **leaf margins (stalks and blades) fringed** with long, simple hairs. It is rare on rocky alpine slopes and **endemic to southern YT.** • Globe-fruited draba (*D. sphaerocarpa*) and **silvery draba** (*D. argyrea*) are mat-forming species **both endemic to central ID.** Globe-fruited draba has smaller (2–6 mm long) **silicles inflated** at least toward the base, with **hairy stalks** and styles 0.2–1 mm long. It is found on granite ridges and outcrops, and rocky slopes in open pine forests in montane to alpine zones. Silvery draba has larger (5–11 mm long) silicles with **hairless stalks** and styles 1–2 mm long. It is a species of rock crevices, ledges and talus slopes in upper montane to alpine zones.

Few-seeded Draba
Draba oligosperma

General: Tufted, **often cushion-forming;** stems 2–8 cm tall, hairless or with comb-like hairs toward the base. **Leaves:** Usually **both surfaces with stalkless, comb-like hairs,** often concentrated toward the tip, margins usually not fringed, **midvein prominent. Flowers:** Petals yellow, 2.5–4 mm long. **Fruits:** Silicles egg- to lance-shaped, **3–6 mm long, somewhat inflated, usually hairy. Where Found:** Rock outcrops, talus and scree, fellfields, gravel benches and fans, meadows and tundra; montane to

alpine zones; frequent in the southern ½ of the region east of the Coast-Cascade Mtns, less frequent northward; cordilleran.

Notes: Few-seeded draba is also known as *Draba andina*. • It is a widespread and highly variable species.

MOSTLY LEAFLESS STEMS, YELLOW FLOWERS AND LOWER LEAF SURFACES MAINLY WITH LONG-STALKED, STAR-LIKE HAIRS

Leeward Draba • *Draba novolympica*

General: Cushion-forming; stems 5–40 cm tall, densely hairy. **Leaves:** Lower surface with long-stalked, star-like hairs, upper surface with simple and forked hairs, **margins strongly fringed. Flowers: Petals yellow, 2–4 mm long. Fruits:** Silicles egg-shaped, **3–5 mm long,** somewhat

inflated, **densely hairy with 2–6-rayed hairs. Where Found:** Rocky slopes, cliffs, ridge crests, outcrops, fellfields, talus, calcium-rich shale scree, dry meadows and open coniferous forests; subalpine and alpine zones; infrequent in the southern ½ of the region.

Similar Species: Payson's draba (*D. paysonii*) has larger silicles (6–9 mm long), with simple and 2-rayed hairs, and **larger flowers (petals 5–6 mm long).** It is found on limestone outcrops, talus and gravelly calcium-rich slopes, in subalpine and alpine zones, and is restricted to southwestern MT and northwestern WY.

Notes: Leeward draba is also known as *Draba barbata* var. *treleasei* and *D. paysonii* var. *treleasei*.

Wind River Draba • *Draba ventosa*

General: Stems 2–6 cm tall, densely covered with 2–6-rayed hairs. **Leaves: Both surfaces with long-stalked, star-like hairs,** margins not fringed. **Flowers: Petals yellow, 4–5.5 mm long. Fruits: Silicles broadly egg-shaped to nearly round, 4–8 mm long, inflated toward the base, densely soft-hairy** with 2–6-rayed hairs. **Where Found:** Cliffs, talus and scree slopes, fellfields and tundra; subalpine and alpine zones; infrequent in the inland southern ¾ of the region.

Similar Species: Coast Mountain draba (*D. ruaxes*; *D. ventosa* var. *ruaxes*) has generally simple hairs on the stems, upper leaf surfaces, leaf margins and silicles (which are **flattened, not inflated**), in addition to few-branched and star-like hairs on the lower leaf surfaces; Wind River draba lacks simple hairs. Coast Mountain draba grows on cliffs, talus and scree slopes, meadows, ridges and summits, often on calcium-rich rock, in subalpine and alpine zones. It is rare in and east of the Coast-Cascade Mtns, from AK and southwestern YT through BC to southwestern AB and northern WA.

STEMS WITH 1 OR 2 TO SEVERAL LEAVES, WHITE FLOWERS AND HAIRLESS SILICLES

Smooth Draba • *Draba glabella*

General: Loosely tufted to matted; **stems 10–35 cm tall. Leaves:** Both surfaces of basal leaves with short-stalked, star-like and comb-like, mostly 4–8-rayed hairs, **margins mostly toothed, stalks fringed; stem leaves 2–17,** hairy. **Flowers: Petals white,** sometimes cream, **4–5.5 mm long. Fruits: Silicles oblong-lance- or egg-shaped, 5–12 mm long, mostly hairless,** the stalks shorter than to about as long as silicles. **Where Found:** Cliffs, rock outcrops and ridges, talus,

meadows, tundra, gravelly shores, sandy streambanks and disturbed soils; lowland (arctic coast) to alpine zones; frequent in the northern ⅓ of the region, infrequent southward; circumpolar, arctic-alpine.

Similar Species: Long-stalked draba (*D. juvenilis*; *D. hirta* var. *tenella*, *D. kananaskis*, *D. longipes*) is shorter (8–20 cm tall) and has fewer (0–3) stem leaves with **mainly cross-like hairs** (or often becoming hairless) and **longer fruit stalks,** the lowest to twice as long as the silicles. It grows on rocky slopes, talus, gravelly shores, streambanks, meadows and tundra, in lowland (arctic coast) to alpine zones. It is an arctic-alpine, amphiberingian species, frequent in AK, YT and NT, south infrequently to southeastern BC and southwestern AB.

Notes: Some authors refer to smooth draba as *Draba hirta*. • Smooth draba seems to favour nitrogen-rich habitats such as around ground squirrel burrows and bird perches.

STEMS WITH 1 OR 2 TO SEVERAL LEAVES, WHITE FLOWERS AND HAIRY SILICLES

Northern Draba • *Draba borealis*

General: Loosely tufted; **stems 10–35 cm tall,** often purplish, often hairy. **Leaves:** Basal leaves egg- to lance-shaped, both surfaces with mostly **4–6-rayed, cross-like or star-like hairs,** margins coarsely toothed; stem leaves usually 3–8, toothed to entire. **Flowers:** Petals white, 4–6 mm long. **Fruits:** Silicles lance-shaped to elliptic, 7–12 mm long, **sparsely hairy** with simple and 2–4-rayed hairs, the **stalks to about as long as the silicles;** styles 0.2–0.8 mm long. **Where Found:** Gravelly terraces, meadows, forest edges and thickets, roadsides, grassy areas, rock outcrops and tundra; montane to alpine zones; frequent in the northern ⅔ of the region; subarctic-alpine, amphiberingian.

Similar Species: Hoary draba or lance-leaved draba (**D. cana**; *D. lanceolata* of some authors, *D. breweri* var. *cana*) has **linear-lance-shaped to oblong basal leaves,** both surfaces densely covered with mostly short-stalked **4–12-rayed, star-like hairs,** smaller flowers (petals 2.5–4 mm long) and **densely hairy silicles** with 3–7-rayed hairs. It occurs on rocky or grassy slopes and  talus, benches and river terraces, roadsides, dry meadows and tundra, in montane to alpine zones. A North American, boreal-subarctic species, it is frequent in the northern ½ of the region, less frequent southward inland of the Coast-Cascade Mtns to CA, NV, UT and NM. • **Tall draba** (p. 222) is a biennial to short-lived perennial with **longer fruit stalks** (the lowest equalling to twice as long as silicles), silicles with a mixture of simple and 2–4-rayed hairs, **styles less than 0.15 mm long** and white to cream petals.

Notes: Northern draba is also known as *Draba maxima*. • Northern draba is highly variable in type of hairs, leaf shape and margin, number of stem leaves and silicle shape, size and twisting. • Apparently the Dene used hoary draba together with other plants such as yarrow and blueberries in bait traps for martens, presumably to mask the human smell.

Grey-leaf Draba • *Draba cinerea*

General: Stems 5–20 cm tall, with mostly star-like hairs. **Leaves: Basal leaves ashy grey on both surfaces with overlapping star-like hairs,** margins entire or rarely with 1 tooth on each side, fringed toward the base and along stalk; stem leaves typically 1–4. **Flowers: Petals white, 3.5–4.5 mm long. Fruits: Silicles oblong to elliptic, plane, 5–8 mm long,** typically grey-green with star-like or cross-like hairs, the stalks about as long as the silicles. **Where found:** Rocky slopes, ridges, meadows, gravel beaches, riverbanks and alluvial fans; montane to alpine zones; frequent in the northern ¼ of the region, infrequent southward; arctic-alpine, circumpolar.

Similar Species: Some **lance-fruited draba** (p. 223), with 1–2 stem leaves and star-like-hairy leaves and stems, could be confused with grey-leaf draba. Lance-fruited draba has silicles that are **longer (6–15 mm), narrowly oblong-lance-shaped** and twisted or plane.

Notes: Remains of grey-leaf draba, or something very much like it, were recovered from 70% of the Late Pleistocene (25,000–30,000 years ago) arctic ground squirrel middens in Yukon's Klondike region, which was ice-free then. • The species name *cinerea* means "ash-coloured."

FLOWERING STEMS WITH 1 OR 2 TO SEVERAL LEAVES AND YELLOW FLOWERS

Ogilvie Mountains Draba • *Draba ogilviensis*

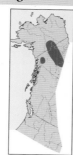

General: Loosely matted perennial with **long, trailing and branching, leafy shoots;** stems 4–15 cm tall. **Leaves:** Basal leaves hairless or sparsely hairy, stalks often sparsely fringed; 1–2 or none on flowering shoots. **Flowers:** Petals golden yellow, 4–6 mm long. **Fruits:** Silicles oblong, 6–9 mm long, hairless. **Where Found:** Meadows, river flats and banks, thickets, gullies, snowbeds, talus slopes and tundra; montane to alpine zones; scattered and locally frequent in the northern ¼ of the region; endemic, subarctic-alpine.

Notes: This species is unmistakeable with its leafy runners.

Tubby Draba • *Draba crassa*

General: Tufted perennial; stems 5–13 cm long/ tall, **sprawling to ascending. Leaves:** Basal leaves **fleshy, hairless except for fringed stalks;** stem leaves 2–6, fringed. **Flowers: Petals yellow, 4–6 mm long.** Fruits: Silicles elliptic-lance-shaped, 8–14 mm long, **hairless,** slightly twisted. **Where Found:** Rocky slopes, ridges, meadows, talus and tundra; subalpine and alpine zones; infrequent in the southeastern corner of the region, in the Rockies of south-central MT to CO; Rocky Mtn endemic.

Golden Draba • *Draba aurea*

General: Stems 10–35 cm tall. Leaves: Basal leaves with **both surfaces densely star-like-hairy,** margins entire or toothed; stem leaves typically **10–20, along length of stem.** Flowers: **Petals yellow, 3.5–5 mm long.** Fruits: Silicles lance-shaped to narrowly oblong, 7–17 mm long, **2–3.5 mm wide, soft-hairy; styles 0.5–1.5 mm long. Where Found:** Rocky slopes and ridges, talus, gullies and meadows, grassy slopes, forest glades, tundra, road cuts and gravelly river terraces; montane to alpine zones; frequent in the southern ¾ of the region, east to Greenland and Labrador; North American.

Similar Species: Pyroclastic draba (*D. aureola*) is a smaller (less than 15 cm tall), stouter-looking plant with numerous **stem leaves crowded toward the base of the stem,** both leaf surfaces with **simple and branched hairs** and **silicles 3–5 mm wide.** It occurs in open coniferous forests, meadows and talus slopes, in subalpine and alpine zones. It is a Pacific Northwest endemic and is infrequent in the Cascades, mostly on the volcanoes, from Mt. Rainier, WA, to Mt. Lassen, CA. • **Slender draba** (p. 222) and **Alaska draba** (p. 222) could be confused with golden draba, but they are both annuals, biennials or short-lived perennials with **fewer (1–4) stem leaves** and **shorter styles (less than 0.15 mm).**

Notes: Golden draba is also known as *Draba luteola*.

Conspectus of Alpine *Draba*

SPECIES	HABIT AND LEAVES	STEMS

FLOWERING STEMS LEAFLESS OR SOMETIMES WITH 1 LEAF

Flowers White

SPECIES	HABIT AND LEAVES	STEMS
lonchocarpa (p. 223)	tufted, sometimes mat-forming; lower leaf surface densely covered (sometimes even felt-like), with tiny, star-like hairs; upper surface hairless or with simple and branched hairs; leaf stalks fringed toward base	hairless or finely felted with tiny, star-like hairs
nivalis (p. 223)	tufted, usually mat-forming; both leaf surfaces greyish, with tiny, short-stalked, overlapping, star-like hairs; leaf stalks not fringed	greyish with tiny, star-like hairs
palanderiana (p. 223)	tufted; both leaf surfaces greyish with overlapping, minutely stalked, star-like hairs; leaf stalks fringed at base	star-like-hairy toward base
lactea (p. 224)	tufted; both leaf surfaces hairless or both with star-like, 4–12-rayed hairs, often concentrated toward apex; leaf stalks usually fringed with simple and forked hairs	hairless or sparsely star-like-hairy toward base
fladnizensis (p. 224)	lower leaf surface mainly with simple and some forked hairs; upper surface often hairless; margins strongly fringed with long, simple hairs	hairless
porsildii (p. 223)	tufted; lower leaf surface with stalked, star-like hairs; upper surface similar or with simple hairs toward base	mostly hairless or nearly so
globosa (p. 224)	densely tufted, cushion-forming; leaves not fleshy; both leaf surfaces hairless; margins fringed with simple hairs	hairless

Flowers Yellow: Lower leaf surfaces with mainly simple or forked to few-branched hairs, or hairless

SPECIES	HABIT AND LEAVES	STEMS
crassifolia (p. 222)	annual, biennial or short-lived perennial; leaves hairless or with a few simple and forked hairs; leaf stalks fringed with unbranched hairs	usually hairless
daviesiae (p. 225)	forming thick, tight cushions; leaves somewhat fleshy; both leaf surfaces hairless; stalks and margins fringed	hairless
pilosa (p. 225)	lower leaf surface with 2–6-rayed hairs; upper surface similar or with simple hairs only; leaf stalks and margins fringed	hairless or with mixture of simple and 2–4-rayed hairs
corymbosa (p. 225)	lower leaf surface with 2–6-rayed hairs (branched, cross-like and long-stalked star-like); upper surface long-hairy with simple and forked hairs; stalks fringed	with simple, forked and 3–5-rayed hairs
macounii (p. 225)	lower leaf surface with short-stalked 2–5-rayed hairs; upper surface hairless or with simple and forked hairs; leaf stalks fringed with long, simple hairs	usually sparsely hairy with simple and 2–4-rayed hairs
stenopetala (p. 225)	cushion-forming; leaves egg- to spoon-shaped; both leaf surfaces with simple and 2–5-rayed hairs or sometimes hairless; stalks and margins fringed	with simple and 2–5-rayed hairs

PETALS	SILICLES (FRUITING PODS)			
	Shape	Length (mm)	Hairs	Stalks
white; 2–4 mm long	linear to lance-oblong to elliptic, somewhat twisted or plane; styles 0.1–0.3 mm long	6–18	hairless or with sparse, simple and forked hairs	hairless or hairy; 2–15 mm long, shorter than silicles
white; 2–4 mm long	oblong to elliptic, plane or twisted; styles 0.1–0.4 mm long	4–9	mostly hairless	hairy; 1–5 mm long, shorter than silicles
white, cream or pale yellow, often drying yellowish; 4.5–5.5 mm long	oblong to elliptic or egg-shaped, plane; styles 0.3–0.8 mm long	4–8	hairless	usually hairless; 4–10 mm long, as long as to slightly longer than silicles
cream to white; 3–5 mm long	oblong to lance-elliptic or egg-shaped, plane; styles 0.1–0.4 mm long	4–8	hairless; dark green	hairless; to about as long as silicles
white; 2–2.5 mm long	oblong to lance-elliptic, plane; styles short, mostly <0.2 mm long	3–8	hairless	hairless; slightly shorter than silicles
white; 2–4 mm long	egg-shaped to oblong, plane; styles 0.1–0.5 mm long	4–8	hairless	hairless; shorter than silicles
white to pale yellow; 2.5–4 mm long	egg-shaped, plane, distinctly veined; styles 0.2-0.6 mm long	4.5–8	hairless	hairless; shorter than silicles
yellow, fading to whitish; 1.5–3 mm long	lance-oblong to elliptic, plane; styles very short, to 0.1 mm long	4–10	hairless	hairless; slightly shorter than silicles
pale to bright yellow; 3.5–4 mm long	egg-shaped to oblong-elliptic, plane, obscurely veined; styles 0.1–0.5 mm long	4–8	hairless	hairless; lowest slightly longer than silicles
yellow; 3.5–6 mm long	elliptic to lance-shaped, plane; styles 0.4–0.9 mm long	5–11	hairless or with simple and forked hairs	hairless or hairy like stems; about as long as silicles
pale yellow; 4–6 mm long	oblong or egg-shaped, plane; styles 0.6–1 mm long	6–12	short, simple and sometimes 2–3-rayed hairs	hairy; to about as long as silicles
pale yellow, drying whitish; 3–4 mm long	somewhat globe- to egg-shaped or ellipsoid; inflated at least toward base, not twisted; styles 0.1–0.5 mm long	4–8	hairless; dark green	hairy like stems; shorter than silicles
yellow (rarely purplish), linear; 2–5 mm long	egg-shaped to somewhat globe-shaped, inflated basally, flattened apically; styles 0.2–0.6 long	3–5	hairless or with simple hairs	hairy like stems; equalling to a bit longer than silicles

SPECIES	HABIT AND LEAVES	STEMS

FLOWERING STEMS LEAFLESS OR SOMETIMES WITH 1 LEAF (cont.)

Flowers Yellow: Lower leaf surfaces with mainly simple or forked to few-branched hairs, or hairless (cont.)

SPECIES	HABIT AND LEAVES	STEMS
densifolia (p. 225)	cushion-forming; leaves linear to oblong; lower leaf surface hairless or with short-stalked 2–4-rayed hairs; upper surface usually hairless; margins fringed with stiff, simple hairs	hairless or rarely hairy with simple and branched hairs
aleutica (p. 225)	densely mat-forming; both leaf surfaces sparsely to densely soft-hairy with mostly simple and few-forked hairs, often hairless on 1 surface; stalks fringed	not much longer than leaves; usually hairy

Flowers Yellow: Lower leaf surfaces short-stalked or stalkless, with mostly star-like or comb-like hairs

SPECIES	HABIT AND LEAVES	STEMS
scotteri (p. 226)	tufted; both leaf surfaces with short-stalked, star-like hairs; stalks and margins fringed with simple hairs	2–8-rayed and some simple hairs
oligosperma (p. 226)	dense cushions; both leaf surfaces with stalkless, comb-like hairs, often concentrated toward tip; margins not fringed	hairless or with comb-like hairs toward base
incerta (p. 226)	tufted, often cushion-forming; both leaf surfaces with short-stalked, comb-like and some star-like hairs; margins fringed	sparse simple, star-like and forked hairs
palanderiana (p. 223)	tufted; both leaf surfaces greyish with overlapping, minutely stalked, star-like hairs; leaf stalks fringed at base	star-like-hairy toward base
argyrea (p. 226)	loosely tufted, matted; both leaf surfaces grey with tiny, short-stalked, star-like hairs; margins not fringed	star-like hairy toward base
sphaerocarpa (p. 226)	loosely tufted, matted; both leaf surfaces grey with tiny, short-stalked, star-like hairs; margins not fringed	densely covered with 2–8-rayed hairs

Flowers Yellow: Lower leaf surfaces with mainly long-stalked, star-like hairs

SPECIES	HABIT AND LEAVES	STEMS
novolympica (p. 227)	cushion-forming; leaves <2 mm wide; lower leaf surface with long-stalked, star-like hairs; upper surface with simple and forked hairs; margins strongly fringed with simple and branched hairs	densely covered with a mixture of simple, forked and star-like hairs
paysonii (p. 227)	cushion-forming; leaves <2 mm wide; lower leaf surface with long-stalked star-like hairs; upper surface with simple and forked hairs; margins strongly fringed with simple and branched hairs	densely covered with a mixture of simple, forked and star-like hairs
ruaxes (p. 227)	tufted; leaves >2 mm wide; lower leaf surface with long-stalked, star-like hairs; upper surface with simple and few-branched hairs; leaf stalks fringed	with simple and a few forked hairs
ventosa (p. 227)	tufted; leaves densely covered on both surfaces with long-stalked, 2–6-rayed hairs, simple hairs lacking; leaf stalks and margins not fringed	densely covered with 2–6-rayed hairs

PETALS	SILICLES (FRUITING PODS)			
	Shape	Length (mm)	Hairs	Stalks
pale yellow, lance- to egg-shaped; 2–5 mm long	egg-shaped to lance-elliptic, plane; styles 0.3–1 mm long	3–7	simple and short-stalked, 2–5-rayed hairs	usually hairless; to as long as or longer than silicles
yellow-green to pale yellow, linear-lance-shaped; 3–4 mm long	egg- to pear-shaped, usually inflated; styles 0.1–0.4 mm long	3–5	hairless or hairy	hairy; to nearly as long as silicles
yellow; 3.5–6 mm long	lance-shaped, plane; styles 0.3–1 mm long	5–11	hairy with simple and a few forked hairs	hairy like stems; mostly shorter than silicles
yellow; 2.5–4 mm long	oval to lance-shaped, somewhat inflated, not twisted; styles 0.1–1 mm long	3–7	simple and forked hairs, rarely hairless	hairless or nearly so; to twice as long as silicles
pale yellow, fading to white; 4–6 mm long	broadly egg- to lance-shaped, plane; styles 0.2–0.9 mm long	5–10	hairless or hairy	hairless or hairy; about as long as silicles
white, cream or pale yellow, often drying yellowish; 4.5–5.5 mm long	oblong to elliptic or egg-shaped, plane; styles 0.3–0.8 mm long	4–8	hairless	usually hairless; as long as to slightly longer than silicles
lemon yellow; 4–6 mm long	lance-egg-shaped, plane or twisted; styles 1–2 mm long	5–11	hairless or minutely hairy or hairless	hairless; about as long as silicles
lemon yellow; 4–6 mm long	ellipsoid to egg-shaped, plane, inflated basally; styles 0.2–1 mm long	2–6	fine, 2–4-rayed hairs	hairy like stems; longer than silicles
yellow; 2–4 mm long	egg-shaped, plane, somewhat inflated basally; styles 0.2–0.8 mm long	3–5	covered with 2–6-rayed and some simple hairs	hairy like stems; mostly shorter than silicles
pale yellow; 5–6 mm long	egg- to lance-shaped, plane, slightly inflated basally; styles 0.6–1.2 mm long	5–9	simple, forked and a few 4–5-rayed hairs	hairy like stems; to about as long as silicles
bright yellow; 4–6 mm long	elliptic to egg-shaped or nearly round, plane; styles 0.5–1 mm long	4–8	soft-hairy at least when young	hairy like stems or hairless; almost as long as silicles
yellow; 3.5–5.5 mm long	broadly egg-shaped to nearly round, plane, inflated basally, flattened apically; styles 0.5–1.4 mm long	4–8	densely short-stalked, 2–6-rayed hairs	hairy like stems; to about as long as silicles

SPECIES	HABIT AND LEAVES	STEMS

FLOWERING STEMS WITH 1–2 TO SEVERAL LEAVES

Flowers White: Silicles hairless

SPECIES	HABIT AND LEAVES	STEMS
glabella (p. 227)	basal leaves loosely tufted to matted; both leaf surfaces with short-stalked, star-like and comb-like, 4–12-rayed hairs; margins usually toothed; stalks fringed; stem leaves 2–17	with simple and 2–8-rayed hairs, or becoming hairless above
juvenilis (p. 227)	loosely tufted or matted; basal leaves have lower surface with stalked, cross-like hairs, upper surface with sparse cross-like and/or simple and forked hairs, often becoming hairless; margins entire to weak-toothed; stalk bases fringed; stem leaves 1–3 (0)	with simple and 2–4-rayed hairs
chamissonis (p. 223)	tufted, sometimes mat-forming; both leaf surfaces densely grey-hairy with short-stalked, 8–12-rayed, star-like hairs; margins often minutely toothed, not fringed; stem leaves 1–2 (to 7)	covered with small, star-like hairs

Flowers White: Silicles hairy

SPECIES	HABIT AND LEAVES	STEMS
borealis (p. 228)	loosely tufted, 10–35 cm tall; both leaf surfaces with forked and 4–6-rayed hairs, margins coarsely toothed; stem leaves usually 3–8	often some long, simple and short, branched hairs
cana (p. 228)	loosely tufted, 10–30 cm tall; both leaf surfaces densely covered with mostly short-stalked, star-like and some simple hairs; margins commonly toothed and partially fringed; stem leaves typically 3–8	densely covered with simple and star-like hairs
praealta (p. 222)	annual or short-lived perennial; loosely tufted, 8–33 cm tall; both leaf surfaces with short-stalked, mostly 3–6-rayed hairs; margins usually toothed; stem leaves typically 3–8	covered with simple and 2–5-rayed hairs
cinerea (p. 228)	densely tufted, 5–20 cm tall; both leaf surfaces ashy-grey with overlapping, star-like hairs; margins entire or with 1 tooth on each side; stem leaves typically 1–4	with star-like hairs mixed with forked or simple hairs
lonchocarpa (p. 223)	densely tufted, 3–11 cm tall; densely covered with short-stalked, star-like hairs; stem leaves 1–2	with star-like hairs

Flowers Yellow: Plants with leafy runners

SPECIES	HABIT AND LEAVES	STEMS
ogilviensis (p. 229)	loosely matted, with leafy runners; both leaf surfaces usually hairless; leaf stalks sometimes fringed; flowering stems with 0–2 leaves	hairless or with simple and 2–3-rayed hairs

Flowers Yellow: Plants tufted, lacking runners

SPECIES	HABIT AND LEAVES	STEMS
crassa (p. 229)	perennial; leaves fleshy, both surfaces hairless, margins fringed; stem leaves 2–6	with simple and forked hairs
albertina (p. 222)	annual, biennial or short-lived perennial; leaves mostly in basal rosette, lower leaf surface with 2–4-rayed hairs, upper surface with simple to forked hairs, margins entire to minutely toothed, fringed with simple hairs; stem leaves 1–4	with coarse, mainly simple hairs, especially near base

PETALS	SILICES (FRUITING PODS)			
	Shape	Length (mm)	Hairs	Stalks
white, sometimes cream; 4–5.5 mm long	oblong to lance- or egg-shaped, plane or rarely twisted, occasionally inflated; styles 0.05–0.5 mm long	5–12	hairless or sometimes sparsely hairy	hairless or hairy like stems; shorter than to as long as silicles
cream to pale yellow or white; 3–5 mm long	elliptic to oblong or narrowly lance-shaped, plane; styles 0.2–0.7 mm long	5–12	hairless or nearly so	hairy like stems; lowest to twice as long as silicles
white; 2–4 mm long	linear to narrowly lance-shaped, plane or slightly twisted; styles 0.1–0.3 mm long	5–11	hairless	hairy like stems; roughly as long as silicles
white to cream; 4–6 mm long	lance-shaped to elliptic, plane or twisted; styles 0.2–0.8 mm long	7–12	sparsely hairy with simple and 2–4-rayed hairs	hairy like stems; shorter than silicles
white; 2.5–4 mm long	narrowly lance-shaped to linear-oblong, often twisted; styles 0.1–0.6 mm long	5–11	usually densely soft-hairy with 3–7-rayed hairs	hairy like stems; shorter than silicles, tight to axis of fruit cluster
white to cream; 3–4 mm long	narrowly lance-shaped, plane; styles 0.03–0.1 mm long	7–14	thinly hairy with simple and 2–4-rayed hairs	hairy like stems; roughly as long as silicles, arching to ascending
white; 3.5–4.5 mm long	oblong to elliptic, plane, slightly flattened; styles 0.2–1 mm long	5–8	typically grey-green with dense, 2–5-rayed hairs	hairy like stems; roughly equalling silicles
white; 2–3.5 mm long	narrowly oblong-lance-shaped, somewhat twisted; 0.1–0.3 mm long	6–15	star-like hairs	hairy like stems; shorter than silicles
golden yellow; 4–6 mm long	oblong, plane; styles 0.4–1 mm long	6–9	hairless	hairless or nearly so; to twice as long as silicles
yellow; 4–6 mm long	lance-egg-shaped, somewhat twisted; styles 0.5–1.5 mm long	8–14	hairless	hairy; about as long as silicles
yellow; 2–3 mm long	linear-oblong to lance-shaped, plane; styles very short, <0.12 mm long	5–12	hairless	usually hairless; about as long as silicles

SPECIES	HABIT AND LEAVES	STEMS

FLOWERING STEMS WITH 1–2 TO SEVERAL LEAVES (cont.)

Flowers Yellow: Plants tufted, lacking runners (cont.)

stenoloba (p. 222)	biennial or short-lived perennial; leaves mostly in basal rosette, lower surface with 3–4-rayed hairs, upper surface with simple and 2–4-rayed hairs, margins toothed to entire; stem leaves 1–3 (or 4)	hairy toward base, mainly with 2–4-rayed hairs
aurea (p. 229)	perennial, 10–35 cm tall; leaves densely star-like-hairy on both surfaces, margins entire to toothed; stem leaves 5–20, along length of stem	with long, simple and 3–6-rayed hairs
aureola (p. 229)	short-lived perennial, 3–15 cm tall; leaves coarse-hairy on both surfaces, with simple and branched hairs; stem leaves to 30, crowded toward base of stem	coarse-hairy with simple and 2–4-rayed hairs

leeward draba

HAIRS AND HAIRY ARCANA

To sort out your drabas, or your cinquefoils or willows or daisies for that matter, you must often focus on their hairs as much as on their flowers and leaves. Are the hairs woolly or cobwebby, long and silky or thick and felted? Are they simple, forked or shaped like stars or combs, stalked or unstalked (see scanning electron microscope photos, p. 221)?

Hairs on the aboveground parts of plants are outgrowths of the surface layer of cells—the epidermis. They can be unicellular or multicellular, simple or variously branched, glandular or nonglandular, colourless or coloured. Some of our alpine plants are not hairy at all. Many others are, and they vary widely in hairiness across genera and families, as well as in the structure of their hairs. Sometimes the hairs are not only diverse within genera, but also remarkably consistent within species. In these cases, they can be used for taxonomic purposes, which they are—and with a vengeance—in *Salix, Draba, Potentilla, Erigeron* and *Poa,* for example.

Why are so many alpine plants hairy? The first and primary contact between plants and their environment is the epidermis. The structure of the epidermis is key to a plant's potential rate of water exchange with the environment and to its defence system against herbivores, pathogens and mechanical damage. A thick cuticle with a tough, waxy finish is part of the surface response, as are epidermal outgrowths (hairs), which can both improve water relations and amplify defences.

PETALS	SILICLES (FRUITING PODS)			
	Shape	Length (mm)	Hairs	Stalks
yellow; 2.5–3.5 mm long	linear-oblong to narrowly elliptic, plane; styles very short, <0.15 mm long	10–17	hairless or nearly so	hairless or nearly so; shorter than to about as long as silicles
yellow; 3.5–5 mm long	oblong to lance-linear, plane or twisted; styles 0.5–1.5 mm long	7–17 × 2–3.5	usually soft-hairy	hairy like stem; mostly shorter than silicles
yellow; 4–6 mm long	oblong to narrowly egg-shaped, plane; styles 1–2 mm long	9–15 × 3–5	coarsely branched-hairy	hairy like stem; mostly shorter than silicles

denseleaf draba and blackish locoweed

Hairs create a layer of still air over a plant's leaf surface. In the reliably windy, cold and often dry alpine environment, this hair layer can reduce drying, water loss and heat loss, allowing pilose plants to photosynthesize and respire in a harsh climate. Dense, woolly hairs can double the effective thickness of the leaves of some willows, cinquefoils, sages and pussytoes. Water vapour escaping from the stomates (breathing pores) travels slowly through the felty barrier. If the hairs are white, as they often are, light will be reflected, moderating internal leaf temperatures and further reducing moisture stress. Hairs also provide protection (physical and sometimes chemical, in the case of some glandular hairs) against grazers and against abrasion from windblown snow and dust. Hairs on reproductive structures can function in pollination (as tactile and visual nectar guides in flowers) and dispersal (as in wind-dispersed fruits or the seeds of *Salix*, *Epilobium* and *Eriophorum*, or in sticktights such as the fruits of *Galium* and some grasses).

Draba, *Potentilla* and *Salix* taxonomists are not necessarily trichophiles (hair lovers). They rely a lot on hairs and other leaf characteristics because the flowers of these genera are rather invariant, and so of limited use in distinguishing species. Do the downy dispositions of drabas truly reflect biological relationships, and so will a hair-based classification prove reliable and stable? Time will tell.

The Genus *Epilobium* (Willowherb)

Our high-elevation *Epilobium* species are perennial herbs from rhizomes, aboveground runners (**stolons**) and fibrous roots or taproots, sometimes with bulb-like offsets (**turions**). The stems are erect or ascending to sprawling. The leaves are opposite or alternate, simple (undivided) and smooth-margined to toothed. The flowers are in a cluster atop a stem or solitary in leaf axils, radially symmetric or nearly so, with 4 pink to magenta or white petals (yellow in 1 species) that are often notched at the tip, 4 sepals and 8 stamens. The 4-chambered ovary is borne below other flower parts (**inferior**) and has a single style with an oblong and unlobed or 4-lobed stigma. The fruits are elongate, club- or spindle-shaped capsules containing tufted, hairy seeds.

Some put the large-flowered species with 4-lobed stigmas in a separate genus, *Chamerion*. The small-flowered species (*Epilobium* in the strict sense) can be difficult to distinguish. You'll need all the plant parts—including those at or below ground level—plus leaves, flowers, fruits and seeds—for identification of these species.

Epilobium is from Greek *epi*, "upon," and *lobos*, "a pod," because the flowers appear to grow out of the top of the capsule (seed pod). The name "willowherb" was originally given to *Epilobium angustifolium* because its leaves resemble those of some species of willow (*Salix* spp.). Willowherb has since been applied to many species of this genus.

Key to *Epilobium*

1a. Petals 8–25 mm long; stigmas 4-lobed **2**

    2a. Petals yellow or cream; leaves opposite below flower cluster . . . . **E. luteum** (p. 240)

    2b. Petals pink to magenta; leaves alternate throughout or opposite toward base and alternate above, including below flower cluster **3**

        3a. Petals notched at tip; ovaries and capsules glandular-hairy; plants somewhat shrubby at base; south of 46° N . . . . **E. obcordatum** (p. 240)

        3b. Petals rounded at tip; ovaries and capsules not glandular; plants not at all shrubby; widespread, especially common north of 48° N **4**

            4a. Plants usually >50 cm tall; leaves 10–15 cm long; flowers usually more than 15; floral bracts linear, much smaller than leaves. . . . . **E. angustifolium** (p. 239)

            4b. Plants usually <40 cm tall; leaves <8 cm long; flowers usually fewer than 12; floral bracts broad, leaf-like. . . . . **E. latifolium** (p. 239)

1b. Petals <10 mm long; stigmas unlobed, oblong or slightly 4-angled. **5**

    5a. Stem leaves narrowly lance-oblong, <3 mm wide; far northern AK, YT and NT. . . . . **E. arcticum** (p. 242)

    5b. Stem leaves broader, lance-shaped to oblong or egg-shaped, usually >3 mm wide; more widespread or southerly. **6**

        6a. Stems hairless, usually glaucous beneath flower cluster . . . . **E. glaberrimum** (p. 242)

        6b. Stems hairy, usually with raised, hairy lines running down stem from leaf bases **7**

            7a. Plants loosely clumped or not; bulb-like, fleshy, scaly offsets present at base; stems erect at base . . . . **E. leptocarpum** (p. 242)

            7b. Plants clumped or tufted, forming short, leafy, aboveground runners; bulb-like offsets lacking; stems curved or angled upward at base. **8**

                8a. Stems 8–35 cm tall; capsules 4–10 cm long; stem leaves toothed or nearly entire (toothless) **9**

                    9a. Petals pink to rose-purple, flower cluster erect in bud; capsules 4–6 cm long, fruiting stalks 5–15 mm long; seeds pimply. . . . . **E. hornemannii** (p. 241)

                    9b. Petals white; flower cluster mostly nodding in bud; capsules 5–10 cm long, fruiting stalks 2–4.5 cm long; seeds net-veined . . . . **E. lactiflorum** (p. 241)

                8b. Stems 3–15 cm tall; capsules 1.5–4 cm long; stem leaves mostly entire **10**

                    10a. Flower cluster nodding in bud, generally hairless; stem leaves oblong-elliptic to lance-shaped; mature fruit about 1 mm wide; seeds 0.7–1.4 mm long, usually net-veined; roots slender, loose. . . . . **E. anagallidifolium** (p. 241)

                    10b. Flower cluster erect in bud, finely stiff-hairy and usually glandular-hairy as well; stem leaves egg-shaped to elliptic; mature fruit 1.5–3 mm wide; seeds 1.5–2 mm long, granular-surfaced; roots wiry, tangled. . . . . **E. clavatum** (p. 241)

River Beauty, Broad-leaved Willowherb
Epilobium latifolium

General: **Clumped** from horizontal roots, **without rhizomes** but often forming colonies via "pseudorhizomes" (a branching complex of persistent shoot bases arising from a common root system); stems sprawling, curved at base to ascending, **10–40 cm long/tall.**

Leaves: Opposite below, alternate above, thickish, **broadly lance-shaped to elliptic or egg-shaped, 1.5–8 cm long,** entire to finely toothed, **bluish green with a bloom,** usually densely short-hairy, nearly stalkless.

Flowers: 3–12 in a cluster at end of stem, **bracts leaf-like,** buds nodding; **petals pink to rose purple,** 1.5–3 cm long; sepals lance-shaped, purplish; style shorter than stamens; stigma deeply 4-lobed.

Fruits: Capsules 3–10 cm long; seeds net-veined, the tuft of hairs white, persistent.

Where Found: Moist river bars, streambanks, meadows and scree slopes; montane to alpine zones; frequent throughout the region except the southwestern corner; arctic-alpine, circumpolar.

Similar Species: Fireweed or rosebay willowherb (*E. angustifolium*; *Chamaenerion angustifolium, Chamerion angustifolium*) is a larger plant, **taller than 50 cm** even at relatively high elevations, with **longer (usually 10–15 cm), narrowly lance-shaped leaves. The flowers are numerous (more than 15),** and the **linear floral bracts are much smaller than the leaves.** The petals are 1–2 cm long, the style longer than the stamens. It grows in mesic open forests, thickets, meadows, burns, roadsides, clearings and on rocky slopes, in all zones. A circumboreal species common throughout, it is merely occasional in the alpine in the north but increasingly of high elevations in the south.

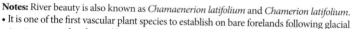

Notes: River beauty is also known as *Chamaenerion latifolium* and *Chamerion latifolium*.
• It is one of the first vascular plant species to establish on bare forelands following glacial retreat or on sand and gravel bars freshly deposited on floodplains. Its primary succession in these challenging habitats is limited by nitrogen, phosphorus and other factors (perhaps the lack of suitable fungi for its roots to associate with). Another of these "other factors" is herbivory by insects. In the Wrangell Mountains of south-central Alaska, the principal herbivore of river beauty is a momphid moth, whose larvae attack the young, rapidly growing shoots. High-intensity attacks by *Mompha* species can seriously reduce the growth and seed production of river beauty clumps, though they also reduce herbivory by voles and porcupines, who like to eat the flowers and fruit pods. • *Epilobium* seeds are well adapted for wind dispersal, with very low rates of fall; a fireweed seed takes about 25 minutes to fall to the ground from 100 metres if the air is completely still. In a Swedish study, wind-blown seeds of fireweed were collected with suction traps on a television tower. Up to 50% of dispersing fireweed seeds were found more than 100 metres above the ground. The researchers suggested that even with very light winds (4 metres per second at 100 metres), fireweed seeds could easily be aloft for 10 hours during a summer day, and that dispersal distances of 100 to 300 kilometres are common. • The Inuit collected young river beauty plants (before they flowered) in early summer and mixed them with other greens, raw or cooked. The Nuxalk ate the central pith of the young stems. • Fireweed is the floral emblem of Yukon.

Yellow Willowherb
Epilobium luteum

General: From widespread rhizomes, often with winter bulblets at the base; stems erect to sprawling, 15–70 cm tall. **Leaves: Mostly opposite,** broadly lance-shaped to elliptic, 2–8 cm long, glandular-toothed, nearly stalkless. **Flowers:** 2–10 along upper leaf axils, nodding in bud, becoming erect in bloom; **petals yellow or cream, 1–2 cm long,** wavy-margined, notched at tip; sepals narrowly lance-shaped, densely glandular and short-hairy; style distinctly longer than petals; **stigma 4-lobed. Fruits:** Capsules 4–8 cm long, glandular-hairy; seeds net-veined, the tuft of hairs rusty, persistent.

Where Found: Streambanks, cascades, shores, springs, seepage areas, moist to wet forest glades and meadows; montane and subalpine to occasionally alpine zones; sporadic but locally frequent in the southern ½ of the region, most frequent in the coastal mountains but absent from the outer Pacific coast between southeastern AK and Vancouver I.; wet cordilleran.

Notes: A late bloomer, yellow willowherb flowers from late July to early September. • Apparent hybrids between *E. luteum* and *E. ciliatum* ssp. *glandulosum* or *E. hornemannii* have pink-purple petals 1 cm or more long and shallowly lobed stigmas, and have been called *E. × treleasianum*. You can occasionally find it in wet subalpine meadows where the 2 parents occur.

yellow willowherb with pink monkeyflower

Rock Willowherb, Rose Willowherb, Rock Fringe • *Epilobium obcordatum*

General: Woody-based, more or less prostrate, mat-forming; stems numerous, **3–10 cm tall. Leaves:** Alternate, crowded, egg-shaped, **5–20 cm long, frosted with a bluish bloom. Flowers:** 1–5 from leaf-like bracts, usually finely glandular-hairy; **petals pink to rose purple,** 1.4–2 cm long, **deeply notched at tip;** sepals purplish; style longer than stamens; **stigma 4-lobed. Fruits:** Capsules 2–4 cm long, **glandular-hairy. Where Found:** In clumps among rocks in dry meadows and on talus slopes, rock ledges, boulder fields and gravelly ridges; subalpine to alpine zones; infrequent in the southernmost part of the region.

Notes: This species is another late bloomer, flowering from August to early September. The heart-shaped petals are stalked at the narrow end, which is what *obcordatum* means.

Alpine Willowherb
Epilobium anagallidifolium

General: Tufted from loose, fibrous roots, often somewhat mat-forming with short, leafy runners and basal offshoots; **stems ascending to erect, curved at the base,** 3–15 cm tall, simple or branched near the base, green or **often reddish,** sparsely hairy in lines. **Leaves:** Opposite, elliptic to lance-shaped, 8–25 mm long, margins smooth or somewhat wavy. **Flowers:** 1–4, **nodding in bud,** the few-flowered cluster **generally hairless; petals pink to rose purple,** 3–6 mm long, notched at tip; sepals mostly hairless; stigma broadly club-shaped. **Fruits:** Capsules 1.5–3.5 cm long, linear-cylindric, **about 1 mm wide,** sometimes arching, red when ripe, nearly hairless; **seeds 0.7–1.4 mm long, net-veined or cross-corrugated, the tuft of hairs dull white, persistent. Where Found:** Moist to wet streambanks, gravel bars, mossy or rocky slopes, scree, seepage areas and meadows; montane to alpine zones; frequent in most of the region except the far north; circumpolar with several large gaps.

Similar Species: At least 3 other partly or largely high-elevation species (considered subspecies or varieties by some taxonomists) are part of the variable *E. alpinum* complex. • **Club-fruited willowherb (*E. clavatum*;** *E. alpinum* var. *clavatum, E. clavatum* var. *glareosum, E. glareosum*) is roughly the same size as alpine willowherb, but has **wiry, tangled roots,** mostly straight stems, **glandular-hairy flower clusters that are erect in bud, club-shaped capsules 2–4 cm long and 2–3 mm wide** and **grainy-surfaced seeds 1.5–2 mm long with an easily detached tuft of hairs.** It grows in moist grassy or rocky meadows and on streambanks and scree slopes, in montane to alpine zones. It is a cordilleran species frequent in most of the region except the far north, in southeastern AK and southwestern YT south through BC and southwestern AB to CA, UT and CO. • **Hornemann's willowherb (*E. hornemannii*;** *E. alpinum* var. *nutans*) is **taller (8–35 cm)** and conspicuously leafy, with rather broad **leaves that are abundant and well formed on the upper stem. The flower clusters are erect in bud,** the flowers with usually **pink to rose purple petals. The capsules are 4–6 cm long, on stalks 5–15 mm long,** with granular-surfaced seeds. It occurs on wet to moist rocky slopes, cliffs and streambanks, and in meadows and thickets, in montane to alpine zones. It is frequent (especially in coastal mountains) in most of the region except the far north, with a distribution much like that of alpine willowherb, and is circumpolar with large gaps. • **White-flowered willowherb (*E. lactiflorum*;** *E. alpinum* var. *lactiflorum*) is also relatively tall (8–35 cm) but has **flower clusters nodding in bud, white to cream petals** (sometimes pinkish) and **capsules 5–10 cm long on stalks 2–4.5 cm long,** with net-veined or finely ridged seeds. It grows in wet to mesic meadows and on streambanks and rocky slopes, in montane to alpine zones, and is frequent from southern AK, southern YT and southwestern NT south through BC and southwestern AB to CA and CO; it is amphi-Atlantic, with a disjunct range in western North America.

Notes: On alpine tundra in the north, grizzly bears in search of arctic ground squirrels dig large, deep (sometimes astonishingly so) holes. Alpine willowherb is significantly more abundant on these bear digs. The ground squirrels are not. • The small flowers seem designed for self-fertilization, with the anthers lying directly on the stigma when the flower is closed. When the flowers open, the petals and anthers are spread wide and cross-pollination can occur. In a Colorado study, flowers opened for only 2 days (closing during the intervening night) before the fruits started to mature. An analysis of proteins revealed strong homozygosity, the genetic uniformity to be expected from a primarily selfing mating

white-flowered willowherb

system. • A big question in plant geography is how plants colonized our region following the retreat of glaciers. Did they exist in northern refugia (areas that somehow escaped glaciation) and recolonize from there? Or did they simply move north from southern areas that were never ice covered? A third explanation may be that some plant species survived by growing on debris-covered glaciers. Researchers documented 41 vascular plant species (including Hornemann's willowherb) growing on Carbon Glacier on Mt. Rainier. Some of our arctic and alpine plants may have ridden out glaciation at uncharacteristically low elevations and latitudes thanks to refrigeration by large mounds of buried ice.

Hornemann's willowherb

Smooth Willowherb, Glaucous Willowherb
Epilobium glaberrimum

General: Generally hairless with a **whitish-waxy bloom;** clumped from branched rhizomes, often somewhat mat-forming with short runners; **stems erect, 8–40 cm tall,** simple or branched. **Leaves:** Opposite, numerous, usually overlapping, clasping stem, lance- to egg-shaped, 1–4 cm long, smooth-margined to finely toothed. **Flowers:** Erect in bud, the few-flowered cluster generally hairless; **petals pink to rose purple, 3–8 mm long,** notched at tip; sepals hairless; stigma club-shaped. **Fruits:** Capsules 3–7 cm long; seeds granular-surfaced in lengthwise rows. **Where Found:** Moist to wet streambanks, rocky slopes, gravel bars and scree slopes; montane to alpine zones; infrequent in the southern ⅓ of the region; cordilleran.

Notes: Smooth willowherb is also known as *Epilobium platyphyllum.*

Slim-pod Willowherb • *Epilobium leptocarpum*

General: Delicate, often loosely clumped from a taproot, with small, fleshy, **bulb-like offsets at base of stem or underground,** sometimes with bulblets in upper leaf axils; stems slender, often reddish, ascending to erect, 8–30 cm tall, **short-hairy in lines below leaf bases. Leaves:** Opposite, lance-shaped to elliptic, 8–40 mm long, mostly hairless, margins entire to toothed. **Flowers:** Nodding in bud, the few-flowered cluster short-hairy but not glandular; **petals white fading to pink, 3–6 mm long;** sepals short-hairy; stigma club-shaped. **Fruits: Capsules 2.5–5.5 cm long, linear-cylindric,** extending beyond top of stem **on long (1.5–4 cm) stalks;** seeds granular-surfaced in parallel lines, the tuft of hairs tawny and persistent. **Where Found:** Moist meadows, streambanks, mossy seepage sites, stony slopes and rocky ledges; montane to alpine zones; infrequent in the southern ⅔ of the region; cordilleran.

Similar Species: Arctic willowherb (*E. arcticum*; *E. davuricum* var. *arcticum*) is a far northern, arctic-alpine, amphi-Atlantic plant, infrequent in moist to wet tundra of mountains in northern AK, northern YT, northwestern NT and eastward. It has **short (5–12 cm),** upright, dark green or purple stems, with **fleshy offsets at the base,** and 2–3 pairs of **narrowly lance-oblong leaves.** The flowers are few, nodding in bud, the **petals whitish to pink** and about 4 mm long. The capsules are 2 cm long, and the seeds granular-surfaced, the tuft of hairs dingy.

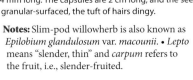

arctic willowherb

Notes: Slim-pod willowherb is also known as *Epilobium glandulosum* var. *macounii.* • *Lepto* means "slender, thin" and *carpum* refers to the fruit, i.e., slender-fruited.

Pea Family (Fabaceae)

The pea family in our region consists of perennial herbs that have mostly basal or alternate, pinnately or palmately compound leaves with **stipules** (appendages at the base of the leaf stalk). In our species, the flowers are bilaterally symmetric, with 5 partially fused sepals, 5 mostly distinct petals, 10 stamens and 1 **superior ovary.** The fruit is a 1- or 2-chambered, variously shaped pod (**legume**) with several to many seeds in 2 alternating rows. The family is also known as Leguminosae. The flowers of our species are butterfly-like, with unequal petals—a large, upright **banner,** a lateral pair of smaller **wings** and 2 inner, joined petals forming a **keel,** which envelops the stamens and ovary (see illustration, right).

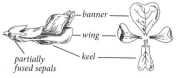

partially fused sepals · banner · wing · keel

Astragalus and *Oxytropis* are the largest genera in our region. With about 17,000 species, the pea family is probably the third largest in the world, after Asteraceae and Orchidaceae, and it is also one of the most economically important. Its species provide food (including nectar for honey), fodder, dyes, gums, resins, oils, medicines and timber. Food products include garden peas (*Pisum*), lentils (*Lens*), peanuts (*Arachis*), beans (*Phaseolus*) and soybeans (*Glycine*); fodder and forage plants include clover (*Trifolium*), alfalfa (*Medicago*), vetch (*Vicia*), bird's-foot trefoil (*Lotus*) and sweet-clover (*Melilotus*).

Key to the Genera of Fabaceae

1a. Leaves palmately compound, with 3 or 5–12 leaflets. **2**
    2a. Leaflets 5–12 or so; flowers in cylindric clusters . . . . ***Lupinus*** (below, p. 244)
    2b. Leaflets 3; flowers in head-like clusters. . . . . ***Trifolium*** (pp. 245–246)
1b. Leaves pinnately compound. **3**
    3a. Pods with constrictions between each of 2–5 seeds, breaking crosswise; keel-petal surpassing wing-petals)
    . . . . ***Hedysarum*** (pp. 247–248)
    3b. Pods not conspicuously constricted between seeds, splitting lengthwise; keel-petal mostly shorter than wing-petals **4**
        4a. Keel-petals blunt; plants (ours) usually with leafy stems. . . . . ***Astragalus*** (pp. 249–252)
        4b. Keel-petals abruptly narrowed to a beak-like tip; plants (ours) usually with leafless flowering stems, the leaves in a basal rosette . . . . ***Oxytropis*** (pp. 253–257)

The Genus *Lupinus* (Lupine)

Our lupines are perennial herbs from taproots and stout, somewhat woody, branching root-crowns. The leaves are palmately compound with 5–12 lance-shaped leaflets. The flowers are several to many in usually elongate clusters atop the stems, ours mostly blue or violet, the wing-petals enclosing the keel-petal. The sepal-tubes are 2-lobed, the lobes toothed or toothless.

Alpine Lupine • *Lupinus lyallii*

General: Sprawling, mat-forming, greyish silky-hairy plants; **flowering stems less than 20 cm long/tall. Leaves:** Long-stalked, sometimes exceeding flower clusters. **Flowers:** In compact, short-cylindric clusters at stem tips; **flowers 7–9 mm long;** petals blue, the bannerpetal often darker blue with a white central blotch. **Where Found:** Dry to mesic, windy meadows, rocky or gravelly slopes, pumice plains and ridges; subalpine and alpine zones; locally frequent in the southern ⅓ of the region, mostly in the Coast-Cascade Mtns and on their leeward slopes.

Similar Species: Silvery lupine (*L. argenteus* var. *depressus*) is erect, greyish-hairy and 15–30 cm tall, with slender, compact clusters of blue to whitish flowers, the **basal leaves mostly withered or fallen by flowering time.** It occurs in meadows and on rocky slopes and grassy balds, and is frequent from central ID to central MT and WY, mostly in subalpine and lower alpine zones.

Notes: Alpine lupine is also known as *Lupinus lepidus* ssp. *lyallii* and var. *lobbii*. • Following the 1980 eruption of Mount St. Helens, alpine lupine was the first vascular plant to successfully colonize the pumice plain and acted as a keystone species in early primary succession.

Arctic Lupine • *Lupinus arcticus*

General: Stems several, **erect to ascending, 20–80 cm tall,** with mostly **short, spreading to appressed hairs.**

Leaves: Mostly basal on long stalks (in the north) to mostly along stem on shorter stalks (in the south), the **stalks mostly 1.5–3 times as long as the blades;** leaflets 2–8 cm long, hairless or sparsely hairy above, stiff-hairy below.

Flowers: Numerous, more or less whorled in elongate clusters 5–15 cm long; petals blue, sometimes with a central white or pinkish area on banner-petal, **14–20 mm long; sepal-tube lower lip slender, lance-shaped,** 5–11 mm long, upper lip 2-toothed at tip.

Fruits: Pods 2–4 cm long, silky to coarse-hairy.

Where Found: Open forests, meadows, gravel bars, clearings, roadsides, heathlands and tundra; lowland to alpine zones; frequent in much of the inland part of the region; cordilleran.

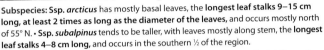

Subspecies: Ssp. *arcticus* has mostly basal leaves, the **longest leaf stalks 9–15 cm long, at least 2 times as long as the diameter of the leaves,** and occurs mostly north of 55° N. • **Ssp. *subalpinus*** tends to be taller, with leaves mostly along stem, the **longest leaf stalks 4–8 cm long,** and occurs in the southern ½ of the region.

Similar Species: Nootka lupine **(*L. nootkatensis*)** also has its longest leaf stalks on the stem, but it has **short-stalked basal leaves, the stalks about as long as the blades are wide,** the leaflets usually shaggy or short-soft-hairy on the lower surface, and the **lower sepal-tube lip is broad and boat-shaped.** It grows in mesic to moist meadows, glades, streambanks, shores, riverbars, thickets and heathlands, in lowland to lower alpine zones. It is a Pacific maritime species and is frequent along the coast, from northern Vancouver I. to southern AK and southwestern YT, and occasional inland to the Rockies.

Notes: Arctic lupine includes *Lupinus latifolius* var. *subalpinus* (=*L. a.* ssp. *subalpinus*). • It is an important food plant for snowshoe hares in Yukon summers and for mother caribou on their Alaskan calving grounds. • Arctic lupine seeds, reportedly at least 10,000 years old, were retrieved from arctic lemming burrows in Yukon in 1967 and successfully germinated to produce healthy plants. Then, 40 years later, radiocarbon dating suggested that the samples were contaminated with modern seeds. The moral—healthy skepticism never gets old. • The flowers of our lupines lack nectar but have plenty of pollen, and they make their insect pollinators (usually bumblebees) work for the energy-rich reward. The single style and 10 stamens are included within the keel-petals, which are fused along their edges except for an opening at the tip. Five longer stamens alternate with 5 shorter ones; the longer 5 have large, elongate anthers that shed pollen into the keel as the flower starts to bloom. The shorter 5 then elongate and push pollen into the keel tip, around the hairy stigma. When visiting a lupine flower, a pollen-collecting bumblebee braces head-first against the banner-petal and depresses the wing- and keel-petals, which forces the stigma piston-fashion through the pollen mass and out the opening at the keel tip, where the bumblebee collects the pollen. • *Lupinus* is Latin from *lupus*, "wolfish" or "wolf-pea"—that is, fit only for wolves and perhaps linked to an early belief that lupines depleted the soil of nutrients. We now know that they do just the opposite by fixing atmospheric nitrogen into a form that they and other plants can use. • **Caution:** All species of lupines should be considered **poisonous,** even though some northern people ate the roots, as do some grizzlies.

L. a. ssp. *subalpinus*

Nootka lupine

The Genus *Trifolium* (Clover)

Plants in this genus grow from taproots and/or rhizomes. The leaves are alternate and palmately compound with 3 leaflets. The pea-shaped flowers are few to many in heads, and in our alpine species are yellowish to reddish or purple. The sepal-tubes are 5-cleft, the lobes or teeth pointy-tipped. The pods are slightly longer than the persistent sepal-tubes, with 1–6 seeds.

Longstalk Clover • *Trifolium longipes*

General: Generally hairy, from a slender tap-root and branched root-crown, **often with rhizomes or runners;** stems single or a few together, ascending to erect, sprawling at the base, **5–30 cm tall,** leafy.

Leaves: Leaflets 3, **lance-shaped,** 2–6 cm long.

Flowers: Numerous (20–70) in dense, rounded or top-shaped heads, **lacking cup of fused bracts** (involucre), atop stalks that usually exceed the leaves; **petals whitish or creamy yellow to purplish,** 10–18 mm long; **sepal-tube about ½ as long as petals.**

Where Found: Meadows, streambanks and rocky slopes; montane to alpine zones; frequent in the southern ¼ of the region; cordilleran.

Varieties: *T. longipes* has perhaps 5 varieties, several of which look very different, scarcely like the same species. Refer to technical manuals for details.

Similar Species: Bigleaf clover or Hayden's clover (*T. haydenii*) also lacks a cup of fused bracts beneath the flower head, but is **tufted** and **hairless,** with a **heavy taproot** and **short (3–10 cm) stems,** the mostly basal leaves with **egg-shaped to roundish leaflets.** Nodding in loose heads, the **5–20 flowers** are 13–17 mm long, **creamy yellow, often tinged with pink or purple, to bright rose,** the sepal-tube ½–⅔ as long as the petals. It is found in dry to mesic meadows and on rocky or gravelly slopes, ridges and fellfields, in subalpine and alpine zones. Bigleaf clover is locally frequent and endemic to southwestern MT, northwestern WY and adjacent ID.

Notes: Longstalk clover is also known as *Trifolium pedunculatum*. • Female yellow sulphur butterflies (*Colias philodice eriphyle*) lay their eggs on longstalk clover. • "Clover" derives from the Anglo-Saxon *cleafer* or *cloefra*—something to do with "clubs" and perhaps the 3-headed club shape of the leaves.

SPECIES WITH A CUP OF FUSED BRACTS BENEATH THE FLOWERHEADS

Dwarf Clover • *Trifolium nanum*

General: Densely matted from a strong taproot; **flowering stems 1–5 cm tall. Leaves:** Tiny, the **leaflets 5–15 mm long;** stipules persistent, lance-shaped. **Flowers:** In heads of **1–4; petals reddish purple or striped reddish** on a paler matrix, 15–22 mm long. **Fruits:** Pods disproportionately large, 5–15 mm long. **Where Found:** Dry to mesic, rocky slopes and ridges, talus, scree and fellfields; subalpine to alpine zones; infrequent in the southeastern portion of the region.

Whip-root Clover
Trifolium dasyphyllum

General: Tufted or somewhat mat-forming, **hairy; flowering stems sprawl-ing, 5–10 cm long.** Leaves: **Leaflets 7–30 mm long,** narrow, often folded; stipules persistent, papery. **Flowers:** 10–20 mm long, in heads of **5–30; flowers often 2-toned,** the banner-petal creamy yellow, the wing- and keel-petals rose to purplish; **sepals hairy. Where Found:** Rocky slopes, ridges, meadows and fellfields; subalpine to alpine zones; infrequent in the south-eastern portion of the region.

Subspecies: Plants with 2-toned flowers and pointy-tipped leaflets are **ssp. *dasyphyllum*.** Those with more uniformly purple-violet flowers and blunt leaflets are **ssp. *uintense*.**

Notes: Many legumes develop root nodules to house nitrogen-fixing bacteria. This mutually beneficial association can be important in the alpine. In Colorado, both soil nitrogen and aboveground biomass were 2 times greater in plant communities with whip-root clover than in surrounding areas. The increased biomass was almost entirely whip-root clover; the benefits of nitrogen-fixation did not automatically and equably "trickle down" to the rest of the community. • *Dasyphyllum* means "shaggy-leaved." The name "whip-root" refers to the plant's long, thin taproot.

Parry's Clover • *Trifolium parryi*

General: Mostly tufted, hairy to hairless plants; flower-ing stems leafless, erect, **4–8 cm tall. Flowers:** 10–20 mm long, in heads of **5–30; petals pinkish magenta to dark reddish purple; sepals hairless. Where Found:** Moist meadows, rocky slopes and streambanks; subalpine to alpine zones; infrequent in the southeastern portion of the region.

Notes: Charles C. Parry (1823–90) was a botanist in Colorado, Utah and Iowa, and worked with the United States and Mexican Boundary Survey.

The Genus *Hedysarum* (Sweetvetch)

Plants in this genus are perennial herbs from woody taproots and stout, branching stem-bases. The leaves are alternate, stalked and pinnately compound, with 7–23 oblong to lance-shaped or elliptic leaflets that are minutely glandular-dotted, at least on the upper surface. The flowers are several to many in usually elongated clusters from the leaf axils, and ours are mostly pink to purple, sweetpea-shaped, with wing-petals shorter than the blunt keel-petal. The sepal-tubes are bell-shaped and 5-toothed. The flattened pods, which look like short, drooping to spreading strings of flattened beads, are pinched in between each of the 2–5 seeds and break crosswise.

Key to *Hedysarum*

1a. Flowers yellow . . . . *H. sulphurescens* (p. 248)

1b. Flowers pink to reddish purple 2

  2a. Leaflets thick, the lateral veins usually not evident; flowers mostly 15–25 mm long, upper teeth of sepal-tube slender, nearly equal to lower teeth; pods cross-corrugated, not wing-margined . . . . **H. boreale (below)**

  2b. Leaflets thin, with prominent lateral veins; upper teeth of sepal-tube triangular, shorter than lower teeth; pods net-veined but not strongly cross-corrugated, wing-margined 3

    3a. Pods 3–7 mm wide, the margins with wings ≤1 mm wide; flowers mostly 10–15 mm long; widespread plants . . . . *H. alpinum* (p. 248)

    3b. Pods 7–12 mm wide, the margins with wings 1–2 mm wide; flowers 16–22 mm long; southern plants . . . . *H. occidentale* (p. 248)

Northern Sweetvetch, Wild Sweetpea
Hedysarum boreale

General: Resembles alpine sweetvetch (p. 248). **Leaves:** Leaflets thick, firm, **lateral veins usually not evident. Flowers:** Generally **larger (mostly 15–25 mm long), deeper-hued flowers** than alpine sweetvetch, reddish purple or magenta to pink; **upper teeth of sepal-tubes linear-lance-shaped, about equal to lower teeth,** unlike the triangular, unequal teeth of alpine sweetvetch. **Fruits:** Pods **hairy, corrugated, with ladder-like ridges, not wing-margined. Where Found:** Mesic to moist gravel bars, river terraces, open forests, thickets, rocky slopes and roadsides; montane to lower alpine zones; frequent in most of the inland northern ⅓ of the region (north of about 57° N), less so southward; subarctic-montane, North American.

Notes: Northern sweetvetch is also known as *Hedysarum mackenzii*. • The **roots are poisonous** and are known to have caused severe illness in the men of John Richardson's arctic expedition, who mistook it for the edible alpine sweetvetch. Chris McCandless, the young man

seeking wilderness in Alaska, could have made the same mistake in 1992, or perhaps he ate sweetvetch seeds (see J. Krakauer's book *Into the Wild*). Northern and alpine sweetvetches could be confused, especially when not in flower. What's more, they often grow in the same northern areas and overlap in blooming time. Flowering time may be synchronized with the arrival of their primary pollinators—in an Alaskan study, a leafcutter bee (*Megachile giliae*) for both species, and a bumblebee (*Bombus flavifrons*) for alpine sweetvetch.

Alpine Sweetvetch, Bear-root
Hedysarum alpinum

General: Stems several, erect to spreading at the base then ascending, 10–90 cm tall, often branched above, short-stiff-hairy.

Leaves: Alternate, leaflets 7–27, lance-shaped to lance-elliptic, abruptly sharp-pointed at tip, **prominent lateral veins,** hairless or nearly so.

Flowers: Several to many (5–50) in elongated to compact clusters, pink to pink-purple (rarely white), paler at the base, **10–15 (to 20) mm long;** upper pair of teeth of sepal-tube **triangular, shorter than lower teeth.**

Fruits: Flattened pods 3–7 mm wide, **narrowly (less than 1 mm) wing-margined, conspicuously net-veined** but not cross-corrugated, **mostly hairless.**

Where Found: Rocky slopes, open forests, roadsides, gravel bars, shores, meadows, heathlands and tundra; lowland (arctic coast) to alpine zones; frequent in the northern mostly inland ½ of the region, less so south of 55° N along the Rockies; broadly amphiberingian.

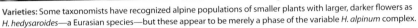

Varieties: Some taxonomists have recognized alpine populations of smaller plants with larger, darker flowers as *H. hedysaroides*—a Eurasian species—but these appear to be merely a phase of the variable *H. alpinum* complex.

Notes: Alpine sweetvetch is also known as *Hedysarum alpinum* var. *grandiflorum* and *H. americanum*. • Generally a tall plant with numerous flowers at lower elevations, alpine sweetvetch grades into smaller plants with fewer flowers at higher elevations or on harsher sites. • The roots are a favourite spring or fall food of grizzly bears, which select this species over northern sweetvetch (p. 247). • *Hedysarum* is from the Greek *hedys*, "sweet," and *saron*, "broom." It is also called wild potato and licorice-root, because the roots of alpine sweetvetch were a major source of starch for northern peoples, including the Dena'ina, Gwich'in, Dene and Inuit. The roots are best (sweet and juicy) in spring and are eaten raw, boiled, roasted or fried in grease. They were stored, often in grease, for winter use, but to forestall rot, they were not washed before storing. • Aboriginal peoples of Siberia gathered edible roots, including those of alpine sweetvetch, from rodent burrows in winter. Sometimes the burrows were completely plundered; other times, some food was left behind for the animals, so that they could survive the winter and, presumably, be raided again next year. In some areas, ceremonies were held to present gifts to the rodents. • **Do not** confuse this plant with northern sweetvetch, the root of which is poisonous.

Western Sweetvetch • *Hedysarum occidentale*

General: Differs from alpine sweetvetch in having **generally larger flowers, 16–22 (to 25) mm long,** and **broader (more than 7 mm wide) pods** with **wider (1–2 mm) wings** along the margins. **Where Found:** Mesic to moist meadows, shrublands, open forests, rocky slopes, scree, talus and tundra; subalpine and alpine zones; scattered but locally frequent in the southern ⅓ of the region; cordilleran.

Similar Species: Yellow sweetvetch (*H. sulphurescens*) differs mainly in its **yellow to whitish yellow flowers,** 14–20 mm long. It grows on grassy slopes, gravel bars, aspen parklands, open forests, meadows, fellfields and turfy tundra, especially on calcium-rich soil, in montane to lower alpine zones. It is scattered but locally frequent in southeastern BC and southwestern AB to WA, OR, ID, MT and WY.

Notes: The root of yellow sweetvetch is an important grizzly bear food in the Rockies.

The Genus *Astragalus* (Milkvetch)

Plants in this genus are perennial herbs from taproots and branching stem-bases or from rhizomes, ours with leafy stems. The leaves are alternate and stalked, and ours are odd-pinnately compound with leaflets that have unlobed, untoothed margins. The flowers are several to many in elongated to compact clusters from the leaf axils, with blunt-tipped keel-petals and cylindric to bell-shaped, 5-toothed sepal-tubes. The fruits are pods of several shapes and textures, and can be hairy or hairless.

Astragalus is a monster genus, the largest in the pea family, with more than 350 species in North America. With 2500 to 3000 species worldwide, it could be the largest genus of flowering plants. It's a big, complex group, but fortunately for identification purposes, there is a manageable number of high-elevation species in our region.

P.A. Rydberg produced the original monograph of North American *Astragalus* in 1929, splitting it into an alarming 28 genera. Fortunately, that "disc" was subsequently "defragmented" by later students of the genus. We've used a 2011 draft *FNA* treatment by Stanley Welsh and Richard Spellenberg. It builds on earlier work by several milkvetch specialists, most notably Rupert C. Barneby (1911–2000), a British-born, classically educated, self-taught botanist, who worked for decades at the New York Botanical Garden. His specialty was Fabaceae, and he was much taken with *Astragalus*. He also apparently was a splendid fellow, a raconteur who loved to hold court on all sorts of topics, engaging in erudite and witty conversation, though perhaps not about basifixed and dolabriform hairs. The *New York Times* obituary noted that he was "… one of the world's top experts on beans." Rupert Barneby definitely knew beans about the peas.

Several species of *Astragalus*, and of the closely related *Oxytropis*, contain toxic chemicals that cause loss of muscle control in livestock, resulting in "blind staggers" and other crazed conditions. Hence some milkvetches are also called "locoweeds." The poisonous agent could be the alkaloid swainsonine (formerly known as locoine) or large amounts of selenium, which some *Astragalus* notoriously accumulate.

Astragalus is from the Greek *astragalos*, "ankle bone." This could allude either to the similarity in shape between the bone and seeds of this genus or to the similarity between the sound made by rattling bones used as dice and that of seeds rattling in dried pods. "Astragalus" is also the name given to archaeological artifacts used in gambling. "Milkvetch" is perhaps because of *gala* (Greek for "milk") in the generic name, or because some species in forage reputedly caused greater milk production in cattle and vaguely resemble true vetches (*Vicia*).

Key to *Astragalus*

1a. Leaflets linear-elliptic, spine-tipped; flowers and fruits small, petals 4–9 mm long, pods 3–8 mm long
....***A. kentrophyta* var. *tegetarius** (p. 250)
1b. Leaflets not spine-tipped; flowers and fruits often larger.. 2

  2a. Stipules distinct, joined to leaf stalk or to both leaf stalk and stem, variably running down or sheathing stem, but not fused opposite leaf stalk 3

    3a. Flowers yellow, 13–19 mm long; stipules 7–30 mm long, leafy, bent downward.... ***A. umbellatus** (p. 250)
    3b. Flowers purplish, 4–8 mm long; stipules 4–9 mm long, not leafy or bent downward ... ***A. eucosmus** (p. 252)

  2b. Stipules of at least lowest nodes fused opposite leaf stalk and sheathing the stem 4

    4a. Mature pods curved.. 5

      5a. Plants prostrate, matted; flowers 1–5 per cluster; pods curved in a semicircle, strongly flattened, 3–5 cm long ....***A. nutzotinensis** (p. 252)
      5b. Plants ascending; flowers 6 to many per cluster; pods crescent-shaped, slightly flattened, 1–3 cm long ....***A. australis** (p. 252)

    4b. Mature pods straight or nearly so.. 6

      6a. Petals all about the same length; plants with tufts of silvery leaves, often nearly stemless
....***A. platyropis** (p. 252)
      6b. Banner-petal longer than keel-petals; leaves along stems, variously hairy but not densely silvery-hairy.. 7

        7a. Flowers mostly <7–8 mm long 8

          8a. Flowers whitish, often with purple highlights; pods ellipsoid, 3–5 mm long, flattened (not inflated) ....***A. vexilliflexus** var. *nubilus** (p. 251)
          8b. Flowers purplish; pods 5–15 mm long 9

            9a. Pods egg- to nearly globe-shaped, somewhat bladdery-inflated, white-hairy
....***A. microcystis** (p. 251)
            9b. Pods egg-shaped to ellipsoid, compressed, brown-hairy.......... ***A. eucosmus** (p. 252)

        7b. Flowers mostly >7–8 mm long 10

10a. Wing-petals deeply notched at tip...*A. australis* (p. 252)

10b. Wing-petals not notched..**11**

11a. Stems 20–30 cm tall or taller; larger leaflets 1–3 cm long; larger stems 1.5–3 mm thick
at the base...*A. robbinsii* (p. 252)

11b. Stems usually <20 cm tall; larger leaflets about 1–1.5 cm long; larger stems 1–1.5 mm
thick at the base...**12**

12a. Stems prostrate, sprawling or weakly ascending **13**

13a. Mature pods not inflated, 0.8–1.5 cm long **14**

14a. Flowers 5–25; pods stalked........................*A. alpinus* (p. 251)

14b. Flowers 1–5; pods unstalked ....*A. molybdenus* (p. 251)

13b. Mature pods bladdery-inflated, 1.5–6 cm long **15**

15a. Flowers 2–5; pods egg-shaped, unstalked; leaflets notched at tip; northern plants..*A. polaris* (p. 251)

15b. Flowers 4–11; pods egg-shaped to spheric, stalked; leaflets blunt to
pointy-tipped; southern plants.......................*A. whitneyi* (p. 251)

12b. Stems ascending-erect, sometimes reclining at the base **16**

16a. Pods ellipsoid, somewhat flattened (not inflated), 1–1.5 cm long; flowers
purplish..*A. bourgovii* (p. 252)

16b. Pods inflated, 2–6 cm long; flowers whitish tinged with pale pink or lavender
....*A. whitneyi* (p. 251)

Prickly Milkvetch, Thistle Milkvetch
Astragalus kentrophyta var. *tegetarius*

General: Prostrate, mat- or cushion-forming, less than 5 cm tall, to 40 cm wide, greyish
green with silky hairs. **Leaves: Leaflets 5–9, linear-elliptic,** 2–9 mm long, barely 1 mm
wide, **spine-tipped. Flowers:** Crouching among leaves, 1–3 per axil;
petals purplish (rarely whitish-tipped pink-purple), **4–9 mm long.**
Fruits: Pods ellipsoid, compressed, 3–8 mm long, grey-short-hairy.
Where Found: Dry, rocky slopes, margins of timberline forests and
shrublands, ridge crests, fellfields and scree; subalpine and alpine
zones; frequent in the southeastern ¼ of the region.

Notes: Prickly milkvetch is also known as *Astragalus tegetarius*
and *A. kentrophyta* var. *implexus*. • This and 2 other *Astragalus*
species in the Utah alpine share primary pollinators, several
species each of mason bees (*Osmia* spp.) and bumblebees
(*Bombus* spp.). • Typical prickly milkvetch is a plant of steppe
and montane zones, the Great Plains and intermontane valleys. • *Kentrophyta* means
"spiny growth"; *tegetarius* may be from *tegetus*, "mat-like."

Tundra Milkvetch • *Astragalus umbellatus*

General: Stems solitary or a few together, soft-hairy, erect to
ascending, 5–30 cm tall; **stipules distinct, 7–30 mm long, leafy,
bent downward. Leaves:** Leaflets oblong to
elliptic, 1–3 cm long, dark green and hairless
above. **Flowers:** 5–11, **drooping** in compact,
umbel-like clusters; **petals yellow with
whitish margins, 13–19 mm long. Fruits:**
Pods ellipsoid to egg-shaped, somewhat
inflated, 1.5–2 cm long, black-hairy, drooping. **Where Found:** Moist to mesic meadows,
heathlands and tundra; lowland
(arctic coast) to alpine zones;
frequent in the northern ⅓ of
the region; arctic-alpine,
amphiberingian.

Alpine Milkvetch • *Astragalus alpinus*

General: Low, less than 20 cm tall, mat-forming, short-appressed-hairy; stems slender, weak, trailing to ascending, 5–35 cm long. **Leaves:** Leaflets mostly 15–25, egg-shaped to oblong-elliptic, rounded to notched at tip. **Flowers:** 5–25 in a short, dense cluster; petals pale bluish to pinkish purple, often white toward the base, 7–15 mm long. **Fruits:** Pods ellipsoid-oblong, not inflated, **8–15 mm long**, grooved below, black-hairy, **drooping on short stalks. Where Found:** Streambanks, river terraces, open forests, meadows, rocky slopes, heathlands, tundra, scree and fellfields; lowland (arctic coast) to alpine zones; frequent in the northern ½ of the region, less so southward; arctic/subarctic-alpine, circumpolar.

Similar Species: Polar milkvetch (*A. polaris*) has deeply notched leaflets, **fewer (2–5) flowers** and **unstalked, egg-shaped pods that are ultimately inflated, papery, bladder-like, 1.5–4.5 cm long** and not grooved below. An amphiberingian species, it is locally frequent in western AK and occurs on gravelly

shores, moraines and rocky slopes, in lowland to alpine zones. **Molly's milkvetch (*A. molybdenus*)** also has **fewer flowers (1–5)** but has erect, egg-shaped, **non-inflated pods, 0.8–1.2 cm long**, unstalked or nearly so. It grows on rocky ridges, scree, talus and tundra in the alpine zone; var. *lackschewitzii* is restricted to Teton County, MT; var. *shultziorum* is found only in the Snake River Range, ID, and the Teton Mtns, WY.

Notes: Alpine milkvetch may be the most widespread species in the genus. • A study in Sweden found that, compared to a subalpine population, flowers of an alpine population were larger and bloomed longer, perhaps because alpine milkvetch (which is self-incompatible and is pollinated mainly by bumblebees) must do more to attract the fewer pollinators available at high elevations. But the abortion rate of fertilized ovules was higher in the alpine, probably because of resource limitations.

Balloon Milkvetch • *Astragalus whitneyi*

General: Stems sprawling to ascending, 5–30 cm long/tall; **stipules 2–9 mm long, not leafy or bent downward. Leaves:** Greyish green with fine, appressed hairs. **Flowers:** 5–16 in compact clusters; **petals cream to whitish tinged with pink, lavender or purple,** 9–17 mm long. **Fruits:** Pods testicle-shaped, greatly inflated, **bladder-like,** usually purplish-mottled, 2–6 cm long, fine-hairy, drooping. **Where Found:** Rocky slopes, ridge crests, sandy and gravelly shrublands and forest openings; montane to alpine zones; scattered but locally frequent (especially on ultrabasic rock) along the eastern side of the Cascades in WA, OR and northeastern CA, east to southern ID and northwestern NV.

Similar Species: Cotton's milkvetch (*A. australis* var. *cottonii*; *A. australis* var. *olympicus*, *A. cottonii*) has flowers of similar colour and size and also has **inflated, membranous pods,** but they are **sausage-shaped,** 2–2.5 cm long and not mottled. It grows on talus slopes and ridge crests in the alpine zone and is rare and

endemic to the Olympic Mtns. • **Least bladdery milkvetch (*A. microcystis*)** has **smaller, much less inflated pods, 0.5–1.5 cm long,** and **purplish flowers, 5–8 mm long.** It occurs in open forests and on rocky-grassy slopes, scree, lakeshores and gravelly flats and bars, in steppe to alpine zones. It is infrequent in southeastern BC, WA, ID and MT. • **White Cloud milkvetch (*A. vexilliflexus* var. *nubilus*)** is densely matted, ashy fine-hairy and has whitish flowers 5–6-mm long, often with purple highlights, and small, ellipsoid **pods 3–5 mm long,** that are **flattened, not inflated.** It grows on rocky ridge crests in the alpine zone and is restricted to the White Cloud Range, ID.

Notes: Balloon milkvetch contains nitrotoxins that are poisonous to livestock. It is also the most important host plant for the small, alpine-adapted butterflies melissa blue (*Lycaeides melissa*) and northern blue (*L. idas*). • *A. whitneyi* honours W.D. Whitney (1819–96), the state geologist of California from 1860 to 1876 and for whom Mt. Whitney was named.

Sickle Milkvetch, Nutzotin Milkvetch
Astragalus nutzotinensis

General: Prostrate, mat-forming; stems slender, 5–40 cm long, minutely appressed-hairy with white and black hairs. **Leaves:** Leaflets mostly 9–15, elliptic to oblong, usually short-appressed-hairy, frequently with purplish spots. **Flowers:** 1–5; petals cream with splashes of pink or rose purple, 12–17 mm long. **Fruits:** Pods at first straight but becoming **curved in a semicircle, 3–5 cm long, flattened,** green with purple dots, ultimately **reddish purple** and semi-transparent, **lying on the ground. Where Found:** Mesic to moist, gravelly terraces, outwash and ridge crests, rocky slopes and scree; montane to alpine zones; locally frequent in the northwestern ¼ of the region; endemic.

Notes: This species is named after the Nutzotin Mtns in Alaska and Yukon.

Subarctic Milkvetch • *Astragalus australis*

General: Tufted, more or less hairy; **stems sprawling to ascending,** 10–40 cm long/tall. **Leaves:** Leaflets lance-shaped to oblong-elliptic, often silvery grey with appressed hairs. **Flowers: 6–40** in compact clusters later elongating; petals white to pale purplish or cream, often tipped or tinged with purple, 7–14 mm long, the **wing-petals notched at tip. Fruits:** Pods narrowly ellipsoid to cylindric, nearly straight to somewhat crescent-shaped, membranous, somewhat bladdery, inflated or not, **slightly flattened but turgid when ripe, 1–3 cm long,** green or purplish red, **usually hairless,** drooping or spreading. **Where Found:** Streambanks, gravel bars, forest openings, meadows, grassy or rocky slopes, tundra, scree and fellfields; lowland to alpine zones; widespread (but infrequent at high elevations) in the northern ⅓ of the region, infrequent southward mostly in the Rockies; circumpolar with large gaps.

Similar Species: Tri-corner milkvetch (*A. robbinsii*) is usually an ascending to erect plant to 60 cm tall, **at high elevations becoming sprawling and 20–30 cm tall.** The **larger leaflets are 1–3 cm long, blunt or notched at the tip.** The **5–25 flowers** are pale purple, pink-purple, lilac or whitish, fading to bluish, 6–11 mm long, the **wing-petals not notched** and the **banner-petal longer than the keel.** The narrowly ellipsoid, compressed pods are **obtusely 3-cornered in cross-section** (like a submarine), sparsely **black- or black-and-white-hairy** and 1–2.5 cm long. It is infrequent and scattered throughout both northern and southeastern portions of the region, mostly at low to middle elevations, occasionally on alpine slopes, in AK, YT and northern BC, disjunct in southern BC, southwestern AB, WA, northern OR, ID, MT and WY to UT, CO and NM. • **Bourgeau's milkvetch** (*A. bourgovii*) somewhat resembles both species above, but **lacks the notched wing-petals** of subarctic milkvetch. It has **fewer (5–10) purplish flowers** and **shorter (1–1.5 cm) pods** than both. Compared to tri-corner milkvetch, it is generally smaller (4–20 cm tall), with **pointy-tipped (not blunt) leaflets** mostly 1–1.5 cm long. It grows on gravel bars, streambanks, rocky slopes, cliffs and talus, typically on limestone, in montane to alpine zones, and is locally frequent in the Rockies of southeastern BC and southwestern AB to ID and MT. • **Elegant milkvetch** (*A. eucosmus*) has small, mostly purplish **flowers 4–8 mm long** and **pods 0.5–1.2 cm long.** It occurs in meadows, heathlands, thickets, open forest, sandy-gravelly bars, stream terraces and tundra, in lowland (arctic coast) to (occasionally) lower alpine zones, and is frequent in the inland portion of the region, in AK, YT and NT through eastern BC and AB to ID, MT, WY, OR and CO. • **Broad-keeled milkvetch** (*A. platyropis*) is very short (2–7 cm tall), with **stems 0–2 cm long,** often reduced to crowns; **leaves in silvery-hairy tufts;** 2–9 flowers in head-like clusters with purplish **petals all about same length;** and egg-shaped to nearly spheric pods 2–3 cm long, **bladdery-inflated and purplish-mottled.** It grows on rocky ridges, talus and scree, in montane to alpine zones, and is rare in west-central MT and north-central ID, but more frequent in NV and CA.

Notes: Subarctic milkvetch is also known as *Astragalus aboriginum*.

The Genus *Oxytropis* (Locoweed)

Plants in this genus are perennial herbs from strong taproots and branching stem-bases, mostly without leafy stems. The leaves are concentrated toward the base in a rosette and are stalked and odd-pinnately compound with leaflets that have unlobed, untoothed margins. The several to many flowers are in elongated to compact clusters atop the flowering stems. The flowers have a pointy-tipped keel-petal; the sepal-tubes are cylindric to bell-shaped and 5-toothed. The fruits are membranous to leathery pods, sometimes inflated and hairy or hairless.

Key to *Oxytropis*

1a. Stipules only shortly fused to base of leaf stalks; pods drooping . . . . ***O. deflexa*** (p. 255)

1b. Stipules fused to base of leaf stalks for more than ½ their length; pods erect or spreading. 2

  2a. Plants glandular-warty and usually sticky 3

    3a. Flowers typically pinkish purple, occasionally whitish or blue-tinged. . . ***O. borealis* var. *viscida*** (p. 255)

    3b. Flowers typically white, occasionally blue-tinged. . . . . ***O. borealis* var. *sulphurea*** (p. 255)

  2b. Plants neither glandular-warty nor sticky 4

    4a. Leaflets (at least some of them) in whorls of 3–4 . . . . ***O. campestris*** (p. 254)

    4b. Leaflets not whorled 5

      5a. Leaflets 1–3 (occasionally 5) . . . . ***O. mertensiana*** (p. 257)

      5b. Leaflets 5 to many. 6

        6a. Flowers cream or yellowish; plants relatively tall, 5–30 cm high 7

        7a. Stipules chestnut brown . . . . ***O. maydelliana*** (p. 255)

        7b. Stipules papery white or yellowish. 8

          8a. Flowers mostly <18 mm long; pods thin-walled, fingertip squeezable. . . ***O. campestris*** (p. 254)

          8b. Flowers >18 mm long; pods thick-walled, leathery, not fingertip squeezable
. . . . ***O. sericea*** (p. 254)

      6b. Flowers pink or purple or blue; dwarf species, <10 cm and often <5 cm tall 9

        9a. Flowers 1–5. 10

          10a. Stipules dark brown. . . . . ***O. kokrinensis*** (p. 257)

          10b. Stipules papery white or yellowish. 11

            11a. Stipules with marginal club-shaped structures; flowers 15–25 mm long
. . . . ***O. arctica*** (p. 257)

            11b. Stipules lacking marginal club-shaped structures; flowers mostly <18 mm long. . . . 12

              12a. Pods inflated, egg-shaped, papery . . . . ***O. podocarpa*** (p. 256)

              12b. Pods not or only slightly inflated or swollen 13

                13a. Flowers and pods held above ground; pods erect. 14

                  14a. Loosely tufted; flowers 12–17 mm long; leaves sparsely hairy or hair-less; north of 59° N. ***O. scammaniana*** (p. 257)

                  14b. Densely tufted; flowers 7–12 mm long; leaves hairy on both surfaces; south of 47° N . . . . ***O. parryi*** (p. 256)

                13b. Flowers and pods spreading, stems ultimately reclining; pods reclining to spreading-ascending 15

                  15a. Pods 2–4 cm long, cylindric, 2-chambered; flowers 12–20 mm long; leaflets usually spreading-hairy above and below
. . . . ***O. nigrescens*** (p. 256)

O. nigrescens

                  15b. Pods 1–2 cm long, ellipsoid, 1-chambered; flowers 11–17 mm long; leaflets nearly hairless below. . . . . ***O. huddelsonii*** (p. 256)

        9b. Flowers mostly 5–20 16

          16a. Plants north of 60° N . . . . ***O. campestris* var. *roaldii*** (p. 254)

          16b. Plants south of 48° N 17

             17a. Sepal-cups inflated, densely mixed black-white-hairy; mature pods mostly not inflated . . . . ***O. lagopus*** (p. 256)

             17b. Sepal-cups not inflated, sparsely white-hairy; mature pods mostly inflated
. . . . ***O. besseyi*** (p. 256)

Field Locoweed, Yellow Locoweed
Oxytropis campestris

General: Densely tufted, mostly with straight, spreading hairs; flowering stems ascending to erect, 5–30 cm tall; stipules straw-coloured to black.
Leaves: 5–30 cm long; leaflets 7–45, **mostly opposite, sometimes in whorls of 3–4,** lance-elliptic to oblong, spreading-hairy on both surfaces to nearly hairless above. **Flowers:** 3–30 in spike- or head-like clusters; **petals yellowish to cream, pink, purplish or sometimes purplish-tinged, 10–17 (to 20) mm long. Fruits:** Pods

oblong-ellipsoid, **thin-walled, membranous,** 1–2 cm long, short-hairy, beaked, erect to spreading. **Where Found:** Sandy, gravelly or rocky sites, including river bars, terraces, rock outcrops, grassy slopes, meadows, forest openings, clearings, roadsides, heathlands, tundra and fellfields; steppe to alpine zones; frequent and widespread throughout the mostly inland part of the region; the species complex circumpolar with large gaps.

Varieties: This is an extremely variable species, subject to all sorts of taxonomic and nomenclatural revisions. High-elevation plants in the south are mostly **var. cusickii,** which are short plants (flowering stems to 15 cm tall) with 7–17 leaflets and yellowish or whitish flowers. In the north (AK, YT, NT and sometimes northern BC), **var. jordalii** is usually shorter than 12 cm,

var. *roaldii*

with 9–17 leaflets and usually fewer than 10 yellowish flowers; **var. varians** is typically taller than 12 cm, with 15–45 leaflets and mostly 12–17 yellowish or whitish flowers; **var. roaldii** is shorter than 12 cm and has **purple flowers.**

Notes: Field locoweed includes *Oxytropis columbiana, O. cusickii, O. alaskana, O. hyperborea, O. roaldii* and *O. varians.*

var. *jordalii*

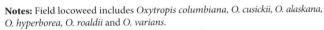

Silky Locoweed • *Oxytropis sericea*

General: Densely tufted, silvery-hairy; flowering stems ascending to erect, 7–25 cm tall; stipules membranous, pale. **Leaves:** Leaflets lance-oblong to oval, **greyish or silvery silky-hairy** on both surfaces. **Flowers:** 5–25 in spike-like clusters; **petals whitish or yellowish,** sometimes tinged with pink or tipped with purple, **18–25 mm long. Fruits:** Pods oblong-egg-shaped to nearly cylindric, 1–2.5 cm long, **leathery or bony when mature,** short-hairy, erect. **Where Found:** Dry, sandy or gravelly bluffs, rocky or grassy slopes, roadsides, river terraces, meadows and ridge crests; steppe to alpine (occasionally) zones, but mostly at low to moderate elevations; locally frequent from southern YT southward, mostly in the Rockies.

Notes: Silky locoweed (and other species of milkvetch and locoweed) often contain the toxic alkaloid swainsonine. This compound is not manufactured by the plants but is synthesized by a fungal endophyte. Some silky locoweed plants have abundant endophytes and lots of swainsonine, whereas others have fewer endophytes and little or no swainsonine. Some species—including field locoweed (above) and alpine milkvetch (p. 251)—appear to lack endophytes (and swainsonine) entirely. • In a Colorado alpine population of silky locoweed, carbohydrates accumulated and stored in the roots and stems peaked in autumn and were used for winter respiration, leaf regrowth in spring and early stages of flowering. But the storage pool wasn't completely drained—a surplus remained. No surprises here—it's a sensible strategy for the unpredictable alpine environment.

Maydell's Locoweed • *Oxytropis maydelliana*

General: Densely tufted; flowering stems erect or ascending, **5–15 cm tall; old, persistent stipules reddish brown.**
Leaves: Leaflets lance-oblong to egg-shaped, 4–17 mm long, sparsely spreading-hairy to nearly hairless.
Flowers: 5–12 in head-like clusters; **petals yellow to whitish yellow, 13–17 mm long. Fruits:** Pods egg-shaped to ellipsoid, papery, 1.5–2 cm long, beaked, black-and-white-hairy. **Where Found:** Meadows, ridge crests, rocky slopes, heathlands and turfy tundra; lowland (arctic coast) to alpine zones; frequent in the northern ⅓ of the region; arctic-alpine, amphiberingian.

Notes: Maydell's locoweed, like most pea family plants, constructs root nodules to house *Rhizobium* and *Bradyrhizobium* bacteria. These bacteria "fix" nitrogen—remove it from the air—and share it with the plants. • This species is named for Baron Gerhard von Maydell (1835–94), a botanical collector in eastern Siberia from 1861 to 1871.

Sticky Locoweed • *Oxytropis borealis* var. *viscida*

General: Densely tufted, **usually glandular;** flowering stems ascending to erect, 5–25 cm tall; stipules membranous, pale. **Leaves:** Leaflets 20–40, lance-shaped to narrowly elliptic, **both surfaces short-hairy to nearly hairless, usually sticky-glandular and often warty. Flowers:** 5–30 in spike- or head-like clusters; **petals typically pink-purple or bluish (occasionally yellowish or cream), 11–16 mm long. Fruits:** Pods oblong-ellipsoid, membranous-papery, 1–2 cm long, beaked, erect, dark short-hairy, often glandular-warty. **Where Found:** Sandy, gravelly and rocky sites, grassy slopes, ridge crests, rock outcrops, talus slopes and tundra; montane to alpine zones; frequent and widespread in the northern ⅓ of the region, locally frequent southward; the variety cordilleran.

Similar Variety: White sticky locoweed (*O. borealis* var. *sulphurea*) has white (occasionally bluish-tinged) flowers. It is found on gravel bars, ridge crests, roadcuts, shrublands and meadows, in montane to subalpine zones, and is scattered but locally frequent in east-central AK, central and southern YT and northern BC.

Similar Species: Stemmed locoweed (*O. deflexa*) is another extremely variable species, beset with many names. It has **stems that are often leafy along the lower part,** with stipules only shortly fused to the leaf stalks, small, **pale to dark blue flowers, 5–11 mm long,** and **drooping pods.** It grows on gravel bars, shores, grassy slopes, meadows, open forest, rocky slopes and fellfields, in lowland to alpine zones. A broadly amphiberingian species, it is scattered but locally frequent in most of the inland part of the region (from AK, YT and NT to CA, NV and NM) but at high elevations only in the southeast.

Notes: Sticky locoweed includes *Oxytropis glutinosa, O. leucantha* var. *depressa, O. sheldonensis, O. verruculosa, O. viscida* and *O. viscidula.* • It is an important food plant for muskoxen, caribou and arctic hares on Banks I., Northwest Territories. • Flower colour is highly and aggravatingly variable in some *Oxytropis,* including sticky, field and arctic locoweeds. Some have questioned its diagnostic reliability within or among these species.

Blackish Locoweed
Oxytropis nigrescens

General: Cushion- or mat-forming, variously hairy; branches prostrate to ascending or erect, **to merely 5 cm tall;** stipules white-papery. **Leaves:** 1–5 cm long; leaflets 5–15, elliptic to egg-shaped, sparsely to densely **spreading-long-hairy,** sometimes snowy-white-silky-hairy, rarely hairless. **Flowers:** 1–4 **(usually 2–3)** on a stalk 1–5 cm long, barely overtopping leaves; **petals pink-purple or blue-purple** (rarely white), **12–20 mm long;** sepal-cups usually black-hairy. **Fruits: Pods sausage-shaped,** membranous, **2–4 cm long, 2-chambered** or nearly so, greyish- to dark-hairy, at maturity often turning spectacularly red and lying on the ground. **Where Found:** Sandy and gravelly ridge crests, rocky slopes, meadows, heathlands, tundra and fellfields; lowland (arctic coast) to alpine zones; frequent throughout the northern ⅓ of the region; arctic-alpine, amphiberingian.

Notes: In southwestern Yukon, blackish locoweed is grazed heavily by collared pikas (*Ochotona collaris*) but can tolerate the removal of up to about 60% of summer leaf production, perhaps because it produces new leaves very early the following spring, before the pikas really start making hay.

Huddelson's Locoweed
Oxytropis huddelsonii

General: Resembles blackish locoweed (above). **Leaves:** Leaflets sparsely hairy on the lower surface. **Flowers:** Usually 1 (sometimes 2–3) per stem. **Fruits: Pods football-shaped, 1–2 cm long, 1-chambered. Where Found:** Grows in the same sorts of habitats as blackish locoweed but less frequently and with a more restricted, endemic range.

Notes: The type specimen was collected near Whitehorse. Yukon being Yukon, the species was named after C.W. Huddelson, a mining engineer.

Stalked-pod Locoweed • *Oxytropis podocarpa*

General: Sort of the southern version of blackish locoweed (above). **Flowers:** 1–3 **(usually 2), 10–17 mm long. Fruits: Pods egg-shaped, papery, bladdery-inflated, prominently beaked, on stalks 2–3 mm long. Where Found:** Rocky ridge crests, scree slopes and turfy tundra, on calcium-rich sites; subalpine and alpine zones; locally frequent inland in the southern part of the region; curiously also in the Canadian eastern arctic.
Similar Species: Parry's locoweed (*O. parryi*) is a similar southern species, but has **shorter (7–12 mm) flowers** and unstalked, sausage-egg-shaped, black-hairy pods. It occupies alpine meadows, ridge crests, fellfields and tundra in the Great Basin area, WY to NM, west to central ID, UT and CA. • Two southern (southwestern AB, MT, WY, ID, UT and CO) species that in some forms occur at high elevations are **hare's-foot locoweed (*O. lagopus*)** and **Bessey's locoweed (*O. besseyi*).** They both have mostly 5–20 pink-purple flowers in head-like clusters atop erect stems. Hare's-foot locoweed has **inflated, mixed black-and-white-hairy sepal-cups** and mostly **scarcely inflated pods,** whereas Bessey's locoweed has **uninflated, sparsely white-hairy sepal-cups** and **mostly inflated pods.**

Notes: *Podocarpa* literally means "foot fruit," probably referring not to a foot fetish, but rather to the stalk-supported pod.

Scamman's Locoweed
Oxytropis scammaniana

General: Loosely tufted; branches spreading-ascending, to 10 cm long, covered with persistent, straw-coloured stipules. **Leaves:** 2–9 cm long; **leaflets 9–13, lance-shaped to elliptic, 4–13 mm long,** sparsely white-hairy to hairless. **Flowers:** 1–5 (usually 2–3) atop an erect stalk 2–8 cm tall, overtopping leaves; petals blue-purple, 12–17 mm long; sepal-cups black-hairy. **Fruits:** Pods oblong-ellipsoid, membranous, 1–2 cm long, more or less 1-chambered, **usually black-hairy, erect and borne aloft. Where Found:** Stony slopes, heathlands and tundra; montane to alpine zones; locally frequent in the northern ⅓ of the region; arctic-alpine, endemic.

Similar Species: Mertens' locoweed (*O. mertensiana*) has merely **1–3 (rarely 5) rather large (7–25 mm long) leaflets,** pink-purple flowers and **erect, black-hairy pods.** It is found on moist, rocky slopes, gravel bars, heathlands and tundra, in lowland (arctic coast) to alpine zones. It is an arctic-alpine, amphiberingian species that is locally frequent in northern, western and east-central AK, rare in northern YT.

Notes: The species is named in honour of Edith Scamman (1882–1967). With advanced degrees in English and comparative literature, and after much church work and caring for her mother, Scamman took up botany seriously in her 50s. She was particularly interested in the plants of unglaciated Alaska and very keen on ferns. From 1949 until her death, she was a research associate at the Gray Herbarium at Harvard University.

Arctic Locoweed • *Oxytropis arctica*

General: Densely tufted; branches prostrate to sprawling, sometimes forming ashy-hairy cushions to 30 cm across; **stipules white-papery, the margins fringed and furnished with tiny, club-shaped structures. Leaves:** 4–20 cm long; leaflets 9–21, lance-oblong to elliptic, white-hairy at least on the lower surface. **Flowers:** 2–10 in a head-like cluster atop a stalk 6–20 cm long, overtopping leaves; petals dark purple, pink-purple, pink, bluish or whitish, **15–25 mm long. Fruits:** Pods narrowly egg-shaped, pointed at both ends, often somewhat sickle-shaped, membranous, 1–3 cm long, hairy, **erect or spreading. Where Found:** Mesic to moist gravel bars, river terraces, sand dunes, rocky ridges, heathlands and tundra; lowland to alpine zones; infrequent in the far northern part of the region, east to arctic Canada; arctic-alpine, amphiberingian.

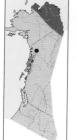

Similar Species: Kokrines locoweed (*O. kokrinensis*) is also densely tufted but has **dark brown, persistent stipules, small leaves (1–5 cm long),** the leaflets rolled-under or folded, **1–2 purple flowers,** 12–15 mm long, **on stalks barely exceeding the leaves,** and oblong-ellipsoid, somewhat inflated, **reclining pods.** It grows on dry, rocky slopes and ridge tops, in subalpine and alpine zones, and is a rare endemic of the Kokrines Mtns and the western Brooks Range of AK.

Notes: Arctic locoweed is also known as *Oxytropis coronaminis*, *O. koyukukensis*, *O. roaldii* in part, *O. uralensis* and *O. arctica* vars. *barnebyana* and *koyukukensis*.
• *Oxytropis* comes from the Greek *oxys*, "sharp," and *tropis*, "a keel," in reference to the pointy-tipped keel-petal of the flowers. Many species are poisonous to livestock, hence the common name "locoweed."

Violet Family (Violaceae)

The violet family is widely distributed, occurring on all continents. It includes shrubs as well as herbs and comprises more than 20 genera. We have but one genus, the well-known *Viola*, which has around 400 species worldwide. Ours are low, perennial herbs with alternate or basal, usually **simple** (undivided) leaves that have **stipules** (appendages at the base of the leaf stalk). The bilaterally symmetric flowers are single atop stalks arising from the rhizome crown or from the leaf axils. There are 5 distinct sepals and 5 distinct petals, the lowest spurred at the base and larger than the others. The 5 stamens form a ring around the single **superior ovary.** The fruits are 1-chambered capsules.

Some violets have an explosive seed-dispersal mechanism, whereby the drying capsules contract and split under pressure, catapulting the seeds into the air. Dispersal can be enhanced by ants—the seeds of some violets have special oil bodies that are attractive to ants, who industriously shift the seeds to their nests.

The leaves and flowers of all violets can be used raw in salads, as potherbs or to make a tea. Candied violets are used as cake decorations. The leaves are added to soups as a thickening agent in the southern U.S. The leaves and flowers have long been part of various herbal remedies. They are used as poultices, as laxatives for children and to relieve coughs and lung congestion, among others. However, **the rhizomes, fruits and seeds are reportedly poisonous.**

Key to *Viola*

1a. Petals yellow 2
  2a. Leaves not distinctly heart-shaped at base, usually squared-off or tapered, blades coarsely few-toothed, mostly <2 cm wide. . . . . *V. purpurea* var. *venosa* (p. 260)
  2b. Leaves heart-shaped at base, blades more finely toothed, mostly >2 cm wide (to 5–9 cm wide). 3
    3a. Side pair of petals not bearded; sepals often with purplish black stripe; style heads smooth. . . . . *V. biflora* (p. 260)
    3b. Side pair of petals bearded; sepals without purplish black stripe; style heads bearded . . . . *V. orbiculata* (p. 260)
1b. Petals purple, violet, blue or lilac 4
  4a. Leafy aerial stems well developed, often exceeding leaves 5
    5a. Leaves kidney-shaped, somewhat fleshy; plants of Olympic Mtns . . . . *V. flettii* (p. 260)
    5b. Leaves heart-shaped, not fleshy; plants widespread along Pacific coast . . . . *V. langsdorffii* (p. 259)
  4b. Leafy aerial stems shorter than leaves or lacking 6
    6a. Plants lacking stems but with stolons (aboveground runners) . . . . *V. epipsila* var. *repens* (p. 259)
    6b. Plants short-stemmed but without stolons. 7
      7a. Stipules jagged or sharp-toothed; lowest petal 7–20 mm long including 5–10 mm long, cylindric spur; style head bearded . . . . *V. adunca* (p. 259)
      7b. Stipules smooth-margined; lowest petal 12–25 mm long including 2–5 mm long, pouched spur; style head smooth . . . . *V. langsdorffii* (p. 259)

Haida twinflower violet

Early Blue Violet, Hooked Violet • *Viola adunca*

General: Tufted from a slender rhizome; stems apparently lacking in spring but developing as season progresses, spreading-ascending, usually hairy, 2–20 cm long/tall.

Leaves: Basal and along stem, **egg- to triangular-egg-shaped**, squared-off or wedge-shaped to somewhat heart-shaped at base; blades 0.5–5 cm long, margins blunt-toothed to nearly entire; stalks 5–9 cm long, **stipules jaggedly toothed.**

Flowers: Single on stalks from leaf axils; **petals 5, blue to violet, the lowest petal 7–20 mm long** including the **5–10 (to 15) mm long, often curved or hooked spur,** the lower 3 petals often whitish with purple veins, the lateral pair white-bearded; style head hairy.

Fruits: Capsules squat, egg-shaped, 6–11 mm long, hairless.

Where Found: Open forests, meadows, roadsides, clearings, streambanks, shores, heathlands and tundra; lowland to (occasionally) alpine zones; frequent in the southern ¾ of the region; boreal North American.

Varieties: The widespread **var. *adunca*** occasionally makes it into the alpine zone, especially in the southern ⅓ of the region. • The compact **dwarf (to 6 cm tall) var. *bellidifolia*** has **hairless leaves and petals,** the **lowest petal 5–14 mm long.** It occurs sporadically at high elevations in the Rockies of southeastern BC, MT and WY.

Notes: *Adunca* means "hooked" or "having hooks," referring to the spur, which is often curved or hooked.

Alaska Violet • *Viola langsdorffii*

General: Stems erect, 2–25 cm tall, sometimes not obvious. **Leaves:** Mostly basal, **heart-shaped to nearly circular;** blades 1–6 cm long and wide; stalks 6–15 cm long, **stipules toothless** but glandular-margined. **Flowers:** Single atop **long stalks from leaf axils;** petals violet, the lowest petal **12–25 mm long** including the short (2–5 mm), **pouched spur,** the lower 3 petals dark-pencilled, the lateral pair white-bearded; style head hairless. **Fruits:** Capsules egg-shaped to oblong, 8–13 mm long. **Where Found:** Bogs, fens, moist meadows, streambanks, snowbeds, talus and scree, heathlands and tundra; lowland (coastal bogs in WA and OR) to alpine zones; frequent in the Pacific coastal mountains, infrequent inland; amphiberingian.

Similar Species: Dwarf marsh violet (*V. epipsila* var. *repens*; *V. epipsiloides*, *V. repens*) **lacks leafy stems but has runners** and violet to lilac flowers on long (to 7 cm) **stalks from a rhizome,** the **lowest petal 12–15 mm long.** It grows in bogs, fens, wet meadows and on mossy streambanks, heathlands and tundra, in lowland to alpine zones. It is an amphiberingian species locally frequent in the northern ½ of the region, AK and YT to central BC, and disjunct in CO.

Notes: The Hawaiian Islands, which are more than 3500 km from the nearest continent, have several endemic violet species, mostly woody—small trees and shrubs—and with flowers in clusters, not singly on stalks. DNA analysis has revealed that the Hawaiian violets are sisters to Alaska violet! Researchers propose the long-distance dispersal of ancestral *V. langsdorffii* from the arctic to Kauai by migrating birds, with subsequent diversification and the development of woody stems and branched inflorescences.

dwarf marsh violet

Olympic Violet • *Viola flettii*

General: Small, hairless perennial; **stems leafy,** 3–15 cm long. **Leaves: Kidney-shaped,** 1.5–4 cm wide, **fleshy, dark green, purple-veined,** margins finely scalloped. **Flowers:** On stalks usually exceeding leaves, **10–15 mm long, lavender to reddish purple,** yellow at base; lower 3 petals veined darker purple, the side pair yellow-bearded, the spur very short, yellow. **Where Found:** Crevices in basalt outcrops, talus and scree slopes; subalpine and alpine zones; infrequent in the Olympic Mtns, WA; endemic.

Notes: This is one of several Olympic endemics threatened by introduced mountain goats. • The species is named for botanist and mountaineer John B. Flett, a Scot who came to Tacoma in 1893, taught biology and geology, and worked as a ranger in Mt. Rainier National Park from 1913 to 1921.

Twinflower Violet • *Viola biflora*

General: Small clumps from a slender rhizome; **stems aerial, obvious,** spreading to ascending, **5–25 cm long/tall. Leaves: Roundish to kidney-shaped,** 1–6 m wide, mostly broader than long, scalloped, hairy on upper surface and on veins below. **Flowers:** Single in leaf axils, **6–15 mm long, yellow;** petals with maroon veins, the **side pair not bearded,** the spur short, 1–2 mm long. **Where Found:** Rock outcrops, ridges, meadows, scree slopes and turfy tundra; montane to alpine zones; locally frequent in the northwestern part of the region, disjunct in CO.

Varieties: Compared to amphiberingian **var. *biflora*,** the more robust **Haida twinflower violet** (*V. biflora* var. *carlottae*) has larger leaves with blades to 6 cm wide (vs. up to 3 cm) and flowers with the lowest petal 11–15 mm long (vs. 6–10 mm). It is endemic to coastal BC, frequent on Haida Gwaii and rare on northwestern Vancouver I.

Notes: Twinflower violet is a rich source of cyclotides, proteins demonstrated to be cytotoxic, antimicrobial and haemolytic. These compounds may help protect the violet against insect grazing. • Most violets produce 2 kinds of flowers: showy summer blooms, then, in autumn, concealed among leaves near the ground, much smaller flowers that don't open but self-fertilize. In this species, there are often 2 such reclusive flowers in the axil of the same leaf, thus the name *biflora*.

Round-leaved Violet, Darkwoods Violet
Viola orbiculata

General: Aerial stems ascending-erect, 3–9 cm tall. **Leaves:** Basal leaves (at least some of them) **evergreen, round, heart-shaped at base,** 1.5–5 cm wide, margins scalloped. **Flowers: Yellow;** lower 3 petals maroon-veined, the lowest 8–17 mm long, including the short, pouched spur. **Where Found:** Open forests, meadows, streambanks and heathlands; montane to lower alpine zones; frequent in the southern ½ of the region; cordilleran.

Similar Species: Goosefoot violet or **purple-veined yellow violet** (*V. purpurea* var. *venosa*) has **egg- or wedge-shaped to round, noticeably veined,** rather **fleshy, coarsely few-toothed leaves,** 0.5–2 cm wide and often tinged or veined purple, and **yellow flowers with purplish-backed upper petals.** It is found in forests, meadows and rocky slopes, in mostly montane and subalpine zones, but occasionally reaches alpine ridges and scree slopes. Goosefoot violet ranges from southernmost BC to CA, east to ID, WY and CO.

Notes: The persistent basal leaves of round-leaved violet are pressed flat to the ground by the winter snowpack. In spring, they remain partly or entirely green after the snow has melted. Mature plants thus have both current and previous years' basal leaves.

Common Butterwort
Pinguicula vulgaris

General: Dwarf perennial, **insect-eating herb** from fibrous roots; flowering stems erect, usually solitary, hairless or minutely hairy, 5–15 cm tall.

Leaves: All basal in a **rosette 3–8 cm wide;** blades tongue-shaped to lance-elliptic, 1.5–5 cm long, **yellowish green, somewhat fleshy, greasy-slimy on upper surface,** margins smooth, **in-rolled.**

Flowers: Single and nodding atop stems, bilaterally symmetric, **violet or purplish, 1.2–2.5 cm long;** petals form funnel-like tube flaring to 2 lips, with white hairs in throat and a **narrow, somewhat pointed spur at the base,** the upper lip 2-lobed, the lower lip 3-lobed.

Fruits: Capsules globe-shaped, erect, 4–6 mm long; seeds numerous, wrinkled.

Where Found: Streambanks, mossy seeps, rocky drip-faces, rocky beaches, bogs and fens; lowland to upper subalpine zones; scattered but locally frequent throughout the region except the south-eastern portion, AK, YT and NT through BC and southwestern AB to WA, OR, northern CA and MT; circumboreal.

Subspecies: Common butterwort has 2 subspecies, the circumboreal **ssp. *vulgaris*** and the coastal-Cascadian, amphi-beringian **ssp. *macroceras*,** which has **larger flowers** (mostly longer than 2 cm) with **blunt spurs** usually longer than 6 mm.

Notes: Butterworts seem to lack mycorrhizae but supplement their sunlight diet through carnivory, the leaves acting as traps for small insects that are held and digested by sticky secretions. In an Alberta study, common butterworts that were force-fed fruit flies grew 60% heftier than unfed plants after a single growing season. In a Swedish experiment, common butterwort captured 21–37 micrograms of insect prey per cm^2 of leaf surface per day, considerably more than the similar but smaller-flowered hairy butterwort (*P. villosa*). The numbers for hairy butterwort were similar to sticky paper, suggesting that hairy butterwort simply captures what happens to land on it, whereas the leaves of common butterwort seem to somehow attract insects. • The flowers of butterworts are showy, but both species are self-fertile and (in Sweden) were infrequently visited by potential insect pollinators, mostly flies (especially hoverflies) to common butterwort and mosquitoes to hairy butterwort. • *Pinguicula* is from the Latin *pinguis*, "fat," in reference to the greasy leaves; *vulgaris* means "the usual one" or "common." The name "butterwort" refers to the leaves, which look as if they were smeared with butter. • Butterwort supposedly encouraged or protected the productivity of milk cows, ensuring a supply of butter. Yorkshire farmwomen anointed the chapped udders of cows with butterwort juice. This plant was also thought to protect cows from elf arrows and humans from witches and fairies.

Figwort Family (Scrophulariaceae)

In our region, the figwort family is represented by herbs with alternate or opposite leaves that have entire or lobed margins. Some species are chlorophyll-containing parasites or partial parasites (*Castilleja*, *Pedicularis*, *Orthocarpus* and *Euphrasia*). The flowers are typically bilaterally symmetric, with an often-conspicuous tube of fused petals (collectively the corolla) that are 2-lipped and 4–5-lobed. *Veronica* and *Synthyris* are weakly bilaterally symmetric, short-tubed exceptions to the rule. *Castilleja* species have brightly coloured bracts that resemble petals. There are commonly 4 fertile stamens; *Veronica*, *Synthyris* and *Lagotis* have only 2. The ovary is single and superior. The fruits are typically 2-chambered capsules; seeds are usually numerous, smooth or variously roughened, and angled or winged.

The family includes the drug plant *Digitalis* but otherwise has little economic importance except as highly valued garden flowers. Notable ornamentals are the snapdragons (*Antirrhinum*), speedwells (*Veronica*), beardtongues (*Penstemon*), monkey-flowers (*Mimulus*), foxgloves (*Digitalis*) and slipperflowers (*Calceolaria*).

You should be warned that the traditional family Scrophulariaceae has been deconstructed and will eventually appear in balkanized but monophyletic form in a forthcoming volume of *FNA*. For the "scroph" genera treated in this guide, recent molecular evidence indicates the following:

- The green root parasites (*Castilleja*, *Pedicularis*, *Orthocarpus* and *Euphrasia*) should be transferred to the broomrape family (Orobanchaceae), traditionally a family of full parasites without chlorophyll.

- *Penstemon*, *Chionophila*, *Synthyris*, *Lagotis* and *Veronica* should be placed in the plantain family (Plantaginaceae).

- *Mimulus* belongs in the lopseed family (Phrymaceae), previously a monotypic family restricted to eastern North America and eastern China.

- Our alpine flora has no representatives of the remnant, strictly defined Scrophulariaceae.

The traditional Scrophulariaceae always was something of a hodgepodge, a beautiful but awkward group without uniquely defining or consistent unifying traits. Still, what a shocker!

Key to the Genera of Scrophulariaceae

1a. Stem leaves mainly alternate (lower ones sometimes opposite or whorled) or leaves chiefly at base of stem **2**

  2a. Stamens 2 . . . . **3**

    3a. Corolla (fused petals) 4-lobed (not lipped), or corolla lacking; plants hairy . . . . . **Synthyris** (pp. 263–264)

    3b. Corolla 2-lipped; plants hairless. . . . . **Lagotis glauca** (p. 264)

  2b. Stamens 4 . . . . **4**

    4a. Upper lip of corolla hooded, rounded at top, squared-off at tip or extending into a narrow beak; leaves basal and along stem, deeply dissected (fern-like) or toothed, upper leaves green . . . **Pedicularis** (pp. 272–278)

    4b. Upper lip of corolla beak-like, more or less straight; leaves all on stem, entire to pinnately lobed, upper leaves bract-like and usually highly coloured. **5**

      5a. Upper corolla lip much longer than lower lip; ours at high elevations are perennial
. . . . **Castilleja** (pp. 265–271)

      5b. Upper corolla lip just slightly longer than lower lip; annual. . . . . . . **Orthocarpus imbricatus** (p. 265)

1b. Stem leaves opposite. **6**

  6a. Calyx (fused sepals) 4-lobed. **7**

    7a. Stamens 2; corolla 4-lobed, somewhat saucer-shaped, not 2-lipped; leaves pinnately veined
. . . . **Veronica** (p. 279)

    7b. Stamens 4; corolla distinctly 2-lipped; leaves palmately veined . . . . **Euphrasia subarctica** (p. 280)

  6b. Calyx 5-lobed. **8**

    8a. Stamens 5 (1 sterile); flowers blue or purple to whitish. **9**

      9a. Flower cluster narrow, 1-sided, with 1 flower per node; stem leaves inconspicuous
. . . . **Chionophila tweedyi** (p. 281)

      9b. Flower cluster open or of compact whorls, with ≥2 flowers per node; stem leaves well developed in most species. . . . . **Penstemon** (pp. 282–287)

    8b. Stamens 4 (all fertile); flowers yellow to pink or red. . . . . **Mimulus** (pp. 280–281)

Key to *Synthyris* (Kittentails)

1a. Leaves at base and along stem 2

    2a. Sepals 4, distinct; corolla deep blue; north of 60° N . . . . ***S. borealis*** (below)

    2b. Sepals 2 (occasionally 3), fused near the base; corolla lacking; stamens dark red or purple; south of 50° N
. . . . ***S. wyomingensis*** (p. 264)

1b. Leaves all or mostly at base 3

    3a. Leaves coarsely toothed; corolla lobes frilly 4

        4a. Corolla 2.5–3.5 mm long; leaves persistent . . . . ***S. platycarpa*** (p. 264)

        4b. Corolla 4–6 mm long; leaves withering . . . . ***S. schizantha*** (p. 264)

    3b. Leaves pinnately cleft or dissected; corolla lobes entire 5

        5a. Leaves heart-egg-shaped, cleft more than halfway to midrib . . . . ***S. canbyi*** (below)

        5b. Leaves lance-oblong, dissected all the way to midrib . . . . ***S. pinnatifida*** (below)

Northern Kittentails
Synthyris borealis

General: Tufted from short rhizomes, **long-hairy throughout; flowering stems leafy,** spreading to erect, 5–20 cm tall. **Leaves: Basal leaves round to heart-shaped,** 4–8 cm long, long-stalked, **margins coarsely blunt-toothed to shallowly lobed;** stem leaves alternate or nearly opposite, progressively smaller upward. **Flowers:** Numerous in a dense, **bracted, spike-like cluster; corolla deep blue, 4-lobed,** upper lobe wider and often longer than lower 3; **sepals 4, distinct; stamens 2,** protruding with styles from spike. **Fruits:** Capsules heart-shaped; seeds 2 to several per chamber. **Where Found:** Tundra and rocky ridges; alpine zone; locally frequent in the northern ⅓ of the region; endemic.

Notes: Based on molecular and genetic evidence, *Synthyris* is closely related to *Veronica* and might best be accommodated in that genus. Stay tuned as the taxonomists duke it out!

Cutleaf Kittentails
Synthyris pinnatifida

Leaves: Basal, pinnately dissected, fern-like, lance-oblong. Flowers: Cluster shorter than leaves at flowering time; corolla deep blue to purplish. **Where Found:** Rocky slopes and gravelly ridges; subalpine and alpine zones; locally frequent in the southern ¼ of the region.

Varieties: Endemic to the Olympic Mtns, **var. *lanuginosa*** is white-woolly all over, noticeably hairier than the other 2 inland varieties (**var. *pinnatifida*** and **var. *canescens***).

Similar Species: Canby's kittentails or Lewis and Clark's kittentails (**S. canbyi**) is an alpine species endemic to the Mission Range of MT. It has **heart-egg-shaped leaves that are deeply cleft but not all the way to the midrib.** The **flower cluster exceeds the leaves** at flowering time.

Notes: *Synthyris* is from the Greek *syn*, "together" or "joined," and *thyris*, "a little door," in reference to the capsule segments. The protruding stamens give the flower cluster a fluffy look, like the tail of a kitten on alert.

Fringepetal Kittentails • *Synthyris schizantha*

General: Rhizomatous perennial 10–30 cm tall.

Leaves: Heart- to kidney-shaped, shallowly lobed, hairy on lower-surface veins, **withering after one year.**

Flowers: Corolla blue-purple, 4–6 mm long, lobes slit into slender, nearly thread-like divisions.

Where Found: Moist, shady cliffs and ledges; sub-alpine and alpine zones; infrequent Pacific Northwest endemic in WA and OR coastal mountains, Saddle Mtn, OR, to the Olympics and Mt. Rainier and a few places in between.

Similar Species: Evergreen kittentails (*S. platycarpa*) has similar leaves that remain on the plant for a couple of years. It also has **frilly corollas,** but they are shorter (2.5–3.5 mm long). Evergreen kittentails grows in open forests and on rocky slopes, in subalpine and alpine zones, in the mountains of north-central ID.

Wyoming Kittentails • *Synthyris wyomingensis*

General: Stems leafy; plants often soft-hairy and greyish when young.

Leaves: Basal leaves egg-shaped to elliptic, coarsely blunt-toothed.

Flowers: Corolla lacking; calyx asymmetric, 3–6 mm long, **2-lobed (occasionally 3), the lobes shortly united at base;** stamens 2, sticking out from spike, 5–12 mm long, **filaments dark red or purple** (sometimes whitish yellow), giving flowers their colour. **Where Found:** Dry, grassy and rocky slopes, savannahs and ridges; montane to alpine zones; infrequent in the south-eastern part of the region; cordilleran–Great Plains.

Notes: Wyoming kittentails is also known as *Besseya wyomingensis*. • DNA studies have found the most genetically diverse populations in the northern part of this species' range. Researchers inferred relatively recent range expansions south-ward out of more northerly ancestral areas.

Weasel Snout • *Lagotis glauca*

General: Hairless, glaucous perennial from a stout rhizome; flowering stems 1 to few, **leafy,** erect, 10–35 cm tall.

Leaves: Basal leaves lance-shaped to elliptic, 2–20 cm long, long-stalked, coarsely blunt-toothed, hairless; stem leaves alternate, unstalked.

Flowers: Numerous in a dense, egg-shaped to cylin-dric, **leafy-bracted spike** atop stem, the bracts tinted blue or purple; **corolla violet-purple to blue, 9–14 mm long, 2-lipped,** the lower lip with 2 lobes; calyx asym-metric, 2-lobed, the lobes fringed; stamens 2.

Fruits: Capsules egg-shaped, 2-lobed, **enclosed in expanded, curved corolla;** seeds 1 in each of the 2 chambers.

Where Found: Tundra, heathlands, stony slopes and seepage areas; lowland (arctic coast) to alpine zones; frequent in the northern ¼ of the region; arctic-alpine, amphiberingian.

Notes: Weasel snout is also known as *Lagotis stelleri*. • *Lagotis* means "hare's ear," from the Greek *lagos*, "hare," and *ous* or *otos*, "ear," maybe referring to the leaf shape. "Weasel snout" is perhaps because of the curved shape of the mature corolla.

Mountain Owl-clover • *Orthocarpus imbricatus*

General: Annual, green, herbaceous **root parasite,** hairless to thinly short-hairy; stems ascending to erect, leafy, 10–35 cm tall.

Leaves: Alternate, linear to narrowly lance-shaped, **entire,** 1–5 cm long, unstalked.

Flowers: Several to many atop stem in a prominently bracted spike; **bracts petal-like,** about as long as flowers, some with **purplish pink tips,** broadly oblong to egg-shaped, blunt to round-tipped, **some narrowly lobed on each side; corolla rose purple, 10–13 mm long, largely concealed by bracts,** 2-lipped, **upper lip beak-like and hooked,** lower lip pouched, yellowish, tipped with 3 tiny teeth; calyx 2-cleft, each segment 2-toothed; stamens 4.

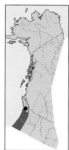

Fruits: Capsules ellipsoid, about 5 mm long; seeds 3–5, with tight-fitting, netted coats.

Where Found: Rocky meadows and scree slopes; subalpine and lower alpine zones; infrequent in the southern coastal mountains; Pacific maritime endemic.

Notes: Orthocarpus is from the Greek *orthos,* "straight," and *karpos,* "fruit," referring to the straight, symmetric capsules; *imbricatus* refers to the overlapping bracts.

The Genus *Castilleja* (Paintbrush)

The paintbrushes are green root-parasites; ours are perennial herbs with clustered, leafy stems that are often somewhat woody at the base. The leaves are usually long and narrow, alternate, unstalked and entire or variously cleft into lobes. The small, tubular flowers are numerous atop stems in dense, bracted, spike-like clusters and are mostly concealed by the brightly coloured, petal-like bracts. The calyx is unequally 4-lobed and generally coloured like the bract tips. The corolla is greenish and 2-lipped, the upper lip (**galea**) elongate and beak-like, the lower lip usually much shorter and 3-toothed. The 4 stamens are enclosed in the galea, and the style usually protrudes beyond the tip of the galea. The fruits are egg-shaped to cylindric capsules; the seeds are usually numerous, with rather loose, net-veined seed coats.

Castilleja has evolved and diversified mostly in the Northwest, where it is a big, taxonomically difficult genus, in part because of frequent hybridization. Long considered too temperamental as a partial parasite to bother trying to cultivate, *Castilleja* has attracted the determined attention of some alpine gardeners, who maintain that several species can be grown from seed without a host and that adequate moisture, not nutrients, is the key factor. These plants are called "paintbrushes" because the showy bracts around the flowers resemble a brush dipped in paint.

Key to *Castilleja*

1a. Beak-like upper corolla lip (galea) relatively short, 3–10 (to 13) mm long, mostly <½ as long as corolla tube; bracts mostly yellowish, sometimes purplish to pink or dull red, rarely scarlet **2**

  2a. Bracts purple, rose, pink, reddish or sometimes whitish **3**

    3a. Leaves mostly entire or occasionally with a pair of lobes **4**

      4a. Stems usually ascending; bracts loosely hairy to long-soft-hairy **5**

        5a. Plants 10–16 cm tall; corolla 12–15 mm long; southern species (Mt. Rainier)
          . . . . *C. cryptantha* (p. 268)

        5b. Plants 5–25 m tall; corolla 20–25 mm long; north of 66° N . . . . *C. elegans* (p. 267)

      4b. Stems usually erect; bracts short-hairy or with coarse-hairy margins; north of 57° N
        . . . . *C. raupii* (p. 267)

    3b. Middle or at least upper leaves lobed **6**

      6a. Lower corolla lip 1–3 (to 4) mm long, the lobes reduced to teeth . . . . *C. parviflora* (p. 267)

      6b. Lower corolla lip (2 to) 3–6.5 mm long, the lobes somewhat petal-like **7**

7a. Corolla 15–25 mm long; ID, MT, WY and UT . . . . ***C. pulchella*** (p. 268)

7b. Corolla 12–15 mm long; restricted to Wallowa Mtns of northeastern OR . . . . ***C. rubida*** (p. 268)

2b. Bracts usually yellowish **8**

8a. Lower corolla lip 3–6 mm long, the lobes somewhat petal-like **9**

9a. Upper corolla lip conspicuously shaggy-long-hairy on the back; bracts densely woolly, green or greenish yellow . . . . ***C. nivea*** (p. 268)

9b. Upper corolla lip glandular short-hairy or obscurely short-hairy; bracts sticky-long-hairy, pale yellow, occasionally purplish or reddish. **10**

10a. Plants spreading at base, (5 to) 10–20 cm tall; calyx 12–20 mm long, equalling or shorter than corolla . . . . ***C. chrysantha*** (p. 268)

10b. Plants erect to ascending, 10–40 cm tall; calyx 12–28 mm long, equalling or longer than corolla **11**

11a. Calyx 22–28 mm long, the segments blunt; stems, leaves and bracts sticky-hairy . . . . ***C. cusickii*** (p. 269)

11b. Calyx 12–25 mm long, the segments pointy-tipped; stems, leaves and bracts hairy but mostly not glandular. ***C. thompsonii*** (p. 268)

8b. Lower corolla lip 1–3 (to 4) mm long, the lobes reduced to teeth. **12**

12a. Plants 6–16 (to 25) cm tall **13**

13a. Leaves unlobed or sometimes the uppermost with a pair of short side lobes; south of 57° N. . . . . ***C. occidentalis*** (p. 269)

13b. Leaves, at least the middle and upper, with 1–2 pairs of slender lobes; north of 59° N. . . . . ***C. hyperborea*** (p. 269)

12b. Plants mostly 20–50 cm tall. **14**

14a. Lateral lobes of calyx 1–4 mm long; south of 57° N. . . . . ***C. sulphurea*** (p. 268)

14b. Lateral lobes of calyx 3–10 mm long; mostly north of 54° N **15**

15a. Upper lip of corolla about 3 times longer than lower lip . . . . ***C. unalaschcensis*** (p. 269)

15b. Upper lip of corolla more than 5 times longer than lower lip . . . . ***C. caudata*** (p. 269)

1b. Beak-like upper corolla lip (galea) relatively long, mostly 10–20 mm, mostly >½ as long as corolla tube; bracts generally red or reddish orange to purplish **16**

16a. Leaves mostly unlobed, upper leaves rarely few-lobed. **17**

17a. Bracts relatively inconspicuous, shorter and broader than leaves, greenish, sometimes red-tipped; calyx lobes conspicuously bright red; restricted to Wallowa Mtns of northeastern OR . . . . ***C. fraterna*** (p. 270)

17b. Bracts conspicuous, mostly bright reddish; not restricted to Wallowa Mountains. . . .**18**

18a. Bracts reddish (scarlet) or red-orange to yellowish; corolla 2–4 cm long; plants mostly >30 cm tall **19**

19a. Leaves usually entire; calyx segments linear to lance-shaped, pointy-tipped . . . . ***C. miniata*** (p. 270)

19b. Upper leaves with 1–3 pairs of linear, spreading side lobes; calyx segments rounded at tip . . . . ***C. hispida*** (p. 270)

18b. Bracts purplish, rose or pinkish to crimson; corolla mostly 2–3 cm long; calyx segments short-pointed to blunt; plants usually <30 cm tall **20**

20a. Plants nearly hairless to obscurely sticky-hairy in flower spike . . . . ***C. rhexifolia*** (p. 270)

20b. Plants conspicuously sticky long-soft-hairy, especially in flower spike . . . . ***C. elmeri*** (p. 271)

16b. Leaves, at least upper ones, with 1–3 pairs of linear, spreading side lobes. **21**

21a. Stems solitary; plants 30–75 cm tall; calyx segments 8–12 mm long . . . ***C. suksdorfii*** (p. 271)

21b. Stems clustered; plants smaller, 6–25 cm tall; calyx segments 1–5 mm long. **22**

22a. Upper corolla lip 7–13 mm long; plants of Rocky Mtns . . . . ***C. covilleana*** (p. 271)

22b. Upper corolla lip 14–21 mm long; plants of Cascade Mtns . . . . ***C. rupicola*** (p. 271)

Small-flowered Paintbrush, Magenta Paintbrush • *Castilleja parviflora*

General: Stems erect or ascending, unbranched, leafy, 10–30 cm tall, nearly hairless to thinly long-soft-hairy. **Leaves:** Lance-shaped, 1.5–5 cm long, **all but lowermost cleft into 3–5 lateral lobes. Flowers: Bracts rose pink, magenta, crimson or sometimes whitish,** lance- to egg-shaped, 3–5-lobed, long-soft-hairy, about as long as flowers; corolla 12–30 mm long, the **lower lip 1–4 mm long,** the **lobes reduced to teeth;** calyx 10–20 mm long. **Where Found:** Meadows, heathlands, streambanks and rocky slopes; sub-alpine and alpine zones; frequent throughout much of the southern ¾ of the region; mostly Pacific maritime.

Varieties: The whitish form has been called *C. parviflora* var. *albida*.

Notes: Small-flowered paintbrush includes *Castilleja henryae, C. oreopola* and *C. parviflora* vars. *albida, olympica* and *oreopola*. • One of the chief threats to whitebark pine (p. 44) survival in our region is white pine blister rust (*Cronartium ribicola*). This introduced fungus needs 2 hosts, usually whitebark pine and some species of *Ribes* (currant or gooseberry), to complete its life cycle. It turns out that small-flowered paintbrush (as well as several other paintbrushes and louseworts) may also support the 2 spore stages usually found on *Ribes* species.

Elegant Paintbrush • *Castilleja elegans*

General: Stems ascending, unbranched, 5–25 cm tall; plants hairy, especially through flower cluster. **Leaves: Entire or upper leaves with a pair of side lobes,** narrowly lance-shaped, 2–6 cm long. **Flowers: Bracts usually purplish or rose purple** (sometimes cream or tipped with yellow), lance- to egg-shaped, entire or with 1–3 pairs of sharp lobes; **corolla 20–25 mm long;** calyx purplish, 15–19 mm long. **Where Found:** Tundra, willow thickets, shores, rocky slopes and fellfields; lowland to alpine zones; frequent in the far north; arctic-alpine, amphiberingian.

Similar Species: Raup's paintbrush (*C. raupii*) is also northern (central AK, YT, NT, northeastern BC and northern AB) but is **taller (20–45 cm),** with **erect stems that are often branched above.** It grows on riverbanks, gravel bars and lakeshores at low to moderate elevations, occasionally to timberline on rocky slopes.

Notes: Elegant paintbrush is also known as *Castilleja pallida* var. *elegans*.

Raup's paintbrush

Showy Paintbrush • *Castilleja pulchella*

General: Sprawling to ascending, 5–20 cm long/tall; plants soft-sticky-hairy, especially through flower cluster. **Leaves:** Linear to lance-shaped, **upper leaves with 1–2 pairs of side lobes.** **Flowers: Bracts purple to yellow,** lance-egg-shaped, **rounded,** with a pair of side lobes; **corolla 15–25 mm long, upper lip 4.5–7 mm long,** lower lip about ½ as long as upper lip; calyx purplish, nearly as long as corolla. **Where Found:** Meadows, tundra and rocky slopes; subalpine and alpine zones; frequent in the south-eastern part of the region.

Similar Species: Obscure paintbrush (*C. cryptantha*) has a **shorter (12–16 mm) corolla, sharp-pointed bracts** and is endemic to the high meadows of Mt. Rainier. • **Purple alpine paintbrush (*C. rubida*)** is even smaller than showy and obscure paintbrushes. The **stems are 2–10 cm long/tall,** the **corolla 12–15 mm long** and the **upper lip 3.5–4 mm long.** It grows on alpine tundra and is endemic to the Wallowa Mtns of northeastern OR.

Sulphur Paintbrush • *Castilleja sulphurea*

General: Stems 20–50 cm tall, often purplish; **plants sticky-hairy** upward. **Leaves:** Linear to lance-shaped, 2–5 cm long, **mostly entire,** sometimes the uppermost leaves with a pair of small side lobes. **Flowers: Bracts pale yellow,** oblong-egg-shaped, entire and rounded or with 1–2 pairs of small lobes near the top; corolla 20–30 mm long, **lower lip short, to 2 mm; calyx lobes pointy-tipped, 1–4 mm long. Where Found:** Moist meadows and rocky slopes; subalpine and alpine zones; locally frequent in the southeastern part of the region; cordilleran.

Similar Species: Snow paintbrush (*C. nivea*) is smaller **(5–15 cm)** and white **cobwebby- or woolly-hairy** with **greenish yellow bracts,** a longer **(3–4 mm) lower corolla lip** and **longer (4–8 mm), pointy-tipped calyx lobes.** It grows in alpine meadows, rocky tundra and fellfields, and is endemic to southwestern MT and northern WY. • **Yellow Wallowa paintbrush (*C. chrysantha*)** is also small **(5–20 cm)** and has **mostly yellowish, pointy-tipped bracts,** a longer **(3–6 mm) lower corolla lip** and **blunt to rounded calyx lobes.** It is found in moist subalpine and alpine meadows in the Wallowa and Blue Mtns of northeastern OR. A form of *C. chrysantha* with dull red bracts, previously known as *C. ownbeyana*, is restricted to the Wallowa Mtns. • **Thompson's paintbrush (*C. thompsonii*)** is 10–30 cm tall and has **upper leaves with 1–2 pairs of linear side lobes, yellowish, 3–5-lobed bracts** and pointy-tipped calyx lobes 1–6 mm long. It grows in dry shrublands and on rocky slopes and ridges, in steppe to subalpine zones. Thompson's paintbrush is locally frequent in inland southern BC and central WA.

Notes: Most paintbrush species (including these) are partial parasites. Although they are green and can make their own food, their roots are also connected to the roots of host plants, and they highgrade their hosts. Paintbrushes generally have high nutrient concentrations in their leaves, a high transpiration rate and small, usually hairless, non-mycorrhizal roots that tap into host plant roots via haustoria (little pegs) to suck carbohydrates and other compounds. The other compounds can be important; sulphur paintbrush, for example, parasitizes larkspurs and lupines, obtaining alkaloids from them that render the paintbrush less tasty to insect herbivores.

Thompson's paintbrush

Western Paintbrush • *Castilleja occidentalis*

General: Stems 5–20 cm tall, often purplish; plants usually sticky-hairy especially through the flower cluster. **Leaves:** Narrowly lance-shaped, 2–5 cm long, **mostly entire, sometimes with a pair of small side lobes. Flowers:** Bracts pale yellow, often with a brownish, purplish or reddish cast, oblong-egg-shaped, entire and rounded or with 1–2 pairs of small lobes near the tip; corolla 15–25 mm long, **lower lip short, to 2 mm long.** Where Found: Meadows and talus slopes; subalpine and alpine zones; infrequent in the Rockies in the southeastern part of the region.

Similar Species: Cusick's paintbrush (*C. cusickii***)** ranges from southwestern AB and southeastern BC to eastern WA, northeastern OR, ID, western MT and WY,

and is locally frequent in meadows, in montane to lower alpine zones. It has **upper leaves with 1–3 pairs of narrow side lobes,** a **longer (3–6 mm) lower corolla lip** and **oblong, yellow (sometimes purplish) bracts** with 2 pairs of lateral lobes.

Notes: Although paintbrushes are parasites, they may ultimately benefit their hosts and neighbours. In the alpine zone of the Colorado Rockies, species near western paintbrush plants grew nearly twice as fast as those farther away. This is likely an effect of the rapid decomposition of nitrogen-rich leaf litter from the paintbrush. In nutrient-poor habitats where decomposition is slow, the surge from the paintbrush litter could outweigh the drag from parasitism. In terms of nutrient cycling, hemiparasites could function as both Dracula and Robin Hood.

Cusick's paintbrush

Unalaska Paintbrush • *Castilleja unalaschcensis*

General: Ascending to erect, **20–80 cm tall,** nearly hairless below, appressed-hairy above. **Leaves:** Lance-shaped, 3–10 cm long, **entire. Flowers:** Bracts greenish yellow to bright yellow (sometimes orange-tinged), lance-, egg- or wedge-shaped, hairy, entire or upper leaves with 1–2 pairs of very short, blunt lobes near the tip; **calyx lobes 3–10 mm long.** Where Found: Moist to mesic meadows, thickets, open forests, heathlands and tundra; lowland to alpine zones; frequent in the west-central part of the region; cordilleran.

Notes: Unalaska, which includes Dutch Harbor, is a city on the Aleutian island of the same name.

Northern Paintbrush • *Castilleja hyperborea*

General: Stems 7–16 cm tall; plants hairy especially through flower cluster. **Leaves:** Narrowly lance-shaped, 1.5–4 cm long, **mostly divided** into 1–2 pairs of slender side lobes. **Flowers:** Bracts yellow to yellowish green, lance-shaped to lance-oblong, usually **deeply lobed; calyx teeth short (to 2 mm). Where Found:** Tundra, stony slopes and ridges; montane to alpine zones; frequent in the northern ⅓ of the region; arctic-alpine, amphiberingian.

Similar Species: Pale paintbrush (*C. caudata***;** *C. pallida*) is **taller (15–50 cm),** with long-tapering, narrowly **lance-shaped, unlobed leaves, greenish yellow** (sometimes whitish), **mostly unlobed bracts** and **longer (3–7 mm) calyx teeth.** It grows on moist, stony shores, gravel bars, meadows, thickets and tundra, in lowland to alpine zones. A subarctic-alpine, amphiberingian species, it is frequent in the northern ⅓ of the region, AK, YT and NT.

Notes: *Castilleja* was named for Don Domingo Castillejo, an 18th-century Spanish botanist.

Scarlet Paintbrush, Common Red Paintbrush
Castilleja miniata

General: Plants 20–80 cm tall, hairless below, hairy above especially in the flower cluster.
Leaves: Entire, narrowly lance-shaped, 3–10 cm long. **Flowers: Bracts bright red or scarlet to orange,** lance-shaped, 1–2 pairs of **sharp lobes** near tip, hairy, often sticky; **corolla 20–40 mm long; calyx segments lance-shaped, long-tapering to pointy tips. Where Found:** Meadows, shores, grassy, rocky or gravelly slopes, fens, thickets and open woods; lowland to subalpine zones; common throughout the southern ⅔ of the region, infrequent northward; cordilleran.

Similar Species: Harsh paintbrush (*C. hispida*) is generally hairy (often bristly-hairy) and has **upper leaves with 1–2 pairs of narrow lobes** above the middle. It grows in meadows, forest openings and on coastal bluffs and grassy slopes, in lowland to subalpine zones. Harsh paintbrush is frequent in the southern ½ of the region, southern BC (from 54° N) and southwestern AB to WA, OR, ID and MT.

Notes: Scarlet paintbrush includes *Castilleja chrymactis, C. dixonii, C. gracillima* and *C. hyetophila.*

• Scarlet, alpine, harsh, sulphur and Unalaska paintbrushes appear to hybridize freely among themselves where their ranges overlap, which they do in many places in our region. Some hybrid swarms display a range of bract colour from magenta to red through orange to yellow, and everything in between. Hybrids are intermediate in character from their parents, but not straightforwardly so. No single characteristic or combination of traits from morphology, cytology (polyploidy is often involved) and genetics can be relied on to sort things out. If you're having difficulty putting a name to a paintbrush, this could be why.

harsh paintbrush

Alpine Paintbrush, Rosy Paintbrush
Castilleja rhexifolia

General: Plants 10–40 cm tall, nearly hairless to fine-sticky-hairy, especially in the flower cluster. **Leaves:** Lance-shaped, **mostly entire** or upper sometimes short-lobed, **veins prominent. Flowers: Bracts crimson to purplish or rose** (rarely scarlet or yellowish), oblong-egg-shaped, usually with 1–2 pairs of short, **blunt side lobes;** corolla 20–35 mm long; **calyx segments blunt. Where Found:** Meadows, fens and rocky slopes; subalpine and alpine zones; frequent in the southern ½ of the region, east of the Coast-Cascade Mtns; cordilleran.

Similar Species: Brotherly paintbrush (*C. fraterna*) is small (**10–15 cm tall**) and **hairy;** the colour of the flower spike comes from the **bright red calyces,** and the **bracts are rather inconspicuous.** It is endemic to the Wallowa Mtns of northeastern OR and grows in alpine meadows and on talus slopes.

Notes: Alpine and scarlet paintbrushes often occur in the same area, with alpine paintbrush typically at higher elevations.

Elmer's Paintbrush, Wenatchee Paintbrush
Castilleja elmeri

General: Plants 15–30 cm tall, generally **sticky-hairy.**
Leaves: Narrowly lance-shaped, **mostly entire,** upper
leaves sometimes with a pair of short lobes. **Flowers:**
Bracts crimson to scarlet (occasionally yellowish), oblong-
egg-shaped, **usually unlobed; calyx lobes blunt, 1–4 mm
long. Where Found:** Mesic meadows; montane to alpine
zones; locally frequent in the south-central part of the
region in the Cascade and Wenatchee Mtns; endemic.

Similar Species: Suksdorf's paintbrush (*C. suksdorfii*)
has **taller (30–75 cm), solitary stems,** upper **leaves
usually with 1–3 pairs of side lobes, bracts scarlet
in the upper part** and green below, and

sharp-pointed
calyx segments
8–12 mm long.
It is found in moist
meadows, glades
and on stream-
banks, in upper
montane and sub-
alpine zones, in the
Cascades from
Mt. Adams in cen-
tral WA to Crater
Lake, OR.

Cliff Paintbrush · *Castilleja rupicola*

General: Plants 6–25 cm tall, generally **soft-hairy. Leaves:** Divided into
3–5 (to 7) linear, spreading lobes. **Flowers: Bracts scarlet or crimson,** mostly
deeply 5-lobed, shorter than the 25–40 mm long corolla, the **upper lip
14–21 mm long; calyx segments 1–5 mm long. Where Found:** Cliffs, ledges,
rocky meadows and talus; upper
montane to alpine zones; locally
frequent in the Cascades.

**Similar Species:
Rocky Mountain
paintbrush
(*C. covilleana*)** has
**shorter (7–13 mm)
upper corolla lips.**
It grows on rocky
slopes and ridges,
in subalpine and
alpine zones,
in central ID
and adjacent MT.

alpine paintbrush hybrids (below)

scarlet paintbrush × Unalaska paintbrush (below)

The Genus *Pedicularis* (Lousewort)

Louseworts are mostly perennial, green, root parasites with erect, mostly unbranched stems. The pinnately toothed, cleft, dissected or compound leaves are alternate, basal or, in one species, whorled. The flowers grow atop stems in bracted, spike-like clusters. The corolla (fused petals) is 2-lipped, the upper lip (**galea**) hood- or helmet-like, the lower lip 3-lobed. The calyx (fused sepals) is tubular with 5 (sometimes 2 or 4) teeth. The 4 stamens are enclosed in the galea. The fruits are somewhat flattened, asymmetric, curved capsules; the several seeds are smooth or have netted coats.

Louseworts are hemiparasites. They make their own food through photosynthesis, but their roots are also connected to the roots of other plants, and they steal food from those host plants. Most louseworts seem capable of parasitizing just about any plant they can reach, though they do have favourites—preferred hosts include grasses and some species of the pea family (Fabaceae), perhaps because peas can fix nitrogen.

Pedicularis derives from the Latin *pediculus*, "louse," because of an early belief that livestock that ingested the European common lousewort (*P. sylvatica*) would become infested with lice. Or perhaps the plant grew in poor pastures in northern Europe that only supported weak, unhealthy, lice-ridden stock. Several lousewort species, including *P. lanata, langsdorffii, oederi, ornithorhyncha* and *sudetica*, are edible. When the flower tops first appear in the spring, they were and are still harvested by northern peoples and fermented with water. They are eaten with oil and sugar, somewhat like sauerkraut. The roots are picked in early spring just as the flowers appear, or in the autumn after the plant has wilted. The young stems and roots can be consumed raw or boiled, or roasted until tender. But louseworts should really only be eaten ceremonially or in an emergency because they can contain enough poisonous compounds to make you really sick if eaten in quantity, and also because several species are uncommon and locally rare.

Key to *Pedicularis*

1a. Stem leaves whorled . . . . *P. verticillata* (p. 274)
1b. Stem leaves alternate or lacking 2
    2a. Leaves merely toothed or short-lobed 3
        3a. Corolla whitish or pink to purplish, hood-like upper lip tapering into a slender, downcurved beak; south of 54° N. . . . . *P. racemosa* (p. 277)
        3b. Corolla light yellow, hood-like upper lip with a short, straight beak; north of 64° N. . . . *P. lapponica* (p. 277)
    2b. Leaves pinnately lobed to twice pinnately cleft 4
        4a. Stems freely branched, or with at least some axillary branches . . . . *P. labradorica* (p. 277)
        4b. Stems unbranched 5
            5a. Plants leafy-stemmed; basal leaves, if present, not markedly larger than stem leaves 6
                6a. Plants usually >30 cm tall; leaves deeply pinnately cleft, blades 5–15 cm long; corollas yellow or tinged with red or purple to wholly purple . . . . *P. bracteosa* (p. 278)
                6b. Plants mostly 5–25 cm tall; leaves pinnately dissected to lobed, blades 2–4 cm long 7
                    7a. Corollas pink to purple; spike many-flowered, elongating. . . . . *P. langsdorffii* (p. 273)
                    7b. Corollas yellow. 8
                          8a. Spike of several to many flowers, head-like at first, then elongating; leaves dissected nearly to midrib; hood-like upper corolla lip (galea) beakless, toothless; calyx 5-lobed . . . . *P. oederi* (p. 276)
                          8b. Spike few-flowered, head-like; leaves merely lobed, blade continuous along both sides of midrib; galea short-beaked, slender-toothed; calyx 2-lobed . . . . *P. lapponica* (p. 277)
                                9
            5b. Plants with leaves mostly at base; stem leaves few and reduced in size 10
                9a. Galea with distinct beak >2 mm long 11
                    10a. Beak of galea straight 11
                        11a. Flower cluster head-like; corolla purple, 1–1.7 cm long; beak of galea 2–4 mm long; mostly Coast-Cascade Mtns . . . . *P. ornithorhyncha* (p. 275)
                        11b. Flower cluster elongate, spike-like; corolla white to cream or yellowish, or purple, 1.5–2 cm long; beak of galea 1–2 mm long; Rocky Mtns . . . . *P. parryi* (p. 275)
                  10b. Beak of galea strongly curved 12
                      12a. Beak of galea curved downward; corolla yellowish white or pink to purple . . . . *P. contorta* (p. 277)
                    12b. Beak of galea curved upward; corolla pink to reddish purple 13

13a. Flower cluster usually hairless; beak of galea 7–18 mm long; outer lobes of lower lip ear-shaped . . . . **P. groenlandica** (p. 275)

13b. Flower cluster white-woolly; beak of galea 3–5 mm long; lower lip fan-like . . . . **P. attollens** (p. 275)

9b. Galea beakless or with pointy tip <1 mm long 14

14a. Corolla yellow or creamy white, sometimes flushed with pink or maroon purple, especially toward tip of galea. 15

15a. Primary lobes of leaves strongly incised. 16

16a. Plants 5–15 cm tall; flowers usually <10 in nearly flat-topped heads; corolla 2.5–4 cm long; north of 53° N . . . . **P. capitata** (p. 276)

16b. Plants 15–40 cm tall; flowers usually >10 in elongate spikes; corolla about 1.5 cm long; Mt. Rainier . . . . **P. rainierensis** (p. 276)

15b. Primary lobes of leaves merely toothed. . . . . **P. oederi** (p. 276)

14b. Corolla pink to purple. 17

17a. Stems leafless or nearly so; flowers spirally arranged; galea twisted, with a pair of short, slender teeth near tip . . . . **P. sudetica** (p. 274)

17b. Stems leafy; flowers not spirally arranged. 18

18a. Primary lobes of leaves merely toothed, leaf axis relatively broad; galea with a pair of small, slender teeth near tip; north of 51° N . . . . **P. langsdorffii** (below)

18b. Primary lobes of leaves deeply cleft or lobed again. 19

19a. Flower spike densely white-woolly; corolla pink to lavender, galea without a pair of teeth near tip; north of 54° N. **P. lanata** (p. 274)

19b. Flower spike hairy but not densely white-woolly; corolla purple, galea with a pair of slender teeth near tip; southwestern MT and northwestern WY. 20

20a. Plants <10 cm tall; bracts not strongly differentiated from upper leaves . . . . **P. pulchella** (below)

20b. Plants 15–40 cm tall; bracts strongly differentiated from upper leaves . . . . **P. cystopteridifolia** (below)

Arctic Lousewort, Langsdorff's Lousewort
Pedicularis langsdorffii ssp. *arctica*

General: Plants from a **yellow taproot** and a sturdy stem-base, **nearly hairless to somewhat long-woolly, especially in flower spike; stems 1 to several,** erect, 5–25 cm tall, **leafy. Leaves:** Basal leaves lance-shaped, 4–7 cm long including winged stalks, **pinnately lobed to cleft (comb-like);** stem leaves similar, not much smaller than basal ones. **Flowers:** Numerous in a dense, bracted spike, compact at first, then elongating; bracts similar to leaves; **corolla pink to purple, 20–25 mm long,** upper lip 8–12 mm long, arched, hood-like, **beakless but with a pair of slender teeth near the tip;** calyx long-woolly, 5-toothed. **Fruits:** Capsules 12–15 mm long, lance-oblong, asymmetric, flattened, curved, hairless. **Where Found:** Tundra, heathlands, rocky meadows, gravelly slopes and ridges; lowland (arctic coast) to alpine zones; frequent in the northern (from 52° N) inland ⅔ of the region; arctic-alpine, ssp. *arctica* mostly North American.

Similar Species: Fernleaf lousewort (*P. cystopteridifolia*), found in meadows and rocky slopes, and **pretty dwarf lousewort (*P. pulchella*),** of fellfields, scree and talus, are both endemic to southwestern MT and northwestern WY. Their flowers are similar to those of arctic lousewort, but their **leaves are more divided and fern-like.** Fernleaf lousewort is taller (**15–40 cm**) with flower bracts very different from the leaves. Pretty dwarf lousewort is shorter (**to 10 cm tall**) with bracts similar to the leaves.

Notes: Arctic lousewort is also known as *Pedicularis arctica*. • This plant blooms very early, partly because it favours windswept habitats with scant snowpack. • This species is named for Prussian aristocrat, physician and naturalist Georg Heinrich von Langsdorff (1774–1852); he accompanied Krusenstern on the circum-navigation of the world in the ships *Nadezhda* and *Neva*.

Woolly Lousewort • *Pedicularis lanata* ssp. *lanata*

General: Similar to arctic lousewort (p. 273); also from a thick, yellow taproot; **stems usually single. Leaves:** Pinnately divided; more deeply divided than arctic lousewort. **Flowers: Flowering spike densely white-woolly; upper corolla lip lacks pair of teeth. Where Found:** Tundra, fellfields, rocky slopes and ridges; montane to alpine zones; frequent in the northern mostly inland ½ of the region, especially on calcium-rich substrates; arctic-alpine, species circumpolar, ssp. *lanata* North American.

Notes: Woolly lousewort is also known as *Pedicularis kanei*. • According to the Fisherman Lake Dene-thah of Saskatchewan, small pieces of woolly lousewort were dried, mixed with tobacco and smoked for headaches. In parts of Russia, the leaves were used to make tea. • The tops are browsed by caribou.

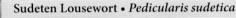

Sudeten Lousewort • *Pedicularis sudetica*

General: Similar to both arctic lousewort (p. 273) and woolly lousewort (above); often grows in the same areas but from stout rhizomes not a yellow taproot. **Leaves: Mostly or all basal;** pinnately divided, more finely divided **(fern-like)** than those of the preceding 2 species. **Flowers:** Flowering spike long-woolly but not densely so; **upper corolla lip with 2 slender teeth;** the best field clue is the **spiral arrangement of the flowers,** which can clearly be seen by looking straight down on the spike. **Where Found:** Meadows, thickets, peaty seepage sites, streambanks, open forests, rocky slopes, heathlands and tundra; lowland (arctic coast) to alpine zones; frequent throughout the inland ⅔ of the region, disjunct as ssp. *scopulorum* from WY to NM; arctic-alpine, circumpolar.

Notes: This is a very variable species. One form with 2-toned flowers, distinguished as var. *albolabiata*, is particularly striking. • A pollination study of 6 *Pedicularis* species (including Sudeten lousewort) in the Kluane Range, Yukon, showed pollination primarily by 14 species of bumblebees (*Bombus*). Captured bumblebees carried pollen from more than one lousewort species about half the time, suggesting some promiscuous pollination. Different nectar tube lengths of the lousewort species are probably related to tongue lengths of the various bumblebee species. • This species was first described from the Sudetes Mountains of the western Czech Republic.

Whorled Lousewort • *Pedicularis verticillata*

Leaves: Unique among our louseworts in having **whorled (not alternate) leaves** along the stem as well as at the base, pinnately divided. **Flowers:** Similar to those of preceding species; **upper corolla lip lacks pair of teeth** near tip. **Where Found:** Moist meadows, thickets, rocky slopes, heathlands and turfy tundra; lowland (arctic coast) to alpine zones; locally frequent in the northern ½ of the region; amphiberingian, also European.

Notes: *Verticillata* means "having whorls" or "a ring around an axis" and describes the arrangement of the leaves.

Bird's-beak Lousewort • *Pedicularis ornithorhyncha*

General: Stems single to several clumped, 5–30 cm tall, hairless except long-hairy in flower head. **Leaves: All or mostly basal,** long-stalked, oblong-elliptic, 3–12 cm long, pinnately lobed and cleft **(fern-like),** the divisions often toothed. **Flowers:** Few to several in a head-like cluster; bracts much smaller than leaves; **corolla purple, 10–17 mm long** including beak, 2-lipped, upper lip 6–8 mm long, **strongly hooded,** prolonged into **straight, conical beak 2–4 mm long;** calyx long-hairy. **Where Found:** Meadows, heathlands, tundra, streambanks and rocky slopes; subalpine and alpine zones; frequent in the Pacific coastal mountains, rare inland; Pacific Maritime endemic.

Similar Species: Parry's lousewort (*P. parryi*) has less-divided leaves, a longer flower spike and **longer (15–20 mm),** purple (var. *purpurea*) to yellowish or cream (var. *parryi*) flowers with **shorter (1–2 mm) corolla beaks.** It grows in dry to mesic meadows and on open, rocky slopes and fellfields, in subalpine to alpine zones, and is locally frequent in the Rockies from southwestern MT and central ID to NM and AZ.

Notes: Some louseworts offer pollinators nectar, whereas others such as bird's-beak lousewort do not. In this and other nectar-less louseworts, pollinators are pollen-eating worker bumblebees and an occasional queen vibrating pollen from the concealed anthers. • *Ornithorhyncha* means "bird beak," from *ornitho,* "bird-like," and *rhyncho,* "beak."

Elephant's-head Lousewort, Pink Elephants
Pedicularis groenlandica

Leaves: Numerous, fern-like, at base and along hairless, sometimes reddish purple stem. **Flowers:** Many in long, **mostly hairless spikes; flowers pink to reddish purple; corolla resembling an elephant's head and trunk,** upper lip strongly hooded and with **long (7–18 mm), upcurved beak,** lower lip with ear-shaped side lobes. **Where Found:** Wet to moist meadows, fens, swamps, thickets, seepage areas and streambanks; montane to subalpine zones; locally frequent in the southern ½ of the region, infrequent northward; boreal North American.

Similar Species: Little elephant's head (*P. attollens*) is noticeably **white-woolly in the flower cluster** and has **shorter (3–5mm) corolla beaks.** It occurs in wet meadows, streambanks and fens, in montane to alpine zones, and is locally frequent from the Cascades of OR to the Sierras.

Notes: Elephant's-head lousewort is a parasite on arrow-leaved groundsel (p. 390), as is towering lousewort (p. 278). In addition to sucking sugars, both louseworts take up the pyrrolizidine alkaloid senecionine from the groundsel. Herbalists using louseworts medicinally should reflect upon the chemicals these plants could be obtaining from their host plants, such as the hepatotoxic, genotoxic and cytotoxic senecionine.

Capitate Lousewort • *Pedicularis capitata*

General: Stems single, 5–15 cm tall, usually hairy in flower cluster. **Leaves:** Basal leaves oblong, 3–7 cm long including long stalk, pinnately dissected and toothed; stem leaves lacking or 1–2 just below flower spike. **Flowers: 1 to several** in a bracted, head-like cluster; bracts similar to leaves but smaller; **corolla cream or yellowish white, often tinged with pink or purple at tip, 25–40 mm long,** upper lip 15–25 mm long, **strongly arched** and hooded, **beakless but usually with pair of slender teeth near tip;** calyx 5-lobed, the lobes broad, 4–10 mm long. **Where Found:** Moist, rocky slopes, meadows, heathlands and tundra; lowland (arctic coast) to alpine zones; frequent in the northern ½ of the region; arctic-alpine, amphiberingian.

Similar Species: Mount Rainier lousewort (*P. rainierensis*) is taller (15–40 cm) and leafier, with more (usually more than 10) but **smaller flowers, the corollas about 15 mm long.** It grows in high-elevation meadows and on streambanks, typically on north slopes, and is endemic to magnificent Mt. Rainier National Park, WA.

Notes: Different sorts of mycorrhizae (fungus-plant root associations) occur on different arctic-alpine plants. Ecto-mycorrhizae and arbutoid mycorrhizae occur to 79° N; capitate lousewort is ectomycorrhizal on Ellesmere Island. Arbuscular mycorrhizae have been found to 82° N. And root- and rhizoid-associated fungi called dark septate endophytes (DSE) are apparently more common than mycorrhizal fungi in the high arctic (and antarctic). We don't know exactly what the DSE are up to, but they are wide-spread and ubiquitous, and appear to help plants grow.

Oeder's Lousewort
Pedicularis oederi

General: Stem 5–25 cm tall, nearly hairless to woolly, especially through flower spike. **Leaves:** Basal and on the stem, oblong to lance-shaped, **pinnately lobed or cleft to midrib. Flowers:** Numerous in spikes; **flowers yellow, often maroon-tipped; corolla 15–25 mm long,** upper lip somewhat arched and hood-like, **beakless, toothless. Where Found:** Meadows, tundra, heathlands, fellfields and rocky slopes; montane to alpine zones; locally frequent in the northern ½ of the region, disjunct in the Rockies of the southeastern part of the region; circumboreal with amphiberingian theme.

Notes: The Asian variety (var. *sinensis*) of Oeder's lousewort flowers from mid-July to the end of August (more than 40 days) at 5180 m on the north slope of Mount Qomolangma (Everest). • The species is named for G.C. von Oeder (1728–91), a professor of botany in Copenhagen, Denmark.

Lapland Lousewort • *Pedicularis lapponica*

General: Resembles Oeder's lousewort (p. 276) but has **leaves merely toothed to lobed, not cleft to midrib. Flowers:** Spike few-flowered, **flat-topped, head-like; corolla pale yellow, 11–15 mm long,** upper lip slightly arched and hood-like, with short, **slender-toothed beak; calyx 2-lobed. Where Found:** Tundra, heathlands and meadows;

montane to alpine zones; infrequent in the northern ⅓ of the region; subarctic-alpine, circumpolar.

Notes: Lapland lousewort keeps open its reproductive options for dealing with different environmental conditions. In a study in Swedish Lapland, this species mated with other individuals (cross-fertilization) at lower elevations but increased in self-compatibility at higher elevations, presumably because there were fewer insect pollinators as elevation increased. In western Greenland, Lapland lousewort primarily reproduced vegetatively by rhizomes.

Coiled-beak Lousewort • *Pedicularis contorta*

Leaves: Mainly basal, pinnately compound with linear, toothed leaflets. **Flowers:** Numerous in long-bracted spikes; **corolla white or cream** with dark spots (occasionally pink to purple in var. *ctenophora*), with **quarter-moon-shaped beaks, curved down but not to 1 side; calyx 5-lobed. Where Found:** Meadows, glades and rocky slopes; subalpine and alpine zones; locally frequent in the southern part of the region.

sickletop lousewort

Similar Species: Sickletop lousewort or ram's-horn lousewort (*P. racemosa*) has **merely toothed,** often coppery green **leaves all on the stem.** The **cream to pinkish white or purplish corolla** has a strongly arched upper lip, hooded and prolonged into a slender, **sickle-shaped beak, curved down and in** toward the prominent lower lip. It occurs in open coniferous forests, glades, rocky slopes and meadows (usually in and around tree clumps), in montane and upper subalpine zones. Sickletop lousewort is frequent in the southern ⅓ of the region, BC and southwestern AB from about 54° N south to CA and NM.

Labrador Lousewort • *Pedicularis labradorica*

General: Biennial or short-lived perennial from a spindly taproot; stems single or several, **usually branched,** 10–30 cm tall, **leafy,** white-hairy typically in lines below leaf bases. **Leaves:** Pinnately cleft or lobed, coarsely toothed, stalked, basal (where smaller) and on stems. **Flowers: Few to several** (5–10), in small, loose clusters at

stem tips or **single in leaf axils; corolla yellow,** often with orange or red markings, 12–17 mm long, upper lip hooded, with **pair of slender teeth near tip,** beakless or short-beaked. **Where Found:** Forests, thickets, bogs and swamps, rocky slopes, meadows, heathlands and tundra; montane to subalpine and sometimes alpine zones; frequent in the northern mostly inland ½ of the region; subarctic-alpine, interruptedly circumpolar.

Notes: The narrowly oblong, pointy-tipped capsules are flattened and held horizontally, splitting open when ripe to form structures similar to sugar scoops, which when jostled flick the seeds out, effectively dispersing them.

Towering Lousewort, Bracted Lousewort, Wood-betony • *Pedicularis bracteosa*

General: Stout stems **30–100 cm tall** from a mix of fibrous and tuberous-thickened roots. **Leaves: Mostly on stem,** finely divided, **fern-like,** double-toothed. **Flowers:** Many in **dense, bracted, elongated spikes; corolla yellow or greenish yellow to red or purplish,** 13–21 mm long, **upper lip hooded, beakless or nearly so. Where Found:** Moist, open forests, glades, thickets and meadows; montane to alpine zones; frequent in most of the southern ½ of the region; cordilleran.

Notes: In the Wyoming alpine at 2945 m, nesting queens of the bumblebee *Bombus kirbyellus* were the most important pollinators of towering lousewort. As elevation declined, queens of other bumblebees (especially *B. flavifrons* and *B. mixtus*) became more important pollinators.
• Towering lousewort is a parasite on arrow-leaved groundsel (see elephant's-head lousewort, p. 275, for details) but also parasitizes Engelmann spruce (p. 40), from which it takes up sugars and the alkaloid pinnidol. • Some claim that "betony" comes from the Latin *bettonica* and is the common name of *Betonica (Stachys) officinalis*, a mint-family herb revered as a charm against evil spirits. Others say that the name comes from an old Gallic word meaning "medicinal plant." • Nlaka'pamux women incorporated the leaf pattern of towering lousewort in basket designs.

POLLINATION IN *PEDICULARIS*

The louseworts owe much of their diversity in species and in flower colour and form to coevolution with pollinators. The two-lipped flowers are most straightforward in species such as towering, Mt. Rainier and capitate louseworts, in which the upper lip forms an arching hood that encloses the style and stamens. These 3, mostly yellow-flowered species are visited primarily by bumblebees foraging for both pollen and nectar. The yellow-flowered Oeder's and the pink-flowered arctic, Sudeten, whorled and woolly louseworts all have beakless flowers as well. Their flowers have a similar gullet construction in which the lower lip forms a landing platform and the upper, hooded lip protects the anthers, which touch the back of any insect visitor that pushes its head down into the basal tube when looking for nectar. But flower tube depth often differs among species and is at least partly related to the tongue lengths of their bumblebee pollinators. The most strongly modified flowers have taken on remarkable—even bizarre—forms, mostly involving elongation of the hood into a pronounced beak variously twisted or curved. Long-beaked flowers occur in the pink/purple-flowered bird's-beak and elephant's-head louseworts, as well as in the yellowish-flowered sickletop and coiled-beak louseworts. The long-beaked species provide pollen but no nectar and are visited by pollen-gathering bumblebees often employing buzz pollination (see box essay on p. 300).

You can often find 5 or 6 different species of louseworts on the same mountain. You might wonder how the species maintain their genetic and ecological identities, given that lousewort species and their bumblebee pollinators are not strictly faithful to each other. One *Pedicularis* species may be visited by several *Bombus* species, and one *Bombus* pollinator may visit different plant species at different times. Reproductive segregation among co-occurring lousewort species is strengthened by differences in pollinator behaviour and floral biology (form, colour, pollinator rewards and blooming time), and is reinforced by different habitat preferences.

Alpine Speedwell • *Veronica wormskjoldii*

General: Flowering stems from a shallow rhizome; erect or bent at base, unbranched, leafy, 7–30 cm tall, **long-wavy-hairy**, also glandular in flower cluster.

Leaves: All on stem, opposite, unstalked, elliptic to lance-shaped, 1–4 cm long, hairless to long-wavy-hairy, margins smooth to blunt-toothed.

Flowers: Few to several atop stem in a bracted cluster, at first compact then elongating; **corolla violet purple to light blue** with cream centre, saucer-shaped, 6–11 mm across, **irregularly 4-lobed,**

lobes much longer than basal tube; **calyx glandular-hairy, deeply 4-lobed; styles short, 1–3 mm long; stamens 2,** protruding, 1–1.5 mm long.

Fruits: Capsules 4–7 mm long, flattened, **longer than wide, heart-shaped,** notched or blunt at the top, glandular-hairy; seeds numerous, flat, about 1 mm long.

Where Found: Moist meadows, seepage areas, streambanks and heathlands; montane to alpine zones; frequent throughout the region except the far north; cordilleran, disjunct in northeastern North America.

Notes: Alpine speedwell was originally considered part of the circumpolar *Veronica alpina* as *V. alpina* var. *wormskjoldii.* • The species is named for Morten Wormskjold (1783–1845), a Danish lieutenant and a member of Kotzebue's first expedition to Alaska.

Cusick's Speedwell
Veronica cusickii

General: Stems erect or bent at base, 5–20 cm tall. **Leaves:** Elliptic to egg-shaped, 1–2.5 cm long, **toothless, hairless. Flowers: Corolla deep blue-violet,** 8–13 mm across; **style 5–10 mm long, sticking way out; stamens 4–8 mm long. Where Found:** Meadows, rocky slopes and streambanks; subalpine and lower alpine zones; frequent in the southern ¼ of the region; cordilleran.

Notes: In the Olympic Mountains of Washington, seed set in Cusick's speedwell appears to be limited by the availability of pollinating insects. In Manning Park, BC, the species is pollinated by hoverflies,

which clasp the protruding stamens and brush the long style as they ease down on the flowers—kind of like a helicopter landing on a bush pad of logs. • *Veronica* is the Latin form of the Greek *berenice* or *beronike*, "bringer of victory." Some say it is a corruption of *Betonica* because the foliage is similar. Others ardently believe the genus is named after the legendary St. Veronica, from the Latin *vera* and *icon* (*iconica*), meaning "a true image." As Jesus lugged the cross to Calvary, a woman offered him a handkerchief with which to wipe his brow. When he returned it to her, it bore a perfect image of his face. She became St. Veronica, whose saint day is February 4. • "Speedwell" could mean "goodbye" or "travel well" because *V. officinalis* (the original speedwell) was used medicinally against coughs and to heal wounds.

Arctic Eyebright • *Euphrasia subarctica*

General: Taprooted **annual**, reputedly a root parasite; stems slender, erect, 3–25 cm tall, leafy, minutely hairy, often also glandular-hairy in the flower spike.

Leaves: Mostly 1–4 pairs, all on the stem, broadly egg-to lance-shaped or nearly circular, 2–15 mm long, **opposite, unstalked, palmately veined,** coarsely toothed, sparsely hairy.

Flowers: Several in a **loose spike of single, small flowers in the axils of leafy bracts; corolla whitish with purple markings and a yellow eye,** about 5 mm long, 2-lipped; calyx bell-shaped, almost as long as corolla, 4-toothed; **stamens 4.**

Fruits: Capsules oblong, flattened, somewhat hairy; seeds numerous, narrowly winged.

Where Found: Streambanks, shores, heathlands and gravelly openings in thickets; montane and subalpine to (rarely) alpine zones; infrequent in the central part of the region; boreal North American.

Notes: Arctic eyebright is also known as *Euphrasia arctica* var. *disjuncta* and *E. disjuncta*. • Some say *Euphrasia* is from the Greek for "delight," maybe in reference to these plants' reputed medicinal powers. Others think it is named for Euphrosyne, one of the 3 Greek Graces. • Based on the Doctrine of Signatures, the dark dot in middle of the flowers of European eyebright (*E. officinalis*) signifies that the plant can be used to clear the eyes, hence it was widely used to strengthen vision and memory, as well as to relieve nasal congestion, sinusitis and conjunctivitis.

Key to *Mimulus* (Monkeyflower)

1a. Plants annual; corolla scarcely 2-lipped, <1 cm long. . . . . *M. suksdorfii* (p. 281)

1b. Plants perennial; corolla strongly to weakly 2-lipped, >1 cm long. 2

   2a. Corolla pink-purple; plants erect, 30–100 cm tall . . . . *M. lewisii* (below)

   2b. Corolla yellow; plants creeping or matted, <20 cm tall 3

      3a. Plants 5–20 cm tall; stems leafy; corolla 2–4 cm long. . . . . *M. tilingii* (p. 281)

      3b. Plants 4-6 cm tall; leaves all near base; corolla 1–2 cm long . . . . *M. primuloides* (p. 281)

Pink Monkeyflower • *Mimulus lewisii*

General: Sticky-soft-hairy perennial from a stout, branching rhizome; stems robust, erect, **30–100 cm tall,** leafy.

Leaves: Large, unstalked, **opposite,** clasping stem, oval, pointy-tipped, 3–7 cm long, 3–5-veined from the base, **margins with widely spaced teeth;** lowest leaves much reduced.

Flowers: Several on long (3–10 cm) stalks in axils of upper leaves; **corolla pink-purple to rose red with yellow markings, trumpet-shaped, 3–5.5 cm long, 2-lipped,** the lips spreading, upper lip 2-lobed, lower lip 3-lobed with 2 yellow-hairy ridges within; calyx bell-shaped, green; **stamens 4.**

Fruits: Capsules narrowly oblong, long-pointed, 10–16 mm long; seeds numerous.

Where Found: In and along streams (especially ice-cold ones), seepage areas, wet meadows, talus slopes and avalanche tracks; montane to lower alpine zones; frequent in the southern ½ of the region; cordilleran.

Notes: Pink monkeyflower does poorly when planted below its natural elevational range.

Mountain Monkeyflower
Mimulus tilingii

General: Dwarf, often mat-forming perennial, **5–20 cm tall,** from creeping rhizomes, sometimes also with runners. **Leaves: Mostly on stems,** elliptic to egg-shaped, **5–25 mm long,** irregularly few-toothed, stalks short or absent. **Flowers:** 1–5 on long stalks from the axils of upper leaves; **corolla broadly funnel-shaped, brilliant yellow with maroon markings in flaring throat, 2–4 cm long, strongly 2-lipped,** lower lip 3-lobed, with 2 ridges having sticky hairs and maroon splotches; calyx pale yellow-green, bell-shaped, asymmetrically swollen in fruit. **Where Found:** Wet, mossy seepage areas, meadows, rivulets and streambanks; subalpine and alpine zones; frequent in the southern ½ of the region; cordilleran.

Similar Species: Primrose monkeyflower (*M. primuloides*) is a small (to 6 cm tall), **densely matted** perennial with **leaves all crowded at or near the base** and **single, yellow flowers, 1–2 cm long and weakly 2-lipped.** It occurs in wet meadows and bogs, in montane to lower alpine zones, in the Cascades of WA and OR and the Olympic Mtns, east to central ID. • **Suksdorf's monkeyflower (*M. suksdorfii*)** is a small (3–10 cm tall), slender, often much-branched **annual** with narrowly lance-shaped leaves and small, **4–8-mm long, yellow, slightly 2-lipped flowers.** It grows in moist to dry openings, in montane and subalpine to (occasionally) lower alpine zones, from Mt. Adams, WA, south to CA and east to WY and CO.

Notes: The lower corolla lip with its hairy, spotted ridges provides a well-marked landing platform for bumblebees. The flowers look almost too big for the stems. • Studies documenting plant succession after glacier retreat have generally focused on aboveground changes. However, a study on Lyman Glacier (North Cascades, Washington) suggests that the availability of soil fungi to form associations with plant roots (mycorrhizae) could be important in determining plant succession. Non-mycorrhizal plants predominated in early successional sites, and species (including mountain monkeyflower) in longer-established plant communities were mycorrhizal.

Tweedy's Snowlover
Chionophila tweedyi

General: From a short rhizome or stem-base; stems slender, mostly single, erect, 5–25 cm tall, stalked-glandular among the flowers.

Leaves: Mostly basal, lance-shaped, 3–9 cm long, toothless; **stem leaves opposite,** much reduced.

Flowers: Several (4–10) on short stalks in a loose, **1-sided, spike-like cluster,** mostly 1 flower per node; corolla pale lavender, tubular, 9–14 mm long, **2-lipped; calyx 5-toothed; stamens 5 (4 fertile, 1 sterile).**

Fruits: Capsules egg-shaped to elliptic; seeds numerous, with net-like coat.

Where Found: Rocky slopes, sandy-gravelly openings, meadows and talus; subalpine and alpine zones; frequent in the mountains of central ID and southwestern MT; cordilleran.

Notes: The name comes from the Greek *chion,* "snow," and *philos,* "beloved" or "loving," referring to this plant's habitat preferences. • Frank Tweedy (1854–1937) was a topographic engineer with the U.S. Geological Survey.

The Genus *Penstemon* (Penstemon)

With about 260 species, *Penstemon* is the largest genus of flowering plants endemic to North America. Pentsemons—also known as beardtongues—are perennial herbs or sometimes low shrubs. The leaves are generally opposite, entire to toothed, the upper ones unstalked. The flowers are typically in spaced-out stacks of whorled clusters atop the stem. The tubular corolla is 2-lipped, usually blue, purple or lavender, but sometimes pink, yellow or whitish. The calyx is 5-lobed, and there are 5 stamens (which is what *Penstemon* means).

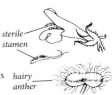

Key to *Penstemon*

1a. Plants woody, at least near the base; anthers densely woolly with long, tangled hairs 2

    2a. Leaves all on stem, not clustered toward the base. . . . . *P. montanus* (p. 284)

    2b. Leaves tending to be clustered near the base of plant or near the base of current year's growth 3

        3a. Plants ascending to erect, usually >15 cm tall, branched above ground surface; leaf clusters elevated, not forming mats; leaf blades 2–10 times as long as wide. . . . .*P. fruticosus* (p. 283)

        3b. Plants usually <15 cm tall, with basal leaf clusters mat-forming on ground surface; leaf blades 1–2.5 times as long as wide 4

            4a. Leaves of erect flowering shoots well developed, usually >1 cm long; Rocky and Columbia Mtns. . . . .*P. ellipticus* (p. 284)

            4b. Leaves of erect flowering shoots small, bract-like, <1 cm long; Coast-Cascade Mtns and westward. 5

                5a. Flowers purple to blue-lavender; leaves hairless, not glaucous. . . . . *P. davidsonii* (p. 283)

                5b. Flowers pink or reddish to rose purple; leaves glaucous, blue-green, often spreading-hairy . . . .*P. rupicola* (p. 283)

1b. Plants not woody; anthers hairless or with short, inconspicuous hairs 6

    6a. Plants glandular-hairy in flower cluster 7

        7a. At least some leaves irregularly and obscurely sawtoothed . . . .*P. albertinus* (p. 284)

        7b. Leaf margins smooth, not toothed. 8

            8a. Ovary and capsule glandular-hairy near tip; corolla 2–3 cm long; calyx >7 mm long; sterile stamen protruding from corolla . . . .*P. whippleanus* (p. 285)

            8b. Ovary and capsule hairless; corolla 1–2 cm long; calyx <7 mm long; sterile stamen included within corolla 9

                9a. Plants 10–25 cm tall; corolla 1–1.3 cm long, with evident guidelines in throat; Wallowa Mtns . . . .*P. spatulatus* (p. 285)

                9b. Plants generally taller, or with longer corolla; guidelines in throat obscure or lacking. 10

                      10a. Leaves hairless; calyx lobes with irregular (as if gnawed), wax-papery margins . . . .*P. attenuatus* (p. 285)

                      10b. Leaves short-hairy; calyx lobes with smooth margins. . . . . *P. humilis* (p. 285)

    6b. Plants not glandular-hairy in flower cluster 11

        11a. Corolla yellow . . . .*P. flavescens* (p. 287)

        11b. Corolla blue to purplish 12

            12a. Corolla 6–10 (to 12) mm long; plants 10–35 cm tall . . . .*P. procerus* (p. 286)

            12b. Corolla mostly >15 mm long; plants 20–70 (to 90) cm tall. 13

                13a. Leaves all along stem, mostly sawtoothed 14

                  14a. Corolla lobes fringed with fine hairs; fertile stamens long-hairy toward anthers; corolla 25–40 mm long. . . . .*P. venustus* (p. 287)

                  14b. Corolla lobes not fringed; fertile stamens hairless; corolla 15–28 mm long . . . .*P. serrulatus* (p. 287)

              13b. Leaves basal and along stem, entire or nearly so 15

                15a. Flowers usually in 1 head-like cluster; corolla bright blue to blue-purple; anthers hairless; central and northern ID, northeastern OR and southwestern MT . . . . .*P. globosus* (p. 286)

                15b. Flowers in 2–8 whorls; corolla deep blue to lavender or violet; anthers hairy; southeastern ID, northeastern UT and adjacent WY . . . .*P. cyananthus* (p. 286)

Woody at Base; Long-Woolly Anthers

Shrubby Penstemon
Penstemon fruticosus

General: Low shrub or at least lower stems woody, **15–40 cm tall;** stems ascending to erect, much-branched, often reddish and brittle, mostly hairless except glandular-hairy in flower cluster. **Leaves:** Mostly opposite, persistent; primary leaves concentrated toward base and on short, sterile shoots, **lance-shaped to elliptic, 1–6 cm long,** margins toothed or smooth; leaves of flowering shoots

reduced and less crowded. **Flowers:** Few to several pairs in a bracted cluster; corolla blue-purple to lavender, **2.5–5 cm long,** 2-lipped, hairless on the outside, lower lip long-hairy within, especially along a pair of ridges; calyx hairy; sterile stamen shorter than fertile stamens, yellow-bearded toward tip; **anthers densely white-woolly. Fruits:** Capsules 8–12 mm long; seeds numerous, angled, narrowly winged, 1–2 mm long. **Where Found:** Well-drained, rocky slopes, cutbanks and open forests; steppe to alpine zones, mostly below treeline; frequent in the southern interior ⅓ of the region; cordilleran.

Davidson's Penstemon • *Penstemon davidsonii*

General: Low semi-shrub but spreading, woody **branches root at nodes and form dense mats 5–10 cm tall.** Leaves: Shorter, broader than shrubby penstemon (above); **primary leaves elliptic to circular, evergreen, thick, firm, hairless** but sometimes glandular-spotted, 5–20 mm long, **margins smooth or minutely sawtoothed;** leaves of flowering shoots few, less

than 1 cm long. **Flowers:** Purple to blue-lavender, **2–3.5 cm long,** similar in shape and structure to those of shrubby penstemon (above); **calyx hairless or nearly so. Where Found:** Dry rock outcrops, slabs, ledges and talus slopes; montane to alpine zones; locally frequent in and west of the Coast-Cascade Mtns from 55° N south to CA; Pacific maritime endemic.

Similar Species: Cliff penstemon or rock penstemon (*P. rupicola*) also forms dense, shrubby mats with oval, evergreen leaves but has **pink or reddish to rose purple flowers** and **glaucous, blue-green, often hairy leaves.** It grows on dry cliffs, ledges and rocky slopes, in montane to alpine zones, and is locally frequent in the Cascades of WA and OR, south to northern CA.

Notes: Davidson's penstemon is pollinated by long-tongued flies, bees and wasps. Most *Penstemon* species are pollinated by bees and wasps, and some also by hummingbirds. Penstemons in general have deeply recessed nectaries that can quickly replenish nectar, and some bloom rather late in summer, when pollinators are abundant and hungry. • This species is named for Dr. Anstruther Davidson (1860–1932), a Scottish dermatologist and botanist who collected the plant in California; he was also the co-author of *Flora of Southern California.*

cliff penstemon

Oval-leaved Penstemon, Rockvine Penstemon
Penstemon ellipticus

General: Similar to the preceding 3 woody species, with spreading or creeping stems forming mats 5–15 cm tall. **Leaves: Primary leaves hairless but not glaucous,** evergreen, thick, firm, elliptic to egg-shaped, 1–2.5 cm long, **margins finely sawtoothed** or occasionally nearly entire; **leaves of flowering shoots usually at least 1 cm long. Flowers:** Light purple to deep lavender, similar in shape and structure to those of shrubby penstemon (p. 283), **calyx glandular-hairy. Where Found:** Dry, rocky slopes, cliff crevices and ledges; subalpine and alpine zones; frequent in the southeastern part of the region; Columbia Mtns and Rockies.

Notes: This and many other penstemon species have a reduced, sterile stamen (called a staminode) that has lost its mojo. It is now a vestigial male organ put to a new use, evolutionarily speaking. In this species, the staminode functions like underthings, hindering bee pollinator access to nectar and increasing bee visitation time and pollinator contact with fully functional stamens and stigmas.

Mountain Penstemon, Cordroot Penstemon
Penstemon montanus

General: Distinguished from others in this shrubby group by having **all leaves on stem,** not clustered toward the base; plants typically **glandular-hairy;** stems several to many, often lax, 10–30 cm long, wholly herbaceous or woody toward the base. **Leaves:** Oval or lance-shaped, mostly 1.5–5 cm long, margins strongly sawtoothed to toothless. **Flowers: Lavender to violet, 2.5–4 cm long,** similar to those of shrubby penstemon. **Where Found:** Dry talus, scree and rock crevices; subalpine and alpine zones; locally frequent in western MT, western WY and eastern ID to UT.

Herbs; Flower Cluster Glandular-hairy

Alberta Penstemon • *Penstemon albertinus*

General: Stems several, clustered, 10–40 cm tall, leafy, **hairless except glandular-hairy in flower cluster. Leaves: Toothed to entire,** bright green, thick, firm, mostly hairless; basal leaves stalked, lance- to spoon-shaped or oval, 4–10 cm long; stem leaves several, well developed. **Flowers:** In an interruptedly spike-like arrangement of 4–8 dense, several-flowered whorls; **corolla blue-violet to light blue, 1.2–2 cm long, hairy on the outside and within at throat;** anthers hairless except bristly on sutures; sterile stamen yellow-bearded toward scarcely expanded tip. **Where found:** Dry, open, gravelly slopes, rocky ridges and forest edges; montane to alpine zones; frequent in the southeastern part of the region; Columbia Mtns and the Rockies.

Thinstem Penstemon, Taper-leaved Penstemon • *Penstemon attenuatus*

General: Stems solitary or a few clumped, slender, erect, **10–70 cm tall. Leaves: Lance-shaped,** to 15 cm long, **hairless, margins mostly entire. Flowers:** In a cluster of 2 to several **dense whorls; corolla 1–2 cm long, dark blue (occasionally pale yellow or whitish), glandular-hairy on the outside;** calyx **4–7 mm long,** lobes with irregular (as if gnawed), wax-papery margins; **ovary and capsule hairless; sterile stamen not protruding** beyond mouth of corolla, bearded on expanded tip. **Where Found:** Meadows, rocky, open or wooded slopes and fellfields; montane to subalpine, occasionally alpine zones; frequent in the southeastern part of the region.

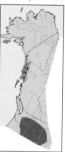

Similar Species: Wallowa penstemon (*P. spatulatus*) is shorter (10–25 cm), with shorter (to 6 cm), **spoon-shaped basal leaves and blue-purple corollas 1–1.3 cm long.** It is a rare endemic of open slopes at moderately high elevations in the Wallowa Mtns, OR. • **Lowly penstemon (*P. humilis*) has** at least **some short-hairy leaves and loose whorls of few flowers. The blue to purplish blue corolla is 1–1.7 cm long,** the calyx lobes smooth-edged. It grows on dry, rocky slopes, in montane to lower alpine zones, and is a southern cordilleran species frequent in WY, central WA and eastern OR to CA, NV, UT and CO.

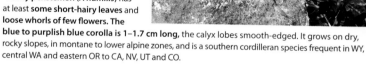

Dusky Penstemon, Whipple's Penstemon
Penstemon whippleanus

General: Stems several, clumped, erect, 20–60 cm tall. **Leaves:** Elliptic to egg-shaped, mostly 5–10 cm long, **margins entire. Flowers:** Longer and wider than other species of this group, in clusters of 2–7 open whorls; **corolla 2–3 cm long,** inflated toward wide (7–11 mm) mouth, ranging in colour from **blue, dark purple or lavender to plum or cream,** lower lip much longer than upper; **calyx 7–11 mm long;**

ovary and capsule glandular-hairy near the top; sterile stamen protruding beyond mouth of corolla. **Where Found:** Well-drained, rocky slopes, open forests and timberline meadows; montane to subalpine, occasionally lower alpine zones; another Rocky Mtn species frequent in the southeastern part of the region.

Notes: The specific epithet honours the spectacularly named Lieutenant Amiel Weeks Whipple (1817–63), a topographical engineer and surveyor, and the commander of the Pacific Railroad Survey.

HERBS; FLOWER CLUSTER USUALLY HAIRLESS, NOT GLANDULAR

Small-flowered Penstemon
Penstemon procerus

General: **Flowering stems 10–35 cm tall, clumped, slender,** leafy, hairless, ascending to erect from stem-base, often with short, leafy mat-forming stems at the base. **Leaves:** Smooth-margined, hairless; basal leaves lance- to spoon-shaped, 3–10 cm long; stem leaves few, opposite, lance-shaped, shorter than basal leaves. **Flowers:** In **1 to several dense whorls; corolla deep purple-blue** (occasionally pinkish or yellowish white), narrowly tubular, **6–12 mm long,** 2-lipped, hairless on the outside, hairy within at the **2–3 mm wide throat;** calyx 3–6 mm long; anthers hairless; sterile stamen about as long as fertile stamens, yellow-bearded at its expanded tip. **Where Found:** Dry to mesic meadows, grassy hillsides, rocky slopes, gravelly ridges and open forests; montane to alpine zones; frequent in the interior southern ⅔ of the region, also the Olympic Mtns; cordilleran.

Notes: Small-flowered penstemon is host to the bug *Orectoderus obliquus,* which feeds on the plant and lays its eggs in the leaves. This plant bug—the female at least—mimics ants in appearance at all life stages, a strategy with the delightful name "myrmecomorphy." Presumably this protects the bug from predation, perhaps by spiders, by tricking the predators into believing the bugs are distasteful or dangerous ants. • Small-flowered penstemon does indeed have small flowers (for a penstemon) that are angled downward and with the lower corolla lip expanded into a bowl-shaped bee landing platform.

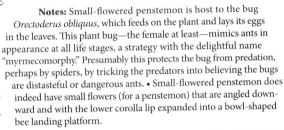

Globe Penstemon
Penstemon globosus

General: Similar to small-flowered penstemon (above) but with **larger flowers usually in 1 head-like cluster; corolla bright blue or blue-purple, 13–22 mm long; anthers hairless. Where Found:** Meadows and moist, open slopes; montane to subalpine zones; locally frequent in the southeastern part of the region.

Similar Species: Wasatch penstemon (*P. cyananthus*) has flowers about the same size (17–25 mm long) as those of globe penstemon but in **2 to several distinct whorls** and with **hairy, green or dark blue anthers.** It grows on scree slopes and rocky ridges above timberline, mostly in the Wasatch Mtns, and is endemic to southeastern ID, northeastern UT and adjacent WY.

Wasatch penstemon (left)

Lovely Penstemon, Blue Mountain Penstemon
Penstemon venustus

General: Stems few to many, clumped, 30–80 cm tall. **Leaves: All along stem,** lance-oblong, **mostly saw-toothed. Flowers:** Numerous in long, 1-sided cluster; **corolla lavender to purple-violet, 25–40 mm long, lobes fringed** with fine hairs; **fertile stamens long-hairy toward anthers.** **Where Found:** Rock outcrops, gravelly ridges and talus slopes; montane to lower alpine zones; locally frequent in the Blue Mtns of southeastern WA and northeastern OR, and in adjacent ID.

Similar Species: Coast penstemon (*P. serrulatus*) has lance-elliptic, usually sawtoothed **leaves all on stems** 20–80 cm tall;

flowers in 1 whorl (sometimes to 5), the **deep blue to dark purple corolla 15–28 mm long,** the lobes not fringed; and **hairless fertile stamens.** It occurs in moist gullies and on streambanks and rocky slopes, in lowland to subalpine zones. A Pacific maritime endemic, it is frequent in and west of the Coast-Cascade Mtns, southeastern AK and west-central BC to OR.

Notes: Slow and steady when climbing uphill seems to be the strategy for lovely penstemon. Plants above treeline in the Wallowa Mountains were older than lower-elevation plants, with smaller annual growth rings. However, they produced many more flowering shoots in the alpine than at lower elevations.

coast penstemon

Yellow Penstemon • *Penstemon flavescens*

Leaves: Lance-shaped, **relatively thick and firm, entire,** blackening when drying. **Flowers: Corolla light yellow,** 12–16 mm long. **Where Found:** Dry, rocky slopes, glades and open forests; montane to lower alpine zones; locally frequent in the Bitterroot Mtns of central ID and southwestern MT.

Bog Bunchberry, Swedish Dwarf Cornel • *Cornus suecica*

General: Perennial herb from a slender, creeping rhizome; stems 4–25 cm tall, erect, 4-angled in cross-section, minutely hairy.

Leaves: Commonly **1–3 pairs of opposite leaves** below a terminal pair or whorl of 4–6 leaves, egg-shaped to elliptic, **unstalked,** sparsely hairy above, hairless and paler below, **lateral veins arising at or near leaf base.**

Flowers: Several in a solitary, **umbel-like cluster** surrounded by **4 white, occasionally yellowish or pink-purple, egg-shaped, petal-like bracts** 5–15 mm long, falling off in fruit; **petals dark purple,** 1–2 mm long, 1 petal with a slender awn to 1 mm long; sepals tiny, also purplish; stamens 4, alternate with petals; ovary 1, inferior, 2-chambered, dark purplish and white-hairy when young; style 1, nearly as long as stamens.

Fruits: Drupes red, egg-shaped, berry-like, 1–2-seeded, 7–12 mm long, in a cluster.

Where Found: Wet to mesic forests, heathlands, meadows and tundra; lowland to alpine zones; locally frequent in AK, rare in northern coastal BC; circumpolar with large gaps.

Similar Species: *C. suecica* forms hybrids with bunchberry (*C. canadensis*), which usually has **merely 1 pair of short-stalked leaves,** with **lateral veins arising from the midvein in the lower ⅓ of the leaf,** and **cream to greenish yellow petals.** The hybrids have been treated by some taxonomists as a separate species, *C. unalaschkensis*.

Notes: These dwarf dogwoods boast explosive pollination. As studied in bunchberry, each stamen is a miniature catapult, held under tension within a cage of developing petals that remain joined at their tips. When an insect touches a trigger hair on one of the mature petals, the flowers burst open and the stamens launch pollen into the air in less than half a millisecond—less time than it takes a bullet to leave a rifle barrel. Some expect the National Rifle Association to adopt bunchberry as its floral emblem. • Most plants have male and female parts in each flower and have evolved different ways of avoiding self-fertilization. In bog bunchberry, stamens extend and anthers open just as the petals open, before the stigma is fully developed. By the time the stigma is receptive, the anthers have spread out to the sides, reducing the chance that their pollen will fall on their own stigma. Pollination is primarily by flies and hoverflies, which are probably guided to the tiny flowers by the large, petal-like bracts. • The berries of *C. canadensis*, though sweet, are dry and pulpy. They were sometimes eaten raw or cooked by coastal peoples and the Stl'atl'imc. The Gitxsan ate them mixed with other berries, and 2 or 3 berries were added during the cooking of other berries (especially saskatoons) being prepared for drying. The bunchberries acted as a kind of glue or thickening agent, holding the berry cake together and preventing it from cracking when drying. Bunchberries were also sometimes steamed and preserved for winter use. Generally, however, many groups did not eat them or only ate them as emergency food; some considered them unpalatable and only good for bears and birds.

Carrot Family (Apiaceae)

Our species are perennial herbs, often aromatic, from taproots often surmounted by stem-bases or from clusters of fleshy or fibrous roots. The leaves are basal and also (and more usually) along the stem and alternate. They are stalked, usually with sheathing bases, and usually compound, much cleft or divided, sometimes fern-like, rarely simple and undivided. The flowers are individually small, radially symmetric and numerous in usually compound umbels (see illustration, right), the spokes (stalks of individual clusters or umbellets) and the umbellets themselves often subtended by bracts and bractlets, respectively. There are 5 distinct petals, usually white or yellow (sometimes purplish), small or obsolete sepals, 5 stamens attached to a disc atop the inferior, 2-chambered ovary and 2 styles, sometimes swollen at the base. The dry fruits split into 2 halves (as in dill or caraway "seeds"), the halves flattened or rounded, often ribbed and sometimes winged or spiny; each half is 1-seeded and suspended after dehiscence on a slender, wiry stalk.

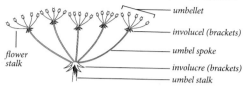

This economically important family produces food, condiments and ornamentals. Food plants include carrot (*Daucus*), parsnip (*Pastinaca*), celery (*Apium*) and fennel (*Foeniculum*). Flavouring comes from anise (*Pimpinella*), caraway (*Carum*), dill (*Anethum*), chervil (*Anthriscus*), coriander and cilantro (*Coriandrum*), cumin (*Cuminum*), fennel, lovage (*Ligusticum*) and parsley (*Petroselinum*). Water-hemlock (*Cicuta*) and poison-hemlock (*Conium*) possess resins or alkaloids in lethally poisonous quantities. Cultivated ornamentals include angelica (*Angelica*), goutweed (*Aegopodium*) and sea-holly (*Eryngium*).

Apiaceae (also known as Umbelliferae) is a large family in our region but relatively few species are true alpines.

Angelica roseana

Bupleurum americanum

Cymopterus glaucus

Heracleum maximum

Ligusticum grayi

Lomatium brandegeei

Lomatium sandbergii

Osmorhiza purpurea

Podistera macounii

Tauschia stricklandii

Key to the Genera of Apiaceae

1a. Leaves all simple (undivided), entire (not toothed or lobed), linear to lance-shaped
.... ***Bupleurum americanum*** (p. 291)

1b. Leaves compound or deeply divided.. 2

   2a. Leaves, or most of them, with well-defined, broad leaflets, not dissected into small, narrow
   segments 3

   3a. Leaflets 3, very large, usually >10 cm long and wide ...... ***Heracleum maximum*** (p. 292)

   3b. Leaflets usually >3, smaller, usually <10 cm long and wide.......................... 4

      4a. Flowers yellow 5

      5a. Fruits unstalked; restricted to northwestern WY and adjacent MT
      .... ***Shoshonea pulvinata*** (p. 294)

      5b. Fruits stalked 6

         6a. Fruits broadly ellipsoid to almost spheric, nearly as wide as long; south of
         48° N .... ***Tauschia stricklandii*** (p. 296)

         6b. Fruits oval, longer than wide; north of 60° N.............. ***Podistera*** (p. 293)

      4b. Flowers white to purplish.. 7

      7a. Leaves all basal .... ***Podistera*** (p. 293)

      7b. Leaves at base and along stem 8

         8a. Fruits narrowly cylindric or club-shaped, stiff-hairy, in open (see-through)
         umbels with few spokes; flowers inconspicuous......... ***Osmorhiza*** (p. 291)

         8b. Fruits oblong to roundish, more or less flattened, in compact umbels with
         many spokes; flowers showy 9

            9a. Stem-base conspicuously fibrous; fruits roundish in cross-section or
            slightly flattened side to side..................... ***Ligusticum*** (p. 293)

            9b. Stem-base not fibrous; fruits strongly flattened front to back.......... 10

               10a. Leaves with well-defined, relatively broad leaflets; fruits tipped with
               a nose cone (swollen base of styles).............. ***Angelica*** (p. 292)

               10b. Leaves with narrower, less-definite leaflets; fruits without a nose
               cone.. ***Lomatium*** (pp. 295–298)

   2b. Leaves dissected into small, narrow, ultimate segments, lacking well-defined leaflets 11

   11a. Fruits slightly flattened side to side; flowers white or sometimes pinkish
   .... ***Ligusticum*** (p. 293)

   11b. Fruits flattened front to back; flowers white or yellow 12

      12a. Fruits winged on the back and sides; bractlets of flower clusters relatively prominent,
      lance-shaped 13

         13a. Plants tufted, with numerous stems arising together in a bouquet-like bunch,
         resinous; leaves yellowish green; flowering stems usually with at least 1 leaf
         .... ***Pteryxia terebinthina*** (p. 297)

         13b. Plants mat-forming or with single or few stems, not tufted, not resinous;
         leaves bluish green or greyish green; flowering stems without leaves
         .... ***Cymopterus*** (p. 294)

      12b. Fruits winged on the sides only; bractlets of flower clusters lance-shaped to elliptic,
      usually not prominent .... ***Lomatium*** (pp. 295–298)

Calder's mountain-lovage

Yukon goldcrown

American Thorough-wax, American Thorowort
Bupleurum americanum

General: Hairless, often glaucous, from a taproot and stem-base clothed with brown leaf bases; stems 5–30 cm tall at high elevations.

Leaves: Basal and along stems, **simple,** 3–20 cm long, linear to oblong-lance-shaped, prominent parallel veins.

Flowers: In a compound umbel with leaf-like bracts; umbellets compact, rounded, with yellow bractlets; **petals yellow** to greenish yellow, sometimes with purplish splotches.

Fruits: Broadly oblong, 3–4 mm long, **somewhat flattened, with raised ribs** but no wings.

Where Found: Meadows, grassy and rocky slopes, gravelly terraces, tundra, talus slopes and fell-fields; montane to alpine zones; frequent in the north, disjunct in the southeast; amphiberingian.

Notes: American thorough-wax is also known as *Bupleurum triradiatum* ssp. *arcticum.* • Alpine plants are small, with few spokes and umbellets, whereas plants of lower elevations are branched, can reach 70 cm tall and have more umbellets. • *Bupleurum* is from the Greek for "ox-rib," probably because of the ribbed fruits. "Thorough-wax" could be a corruption of "thoroughwort"—the common name for *Eupatorium perfoliatum*—so called because the stem appears to grow right up through the leaves (i.e., the leaves are perfoliate). It was also called "thorow-wax" or "throw-wax'"—the name originally given to *B. rotundifolium*—because "the stalke waxeth throw (or throwe) the leaves" (Prior, 1879, quoting William Turner's 16th-century herbal).

Purple Sweet-cicely • *Osmorhiza purpurea*

General: Slender, from a well-developed taproot; stems 20–60 cm tall.

Leaves: Basal and stem leaves deltoid in general outline, twice divided into 3s; leaflets coarsely toothed, thin, yellowish green, **usually hairless.**

Flowers: Several to many in 2–6 spreading heads in a **loose, compound umbel** without bracts; **petals usually pink to purplish,** sometimes greenish white.

Fruits: Spindle-shaped, **8–13 mm long, bristly-hairy,** constricted below the **beaked tip, which is shaped like a "plumber's helper" and broader than tall.**

Where Found: Open forests and glades, streambanks, meadows, thickets and avalanche tracks; montane to subalpine and occasionally lower alpine zones; frequent in the southern ⅔ of the region; cordilleran.

Similar Species: **Blunt-fruit sweet-cicely** (*O. depauperata*) has **hairy, club-shaped fruits** that are **rounded or blunt (not beaked) at the tip** and **greenish white flowers.** It occurs in open forests, glades and forest margins, mostly in lowland to montane zones, occasionally to timberline. A cordilleran species, it is frequent throughout the mostly inland southern ¾ of the region, southern AK, southeastern YT and southwestern NT south through BC and AB to CA and NM. • **Western sweet-**

cicely (*O. occidentalis*) has **hairless fruits 12–20 mm long and shaped like English cucumbers, yellow or greenish white flowers** and is **usually shaggy around the leaf bases.** It grows in open forests, glades, avalanche tracks, rocky slopes and streambanks, in montane and subalpine zones. Western sweet-cicely is locally frequent in the southeastern part of the region, south-central to southeastern BC, southwestern AB and northwestern WA to CA and CO.

Notes: Grizzly bears like to eat sweet-cicely roots in spring and can be remarkably deft at prying them from the soil. The roots were dug up in early spring by interior peoples and either steamed or boiled. They reportedly have a delicate, sweet flavor reminiscent of carrots. The roots were also chewed as a cold remedy. • *Osmorhiza* means "scented root" because the roots have a sweet, licorice or anise-like smell when crushed, as do the green fruits. "Cicely" is from Latin and Greek *sesili*—the name for a carrot-family medicinal plant—somehow conflated with the girl's name Cicely.

Cow-parsnip • *Heracleum maximum*

General: Robust, hairy, from a stout taproot or cluster of fleshy roots; stems single, erect, hollow, **to 1.5 m tall.**

Leaves: Leaflets 3, 10–30 cm long/wide, palmately lobed, often maple-leaf-like, coarsely sawtoothed, hairy, the leaf stalks inflated and winged at the base.

Flowers: Numerous in flat-topped, compound umbels, 10–30 cm across, the bracts soon dropped; outer flowers larger than central flowers; petals white, often 2-lobed.

Fruits: Egg- to heart-shaped in outline, **7–12 mm long,** aromatic, strongly flattened front to back, ribbed, the **2 lateral ribs broadly winged.**

Where Found: Moist, rocky slopes, gullies, forest openings, meadows, seepage areas and streambanks; lowland to alpine zones; frequent throughout the southern ¾ of the region, less so at high elevations; amphiberingian, transcontinental in North America.

Notes: Cow-parsnip is also known as *Heracleum lanatum* and *H. sphondylium.* • It was eaten as a green vegetable by most First Nations groups in our region, though some consider it poisonous. The young stems and leaf stalks, before the flowers matured, were peeled and eaten raw or occasionally boiled. This plant is sometimes called "Indian celery" because the peeled young stems taste mild and sweet, despite the strong odour of the leaves and outer skin. Alaskan peoples often dipped the stems in seal oil before eating them. The Dena'ina and Gitxsan, among others, used the roots medicinally; they were chewed raw, pulverized or boiled to make a tea to treat colds, sore throats, mouth sores, tuberculosis, arthritis and swelling, as well as for drawing pus, as a poultice on infected areas and for bathing to soothe aching limbs. Gitxsan children fashioned drinking tubes and blowguns from the hollow stems. • **Caution:** Cow-parsnip contains compounds called furanocoumarins, which can cause blistering, severe dermatitis and skin damage, especially in people with light-sensitive skin. The stalks should be peeled before handling or eating.

Rose's Angelica • *Angelica roseana*

General: Stout, from a well-developed taproot; stems 15–60 cm tall, often glaucous.

Leaves: 2–3 times divided into 3s; leaflets sharp-toothed, **1–3 cm long,** firm, hairless or rough-hairy; leaf stalks swollen, strongly sheathing at the base.

Flowers: Numerous in 2–3 loose, compound umbels with **15–35 spokes of unequal length** and without bracts; petals dingy white, sometimes pink.

Fruits: Elliptic-oblong, 4–7 mm long, **rough-hairy,** flattened front to back, ribbed, the **ribs winged.**

Where Found: Rocky slopes, talus and fellfields; subalpine and alpine zones; infrequent in the southeastern corner of the region; Rocky Mtn endemic.

Similar Species: Seacoast angelica or sea-watch (**A. lucida**) has **umbel spokes all roughly the same length** and **hairless fruits with thin-edged but scarcely winged ribs.** It is an amphiberingian species most typically and frequently found on beaches and coastal bluffs from AK to CA, but also ranges inland to subalpine and lower alpine zones in moist meadows, especially north of 54° N.

Notes: Traditional medicine, especially in Asia, employs more than 60 species of *Angelica.* They are used as remedies for colds, flu, arthritis and hepatitis; to reduce swelling and induce phlegm; and to combat bacterial and fungal infections. Some sanguine Siberians carry seacoast angelica root as an amulet against polar bears; the Siberian Inuit inhaled fumes of the roasted root as a seasickness remedy.

seacoast angelica

Gray's Mountain-lovage • *Ligusticum grayi*

General: Stout, hairless, taprooted; stems 20–60 cm tall, clothed at the base with fibrous remains of old leaf sheaths.

Leaves: Mostly basal, divided (similar to Italian parsley) into many toothed or cleft, **lance-shaped leaflets** to 3 cm long; **stem leaves 1–2, much reduced.**

Flowers: Numerous in 1–3 compound umbels with **7–14 spokes of equal length** and without bracts; petals white, sometimes pink to purplish.

Fruits: Elliptic-oblong, 4–6 mm long, slightly flattened side to side; **ribs narrowly winged.**

Where Found: Moist to dry, open, rocky slopes, forest openings and meadows; montane to subalpine and occasionally lower alpine zones; frequent in the southern mostly inland ¼ of the region.

Similar Species: Calder's mountain-lovage (**L. calderi**) shares the fibrous root crowns, mostly basal leaves and narrowly winged fruit ribs of Gray's mountain-lovage, but has **more finely divided leaflets** and is **restricted to the outer north coast**, northern Vancouver I. (Brooks Peninsula) to Haida Gwaii and southeastern AK. It grows in wet, rocky, exposed habitats—boggy slopes, meadows and heathlands, from lowland to alpine zones—and is a scattered, locally frequent, insular endemic of our north Pacific coast. • **Canby's mountain-lovage** (**L. canbyi**) is **more robust**, to 1 m tall, and has **15–40 spokes** per terminal umbel. It is found in moist meadows and on rocky slopes and streambanks, in montane and subalpine zones. Canby's mountain-lovage is locally frequent in south-central and southeastern BC, and the Cascade and Wenatchee mountains of WA to northeastern OR, ID and MT. • **Fernleaf mountain-lovage** (**L. filicinum**) has finely divided, **fern-like leaves**, the **ultimate segments linear** and mostly 1–3 mm wide. It grows in open forests, rocky slopes and meadows, in montane and subalpine zones, and is frequent in the southeastern corner of the region, eastern ID, western MT and western WY to UT and CO.

Notes: The roots of Gray's mountain-lovage have been used medicinally by Aboriginal peoples to treat a variety of ailments. Recent medical research has demonstrated that extracts from the roots kill breast cancer cells. Other lovage species are routinely used by herbalists to combat viral and bacterial infections. Grizzly bears have been observed to chew the root of (probably) beach lovage (*L. scoticum*), spit the mixture of saliva and juice on their paws and rub it into their fur, perhaps as an attempt at self-medication. • "Lovage" appears to be from the Old French *luvesche* or *levesche*, a corruption of the Latin *ligusticum*, meaning "from Liguria," because culinary lovage (*Levisticum officinale*), a garden vegetable, grows wild in mountains of Liguria in northwestern Italy. • Gray's lovage was named for Asa Gray (1810–88), a professor of botany at Harvard and a preeminent, prolific botanical author.

Macoun's Woodroot • *Podistera macounii*

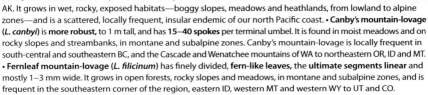
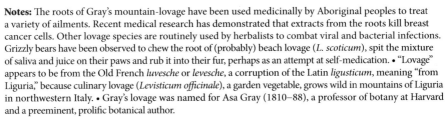

General: Hairless, from a taproot and branching, **fibrous stem-base;** stems 4–20 cm tall.

Leaves: **All basal**, broadly oblong in general outline, pinnately divided into egg-shaped, **coarsely toothed or cleft leaflets** 4–15 mm long.

Flowers: Several to many in compound umbels with 5–20 short spokes, with linear-lance-shaped, often toothed or lobed bracts; **petals purplish, white or yellowish.**

Fruits: Oval, 4–5 mm long, somewhat flattened side to side, with **prominent, unwinged ribs.**

Where Found: Dry, turfy tundra, heathlands and stony slopes; lowland (Bering coast) to alpine zones; frequent in the northern ⅕ of the region; arctic-alpine, amphiberingian.

Related Species: Yukon goldcrown (*P. yukonensis*) has mostly entire leaflets and smaller umbellets with greenish to yellowish white flowers. It grows on talus, scree and cliffs, in montane to alpine zones, and is a rare endemic of west-central YT and adjacent AK.

Notes: Macoun's woodroot is also known as *Ligusticum macounii* and *L. mutellinoides* ssp. *alpinum*. • *Podistera* is from the Greek *podus*, "foot," and *stereos*, "solid," perhaps in reference to the stout stem-base. • *P. macounii* honours John Macoun (1832–1920), a government of Canada naturalist, as well as an explorer and an excellent field botanist.

Snowbank Spring-parsley, Snowline Spring-parsley
Cymopterus nivalis

General: From a stout taproot and branching **stem-base covered with persistent leaf stalks;** flowering stems 5–25 cm tall.

Leaves: All basal, lance-oblong, 2–10 cm long, pinnately **finely dissected** (parsley-like) into numerous **tiny, crowded, narrow, glaucous segments.**

Flowers: Numerous in dense, compact umbels without bracts; **petals white.**

Fruits: Oblong-egg-shaped, 3–6 mm long, flattened front-to-back; **ribs narrowly winged.**

Where Found: Dry, rocky, exposed slopes; montane to alpine zones; scattered but locally frequent in the southeastern part of the region.

Similar Species: Greyish spring-parsley (*C. glaucus*) also has pale bluish green, finely divided leaves, but they are borne in a **whorl on the stems** near ground level, and the **yellow flowers** are in umbels with bracts. It grows on dry, gravelly or rocky slopes, in montane to alpine zones, in northwestern MT to central ID. • **Henderson's spring-parsley** or wavewing (*C. hendersonii*) is **smaller,** the lax to erect **flowering stems 1–8 cm tall.** It occurs on dry, rocky slopes, ridge crests and talus, in subalpine and alpine zones, and is infrequent and restricted to western MT and east-central ID. • **Rocky Mountain spring-parsley (*C. longilobus*) has a stem-base covered with old leaf stalks** and yellow flowers borne in **umbels with conspicuous green bractlets.** It occurs on dry, open, rocky slopes, ledges and fellfields, in montane to alpine zones, and is a Rocky Mountain endemic frequent in the southeastern corner of the region. • **Shoshone carrot (*Shoshonea pulvinata*)** forms shiny, green mats or cushions. The leaves are all basal, **once pinnately divided** into 2–5 pairs of leaflets, the **flowers yellow** and the **fruits oblong and unstalked.** It grows on limestone outcrops, rimrock, ridge crests and talus, in montane and subalpine zones. Shoshone carrot is a rare endemic species of the Absaroka and Owl Creek Mtns of northwestern WY and adjacent MT.

Henderson's spring-parsley

Notes: Snowbank spring-parsley is also known as *Cymopterus bipinnatus.* • Genetic studies suggest that the species currently accommodated in *Cymopterus* are a motley assortment, with several more closely related to species in other genera than to each other. Fruit characteristics, traditionally important in delineating genera of the carrot family, may not reflect actual genetic relationships very well—in this group, anyway—or may have been misinterpreted. • *Cymopterus* is from the Greek *kyma*, "wave," and *pteron*, "wing," referring to the fruit ribs, which have wavy wings in most species. • Spring-parsley? These plants tend to bloom early. Parsley is from the French *persil* and the Latin *petroselinum*, the latter derived from the Greek *petros*, "rock," and *selinon*, "an umbelliferous plant." It is thought that the word was gradually corrupted to *petersylinge*, then *persele* and *persely*, whence parsley.

The Genus *Lomatium* (Desert-parsley, Biscuit-root)

Lomatium is a substantial genus, with about 80 species, found only in western North America and mostly cordilleran or Great Plains. The alpine flora of our region includes 10 or so desert-parsley or biscuit-root species. They are all taprooted, perennial herbs, the stems mostly short or lacking. The leaves are mostly basal and compound, pinnately divided into either relatively large leaflets or very small, narrow, ultimate segments. The flowers are mostly yellow or white, in compound umbels without bracts; the umbellets may or may not have bracts. The fruits are narrow to roundish, flattened front to back and with evident lateral wings.

Both coastal and interior First Nations peoples used several species of *Lomatium*. The roots were dug and eaten raw or boiled, or pounded to make a type of flour. The young leaves of some species were eaten as a spring vegetable. The seeds, leaves and upper stems flavoured stews, soups and teas and served as a tobacco substitute. Infusions and teas were widely used for treating tuberculosis, and the seeds were chewed for colds, sore throats and tuberculosis.

Lomatium comes from the Greek *loma*, "border," in reference to the winged margins of the fruit.

Key to *Lomatium*

1a. Ultimate segments of leaves relatively large, mostly ≥1 cm long. 2
    2a. Ultimate segments of leaves forming definite leaflets usually >5 mm wide. 3
        3a. Leaflets strongly toothed or cleft; flowers usually white or cream, sometimes yellow (Vancouver I. and Olympic Mtns) . . . . ***L. martindalei*** (p. 296)
        3b. Leaflets mostly entire or shallowly toothed; flowers yellow . . . . ***L. brandegeei*** (p. 298)
    2b. Ultimate segments of leaves usually <5 mm wide, not forming definite leaflets 4
        4a. Umbellet bractlets and ultimate leaf segments egg-shaped to elliptic. . . . . ***L. cous*** (p. 297)
        4b. Umbellet bractlets linear-lance shaped or lacking; ultimate leaf segments linear 5
            5a. Flowers white or yellowish white to occasionally purplish; stems numerous, arising singly from subterranean branches of a root crown . . . . ***L. cusickii*** (p. 296)
            5b. Flowers yellow or sometimes purple; stems few or numerous, all arising in a tight bunch from the top of a taproot 6
                6a. Umbellets without bractlets; flowering stems mostly lacking leaves . . . . . . ***L. idahoense*** (p. 296)
                6b. Umbellets with bractlets; flowering stems mostly with at least 1 leaf. . . . . . ***L. dissectum*** (p. 297)
1b. Ultimate segments of leaves relatively small, rarely as long as 1 cm. 7
    7a. Umbellet bractlets and ultimate leaf segments egg-shaped to elliptic . . . . ***L. cous*** (p. 297)
    7b. Umbellet bractlets linear or lance-shaped or lacking; ultimate leaf segments linear or lance-shaped to oblong. 8
        8a. Dwarf (<10 cm high), high-elevation species; mountains of northeastern OR. 9
            9a. Ultimate segments of leaves hairy, 1–5 mm long; ovaries and fruits hairy . . . . . ***L. oreganum*** (p. 296)
            9b. Ultimate segments of leaves hairless, 3–8 mm long: ovaries and fruits hairless . . . ***L. greenmanii*** (p. 296)
        8b. Plants generally taller than 10 cm. 10
            10a. Wings of fruit corky-thickened; flowers yellow or purplish 11
                 11a. Leaves short-hairy; flowers yellow or chocolate red. . . . . ***L. dissectum*** (p. 297)
                 11b. Leaves hairless 12
                      12a. Leaves with ultimate segments sharply pointy-tipped; flowers purple; restricted to Wenatchee Mtns of north-central WA . . . . ***L. cuspidatum*** (p. 298)
                      12b. Leaves with ultimate segments blunt; flowers yellow; restricted to southwestern MT and northwestern WY. . . . . ***L. attenuatum*** (p. 297)
            10b. Wings of fruit thin; flowers yellow or white 13
                 13a. Leaves not much dissected, rather with toothed or cleft leaflets; flowers white to cream or sometimes yellow; southwestern part of region . . . . ***L. martindalei*** (p. 296)
                 13b. Leaves more dissected, with small, narrow ultimate segments that do not resemble leaflets; flowers yellow; southeastern part of region . . . . ***L. sandbergii*** (p. 297)

Martindale's Biscuit-root, Few-fruited Lomatium • *Lomatium martindalei*

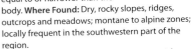

General: From an elongated tap-root; stems several, prostrate to ascending, 5–25 cm long/tall. **Leaves:** Mostly basal, **shiny, green to blue-green,** divided into **rather large (1–3 cm long), crowded, oblong, cleft or toothed, round-tipped leaflets.** **Flowers: White, cream or bright yellow;** umbellets short-stalked, with a few small bractlets, or none. **Fruits:** Oblong-elliptic, 8–16 mm long; wings thin, equal to or narrower than the body. **Where Found:** Dry, rocky slopes, ridges, outcrops and meadows; montane to alpine zones; locally frequent in the southwestern part of the region.

Similar Species: Two dwarfed (shorter than 10 cm), narrowly endemic species occur in rocky, windswept, high ele-vation habitats of the **Wallowa and Blue Mtns in northeastern OR.** They both have lance-elliptic leaflets less than 1 cm long and yellow flowers in very small (less than 1 cm long), compact umbels. **Blue Mountain biscuit-root (*L. oreganum*)** has hairy leaflets, ovaries and fruits. Greenman's biscuit-root (*L. greenmanii*) is **hairless.** • Strickland's tauschia (*Tauschia stricklandii*) is 5–20 cm tall and has long-stalked basal leaves with **undivided, elliptic leaflets 1–3 cm long, yellow flowers** and **rugby-ball-shaped fruits.** It is found on Mt. Rainier, WA, in moist high-elevation meadows, and also occurs on high slopes above the Columbia River Gorge, OR.

Idaho Desert-parsley
Lomatium idahoense

General: Low plant from a taproot; flowering stems to 15 cm tall. **Leaves:** Greenish, mostly basal but often 1–2 along stem, 2–3 times dissected into **long (1–5 cm) linear seg-ments. Flowers:** Yellow or becoming purplish with age; **umbellets mostly lacking bractlets.**

Fruits: Narrowly elliptic, 6–11 mm long; **wings less than ½ as wide as body. Where Found:** Dry, rocky slopes, ridges and meadows; montane to alpine zones; infre-quent in central ID and adjacent OR; endemic.

Similar Species: Cusick's desert-parsley (*L. cusickii*) has white flowers (occasionally purplish) and grows from a branching root crown. It is found in dry, open forests and on rocky slopes, ridges and outcrops, in montane to alpine zones, and is a cordilleran species, infrequent in the southeastern corner of the region.

Cous Biscuit-root • *Lomatium cous*

General: Low-spreading, hairless plant, from a **usually tuberous-thickened taproot;** flowering stems 10–20 cm tall. **Leaves:** Mostly basal, 3–4 times divided into small, narrowly elliptic, **finger-shaped segments, withering as blooming finishes. Flowers:** Yellow; umbellets 5–20 on spokes of unequal length, with **oval bractlets. Fruits:** Oblong-elliptic, 5–8 mm long, on stalks 1–3 mm long; wings about as wide as body. **Where Found:** Dry, open, rocky slopes, flats, ridges and outcrops; steppe to alpine zones, mostly at lower elevations but occasionally ascending above treeline; infrequent at high elevations in the southeastern corner of the region; cordilleran.

Similar Species: The related **taper-tip desert-parsley** or Absaroka biscuit-root (***L. attenuatum***) has **narrower, linear bractlets** and **fruits on stalks 3–10 mm long.** It grows on dry, rocky or gravelly slopes, ridges, scree and talus, in subalpine and alpine zones. It is an infrequent endemic in the Tendoy Mtns of southwestern MT and the Absaroka Mtns of northwestern WY.

Notes: The earliest umbels of cous biscuit-root bear a mix of flowers with both male and female organs ("perfect" flowers) and some with male organs only. As later umbels bloom, the ratio of perfect to male-only flowers increases. • "Cous" (also "couse" or "cows") is said to be a Native American name for several species of *Lomatium* whose thick, fleshy roots were processed into a kind of flatbread. • The journals of Meriwether Lewis and William Clark describe the tuberous roots of the lower-elevation Geyer's biscuit-root (*L. geyeri*) as being ground into meal and shaped into large, flat cakes, which some claim taste like dry biscuits. Evidently, this is why the genus got the name "biscuit-root." The roots could also be eaten raw and are said to taste like celery. • Beds of size-sorted stones sometimes form conspicuous stripes perpendicular to contours in the Blue Mountains of Oregon. Some have proposed that these distinctive features result from the activities of pocket gophers digging for cous biscuit-root and other roots, followed by weathering. Others suggest that frost action in late winter and early spring is more likely responsible.

Sandberg's Desert-parsley • *Lomatium sandbergii*

General: Plants from a **long, slender taproot; often branched near base,** 7–25 cm tall. **Leaves:** Basal and low on stem, small (blade 2–7 cm long), dissected into numerous, linear segments 1–5 mm long, **all lying in a single plane,** withering as fruits ripen; **leaf stalk sheath white-margined. Flowers:** Yellow; umbellets on spokes of unequal length, with several slender bractlets. **Fruits:** Elliptic, 5–8 mm long; wings much narrower than body. **Where Found:** Dry, open, rocky slopes, ridges and outcrops; subalpine and alpine zones; frequent in the southeastern part of the region.

Similar Species: Fern-leaved desert-parsley (*L. dissectum*) is a more robust plant, **greater than 40 cm tall,** with **yellow or purple** (to chocolate red) **flowers** and **fruits 8–18 mm long,** with **corky, thickened** narrow wings. It occurs on dry, rocky slopes and in shrublands, open forests, meadows and talus, in steppe to subalpine zones, occasionally to timberline, and is frequent in the southern ⅓ of the region, southern BC and southwestern AB to CA, AZ and CO. • **Turpentine spring-parsley** (*Pteryxia terebinthina* var. *foeniculacea*; *Cymopterus terebinthinus* var. *albiflorus* and var. *foeniculaceus*) also has very dissected leaves and yellow flowers, but the **fruits are winged on the back as well as the sides.** It grows on dry, open, rocky or gravelly slopes and ridges; this variety is locally frequent at high elevations in WA and MT south to CA and CO, and disjunct on Mt. Adams, WA.

turpentine spring-parsley

Notes: In Glacier National Park, Montana, the roots of Sandberg's desert-parsley are eaten by grizzly bears. • John H. Sandberg (1848–1917), a Swedish-born agronomist and forester, was a field agent for the U.S. Department of Agriculture and collected plants in the Midwest and in Washington, Idaho and Montana.

Brandegee's Desert-parsley
Lomatium brandegeei

General: Mostly hairless; stems 20–50 cm tall. **Leaves:** Mostly at or near the base, divided into several **long (1–5 cm), linear to lance-shaped leaflets.**
Flowers: Yellow; umbellets on spokes of unequal length, with several narrow bractlets. **Fruits:** Narrowly elliptic, 8–12 mm long, **bent down;** wings narrower than to nearly as wide as the body. **Where Found:** Dry to mesic grasslands, shrublands, open forests and rocky slopes; montane to sub-alpine zones; infrequent from extreme south-central BC to central WA.

Similar Species: Wenatchee desert-parsley (*L. cuspidatum*) has leaves dissected into numerous small, crowded, **firmly sharp-pointed segments** and **purple flowers.** It grows on open, rocky slopes, often on serpentine, in montane to alpine zones, and is endemic to the Wenatchee Mtns, WA.

Notes: The specific epithet honours the improbably named Townshend Stith Brandegee (1843–1925), a California botanist and a student of Mexican flora.

Arctic Wintergreen • *Pyrola grandiflora*

General: Perennial from a slender rhizome; flowering stems single, erect, 5–20 cm tall.

Leaves: All basal, evergreen, leathery, shiny, egg-shaped to circular; blades 1–4 cm long, green above, often somewhat reddish beneath, margins smooth to wavy or toothed; stalks 1–7 cm long.

Flowers: Several (4–12) in a cylindric cluster atop stem, short-stalked, bowl-shaped but weakly bilaterally symmetric; **petals 5, distinct, creamy white with some pink,** 6–11 mm long, broadly rounded; stamens 10; anthers yellow, inverted, opening by apparently terminal pores; ovary 1, superior, 5-chambered; **style 1, curved,** longer than stamens, with a collar below the stigma.

Fruits: Capsules globe-shaped, 4–6 mm wide; seeds tiny, numerous.

Where Found: Moist, open forests, thickets, heathlands and tundra; lowland (arctic coast) to alpine zones; frequent north of 60° N, infrequent southward; arctic-alpine, circumpolar.

Notes: The wintergreens (*Pyrola*) have often been placed in a separate family (Pyrolaceae) based on herbaceous habit and separate (not fused) petals. Molecular evidence supports inclusion of wintergreens and their chlorophyll-lacking cousins—such as Indian-pipe (*Monotropa*) and pinedrops (*Pterospora*)—in the heather family, albeit in their own subfamily (Monotropoideae). • Arctic wintergreen produces no nectar and is buzz-pollinated (as are other *Pyrola* species) by pollen-collecting insects, especially bees. • Arctic wintergreen roots on eastern Ellesmere I. were found to form with fungi an association called an "arbutoid mycorrhiza." The fungal partner in this mycorrhiza helps the wintergreen gather water and some minerals, in exchange for sugars. But the fungal filaments are also attached to the roots of other plants and may transfer sugars from those plants to the wintergreen, a sort of indirect parasitism. • *Pyrola* leaves are evergreen and often pear-shaped in outline, hence the common name "wintergreen" and the scientific name from the Latin *Pyrus*, "pear."

Arctic Starflower • *Trientalis europaea*

General: Hairless perennial from slender **rhizomes** with small, horizontal **tubers;** stems erect, unbranched, leafy, 5–25 cm tall.

Leaves: Main leaves **5–6 in a whorl** at top of stem, **oval-elliptic to broadly lance-shaped,** 2–6 cm long, rounded at tip; **lower leaves few to several,** much smaller, alternate.

Flowers: Single on each of 1–3 thin stalks arising from centre of leaf whorl, **saucer-shaped, star-like,** 1–2 cm across, the glandular **stalks equalling or usually longer than leaves;** petals 5–9 (usually 7), **white** (sometimes pink-tinged), pointy-tipped, fused at the base; sepals same number as petals but shorter, green; stamens 5–9, attached at base of ovary; ovary 1-chambered; styles 1.

Fruits: Capsules spheric, splitting into 5 segments when dry; seeds several to many.

Where Found: Moist to wet coniferous forests, thickets, meadows, streambanks, swamps, bogs, heathlands and tundra; lowland to lower alpine zones; frequent (less so at high elevations) in most of the region except the far north and the southeastern corner; broadly amphiberingian.

Notes: Arctic starflower is also known as *Trientalis arctica* and *T. europaea* ssp. *arctica*.
• In Sweden, arctic starflower behaves as a clonal "pseudo-annual"; the mother plant dies at summer's end after having produced rhizomes with daughter tubers, which detach and then become mothers themselves the following summer. Most reproduction in the study population was vegetative, and seedling recruitment was rare. • *Trientalis* used to be placed in Primulaceae (the primrose family) but now has been shifted, along with *Lysimachia* (loosestrife, which now also includes *Glaux*, sea milkwort) and *Anagallis* (pimpernel), to Myrsinaceae. The reason for this is that their leaves are not in basal rosettes, and they have very short, fused sections of petals. Molecular evidence supports the realignment.
• *Trientalis* is from Latin and means "one-third of a foot," referring to the plant height (about 10 cm or 4 in).

Primrose Family (Primulaceae)

Our primrose family species are perennial herbs with **simple** (undivided) leaves all in a rosette at the base of the plant. The radially symmetric flowers have 4–5 sepals and petals, both fused in the lower part into **calyx** (sepals collectively) and **corolla** (petals collectively) tubes, respectively; the corolla lobes are flaring or bent back above the tube, and the 5 stamens are attached to the petal tube. The 1-chambered, **superior ovary** has 1 style and 1 stigma. The fruits are capsules that open by segments or sometimes lids.

Key to the Genera of Primulaceae

1a. Corolla lobes sharply bent back; stamens protruding; flowers nodding . . . . *Dodecatheon* (below, p. 301)

1b. Corolla lobes spreading to erect, not bent back; stamens not protruding; flowers erect or spreading 2

   2a. Forming dense cushions or mats of small, narrow leaves; sepals keeled, at least on calyx tubes, hairless or with star-shaped hairs; flowers pink or purple . . . . *Douglasia* (pp. 303–305)

   2b. Mostly not forming cushions or mats; sepals mostly not keeled, hairless or soft-hairy, but not with star-shaped hairs; flowers white or pink to purple 3

      3a. Flowers white, usually <5 mm long; corollas constricted at throat . . . . *Androsace* (p. 302)

      3b. Flowers pink to magenta in our high-elevation species, >5 mm long; corollas not constricted at throat . . . . *Primula* (pp. 306–307)

The Genus *Dodecatheon* (Shootingstar)

Shootingstars arise from a single basal rosette of leaves and have erect stems. The leaves are lance-shaped to oval, unlobed, with smooth or blunt-toothed margins. The flowers are few to several in a bracted, compact umbel atop the stems, nodding on slender stalks in bloom, then becoming erect in fruit. The magenta to pink-purple corolla is yellowish or whitish at the base of the usually 5 lobes, which are long and strongly swept back from short, yellowish tubes. The short-tubular, cup-shaped calyx is 4–5-lobed. There are 4–5 stamens, and the anthers are confluent in a sleeve around the single protruding style. The fruits are egg-shaped to cylindric capsules.

BUZZ POLLINATION

Bumblebees and some species of solitary bees can sonicate pollen from certain types of flowers. The bees clutch the flowers and contract their indirect flight muscles very rapidly, causing the anthers to vibrate resonantly, dislodging pollen. For example, when visiting a shootingstar (*Dodecatheon*) flower, a bumblebee grasps the base of the cone of anthers with her mandibles and curls her inverted body under the anther cone. The muscular vibrations dislodge pollen from the anthers onto her hairy chest and belly—and produce an audible buzz. This process is called *buzz pollination*.

Typical buzz-pollinated flowers hang down, often lack nectar and have protruding anthers with small pores (like the holes in a saltshaker) or slits at the tip. Although this pollination strategy was discovered relatively recently, it is estimated that about 8% of the world's flowering species are primarily buzz pollinated. In our alpine flora, buzz pollination has been reported in all shootingstars, some species of *Vaccinium* (blueberries, cranberries), arctic wintergreen (*Pyrola grandiflora*), tall bluebells (*Mertensia paniculata*) and several species of lousewort (*Pedicularis*).

Honeybees can't do it, thus cannot pollinate some important crops and wildflowers. In fact, buzz pollination is essential for some crop plants, notably tomatoes and blueberries. Commercial greenhouse tomatoes were traditionally pollinated by handheld electric vibrators with names such as "Electric Bee" or "Pollinator II." Buzz-pollinating bumblebees pulse a distinctive, middle-C buzz, noticeably higher pitched than the flight buzz.

tall mountain shootingstar

Northern Shootingstar
Dodecatheon frigidum

General: Roots reddish brown; flowering stems 8–30 cm tall. **Leaves:** Spade- to egg-shaped, squared-off at base, **tapering abruptly to stalks. Flowers:** 2–7; corollas magenta to pink or lavender, the 5 lobes 8–15 mm long; **filaments less than 1 mm long, free or slightly fused, maroon;** anthers 4–6 mm long, purplish; stigma not conspicuously enlarged. **Fruits:** Capsules red to purple, **cylindric. Where Found:** Moist to wet meadows, heathlands, rocky slopes, streambanks and tundra snowbeds; lowland (arctic coast) to alpine zones; frequent in the northern mostly inland ⅓ of the region; amphiberingian.

Notes: Evidence from genetics, cytology and morphology has been used by some taxonomists as a rationale for transferring all *Dodecatheon* species into the genus *Primula*. Uh-huh. • *Dodecatheon* comes from the Greek *dodeka*, "twelve," and *theos*, "god," giving "twelve gods," which can be interpreted to mean a plant protected by the pantheon. Revisionist taxonomists take note. • The name "shootingstar" makes reference to the backward-pointing petals, which stream behind the forward-pointing stamens like a meteor trail.

Pretty Shootingstar
Dodecatheon pulchellum

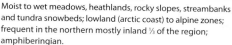

General: Roots whitish; flowering stems 10–40 cm tall. **Leaves:** Narrowly elliptic to spoon-shaped, narrowing gradually to stalks. **Flowers:** 2–8; corolla rose pink to magenta, the 5 lobes 5–15 mm long; **filaments united in yellow-orange tube longer than 1 mm;** anthers 2–7 mm long, dark purple; stigma not enlarged. **Fruits: Capsules reddish purple, cylindric, splitting by segments downward from tip. Where Found:** Moist meadows, rocky slopes and streambanks; lowland to alpine zones; frequent and widespread (merely scattered at high elevations) in the southern ½ of the region, infrequent northward at low elevations; western North American.

Similar Species: Tall mountain shootingstar (*D. jeffreyi*) is 10–60 cm tall, with **4–5 petals, lance-shaped leaves, enlarged stigmas and egg-shaped capsules usually opening at the top by a lid and splitting downward.** It is found in wet meadows, streambanks, bogs, fens and pool margins, in lowland to subalpine zones. A cordilleran species, it is frequent especially along the coast and in the coastal mountains from AK to CA, scattered inland to southeastern BC, ID, MT and WY. • **Alpine shootingstar (*D. alpinum*)** is 8–40 cm tall, with **4 petals, linear-lance-shaped leaves, enlarged stigmas and barrel-shaped capsules splitting by segments from tip.** It grows in moist to wet meadows and on streambanks, in montane to (occasionally) alpine zones. Alpine shootingstar is scattered but locally frequent in the southern part of the region, in southern WA and the OR Cascades to CA, east to northeastern OR, NV, UT and AZ.

Notes: Pretty shootingstar is an extremely variable and wide-ranging species; *FNA* describes 7 varieties.

Rock-jasmine • *Androsace chamaejasme* ssp. *lehmanniana*

General: Perennial from a branched stem-base, forming **tufts or mats** to 10 cm across; **flowering stems single** from each rosette, ascending to erect, 3–10 cm tall, covered with long, soft, shaggy hairs.

Leaves: In multiple, **dense, basal rosettes,** lance-shaped, 3–15 mm long, grey soft-hairy to hairless, margins fringed with hairs.

Flowers: Fragrant, 2–6 in compact umbels atop stems, on **stalks shorter than the flowers; corolla cream to whitish (fading pinkish) with yellow to pink eye, 5–8 mm across,** the short tube constricted at the throat, spreading flat to 5 lobes; calyx 2–3 mm long, the 5 teeth about as long as the tube, **not keeled, long-hairy;** stamens 5; ovary 1-chambered; styles 1, stigma head-shaped.

Fruits: Capsules nearly spheric, 2–3 mm long.

Where Found: Rocky or gravelly slopes and ridges, stony heath-lands and tundra; lowland (arctic coast) to alpine zones; frequent in the northern ¼ of the region, disjunct in the Rockies of the southeast; arctic-alpine, amphiberingian, the entire species complex circumpolar.

Notes: *Chamaejasme* is from *chamae*, "dwarf" or "on the ground," and *jasmin*, presumably indicating a very small plant with flowers like those of true jasmine.

Northern Fairy-candelabra *Androsace septentrionalis*

General: Annual or biennial, not mat-forming; leaves in a **single rosette** with **several (1–10) flowering stems** from the centre. **Leaves:** Lance-shaped, 1–3 cm long, sparsely to densely hairy, entire to toothed toward tip. **Flowers:** 5–20 in umbels, on **stalks much longer than the flowers; corolla white, small (3–4 mm long),** 5-lobed, **2–3 mm across; calyx top-shaped, keeled,** the 5 triangular teeth shorter than the tube. **Where Found:** Dry, rocky slopes, sandy-gravelly terraces, balds, ridge crests and tundra; lowland to alpine zones; frequent throughout the region inland of the coastal mountains; circumpolar.

Notes: In the Colorado alpine, both timing and the abundance of flowering of northern fairy-candelabra were highly variable. Dates of flowering were primarily determined by the date of snowmelt. Flower abundance was associated with climatic factors (the previous summer's precipitation and the current year's average minimum May temperature) in rocky meadows, but not on wetter sites. As climates warm, it will be interesting to observe the effect on alpine annuals whose flowering is so closely tied to snowmelt and other climatic factors. • The Fisherman Lake Dene-thah report using the whole plant to make a decoction for washing hair or other affected body parts to get rid of lice. • *Androsace* is from the Greek *andros*, "male," and *sakos*, "shield," alluding to the shape of the anthers; *septentrionalis* means "northern."

The Genus *Douglasia* (Dwarf-primrose)

Douglasia or dwarf-primrose is related to both *Androsace* and *Primula*. Except for 1 biennial species, ours are perennial herbs, mat- or cushion-forming from multiple rosettes, with prostrate to ascending stems from a taproot and generally with some star-shaped hairs. The small, lance-shaped leaves are in overlapping rosettes. The flowers are solitary or in 2–10-flowered umbels, stalked from the terminal rosettes, the stalks very short in early bloom but elongating until fruiting. The primrose-shaped flowers have a pink, rose, magenta or occasionally white corolla with a short tube flaring to 5 lobes and a constricted throat with 5 crests. The calyx is broadly bell-shaped and also 5-lobed. There are 5 stamens and 1 style. The fruits are egg- to globe-shaped capsules.

Douglasia is mostly North American, and 2 areas house most of its diversity: far northwestern North America (also known as Beringia) and the Pacific Northwest (northwestern contiguous U.S. and adjacent southwestern Canada). The genus is nearly absent from the large gap between these northern and southern centres of its species diversity. The gap was occupied by Pleistocene ice during the last glacial maximum. You could conclude that species of *Douglasia* do not colonize new territory rapidly. All of our species are regionally or narrowly endemic, restricted to globally small ranges.

The genus name honours David Douglas (1798–1834), an intrepid Scottish plant explorer of the Pacific Northwest. Douglas introduced many Northwest plants into European gardens. He arrived in Fort Vancouver, Washington, in 1825 for a two-year botanical expedition and came back for more in 1830. Since 1977, *Douglasia* has been the journal of the Washington Native Plant Society. With their compact form and pretty pink flowers, dwarf-primroses are big favourites of rock gardeners.

Coeur d'Alene dwarf-primrose

Key to *Douglasia*

Alaska Dwarf-primrose • *Douglasia alaskana*

General: Biennial from a **single, dense rosette**; flower stalks 4–20 or more, very short in early bloom, **later elongating and ultimately sprawling,** 2–10 cm tall/long, hairy upward. **Leaves:** Wedge-shaped, 5–15 mm long, **densely hairy above,** entire to 3-toothed at tip. **Flowers: 1–2 on each leafless stem; corolla purple at first, white with age,** 3–5 mm long, the lobes 1–3 mm long; calyx often purplish, hairless, 3–6 mm long. **Where Found:** Dry, rocky slopes, scree and stony tundra; subalpine and alpine zones; infrequent in southern AK and southwestern YT; endemic.

Notes: Alaska dwarf-primrose is also known as *Androsace alaskana.* • This is the only species of *Douglasia* with a single rosette of leaves, and for that reason, it was previously considered an *Androsace.* Moreover, no single or combination of morphological characteristics can clearly separate *Douglasia* from *Androsace.* Genetic analysis suggests that species of *Douglasia* are closely related, DNA-wise, to *Androsace,* and also that some species of *Androsace* are not closely related to other species in the genus. So don't be surprised to see both genera deconstructed in the future.

Mackenzie River Dwarf-primrose • *Douglasia arctica*

General: Loosely tufted cushions to 20 cm across, with many prostrate to ascending stems, 2–10 cm long/tall, clothed with reddish brown, dead but persistent leaves below and with green leaf rosettes above. **Leaves:** Linear to narrowly lance-shaped, 3–10 mm long, ascending, overlapping, **hairless on both surfaces but fringed with unbranched hairs. Flowers:** Solitary atop stalks that are short in early bloom, later elongating to 2–4 cm; corolla rose pink, whitish with age, **4.5–6 mm long,** the lobes 2.5–6 mm long. **Where Found:** Scree slopes and stony tundra; lowland (arctic coast) to alpine zones; frequent in the far north; arctic-alpine, endemic.

Notes: Mackenzie River dwarf-primrose forms looser cushions with simple-fringed but otherwise hairless leaves and has larger flowers than the very similar Yukon dwarf-primrose (below), which also has a more southerly distribution, though still mostly north of 60° N.

Yukon Dwarf-primrose
Douglasia gormanii

General: Forms **tightly tufted cushions**. **Leaves: Erect,** linear to narrowly lance-shaped, **branched-hairy on both surfaces, fringed with forked hairs. Flowers:** Solitary atop stalks 1–2 cm long; corolla rose pink, **3–4 mm long,** the lobes 2–4 mm long. **Where Found:** Rocky slopes, gravelly ridges, scree and stony tundra; montane to alpine zones; frequent in central AK and southwestern YT, rare in northwestern BC; endemic.

Similar Species: Northern dwarf-primrose (*D. ochotensis*) differs in having **down-curved leaves** with **unbranched hairs only.** It is found on scree slopes and rocky tundra, in lowland (arctic coast) to alpine zones. It is an arctic-alpine, amphiberingian species, locally frequent across northern AK, northern YT and northwestern NT.

Notes: All 3 of these northern perennial dwarf-primroses flower very early; the mass of blooms can completely conceal the leafy cushion. The unwary could mistake them for moss campion (p. 135). • Martin Woodlock Gorman (1853–1926) was a plant collector in western North America.

Cliff Dwarf-primrose • *Douglasia laevigata*

General: Loosely tufted, sometimes forming extensive mats; prostrate to ascending stems beset with leaf rosettes. **Leaves:** Lance-oblong to spoon-shaped, **hairless** except often with short-fringed margins, usually few-toothed.

Flowers: 2–10, short-stalked (2–15 mm), in compact, bracted umbels atop stems 2–7 cm long; **corolla deep pink to rose pink fading to lavender,** 6–7 mm long, lobes 4–5 mm long. **Where Found:** Moist rock outcrops, cliffs, ledges, talus slopes and ridges; lowland to alpine zones; frequent in the southwestern part of the region, rare northward to Haida Gwaii.

Notes: *Laevigata* means "smooth," acknowledging the hairless leaf surfaces.

Snow Dwarf-primrose • *Douglasia nivalis*

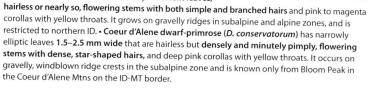

General: Loosely tufted, mat-forming. **Leaves:** Linear to lance-shaped, **1.5–4 mm wide, greyish** with fine, dense, **branched and star-shaped hairs. Flowers: 2–8,** short-stalked (2–30 mm), in compact, bracted umbels atop stems 1–7 cm long; **corolla purplish pink, usually with dark markings near throat,** 6–7 mm long, lobes 3–5 mm long. **Where Found:** Dry, rocky slopes, talus and ridges; montane to alpine zones; locally frequent in north-central WA, especially the Wenatchee Mtns.

Similar Species: Idaho dwarf-primrose (*D. idahoensis*) has **narrow (1–2 mm wide),** distinctly **succulent leaves, hairless or nearly so, flowering stems with both simple and branched hairs** and pink to magenta corollas with yellow throats. It grows on gravelly ridges in subalpine and alpine zones, and is restricted to northern ID. • **Coeur d'Alene dwarf-primrose (*D. conservatorum*)** has narrowly elliptic leaves **1.5–2.5 mm wide** that are hairless but **densely and minutely pimply, flowering stems with dense, star-shaped hairs,** and deep pink corollas with yellow throats. It occurs on gravelly, windblown ridge crests in the subalpine zone and is known only from Bloom Peak in the Coeur d'Alene Mtns on the ID-MT border.

Notes: Snow dwarf-primrose was first collected by David Douglas. Based on this collection, English botanist John Lindley erected the genus in 1827 and named it after Douglas. But Lindley indicated the collecting locality as the BC-Alberta Rockies near Mount Robson and the headwaters of the Columbia River, which is almost certainly an error. The species hasn't been seen in Canada since, if ever.

Rocky Mountain Dwarf-primrose
Douglasia montana

General: Distinguished from other southern dwarf-primroses by having **only 1–2 flowers per stem. Leaves:** Narrowly lance-shaped, hairless except for short-fringed margins. **Where Found:** Rocky slopes, scree, fellfields and stony tundra; montane to alpine zones; frequent in the south-eastern part of the region.

The Genus *Primula* (Primrose)

Primroses are perennial herbs from a single basal rosette of leaves, with ascending to erect stems. The leaves are lance- to wedge-shaped, unlobed, usually hairless and often with a whitish, mealy or floury coating. The flowers are in a bracted umbel atop leafless stems. The corolla is magenta, pink, rose, lilac or white, often with a yellow eye, the tube flaring to 5 often notched lobes, the throat not constricted and without obvious crests. The tubular calyx is also 5-lobed. There are 5 stamens and 1 style. The fruits are cylindric to ellipsoid or globe-shaped capsules.

Some primrose species are heterostylous, with different lengths of styles in flowers of different individuals. Cusick's primrose (p. 307) is "distylous"—that is, there are 2 arrangements of floral parts in populations of the species. The "pin" morph has a long style, stamens located low in the corolla tube and small pollen grains; the "thrum" morph has a short style, stamens located high in the corolla tube and larger pollen grains. Pin morph styles can only be fertilized by thrum morph pollen and vice versa, requiring insect pollinators and ensuring outcrossing.

Primula is from the Latin *primus,* "first," alluding to the primrose habit of blooming early.

Key to *Primula*

1a. Flowers with corolla lobes distinctly notched at tip; capsule ellipsoid-egg-shaped to barrel-shaped or nearly spheric, equalling or shorter than calyx **2**

    2a. Leaves erect, 10–30 cm long, finely blunt-toothed to nearly toothless; plants of U.S. Rocky Mtns
. . . . **P. parryi (p. 307)**

    2b. Leaves spreading, <10 cm long. **3**

        3a. Leaves lance- to spoon-shaped, nearly entire to vaguely blunt-toothed; capsule ellipsoid, about as long as calyx; plants of ID and OR in our region. . . . . **P. cusickiana (p. 307)**

        3b. Leaves wedge-shaped, coarsely blunt-toothed toward tip; capsule nearly spheric, shorter than calyx; plants of AK and coastal BC. . . . . **P. cuneifolia ssp. saxifragifolia (below)**

1b. Flowers with corolla lobes entire to slightly notched; mature capsules broadly cylindric, 2–3 times length of calyx . . . **4**

    4a. Flowers homostylous (styles all about same length); plants usually somewhat white-mealy at least when young; leaves elliptic to wedge-shaped . . . . **P. pumila (p. 307)**

    4b. Flowers heterostylous (styles of 2 distinctly different lengths); plants not white-mealy; leaves narrowly lance-shaped. . . . . **P. tschuktschorum (p. 307)**

Pixie-eyes, Wedgeleaf Primrose
Primula cuneifolia ssp. *saxifragifolia*

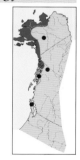

General: Flowering stems short, 2–6 cm tall, from a single rosette of leaves. **Leaves:** Basal, rather thick, hairless, **lance- to wedge-shaped,** with 5–11 coarse, blunt teeth toward tip. **Flowers:** 1–4; corollas deep pink to rose with yellow eye, 1–2.5 cm across, the lobes deeply 2-cleft. **Where Found:** Moist meadows, heathlands and tundra, typically on acidic bedrock; lowland to alpine zones; scattered but locally frequent in the **northwestern coastal mountains;** the species amphiberingian, ssp. *saxifragifolia* primarily northwestern North American.

Notes: The flowering date of pixie-eyes, like that of many alpine plants, is determined largely by the date of snow-melt. This can vary considerably even in relatively small areas. Around one Japanese snow patch, the flowering season of *P. cuneifolia* ssp. *cuneifolia* varied by more than 50 days, though individual blooms lasted fewer than 10 days. These phenological differences were reflected in the genetics of the plant's population.

Parry's Primrose • *Primula parryi*

General: Tall and **cabbagy, rather rank** and **greasy to the touch; flowering stems 15–50 cm tall**, from a single but often clumped rosette of leaves. **Leaves:** Hairless, **broadly lance-shaped**, finely blunt-toothed to toothless, **erect-ascending, 10–30 cm long** (sometimes almost as long as stems). **Flowers:** 5–25; **corolla magenta**

with yellow eye, 1.5–2.5 cm across. **Where Found:** Wet meadows, fens, streambanks, seepage areas, talus in the drip line of large boulders, weeping cirque walls, ledges and fellfields; sub-alpine and alpine zones; frequent in the southeastern part of the region.

Notes: Parry's primrose is the largest and one of the showiest of the native North American primroses. Handsome as it is, it has a distinctive skunky odour.

Cusick's Primrose
Primula cusickiana var. *cusickiana*

General: Flowering stems 3–10 cm tall, from a single rosette of leaves. **Leaves:** Hairless, **spreading, 1–5 cm long, lance- to spoon-shaped, entire or vaguely blunt-toothed. Flowers:** 1–3 (to 8); corolla rose to magenta purple, 1–2 cm across. **Where Found:** Moist meadows, swales in shrublands, rocky slopes and seepage areas; montane to alpine zones; scattered but locally frequent from central ID to northeastern OR and NV; an **intermontane species.**

Notes: The species is named for plant collector William Conklin Cusick (1842–1922).

Arctic Primrose • *Primula pumila*

General: Stocky plants, with a **white-floury coating at least when young;** flowering stems 8–25 (to 40) cm tall, from single or clustered rosettes of leaves. **Leaves: Broadly lance-shaped to elliptic,** somewhat fleshy, hairless, entire to weakly toothed. **Flowers:** 3–15, homostylous; **corolla rose magenta with whitish eye, 1–2 cm across,** the lobes usually rounded at tip. **Where Found:** Wet meadows, tundra, streambanks, seepage areas, snowbeds and solifluction terraces; lowland to alpine zones; scattered but locally frequent in the far north-western part of the region; arctic-alpine, amphiberingian.

Similar Species: Chukchi primrose (*P. tschuktschorum*) is distinguished from its close relative arctic primrose by its **heterostylous flowers, linear-lance-shaped leaves** and the **lack of a white-floury coating.** It is an arctic-alpine, amphiberingian species found on wet streambanks, frost boils and late snowbeds in tundra, in western AK (Bering Strait region).

Notes: Arctic primrose is also known as *Primula eximia* and *P. tschuktschorum* in part. • It is homostylous (the styles are about the same length in all plants, and mature stigmas and anthers are close together), whereas Chukchi primrose is distylous.

DISJUNCT OCCURRENCES

The isolated, small occurrence of pixie-eyes on a mountaintop on Vancouver Island is 1500 km away from the next closest occurrence of this species and nearly twice as far from its main distribution in the north.

Disjunctions—occurrences that are far removed from main distributions—have always fascinated naturalists and early explorers, including such renowned botanists as Charles Darwin, Adolf Engler, Asa Gray and Joseph Dalton Hooker. Disjunctions have been linked to past geologic events, floras as relics of bygone eras and plant migrations.

Often these outlier occurrences either have climatic similarities or occur on similar substrates to those of the main distribution. For example, western disjunct populations of curly sedge occur along the leeward flanks of the Coast Mountains on isolated areas of limestone or other calcium-rich bedrock, the same substrates as in its primary range in the Rockies.

Curiously, 2 other members of the primrose family, rock-jasmine and cliff dwarf-primrose, also show disjunctions, the former between high latitudes and the Rockies and the latter among the Olympic Mountains, Vancouver Island and Haida Gwaii (Queen Charlotte Islands). Other alpine examples involve longstem sandwort, rock-dwelling sedge, three-forked mugwort, nodding campion, pink campion, whitish gentian, fellfield springbeauty and arctic wood-rush, to name just a few.

Another pattern of disjunctions has species present in the north (northern BC northward), on the Beartooth Plateau (on the Montana-Wyoming border) and in northern Colorado, with extensive areas of suitable but unoccupied habitat in between. Species that display this distribution include icegrass, Iceland koenigia, alpine avens, yellow marsh saxifrage, sooty sedge, northern alpine-sedge and two-flowered rush. Perhaps these arctic-alpine species were much more widespread in western North America during the Pleistocene, but then became locally extinct in many areas as climate warmed during the Holocene.

cliff dwarf-primrose

Phlox Family (Polemoniaceae)

Our phlox family species are annual, biennial or perennial herbs with opposite or alternate, entire to pinnately compound or variously divided leaves. The radially symmetric flowers are solitary or in open to compact clusters, with 5 partially fused petals (collectively the corolla) and 5 sepals (collectively the calyx), united toward the base. The corollas are trumpet-, bell- or phlox-shaped (narrowly tubular below, abruptly flaring above to 5 lobes). The 5 stamens are attached to the corolla tube, usually not sticking out much beyond the corolla. The superior ovary (attached to the top of the flower stalk, above the attachment of other flower parts) has 1 style and 3 stigmas. The fruits are egg-shaped to ellipsoid, 3-chambered capsules that open along the midline of each chamber wall.

Key to the Genera of Polemoniaceae

1a. Leaves opposite, sometimes the uppermost alternate **2**
   2a. Leaves entire or nearly so . . . . ***Phlox*** (pp. 312–314)
   2b. Leaves palmately 5–9-cleft nearly to the base. . . . . ***Linanthus nuttallii*** (p. 316)
1b. Leaves alternate, sometimes the lowermost opposite. **3**
   3a. Calyx tubes uniformly textured, not ruptured by the developing capsules **4**
      4a. Leaves mostly basal (ours), pinnately compound with definite leaflets . . . . ***Polemonium*** (pp. 309–311)
      4b. Leaves mostly along the stem, entire or few-lobed but without definite leaflets . . . . . . ***Collomia*** (p. 315)
   3b. Calyx tubes with green ribs separated by transparent tissue, usually ruptured by the developing capsules. **5**
      5a. Perennials or biennials, not prickly; calyx lobes all about the same size . . . . ***Ipomopsis*** (p. 315)
      5b. Prickly annual; calyx lobes unequal in size. . . . . ***Navarretia divaricata*** (p. 316)

The Genus *Polemonium* (Jacob's-ladder, Sky Pilot)

Ours are perennial herbs from a rhizome or a taproot surmounted by a branched stem-base, with alternate, pinnately compound leaves, the leaflets entire or deeply 2–5-cleft. The plants are generally glandular-hairy, at least in the flower cluster, and often have a skunky smell. The showy flowers are mostly blue, purple or occasionally white, in clusters atop stems or from the leaf axils. The corolla is broadly bell-shaped to funnel-shaped. The calyx is green throughout, enlarging in fruit and not ruptured by the ripening capsule. The stamens are inserted equally on the corolla tube. Each capsule chamber has 1–10 black or brown, angled or winged seeds that sometimes become sticky when moistened.

sky pilot

Key to *Polemonium*

1a. Leaflets numerous and 2–5-cleft, appearing whorled . . . . ***P. viscosum*** (p. 310)
1b. Leaflets undivided, appearing as pairs. **2**
   2a. Corollas funnel-shaped, longer than wide; plants strongly glandular and skunky . . . . ***P. elegans*** (p. 310)
   2b. Corollas bell-shaped to nearly saucer-shaped, wider than long; if glandular, then only in the flower cluster **3**
      3a. Stems several from a branched stem-base atop a taproot; flowers 7–13 mm long. . . . ***P. pulcherrimum*** (p. 311)
      3b. Stems solitary from a short, unbranched, horizontal rhizome; flowers 15–20 mm long **4**
         4a. Stems 8–30 cm tall; leaflets hairy (at least when young); petals with rounded tips. . . . ***P. boreale*** (p. 311)
         4b. Stems 20–60 cm tall; leaflets mostly hairless; petals tapering to somewhat pointed tips. . . . .
         . . . . ***P. caeruleum*** (p. 311)

Sky Pilot, Skunk Jacob's-ladder, Sticky Jacob's-ladder • *Polemonium viscosum*

General: Low, **strongly glandular-hairy, skunky,** from a stout taproot and branching stem-base; **stems single to several, erect,** 10–30 cm tall. **Leaves:** Mostly near the base, to 15 cm long including short stalks; leaflets numerous, crowded, 2–6 mm long, **deeply cleft** into 2–5 elliptic to spoon-shaped segments, **appearing whorled. Flowers:** In **dense, head-like clusters** atop stems; **corolla blue-purple, funnel-shaped,** 1.5–3 cm long, the rounded lobes shorter than the tube; stamens shorter than to sometimes as long as corolla, anthers orange. **Where Found:** Rocky ridges, talus, scree, cliffs, ledges and fellfields; subalpine and alpine zones; locally frequent in the southern ⅓ of the region; cordilleran.

Notes: Sky pilot is also known as *Polemonium confertum.* • In the Colorado alplands, sky pilot is pollinated primarily by flies at timberline and by bumblebees at higher elevations. Skunky-smelling flowers, more attractive to flies, set more seed at lower elevations, whereas sweet-smelling flowers, more attractive to bees, set more seed at higher elevations. Two flower characteristics, size and smell, are related: sweet-smelling flowers have wider corolla lobes, longer corolla tubes and longer sepals. Perhaps not surprisingly, flower size and height both increase with elevation. What's more, nectar-thieving ants prefer flowers with larger, broadly flared corollas and cause more damage and reduce seed production more in showier flowers than in narrower forms, to some extent counteracting the positive selection pressure from bumblebee pollinators, who also prefer showier, more sugary flowers.

Elegant Sky Pilot, Elegant Jacob's-ladder • *Polemonium elegans*

General: Low, glandular-hairy, **skunky;** stems clustered, **to 15 cm tall. Leaves:** Mostly basal, the **crowded leaflets undivided. Flowers:** In compact clusters; corolla funnel-shaped, **blue but paler and shorter (1.2–1.5 cm)** than that of *P. viscosum;* stamens protrude slightly beyond corolla tube. **Where Found:** Cliffs, crevices and ledges, talus and scree slopes; subalpine and alpine zones; infrequent in the southwestern ¼ of the region, mostly in the Coast-Cascade Mtns.

Notes: Sky pilots are stinky plants, but their flowers can be sweet smelling. • "Sky pilot" is military slang for a chaplain. Also, in anti-war circles, it's a favourite song by Eric Burdon and the Animals. We botanists surmise that the name was given to these stunning plants because they mark skyways along high ridges. • The origin of *Polemonium* is not clear. Some say the genus is named for Polemon of Cappadocia, a Greek philosopher and the king of Pontus. Others argue that it is derived from the Greek *polemos,* meaning "war" or "strife," because the discovery of its supposed medicinal properties is reported to have caused a war between 2 kings. Or perhaps *polemos* refers to the lance-shaped leaflets, thought to resemble spearheads. It has also been reported that the plant was originally called *machebate* or *makebate* because, if placed under the bed of a married couple, it would cause them to quarrel (engage in polemics).

Showy Jacob's-ladder • *Polemonium pulcherrimum* var. *pulcherrimum*

General: Plants glandular-hairy especially in flower cluster; **stems several** from a branched stem-base atop a taproot, clustered, **loosely erect to sprawling,** 5–20 (to 30) cm tall. **Leaves:** Mostly near the base, the leaflets egg-shaped to circular. **Flowers:** In compact clusters atop stems; **corolla blue (rarely white) with yellow centre, bowl-shaped, 7–13 mm long,** 2–3.5 cm across, the **rounded lobes** equalling to nearly twice as long as the tube. **Where Found:** Dry to mesic, gravelly-sandy terraces, roadsides, open forests, meadows, rocky slopes and ridges; montane to alpine zones; frequent in most of the region.

Similar-flowered Species: Although it's in the flax (Linaceae) not the phlox family, **wild blue flax** (*Linum lewisii*; *L. perenne* var. *lewisii*) also has **blue, saucer-shaped flowers 2–4 cm across;** however,

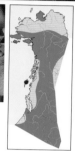

the **petals are not fused at the base** and the **leaves are simple, linear** and alternate along the 20–50 cm tall stems. It is found on dry, rocky or grassy slopes and ridges, in montane to alpine zones. Wild blue flax is widespread but infrequent at high elevations mostly in the southern ½ of the region. • **Alpine Lewis' flax** (*L. lewisii* var. *alpicola*), a smaller, mostly alpine variety with flowers 1.5–2 cm across, occurs from central ID to CA, NV and UT.

wild blue flax

Notes: The name Jacob's-ladder refers to the ladder-like arrangement of the leaflets beneath the blue flowers; the name also alludes to Jacob of religious legends, who dreamed of a ladder to heaven with angels ascending and descending.

Tall Jacob's-ladder *Polemonium caeruleum*

General: Stem single, erect from a curved base and **rhizome,** glandular-hairy especially above, 20–60 cm tall. **Leaves: Hairless** or nearly so, the leaflets lance-shaped to elliptic, **pointy-tipped. Flowers:** Short-stalked in head-like or somewhat elongated clusters atop stem or in upper leaf axils; **corolla blue, lavender or purple, rarely white, bell-shaped, 1.5–2 cm long,** the **pointed lobes** twice as long as the tube. **Where Found:** Wet to moist thickets, heathlands, meadows and streambanks; lowland (arctic coast) to alpine zones; frequent in the northern ½ of the region; arctic-alpine, species complex circumpolar.

Similar Species: Northern Jacob's-ladder (*P. boreale*) is another northern species but is **smaller (8–30 cm tall),** with **hairy leaflets** and **rounded corolla lobes.** It is found in mesic to dry meadows

and on scree slopes, rocky ridges and sandy tundra, in lowland (arctic coast) to alpine zones. It is an arctic-alpine, interruptedly circumpolar species infrequent in the northern ½ of the region, AK, YT and western NT south through inland BC to about 53° N.

Notes: Tall Jacob's-ladder is also known as *Polemonium acutiflorum*.

northern Jacob's-ladder

The Genus *Phlox* (Phlox)

Our phloxes are low, tufted, taprooted, perennial herbs, often somewhat woody at the base, with opposite (or upper-most alternate), undivided, often narrow and needle-like leaves. The showy flowers are pink, white or blue, and are solitary or in few-flowered clusters atop the stems. The corolla is a slender tube below, spreading abruptly above to horizontal lobes. The calyx has wax-papery intervals between green ribs and is ruptured by the developing capsule. The stamens are inserted unequally on the corolla tube; the ovary has 1 style with 3 stigmas. The seeds are few (1–4) per chamber and do not become sticky when moistened.

Key to *Phlox*

1a. Flowers on stalks to 5 mm long; northern mountains of AK, YT and NT. . . . . *P. alaskensis* (p. 313)
1b. Flowers unstalked or on very short stalks; plants mostly in southern ⅓ of the region 2
   2a. Styles 1–5 mm long; leaves firm, 0.5–1.5 mm wide 3
      3a. Leaves linear, generally about 0.5 mm wide and 4–10 mm long, cobwebby-hairy, firmly sharp-pointed
      . . . . *P. hoodii* (p. 314)
      3b. Leaves narrowly lance-shaped, 1–1.5 mm wide near midleaf, hairy or glandular-hairy to hairless but not cobwebby, pointy-tipped but not prickly 4
         4a. Styles 1–2 mm long; Cascade Mtns. . . . . *P. hendersonii* (p. 314)
         4b. Styles 2–5 mm long; range east of the Cascades 5
            5a. Calyx usually glandular-hairy. . . . . *P. pulvinata* (p. 314)
            5b. Calyx hairless. . . . . *P. austromontana* (p. 313)
   2b. Styles mostly >5 mm long; leaves firm or not, 1–5 mm wide. 6
      6a. Leaves 10–20 mm long, 2–5 mm wide; styles 6–12 mm long . . . . *P. variabilis* (p. 314)
      6b. Leaves 2–12 mm long, 1–2.5 mm wide; styles 4–10 mm long 7
         7a. Styles 5–8 mm long; leaves firm. 8
            8a. Leaves mostly 2–5 mm long and 1–2.5 mm wide, margins thickened and whitish, fringed toward the base. . . . . *P. albomarginata* (p. 314)
            8b. Main leaves 12–30 mm long and 1–2 mm wide, finely stubbled but otherwise hairless, margins not thickened or whitish. . . . . *P. multiflora* (p. 313)
         7b. Styles 4–10 mm long; leaves soft, 5–20 mm long, 1–2 mm wide, hairless except usually with cobwebby-fringed margins toward the base . . . . *P. diffusa* (p. 313)

spreading phlox

Alaska Phlox • *Phlox alaskensis*

General: Cushion- or mat-forming; stems much-branched. **Leaves:** Crowded, linear to lance-shaped, flattened, sharp-tipped, 8–22 mm long, 1–2.5 mm wide, **glandular-hairy,** fringed with long hairs. **Flowers:** Single (sometimes 2–3) at branch ends, on **stalks to 5 mm long,** sticky-hairy; **corolla pink or whitish to lilac, 2–3 cm across,** the tube 6–12 mm long; calyx sticky-hairy; about as long as corolla tube. **Where Found:** Calcium-rich rock outcrops, dry, rocky slopes and tundra; lowland to alpine zones; frequent in AK, YT and northwestern NT **north of 64° N;** endemic.

Notes: Alaska phlox is also known as *Phlox sibirica*, *P. sibirica* ssp. *alaskensis* and *P. richardsonii* ssp. *alaskensis*. • *Phlox* is Greek for "flame"; the flowers of many species in this genus burn brightly.

Spreading Phlox • *Phlox diffusa*

General: Stems usually mat-forming, 5–10 cm tall. **Leaves:** Linear, pointy-tipped but not spiny, fused at the base in pairs, hairless except margins cobwebby-fringed toward the base, **5–20 mm long, 1–2 mm wide. Flowers:** Single at leafy branch tips, **stalkless; corolla pink to lavender or whitish, 1–2 cm across,** the tube 9–17 mm long, less than 2 times as long as the calyx; calyx long-woolly-hairy or cobwebby-hairy, the teeth thickened; **styles 4–10 mm long. Where Found:** Mesic to dry, rocky or gravelly slopes and ridges, rock outcrops in open forests; montane to alpine zones; frequent in the southwestern part of the region.

Similar Species: Great Basin phlox or desert phlox (*P. austro-montana*) is sort of an intermontane equivalent of the largely Cascadian spreading phlox , but has **white or (less often) bluish or pink flowers** with **shorter styles 2–5 mm long.** It is locally frequent in central and northeastern OR and central ID to CA, NV, UT and AZ. • **Rocky Mountain phlox** or many-flowered phlox (*P. multiflora*) has **very finely stubbled,** typically **longer (12–30 mm) leaves** and **white (occasionally bluish or pinkish) flowers.** It grows on rocky slopes and dry meadows, in subalpine and alpine zones, and is frequent in southwestern MT and adjacent ID to NV, UT and NM.

White-edged Phlox • *Phlox albomarginata*

General: Cushion-forming. **Leaves:** Awl-shaped, **short**, mostly 2–5 mm long and 1–2.5 mm wide, firm, margins thickened and whitish. **Flowers:** Single; **corolla pink or purplish to white,** 1.3–2 cm across; styles 5–8 mm long. **Where found:** Open, rocky slopes and ridges; montane to alpine zones; locally frequent in southwestern MT and adjacent ID.

Notes: Doctor Phlox is a Denobulan character in the television series *Star Trek: Enterprise*. Perhaps in an elliptic nod to the generally outcrossing nature of *Phlox* species, Dr. Phlox has 3 wives, each of whom has 2 other husbands.

Cushion Phlox • *Phlox pulvinata*

General: Cushion- or mat-forming. **Leaves:** Crowded, narrowly lance-shaped, **5–12 mm long, about 0.5 mm wide,** firm, margins slightly thickened. **Flowers:** Single (usually), stalkless or short-stalked; **corolla white or light blue,** 1–1.5 cm across, the tube 9–13 mm long, about 2 times as long as the calyx; calyx usually glandular-hairy, sometimes smooth, not thickened; **styles 2–5 mm long. Where Found:** Fellfields, windswept ridges and rocky slopes; montane to alpine zones; frequent in the southeastern part of the region.

Similar Species: Henderson's phlox (*P. hendersonii*) has nearly linear leaves, often in **groups of 3 and very glandular-hairy,** and **shorter (1–2 mm) styles.** It occurs in similar habitats, rather infrequently in the Olympic Mtns and Cascades from central WA to northern OR. • Hood's phlox (*P. hoodii*) forms **tight cushions** and has **narrowly linear** (about 0.5 mm wide), firm, almost spiny, cobwebby leaves and white to lavender or pinkish flowers 1–1.5 cm across. It is found typically at low to moderate elevations but also fairly frequently occurs on rocky or grassy slopes and exposed ridges, in subalpine and alpine zones, in eastern AK and southwestern YT, then again in southwestern AB and east of the Cascades in WA, OR, ID, MT, WY and UT. • Foothills phlox (*P. variabilis*, *P. alyssifolia*) has prostrate stems; **linear-oblong leaves (10–20 mm long, 2–5 mm wide)** with hard, **white margins** and **white to blue flowers** 1.5–2.5 cm across. It grows on dry, rocky, gravelly or grassy slopes, in montane to alpine zones, and is infrequent on the eastern slope of the Rockies, southwestern AB to CO and east to SK and SD.

Notes: Cushion phlox is also known as *Phlox caespitosa* in part.

Henderson's phlox   Hood's phlox

Alpine Mountain-trumpet, Alpine Collomia • *Collomia debilis* vars. *debilis* and *ipomaea*

General: Prostrate perennial from a taproot, **forming mats** to 30 cm across; stems numerous, slender, simple or branched, **sprawling,** 10–30 cm long, the tips ascending.

Leaves: Alternate, tending to be **crowded toward stem tips,** oval to spoon-shaped, **entire to often 3–5-lobed.**

Flowers: Several in leafy-bracted clusters at ends of stems; **corolla blue or lavender to rose pink, whitish or cream, trumpet-shaped, to 2 cm across,** 1.5–3.5 cm long, **tube much longer than flaring lobes;** stamens protruding slightly.

Fruits: Capsules 3-chambered; seeds 1 per chamber, **sticky when moistened.**

Where Found: Talus and scree slopes; subalpine and alpine zones; infrequent in the southern ¼ of the region.

Similar Species: Talus collomia (*C. larsenii,* *C. debilis* var. *larsenii*) has primary leaves deeply divided into 3–7 lobes and purplish flowers. It grows on high, rocky slopes in the Olympic Mtns and Cascades from WA to northern CA.

Notes: *Collomia* is from the Greek *kŏlla,* "glue," because the seeds are mucilaginous when wet; *debilis* means "weak" or "feeble," in reference to the sprawling stems.

talus collomia

Spike Fairy-trumpet • *Ipomopsis spicata* var. *orchidacea*

General: Cobwebby or thinly woolly perennial from a taproot; stems erect, **5–10 cm tall.**

Leaves: Basal leaves tufted, **pinnately 5-cleft; stem leaves alternate,** cleft or upper ones entire.

Flowers: Numerous in **dense, bracted, head-like to spike-like clusters** atop stems; **corolla white, phlox-like, to 1 cm across,** 5–9 mm long, **tube longer than flaring lobes;** stamens attached to and protruding slightly from tube.

Fruits: Capsules 3-chambered; seeds 1–2 per chamber, **sticky when moistened.**

Where Found: Dry, rocky slopes, ridges and meadows; subalpine and alpine zones; infrequent in the southeastern part of the region.

Similar Species: Ballhead fairy-trumpet (*I. congesta,* Gilia congesta) is low and spreading at high elevations and has **round balls of smaller white flowers to 5 mm across and 3–4 mm long.** It occurs on dry, rocky slopes, in montane to alpine zones, and is infrequent in southern and eastern OR to CA, east to the Rockies of MT, WY and CO. Our high-elevation forms are mostly vars. *montana* and *viridis.* • **Slendertube skyrocket (*I. tenuituba,* Gilia aggregata var. *tenuituba*)** has **really long (25–45 mm), white to pale pink or lavender flowers.** It grows on open, rocky or gravelly slopes and in shrublands, glades and meadows, in upper montane to alpine zones. Slendertube skyrocket is locally frequent in the southern fringe of the region, northeastern OR, southern ID and WY, and more frequent south to CA, CO, AZ and NM.

Notes: Spike fairy-trumpet is also known as *Gilia spicata* var. *orchidacea.*

Nuttall's Flaxflower
Linanthus nuttallii

General: Perennial from a taproot and branched, woody stem-base, fragrant (not skunky); stems numerous, simple or branched, **erect,** hairy at least above, **10–30 cm tall.**

Leaves: Opposite, palmately divided into 5–9 linear, bristle-tipped segments, appearing whorled.

Flowers: In compact clusters atop stems; **corolla white or cream, about 1 cm across, trumpet-shaped, 6–9 mm long,** the throat yellow, the hairy tube longer than the lobes; stamens equally inserted on flaring mouth of trumpet, included or protruding slightly.

Fruits: Capsules 3-chambered, **rupturing calyx when mature;** seeds 1 (to 4) per chamber, **not becoming sticky when moistened.**

Where Found: Open, rocky slopes, talus and forest openings; montane (typically) to lower alpine zones; infrequent in the southern ¼ of the region.

Related Species: Prickly miniphlox (*Navarretia divaricata*) is a **tiny annual** that occasionally reaches the alpine. The stems are **spreading** and branched, with **alternate leaves pinnately divided into**

very narrow, bristle-tipped segments. The flowers are in bracted clusters and **white to pale pink or lavender, 3.5–5 mm long,** with 2–3 calyx lobes longer than the others. It grows on dry, open, rocky or gravelly sites, often on volcanic slopes, in montane to alpine zones, and is frequent in the southern inland ¼ of the region, southern WA to central ID and northwestern MT, south through eastern OR to CA.

Notes: Nuttall's flaxflower is also known as *Linanthastrum nuttallii.* • *Linanthus* comes from the Greek *linon,* "flax," and *anthos,* "flower," hence flax-flower. • The species is named for Thomas Nuttall (1786–1859), a Philadelphia botanical collector and author, and a noted ornithologist.

THOMAS NUTTALL

"Privations to [the naturalist] are cheaply purchased, if he may but roam over the wild domain of primeval nature … For thousands of miles my chief converse has been in the wilderness with the spontaneous productions of Nature and the study of these objects and their contemplation has been to me a source of constant delight."

–Thomas Nuttall, from *North American Sylva: Trees not described by F.A. Michaux* (1841)

prickly miniphlox

Gentian Family (Gentianaceae)

Our gentians are annual, biennial or perennial herbs, usually hairless, with simple, entire, opposite or whorled leaves. The often-showy flowers are radially symmetric, with 4–5 fused petals (collectively the corolla) and 4–5 sepals, also often fused (collectively the calyx). The corollas are tubular or funnel-, saucer- or star-shaped; there are as many stamens as corolla lobes. The superior ovary (attached to the top of the flower stalk, above the attachment of other flower parts) is 1-chambered, the style 1 or none and the stigma single or 2-lobed. The fruits are capsules that split down seams into 2 segments, and the numerous seeds are often winged.

Plants in the gentian family are well known for their pharmacological properties. They are generally bitter because of the presence of certain glycosides and have long been used (in the form of "medicinal bitters") for digestive ailments. They also contain a host of other interesting chemicals (e.g., amarogentin, bellidifolin, gentianine and swerchirin) reported to be useful for everything from treating amoebic infections to regulating blood sugar levels.

Key to the Genera of Gentianaceae

1a. Flowers tubular to funnel- or bell-shaped; corolla lobes shorter than tube **2**

    2a. Corolla lobes fringed or irregularly cut or toothed on margins; petals and sepals 4 . . ***Gentianopsis*** **(p. 321)**

    2b. Corolla lobes not fringed or raggedy on margins; petals and sepals 4–5. . . . . **3**

        3a. Corolla pleated, with folds between lobes. . . . . ***Gentiana*** **(pp. 318–321)**

        3b. Corolla not pleated, without folds between lobes . . . . ***Gentianella*** **(p. 322)**

1b. Flowers star-shaped, opening flat; corolla lobes about twice as long as tube **4**

    4a. Leaves opposite; petals 5, bluish purple; style inconspicuous, scarcely 1 mm long . . . . ***Swertia*** **(p. 323)**

    4b. Leaves whorled; petals 4, green or white; style evident, at least 2 mm long. . . . . ***Frasera*** **(p. 323)**

WHY ARE THERE MORE BLUE FLOWERS ABOVE TIMBERLINE THAN BELOW?

Biologists think that flower colour in plants is largely a co-evolutionary response to pollinator preferences. If you can't get your pollen transferred to someone else's stigma, and vice versa, the long-term prospects for your genome are poor. (This also applies to botanists.) At high, open elevations, there are lots of insect pollinators, many of them bees, who see best at the blue and ultraviolet end of spectrum and are sensitive to colour contrasts. They are also attracted to sweet smells and large, deep flowers or flower clusters. In response to this selection pressure, evolution has provided many large, aromatic, blue or purple blooms, often with darker or ultraviolet nectar guides.

Now, bees are not the only insect pollinators of alpine flowers. Flies generally prefer white or yellow, bowl-shaped flowers with easily accessible nectar and pollen, such as buttercups and mountain-avens. Butterflies favour brightly coloured but not necessarily blue flowers that provide them with a landing platform, so they can probe for nectar while alight, not aloft. Moss campion, arnicas and phloxes are all non-blue, butterfly-friendly flowers; Jacob's-ladders and asters are both blue and butterfly-friendly.

Some flowers are structurally complex and restrict access to nectar or pollen rewards to all but the largest, strongest or longest-tongued insects, or those with just the right frequency of wing vibrations—often bumblebees. Some of these bee flowers are blue (gentians, lupines and larkspurs), some purple (penstemons and locoweeds), some pink (alpine clovers and woolly lousewort) and others yellow (mountain monkey-flower and yellow paintbrushes). Some alpine flowers are strikingly blue but not strongly specialized for bee pollination, for example, star gentian, speedwells, northern geranium, alpine forget-me-not and harebells.

arctic lupine
explorer's gentian

Olympic harebell

northern Jacob's-ladder

The Genus *Gentiana* (Gentian)

Our high-elevation gentians (i.e., *Gentiana* in the strict sense) are mostly hairless perennials from rhizomes or thick, fleshy roots, except for 2 annual/biennial species from taproots. The stems are usually erect to ascending, sometimes prostrate, and usually unbranched. The leaves are all on the stem or both at the base and opposite along the stem. The flowers can be large or small, solitary or several to many in flat-topped to elongate clusters. The corolla is blue to purplish, greenish or yellowish to white, tubular to funnel-shaped, flaring to 5 (sometimes 4) lobes and with folds or pleats in the throat between the lobes. The calyx is mostly 4–5-toothed (2-lobed in one species), the 4–5 stamens are attached to the base of the corolla tube, the single style is short and stout, and there are 2 stigmas.

Gentiana includes some of our showiest, most resplendent alpines, which typically bloom late and are among the last flowers of the season in the high country. Gentians (in the broad sense, including *Gentiana*, *Gentianella* and *Gentianopsis*) tend to open their flowers fully only in bright sunshine, closing up in cloudy conditions. They are named for King Gentius of Illyria (an ancient country east of the Adriatic Sea), who in the 2nd century BC discovered the medicinal properties of the European yellow gentian.

Key to *Gentiana*

1a. Annuals or biennials from slender taproots; stems prostrate to ascending or erect; flowers 1 to several **2**

    2a. Stems repeatedly branched above the base; flowers bright white with purplish markings; coastal mountains . . . . **G. douglasiana** (p. 319)

    2b. Stems simple or few-branched at the base; flowers blue or bluish white; interior mountains **3**

        3a. Stem leaves spreading, not distinctly white-margined; corolla lobes blue on both sides . . . . **G. prostrata** (p. 319)

        3b. Upper stem leaves ascending, conspicuously white-margined; corolla lobes whitish to pale blue, often dark blue on the outside . . . . **G. fremontii** (p. 319)

1b. Perennials from rhizomes or stem-bases; stems upright or ascending; flowers usually several, sometimes solitary **4**

    4a. Flowers whitish or cream to yellowish green with purple stripes or flecks, 3.5–5 cm long; leaves linear to narrowly lance-shaped. . . . . **G. algida** (p. 319)

    4b. Flowers purple, blue or blue-green, often with green stripes or flecks, if yellowish, then <3 cm long; leaves lance- to egg-shaped **5**

        5a. Stems <15 cm tall/long; stem leaves 0.5–1 cm long; flowers 1–2 cm long, inky blue to blue-green, occasionally yellowish . . . . **G. glauca** (p. 320)

        5b. Stems 10–35 cm tall/long; stem leaves 1–7 cm long; flowers 1.5–4.5 cm long, deep blue **6**

            6a. Leaves lance-elliptic; flowers several per stem in upper leaf axils; stems finely hairy below nodes . . . . **G. affinis** (p. 320)

            6b. Leaves egg-shaped; flowers mostly 1 per stem and terminal; stems hairless **7**

                7a. Calyx always 2-parted, the segments with 2–3 narrow teeth at the tip; flowers broadly funnel- to bell-shaped; coastal mountains. . . . . **G. platypetala** (p. 321)

                7b. Calyx variably 2–5-parted, if 2-parted, then the segments lacking teeth; flowers narrowly funnel-shaped; interior mountains . . . . **G. calycosa** (p. 320)

G. calycosa

G. douglasiana

G. glauca

G. platypetala

G. prostrata

Gentianella propinqua

Gentianella tenella

Pygmy Gentian • *Gentiana prostrata*

General: **Annual or biennial** from a slender taproot; stems several, **prostrate to ascending,** usually branched from the base, 2–10 (to 15) cm long. **Leaves:** Basal leaves spoon-shaped; stem leaves egg-shaped to oblong, **spreading,** sheathing stem at the base, **2–7 mm long, light green. Flowers:** Solitary and short-stalked at branch tips; **corolla clear blue,** narrowly funnel-shaped, **0.7–2 cm long,** with **triangular pleats** between the 5 (sometimes 4) lobes; calyx 4–5-toothed. **Where Found:** Moist meadows, seepage sites, streambanks, animal trails, grassy ridges, heathlands and tundra; subalpine and alpine zones; widespread but scattered and locally frequent in most of the interior part of our region; arctic-alpine, amphiberingian.

Similar Species: Moss gentian (*G. fremontii*; *G. humilis*) is **spreading to erect,** with **white-margined leaves,** the **upper leaves narrowly lance-shaped and strongly ascending.** The **whitish to pale blue corolla lobes** are often dark blue on the outside. It grows in wet meadows, fens and moist, sandy flats, in montane to alpine zones, and is infrequent from CA to CO, north to southwestern AB and south-central SK.

Other Species: Swamp gentian (*G. douglasiana*) is a **white-flowered annual** of bogs, fens, swamps, bog forests and wet meadows, frequent **along the coast** from southern AK to WA. It is a Pacific maritime endemic found in lowland to alpine zones but mostly at low to medium elevations, occasionally attaining summits in hypermaritime mountains.

Notes: The flowers of pygmy gentian open only in bright sunshine and *quickly* close if shaded (just pass your hand over them) or touched.

Whitish Gentian, Arctic Gentian *Gentiana algida*

General: Tufted perennial with several erect to ascending, yellowish green or purplish stems 8–20 cm tall. **Leaves:** Long (3–12 cm), **narrow (linear to lance-oblong),** yellowish green. **Flowers:** Solitary or several; **corolla white or cream to yellowish green,** striped and/or mottled with purple, **3.5–5 cm long,** strongly pleated between the 5 short-flaring lobes; calyx green with purplish blotches, usually ½ as long as corolla. **Where Found:** Moist to wet meadows, seeps, heathlands, tundra and fellfields; subalpine and alpine zones; locally frequent in AK and YT, disjunct and occasional in MT, WY and CO; amphiberingian.

Notes: Whitish gentian is also known as *Gentiana frigida* and *G. romanzovii*. • In a study in the Wyoming Rockies, whitish gentian closed its flowers before thunderstorms, apparently to prevent rain from washing away its pollen. The corolla mouth narrowed about 10% per minute in advance of storms in response to declining air temperature.

Inky-blue Gentian, Glaucous Gentian
Gentiana glauca

General: Perennial from a slender rhizome; stems erect, solitary, unbranched, 4–15 cm tall, yellow-green. **Leaves:** Mostly basal in a small rosette, elliptic to oval, **somewhat fleshy,** 1–2 cm long; stem leaves in 2–4 pairs, **5–10 mm long. Flowers:** Few to several in erect, flat-topped clusters atop stems; **corolla deep blue, blue-green or occasionally yellowish,** tubular, 1–2 cm long, with pale pleats between the 5 short lobes. **Where found:** Moist to mesic meadows, heathlands and tundra; subalpine and alpine zones; frequent in most of the northern, mostly inland ¾ of the region; arctic-alpine, amphiberingian.

Notes: The typical inky, greenish blue colour of the flowers is distinctive and striking. • The density of inky-blue gentian rosettes declined by 44% between 1989 and 2002 at sample sites in Glacier National Park, Montana. During this period, mean annual and growing season temperatures were 0.4°C and 0.6°C, respectively, higher than the preceding four decades. It's predicted that climate change will cause the extirpation of alpine plants at the southern edges and lower limits of their ranges. We might also project that populations of native alpine species, given time, will migrate northward and higher in elevation—but chances are they won't because the climate is changing too fast.

Explorer's Gentian, Mountain Bog Gentian • *Gentiana calycosa*

General: Rather shiny, **hairless** perennial from thick, fleshy roots; stems erect to bent at the base, usually several and clumped, unbranched, **10–35 cm tall. Leaves:** Crowded along stem in 7–9 pairs, **broadly egg-shaped,** 1–3 cm long. **Flowers:** Erect, **solitary or occasionally 3** atop stems; **corolla deep blue,** sometimes streaked or mottled with green or yellow, speckled greenish yellow inside, tubular-funnel-shaped, **2–4 cm long,** with **frilly pleats** between the 5 spreading lobes. **Fruits: Seeds not winged. Where Found:** Wet to moist meadows, fens, streambanks and fellfields; subalpine and alpine zones; frequent in the southern ¼ of the region; cordilleran.

Similar Species: Rocky Mountain pleated gentian or prairie gentian (**G. affinis; G. parryi**) has **narrower, lance-shaped leaves,** stems that are **finely hairy** in lines below nodes, usually **2–5 flowers** and **wing-margined seeds.** It is a widespread, very variable species in the southern ¼ of the region, mostly at low to moderate elevations, but occurs occasionally in timberline meadows and on rocky ridges in the lower alpine zone, in south-central and south-eastern BC to southwestern AB, south in the eastside Cascades and Rockies to CA and AZ.

Notes: Explorer's gentian has also been known as *Gentiana cusickii, G. gormani, G. idahoensis, G. myrsinites* and *G. saxicola.* • This is a big, dazzlingly beautiful gentian.

Broad-petalled Gentian
Gentiana platypetala

General: Perennial from a short, thick rhizome; stems erect to ascending, usually several and clumped, unbranched, **10–35 cm tall. Leaves:** Basal leaves few, small; stem leaves crowded in 6–9 pairs, **egg-shaped to lance-elliptic,** 1.5–3 cm long, **becoming larger upward. Flowers:** Erect, **solitary; corolla bright blue,** green-speckled, broadly funnel-shaped, **2.5–4 cm long, with small pleats** between the roundish, spreading lobes; **calyx 2-lipped,** 1 lip with 2 teeth, the other with 3 teeth. **Where Found:** Moist, grassy meadows, lake-shores, grassy ridges, weathered rock outcrops and talus

slopes; subalpine and alpine zones, sometimes descending to low elevations on the exposed outer coast; frequent in the insular mountains, southern AK to northern Van. I., rare on the adjacent coastal mainland; north Pacific Maritime endemic.

Notes: Broad-petalled gentian is also known as *Gentiana covillei.* • This is another absolutely fabulous gentian. No wonder the gentians are highly prized by alpine gardeners.

Rocky Mountain Fringed Gentian
Gentianopsis detonsa

General: Hairless **annual or biennial** from a slender taproot; stems several, **often branched from the base,** erect, 15–50 cm tall.

Leaves: Basal leaves soon deciduous; stem leaves opposite, 2–4 pairs, **lance-shaped to oblong,** 1.5–5 cm long.

Flowers: Single on long stalks atop stems, sometimes from leaf axils; **corolla deep blue to purplish,** funnel-shaped, **without pleats or fringes in the throat,** 3–5 cm long, flaring to **4 lobes** 3–6 mm long, **minutely jagged and fringed** on margins, commonly twisting as they close; calyx with 4 pointed lobes; style 1, stigma 2-lobed and fringed.

Fruits: Capsules cylindric, as long as corolla tube.

Where Found: Moist to wet, **calcium-rich** meadows, fens, forest edges, streambanks, heathlands and tundra; montane to lower alpine zones (usually not at high elevations in the north); scattered but locally frequent throughout much of the inland portion of the region; circumboreal.

Similar Species: Perennial fringed gentian or fragrant gentian (**G. barbellata**; *Gentiana barbellata*) ranges from WY and UT to NM and AZ, in meadows and on rocky slopes and ridges in the alpine zone. Unlike Rocky Mountain fringed gentian, it is **perennial** and has **unstalked flowers.**

Notes: Rocky Mountain fringed gentian is also known as *Gentiana detonsa, G. barbata, G. elegans, G. macounii, G. raupii, G. richardsonii, G. thermalis; Gentianella crinita* ssp. *macounii.* • Rocky Mountain fringed gentian is the official flower of Yellowstone National Park, where it is abundant and has been known as *Gentiana thermalis,* presumably because of an affinity for habitats near the park's hot springs and geysers. • We're not sure why the name *detonsa,* which means "shaved"—perhaps it refers to the short fringe (appearing trimmed) on the petal margins.

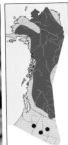

Four-parted Gentian
Gentianella propinqua

General: Annual from a taproot; stems ascending to erect, several, 4–30 cm tall, simple or branched from the base.

Leaves: Basal leaves in a rosette, spoon-shaped to elliptic; stem leaves narrowly egg-shaped to oblong, 5–35 mm long.

Flowers: Few to many, stalked from leaf axils and atop stem, in **loose clusters; corolla blue, purplish pink, lavender** or rarely whitish, tubular to narrowly funnel-shaped, 1–2 cm long (topmost flower usually the largest), **lacking pleats** between the **4 pointy-tipped lobes,** the **lobes not fringed** marginally or within; calyx 4-lobed; stamens 4.

Where Found: Moist meadows, open forests, roadsides, heathlands and tundra; lowland to alpine zones; frequent throughout much of northern inland ¾ of the region; basically amphiberingian.

Variety: Var. *aleutica* (*G. aleutica*) has **smaller (8–13 mm long), yellowish or pale pink-purple to whitish flowers** and occurs in the Aleutians and coastal southern AK.

Similar Species: Northern gentian (G. amarella) is another annual. It usually doesn't occur in the alpine, but you can find it in subalpine meadows and grasslands over most of the region except the far north. The **corolla lobes fringed in the throat** distinguish it from four-parted gentian.

northern gentian

Notes: Four-parted gentian is also known as *Gentiana propinqua* and *G. propinqua* ssp. *arctophila*.

Delicate Gentian, Slender
Gentian • *Gentianella tenella*

General: Small annual usually **branched from the base. Flowers:** With **fringes in the throat** similar to northern gentian (above) but **longer-stalked** (to 10 cm vs. to 2 cm in northern gentian); **corolla blue to white,** 0.8–1.5 cm long; sepals 4–5, **nearly distinct, not fused. Where Found:** Gravelly slopes and meadows, heathlands and tundra; montane to alpine zones; rare in the north, disjunct and sporadic in southern BC, ID and MT to CA, AZ and NM; arctic-alpine, circumpolar with many large gaps.

Notes: Delicate gentian is also known as *Gentiana tenella* and *Lomatogonium tenellum*. • In a California alpine study, the annual or biennial delicate gentian and moss gentian (p. 319) both self-pollinated and allocated a relatively high proportion of their biomass to reproductive structures. Consequently, they produced many fruits and lots of seed. The perennial Newberry's gentian (*Gentiana newberryi*), in contrast, generally outcrossed, allocated less biomass to reproduction and produced fewer seeds each year.

Star Gentian, Alpine Bog Swertia, Star Felwort • *Swertia perennis*

General: Hairless perennial from a rhizome; stem single, unbranched, erect, **10–40 cm tall.**

Leaves: Mostly in a tuft at the base, egg-shaped to oblong-elliptic, long-stalked, **4–12 cm long; stem leaves in a few pairs,** reduced in size upward.

Flowers: Solitary or several atop stem and in upper leaf axils; **corolla usually dull bluish purple, often with dark green streaks or spots, 1–1.5 cm across, star-shaped; petals 5,** nearly distinct, each with 2 fringed, glandular pits at the base; sepals 5, nearly distinct; stamens 5; style 1, very short.

Fruits: Capsules ellipsoid, somewhat flattened; seeds irregularly winged.

Where Found: Moist to wet meadows, fens, streambanks, thickets and snowbeds; montane to lower alpine zones; frequent in the north Pacific maritime part of the region, disjunct and locally frequent south of 47° N; interruptedly circumpolar.

Notes: In a Swiss study, smaller, more isolated populations of star gentian in alpine fens had higher rates of inbreeding and reduced genetic variability, which was associated with increased susceptibility to herbivore damage, less vigour (e.g., fewer, smaller leaves and shorter stems) and lower fitness. These smaller, more isolated populations were also more likely to disappear over time. Worryingly, many of the star gentian populations in our region are small and isolated. • The genus is named after Emanuel Sweert (1552–1612), a Dutch herbalist and gardener.

Monument Plant, Elkweed, Green Gentian • *Frasera speciosa*

General: Perennial from a **heavy taproot** and stem-base; stem single, unbranched, erect, to **50–70 cm tall** at high elevations.

Leaves: Basal leaves tufted, elliptic-oblong to spoon-shaped, **20–30 cm long; stem leaves whorled, mostly in 4s,** becoming smaller and lance-shaped upward, strongly veined.

Flowers: Numerous from upper leaf axils in conical clusters; **corolla yellowish green to greenish white,** purple-flecked, saucer- to wheel-shaped; **petals 4,** oval, **1–2.5 cm long,** each with a **pair of elongate, pink-fringed, glandular pits** at the base and with a broad, frilly, basal appendage; **sepals 4, nearly distinct, slightly longer than petals;** stamens 4; style 1, about ½ as long as ovary.

Fruits: Capsules leathery, ellipsoid, 2–2.5 cm long, slightly flattened.

Where Found: Vernally moist to mesic meadows and grassy slopes; montane to lower alpine zones; frequent in the southern inland ⅓ of the region, both sides of the Rockies and the eastside Cascades; southern cordilleran.

Notes: Monument plant populations reportedly flower synchronously every 2–4 years, and then the plants die. It's not clear what environmental cues are important in these coordinated flowerings, but they happen well ahead of time—flowers in this species are pre-formed at least 3 years in advance of blooming. In dense flowerings, seed set is increased and seed predation rate is reduced—both potential advantages to a mass-flowering strategy. • The alpine can be a harsh environment, especially for young plants, but parents can help. Monument plant seeds buried in leaf litter from their parents are much more likely to germinate and survive than seeds not "nursed" by their larger "mother."

Buckbean Family (Menyanthaceae)

The buckbean family (Menyanthaceae) has been considered closely related to the gentian family (Gentianaceae) on the basis of generally similar flowers and fruits. Although sometimes combined with Gentianaceae, Menyanthaceae is distinguished in most manuals by alternate leaves, a partially inferior ovary, large, smooth seeds and a general preference for wetter habitats. The distinction is supported by more recent biochemical and molecular studies, and much evidence now points to a close relationship to the aster family (Asteraceae)!!

Deer-cabbage
Nephrophyllidium crista-galli

General: Hairless, somewhat fleshy perennial from a thick, shallow rhizome covered with old leaf bases; flowering stems erect, unbranched, leafless, **10–40 cm tall.**

Leaves: Numerous, **clustered at the base, long-stalked** (stalks 5–30 cm long); **blades kidney-shaped,** broader (5–12 cm) than long, margins evenly blunt-toothed.

Flowers: Few to several in small clusters atop long stems; **corolla white,** top-shaped, short-tubular at the base, spreading above into 5 lobes, the lobes 5–7 mm long, with **wavy flanges** along the mid-vein and margins; calyx conic, joined to base of ovary, with 5 spreading lobes; stamens 5.

Fruits: Capsules conehead-shaped, elongated at maturity, 1-chambered; seeds smooth, shiny.

Where Found: Bogs, fens, swamps, seepage areas in open forests and wet meadows; lowland to subalpine and sometimes lower alpine zones; frequent along the coast from southern AK to the Olympic Peninsula, WA; amphiberingian.

Similar Species: When not in flower or fruit, deer-cabbage could be confused with twin-flowered mountain marsh-marigold (p. 185), which often occurs in similar habitats. However, the lobes at the base of deer-cabbage's leaves **tend not to touch,** whereas the lobes of twin-flowered mountain marsh-marigold leaves usually touch or overlap. Deer-cabbage also has **grooved leaf stalks.**

Notes: Deer-cabbage is also known as *Fauria crista-galli* and *Menyanthes crista-galli*. • The attractively fringed white flowers have a rank odour, similar to mildewed laundry or sour milk, which attracts pollinating flies.

• The genus name indicates that this plant is similar to *Nephrophyllum*, another genus with kidney-shaped leaves (from the Greek *nephros*, "kidney"). The species name *crista-galli* means "comb of the cock" and refers to the crest-like ridges on the petals.

The Genus *Campanula* (Harebell)

Our *Campanula* are perennial herbs, with stems spreading at the base to ascending or erect. The leaves are chiefly basal or mostly along the stem and alternate, linear to elliptic, lance-shaped or egg-shaped. The radially symmetric, relatively large flowers are solitary or 2 to several in small clusters. The blue or rarely white corolla (fused petals, collectively) is mostly bell-shaped, flaring to 5 lobes. The calyx (basally fused sepals, collectively) is also 5-lobed. There are 5 stamens, 1 style and a 3-lobed stigma. The 3-chambered ovary is inferior. The fruits are capsules, opening by pores and bearing numerous seeds.

Campanula, the diminutive of the Latin *campana*, "bell," refers to the shape of the flowers.

Key to *Campanula*

1a. Corolla 15–35 mm long, the lobes much shorter than the tube **2**
  2a. Calyx hairless, the lobes entire; capsules nodding, opening by pores near the base; basal leaves oval or roundish, stem leaves linear-lance-shaped . . . . **C. rotundifolia (below)**
  2b. Calyx hairy, the lobes with a few slender teeth; capsules erect, opening by pores near the top; leaves elliptic to lance-shaped . . . . **C. lasiocarpa (below)**
1b. Corolla 5–18 mm long, the lobes slightly shorter than to nearly as long as the tube **3**
  3a. Leaves sharply toothed; capsules nearly globe-shaped, 3–5 mm long; Olympic Mtns only . . **C. piperi (p. 326)**
  3b. Leaves toothless or nearly so **4**
    4a. Flower 1, the anthers 1–2.5 mm long; capsules 12–20 mm long . . . . **C. uniflora (p. 326)**
    4b. Flowers 1–3 (to 5), the anthers 3–5 mm long; capsules 5–11 mm long **5**
      5a. Plants minutely spreading-hairy throughout; capsules 5–7 mm long . . . . **C. scabrella (p. 326)**
      5b. Plants mostly hairless except for fringed bases of lower leaves; capsules 7–11 mm long **6**
        6a. Corolla lobes erect, equalling to ½ as long as tube; southern plants . . . . **C. parryi (p. 326)**
        6b. Corolla lobes spreading to bent back, longer than tube; northern plants . . . . . . **C. aurita (p. 326)**

Mountain Harebell
Campanula lasiocarpa

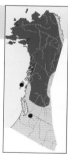

General: Stems spreading to ascending or erect, 1 to several, **2–15 cm tall. Leaves: Chiefly basal,** elliptic to lance-shaped, 1–6 cm long, **sawtoothed,** stalked; stem leaves few, reduced in size upward. **Flowers: Usually solitary,** rarely 2–5, large, showy; corolla blue (rarely white), bell-shaped, **1.5–3.5 cm long,** broad lobes much shorter than tube; **calyx hairy,** deeply 5-lobed, the lobes narrowly lance-shaped, usually with **a few slender teeth. Fruits: Capsules erect,** roughly cylindric, **hairy. Where Found:** Meadows, rocky slopes, heathlands and tundra; subalpine and alpine zones; frequent mostly inland in the northern ⅔ of the region, less frequent southward; amphiberingian.

Similar Species: Common harebell or bluebells-of-Scotland (*C. rotundifolia*) has similar flowers, usually more of them than

mountain harebell, but alpine forms are often 1-flowered. Common harebell is generally **taller** and has roundish, basal leaves (often withered), **narrower (lance-linear) stem leaves,** a **hairless calyx** with untoothed lobes and **nodding, hairless capsules.** It is frequent throughout the region south of about 62° N, from lowland to upper montane zones, ascending to the alpine on dry, rocky slopes and outcrops mostly in the southern ⅓ of the region.

common harebell

Notes: Mountain harebell is a brave plant, bearing disproportionately large flowers, often in the most exposed and extreme alpine sites.

Arctic Harebell • *Campanula uniflora*

General: Stems several, spreading to ascending, **3–10 (to 20) cm tall. Leaves:** Dark green, some-what leathery; basal leaves few; **stem leaves more numerous, elliptic to lance-shaped or linear,** 5–45 mm long. **Flowers: Solitary, erect; corolla blue to purplish, funnel-shaped, 5–12 mm long,** lobes about as long as tube; calyx sparsely hairy; **anthers 1–2.5 mm long. Fruits:** Capsules long-cylindric, tapering to the base, 12–20 mm long. **Where Found:** Rocky slopes, cliffs, scree, meadows, heathlands, tundra and fellfields; subalpine and alpine zones; infrequent in the north, sporadic southward especially in the Rockies; arctic-alpine, circumpolar with large gaps.

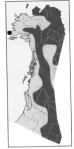

Notes: Most *Campanula* species are outcrossing—individual plants don't fertilize themselves. In Greenland and Iceland, however, arctic harebell plants usually *do* fertilize themselves, with pollen being released before the flower even opens. Still, seed set and germination are good in these plants, and selfing (though it can, if overdone, have undesir-able genetic consequences) is, after all, reproduction with someone you truly love.

Parry's Harebell • *Campanula parryi*

General: From a slender **rhizome;** stems ascending to erect, to 25 cm tall. **Leaves: Mostly untoothed;** basal leaves few, elliptic to lance-shaped; stem leaves several, narrower, 2–5 cm long, margins of **lower stem leaves fringed toward the base. Flowers:** Typically single, sometimes 2–4, erect; **corolla blue to blue-purple, broadly bell-shaped, 1–1.5 cm long, lobes equalling to ½ as long as tube;** anthers 4–5 mm long. **Fruits:** Capsules somewhat cylindric, tapering to the base, 7–11 mm long. **Where Found:** Meadows, gravelly ridges and scree slopes; subalpine and alpine zones; locally frequent in the inland southern ¼ of the region; cordilleran.

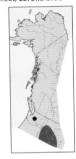

Similar Species: Rough harebell (*C. scabrella*) looks rather like Parry's harebell, with similar leaves, but has a **taproot,** is minutely **spreading-hairy throughout** and has **smaller (6–12 mm long), more openly bell-shaped flowers** with **corolla lobes about as long as the tube** and shorter **capsules, 5–7 mm long.** It grows on rocky ridges and talus slopes, in subalpine and alpine zones, in the Cascades from central WA to northern CA and in the Rockies of central ID and western MT.

Yukon Harebell • *Campanula aurita*

General: Stems spreading to erect, **10–30 cm tall. Leaves:** Along stem, entire to weakly toothed, **linear to lance-shaped. Flowers:** Solitary, or more typically 2–7 (at lower elevations); **corolla deep blue,** broadly bell-shaped, **cleft nearly to the base into lance-shaped, spreading to bent-back lobes; anthers 3–5 mm long. Fruits:** Capsules roughly cylindric, 7–11 mm long. **Where Found:** Meadows, open forests, rocky slopes, gravelly ridges, cliff ledges and rock outcrops, usually on calcium-rich substrates; montane to lower alpine zones; scat-tered but locally frequent in the northern ⅓ of the region; endemic.

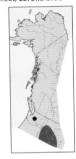

Similar Species: The **much shorter, cushion-forming Olympic harebell (*C. piperi*),** photo p. 317, has 1–3 **bowl-shaped flowers,** a **paler blue corolla** with **egg-shaped, spreading lobes, spoon-shaped, sawtoothed leaves** and **short (3–5 mm), nearly spheric capsules.** It occurs on rocky slopes and cliff crevices, in subalpine and alpine zones, and is endemic to the Olympic Mtns of WA.

Notes: The stamens of Yukon harebell deposit some of their pollen on their flower's own hairy style. After the stamens have shed all the pollen and shrivelled up, the stigma opens into 3 lobes, ready to receive pollen from other plants, usually via bumblebees. If the plant's stigma isn't fertilized by another plant's pollen, however, the stigma lobes spread wider still, bringing them into contact with homegrown pollen on the style and enabling self-fertilization.

Waterleaf Family (Hydrophyllaceae)

Ours are perennial herbs, often hairy, with alternate, entire to toothed, lobed or pinnately compound leaves. The flowers are several to many in clusters, radially symmetric, with 5 fused petals (collectively the corolla) and 5 sepals, united toward the base (collectively the calyx). The corollas are tubular, bell- or saucer-shaped, flaring to 5 lobes and often appendaged at the base. The 5 stamens are attached to the corolla tube and usually protrude beyond the corolla. The ovary is superior and the single style is entire or 2-cleft. The fruits are capsules.

Key to the Genera of Hydrophyllaceae

1a. Leaves chiefly basal, kidney-shaped to nearly circular, deeply palmately toothed; style entire or nearly so
.... *Romanzoffia* (below)

1b. Leaves mostly entire and lance-shaped, or pinnately divided; style 2-cleft 2

    2a. Flower clusters forking-branched without a central axis; roots fleshy-fibrous .... *Hydrophyllum* (p. 328)

    2b. Flower clusters more or less helically coiled; taproots .... *Phacelia* (pp. 328–329)

Sitka Mist-maiden
Romanzoffia sitchensis

General: Stems several, ascending, 8–30 cm tall, sparsely hairy to nearly hairless.

Leaves: Mostly from the base, numerous, **round to kidney-shaped**, 1–4 cm wide, rather fleshy, palmately veined, with **5–9 coarse teeth,** on **long (1–6 cm) stalks** with swollen, overlapping bases and fringed margins; stem leaves few, similar but reduced in size.

Flowers: Few to several, stalked, in a **loose, rather lax cluster** atop stem; **corolla white to cream, usually with yellow eye, bell-shaped,** 6–10 mm long and wide; calyx lobes linear-lanceolate, 2–4 mm long; **stamens shorter than corolla;** style 1, not lobed.

Fruits: Capsules narrowly egg-shaped, 2-chambered; seeds numerous.

Where Found: Moist to wet streambanks, gravel bars, shady rock crevices, cliff bases and talus slopes; lowland (especially in the north) to lower alpine zones; frequent in and west of the Pacific coastal mountains, inland sporadically to the Rockies.

Similar Species: The leaves could be mistaken for those of a saxifrage (e.g., Nelson's saxifrage, p. 151) of similar habit and habitats, but the petals of Sitka mist-maiden are fused at the base into a 5-lobed funnel with a yellow eye and its fruits are egg-shaped capsules; saxifrages have separate petals, lack a yellow eye and have 2-beaked capsules.

Notes: The genus is named for Count Nikolai Romanzoff (1754–1826), a Russian patron of botany who sponsored Kotzebue's expedition to the Pacific coast of North America.

Ballhead Waterleaf
Hydrophyllum capitatum

General: From a very short rhizome with slender, **fleshy-fibrous roots;** stems single or few, spreading to ascending, 10–30 cm tall.

Leaves: Mostly from the base, some attached below ground, rather few but **large, 10–15 cm long,** long-stalked, **pinnately cleft** into (5 to) 7–11 **rounded leaflets,** often lobed or toothed.

Flowers: Numerous in stalked, **ball-shaped clusters** near the ground and **overtopped by leaves; corolla lavender to purplish blue,** occasionally whitish, cup-shaped, 5–10 mm long, lobes 2–6 mm long; calyx lobes linear-oblong, **bristly-hairy;** stamens and 2-cleft style protruding well out from corolla.

Fruits: Capsules globe-shaped; seeds 1–4.

Where Found: Mesic to dry meadows, forest openings and grassy slopes, often in disturbed soil; montane to subalpine zones; frequent in the inland southern ⅓ of the region; cordilleran.

Similar Species: Fendler's waterleaf (*H. fendleri*) has **white or occasionally lavender or purplish flowers** in long-stalked **clusters usually not overtopped by the spreading leaves,** which are pinnately divided into **sharp-toothed, pointy-tipped leaflets.** It occurs in moist to mesic forest openings, thickets and meadows, in montane to subalpine zones, and is frequent from southwestern BC to CA in the Cascades and Olympics, and in the Rockies from ID and WY to UT and NM.

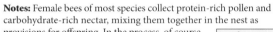

Notes: Female bees of most species collect protein-rich pollen and carbohydrate-rich nectar, mixing them together in the nest as provisions for offspring. In the process, of course, they transfer pollen from one plant to another. Bees that don't remix their collections, such as the mason bee (*Osmia lignaria*), must collect both pollen and nectar on each flight. In one Utah study, the mason bees collected pollen preferentially from various willows (*Salix* spp.)

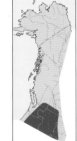

Fendler's waterleaf

and nectar primarily from the nectar-rich ballhead waterleaf, though pollen and nectar were collected from both. • Some First Nations groups ate the boiled or steamed roots of ballhead waterleaf, sometimes with yellow glacier-lily (p. 405) bulbs. The young shoots and leaves were boiled and eaten as vegetables by Native peoples and settlers.

Key to *Phacelia* (Phacelia)

1a. Leaves mostly entire, larger ones sometimes with a pair of side lobes. . . . . ***P. hastata*** (p. 329)

1b. Leaves coarsely toothed or lobed to pinnately divided. 2

    2a. Corolla cream to yellowish, 8–10 mm long, 10–14 mm wide; plants with long-soft hairs mixed with glandular hairs; north of 59° N. . . . . ***P. mollis*** (p. 329)

    2b. Corolla purple to dark blue, 5–9 mm long and wide; plants variously hairy; mostly south of 54° N (*P. sericea* reportedly rare in AK). 3

        3a. Leaves with lance-shaped to triangular lobes or coarse teeth; corolla deciduous; stamens 1–2 times as long as corolla; plants long-hairy in flower cluster, otherwise greenish and usually glandular, sparsely hairy . . . . ***P. lyallii*** (p. 329)

        3b. Leaves pinnately divided into linear-oblong lobes; corolla persistent; stamens 2–3 times as long as corolla; plants hairy throughout, not evidently glandular. . . . . ***P. sericea*** (p. 329)

Silverleaf Phacelia • *Phacelia hastata*

General: From a **stout taproot** with branching stem-base; stems erect to spreading or prostrate, 10–40 cm tall. **Leaves: Often finely silvery-hairy and smooth-margined;** basal leaves tufted, **lance-shaped,** 4–8 cm long; stem leaves similar but smaller. **Flowers:** Numerous in **several 1-sided coils in a compact cluster** atop stem; **corolla whitish to lavender, bell-shaped,** 4–7 mm long; **calyx deeply lobed,** the lobes linear and coarse-hairy; **stamens protruding,** nearly twice as long as corolla. **Where Found:** Dry meadows, forest openings, rocky or grassy slopes, talus and scree; lowland to alpine zones; frequent in the southern mostly inland ⅓ of the region; cordilleran.

Varieties: Subalpine-alpine **timberline phacelia (var. *compacta*)** of the Cascades from central WA to CA and NV is **often prostrate,** usually **less than 15 cm tall** and has **whitish flowers.** • **Alpine phacelia (var. *alpina*)** is also prostrate to ascending, with **lavender or purplish flowers,** and occurs in the mountains of the Great Basin and the Rockies, from UT to northeastern OR, central ID and MT. • **Narrow-sepal phacelia (var. *leptosepala*)** is usually **upright, to 40 cm tall,** with broadly lance-shaped, **loosely coarse-hairy leaves, often with 2 side lobes.** It is found in montane to lower alpine zones, and is frequent in the southern ¼ of the region, especially in the coastal mountains, southernmost BC, WA, OR, northern ID and northwestern MT.

timberline phacelia

Notes: Silverleaf phacelia is also known as *Phacelia leucophylla* var. *compacta*, *P. alpina* and *P. leptosepala*. • *Phacelia* is from the Greek *phakelos*, "bundle" or "cluster," in reference to the bunched flowers.

narrow-sepal phacelia

Silky Phacelia • *Phacelia sericea*

General: Silvery-silky-hairy plants, taprooted with branching stem-base; stems usually several, clustered, erect to ascending, 10–30 cm tall. **Leaves:** Oblong to lance-shaped, 2–6 cm long, **pinnately divided** into numerous linear-oblong lobes. **Flowers:** Numerous in a **spike-like, bottlebrush cluster; corolla dark blue or purple,** bell-shaped, hairy, 5–7 mm long and wide; **stamens purple, anthers yellow-orange and protruding,** 2–3 times as long as corolla. **Where Found:** Dry meadows, glades, rocky slopes, gravelly terraces, talus, scree and fellfields; montane to alpine zones; frequent in the southern mostly inland ⅓ of the region; disjunct in AK.

Similar Species: Silky phacelia has 2 sister species, both with **leaves merely lobed or coarsely toothed less than ⅔ of the way to the midvein.** • **Lyall's phacelia (*P. lyallii*)** has slightly larger flowers (5–9 mm long) than silky phacelia, with stamens 1–2 times as long as the corolla. It also tends to be **greenish and less hairy, often with some glandular hairs.** Lyall's phacelia grows in meadows and gullies and on rocky slopes, scree and cliffs, in subalpine and alpine zones. Endemic to the Rockies, it is locally frequent in southeastern BC, southwestern AB, ID and western MT. • **Soft phacelia (*P. mollis*)** has yet **larger flowers,** 8–10 mm long and 10–14 mm wide, **cream to yellowish** often tinged with blue, and tends to be **greenish but densely long-soft-hairy and glandular.** It occurs on sandy or gravelly roadsides, open forests, rocky ridges and tundra, in montane to alpine zones. An endemic species, it is scattered but locally frequent in east-central AK (rare in southeastern AK around Haines and Skagway), central and southwestern YT and northwestern BC.

soft phacelia

Notes: Silky phacelia apparently can concentrate gold from mineralized areas, up to 55 parts per billion. Thus, prospectors can search for subsurface gold deposits by analyzing silky phacelia plants, a process called biogeochemical prospecting.

Borage Family (Boraginaceae)

Our high-elevation members of this family are hairy perennial herbs with alternate, simple leaves. The radially symmetric flowers are in often-coiled clusters atop the stems. The petals are joined below into a tube that spreads or flares to 5 lobes; the corolla (petals collectively) is tubular-bell-shaped, funnel-shaped or phlox-shaped, usually with 5 appendages or bulges in the throat. The sepals are mostly distinct, joined a bit at the base, the calyx (sepals collectively) thus 5-parted. The 5 stamens are attached to the corolla tube, the anthers not extending beyond the throat. The superior ovary is deeply 4-lobed and appears 4-chambered. The single style arises from the base of the ovary between the 4 lobes—the renowned "gynobasic" style, as it is known in the trade. At maturity, the fruit separates into commonly 4 single-seeded nutlets, which are smooth or variously ornamented.

Key to the Genera of Boraginaceae

1a. Corolla tubular or funnel-shaped, the lobes ascending to erect; bulges in corolla throat moderately developed, not closing the throat. . . . . *Mertensia* **(pp. 333–334)**

1b. Corolla phlox-shaped, the lobes spreading perpendicular to the tube; bulges in corolla throat well developed, nearly closing the throat. **2**

    2a. Nutlets with conspicuous, barbed prickles along margins; fruiting stalks bent down . . . . *Hackelia* **(p. 332)**

    2b. Nutlets smooth or with inconspicuous bumps or hairs; fruiting stalks not bent down **3**

        3a. Flowers white; front of nutlet with a groove running down the middle . . . . *Cryptantha* **(p. 332)**

        3b. Flowers blue (occasionally white in albino forms); nutlets not grooved down the middle. . . . **4**

            4a. Plants densely tufted, cushion-forming; nutlets sharply angled . . . . *Eritrichium* **(pp. 330–331)**

            4b. Plants loosely tufted, not cushion-forming; nutlets rounded, without sharp angles . . . . *Myosotis* **(p. 332)**

The Genus *Eritrichium* (Mountain Sapphire)

Eritrichium is a genus of dwarf perennials that are strongly tufted, mat- or cushion-forming, from a taproot and a branching stem-base covered with persistent dead leaves. The plants are virtually stemless or have short, leafy, erect flowering stems. The leaves are small, hairy and mostly on numerous, crowded, short shoots or toward the base of the longer flowering stems. The flowers are shaped like forget-me-nots, in compact to somewhat expanded clusters. The corolla is **intensely blue**, rarely white, commonly with a yellow or whitish eye (bulging in the throat), the short tube flaring to 5 lobes. The calyx is also 5-lobed, cleft nearly to the base. The fruits are 1–4 sharply angled nutlets, with a flange or crown on the back. The mountain sapphires are legendary among alpine gardeners for both unparalleled beauty and difficulty of cultivation. In bloom, mountain sapphire is a dazzling, unforgettable sight, especially when the cushions are covered in masses of flowers. The flowers bloom very early and are very fragrant.

Eritrichium is from the Greek *erion*, "wool," and *trichos*, "hair," and refers to the woolly hairs of *E. nanum*, the original species described.

Key to *Eritrichium*

1a. Flowers 9–13 mm across; leaves linear to narrowly lance-shaped, with short, stiff, appressed hairs . . . . *E. splendens* **(p. 331)**

1b. Flowers 4–8 mm across; leaves oblong to lance- or egg-shaped, with soft or stiff, spreading hairs **2**

    2a. Mature leaves loosely long-soft-hairy, the surface visible between the hairs, which often form a fringe or apical tuft . . . . *E. nanum* **(p. 331)**

    2b. Mature leaves densely and coarsely grey- or silvery-hairy, the surface mostly hidden by the coarse hairs, which do not form a pronounced fringe or apical tuft. **3**

        3a. Leaves narrowly lance-shaped, covered by straight, silvery hairs without blister-like bases; nutlets with low, smooth flange or crown; MT and WY . . . . *E. howardii* **(p. 331)**

        3b. Leaves egg-shaped, covered by dense, grey hairs mostly with blister-like bases; nutlets with jaggedly toothed crown; AK and YT. . . . . *E. chamissonis* **(p. 331)**

Mountain Sapphire
Eritrichium nanum

General: Forming dense tufts, cushions or mats; flowering short shoots or erect stems typically numerous, 5–10 cm tall. **Leaves:** Oblong to lance-shaped, 4–10 mm long, loosely covered with long, soft, often wavy hairs, crowded. **Flowers:** Numerous, crowded; **corolla 4–8 mm across,** with rounded lobes; calyx lobes very hairy. **Fruits:** Nutlets rather cone-shaped, hairless, with **toothed or smooth crowns.**

Where Found: Dry, rocky slopes, gravelly ridges, meadows and stony tundra; alpine zone; widespread but scattered, locally frequent in the northern ¼ of the region, disjunct south of 49° N; arctic-alpine, incompletely circumpolar.

Similar Species: Bering mountain sapphire (*E. chamissonis*; *E. nanum* var. *chamissonis*) has flowers that **scarcely exceed the leaves,** which are **egg-shaped and densely covered with grey hairs, mostly with blister-like bases,** and nutlets with **jaggedly toothed crowns.** It is an arctic-alpine, amphiberingian species found on dry tundra, limestone barrens and exposed rocky or sandy ridges in the far north, rare in northern YT, northern and western AK and islands in the Bering Sea. • **Silvery mountain sapphire (*E. howardii*)** also has densely **silvery-hairy leaves,** but they are **narrower (linear-lance-shaped)** and the **hairs do not have blister-like bases; the smooth-flanged nutlets** are often **short-whiskery on the back.** It grows on dry, open, rocky slopes, on limestone, in montane to alpine zones, and is an endemic species infrequent in west-central and southwestern MT to northern WY, east of the Continental Divide.

Notes: Mountain sapphire is also known as *Eritrichium aretioides* and *E. argenteum.* • It is generally assumed that "selfing"—sex with oneself—increases with elevation in alpine plants because there are fewer pollinators higher up. However, one study of mountain sapphire in the Alps showed the opposite; there, selfing decreases with elevation. So who's transferring the pollen? In another study, flower visitors represented 12 insect families, mostly Diptera (true flies). • It has been suggested that ants, frequent visitors to mountain sapphire flowers in Colorado, also pollinate the flowers. Evidence indicates otherwise, that the ants chew on the lipid-rich throat bulges and do not forage deeper in the flower for nectar or pollen.

Showy Mountain Sapphire
Eritrichium splendens

General: Forming small, rather **loose tufts or cushions;** flowering stems erect or ascending, 5–20 cm tall. **Leaves:** Linear to lance-shaped, 1–4 (to 5) cm long, with **short, stiff, appressed hairs,** the stem leaves few. **Flowers:** Few to several in loose clusters; corolla 9–13 mm across. **Fruits:** Nutlets with **jaggedly toothed crowns. Where Found:** Dry, rocky slopes, crevices and ledges; alpine zone; rare in the north; arctic-alpine, endemic.

Mountain Forget-me-not
Myosotis alpestris ssp. *asiatica*

General: Spreading-hairy; stems several, tufted, erect to spreading, **5–40 cm tall.**

Leaves: Basal leaves lance- to spoon-shaped, 5–11 cm long; stem leaves several, oblong to lance-elliptic.

Flowers: Erect (**flower stalks remaining erect in fruit),** several to many in small, coiled, rather compact clusters (elongating in fruit); **corolla usually electric blue,** rarely white, with **yellow or orangey eye** (5 bulges in throat), the **tube about as long as the sepals,** spreading flat to 5 lobes **4–10 mm across; anthers concealed** in corolla tube.

Fruits: Nutlets egg-shaped, 1–2 mm long, **smooth, black, shiny.**

Where Found: Meadows, streambanks, forest openings, thickets, rocky slopes, snowbeds, tundra and fellfields; lowland (arctic coast) to alpine zones; common in the northern ½ of the region, less frequent southward; arctic-alpine, amphiberingian, entire species complex circumpolar.

Similar Species: Blue stickseed (*Hackelia micrantha*) and **western stickseed (*H. floribunda*)** look a lot like vigorous mountain forget-me-not, but they have **downward-curved flower stalks** in fruit, **nutlets with barbed prickles** and do not usually attain high elevations. However, a recently described species, **Taylor's stickseed (*H. taylori*)** occurs in subalpine and alpine zones, on rocky or sandy, granitic slopes, and is endemic to north-central WA (Chelan Co.).

Notes: Mountain forget-me-not is also known as *Myosotis asiatica* and *M. sylvatica* var. *alpestris*. • It is the state flower of Alaska. • Small *Myosotis* plants at high elevations could be confused with *Eritrichium*. • The origin of the name "forget-me-not" is unclear. One story dates back to the 1500s, when forget-me-not was attached to *Myosotis* because a blue flower was traditionally worn to retain a lover's affection. Another source says the name was origi-nally given to another plant, yellow-flowered ground-pine (*Ajuga chamaepitys*)—a mint that smells of pine resin and does not at all resemble *Myosotis*—because of the nauseating taste it left in one's mouth, and the name was somehow transferred to *Myosotis*.

Alpine Cryptantha, Waterton Lakes Cryptantha, Miner's Candle • *Cryptantha sobolifera*

General: Strikingly bristly-hairy; stems erect, 3–15 cm tall.

Leaves: Basal leaves tufted, broadly **spoon-shaped, to 3.5 cm long;** stem leaves lance-shaped, reduced in size upward.

Flowers: In small, tight coils, aggregated into dense **head-like or spike-like cluster; corolla white with yellow eye** (bulges in throat), **4–8 mm across,** the tube about as long as the sepals; **calyx lobes conspicuously bristly-hairy.**

Fruits: Nutlets lance-shaped, grooved, 3–4 mm long, smooth on inside surface, bumpy with low ridges on outside surface.

Where Found: Rocky slopes and exposed gravelly or pumice ridges; montane to alpine zones; locally frequent in the inland southern ⅕ of the region.

Similar Species: Thompson's cryptantha or cat's-eye **(*C. thompsonii*)** is **taller (10–30 cm),** with **longer, blue-green leaves,** the larger basal ones 4–7 cm long. It grows on open, rocky slopes, cliffs and talus, often on serpentine, in montane to alpine zones, and is infrequent in the Wenatchee Mtns of WA and report-edly also in OR.

Notes: Alpine cryptantha is also known as *C. nubigena* by some, *C. hypsophila* and *C. celosioides* in part.

The Genus *Mertensia* (Bluebell)

Our bluebells (also known as chiming bells) are hairy to hairless perennial herbs, with usually multiple, erect stems and alternate, entire, lance-shaped to elliptic leaves. The flowers are in short, open or compact clusters atop leafy stems, often drooping in bloom. The blue corollas are often pinkish in bud, with short, erect or ascending lobes from tubes with evident but not strongly developed bulges in the throat. The nutlets are erect and wrinkled when dry.

The genus is named for Franz Karl Mertens (1764–1831), a German botanist.

Key to *Mertensia*

1a. Stem leaves with evident lateral veins; stems usually >30 cm tall **2**

    2a. Principal stem leaves mostly rounded at the base and short-stalked, hairy at least on lower surface; sepals 3–7 mm long; corolla limb (expanded part of corolla, above throat) usually about 1.5 times as long as tube; anthers 2.3–3.5 mm long. . . . . ***M. paniculata*** (below)

    2b. Principal stem leaves tapering to the base, often unstalked, hairless or hairy on lower surface; sepals 1–3 mm long; corolla limb about as long as tube; anthers mostly about 2 mm long . . . . ***M. ciliata*** (below)

1b. Stem leaves without evident lateral veins; stems usually <30 cm tall. **3**

    3a. Filaments short, about 1 mm; anthers hidden in corolla tube, not projecting beyond throat. . . ***M. alpina*** (p. 334)

    3b. Filaments longer, 1.5–3 mm; anthers projecting beyond throat of corolla **4**

        4a. Corolla tube usually a little longer than "limb" (expanded part of corolla, above throat), with a ring of hairs within . . . . ***M. viridis*** (p. 334)

        4b. Corolla tube to twice as long as limb, hairless within . . . . ***M. oblongifolia*** (p. 334)

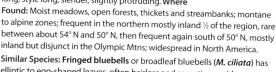

Tall Bluebells • *Mertensia paniculata*

General: From a taproot surmounted by a stout, branched stem-base, stems 20–70 cm tall. **Leaves:** Strongly veined, rough-hairy usually on both surfaces; basal leaves long-stalked, egg- to heart-shaped; stem leaves numerous on short, winged stalks, lance-shaped to broadly egg-shaped, 3–15 cm long. **Flowers:** Few to many in open to compact, drooping clusters atop stem, sometimes from upper leaf axils; **corolla 10–19 mm long,** short tube flaring to **longer, bell-shaped limb** with 5 short lobes, **bright blue to lavender or pinkish** (pink in bud and early bloom); **sepals 3–7 mm long;** anthers 2.3–3.5 mm long; style long, slender, slightly protruding. **Where Found:** Moist meadows, open forests, thickets and streambanks; montane to alpine zones; frequent in the northern mostly inland ½ of the region, rare between about 54° N and 50° N, then frequent again south of 50° N, mostly inland but disjunct in the Olympic Mtns; widespread in North America.

Similar Species: Fringed bluebells or broadleaf bluebells (***M. ciliata***) has elliptic to egg-shaped leaves, often hairless and sometimes with a waxy sheen, the **stem leaves tapering to an often unstalked base.** The **sepals are shorter (1–3 mm)** with fringed lobes, the bell-shaped limb of the corolla is **about as long as the tube,** and the anthers are about 2 mm long. It is found on streambanks and rocky ledges, and in wet meadows, thickets, seepage areas and wetlands, in montane to alpine zones. A cordilleran species, it is frequent in the southeastern corner of the region, MT, ID, central WA and central OR south to CA, CO and NM.

Notes: Bumblebees visit the young, pinkish flowers of tall bluebells for pollen and the older, blue flowers for nectar. When visiting young, pollen-rich flowers, the bees buzz-pollinate them. When visiting older, nectar-loaded flowers, the bees mostly don't accomplish pollination but tend to "go sideways," biting holes in the floral tube to get at the nectar. This behaviour is sometimes described as "nectar robbery" because there's no obvious benefit to the plant in having its older flowers visited. However, studies in Alaska's Wrangell Mountains suggest that providing nectar in older flowers may increase visits to nearby younger flowers, and occasional "legitimate" bumblebee visits to older flowers can also contribute to seed set in those blossoms.

Greenleaf Bluebells
Mertensia viridis

General: Stems lax, 5–30 cm tall.
Leaves: Stem leaves lance-shaped
to narrowly elliptic, with obscure
lateral veins. **Flowers:** Corolla blue,
the bell-shaped **limb a little shorter
than the tube,** which has conspicuous bulges in the throat and a **ring
of hairs inside** and below the
middle; anthers 1.3–3 mm long.
Where Found: Dry meadows and
open, rocky or grassy slopes; montane to lower alpine zones; frequent
in the southeastern portion of
the region; cordilleran.

**Similar Species: Oblongleaf
bluebells** or sagebrush bluebells

(**M. oblongifolia**) has narrower leaves
(lance-oblong) and a **corolla limb
1–2 times longer than the tube,** which
is **hairless within.** It occurs in dry
meadows, shrublands and on rocky
and grassy slopes, in steppe to subalpine zones, occasionally in the alpine
zone, and is frequent in the southeastern part of the region, eastside WA to
MT, south to NV, UT and CO.

Notes: Greenleaf bluebells is also
known as *Mertensia lanceolata* var.
viridis, M. oblongifolia var. *amoena*
and *M. paniculata* var. *nivalis.*

oblongleaf bluebells

Alpine Bluebells
Mertensia alpina

**General: Stems sprawling to ascend-
ing, to 20 cm tall. Leaves:** Lance-
shaped, hairy above, hairless below,
**lateral veins obscure. Flowers: Corolla
deep blue, 7–11 mm long,** the tube
upright (not drooping), hairless within
and about as long as the limb, which
flares abruptly, the flowers thus
tubular-saucer-shaped and **somewhat resembling a *Myosotis*** (p. 332);
anthers enclosed
by the corolla
tube and con-
cealed in the
throat, which
has conspicuous
bulges within.

Where Found: Meadows, rocky slopes and fellfields; subalpine and alpine zones; frequent in
the southeastern part of the region; Rocky Mtn endemic.

Similar Species: Obscure bluebells (*M. perplexa*) has **anthers that peek out** from the mouth
of the corolla tube, which is **9–14 mm long and hairy within.** It grows on open, rocky slopes
and ridges, in subalpine and alpine zones, and is a Rocky Mountain endemic infrequent from
southwestern MT to CO.

Mint Family (Lamiaceae)

Mints characteristically have stems that are square in cross-section, opposite leaves and aromatic oils. The flower cluster usually appears to be whorled and often spike-like or head-like at the top of the stem. The flowers are normally bilaterally symmetric with 5 fused sepals and 5 petals (collectively the "corolla") joined into a 5-lobed, 2-lipped tube. There are 2 or 4 stamens and a superior, 4-lobed ovary with a single style arising from the navel of the lobes. The fruits are 4 nutlets (hard-coated seeds). The mint family shares its distinctive 4-lobed ovary and **gynobasic** style with the borage family (Boraginaceae), but borages typically have round stems, alternate leaves and radially symmetric flowers.

Western Mountain Balm, Coyote Mint, Cloverhead Horsemint • *Monardella odoratissima*

General: **Strongly aromatic** perennial from a stout tap-root and branching stem-base; stems clustered, ascending to erect, unbranched, **10–40 cm tall, 4-angled,** hairy.

Leaves: Opposite, firm, **lance- to egg-shaped, 1–3.5 cm long,** short-stalked or nearly unstalked, **densely to sparsely short-hairy** and accordingly greyish to green, often purplish-tinged, **margins untoothed.**

Flowers: Many in a **flat-topped head** set in a bowl of **papery purplish bracts,** the outer bracts spreading or bent down, the **head 1–4 cm across; flowers pink-purple or lavender to whitish, 1–2 cm long;** corolla tubular, **obscurely 2-lipped,** the upper lip erect and 2-lobed, the lower lip bent back somewhat and 3-lobed; stamens 4.

Fruits: Nutlets 4, hard, brownish, hairless, 1-seeded.

Where Found: Open forests, shrublands, rocky slopes, gravelly ridges, meadows, scree and talus; montane to lower alpine zones; frequent in the mostly inland southern ¼ of the region; cordilleran.

Notes: Western mountain balm is mainly pollinated by butterflies. • *Monardella* is the diminutive of *Monarda*, which was named for Nicolas Monardes (1493–1588), a Spanish physician and botanist. He published a book on American products that was translated into English with the title *Joyfull Newes out of newe founde Worlde.*

Northern Bedstraw • *Galium boreale*

General: Perennial from a creeping rhizome; **stems usually numerous,** clustered, erect or ascending, **20–50 cm tall, 4-angled.**

Leaves: Along stem in several **whorls of 4, lance-shaped to oblong or linear,** unstalked, **1.5–4 cm long,** pointed but **blunt-tipped.**

Flowers: Small, numerous, stalked, on branchlets in upper leaf axils, the whole a **showy terminal cluster;** parts in 4s (4 petals, sepals and stamens); **corolla cream or white;** petals fused toward base, **topped by spreading lobes, star-shaped, 3–7 mm across;** ovary inferior; styles 2.

Fruits: Nutlets 2-lobed, 2-seeded, rounded, about 2 mm long, usually **short-hairy.**

Where Found: Meadows, open forests, thickets, river terraces, rocky or grassy slopes and tundra; lowland to subalpine and occasionally lower alpine
zones; frequent in most of the region but usually not at high elevations; circumpolar.

Notes: The Dena'ina used this species in hot packs for aches and pains. A liquid decoction was applied to sores and infections. The roots are a source of dyes. • The flowers have a lovely scent, but the name "bed-straw" was originally given to the yellow-flowered, aromatic European species *Galium odoratum*, which was strewn on floors, hung in linen cupboards and churches, and stuffed into pillows for its soothing scent and supposed soporific properties.

The Genus *Valeriana* (Valerian)

Our valerians are perennial herbs from aromatic taproots or rhizomes, the stems erect or ascending. The leaves are chiefly at the base or both basal and opposite along the stem, and entire to pinnately divided. The small flowers are often in dense, showy clusters atop the stems, the clusters expanding and becoming more diffuse in fruit. The corolla (petals collectively) is white to pinkish, tubular to funnel-shaped and flaring to 5 lobes; the sepals are lacking or modified into feathery bristles. There are commonly 3 stamens that usually stick out beyond the corolla. The inferior ovary has a single style and a 3-lobed stigma. The fruits are achenes surrounded by a persistent, feathery "calyx"—bristles much like the pappus plumes of the aster family.

Key to *Valeriana*

1a. Plants from a taproot; basal leaves narrowly oblong, tapering gradually to the base; leaves thickish, firm, nearly parallel-veined; flower cluster long and open. . . . . **V. edulis** (p. 337)

1b. Plants from a rhizome or stem-base and numerous fibrous roots; basal leaves egg- to spoon-shaped, rather abruptly stalked; leaves relatively thin, net-veined; flower cluster compact 2

  2a. Corolla small, usually 2–4 mm long, the spreading lobes about equalling the tube 3

    3a. Plants 10–40 cm tall; stem leaves few, the lateral lobes strap-shaped, <1 cm wide; achenes hairless . . . . .
. . . . **V. dioica** (p. 337)

    3b. Plants 20–80 cm tall; stem leaves several, the lateral lobes egg-shaped, some 1–2 cm wide; achenes commonly short-hairy . . . . **V. occidentalis** (p. 337)

  2b. Corolla larger, 4–18 mm long, the ascending lobes much shorter than the tube 4

    4a. Stamens not protruding from the 11–18 mm long corolla . . . . **V. columbiana** (p. 338)

    4b. Stamens extending much beyond the 4–9 mm long corolla 5

      5a. Upper stem leaves distinctly stalked, with 1–3 pairs of lateral lobes; fruits egg-shaped
. . . . **V. sitchensis** (p. 338)

      5b. Upper stem leaves unstalked or nearly so, usually with 1 pair of lateral lobes; fruits lance-oblong . . . 6

        6a. MT south . . . . **V. acutiloba** (p. 338)

        6b. Northern BC north. . . . . **V. capitata** (p. 338)

Edible Valerian, Tobacco Root
Valeriana edulis

General: From a stout **taproot** and branching stem-base; stems erect, solitary, **10–70 cm tall. Leaves:** Thickish, firm, **nearly parallel-veined; basal leaves linear to lance-oblong,** entire to sometimes pinnately lobed; **stem leaves 2–6 pairs, pinnately divided into narrow, strap-shaped lobes. Flowers:** In clusters at first compact, **later becoming longer and more open;** flowers bisexual and unisexual; corolla white to cream, **1.5–4 mm long,** the tube not much longer than the lobes; stamens protrude slightly beyond corolla. **Fruits:** Achenes egg-shaped, short-hairy to nearly hairless. **Where Found:** Moist to mesic shrublands, saline swales, meadows, open slopes and ridges; steppe to lower alpine zones; frequent in the southeastern part of the region; cordilleran–Great Plains.

Other Species: Marsh valerian (*V. dioica* ssp. *sylvatica*) is **10–40 cm tall, with spoon- to egg-shaped basal leaves** and 2–4 pairs of stem leaves that are pinnately cleft with **strap-shaped lateral lobes less than 1 cm wide.** It occurs in moist to wet meadows, thickets, fens, forest openings, lakeshores and streambanks, in montane to upper subalpine zones. Marsh valerian is frequent in the southern inland ⅔ of the region, south of about 62° N, in southern YT and southwestern NT through BC and western AB to WA, ID and WY, and is widespread in North America. • **Western valerian (*V. occidentalis*; *V. sylvatica*, *V. septentrionalis*)** resembles marsh valerian but is **20–80 cm tall** and has stem leaves with **broader, egg-shaped lateral lobes, some 1–2 cm wide.** It grows in moist meadows, thickets, open forests, parkland and talus slopes, in montane to upper subalpine zones, and is a cordilleran species frequent in the southeastern part of the region, MT and ID to CA, AZ and CO.

Notes: Edible valerian hosts entire agricultural systems in some alpine meadows. Aphids feed on the valerian, especially on female plants, extracting sweet plant juices, and ants tend the aphids, feeding indirectly on the sugars they extract. Sometimes (likely when the ants are low on protein) the ants feed on the aphids themselves. • Some Native American groups cooked and ate the roots of edible valerian, and presumably they also dried and smoked it.

marsh valerian

Sitka Valerian • *Valeriana sitchensis*

General: Perennial from a stout, branching rhizome or stem-base with fibrous roots; stems erect, solitary, **30–120 cm tall. Leaves:** Mostly **along stem, 2–5 pairs,** long-stalked, pinnately divided into **3–7 broad, coarsely toothed segments,** the top segment largest. **Flowers:** Numerous in compact, hemispheric to somewhat flat-topped clusters; corollas white or pinkish, **5–8 mm long,** the tube 2 times the length of the lobes. **Fruits:** Achenes egg-shaped, 3–6 mm long, hairless. **Where Found:** Moist to wet meadows, thickets, streambanks, open forests, glades and avalanche tracks; montane to alpine zones; frequent throughout most of the region south of about 64° N; cordilleran.

Similar Species: Capitate valerian (*V. capitata*) is smaller, usually **10–50 cm tall,** the **upper stem leaves unstalked** or nearly so and with **just 1 pair of lateral segments.** It is found in moist meadows, thickets, streambanks, heathlands and tundra, in montane to alpine zones, and is an amphiberingian species frequent in the northern ⅓ of the region, most of AK and YT to northwestern NT, but rare in northern BC. • **Sharpleaf valerian (*V. acutiloba*;** *V. capitata* ssp. *acutiloba*) is basically a southern version of capitate valerian. It grows on rocky slopes, meadows and the edges of krummholz, in montane to alpine zones, and is locally frequent from southwestern MT to southern OR, CA, AZ and NM. • **Wenatchee valerian (*V. columbiana*)** is the showiest of our valerians, with **white corollas 11–18 mm long** and stamens that do not stick out beyond the corolla. It occurs on open, rocky slopes, in montane to upper subalpine zones, and is endemic to the Wenatchee Mtns of WA.

Notes: Sitka valerian is one of the most constant and abundant elements of the signature subalpine meadows of Cascadia, and it is responsible for the strong, sour odour detected in subalpine meadows after the first autumn frost. Whereas some find the smell disagreeable, we hang on its bracing pungency. • First Nations peoples used the roots of Sitka valerian medicinally. They rubbed chewed roots onto their heads to relieve headaches, prepared poultices from them for earaches, cuts and wounds, and applied them to people suffering seizures. The Alaskan Tlingit called it "the medicine that stinks." Crushed roots were applied to mothers' nipples when it was time to wean a child, rubbed on sore muscles and blown into animal traps for luck. Powdered roots were added to smoking mixtures to relieve cold symptoms. Some used the roots in perfumes, disinfectants, skin creams and hair oils. • Valerian roots have been used in Europe for centuries as a tranquilizer with few side effects. Sitka valerian is much stronger than the European species. The root functions as an antispasmodic and a sedative when a person is agitated, but as a stimulant when a person is fatigued. The roots are said to have antibacterial, anti-diuretic and liver-protective properties. • One survey of commercial valerian products failed to detect valerian compounds in 4 of 17 products sampled, found only half of the expected levels in another 4 and discovered lead contamination in 2 more products and cadmium contamination in one. Low levels of valerian compounds are probably related to the instability of these compounds during extraction and storage. Bottom line: gather your own valerian for tea. • **Caution:** Large doses of valerian tea can cause vomiting, stupor and dizziness. The tea should never be boiled, and roots should be cooked for at least 2 days. • In the North Cascades, plant communities dominated by Sitka valerian generally occur on windward (western) sites where snowmelt is earliest (June to mid-July) and soils are warmest.

capitate valerian

Aster Family (Asteraceae)

The composites, or plants of the aster family (Asteraceae), form the largest plant family in the world (or perhaps the second largest, after the orchids), with over 23,000 species. Composites are easily recognized by their inflorescence (**flowerhead**), which is often mistaken for a single, large flower, but is actually made up of numerous, small, individual flowers (**florets**) attached to the broadened top of the stem (the **receptacle**). These florets can be of 2 forms—tubular and sitting on the stem top (**disc florets**) or strap-shaped and arranged around the edges of the stem top (**ray florets**). When you play "loves me, loves me not," you are plucking ray florets. A plant may have ray florets only, disc florets only or both. Each floret has 5 united petals that form a 5-toothed **corolla**, 5 stamens united at the anthers and an inferior, 1-chambered ovary. What originally were the sepals are interpreted to have been modified into hairs, or less commonly into scales, awns or hooks (collectively called the **pappus**), which crown the summit of the single-seeded fruits (**achenes**) and assist in wind-dispersal, as in the downy parachutes of dandelions. Attached to the rim of the head is an **involucre** consisting of scale-like or somewhat leaf-like bracts, called **involucral bracts.**

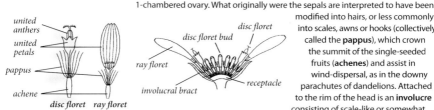

Parts of an Aster Flowerhead

The aster family is nearly cosmopolitan in range but is especially well adapted to dry, temperate to subtropical climates. It has considerable economic importance through food plants such as lettuce (*Lactuca*), globe artichoke (*Cynara*), endive and chicory (species of *Cichorium*), salsify (*Tragopogon*) and sunflower (*Helianthus*). Many species are noxious weeds (e.g., Canada thistle, *Cirsium canadense*, and knapweeds, *Centaurea* spp.), whereas others are used in medicinal preparations or herbal teas. Many genera provide ornamentals; some favourites of alpine gardeners include species of daisy and fleabane (*Erigeron*), alpinegold (*Hulsea*), rubberweeds (*Hymenoxys*) and the incomparable Easter daisies (*Townsendia*).

Key to the Groups of Genera of Asteraceae

1a. Heads of strap-shaped ray florets only; plants with milky juice . . . . **Group I (pp. 340–344)**

1b. Heads of florets that are not all strap-shaped, some or all of them tubular; plants mostly with watery juice . . . **2**

    2a. Heads of tubular disc florets only; ray florets lacking . . . . **Group II (pp. 345–360)**

    2b. Heads of both ray and disc florets **3**

        3a. Ray florets white, pink, purple, reddish or blue (not yellow or orange) . . . . **Group III (pp. 361–379)**

        3b. Ray florets yellow or orange . . . . **Group IV (pp. 380–400)**

clasping arnica and pink monkeyflower

Key to Group I: Flowers All Strap-shaped; Juice Milky (Dandelion Tribe)

1a. Flowerheads few to several or many; some leaves along stem 2

    2a. Pappus straw-coloured to dingy white; achenes <4 mm long; plants with short rhizomes and fibrous roots . . . . ***Hieracium triste*** (p. 341)

    2b. Pappus bright white; achenes >4 mm long; plants with a taproot. . . . . ***Crepis nana*** (below)

1b. Flowerheads solitary atop stems; leaves all basal 3

    3a. Involucral bracts in distinct rings of short and long; achenes minutely spiny or prickly, at least toward top . . . . ***Taraxacum*** (p. 343)

    3b. Involucral bracts not in distinct rings, all of more or less equal length, or grading from short to long; achenes smooth or at least not minutely spiny or prickly 4

    4a. Involucral bracts mostly hairy; achenes beaked at maturity . . . . ***Agoseris*** (p. 342)

    4b. Involucral bracts mostly hairless; achenes beakless. . . . . ***Nothocalaïs*** (p. 344)

Dwarf Alpine Hawksbeard
Crepis nana

General: Low, tufted, **hairless** perennial with milky juice, **mostly less than 15 cm tall,** from a **slender taproot** often surmounted by a short stem-base, sometimes with rhizomes as well; **stems several to many in dense clumps,** often branched, ascending to erect.

Leaves: Mostly basal, 1–8 cm long, stalked, **egg- to spoon-shaped, often purplish below and glaucous green above, margins mostly entire,** occasionally toothed or pinnately lobed; stem leaves similar to basal ones, becoming smaller upward, sometimes not obvious.

Flowerheads: Yellow, few to many, borne **erect among or a bit beyond leaves,** 9–12-flowered, of ray florets only; involucres cylindric, about 1 cm long, outer bractlets lance-shaped, shorter than the 8–10 oblong, often purplish inner bracts.

Fruits: Achenes golden brown, columnar, ribbed, **4–7 mm long,** tapering to the tip but not beaked; **pappus bright white.**

Where Found: Rocky slopes, scree, talus, streambanks and gravel bars; subalpine and alpine zones; infrequent in most of the region; arctic-alpine, North American (especially the west) and northern Russian.

Notes: Typically the plants are tufted and the flowerheads occur among the leaves. • *Crepis* is a name used by Theophrastus and is derived from the Greek *krepis,* "slipper" or "sandal," referring to the achene shape or for the resemblance of the highly divided leaves of other species to the thongs of a sandal; *nana* means "dwarf." • "Hawksbeard" is a name coined without explanation by S.F. Gray, a British botanist and the author of *Natural Arrangement of British Plants* (1821), for the genus *Crepis.* Reportedly no longer a *Crepis,* dwarf alpine hawksbeard has been punted to the genus *Askellia* based on distinctive DNA and morphology. Whatever the name, this species is a striking plant and one of our Top 10 favourite alpines.

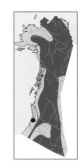

Woolly Hawkweed
Hieracium triste

General: Perennial with milky juice, from a **short rhizome with fibrous roots; stems 1 to few,** erect, unbranched, **usually hairy especially toward the top, 5–30 cm tall.**

Leaves: Mostly in a tuft at the base, 5–12 cm long, tapering to slender stalks, spoon- to lance-shaped, usually hairless above, **margins mostly entire,** rarely tiny-toothed; stem leaves absent or few, reduced.

Flowerheads: Yellow, few to several (2–8, occasionally 1), on hairy stalks, of ray florets only; involucres bell-shaped, 7–10 mm long, bracts roughly the same size, **densely hairy** with mix of **greyish or blackish,** fine, star-shaped, straight-spreading and gland-tipped hairs.

Fruits: Achenes reddish brown to black, columnar, ribbed, **2–3.5 mm long; pappus straw-coloured to dingy white,** the bristles minutely barbed.

Where Found: Meadows, heathlands, forest edges, rocky slopes, snowbeds and streambanks; subalpine and alpine zones; frequent throughout except the far north; arctic-alpine, amphiberingian.

Varieties: Two taxa have often been recognized, but not by *FNA*: amphiberingian *H. triste* **var. triste,** woolly hawkweed, and cordilleran *H. gracile* (*H. triste* var. *gracile*), slender hawkweed. Compared to slender hawkweed, woolly hawkweed has larger heads and longer, greyish black hairs (its heads and stalks look quite shaggy), but no glands.

Notes: *Hieracium* is a large genus of herbaceous perennials, with between 90 and 10,000 species, depending on what you call a "species." Woolly hawkweed is reasonably straightforward—a diploid, sexual, self-compatible and largely outcrossing species—but other hawkweeds often reproduce by **apomixis,** producing seeds without bothering with fertilization, meiosis and all the rest. Seeds produced by apomixis, then, are genetically identical to the parent. The result in *Hieracium* is a very large number of slightly different taxa, sometimes called "microspecies" or alternatively members of (far fewer) "species complexes." • North America north of Mexico has 36 species of *Hieracium*: 23 native and 13 introduced Eurasian. The introduced species

are often invasive, and some can rapidly take over open habitats and displace native vegetation. Scientists are investigating biological control for these invasive species—that is, finding insects or fungi that will kill them, or at least slow their spread. But it's a tricky business with *Hieracium*, because the invasive species often grow side by side with natives and can also be closely related. The trick is to find an insect or fungus that kills the invaders without causing collateral damage to the natives. • *Hieracium* is from the Greek *hierakion*, which in turn comes from *hierax*, "hawk." This plant was allegedly fed to hawks in the days when falconry was popular among the gentry, in the belief that hawks ate the sap of the plants to sharpen their eyesight. Thus the plant became associated with clear-sightedness and was used in early medicine to help a person "see like a hawk" (hence the common name). The specific epithet *triste* means "bitter, gloomy, dull-coloured," in reference to the greyish black hairs.

Orange Mountain-dandelion, Orange Agoseris
Agoseris aurantiaca var. *aurantiaca*

General: Perennial from a taproot; flowering stems hairless or hairy toward the top, erect, 5–40 cm tall.

Leaves: All basal, lance-shaped, margins entire or coarsely toothed or jaggedly pinnately cut, 5–30 cm long.

Flowerheads: Usually burnt orange, sometimes yellowish, drying pinkish or purple, **solitary,** large, of ray florets only; involucres cylindric to bell-shaped, 2–3 cm long, bracts green, often with dark purple splotches, long-pointy-tipped.

Fruits: Achenes brown, columnar, ribbed, **abruptly tapering to slender beaks about as long as the body;** pappus white, the bristles minutely barbed.

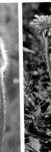

Where Found: Meadows, streambanks, thickets and forest openings; montane to alpine zones; frequent in the southern ¾ of the region; cordilleran.

Similar Species: Some taxonomists recognize as a separate species **pink mountain-dandelion (*A. lackschewitzii*),** which has pink flowerheads, fewer involucral bracts that are broader and more abruptly pointed at the tip and wider leaves. It grows in moister meadows in subalpine and alpine zones, and is infrequent in south-central and southeastern BC and southwestern AB to northern ID and northwestern MT.

Notes: *Agoseris* may mean "goat chicory," from the Greek *aix*, "goat," and *seris*, "chicory," perhaps because this plant is a type of chicory eaten, or only suitable for eating, by goats. Chicory in this instance probably refers to endive (*Cichorium endivia*); *aurantiaca* means "golden" or "orange."

pink mountain-dandelion

Short-beaked Mountain-dandelion, Pale Mountain-dandelion • *Agoseris glauca* var. *dasycephala*

General: Taprooted perennial; flowering stems usually somewhat hairy when young, often becoming hairless at least toward the base, erect, usually 10–50 cm tall.

Leaves: All basal, usually **erect, linear to lance-shaped,** 5–30 cm long, **usually somewhat hairy, margins usually entire, often wavy,** occasionally toothed or lobed.

Flowerheads: Yellow, solitary, large, of ray florets only; involucres conic to hemispheric, 1–3 cm long.

Fruits: Achenes spindle-shaped to narrowly conic, **gradually tapering to a stout, grooved beak less than ½ as long as the body;** pappus white.

Where Found: Grassy and rocky slopes, shrublands, open forests, meadows and scree slopes; grassland to alpine zones; frequent in the mostly inland southern ¾ of the region; cordilleran.

Similar Species: Sierra Nevada mountain-dandelion (*A. monticola*; *A. glauca* var. *monticola*) differs in its flowering stems, which are **hairy to the base,** and **spreading leaves** with **usually toothed or lobed margins.** It occurs in meadows, open forests, rocky slopes and tundra, in subalpine and alpine zones. Sierra Nevada mountain-dandelion is sporadic but locally frequent in the Cascades-Sierras from Mt. Adams south and also in the Blue Mtns, from southern WA and OR to CA and NV.

Notes: Short-beaked mountain-dandelion and tufted fleabane (p. 374) are favourite nectar flowers for butterflies in alpine meadows of Kananaskis Country, Alberta. • The Okanagan-Colville dried the latex of this species and used it as chewing gum. They also made an infusion of the plant to wash sores and rashes, rubbed the stem latex into sores and steeped the roots for use as a laxative.

Horned Dandelion • *Taraxacum ceratophorum*

General: Perennial from a branching taproot; flowering stems ascending to erect, **3–30 cm tall, long-hairy** at least when young.

Leaves: All basal, lance-shaped to narrowly oblong, 4–25 cm long, mostly hairless, **margins usually lobed, coarsely toothed or jaggedly cut.**

Flowerheads: Yellow, solitary, of ray florets only; florets 1–2 cm long, drying cream to whitish; **involucres about 1–2 cm long**, bell-shaped to hemispheric, **bracts dark green,** the **inner strongly horned** at tip.

Fruits: Achenes brownish, lance-shaped in outline, 3–6 mm long not including beak, **tipped with nose cone plus long (5–14 mm), slender beak,** ribbed and usually warty or spiny above; pappus of numerous, white to cream, hair-like bristles.

Where Found: Meadows, shores, roadsides, rocky slopes, scree and fellfields; lowland (arctic coast) to alpine zones; scattered throughout the region, infrequent in the outer coastal mountains; low arctic-alpine, circumpolar.

Notes: Horned dandelion is also known as *Taraxacum eriophorum, T. hyperboreum* and *T. lacerum.* • The most widespread native dandelion in North America, this species complex "has been subdivided into many microspecies in North America, most of which appear unworthy of recognition" (*FNA*). • Our native horned dandelion can sometimes be found growing with the introduced common dandelion (*T. officinale*). Where they grow together, they flower at the same time and share insect pollinators, which suggests that pollen transfer between species is likely to occur. Now, horned dandelion normally cannot fertilize itself—it is an outcrosser. And the non-native dandelion doesn't bother with fertilization at all—it simply sets seed that's genetically identical to the parent (apomixis). When the 2 species are experimentally "crossed" in the greenhouse, about one-third of the horned dandelion offspring are hybrids, and the rest are "selfed" and inbred (horned dandelion fertilizing itself; its self-incompatibility sometimes breaks down when common dandelion pollen is in the mix). In time, this "asymmetrical hybridization" could lead to the genetic assimilation of horned dandelion by the introduced common dandelion.

Alpine Dandelion • *Taraxacum scopulorum*

General: Diminutive perennial from a branching taproot; flowering stems ascending to erect, **1–5 cm tall, hairless.**

Leaves: All basal, **narrowly lance-shaped,** 1.5–4 cm long, mostly hairless, **margins regularly deeply lobed.**

Flowerheads: Yellow, solitary, of ray florets only; **florets 7–9 mm long; involucres about 1 cm long,** narrowly bell-shaped to cylindric, bracts dark green, **hornless at tip.**

Fruits: Achenes reddish brown to grey, 3.5–4 mm long not including beak, **tipped with nose cone plus stout, 3–4.5 mm long beak,** ribbed and often warty or spiny above; pappus of numerous, white, hair-like bristles.

Where Found: Ridges, shores, rocky slopes, fellfields and tundra; lowland (arctic coast) to alpine zones; infrequent in the Rockies of the southeastern part of the region; arctic-alpine, North American.

Similar Species: Alaska dandelion (*T. alaskanum; T. kamtschaticum*) has been lumped with alpine dandelion in some treatments, but it is **larger (3–10 cm tall),** with **broader, lance-oblong leaves** and **longer (1–2 cm) ray florets.** It grows on rocky slopes, bluffs and tundra, in lowland (eastern arctic coast) to alpine zones. An arctic-alpine, amphiberingian species, it is frequent in AK and YT, rare in northern BC. • **Pink dandelion** (*T. carneocoloratum*) is distinguished by pink to bronzy flowerheads. It occurs on high, dry, gravelly ridges, crests and scree slopes, in subalpine and alpine zones, and is rare or infrequent in Beringia (the part of AK and YT that escaped Pleistocene glaciation). • In the north, watch also for **high-arctic dandelion** (*T. hyparcticum*), which has whitish to cream flowerheads.

Notes: *Taraxacum* possibly comes the Arabic *tarakhshaqun,* "wild chicory," or the Persian *talkh chakok,* "bitter herb." "Dandelion" is from *dent de lion,* French for "lion's tooth," an allusion perhaps to the jagged leaf margins.

Alpine False Dandelion
Nothocalaïs alpestris

General: Perennial from a stout **taproot**, essentially **hairless throughout;** flowering stems erect, 5–30 cm tall.

Leaves: All basal, narrowly lance-shaped, usually **coarsely toothed to pinnately lobed,** 3–15 cm long, margins sometimes entire.

Flowerheads: Yellow, solitary, of ray florets only; florets 1–2 cm long, withering early; involucres 1–2 cm long, **green bracts evenly purple dotted.**

Fruits: Achenes brown, columnar, ribbed, sometimes tapering but **not beaked** at tip; pappus white, the bristles minutely barbed.

Where Found: Rocky slopes, pumice flats and meadows; subalpine and alpine zones; infrequent in the southwestern part of the region; Pacific Northwest endemic.

Similar Species: Speckled false dandelion (N. nigrescens; *Microseris nigrescens*) has **entire (not toothed or lobed) leaves** and a **pappus of awned scales (not bristles).** It occurs in the Rockies of ID, MT and WY, in meadows and glades, on grassy and rocky slopes and in open, coniferous forests, in montane to lower alpine zones.

Notes: Alpine false dandelion is also known as *Microseris alpestris* and *Agoseris alpestris.* • *Nothocalaïs* is from the Greek *notho,* "false," and *Calaïs,* a one-time genus now part of *Microseris* (the silverpuffs).

APOMIXIS AND TAXONOMY

Seeds are usually produced when female ovules are fertilized by sperm from pollen, and the fertilized embryo develops within the seed. This is sexual reproduction. However, many alpine plants can also produce seed without bothering with fertilization; this asexual reproduction is called "apomixis," and the plants that can pull it off are called "apomicts." As far as we know, all species that reproduce asexually through apomixis also reproduce sexually, at least occasionally. Interestingly, most sexually reproducing plants have the regular 2 sets of chromosomes ("diploid," like you), whereas most apomictic plants have more than 2 ("polyploid"). These diploid, sexually reproducing plants often grow side by side with polyploid apomicts of the same species in the same alpine meadows.

Apomixy is most common in the aster, rose, mustard and grass families, but it's been recorded in at least 17 other plant families. And it's particularly important and widespread in some genera, including *Potentilla, Poa, Antennaria, Arnica, Hieracium* and *Taraxacum.* Seeds produced asexually through apomixis initially are genetically identical to their parent. This can result in a very large number of slightly different taxa, sometimes called "microspecies." Some taxonomists recognize these microspecies as separate species, and some do not. As a result, for example, in the hawkweeds (*Hieracium*), there are between 90 and 10,000 species, depending on what you call a species! Pursuing the microvariation and partitioning it among numerous entities may or may not have taxonomic value. A field guide must acknowledge that apomixis is an important actor in the "ecological theatre and the evolutionary play," but must also judge how far to go in recognizing the microvariation that results and to what degree the discrimination advances general understanding and effective conservation of the plants involved.

Sexual reproduction is considered critical for long-term maintenance of genetic diversity in populations, and thus adaptability in changing environments. Even in hardcore apomicts, occasional sexual reproduction and hybridization periodically produce new and variable combinations of genes, and the best new genotypes can then be carried forward by continued apomixis. Whatever the reason, apomixy has proven spectacularly successful, at least in contemporary if not geologic time. In general, asexually reproducing species of plants (and animals) have more widespread distributions. This is certainly the case in plant groups with apomictic and sexually reproducing members—the apomicts have larger ranges, often to higher elevations and latitudes.

Key to Group II: Heads of Tubular Disc Florets Only; Ray Florets Usually Lacking

The Genus *Cirsium* (Thistle)

Ours are perennial or biennial spiny herbs from a taproot, with alternate, toothed to pinnately lobed leaves. The flowerheads are large, the florets all tubular; the corollas are pink-purple to yellowish or white. The involucres are egg- to bell- or bowl-shaped, the bracts in several series, shingled and at least some of them spine-tipped. The achenes are quadrangular or flattened, hairless and several-nerved, with a pappus of numerous feathery bristles, falling in a ring.

The roots of many thistles are edible when cooked and can provide nutritious food in an emergency. The Secwepemc and Nlaka'pamux name for the roots means "flatulence" because eating too many can cause excessive gas. Some groups believed thistles had protective properties because of their prickles, so pieces were placed in the bath or carried as talismans.

Cirsium is the ancient Greek name (*kirsion*) for a thistle, from *kirsos*, "swollen vein." Thistles were a reputed remedy for swollen veins; nowadays, they are used to treat gout. "Thistle" is from the Anglo-Saxon *thistel* or *distel*, of unknown meaning. Watts (2000) says "thistle" is from *thydan*, "to stab."

edible thistle

Edible Thistle • *Cirsium edule* var. *macounii*

General: Stems usually 1, stout, erect, leafy, thick and rather succulent in the lower portion but tapering and becoming slender above, fairly hairy, **0.4–1.4 m tall.**

Leaves: Basal and along the stem, lance-shaped to narrowly elliptic or oblong, **irregularly lobed or coarsely toothed, spiny,** hairy when young, becoming green and sparsely hairy; basal leaves to 40 cm long but often absent at flowering; **stem leaves 10–15 cm long.**

Flowerheads: Pinkish purple, 1 to many in clusters at branch tips, **nodding when young;** florets 2–2.5 cm long; styles exceed corollas by at least 3 mm; **involucres 1.5–4 cm high, cobwebby-hairy,** bracts slender, tapering, loose or spreading, **outer bracts tapering to short spines.**

Fruits: Achenes 4–6 mm long; **pappus white or buff, shorter than florets.**

Where Found: Meadows, forest openings, gullies, avalanche tracks; lowland (occasionally) to lower alpine zones; frequent in the Pacific coastal mountains, less frequent inland in snowy mountains; primarily Pacific maritime.

Similar Species: Leafy thistle or elk thistle (*C. foliosum*) has **white to pale pink flowerheads** in dense, woolly clusters enveloped and overtopped by leafy bracts, the **tawny pappus hairs exceeding the florets.** It occurs in meadows, forest edges and openings, in montane to lower alpine zones. Leafy thistle is scattered but locally frequent inland from southern YT and southwestern NT south in the Rockies through BC and adjacent AB, and is also found in WY.

leafy thistle

Notes: Edible thistle seeds were soaked for 140 days in fresh and salt water to simulate the effects of the biblical Great Flood, but the seeds failed to germinate. The author concluded that edible thistle seeds must have survived the Deluge on Noah's ark, or perhaps floating on logs (Howe, 1968). • The stems of *C. edule* (meaning "edible") can be eaten if peeled. The Secwepemc and Nlaka'pamux ate the roots of first-year, non-flowering plants, which are said to taste like sunflower roots.

Mountaintop Thistle
Cirsium eatonii var. *murdockii*

General: Stems 10–75 cm tall, very leafy. **Leaves:** Oblong, 15–30 cm long, deeply toothed to lobed, viciously spiny, mostly hairless on the undersurface. **Flowerheads:** White to pink or lavender, few in spike-like or sometimes head-like clusters; florets about 2 cm long; involucres 2–3 cm long, densely woolly-hairy, bracts spine-tipped. **Where Found:** Talus and scree, rocky ridges, meadows and forest openings; subalpine and alpine zones; this variety frequent in the southeastern part of the region.

Similar Species: White thistle or Hooker's thistle (*C. hookerianum*) also has **creamy white flowerheads** but with **florets 2–3 cm long** and **leaves merely toothed or shallowly lobed, moderately spiny and white-woolly beneath.** It grows in meadows, aspen parkland, forest openings, krummholz edges and on grassy or rocky slopes, in montane to alpine zones, and is frequent mostly in the inland southern ⅓ of the region, southern BC and southwestern AB to WA, ID, MT and WY.

Notes: Mountaintop thistle includes *Cirsium murdockii*, *C. polyphyllum* and *C. tweedyi*.

white thistle

The Genus *Saussurea* (Saw-wort)

These are perennial, non-spiny herbs from rhizomes, with alternate, entire to toothed leaves. The flowerheads are of tubular florets only and are blue, lavender or pinkish purple, rarely whitish, the receptacles scaly-bristly to naked. Involucres are egg- to bell-shaped, the bracts in several series and shingled. The prismatic or flattened achenes are hairless, 5-nerved and beakless, with a pappus of 2 series, the outer of short bristles, the inner of numerous feathery bristles.

Key to *Saussurea*

1a. Lower leaves triangular-egg-shaped to lance-shaped, usually >3 cm wide, heart-shaped to squared off at the base; plants usually >50 cm tall . . . . **S. americana** (p. 347)

1b. Lower leaves linear to elliptic, <2.5 cm wide, tapering to the base; plants 3–40 cm tall 2

   2a. Involucral bracts about equal in size, linear to lance-shaped; receptacles naked . . . . **S. nuda** (p. 347)

   2b. Involucral bracts very unequal, the outer egg- to lance-shaped; receptacles scaly 3

      3a. Outer involucral bracts pointy-tipped; northern (AK and northwestern Canada)
. . . . **S. angustifolia** (p. 348)

      3b. Outer involucral bracts with rounded tips; southern (U.S. Rocky Mtns) . . . . **S. weberi** (p. 348)

American Saw-wort • *Saussurea americana*

General: Stems erect, loosely woolly when young, becoming hairless, **30–120 cm tall. Leaves: Well-distributed along stem,** usually more than 20, **broadly triangular, heart-shaped to squared-off at the base, coarsely sawtoothed, 5–15 cm long,** pale and hairy on lower surface, green above. **Flowerheads: Dark blue-purple to lavender blue,** in usually tight clusters atop stem; florets 11–13 mm long; involucres 10–15 mm long, loosely woolly, **bracts strongly unequal;** receptacles naked. **Fruits:** Achenes 4–6 mm long; **pappus brownish.**

Where Found: Moist to wet meadows, thickets, fens, gullies, canyons, streambanks and avalanche tracks; montane to lower alpine zones; sporadic but locally frequent in the southern ⅓ of the region, infrequent northward; cordilleran with maritime leanings.

Similar Species: If not in bloom, American saw-wort could be confused with arrow-leaved groundsel (p. 390).

Notes: *Saussurea* is named after father and son Swiss naturalists Horace B. (1740–99) and Nicholas T. (1767–1847) de Saussure. The name "saw-wort" was originally given to *Serratula tinctoria* (a medicinal European mint-family species, also known as *Stachys officinalis*) because its leaves are "somewhat snipt about the edges like a sawe" (Gerard, 1597).

Dwarf Saw-wort • *Saussurea nuda*

General: Stems 5–30 cm tall, solitary, erect, loosely woolly when young, becoming hairless. **Leaves:** Basal and crowded along stem, **lower leaves tapering to winged stalks and lance-shaped to elliptic, margins irregularly toothed to nearly entire. Flower-heads: Pinkish purple,** occasionally whitish, in tight clusters; **involucral bracts nearly equal,** woolly-hairy; receptacles naked. **Fruits:** Achenes 6–7 mm long; pappus bristles white to brownish. **Where Found:** Rocky slopes, scree, meadows, heathlands and tundra; lowland (coastal northwestern AK) to alpine zones; infrequent in the southeastern part of the region, disjunct and rare in the north; arctic-alpine, amphiberingian.

Notes: Dwarf saw-wort is also known as *Saussurea alpina*, *S. densa* and *S. nuda* ssp. *densa*. • *Nuda* refers to the naked receptacles; the stems are hairy, at least when young.

Narrow-leaved Saw-wort
Saussurea angustifolia

General: Stems 3–40 cm tall, ascending, loosely woolly when young, becoming hairless. **Leaves: Basal and along stem**, stalkless, **linear to narrowly elliptic, margins entire to vaguely toothed. Flowerheads: Purple to dark blue;** florets 11–15 mm long; **involucral bracts very unequal, pointy-tipped;** receptacles scaly. **Fruits:** Achenes 3–4 mm long; pappus brownish. **Where Found:** Rocky slopes, thickets and tundra; lowland (arctic coast) to alpine zones; frequent in the northern ⅓ of the region; arctic-alpine, amphiberingian.

Varieties: Var. *angustifolia* is taller (usually **more than 15 cm**), more slender, with narrower (2–8 mm), **hairless or sparsely cobwebby leaves** with smooth or vaguely toothed margins. • **Var. *yukonensis*** is **shorter (3–15 cm)** and more compact, with toothed, **cobwebby-woolly leaves often wider than 8 mm.** It seems to prefer drier tundra.

Similar Species: Weber's saw-wort (*S. weberi*) is similar, especially to *S. angustifolia* var. *yukonensis*, but has **involucral bracts with rounded tips.** It occurs on scree slopes, gravelly ridges and stony tundra, especially on limestone, in subalpine and alpine zones. This endemic species is scattered but locally frequent in the Rockies of MT, WY and CO.

Notes: *Saussurea weberi* is named after William A. Weber (1918–), a University of Colorado botanist specializing in Rocky Mountain flora. He does not approve of common names, so we won't use "Weber's saw-wort" again.

The Genus *Artemisia* (Sage, Sagebrush, Sagewort, Mugwort, Wormwood)

Our *Artemisia* are perennial herbs, subshrubs (woody at the base) or shrubs, usually aromatic, from a taproot or rhizomes, with alternate or all basal leaves, entire to toothed, lobed or dissected. The flower clusters are long and narrow, spike-like to open but rarely head-like. The several to many flowerheads are small, of disc florets only, the florets bisexual, or sometimes the central ones sterile and the marginal ones female. The involucral bracts are shingled in several series, dry, at least the inner ones with wax-papery margins. The receptacle is naked or long-hairy, and often glandular. The generally hairless achenes are rounded or angled in cross-section, with the pappus lacking or a very short crown.

Artemisia was named after Artemis, Apollo's twin sister (known as Diana to the Romans), Greek goddess of the moon, wild animals and the hunt, vegetation and childbirth. She protected all mortal beings from pestilence and disease because she discovered the medicinal value of these plants. Or maybe more directly, the name honours Queen Artemisia of Anatolia, who lived about 350 BC and was reputedly a botanist and medical researcher.

"Wormwood," the name originally applied to some European species because they were used as vermifuges, is a corruption of the Anglo-Saxon and Old English *wermod*, which in turn is compounded from the German *wehren* or the Old English *werian*, "to fend off," and *mod*, "maggot"—in other words, a herb used for protection from maggots and as a worm medicine. Another explanation is that it's from the German *Wermut*, derived from the Old High German *Werimuota*, which is also the origin of the French word "vermouth" (certain white wines flavoured with herbs such as wormwood). Others claim that the strong odour indicates the plant can protect woollen clothes from "worms," actually moth larvae.

"Mugwort" comes from the Old Saxon *muggia*, "midge," or from the Old English *mough, moghe* or *moughte*, meaning "maggot" or "moth." The name was originally given to the European *A. vulgaris*, which was used like a "no-pest strip" to attract and kill "all such insects, including ants in the pantry." According to one source, bunches of the plant hung in a house would attract hundreds of midges. The bunches would then be bagged and beaten, killing the insects.

Key to *Artemisia*

1a. Shrubs 2

  2a. Leaves linear to narrowly lance-shaped, 2–4 cm long, 2–6 mm wide, usually entire, sometimes lobed, densely to sparsely grey-hairy . . . . *A. cana* (p. 350)

  2b. Leaves lance- to wedge-shaped, 2.5–5.5 cm long, 8–12 mm (or more) wide, usually lobed, sometimes entire, very hairy. . . . . *A. spiciformis* (p. 350)

1b. Herbs or subshrubs. 3

  3a. Receptacle covered with long hairs. 4

    4a. Leaves bright green, hairless or sparsely hairy, sticky-glandular dotted . . . . *A. rupestris* (p. 351)

    4b. Leaves grey-green or silvery, silky-hairy, not glandular. 5

      5a. Mat- or mound-forming perennial, woody at the base; flowerheads numerous, mostly >25; stem leaves numerous; leaf blades 0.5–2 cm long . . . . *A. frigida* (p. 351)

      5b. Herb, not woody or mat-forming; flowerheads fewer (5–22); stem leaves few; basal leaf blades mostly >2 cm long. . . . . *A. scopulorum* (p. 351)

  3b. Receptacle hairless 6

    6a. Flowerheads in head-like clusters; plants mostly 4–15 cm high. 7

      7a. Involucres 3.5–6 mm long, 6–11 mm wide, the bracts with brown margins; florets reddish black, hairless. . . . . *A. globularia* (p. 350)

      7b. Involucres 3–4 mm long, 3.5–5 mm wide, the bracts with white margins; florets yellow, hairy or not . . . . *A. glomerata* (p. 350)

    6b. Flowerheads in elongate or more open clusters; plants usually taller 8

      8a. Leaves mainly along stem, usually bicoloured (white-woolly below, green or greenish above, except *A. ludoviciana*) 9

        9a. Leaves partly palmately lobed; leaf mid-blade about as wide as the lobes; plants scented like perfume, not like sagebrush . . . . *A. michauxiana* (p. 351)

        9b. Leaves always pinnately lobed; leaf mid-blade mostly wider than the lobes; plants scented like sagebrush 10

          10a. Involucres bell-shaped; inflorescence very dense in bud (like a head of broccoli); leaves 2–5 cm wide; plants mostly in cool, humid (micro)climates . . . . *A. tilesii* (p. 352)

          10b. Involucres cup- to wineglass-shaped; inflorescence stretched out and sparse in bud (not dense like a head of broccoli); leaves (ours) 0.5–2 cm wide; plants mostly in dry, warm (micro)climates . . . *A. ludoviciana* (p. 351)

      8b. Leaves mainly at base of stem, upper and lower surfaces more or less uniformly coloured 11

        11a. Basal leaves 1–3 times pinnately compound or divided, often with ultimate segments again toothed. 12

          12a. Flowerheads 5–10 mm wide, nodding. . . . . *A. norvegica* (p. 352)

          12b. Flowerheads smaller, <5 mm wide, spreading to nodding . . . . *A. borealis* (p. 353)

        11b. Basal leaves 1–2-times divided into 3s or palmately divided. 13

          13a. Flowering stems arising from woody branches of previous season; plants 15–60 cm tall; lower leaves palmately 3-lobed or twice divided into 3s . . . . *A. alaskana* (p. 353)

          13b. Flowering stems arising directly from a non-woody rhizome or stem-base; plants 7–35 cm tall; lower leaves palmately or pinnately divided. 14

            14a. Leaves 1–3 times palmately lobed, the ultimate segments lacking tufts of hair at the tips . . . . *A. furcata* (p. 353)

            14b. Leaves 2–3 times pinnately lobed, the ultimate segments commonly with long tufts of hair at the tips . . . . *A. borealis* (p. 353)

Silver Sagebrush • *Artemisia cana*

General: Medium-sized, **much-branched, aromatic shrub, 50–70 cm tall; stems white-woolly or brownish and sparsely hairy,** branched from the base, the branches erect. **Leaves:** Deciduous, linear to narrowly lance-shaped, **mostly entire,** 2–4 cm long, densely to sparsely hairy. **Flowerheads:** 2–3 per branch cluster in long, narrow, sparsely leafy arrays; involucres bell-shaped, 3–4 mm long, bracts narrowly lance-shaped, hairy. **Fruits:** Achenes resinous. **Where Found:** Wet meadows, streambanks and rocky snowbeds; subalpine and alpine zones; frequent in the southeastern part of the region.

Similar Species: Snowfield sagebrush (*A. spiciformis*; *A. tridentata* ssp. *spiciformis*) is also a medium-sized shrub but has broader (8–12 mm wide), lance- to wedge-shaped, usually lobed leaves. It occurs on moist

slopes, rocky meadows, streambanks, open forests and snowbeds, in subalpine and alpine zones, and is frequent in the inland southern ⅓ of the region.

Notes: Many species of *Artemisia* contain numerous essential oils, some with medicinal properties. Silver sagebrush, for example, contains significant amounts of 1,8-cineole and camphor in its leaves and flowers. These oils can inhibit the growth of bacteria, yeasts and dermatophytes. • The "sagebrush steppe" of western North America is dominated by 10–13 species of *Artemisia*, all woody perennials adapted to a dry environment. Some of these shrubs are remarkably long-lived—the most common lower-elevation species, big sagebrush (*A. tridentata*), can live more than 200 years and some of our alpine species perhaps longer.

Bering Sagewort
Artemisia globularia
ssp. *globularia*

General: Plants mostly **3–15 cm tall;** stems erect, whitish grey, woolly. **Leaves:** Greenish to whitish green, sparsely hairy, **1–2 times palmately lobed or divided into 3s,** ultimate segments oblong to linear, blunt. **Flowerheads: Head-like clusters; florets reddish black or purplish;** involucres hemispheric, 3.5–6 mm long, 6–11 mm wide. **Where Found:**

Rocky slopes and tundra; montane to alpine zones; sporadic but locally frequent in the northern ¼ of the region; amphiberingian.

Similar Species: Congested sagewort (*A. glomerata*; *A. norvegica* ssp. *glomerata*) has **hairier, whitish leaves** and smaller flowerheads (**involucres 3–4 mm long, 3.5–5 mm wide**) in head-like to more expanded and elongate clusters, the **florets yellowish and often hairy.** It occurs on sandy and rocky slopes and tundra, in lowland to alpine zones. An amphiberingian species, it is sporadic but locally frequent in western AK, also in the arctic mountains and on the north slope of AK and YT.

Notes: Bering sagewort is also known as *Artemisia norvegica* ssp. *globularia*.

congested sagewort

Rocky Mountain Sage, Alpine Sage
Artemisia scopulorum

General: Tufted perennial **herb**; stems erect, unbranched, grey-green but often reddish, becoming hairless. **Leaves: Mostly basal**, persistent, **grey-green, silky-hairy above; blades 2–5 cm long**, mostly 2 times pinnately lobed, **ultimate segments linear to oblong. Flowerheads:** Yellow, 5–22 in long, narrow arrays; **receptacles with long, white hairs** among florets; involucres globe-shaped, 4 mm long, bracts green,

trimmed with black, densely hairy. **Fruits:**

Achenes about 1 mm long, hairless. **Where Found:** Meadows, talus and scree slopes, rocky streambanks, among boulders and in fellfields; subalpine and alpine zones; frequent in the southeastern part of the region.

Similar Species: Prairie sagewort, pasture sage or fringed sage (*A. frigida*) is a low perennial, **often woody at the base,** forming silvery mats or mounds 10–40 cm tall, with **silvery-silky-hairy leaves at the base and along the stem, the blades 0.5–2 cm long,** 2–3 times divided into 3s, the **ultimate segments fine-linear.** It occurs in dry grasslands, rocky slopes, sandy cutbanks and gravelly terraces and ridges, in montane and subalpine zones. An interruptedly circumboreal species, it is frequent throughout the inland part of the region (except OR), AK, YT and NT south to WA, AZ and NM. • **Siberian sage** (*A. rupestris*) is also mat-forming but is **sticky-glandular** throughout, with **bright green,** deciduous, **pinnately**

Siberian sage

dissected leaves that are **hairless** or nearly so. It grows on dry, boreal steppe and steep, south-facing, rocky slopes, in montane to alpine zones. Restricted in North America to the leeward mountains of southwestern YT, it is frequent on Dall's sheep range—a remarkable disjunction from the central Asian home range of this sage.

Notes: *Scopulorum* means "of cliffs and rock faces."

Salon Sagewort, Michaux's Mugwort
Artemisia michauxiana

General: Perfume-scented perennial from a somewhat woody base; **stems green, hairless,** erect, 20–70 cm tall. **Leaves: Along stem, green or silvery above, usually white-woolly below,** spoon- to egg-shaped, **usually 2–5 cm long,** 2 times lobed (more palmately than pinnately lobed), **ultimate segments toothed, narrower than 5 mm. Flowerheads:** Numerous in long, narrow arrays; florets yellow; involucres

typically bowl-shaped, 3–4 mm long; receptacles hairless. **Where Found:** Rocky slopes, talus, scree and meadows; montane to alpine zones; frequent in the inland southern ¾ of the region; cordilleran.

Similar Species: Mountain wormwood (*A. ludoviciana* ssp. *incompta*) has **narrower, bell-shaped involucres, pinnately lobed leaves** that are **green on both sides,** and is **aromatic like sagebrush.** It occurs in meadows and on rocky slopes, in montane to alpine zones, and is frequent from eastern OR, central ID and southwestern MT to CA, NV, UT and CO.

Notes: *Artemisia michauxiana* is named for André Michaux (1746–1802), a French botanist and the author of *Flora Boreali Americana*.

Caribou Weed, Aleutian Mugwort • *Artemisia tilesii*

Leaves: Usually bicoloured, tending to be **larger** (mostly 5–15 cm long and 2–5 cm wide) and **broader-lobed** than those of the species on p. 351, 1–2 times coarsely pinnately divided, the ultimate **segments mostly wider than 5 mm. Flowerheads: Involucres bowl-shaped. Where Found:** Streambanks, gravel bars, open forests, rocky slopes, meadows and tundra; lowland (in the north) to alpine zones; frequent throughout the northern ½ of the region, less so southward; circumpolar or amphiberingian.

Notes: Caribou weed includes *Artemisia tilesii* vars. *aleutica*, *elatior* and *unalaschcensis*, as well as *A. t.* ssps. *gormanii* and *hultenii*. • It is called "caribou weed" because the leaves look somewhat like caribou antlers. • A very important healing herb for many northern First Nations, caribou weed is still widely used as an anti-tumour agent by some (e.g., Tahltan and Tlingit). The Gwich'in, Tahltan and Alaskan peoples made a tea that was used to treat sore throats and colds, relieve constipation, purify blood, stop internal bleeding and treat kidney problems. Also, they burned the plant on smudge fires to repel mosquitoes and inhaled the fumes to clear nasal passages. Caribou weed has also been used by Alaskan peoples as a hot pack for sore muscles, skin tumours and infections. The Dena'ina made a tea as a wash for skin rashes, athlete's foot, cuts, blood-poisoned areas, toothaches and sore eyes from snow blindness. Crushed leaves could relieve itching and repel mosquitoes. Midwives applied poultices of hot leaves to a woman's stomach before changing the position of an incorrectly placed fetus. • **Caution:** This plant contains absinthol, which can cause tremors, convulsions and coma if taken in large doses. • The Smoking Hills, near Cape Bathurst, Northwest Territories, are seacoast cliffs with exposures of bituminous shale. The shale spontaneously ignited, fumigating the surrounding tundra with plumes of sulphur dioxide and sulphuric acid. Areas closest to the source have been devegetated, but slightly farther away, the first plants to appear are the tolerant caribou weed and reed polargrass (p. 460).

Mountain Sagewort • *Artemisia norvegica* ssp. *saxatilis*

General: Plants 20–50 cm tall. **Leaves:** Mostly basal, **bright green,** hairless to long-hairy, 1–3 times pinnately lobed, the ultimate segments linear, tapering to pointed tips. **Flowerheads: Relatively large, nodding; involucres globe-shaped, 5–10 mm wide. Where Found:** Meadows, open forests, thickets, rocky slopes, heathlands and tundra; lowland (arctic coast) to alpine zones; frequent throughout most of the region except the far south, rare along the Pacific coast; amphiberingian.

Notes: Mountain sagewort is also known as *Artemisia arctica*. • This sage is scarcely aromatic.

Boreal Sage • *Artemisia borealis*

General: Plants 8–30 cm tall. **Leaves:** Mostly basal, **grey-green to white,** densely to sparsely **silky-hairy,** 2–3 times pinnately lobed, the **ultimate segments linear to narrowly oblong,** the long, pointy **tips commonly with long tufts of hair. Flowerheads:** Relatively

small; **involucres hemispheric, 3–4 mm wide.
Where Found:** Meadows, grasslands, rocky slopes, river terraces and tundra; lowland (arctic coast) to alpine zones; frequent in much of the inland part of the region; western North American and Eurasian.

Subspecies: The widespread **ssp. *borealis*** is less hairy and has **yellow-orange florets.** • In arctic mountains and on the North

ssp. *richardsoniana*

Slope of AK, YT and NT, one can find **ssp. *richardsoniana*,** which is **shorter** (mostly 8–15 cm) and **densely white-hairy,** with **reddish purple florets.**

Notes: Boreal sage is also known as *Artemisia campestris* ssp. *borealis.*

Alaskan Sagebrush • *Artemisia alaskana*

General: Subshrubs or perennial herbs **from a woody base,** 15–60 cm tall; **stems sprawling to ascending,** densely grey-woolly, sometimes becoming nearly hairless with age. **Leaves:** Mostly basal but also along stem, **grey-green and woolly-hairy on both surfaces, palmately 3-lobed or twice divided into 3s,** the **ultimate segments broadly linear to oblong, blunt. Flowerheads:** Nodding; involucres bowl-shaped, woolly. **Where Found:** Dry streambanks, gravel bars, river terraces, roadsides, grassy or rocky slopes, scree and tundra; montane to alpine zones; frequent in the northern ⅓ of the region; endemic.

Similar Species: Prairie sagewort (p. 351) is mat-forming and has more finely divided leaves. • **Three-forked mugwort (below)** is generally smaller and **not woody at the base,** with stems that are at most **lightly hairy, not grey-woolly.**

Notes: Alaskan sagebrush is also known as *Artemisia tyrrellii.*

Three-forked Mugwort, Silver Wormwood
Artemisia furcata

General: Plants 7–35 cm tall. **Leaves:** Mostly basal, **grey-green on both surfaces, silky-hairy, 1–3 times palmately lobed,** ultimate segments linear to oblong, **abruptly pointed or blunt. Where Found:** Rocky slopes and tundra; subalpine and alpine zones; infrequent and sporadic in the northern ⅓ of the region, rare southward in western BC, western AB, the Olympic Mtns and Mt. Rainier, WA; amphiberingian.

Notes: Three-forked mugwort is also known as *Artemisia furcata* var. *heterophylla, A. hyperborea* and *A. trifurcata.*

Whitestem Goldenbush, Sharp-scale Goldenweed • *Ericameria discoidea*

General: Low, rounded shrub, 10–40 cm tall; stems much branched, **white-woolly.**

Leaves: Numerous along stems, persistent, ascending to spreading, **oblong or lance-shaped, 1–3.5 cm long, glandular-hairy, resinous,** margins often wavy or crisped.

Flowerheads: Solitary or few on each branch, of disc florets only; **florets yellow,** the styles sticking out well beyond floret tube; involucres top- to bell-shaped, 9–13 mm long, **bracts glandular-hairy.**

Fruits: Achenes 5–6 mm long, brown, hairy; **pappus bristles tan.**

Where Found: Rocky slopes and ridges, open forests, talus and scree; subalpine and alpine zones; frequent in the inland southernmost part of the region.

Similar Species: Dwarf rabbitbrush (*E. nauseosa* var. *nana*; *Chrysothamnus nauseosus* var. *nanus*) has **narrower (hair-like to linear), hairier, greyish to silvery leaves** and **mostly hairless, blunt or pointy-tipped involucral bracts.** It grows on dry, rocky ridges, cliffs and ledges in montane and subalpine zones, and is locally frequent in southeastern WA, northeastern OR (Blue and Wallowa Mtns) and west-central ID. • **Mountain rabbitbrush (*E. parryi* var. *montana*;** *C. parryi* ssp. *montanus*) is **smaller (10–20 cm tall), with green, hairless but somewhat greasy leaves** and **long-pointy-tipped involucral bracts.** It occurs on rocky slopes near timberline and is restricted to the Red Conglomerate Peaks along the ID-MT border.

Notes: Whitestem goldenbush is also known as *Haplopappus macronema* and *Macronema discoidea*.

Singlehead Goldenbush, Singlehead Goldenweed • *Ericameria suffruticosa*

General: Squat shrub 10–40 cm tall; stems, brittle twigs and leaves **glandular-hairy. Leaves:** Lance-shaped, margins usually wavy or crisped. **Flowerheads: Solitary or few per branch,** usually of **both ray (1–8) and disc florets;** florets yellow; involucres bell-shaped, bracts glandular-hairy. **Where Found:** Rocky slopes, ridges, open forests, scree and talus; subalpine and alpine zones; frequent in the inland southernmost part of the region.

Similar Species: Also a low shrub with sticky or greasy stems and leaves, **sticky-leaf rabbitbrush (*Chrysothamnus viscidiflorus* var. *viscidiflorus*)** has **numerous flowerheads in crowded clusters atop the stems,** the heads of **disc florets only.**

It occurs on rocky slopes, scree and talus, in subalpine and alpine zones, from ID and MT to OR, CA, AZ and NM.

Notes: Singlehead goldenbush is also known as *Haplopappus suffruticosus* and *Macronema suffruticosa*. • *Ericameria* is from *Erica*, the genus name of heather, and *meros*, "part or portion," because the leaves supposedly look similar to those of *Erica* species; *suffruticosa* means "somewhat shrubby."

sticky-leaf rabbitbrush

The Genus *Antennaria* (Pussytoes)

Our *Antennaria* are perennial herbs, generally white-woolly, with rhizomes, stolons (runners) or stem-bases and ascending to erect, unbranched stems. The leaves are entire, in conspicuous rosettes at the base and also alternate along the stem. The stem leaves are usually reduced in size upward, the upper ones sometimes with **flags** (flat, linear, wax-papery appendages at the leaf tips). The flower clusters are usually compact and somewhat rounded. The solitary to many flowerheads are small and composed of disc florets only, the numerous florets unisexual, the sexes typically on separate plants. The involucral bracts are shingled in several series, dry and wax-papery at least on the margins, often coloured and woolly-hairy toward the base; the receptacle is naked. The tiny, hairless, ellipsoid to egg-shaped achenes have pappus bristles that are usually baseball-bat-shaped in male florets, numerous and hair-like in female florets.

Antennaria is notoriously difficult taxonomically. This is likely because of its tendency toward polyploidy (extra sets of chromosomes), hybridization and apomixis (asexual production of seeds), in addition to usually having separate male and female plants. In North America, most *Antennaria* species (there are 32) primarily reproduce sexually and are diploid (with 2 sets of chromosomes, 2n=28), often with narrow ranges in unglaciated areas. These tend to be fairly well-defined species. But there are also 8 quite variable polyploid, apomictic species complexes (including in our flora *A. alpina*, *A. friesiana* in part, *A. media*, *A. monocephala* and *A. rosea*) with 4–12 sets of chromosomes and wider geographic ranges, often in glaciated areas. These species complexes evidently originated when sexual, diploid species fertilized themselves and doubled their chromosome numbers, then mated back with themselves or with other, occasionally sexual apomicts. And that's just the simplified, family-friendly version of the story.

The genus *Antennaria* is particularly diverse in western North America. In west-central Montana, for example, up to 6 or 7 species can occur on a single mountain, each in a different habitat, including racemose pussytoes (p. 357) and umber pussytoes (p. 357) in montane and subalpine forests, scented pussytoes (p. 358) and flat-top pussytoes (p. 359) around timberline, and Rocky Mountain pussytoes (p. 358) in alpine tundra.

Antennaria is from the Latin *antenna*, "feeler," and *aria*, "possession of," referring to the male floret's club-shaped pappus bristles, which resemble a butterfly's feeler or antenna. "Pussytoes" refers to the soft-hairy appearance of the flowerheads.

Key to *Antennaria*

1a. Flowerheads solitary, very rarely 2–3, atop stems . . . . *A. monocephala* (p. 356)

1b. Flowerheads 2 to many atop stems 2

  2a. Basal leaves 10–40 mm wide, upper surface green, hairless; inflorescence (array of flowerheads) diffuse, the heads mostly much smaller than the spaces between them . . . . *A. racemosa* (p. 357)

  2b. Basal leaves mostly narrower, equally hairy above and below, or nearly so; inflorescences tight, the heads larger than the spaces between them 3

    3a. Plants tufted, not mat-forming; upper stem leaves usually flagged (with flat, linear, wax-papery appendages at leaf tips). 4

      4a. Plants a bit shrubby, stolons (runners) mostly lifted off the ground (not just at the tips) and somewhat woody at the base; involucral bracts mostly dingy or brownish cream; plants of well-drained soil in rather dry climates . . . . *A. umbrinella* (p. 357)

      4b. Plants not at all shrubby, lacking woody stems, stolons remaining close to the ground except at the tips; involucral bracts of various colours 5

        5a. Plants without stolons, growing from a branched root crown; basal leaves narrowly lance-shaped; stems not glandular; plants mostly temperate to boreal. 6

          6a. Stems 5–25 cm tall; basal leaves 1–6 cm long; involucral bracts whitish or light brown in upper papery portions; plants south of 54° N . . . . *A. lanata* (p. 357)

          6b. Stems 20–50 cm tall; basal leaves 5–15 cm long; involucral bracts brown to blackish in upper portions; plants mostly south of 65° N . . . . *A. pulcherrima* (p. 357)

        5b. Plants with short stolons; basal leaves linear to narrowly lance-shaped; stems glandular; plants mostly high boreal to arctic, mostly north of 60° N . . . . *A. friesiana* (p. 358)

    3b. Plants mat-forming, with leafy rosettes at ends of trailing stolons (runners); upper stem leaves flagged or not 7

      7a. Involucral bracts brown, dark green, olive, or blackish, at least toward tip. 8

        8a. Stolons short (0.5–2.5 cm long), prostrate; basal leaves spoon- to wedge-shaped, 1–2 times as long as wide; restricted to rocky, calcium-rich sites. 9

9a. Basal leaves mostly 5–15 mm long; upper stem leaves not flagged; living plants with odour of citronella when crushed; stems and leaves stalked-glandular; plants south of 50° N .... *A. aromatica* (p. 358)

9b. Basal leaves mostly 3–7 mm long; upper stem leaves flagged; living plants not aromatic; stems and leaves not glandular; plants mostly north of 60° N, rare southward in the Rockies .... *A. densifolia* (p. 358)

8b. Stolons longer (1–15 cm long), ascending or trailing then turning up toward tip; basal leaves lance- to spoon- to narrowly wedge-shaped, 2–6 times as long as wide; not restricted to rocky, calcium-rich sites **10**

   10a. Upper stem leaves not flagged .... *A. media* (p. 358)

   10b. Upper stem leaves flagged **11**

      11a. Stolons short (0.1–4 cm long); stems, leaves and bracts with mixed glandular and non-glandular hairs .... *A. friesiana* (p. 358)

      11b. Stolons longer (1–7 cm long); plants hairy, without glands .... *A. alpina* (p. 358)

7b. Involucral bracts white, cream, pink, red, green, grey and light brown, or combinations thereof, at least toward tip. **12**

   12a. Stolons somewhat woody, ascending; upper papery portions of involucral bracts usually pale brownish, sometimes whitish or cream, sometimes streaked with pink .... *A. umbrinella* (p. 357)

   12b. Stolons not woody, trailing then turning up at tip; involucral bracts usually whitish, cream or pink. **13**

      13a. Upper papery portions of involucral bracts (combinations of) white, cream, pink, green, light brown; plants in dry, mostly well-drained sites, never in fens .... *A. rosea* (p. 359)

      13b. Upper papery portions of involucral bracts white or light brown, with distinct dark brown spot near base of papery portion; plants in wet sites, especially fens... *A. corymbosa* (p. 359)

Pygmy Pussytoes, One-headed Pussytoes
Antennaria monocephala

General: Mat-forming with stolons 2–4 cm long; stems erect, 3–13 cm tall, usually glandular-hairy. **Leaves:** Basal leaves spoon-shaped, to 1.5 cm long, usually green becoming hairless on upper surface; stem leaves linear, flagged. **Flowerheads:** Solitary; upper papery portions of involucral bracts dark brown, olive or blackish. **Where Found:** Meadows, gravelly slopes, heathlands and tundra; lowland (arctic coast) to alpine zones; frequent in the northern ½ of the region, infrequent southward mostly in the Rockies; arctic-alpine, amphiberingian.

Notes: Pygmy pussytoes is also known as *Antennaria angustata, A. pygmaea, A. exilis* and *A. philonipha*. • Species that reproduce asexually generally have wider distributions, often to higher elevations and latitudes, than species that reproduce sexually. So it is in pygmy pussytoes; ssp. *angustata*, which produces seed without fertilization (apomixis), has a much broader range than ssp. *monocephala*, which reproduces sexually.

Racemose Pussytoes • *Antennaria racemosa*

General: Mat-forming with stolons 3–8 cm long; stems erect, **12–40 cm tall,** usually glandular-hairy toward the top. **Leaves:** Basal **leaves elliptic,** to 10 cm long, green and hairless on upper surface, white-woolly below; stem leaves linear, not flagged. **Flowerheads:** Several in **loose, elongate arrays;** upper papery portions of involucral bracts whitish or light brown. **Where Found:** Open forests, cutbanks, meadows, grassy slopes and shrublands; montane to alpine zones; frequent in the southern ½ of the region; cordilleran.

Umber Pussytoes • *Antennaria umbrinella*

General: Mat-forming with slightly woody, **ascending stolons 7–15 cm long;** stems erect, **7–20 cm tall,** densely woolly-hairy. **Leaves:** Basal leaves spoon- to lance-shaped, **grey-hairy to white-woolly on both surfaces;** stem leaves linear, **not flagged. Flowerheads:** In compact clusters; involucral bracts blunt (male) or sharp-pointed (female), the **upper papery portions usually pale brown,** sometimes whitish or yellowish, or streaked with pink. **Where Found:** Open forests, shrublands, meadows, rocky or grassy slopes and fellfields; steppe to alpine zones; frequent in the mostly inland southern ⅔ of the region; cordilleran.

Woolly Pussytoe
Antennaria lanata

General: Tufted, not mat-forming, woolly-hairy throughout; stems erect, 5–25 cm tall. **Leaves:** Basal leaves narrowly lance-shaped, to 6 cm long, **white-woolly above and below;** stem leaves linear, **flagged. Flowerheads:** Several in **compact, rounded clusters;** involucral bracts whitish or light brown in upper papery portions. **Where Found:** Forest glades, edges of krummholz, meadows, rocky slopes and snowbed sites; subalpine and alpine zones; frequent in the inland southern ⅓ of the region; cordilleran.

showy pussytoes

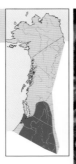

Similar Species: Showy pussytoes (*A. pulcherrima*) tends to be **taller** (20–50 cm) with longer (5–15 cm) basal leaves and involucral bracts that are **brown to blackish in the upper portions,** with a large, **black spot at the base.** It occurs in open forests, meadows, river terraces and thickets, in montane to lower alpine zones. A boreal/subarctic-alpine, North American species, it is scattered but locally frequent through much of the inland part of the region, eastern AK, southern YT and western NT to WA, ID, MT, WY, UT and CO.

Notes: *Lanata* means "woolly"; *pulcherrima* means "very pretty."

Tidy Pussytoes, Denseleaf Pussytoes
Antennaria densifolia

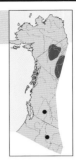

General: Mat-forming with short (1–2 cm long) stolons; stems 3–15 cm tall. **Leaves:** Basal leaves very small (3–7 mm long), crowded, spoon- to wedge-shaped, **grey-woolly on both surfaces;** stem leaves linear, **flagged. Flowerheads:** Few to several; upper papery portions of involucral bracts light brown, dark brown or black. **Where Found:** Calcium-rich, rocky slopes (especially limestone talus) and ridges; subalpine and lower alpine zones; scattered but locally frequent in the northern ⅓ of the region, disjunct in MT and possibly southeastern BC.

Similar Species: Scented pussytoes (*A. aromatica*) is **glandular-hairy, smells of citronella** when crushed, has **larger (5–15 mm long) basal leaves** and the **stem leaves are not flagged.** It is restricted to rocky, calcium-rich sites in the subalpine zone of southwestern AB, MT, ID and WY.

Alpine Pussytoes • *Antennaria alpina*

General: Mat-forming with stolons 1–7 cm long; stems 3–18 cm tall, hairy. **Leaves:** Basal leaves spoon- to lance-shaped, to 2.5 cm long, **upper surface grey-hairy to greenish becoming hairless, white-woolly below;** stem leaves linear, the **upper flagged. Flowerheads:** Either of female florets only (usually) or male florets only (occasionally); **involucral bracts dark brown, olive or blackish in upper papery portions. Where Found:** Meadows, rocky slopes, gravelly ridges, heathlands, tundra, scree and fellfields; montane to alpine zones; frequent in much of the region, infrequent west of the coastal mountains, absent from WA, OR and ID; arctic-alpine, circumpolar.

Alaskan pussytoes

Similar Species: Alaskan pussytoes (*A. friesiana*; *A. alpina* var. *friesiana*, *A. ekmaniana*, *A. alaskana*, *A. neoalaskana*) is related to alpine pussytoes but has **glandular-hairy upper stems,** and 2 of its 3 subspecies do not form mats. It occurs in fellfields, frost boils, rock outcrops, sandy-gravelly ridges and tundra, in lowland (arctic coast) to alpine zones. An arctic-alpine species, it is frequent in northern AK, YT and NT, mostly north of 64° N; the species complex is circumpolar.

Notes: Alpine pussytoes includes *Antennaria compacta*, *A. glabrata*, *A. pallida*, *A. pedunculata* and *A. stolonifera*.

Rocky Mountain Pussytoes • *Antennaria media*

General: Mat-forming with stolons 1–4 cm long; stems 5–13 cm tall. **Leaves:** Basal leaves spoon- to lance-shaped, to 2 cm long, **grey-hairy on both surfaces;** stem leaves linear, pointy-tipped but **not flagged. Flowerheads:** Involucral bracts dark brown, olive or blackish in upper part. **Where Found:** Meadows, rocky slopes, gravelly ridges, heathlands and tundra, scree and fellfields; subalpine and alpine zones; frequent in the southern ¾ of the region except the north Pacific coast; cordilleran.

Notes: Rocky Mountain pussytoes is also known as *Antennaria alpina* var. *media*. • Most of its populations are wholly female; populations with both male and female plants occur in OR and CA.

Rosy Pussytoes • *Antennaria rosea*

General: Mat-forming with stolons 1–7 cm long; stems 5–30 cm tall, densely woolly-hairy.
Leaves: Basal leaves spoon- to lance-shaped, to 4 cm long, 2–10 mm wide, **grey-hairy to white-woolly on both surfaces;** stem leaves linear, **usually not flagged. Flowerheads:** In compact, rounded clusters; involucral bracts mostly pointy-tipped, the **upper papery portions combinations of white, pink, green, pale yellow or light brown.**

Where Found: Rocky and grassy slopes, gravelly ridges and terraces, open forests, shrublands, meadows, rock outcrops and tundra; lowland to alpine zones; frequent throughout the region except the far north and the northern Pacific coast; North American.

Similar Species: Flat-top pussytoes (*A. corymbosa*) has **narrower (2–4 mm)** basal leaves and **white- or light-brown-tipped involucral bracts** with a **dark brown spot** at the base of the papery portion. It occurs in fens, moist meadows and willow thickets, in subalpine and alpine zones, and is infrequent in the southern ⅓ of the region, southern BC, WA, ID and MT to CA, NV, UT and NM.

Notes: Rosy pussytoes includes *Antennaria alborosea, A. arida, A. confinis, A. elegans, A. isolepis* and *A. pulvinata*, among others. It is the most widespread species of pussytoes in North America. • What we call rosy pussytoes is an extremely variable, apomictic polyploid complex believed to have been derived multiple times from the creative reproductive behaviour (selfing and crossing and chromosome doubling) of several sexual *Antennaria* species (including racemose, umber and flat-top pussytoes) from more southerly, unglaciated areas.

Alpine Dustymaidens, Alpine Pincushion
Chaenactis douglasii var. *alpina*

General: From a taproot, tufted to somewhat matted; flowering stems spreading to erect, **5–15 cm tall.**

Leaves: All basal, **twice pinnately divided and fern-like,** somewhat **3-dimensional** (lobes not disposed in one plane, somewhat contorted and curly-edged), 2–6 cm long, thinly grey-cobwebby-woolly to nearly hairless.

Flowerheads: White or cream to lavender, 1 or sometimes 2 per stem, of disc florets only; **style and anthers protruding well beyond corolla;** receptacles naked; involucres conic to hemispheric, **bracts stalked-glandular and/or cobwebby-hairy,** roughly equal, in 1 series.

Fruits: Achenes hairy, glandular; **pappus of 10–20 translucent scales.**

Where Found: Open, rocky slopes, gravelly ridges, talus, scree, rock crevices and fellfields; alpine zone; infrequent in the inland southern-most part of the region.

Similar Species: Evermann's pincushion (*C. evermannii*) has once-pinnately lobed, plane leaves and closely hairy (not glandular) involucres. It is endemic to central ID, on granitic talus, scree, sandy-gravelly ridges and forest openings, in subalpine and lower alpine zones.

Notes: Alpine dustymaidens is also known as *Chaenactis alpina*. • "Dustymaidens" refers to the ruffled, greyish leaves, which look like petticoats after a hoedown. "Pincushion" acknowledges the appearance of the flower-head with exserted styles and anthers.

Rainiera • *Rainiera stricta*

General: From a fibrous-rooted rhizome; **stems usually 1**, erect, **30–100 cm tall.**

Leaves: Basal and alternate along stem, large below, progressively smaller upward, spoon- to lance-shaped, **10–35 cm long, hairless or nearly so, margins mostly entire.**

Flowerheads: Yellow, rarely tinged with purple, numerous in **long, narrow, spike-like clusters** atop stems, of disc florets only; **florets 5 or so,** 10–12 mm long; receptacles naked; involucres top-shaped to cylindric, thinly cobwebby-woolly, **bracts roughly equal,** in 1 series.

Fruits: Achenes 5–6 mm long; pappus bristles white or straw-coloured.

Where Found: Moist meadows and open, rocky slopes; montane to lower alpine zones; infrequent in the Cascades, from Mt. Rainier, WA, to Lane Co., OR; endemic.

Notes: Rainiera is also known as *Luina stricta.* • *Stricta* means "erect" or "upright."

Silverback Luina, Littleleaf Luina
Luina hypoleuca

General: From a branched stem-base; **stems several to many, clumped,** spreading to erect, 15–40 cm tall, white-woolly.

Leaves: Alternate and unstalked along stem, elliptic to egg-shaped, **2–6 cm long, white-woolly below, green and sparsely hairy or nearly hairless above, margins entire.**

Flowerheads: Pale yellow, several in **flat-topped clusters** atop stems, of disc florets only; **florets 11–20;** receptacles naked; involucres top-shaped to cylindric, long-hairy, **bracts roughly equal,** in 1 series.

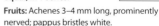

Fruits: Achenes 3–4 mm long, prominently nerved; pappus bristles white.

Where Found: Open, rocky slopes, outcrops and talus; lowland to lower alpine zones; frequent in the southwestern part of the region, mostly in and west of the Cascades; Pacific maritime.

Notes: *Luina* is an anagram of *Inula* (elecampane, another aster family genus); *hypoleuca* means "whitish" or "pale," alluding to the silvery colour on the underside of the leaves.

Key to Group III: Heads with Both Ray and Disc Florets; Ray Florets White, Pink, Purple, Reddish or Blue

1a. Leaves dissected, fern-like; pappus lacking; receptacles with papery scales ...... **_Achillea millefolium_** (below)

1b. Leaves not dissected and fern-like; pappus present; receptacles naked 2

  2a. Pappus of flattened, papery, bristle-like scales or a mere crown.................................... 3

    3a. Pappus a short crown of 6–12 irregular teeth.........................**_Hulteniella integrifolia_** (p. 364)

    3b. Pappus of 12 or more flattened, bristle-like scales .... **_Townsendia_** (pp. 362–363)

  2b. Pappus of hair-like (not flattened) bristles 4

    4a. Stems leafless but with bracts; basal leaves triangular to heart-shaped, coarsely toothed or palmately lobed, white-woolly beneath... **_Petasites frigidus_** (p. 365)

    4b. Stems with ordinary leaves; basal leaves otherwise.. 5

      5a. Involucral bracts narrow, linear-lance-shaped, mostly nearly equal in length, sometimes overlapping but usually in few series, green (but not leaf-like) or wax-papery throughout, not a combination of green above with a whitish, wax-papery base; plants seldom with rhizomes; flower buds often nodding, becoming erect on opening .... **_Erigeron_** (pp. 369–379)

      5b. Involucral bracts mostly broader, lance-elliptic to egg-shaped, usually in several series of unequal length, overlapping like shingles on a roof, the outer ones often progressively shorter, usually green at the tip and wax-papery at the base, sometimes green throughout and somewhat leaf-like; plants often with rhizomes; buds usually erect 6

        6a. Achenes conic or egg-shaped, flattened, margins ribbed 7

          7a. Leaves all along stem, increasing in size to midstem; involucral bracts keeled .... **_Eucephalus_** (p. 367)

          7b. Leaves basal and along stem; involucral bracts not keeled .... **_Aster alpinus_** (p. 366)

        6b. Achenes lance-shaped or lance-oblong in outline, compressed or rounded in cross-section, nerved or ribbed on faces but not margins 8

          8a. Plants from a taproot; leaves all or mostly in a basal rosette.... **_Oreostemma alpigenum_** (p. 367)

          8b. Plants mostly from rhizomes; well-developed leaves along the stem as well as basal 9

            9a. Stem leaves rough-hairy, clasping at the base; disc corollas with tube as long as or longer than limb (the flaring upper part, including lobes)...................... **_Eurybia_** (p. 366)

            9b. Stem leaves usually hairless, occasionally sparsely hairy, often not clasping at the base; disc corollas with tube shorter than limb .... **_Symphyotrichum foliaceum_** (p. 368)

Yarrow • _Achillea millefolium_

General: Aromatic, usually with rhizomes; stems erect, 5–50 cm tall.

Leaves: Basal and alternate along stem, 1–2-times **pinnately dissected, fern-like,** densely hairy to nearly hairless.

Flowerheads: Numerous in **compact, flat or rounded clusters;** ray florets usually 5–8, **white or sometimes pink; disc florets 10–20, cream; receptacles scaly or chaffy;** involucres bell-shaped to hemispheric, glandular-hairy and/or cobwebby, bracts overlapping in 3 series, dry, **green, often dark-margined.**

Fruits: Achenes oblong, hairless, flattened and winged; **pappus lacking.**

Where Found: Wide range of open habitats including meadows, rocky slopes and ridges; lowland to alpine zones; frequent throughout; species complex widespread in the Northern Hemisphere.

Notes: Yarrow in our broad concept of the species includes _Achillea alpicola, A. borealis, A. lanulosa, A. nigrescens, A. pacifica_ and _A. subalpina,_ among others. • _A. millefolium_ is extremely variable. Taxonomists have either recognized the variations as several distinct species or as varieties of a single species, or enveloped them in their concept of one variable super-species. Plants of higher elevations and higher latitudes—in general, those treated in this book—tend to be hairier and have darker margins on the involucral bracts. • First Nations peoples had a variety of medicinal uses for yarrow. Yarrow from high elevations is considered more potent than that from low elevations. • The genus is named after Achilles, who used the plant to stop the bleeding of his soldiers wounded in the Siege of Troy; hence, it is sometimes called the "military plant."

The Genus *Townsendia* (Easter Daisy)

Ours are perennial herbs from a taproot, often surmounted by a stem-base, the stems spreading to erect. The leaves are all at the base or basal and alternate along the stem, spoon- to lance-shaped or linear, the margins not toothed or lobed. The flowerheads, of both ray and disc florets, are solitary atop the stems or unstalked among a basal rosette of leaves. The ray florets are white, pink, bluish or lavender; the numerous disc florets are yellow. The involucral bracts are narrow, unequal, overlapping in several series and generally with a green central stripe and fringed or ragged margins; the receptacles are naked. The achenes are flattened and 2-nerved, with a pappus of whitish, bristle-like scales.

Key to *Townsendia*

1a. Plants biennial or perennial, not cushion-forming, mostly >7 cm tall; leaves basal and along stem; flowerheads very showy, about 3–4 cm wide, at tips of leafy stems. . . . . **T. parryi** (below)

1b. Plants perennial, cushion-forming, <5 cm tall; flowerheads showy but smaller, about 1.5–3 cm wide, atop very short, leafless or few-leaved stems, or stalkless and nestled among basal rosette leaves. **2**

    2a. Involucral bracts in 5 or more overlapping series, each bract at least 9 mm long and at least 5 times as long as wide, narrowly lance- to awl-shaped; basal leaves 1–3 mm or more wide; pappus readily dropping from achenes . . . . **T. condensata** (p. 363)

    2b. Involucral bracts in 3–4 overlapping series, each bract up to 9 mm long and up to 5 times as long as wide, lance-shaped; basal leaves 1–2 mm wide; pappus persistent **3**

        3a. Involucral bracts blunt-tipped; ray florets usually glandular-hairy on lower surface. . . **T. montana** (p. 363)

        3b. Involucral bracts long-tapered to pointy tip; ray florets hairless beneath . . . . **T. leptotes** (p. 363)

Parry's Easter Daisy • *Townsendia parryi*

General: Biennial or short-lived perennial; stems spreading to erect, **5–25 cm long/tall,** short-stiff-hairy. **Leaves:** **Basal and along stem,** narrowly spoon-shaped, 2–6 cm long. **Flowerheads:** Solitary atop stems, **3–5 cm across; ray florets usually blue or purple** (rarely white or pinkish); involucres hemispheric, stiff-hairy or hairless. **Where Found:** Meadows, grassy and rocky slopes, gravelly benches, talus and fellfields; upper montane to alpine zones; sporadic but locally frequent in the southeastern part of the region; cordilleran.

Notes: This species is named for Charles Parry (1923–90), a British American botanist and surveyor.

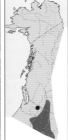

Cushion Easter Daisy
Townsendia condensata

General: Cushion-forming, 1–2 cm tall, stemless or nearly so, generally **woolly or shaggy-hairy. Leaves:** Mostly basal, crowded, spoon-shaped, mostly **1–3 cm long. Flowerheads:** Solitary, 2–3 cm across, unstalked or atop very short stems; **ray florets white** (occasionally pinkish); involucres soft-hairy. **Where Found:** Rocky slopes, talus and fellfields; alpine zone; sporadic but locally frequent in the southeastern part of the region, southwestern AB, MT, ID, WY, UT and CA.

Notes: David Townsend (1787–1858), a banker and talented amateur botanist from Pennsylvania, is the namesake for this genus.

Mountain Easter Daisy • *Townsendia montana*

General: Cushion-forming, 1–5 cm tall, dotted with short, stiff hairs or nearly hairless. **Leaves:** Basal and along short stems, spoon- to lance-shaped, 1–4 cm long. **Flowerheads:** solitary, 2–3 cm across, usually **atop short stems; ray florets usually white,** sometimes lavender, pink or blue, **usually glandular-hairy** on lower surface; **involucral bracts broadly lance- to egg-shaped. Where Found:** Rocky and gravelly meadows, slopes and ridges, talus and fellfields; alpine zone; sporadic but locally frequent in the southeastern part of the region.

Notes: Mountain townsendia is also known as *Townsendia alpigena.* • Rock gardeners consider Easter daisies "the elite of the daisies," on account of their large flowerheads relative to the small size of the plants. However, cultivation is a challenge, especially where winters are mild and wet.

Common Easter Daisy
Townsendia leptotes

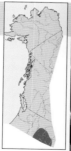

General: Cushion-forming, **1–3 cm tall,** dotted with short, stiff hairs or nearly hairless. **Leaves: Basal and along very short stems,** narrowly spoon-shaped to oblong, 1–4 cm long. **Flowerheads:** Solitary, **1.5–2.5 cm across, usually unstalked; ray florets usually white or pinkish, usually hairless on lower surface; involucral bracts linear to narrowly lance-shaped. Where Found:** Rocky slopes and ridges; alpine zone; sporadic but locally frequent in the southeastern part of the region.

Notes: *Leptotes* is Greek for "delicateness."

Entire-leaved Daisy
Hulteniella integrifolia

General: From a rhizome and branched stem-base; **stems solitary to few,** erect, unbranched, **5–15 cm tall,** hairy toward top.

Leaves: Mostly basal, 5–20 (to 30) mm long, **linear to oblong, margins not toothed or lobed but fringed** with long hairs; stem leaves 1 to few, alternate, smaller.

Flowerheads: Solitary atop stems, 1–1.5 cm across; ray florets 10–20, **white;** disc florets numerous, yellow; receptacles naked; involucres hemispheric, 4–8 mm high, bracts overlapping in 2 series, green with wide, brownish, wax-papery and frilly or eroded margins.

Fruits: Achenes 1.5–2 mm long, prismatic, 5-ribbed, hairless; **pappus a crown of 6–12 tiny teeth.**

Where Found: Rocky slopes, gravelly ridges and flushes, stony barrens and tundra, often on calcium-rich substrates; lowland (arctic coast) to alpine zones; frequent in the far north, rare in northeastern BC; arctic-alpine, broadly amphiberingian.

Notes: Entire-leaved daisy is also known as *Chrysanthemum integrifolium* and *Leucanthemum integrifolium*. • It is a strong candidate for the most poly-syllabic scientific name in our alpine flora. • Eric Hultén (1894–1981) was a professor of botany in Stockholm. He was a Swedish student of American arctic floras and circumpolar flora in general and the author of *Flora of Alaska and Neighboring Territories*, among others. In addition to taxonomic manuals, Hultén is probably best known for studies on plant geography (*The Amphi-Atlantic Plants, The Circumpolar Plants I & II*) and insights into Beringian biota.

Arctic Sweet Coltsfoot, Arctic Butterbur • *Petasites frigidus*

General: From branched, cord-like, creeping rhizomes, often forming clones; **flowering stems erect, unbranched, 10–60 cm tall, leafless but with alternate bracts,** white-woolly, **appearing early in season** before leaves; stems of "male" plants wither soon after flowering, stems of "female" plants elongate after flowering.

Leaves: All basal, long-stalked; blades variable in shape, heart- to kidney-shaped or triangular, palmately veined, **2–20 cm long/wide, margins coarsely toothed or lobed, usually white-woolly on lower surface,** green and hairless or thinly hairy above.

Flowerheads: 1–2 cm across, 4–20 in rounded clusters atop stems; "male" and "female" heads on separate plants, the male heads with outer sterile florets and inner, usually functionally male florets, the female heads with outer, fertile, female florets and functionally male inner florets; **ray florets few to numerous, sometimes lacking, white or pinkish to purplish;** disc florets few to many, white or reddish-tinged; **involucral bracts roughly equal in size,** in 1 series or with a few shorter outer bracts, green or purple-tinged, hairy at base.

Fruits: Achenes cylindric, 5–10-ribbed; **pappus bristles white.**

Where Found: Streambanks, seepage areas and flushes, forest edges, cutbanks, wet meadows, thickets and wet tundra; lowland (arctic coast) to alpine zones; frequent throughout the northern ¾ of the region, less so southward; arctic-alpine, circumboreal.

Subspecies: Our concept of *Petasites frigidus*, unlike that of *FNA*, includes neither *P. palmatus* nor *P. sagittatus*. • Some taxonomists have recognized different species or subspecies within the *P. frigidus* complex, based primarily on leaf shape, which is not the most reliable characteristic, but the variation is striking. The circumpolar **ssp. frigidus** has merely coarsely toothed leaves. The amphiberingian **ssp. nivalis** has deeply palmately lobed leaves. So, too, does **ssp. arcticus**, but its leaves are nearly hairless, not white-woolly on the lower surface; it is a spectacular endemic of the Richardson and Mackenzie mountains of western NT and northeastern YT.

ssp. *arcticus*

Notes: Arctic sweet coltsfoot is also known as *Petasites alaskanus*, *P. arcticus*, *P. nivalis*, *P. hyperboreus* and *P. vitifolius*. • The Alaskan swallowtail butterfly (*Papilio machaon aliaska*) lays its eggs in (and feeds on) its traditional host, a snowparsley (*Cnidium cnidiifolium*), but also on novel hosts arctic sweet coltsfoot and mountain sagewort (p. 352). Butterfly larvae survive and grow better on snowparsley when predators are absent, but survival is better on the aster family plants when there are larval predators (ants and ichneumonid wasps) around. This could represent the latest battle in a coevolutionary war in which the butterflies have switched strategies, but the ants and ichneumonids haven't figured it out … yet. • This plant is reputed to be a tried-and-true cough remedy. Some Alaskan peoples chewed the rhizomes to treat a sore throat. The leaves are used by modern herbalists in teas for menstrual cramps, asthma and croup. The Inupiat eat the young leaves; large leaves (as well of Alaska wild-rhubarb, p. 111) are used to cover berries in barrels and to combat mould. • **Caution:** Arctic sweet coltsfoot contains pyrrolizidine alkaloids, which can cause liver irritation and may be carcinogenic, so it should only be used in small amounts. • The name "coltsfoot" was originally given to the European *Tussilago farfara* because of the shape of its leaves, which are roughly triangular to heart-shaped with lobes. "Butterbur" refers to the large leaves, which were used to wrap butter. *Petasites* is from the Greek *petasos*, "a broad-brimmed hat," because the leaves were considered big enough to protect a person's head from the sun.

ssp. *frigidus*   ssp. *nivalis*

Alpine Aster • *Aster alpinus* ssp. *vierhapperi*

General: From **rhizomes** and a woody stem-base; stem 1 per tuft of leaves, erect or ascending, **5–30 cm tall, grey-hairy and stalked-glandular** especially toward the top.

Leaves: Basal leaves lance- to spoon-shaped, stalked, 1–10 cm long; **stem leaves narrowly oblong,** stalkless, progressively smaller upward, **long-hairy, often stalked-glandular, margins entire, fringed with long hairs.**

Flowerheads: Solitary atop stems, 3–4.5 cm across; ray florets white, pink or lavender; involucres densely hairy, **bracts about equal** in size, **overlapping** in 2–3 series, mostly **green and leaf-like in texture.**

Fruits: Achenes egg-shaped, **flattened, 2-ribbed,** whiskery; pappus bristles white to tan.

Where Found: Rocky and grassy slopes, bluffs, forest edges, stony meadows, talus and tundra, often on calcium-rich substrates; montane to alpine zones; widespread but scattered from the northern interior part of the region south along the Rockies; arctic-alpine, amphiberingian.

Similar Species: Alpine aster could be confused with **tufted fleabane** (p. 374).

Notes: Alpine aster is the only species of the strictly defined *Aster* genus that is native to North America and is our only alpine aster left standing as *Aster*. • *Aster* is named for the stars.

Arctic Aster • *Eurybia sibirica*

General: From **rhizomes;** stems 1–5, often branched, **ascending to sprawling, 5–50 cm tall,** long-hairy but **not glandular.**

Leaves: Along the stem, midstem leaves largest, **lance- to egg-shaped,** 2–10 cm long, **firm,** dark green beneath, paler grey-green and **long-hairy above, margins coarsely toothed;** leaves (or stalks) clasping at base.

Flowerheads: Solitary to many in open arrays atop stems, 2.5–5 cm across; **ray florets purple to pale violet** (occasionally white); disc florets numerous, yellow becoming purplish; involucres hairy, **bracts mostly nearly equal in size and overlapping** in several series, typically **leafy textured,** often purplish with green tips.

Fruits: Achenes compressed-cylindric, 7–10-ribbed, whiskery; **pappus red-brown.**

Where Found: Rocky slopes, sandy forest openings, thickets, gravel bars, shores, bluffs, sand dunes and meadows; lowland to alpine zones; frequent in the northern ½ of the region, less frequent southward in the Rockies; arctic-alpine, amphiberingian.

Similar Species: Thickstem aster (*E. integrifolia*; *Aster integrifolius, A. amplexifolius*) is generally **larger (15–70 cm tall)** and **stalked-glandular, with erect stems** and **smooth-margined leaves 3–14 cm long.** It occurs in meadows, open forests and thickets, in montane to lower alpine zones, and is frequent in the inland southern part of the region, from WA, ID and MT to CA, NV and UT.

Notes: Arctic aster is also known as *Aster sibiricus, A. giganteus, A. montanus* and *A. richardsonii*. • Genetic analyses suggest that arctic aster and thickstem aster are close relatives, but the 23 species currently in *Eurybia* are not all closely related to each other. More taxonomic reassignments could be coming! • *Eurybia* is from the Greek *eurys*, "wide," and *baios*, "few," perhaps because of the few, widely spreading ray florets.

Olympic Mountain Aster
Eucephalus paucicapitatus

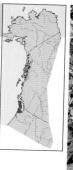

General: From a stout, **woody stem-base;** stems several, ascending to erect, **20–55 cm tall,** soft-hairy or glandular-hairy.

Leaves: Mostly along stem, midstem leaves largest, elliptic-oblong, **2–4 cm long,** stalked-glandular above, margins entire or nearly so.

Flowerheads: Solitary or **2–4** at ends of stems, 3–4.5 cm across; **ray florets white,** mostly 7–13; involucres glandular-hairy, **bracts unequal in size, weakly overlapping, keeled, greenish above** whitish wax-papery base, narrowly **purple-margined.**

Fruits: Achenes conic, 4-nerved, flattened, soft-hairy; **pappus bristles** white to tawny.

Where Found: Meadows, rocky ridges, outcrops and scree slopes; montane to subalpine zones; infrequent endemic of southern Vancouver I. and the Olympic Peninsula.

Similar Species: Engelmann aster (*E. engelmannii*; *Aster engelmannii*) is **larger (50–120 cm tall),** with **larger leaves** (5–10 cm long) and **white to pink ray florets.** It grows in meadows, open forests and on avalanche tracks, in montane and subalpine zones. A cordilleran species, it is frequent in the inland southern ⅓ of the region, southern BC and southwestern AB south to WA, NV and CO.

Notes: Olympic Mountain aster is also known as *Aster paucicapitatus*. • *Eucephalus* is from the Greek *eu,* "good" or "proper," and *kephalotos,* "with a head," in reference to the "elegant qualities of the calyx" (T. Nuttall, 1840).

Engelmann aster

Cascade Mountaincrown, Alpine Cookie Aster
Oreostemma alpigenum

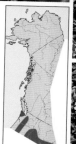

General: Small perennial from a **stem-base and taproot;** stems ascending, unbranched, **4–30 cm tall.**

Leaves: Mostly in a basal rosette, linear to lance-shaped, **3–15 cm long,** often hairy when young but **becoming nearly hairless and shiny, margins entire.**

Flowerheads: Solitary, **2–4 cm across;** ray florets several to many, **lavender, purple or occasionally white;** involucres often woolly-hairy, **bracts unequal in size** and **overlapping** in several series, **papery at base but otherwise leaf-like in texture,** green, often tinted purplish.

Fruits: Achenes narrowly cylindric, the faces **5–10-ribbed; pappus bristles whitish to tawny.**

Where Found: Meadows, shores, bogs, fens, forest openings, rocky slopes and ridges near snowbanks, talus, fellfields and tundra; montane to alpine zones; locally frequent in the southern ¼ of the region, Cascade, Olympic, Blue, Wallowa and Rocky mountains.

Similar Species: Eaton's fleabane or Eaton's shaggy daisy (*Erigeron eatonii*) could be mistaken for Cascade mountaincrown but has **more prominent stem leaves** and **usually white ray florets.** It is found on grasslands, shrublands, meadows and rocky slopes, in montane and subalpine zones, and is infrequent in WA, ID and MT south to CA, AZ and CO.

Notes: Cascade mountaincrown is also known as *Aster alpigenus* and *Haplopappus alpigenus*. • *Oreostemma* is from the Greek *oreo,* "mountain," and *stemma,* "crown."

Leafybract Aster
Symphyotrichum foliaceum

General: Colonial from rhizomes; stems ascending to erect, **10–60 cm tall**, often reddish purple, **hairless or sparsely hairy.**

Leaves: Basal and along stem; midstem leaves elliptic to lance- or egg-shaped, stalkless, sometimes clasping at base, 4–12 cm long, **usually hairless, margins usually entire.**

Flowerheads: **Solitary or several,** on hairy stalks in short, leafy-bracted arrays, 3–6 cm across; ray florets **rose-purple to violet or blue;** involucres bell-shaped, **bracts relatively large, unequal** in size (**some outer ones somewhat leaf-like** and enlarged), **graduated and overlapping** in several series, the inner green and white-margined at base.

Fruits: Achenes cylindric to egg-shaped, not compressed, 3–4-nerved, hairy; **pappus bristles white to tawny.**

Where Found: Open forests, glades, grassy slopes, streambanks, thickets and moist meadows; montane to lower alpine zones; frequent mostly throughout the southern ½ of the region; cordilleran.

Varieties: This species is widespread and variable in size, hairiness, number of heads and shape of involucral bracts; 4 varieties have been recognized (see *FNA* for details).

Similar Species: Leafybract aster could be confused with **subalpine daisy** (p. 372), and **wandering daisy** (p. 372), especially when growing together in subalpine meadows, but **fleabanes and daisies have mostly equal-sized, non-graduated involucral bracts.**

Notes: Leafybract aster is also known as *Aster foliaceus.* • *Symphyotrichum* is from the Greek *symphysis,* "junction," and *trichos,* "hair," maybe alluding to the apparently fused bristles in some species (but not in this one); *foliaceum* means "leaf-like," referring to the outer involucral bracts.

WHERE HAVE ALL THE ASTERS GONE?

Aster used to be one of the larger genera of flowering plants, with 400 to 600 species mostly in the Northern Hemisphere. Over the last 2 decades, the genus has been reduced to fewer than 200 species, with only a single native taxon—*A. alpinus* ssp. *vierhapperi* (p. 366)—remaining in North America. North American species previously in *Aster* now occupy some 10 segregate genera, with our alpine plants variously disposed in *Eucephalus, Eurybia, Oreostemma* and *Symphyotrichum.* What the heck happened to *Aster* and the species that were dis-*Aster*-ed?

Once technologies were developed in the 1990s to peer into the genes of vascular plants, an *Aster*-oid belt of unevenly related species with different chromosome numbers (x = 4–13) and gene sequences became apparent. The North American members of the tribe Astereae (including *Aster*) are mainly annuals and (in the alpine) herbaceous perennials, and are well defined genetically. However, our species evidently are only distantly related to Astereae from South America, Europe and Africa, which are mostly woody perennials. Furthermore, our species formerly known as *Aster* are not closely related to Eurasian asters. And because the first species placed in the genus—Michaelmas daisy (*A. amellus*)—was European, the name *Aster* remains mostly in the Eurozone.

The alpine genera formerly known as *Aster* are largely (*Eurybia, Symphyotrichum*) or entirely (*Eucephalus, Oreostemma*) North American. And although the current classification owes much to molecular and chromosome evidence, it also reflects long-recognized morphological differences; for example, *Eurybia* was first described as a subgenus of *Aster* in 1818.

The Genus *Erigeron* (Fleabane, Daisy)

Ours are perennial herbs that bloom relatively early (compared to many other aster-family species), growing mostly from a taproot and stem-base, occasionally from a rhizome, the stems sprawling to erect. The leaves are basal and/or alternate along the stem, spoon- to lance-shaped or linear, the margins often entire (not toothed or lobed). The flowerheads are solitary to many atop the stems, composed of both ray and disc florets (occasionally of disc florets only). The several to many ray florets are often narrow, pink, lilac, purplish or white, rarely yellow; the numerous disc florets are yellow. The narrow involucral bracts are mostly of similar length, sometimes unequal and overlapping, often green but not distinctly leaf-like in texture, and sometimes mostly wax-papery; the receptacles are naked. The oblong, flattened achenes are nerved and usually hairy, with a pappus of hair-like, often fragile bristles.

It's easy to confuse fleabanes or daisies (*Erigeron*) and asters (i.e., *Aster* plus the plants formerly known as *Aster—Eurybia, Eucephalus, Oreostemma* and *Symphyotrichum*). The involucral bracts of asters are generally broader, lance-elliptic to egg-shaped, mostly unequal in length and overlapping like shingles, whereas the bracts of fleabanes and daisies are narrower, linear-lance-shaped, more nearly equal in length and sometimes also overlapping but usually in fewer series.

Erigeron is from the Greek *eri*, "early," and *geron*, "old man," literally "early old man," perhaps because some species have white-woolly flowerheads or greyish pappus bristles and they tend to flower and fruit relatively early in summer, thus appearing prematurely old.

Key to *Erigeron*

1a. Plants with erect to ascending stems; stem leaves ample, gradually reduced in size upward, usually lance-shaped or wider, clasping at the base **2**

  2a. Leaf margins coarsely toothed; leaves coarsely hairy; ray florets 10–15 mm long . . . . *E. aliceae* (p. 372)

  2b. Leaf margins not toothed; leaves often hairless; ray florets 8–25 mm long **3**

    3a. Involucral bracts usually hairless but densely and evenly stalked-glandular . . . . *E. glacialis* (p. 372)

    3b. Involucral bracts hairy and with fringed margins, usually sparsely glandular toward tip . . . . *E. peregrinus* (p. 372)

1b. Plants usually low and spreading; stem leaves usually much reduced or lacking, mostly linear or lance-shaped **4**

  4a. Ray florets very narrow (thread-like), short, erect **5**

    5a. Leaves all entire; pappus bristles whitish to rusty or tan **6**

      6a. Stems often branched; flowerheads often more than 1; involucral bracts hairless or sparsely hairy . . . . *E. nivalis* (p. 372)

      6b. Stems unbranched; flowerhead 1; involucral bracts very hairy **7**

        7a. Hairs of involucral bracts with purplish crosswalls . . . . *E. humilis* in part (p. 376)

        7b. Hairs of involucral bracts with clear or sometimes reddish crosswalls . . . *E. uniflorus* in part (p. 376)

    5b. At least some leaves 3-forked or 3–5-toothed or lobed at tip **8**

      8a. Pappus bristles tawny white to yellowish; leaves entire or shallowly 3-lobed at tip; southeastern BC and southwestern AB . . . . *E. pallens* in part (p. 378)

      8b. Pappus bristles usually purplish; leaves entire, or toothed or lobed; north of 57° N **9**

        9a. Plants 1–5 cm tall; leaves spoon-shaped, 2–5 mm wide; involucral bracts densely hairy . . . . *E. denalii* in part (p. 379)

        9b. Plants 3–12 cm tall; leaves linear to narrowly lance-shaped, 1–3 mm wide; involucral bracts sparsely hairy or hairless. . . . . *E. purpuratus* in part (p. 379)

  4b. Ray florets usually well developed, strap-shaped, spreading; occasionally reduced, narrow, erect; rarely lacking **10**

    10a. Leaves divided or at least some 3-forked or 3–5-toothed or lobed at tip. **11**

      11a. Leaves (1 to) 2–4 times divided into 3s. . . . . *E. compositus* (p. 373)

      11b. At least some leaves 3-forked or 3–5-toothed or lobed at tip **12**

        12a. Oldest and largest leaves mostly entire, younger smaller leaves often toothed or lobed **13**

          13a. Pappus bristles whitish to tawny, often twisted; in the Rockies south of about 54° N . . . . *E. lanatus* in part (p. 378)

          13b. Pappus bristles usually purplish, not twisted; leaves entire or toothed or lobed at tip; north of 57° N. **14**

28b. Ray florets white to pinkish, bluish or lavender; basal leaves 4–12 cm long; involucral bracts glandular and long-white-hairy, the hairs without dark crosswalls; pappus bristles 12–15 .... ***E. ochroleucus*** (p. 375)

17b. Involucres densely woolly-long-hairy (except sparsely so in *E. fletti* and *E. purpuratus*), the hairs multicellular (with crosswalls) **29**

29a. Ray florets yellow .... ***E. aureus*** (p. 379)

29b. Ray florets white, pink, blue, or purple **30**

30a. Ray florets relatively short and narrow, erect, 3–8 mm long, 0.3–1 mm wide **31**

31a. Pappus bristles purplish **32**

32a. Plants 1–5 cm tall; leaves spoon-shaped, 2–5 mm wide; involucral bracts densely hairy................................... ***E. denalii*** in part (p. 379)

32b. Plants 3–12 cm tall; leaves linear to narrowly lance-shaped, 1–3 mm wide; involucral bracts sparsely hairy or hairless..... ***E. purpuratus*** in part (p. 379)

31b. Pappus bristles white to tawny **33**

33a. Hairs of involucral bracts and upper part of stems with dark reddish to purplish black crosswalls .... ***E. humilis*** in part (p. 376)

33b. Hairs of involucral bracts with clear or sometimes reddish crosswalls...... **34**

34a. Plants with at least a few well-developed stem leaves; leaves not lobed or toothed; north of 57° N .... ***E. uniflorus*** in part (p. 376)

34b. Plants without stem leaves or with only a few reduced ones; some earlier, smaller leaves 3-lobed at tip; southeastern BC and southwestern AB .... ***E. pallens*** in part (p. 378)

30a. Ray florets conspicuous, spreading, 5–13 mm long, about twice as long as pappus or longer, mostly 1–2 mm wide **35**

35a. Some smaller, young leaves 3-lobed or 3-toothed at tip; southeastern plants, in the Rockies south of about 54° N .... ***E. lanatus*** in part (p. 378)

35b. Leaves not toothed or lobed; distributions various **36**

36a. Leaves densely clothed with interwoven woolly hairs; entire plant appears grey-green.. ***E. muirii*** (p. 377)

36b. Leaves otherwise hairy, not tightly woolly............................... **37**

37a. Hairs of involucral bracts with blackish or dark purple crosswalls .... ***E. hyperboreus*** (p. 377)

37b. Hairs of involucral bracts with clear or reddish to reddish purple crosswalls **38**

38a. Lower leaves narrowly lance-shaped, 4–16 cm long; flowerheads 1–2 (to 4) from midstem branches .... ***E. yukonensis*** (p. 377)

38b. Lower leaves lance-oblong to egg- or spoon-shaped, 1–12 cm long; flowerheads 1 .... **39**

39a. Basal leaves lance-oblong to narrowly egg-shaped, pointy-tipped; hairs of involucral bracts whitish, without coloured crosswalls; ray florets 13–17 mm long .... ***E. porsildii*** (p. 377)

39b. Basal leaves lance- to egg- or spoon-shaped, with rounded tips; hairs of involucral bracts glassy, often with reddish crosswalls; ray florets 5–15 mm long **40**

40a. Ray florets 50–130, blue to pink, rarely white; involucral bracts woolly-long-hairy; plants primarily of Rocky Mtns .... ***E. grandiflorus*** (p. 377)

40b. Ray florets 25–40, white; involucral bracts coarsely long-hairy; plants of Olympic Mtns .... ***E. flettii*** (p. 378)

achene

crosswalled hairs

involucral bracts

E. humilis

Subalpine Daisy, Subalpine Fleabane
Erigeron glacialis var. *glacialis*

General: From **rhizomes; stems erect to ascending, 10–70 cm tall,** hairy.

Leaves: Basal and ample along stem, lance- to spoon-shaped; **stem leaves somewhat clasping at base, 3–16 cm long, margins entire.**

Flowerheads: Solitary or several, 3–6 cm across; ray florets 30–80, usually **pink to rose purple or blue,** sometimes white to pale blue, 1.5–3 mm wide; involucral bracts mostly equal in size, in 2–4 series, usually **hairless but densely stalked-glandular.**

Fruits: Achenes oblong, 4–7-nerved; pappus bristles white.

Where Found: Moist meadows, open forests, glades, rocky slopes and streambanks; montane to lower alpine zones; frequent throughout most of the southern ¾ of the region, uncommon along the outer Pacific coast; cordilleran.

Similar Species: Wandering daisy (*E. peregrinus*) has **hairy involucral bracts** that are sparsely stalked-glandular and have **fringed margins.** It is found in moist to wet meadows, thickets, fens, streambanks and forest openings, in montane to alpine zones. Wandering daisy is frequent in and west of the coastal mountains and infrequent inland from southern AK and southwestern YT through western BC to WA. • Alice Eastwood's daisy (*E. aliceae*) usually has **coarsely toothed, generally hairier leaves** and slightly smaller, white to pinkish purple flowerheads with **involucral bracts that are white-hairy toward the base** and **stalked-glandular toward the tip.** It occurs in meadows and open forests, on rocky slopes, ridges and talus, in montane and subalpine zones, and is infrequent in the Cascade and Olympic Mtns, western WA and OR to northern CA.

Notes: Subalpine daisy is also known as *Erigeron peregrinus* ssp. *callianthemus.*

Snowbed Bitter Fleabane • *Erigeron nivalis*

General: Biennial or short-lived perennial from fibrous roots or sometimes a taproot; stems erect to ascending, **5–30 cm tall,** minutely **glandular-hairy.**

Leaves: Basal and along stem, spoon- to lance-shaped, 2–6 cm long, sparsely hairy, margins usually smooth except for the frilly-edged stalks.

Flowerheads: Solitary to few on glandular stalks, 1.5–2 cm across; ray florets numerous, **very narrow (thread-like), erect-ascending, white to pinkish;** involucral bracts mostly equal in size, minutely stalked-glandular.

Fruits: Achenes oblong, 2-nerved; pappus white to somewhat rusty.

Where Found: Gravel bars, streambanks, fens, wet meadows, open forests and glades; montane to lower alpine zones; frequent in most of the region except the far north and the Pacific coast; cordilleran.

Notes: Snowbed bitter fleabane has previously often been treated as a subspecies or variety of bitter fleabane (*Erigeron acris*) and is also known as *E. acris* ssp. *debilis*, *E. debilis* and *Trimorpha acris* var. *debilis.*

LEAVES DIVIDED, 3-FORKED OR 3–5-LOBED AT TIP

Cut-leaf Daisy, Dwarf Mountain Fleabane
Erigeron compositus

General: Densely tufted, taprooted; stems erect, **5–20 cm tall,** hairy to nearly hairless, minutely glandular. **Leaves:** Mostly basal, blades 1–8 cm long, long-stalked, **1–4 times divided into 3s;** stem leaves few, bract-like. **Flowerheads:** Solitary, 1–3 cm across; **ray florets white to pink or blue or lacking;** involucres 5–10 mm high, bracts hairy, **stalked-glandular, purple-tipped. Where Found:** Grassy and rocky slopes, gravelly benches and ridges, meadows, scree, talus and fellfields; lowland to alpine zones; frequent throughout the region; essentially cordilleran.

Notes: Cut-leaf daisy has been divided by some into several varieties, including the rayless var. *discoideus.*

Alberta Fleabane, Three-lobed Daisy
Erigeron trifidus

General: Stems 2–7 cm tall, hairy, minutely glandular. **Leaves:** All basal, blades 1–3 cm long, mostly 3-lobed; lobes 3–8 mm long, lance-shaped, pointy-tipped, coarsely hairy; **stalks 1–2 mm wide, wider toward top. Flowerheads:** Solitary, 1–2 cm across; ray florets white to pinkish, **10–15 mm long; involucres 8–12 mm high,** bracts coarse-hairy, **stalked-glandular, purplish or purple-tipped. Where Found:** Dry scree and talus slopes; alpine zone; infrequent in the Rockies of eastern BC and western AB; endemic.

Notes: Alberta fleabane is also known as *Erigeron compositus* var. *trifidus.*

Salish Fleabane, Salish Daisy
Erigeron salishii

General: Cushion-forming, resembling the preceding 2 species; **stems 2–7 cm tall. Leaves:** All basal, blades 0.3–1.5 cm long, mostly 3-lobed; lobes 2–6 mm long, oblong to egg-shaped, **blunt,** coarsely hairy; **stalks linear, parallel-sided, 0.5–1 mm wide. Flowerheads:** Solitary, 1–2 cm across; ray florets white to bluish, **6–10 mm long; involucres 5–7 mm high,** bracts hairy and glandular. **Where Found:** Cliffs, ledges, gravelly ridges, scree and talus slopes; alpine zone; infrequent endemic of central Vancouver I. and northwestern WA.

Notes: The Puget Sound–Strait of Georgia area First Nations are sometimes collectively called Coast Salish.

Fanleaf Fleabane, Fanleaf Daisy
Erigeron flabellifolius

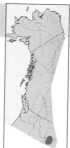 

General: Resembles preceding 2 species but **stems, leaves and involucres are hairless but glandular. Leaves:** Mostly basal, blades wedge- to spoon-shaped, **1–4 cm long, 3–5-lobed, lobes again 3-toothed or lobed. Flowerheads:** Solitary, 2–3 cm across; ray florets white to lavender or pale pink; **involucres 7–8 mm high. Where Found:** Rocky meadows, gravelly ridges, cliffs, scree and talus slopes; alpine zone; infrequent in southwestern MT and northwestern WY; endemic.

Notes: *Flabellifolius* means "fan-like leaves."

Leaves Mostly Entire; Involucres Variously Hairy but Not Woolly

Tufted Fleabane, Tufted Daisy • *Erigeron caespitosus*

General: From a stout taproot surmounted by a stem-base; stems several, spreading to ascending, 5–30 cm tall, **grey-spreading-hairy**, not glandular. **Leaves:** Basal leaves lance- to spoon-shaped, 3-nerved, 2–12 cm long, **hairy like stems, blunt or rounded at tip**; stem leaves several to many, oblong-elliptic, reduced in size upward. **Flowerheads:** 1–4, **3–5 cm across**; ray florets white, blue or sometimes pink; involucres 4–7 mm high, **bracts glandular and grey-hairy**. **Where Found:** Rocky and grassy slopes, outcrops, sandy-gravelly cutbanks and terraces, forest openings, meadows and fellfields; montane to alpine (in the south) zones; widespread but scattered, occasionally locally frequent in the inland part of the region; cordilleran–Great Plains.

Similar Species: Slender fleabane or thin daisy (*E. tener*; *E. caespitosus* var. *tenerus*) has **appressed hairs, 1-nerved, pointy-tipped leaves** and **smaller (1–2 cm across) flowerheads** with blue to purple ray florets. It occurs on rocky slopes, talus, gravelly ridges, cliff ledges and crevices, and forest edges, in montane to alpine zones, and is infrequent inland in the southern ¼ of the region, OR, ID and MT south to CA, NV, AZ and WY.

Leiberg's Fleabane, Leiberg's Daisy *Erigeron leibergii*

General: Stems ascending to erect, **6–25 cm tall, moderately long-hairy and glandular. Leaves:** Basal leaves egg- to spoon-shaped, **hairy and glandular like stems**; stem leaves several to many, smaller and narrower than basal leaves but **not strongly reduced in size upward. Flowerheads: Usually 1** (sometimes up to 5), 2–4 cm across; **ray florets blue to purplish** (occasionally pink or white); **involucral bracts hairy, stalked-glandular. Where Found:** Rocky slopes, cliffs, ledges, scree and talus slopes; montane to alpine zones; infrequent in south-central BC and north-central WA (Cascade and Wenatchee Mtns).

Similar Species: Cascade fleabane (*E. cascadensis*) has **mostly hairless and sparsely glandular stems, leaves and involucres**, and **usually white ray florets**. It grows on cliffs, crevices, talus, outcrops and in meadows, in the subalpine zone, and is infrequent in the Cascades of OR.

Notes: John B. Leiberg (1853–1913) was a bryologist, forester and botanical explorer of Idaho and Washington.

Rockslide Fleabane, Smooth Daisy • *Erigeron leiomerus*

General: Stems spreading to ascending, 4–15 cm tall, hairless or sparsely appressed-hairy. **Leaves:** Basal leaves lance- to spoon-shaped, 1.5–7 cm long, **rounded at tip,** hairless or sparsely hairy, not glandular; **stem leaves several,** much smaller and narrower than basal leaves, reduced in size upward. **Flowerheads: Solitary,** 2–3.5 cm across; **ray florets white, blue or purplish, bending downward;** involucres 4–6 mm high, **bracts hairless** or occasionally sparsely hairy, **minutely glandular. Where Found:** Rocky slopes, forest edges, boulder fields, scree and talus slopes, fellfields and tundra; subalpine and alpine zones; frequent in the southeastern part of the region.

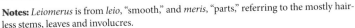

Notes: *Leiomerus* is from *leio*, "smooth," and *meris*, "parts," referring to the mostly hairless stems, leaves and involucres.

Evermann's Fleabane • *Erigeron evermannii*

General: Resembles rockslide fleabane (p. 374) but has **fewer (or no) stem leaves, involucral bracts hairy** as well as sometimes glandular and **white ray florets that spread**

horizontal. Where Found: Rocky slopes, meadows, gravelly ridges, cliffs, scree and talus slopes, often with whitebark pine; subalpine and alpine zones; infrequent in southwestern MT and central ID; endemic.

Similar Species: Idaho fleabane (*E. asperugineus*) is hairier (**spreading hairs**) overall than each of the 2 preceding species, with **pointy-tipped basal leaves, hairy and glandular involucres** and mostly **deep blue to purple ray florets** that **spread upward,** the flowerhead thus top-shaped overall. It grows on rocky slopes, meadows, forest edges, gravelly ridges and talus, often with whitebark or limber pines, in subalpine and alpine zones. Idaho fleabane is scattered but locally frequent in ID, MT, NV and UT.

Buff Fleabane, Pale Daisy • *Erigeron ochroleucus*

General: Stems ascending, **5–25 cm tall**, appressed-hairy, sometimes glandular. **Leaves: Basal leaves linear to narrowly lance-shaped,** 4–12 cm long, **appressed-hairy, pointy-tipped;** stem leaves several, similar to but smaller than basal leaves, often bract-like. **Flowerheads:** 1 (sometimes 2–3), 2.5–4 cm across; **ray florets white, pinkish or bluish;** involucral bracts mostly equal, **long-hairy and minutely glandular,** the whitish **hairs without coloured crosswalls.** Where Found: Rocky slopes, outcrops, cliffs, ledges, scree and talus slopes (often in limestone terrain), dry meadows, forest edges and tundra; montane to alpine zones; frequent in the southeastern part of the region, infrequent and disjunct in northern AK and northwestern YT.

Similar Species: Lackschewitz fleabane (*E. lackschewitzii*) also has densely glandular and hairy involucres, the **hairs sometimes with blackish purple crosswalls,** and **blue to purple ray florets.** It is found on dry, often calcium-rich, rocky slopes, ridges, terraces, meadows and talus, in subalpine and alpine zones, and is infrequent in southwestern AB and MT. • **Bigroot fleabane** or bigroot daisy (*E. radicatus*) is typically **smaller (2–10 cm tall)** than buff fleabane, with a thicker taproot and stem-base, **long-hairy stems, blunt to rounded leaves,** white to sometimes purplish ray florets and **involucral hairs with coloured crosswalls.** It grows on rocky slopes, outcrops, ridges, ledges and talus, usually on limestone, in montane to alpine zones. A Great Plains–cordilleran species, it is infrequent in the southeastern part of the region, southern AB to ID, UT and CO, east to SK, the Dakotas and NE.

Notes: Buff fleabane is also known as *Erigeron laetevirens*, *E. montanus*, *E. scribneri* and *E. tweedyanus*.

Rydberg's Fleabane, Rydberg's Daisy
Erigeron rydbergii

General: From a thick taproot and branched stem-base; stems erect, **2–6 cm tall,** finely hairy, not glandular. **Leaves: Mostly basal,** narrowly lance- to spoon-shaped, 1–5 cm long, **hairless** or nearly so, **blunt or rounded at tip. Flowerheads: Solitary,** 2–3 cm across; **ray florets blue to purplish,** rarely white; involucres 5–6 mm high, bracts fine-hairy and minutely glandular, the **hairs without coloured crosswalls.** Where Found: Rocky slopes, scree and talus; subalpine and alpine zones; infrequent in the southeastern part of the region.

Similar Species: Bigroot fleabane or bigroot daisy (*E. radicatus*) has usually **white ray florets** and **fewer pappus bristles** (6–12 vs. 15–20).

LEAVES MOSTLY ENTIRE; INVOLUCRES USUALLY WOOLLY WITH MULTICELLULAR, CROSSWALLED HAIRS

Arctic-alpine Fleabane, Arctic Daisy • *Erigeron humilis*

General: Fibrous-rooted, from a taproot-like stem-base and occasionally rhizomes; stems lax, ascending to erect, **2–20 cm tall, spreading long-hairy, minutely glandular. Leaves: Mostly basal,** lance- to spoon-shaped, 1–8 cm long, hairy like stems; stem leaves several, smaller and narrower than basal leaves and reduced in size upward. **Flowerheads: Solitary, 1–2 cm across; ray florets whitish to lavender or purplish, thread-like,** 0.3–1 mm wide, **ascending-erect;** involucres 6–9 mm high, **bracts usually dark purple and long-woolly-hairy, the hairs with dark purplish crosswalls. Where Found:** Rocky slopes, meadows, seepage areas, streambanks, edges of snowbeds, heathlands and tundra; lowland (arctic coast) to alpine zones; frequent in most of the northern ½ of the region, less so southward; arctic-alpine, circumpolar.

Notes: Arctic-alpine fleabane is also known as *Erigeron unalaschkensis.* • *Humilis* means "low growing."

One-flower Fleabane, Northern Daisy • *Erigeron uniflorus* var. *eriocephalus*

General: Much like arctic-alpine fleabane (above) but has slightly larger flower-heads with **reddish purple involucral bracts** that have **hairs with clear or bright reddish crosswalls. Where Found:** Rocky and gravelly slopes, ridges, terraces, scree, meadows, snowbed edges, fellfields and tundra; montane to alpine zones; infrequent in the northern ⅓ of the region; arctic-alpine, circumpolar.

Notes: One-flower fleabane is also known as *Erigeron eriocephalus.*

Tundra Fleabane, Tundra Daisy
Erigeron hyperboreus

General: Stems erect or curved at base, 3–13 cm tall, long-spreading-hairy (the hairs with purplish black crosswalls) and minutely glandular, especially near the top. **Leaves:** Mostly basal, lance-shaped, 1–6 cm long, spreading-hairy; stem leaves few to several, linear, reduced in size upward. **Flowerheads:** Solitary, 2.5–4 cm across; **ray florets blue, purplish or white, strap-shaped, 1–2 mm wide, spreading;** involucres 5–8 mm high, bracts usually dark purple, long-woolly-hairy and glandular, the **hairs with purplish black crosswalls. Where Found:** Rocky slopes, meadows, scree and talus, fellfields, heathlands and tundra, often in limestone or ultrabasic (serpentine) terrain; lowland to alpine zones; locally frequent in the northern ¼ of the region; arctic-alpine, endemic.

Similar Species: Yukon fleabane or Yukon daisy (**E. yukonensis;** *E. glabellus* var. *yukonensis*) typically is larger (**10–40 cm tall**), with **lower leaves 4–15 cm long,** 1 (sometimes 2–4) flowerheads with **pink to purplish ray florets** and involucral bracts with **crinkly, whitish hairs with clear crosswalls.** It occurs on rocky slopes and in stony meadows, often on calcium-rich substrates, in subalpine and alpine zones. Yukon fleabane is an endemic species, scattered but locally frequent in eastern AK, YT and NT.

Notes: Tundra fleabane is also known as *Erigeron alaskanus.*

Large-flower Fleabane
Erigeron grandiflorus

General: From a rhizome or crown-like stem-base; stems erect to ascending, solitary, 4–25 cm tall, soft-hairy, often stalked-glandular as well. **Leaves: Basal leaves lance- to spoon-shaped, rounded at tip, 1–9 cm long,** usually long-hairy; stem leaves narrowly lance-shaped, reduced upward. **Flowerheads:** Solitary, 2.5–4.5 cm across; ray **florets 50–130, blue to pink or lavender** (rarely white), spreading; **involucral bracts densely long-woolly-hairy** and minutely glandular at least at tips, the hairs with **clear or sometimes reddish crosswalls. Where Found:** Dry, rocky slopes, meadows and fellfields; subalpine and alpine zones; frequent in the southeastern part of the region (mostly the Rockies), infrequent northward; cordilleran.

Similar Species: Porsild's fleabane or Porsild's daisy (**E. porsildii;** *E. grandiflorus* ssp. *arcticus*) has **narrower** (oblong-lance-shaped to narrowly egg-shaped), **pointy-tipped leaves** and somewhat **larger flowerheads, 3.5–5.5 cm across.** It is found on rocky, often calcium-rich slopes, cliffs, talus, shaly scree, grassy gullies and tundra, in montane to alpine zones. It is an arctic-alpine endemic that is scattered but locally frequent in the northern ⅓ of the region, central and eastern AK, southwestern and northern YT and NT. • **Muir's fleabane** (**E. muirii;** *E. grandiflorus* ssp. *muirii*) is densely white-cobwebby all over, appearing greyish green. It grows on rocky outcrops and slopes, gravelly ridges and tundra, and is a rare endemic in northern AK and northern YT (Herschel I.).

Notes: Large-flower fleabane is also known as *Erigeron simplex.*

Olympic Mountain Fleabane, Flett's Daisy • *Erigeron flettii*

General: Similar to large-flower fleabane (p. 377) but has **basal leaves with stalks longer than or equal to blades, fewer (25–40), consistently white ray florets, moderately spreading-hairy** (not woolly) involucral bracts and a very different distribution. **Where Found:** Rocky and gravelly slopes, ridges, ledges and crevices, scree and meadows; subalpine and alpine zones; endemic to the Olympic Mtns, WA.

Notes: This species is named for John B. Flett, botanist and mountaineer, a Scot who came to Tacoma in 1893. He taught biology and geology, and worked as a ranger in Mt. Rainier National Park from 1913 to 1921.

Woolly Fleabane, Woolly Daisy *Erigeron lanatus*

General: From a taproot and slender, branching stem-base; **stems erect, 2–5 cm tall,** loosely long-hairy and minutely glandular. **Leaves: All basal,** lance-oblong, 5–30 mm long, loosely long-hairy, usually entire, the **earliest and smallest sometimes 3-toothed at tip. Flowerheads:** Solitary, **2.5–4 cm across; ray florets white or lavender,** strap-shaped, **1.5–2 mm wide, spreading;** involucres 9–13 mm high, bracts purple or purple-tipped, moderately to densely long-woolly-hairy, the **hairs sometimes with purplish crosswalls. Fruits:** Pappus mostly whitish. **Where Found:** Rocky slopes, meadows, scree and talus, often on limestone; subalpine and alpine zones; locally frequent in the Rockies of the southeastern part of the region.

Pale Fleabane, Pale Daisy *Erigeron pallens*

Flowerheads: 1–2 cm across; ray florets thread-like, ascending to erect; involucral bracts sparsely hairy. **Fruits:** Pappus tawny white to yellowish. **Where Found:** Dry, rocky slopes, scree and talus; alpine zone; infrequent and restricted to southeastern BC and southwestern AB.

Notes: Northern plants previously identified as *E. pallens* are mostly *E. denalii*, according to *FNA*.

Denali Fleabane, Denali Daisy
Erigeron denalii

General: Similar to pale fleabane (p. 378) but has **densely long-hairy involucral bracts,** the hairs often with dark purple crosswalls, and **purplish red pappus bristles.** **Where Found:** Rocky slopes, scree, forest openings and tundra; montane to alpine zones; scattered but locally frequent in the **northern ⅓ of the region.**

Similar Species: Purple fleabane or purple daisy (*E. purpuratus*) also has **pink to purple pappus bristles,** but compared to Denali fleabane is **taller** (3–12 cm vs. 1–5 cm), with **narrower leaves** (linear-lance-shaped vs. spoon-shaped) and sparsely spreading-hairy (with dark purple crosswalls) or hairless involucral bracts. It is found on gravel bars, sandy-gravelly shores and

cutbanks, rocky slopes and tundra, in lowland to alpine zones, and is an arctic-alpine, endemic species, scattered but locally frequent in the north, in AK and YT west of 137° W.

Notes: Denali fleabane is also known as *Erigeron mexiae* and *E. purpuratus* var. *dilatatus.*

purple fleabane

Golden Fleabane, Golden Daisy • *Erigeron aureus*

General: From a fibrous-rooted, stout, stem-base; **stems several, erect to ascending from a curved base, 3–15 cm tall,** loosely or appressed-hairy, minutely glandular. **Leaves:** Basal leaves spoon-shaped, **triple-nerved,** 2–6 cm long, hairy like stems but not glandular, blunt or rounded at tip; stem leaves several, strongly reduced in size upward. **Flowerheads:** 1 per stem, 2–3.5 cm across; **ray florets yellow, strap-**

shaped, 1.5–2.5 mm wide; involucres 5–8 mm high, bracts of equal size, purplish, **woolly-hairy,** sparsely glandular. **Where Found:** Rocky slopes and ridges, outcrops, meadows, talus and fellfields; montane to alpine zones; frequent over a relatively small part of the southern interior of the region, southern BC to southwestern AB and northern WA.

Notes: Golden fleabane is also known as *Haplopappus brandegeei.*

Key to Group IV: Heads with Both Ray and Disc Florets; Ray Florets Yellow or Orange

1a. Pappus of bracts or scales (chaffy) or of firm awns, or absent 2

   2a. Involucral bracts few (5–13), nearly equal in size, in 1 or apparently 2 series; pappus of 6–12 transparent scales or a merely toothed crown; plants white-woolly . . . . ***Eriophyllum lanatum*** (p. 382)

   2b. Involucral bracts many (20+), in 2–3 series; plants aromatic and glandular or gland-dotted, variously hairy but usually not white-woolly 3

      3a. Achenes lance-linear or lance-oblong, at least 4 times as long as wide; receptacle flat; pappus of 4 transparent scales, fused at base into a leathery ring . . . . ***Hulsea*** (p. 383)

      3b. Achenes wedge-shaped, 2–3 times as long as wide; receptacle convex; pappus of 5–7 scales, often bristly or awned . . . . ***Hymenoxys grandiflora*** (p. 383)

1b. Pappus of hair-like or feathery bristles 4

   4a. Leaves opposite . . . . ***Arnica*** (pp. 384–388)

   4b. Leaves alternate or all basal 5

      5a. Involucral bracts in 2 or more series, equal or unequal and overlapping like shingles 6

         6a. Pappus double; bristles of outer series distinctly shorter than those of inner series . . . . ***Erigeron aureus*** (Group III, p. 379)

         6b. Pappus single; bristles sometimes variable in length but not partitioned into an inner and an outer series 7

            7a. Flowerheads numerous in dense, rounded or wand-shaped arrays . . . . ***Solidago*** (p. 382)

            7b. Flowerheads solitary or few (2–5) in loose arrays 8

               8a. Stems sparsely leafy, the linear stem leaves greatly reduced in size from basal leaves; ray florets 5–17 . . . . ***Stenotus*** (p. 381)

               8b. Stems leafy, the oblong-lance-shaped stem leaves not much reduced in size from basal leaves; ray florets 10–20 (to 30) . . . . ***Tonestus*** (p. 381)

      5b. Involucral bracts in 1 series (or in 2 series in some *Senecio* and *Packera*), mostly equal in size, often with a few much shorter outer ones 9

         9a. Leaf blades egg- to kidney-shaped, palmately veined . . . . ***Sinosenecio newcombei*** (p. 400)

         9b. Leaf blades otherwise, mostly linear to lance- or egg-shaped, pinnately veined 10

            10a. Style branches with "stigmatic areas" (i.e., surfaces receptive to pollen) in 2 lines; stamen filaments expanded toward the top into swollen collars 11

               11a. Leaves basal and/or along stem; roots often fleshy, seldom branched and/or leaf margins with "callous teeth" (hardened, thickened teeth) . . . . ***Senecio*** (pp. 389–392)

               11b. Leaves basal and along stem; roots seldom fleshy, often branched; leaf margins with few or no "callous teeth" . . . . ***Packera*** (pp. 393–397)

            10b. Style branches with continuous "stigmatic areas"; stamen filaments cylindric, not widened toward the top . . . . ***Tephroseris*** (pp. 398–399)

Lyall's serpentweed

Stemless Goldenweed
Stenotus acaulis

General: Tufted or mat-forming, from a stout taproot and branched stem-base; **stems numerous, erect,** 3–20 cm tall, sometimes sticky- or stalked-glandular.

Leaves: Basal and along stem, crowded at ends of short branches of stem-base, **rigid, linear to broadly lance-shaped,** 0.5–8 cm long, **margins roughened and stiff-fringed;** stem leaves few, much smaller than basal ones.

Flowerheads: Usually 1 (sometimes 2–4), 2–4 cm across; **ray florets 5–13,** 2–6 mm wide, **spreading, yellow; involucral bracts unequal** in size, in 2–3 series, hardened at base, wax-papery upward, green toward tip, usually hairless, sometimes sticky or stalked-glandular.

Fruits: Achenes narrowly lance-shaped, 6–12-nerved; **pappus bristles whitish,** minutely barbed.

Where Found: Dry shrublands, forest openings, rocky slopes and meadows; montane to alpine zones; frequent in the inland southernmost part of the region; cordilleran.

Similar Species: Woolly goldenweed (*S. lanuginosus*; *H. lanuginosus*) has **long-hairy to woolly stems and leaves,** the **leaves all basal, pliable,** linear to narrowly lance-shaped, 2.5–10 cm long, with **smooth margins.** It is found on dry, rocky slopes and in shrublands, forest openings and meadows, in steppe to alpine zones, and is scattered but locally frequent in the inland southern ¼ of the region, from central WA, eastern OR, ID and western MT to CA and NV.

Notes: Stemless goldenweed is also known as *Chrysopsis acaulis* and *Haplopappus acaulis*. • *Stenotus* is from the Greek *stenotes*, "narrowness," in reference to the narrow leaves.

Lyall's Serpentweed
Tonestus lyallii

General: Loosely tufted perennial from a branched stem-base on a weakly developed taproot or short rhizome; **stems few to several, erect,** unbranched, 4–15 cm tall, **hairless but densely stalked-glandular.**

Leaves: Basal and along stem, upper surfaces stalked-glandular, margins smooth, not fringed; **basal leaves lance-oblong to spoon-shaped; stem leaves similar,** gradually reduced upward.

Flowerheads: Usually 1 (sometimes 2), 2–3 cm across; **ray florets 11–23,** 1–3.5 mm wide, **spreading, yellow involucral bracts roughly equal** in size, in 3–5 series, stalked-glandular, **oblong to lance-shaped, pointy-tipped.**

Fruits: Achenes linear, 8–12-nerved; pappus bristles whitish or tawny, minutely barbed.

Where Found: Open forests, rocky slopes, sandy-gravelly ridges and shores, meadows, talus and fellfields; subalpine and alpine zones; frequent in the inland southern ⅓ of the region; cordilleran.

Similar species: Pygmy serpentweed (*T. pygmaeus*; *H. pygmaeus*) is at most **sparsely stalked-glandular,** with a stout taproot, **densely hairy stems** and **oblong to egg-shaped, blunt or rounded outer involucral bracts.** It grows on rocky slopes and in meadows, elfin forests, talus and fellfields, in subalpine and alpine zones, and is infrequent in the Rockies of MT, WY, CO and NM.

Notes: Lyall's serpentweed is also known as *Haplopappus lyallii*. • The genus name is an anagram of *Stenotus*.

Northern Goldenrod
Solidago multiradiata

General: Stems 1 to several, erect or curved at the base, branched above, 5–50 cm tall, hairy at least in flower cluster.

Leaves: Basal and along stem, **lance- to spoon-shaped,** 1–15 cm long, **lower leaves wing-stalked, margins usually toothed (especially toward tip) and hairy-fringed,** at least along stalks.

Flowerheads: Several to many (to 75 or more) in a **compact, rounded array,** individual heads about 1 cm across; ray florets 12–18 **(mostly 13** in ours), yellow; **involucral bracts unequal to roughly equal** in size, in 3–5 series, **pointy-tipped.**

Fruits: Achenes cylindric-ellipsoid, 8–10-ribbed, short-hairy; pappus bristles white.

Where Found: Meadows, rocky slopes and ridges, gravel bars, open forests, fellfields and tundra; lowland to alpine zones; frequent throughout the region but less so in the south; arctic-alpine, North American, barely entering eastern Siberia.

Similar Species: Sticky goldenrod or spike-like goldenrod (**S. simplex,** S. decumbens, S. glutinosa and S. spathulata in part) has **spoon-shaped or elliptic to nearly round leaves** that are blunt-toothed and **hairless, not fringed;** several to many flowerheads in **long, narrow arrays,** the ray florets 7–16 (**mostly 8** in ours); and **unequal, sticky-resinous involucral bracts, the inner bracts blunt to rounded** at the tip. It is found on rocky slopes, grasslands, shrublands, meadows, open forests, shores and fellfields, in lowland and steppe to lower alpine zones. Sticky goldenrod is frequent throughout the region except the far north and outer Pacific coast; the species complex is widespread in North America.

Notes: *Solidago* is from the Latin *solidus* and *-ago,* meaning "to make whole," alluding to the healing properties of these plants; *multiradiata* means "with many rays." • The European species was applied externally as a wound herb and taken as a drink for internal injuries.

sticky goldenrod

Woolly Sunflower • *Eriophyllum lanatum*

General: White-woolly herb or subshrub from a taproot; **stems several, branched,** 10–50 cm tall. **Leaves: Mostly along stem,** alternate, **entire to pinnately lobed. Flowerheads:** Sunflower-like, **3–5 cm across, single on long stalks;** ray florets 5–13; involucral bracts relatively few (5–15). **Fruits:** Pappus of 6–12 transparent scales or sometimes a toothed crown. **Where Found:** Essentially a species of low to moderate elevations but climbs to subalpine and alpine habitats—rocky slopes, outcrops, fellfields—fairly frequently in the southern ¼ of the region.

Varieties: Woolly sunflower has many varieties. **Var. *integrifolium*,** with mostly entire leaves, is the one most likely to be encountered at high elevations in our region.

Pacific Alpinegold • *Hulsea algida*

General: Aromatic, tufted from a taproot surmounted by a branched, rhizome-like stem-base; stems 1 to several, ascending to erect, 10–40 cm tall, somewhat hairy.

Leaves: Mostly basal, lance-shaped to narrowly spoon-shaped, broadly stalked; blades 5–10 cm long, rather **fleshy, moderately woolly and stalked-glandular, margins scalloped** with triangular, coarse teeth or shallow lobes; **stem leaves few.**

Flowerheads: Solitary, large, 3–5 cm across; ray florets 25–60, deep yellow; involucral bracts many (20 or more), **roughly equal,** in 2–3 series, **lance-linear,** pointy-tipped, margins hairy.

Fruits: Achenes linear, compressed, silky-hairy; **pappus of 4 transparent, ragged scales,** joined at base in a leathery ring.

Where Found: Rocky slopes, crevices, talus and scree; subalpine and alpine zones; infrequent inland in the southern fringe of the region.

Similar Species: Dwarf alpinegold (*H. nana*) is smaller, **mostly 5–15 cm tall,** and has **usually all basal,** spoon-shaped leaves, **the blades mostly shorter than 6 cm,** with **oblong, rounded lobes, smaller flowerheads (2–3 cm across)** with about ½ as many ray florets and broader, **lance-oblong involucral bracts.** It is scattered but locally frequent in high volcanic terrain—talus, cinder cones, pumice slopes—in subalpine and alpine zones, in the Cascades of WA, OR and CA, the Wallowa Mtns in OR and Seven Devils Mtns in ID.

Notes: The genus is named after Gilbert White Hulse (1807–83), a U.S. Army surgeon and botanist. • *Algida* means "cold"; *nana* means "small" or "dwarf."

Old-man-of-the-mountains, Alpine Sunflower, Greylocks Rubberweed • *Hymenoxys grandiflora*

General: Plants aromatic, generally **cobwebby to woolly,** from a stout taproot and stem-base; stems 1 to several, erect, 8–30 cm tall.

Leaves: Basal leaves deeply cut into narrow, blunt segments, hairy and gland-dotted; stem leaves few.

Flowerheads: Usually 1 (occasionally several per plant), **large, 5–10 cm across, sunflower-like;** ray florets 15–35, **pale yellow,** 3-lobed at tip; **involucral bracts numerous** (30 or more), **similar,** in 2–3 series, lance-linear, densely hairy.

Fruits: Achenes wedge-shaped, 5-sided, hairy; **pappus of 5–7** slender, tapered, **bristle-like scales.**

Where Found: Rocky slopes, meadows, talus and tundra; subalpine and alpine zones; frequent in the southeastern corner of the region; Rocky Mtn endemic.

Notes: Old-man-of-the-mountains is also known as *Actinella grandiflora*, *Rydbergia grandiflora* and *Tetraneuris grandiflora*. • The flowers appear too big for the rest of the plant and reportedly always face the rising sun. • *Hymenoxys* is from the Greek *hymen*, "membrane," and *oxys*, "sharp," in reference to the membranous, bristle-tipped pappus scales. "Old-man-of-the-mountain" probably refers to the plant's hairiness; ditto "greylocks." It is probably called "rubberweed" because several species of this genus contain latex. Colorado rubberweed (*H. richardsonii*) was investigated as an emergency source of rubber during World War II.

The Genus *Arnica* (Arnica)

Arnicas are perennial herbs, fibrous-rooted from rhizomes or stem-bases, the stems usually erect. The leaves are basal and/or (mostly) opposite along the stem, stalked or unstalked, the margins entire or toothed. The flowerheads are yellow, solitary or few to several in arrays atop the stems, comprised of both ray and disc florets (sometimes disc florets only). The involucral bracts are narrow, more or less equal in size, in 1 or 2 series, not overlapping; the receptacles are naked. The roughly cylindric achenes are several-nerved, hairy, glandular or hairless, with a pappus of hair-like, white to straw-coloured or tawny bristles, somewhat feathery or minutely barbed.

Key to *Arnica*

1a. Anthers purple or purplish black . . . . **A. lessingii** (p. 385)

1b. Anthers yellow 2

  2a. Flowerheads lacking ray florets; a few marginal disc florets sometimes appear ray-like . . . **A. parryi** (p. 385)

  2b. Flowerheads typically with both ray and disc florets, ray florets rarely lacking 3

    3a. Midstem leaves stalked. 4

      4a. Main stem leaves narrow, 3–10 times as long as wide, lance-, egg- or spoon-shaped to linear or elliptic 5

        5a. Flowerheads 1–15, erect 6

          6a. Heads 1–3 (to 5); leaves linear to broadly lance-shaped, margins entire to irregularly toothed . . . . **A. angustifolia** (p. 386)

          6b. Heads usually 3–9; leaves egg-shaped to broadly lance-shaped, margins irregularly saw-toothed, sometimes nearly entire . . . . **A. gracilis** (p. 387)

        5b. Flowerheads 1–3, nodding (at least when young) 7

          7a. Leaves rarely stalked-glandular, margins usually toothed; involucral bracts lacking stalked glands. . . . . **A. griscomii** ssp. **frigida** (p. 385)

          7a. Leaves densely stalked-glandular, margins usually entire; involucral bracts covered in stalked glands. . . . . **A. louiseana** (p. 385)

      4b. Main stem leaves broad, 1–3 times as long as wide, heart- or egg-shaped to deltoid or elliptic 8

        8a. Pappus bristles straw-coloured to tawny, somewhat feathery; plants without sterile leafy shoots with leaf rosettes at the base. . . . . **A. ovata** (p. 387)

        8b. Pappus bristles white, usually minutely barbed; plants with sterile leafy shoots with leaf rosettes at the base 9

          9a. Stems usually branched above, often in dense clumps; flowerheads usually 3–9; main leaves egg-shaped to broadly lance-shaped . . . . **A. gracilis** (p. 387)

          9b. Stems not branched; flowerheads usually 1 or 3–5 10

            10a. Main leaves heart- to egg-shaped, coarsely toothed. . . . . **A. cordifolia** (p. 386)

            10b. Main leaves elliptic to egg-shaped, untoothed or minutely toothed . . . . **A. nevadensis** (p. 387)

    3b. Midstem leaves unstalked. 11

      11a. Pappus bristles white, minutely barbed 12

        12a. Leaves lance- to spoon-shaped, 2–7 cm long, 0.5–2.5 cm wide, margins usually untoothed, sometimes with tiny teeth. . . . . **A. rydbergii** (p. 387)

        12b. Leaves egg-shaped to lance-elliptic, 2–10 cm long, 1–6 cm wide, margins sawtoothed, often coarsely so. . . . . **A. latifolia** (p. 386)

      11b. Pappus bristles straw-coloured or tawny, usually somewhat feathery 13

        13a. Stem leaves 2–4 pairs. . . . . **A. mollis** (p. 388)

        13b. Stem leaves usually 4–10 pairs. 14

          14a. Involucral bracts linear-lance-shaped, the tips with tufts of white hairs . . . . **A. chamissonis** (p. 388)

          14b. Involucral bracts narrowly to broadly lance-shaped, the tips lacking tufts of white hairs . . . 15

            15a. Leaves lance-elliptic or egg-shaped, margins usually sawtoothed, sometimes nearly entire; basal leaves present at time of flowering . . . . **A. lanceolata** (p. 388)

            15b. Leaves lance-shaped to lance-elliptic, margins usually entire; basal leaves withered by time of flowering. . . . . **A. longifolia** (p. 388)

Nodding Arnica • *Arnica lessingii*

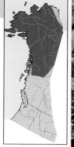

General: Stems usually solitary, sometimes 2- or 3-clumped, **8–35 cm tall, long-hairy**, the hairs with purple crosswalls. **Leaves: 2–6 pairs, crowded toward stem-base** (true basal leaves mostly withering); **blades lance-shaped to elliptic,** 3–10 cm long, margins toothed toward tip. **Flowerheads: 1, nodding, 3–5 cm across;** ray florets yellow, 8–14, conspicuously toothed at tip; **involucral bracts brown-hairy toward base; anthers dark purple. Fruits:** Achenes brown, 5–6 mm long; **pappus bristles yellowish brown, minutely barbed. Where Found:** Moist snowbed and seepage sites, streambanks, meadows, heathlands and peaty tundra; lowland (arctic coast) to alpine zones; frequent in the northern ⅓ of the region; arctic-alpine, amphiberingian.

Similar Species: Nodding arnica could be confused with snow arnica (below), which has yellow, not purple, anthers.

Notes: This species is named after the Lessings: C.F. Lessing (1809–62), a German-born physician and a student of Asteraceae, his nephew K.F. Lessing and his grandfather G.E. Lessing.

Snow Arnica • *Arnica griscomii* ssp. *frigida*

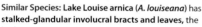

General: Stems 8–40 cm tall, long-hairy, sometimes glandular. **Leaves: Mostly along stem, 1–4 pairs, short-stalked,** lance-shaped to elliptic; blades 1–10 cm long, **hairless or sparsely hairy on upper surface, margins usually toothed. Flowerheads: Usually 1 (rarely 2–3), nodding when young,** becoming erect, 3–5 cm across; **involucral bracts densely yellow-hairy at base,** not stalked-glandular. **Fruits: Pappus bristles white,** minutely barbed. **Where Found:** Rocky slopes, meadows, snowbeds and tundra; lowland (arctic coast) to alpine zones; frequent in the northern ⅓ of the region; arctic-alpine, amphiberingian.

Similar Species: Lake Louise arnica (*A. louiseana*) has **stalked-glandular involucral bracts and leaves,** the leaf **margins usually entire.** It occurs on rocky, calcium-rich slopes, in meadows and stony tundra, in the alpine zone, and is endemic and infrequent in southwestern AB and adjacent BC.

Notes: Snow arnica is also known as *Arnica frigida* and *A. louiseana* ssp. *frigida*.

Parry's Arnica • *Arnica parryi*

General: Stems solitary, erect, 15–50 cm tall, hairy and stalked-glandular especially toward the top. **Leaves: Mostly along stem, 2–4 pairs, lance- to oblong-egg-shaped; blades 4–20 cm long, margins usually entire, occasionally with a few teeth. Flowerheads: Several (3–12, occasionally 1), nodding in bud, of disc florets only,** 1–2 cm across; **involucral bracts sparsely hairy and glandular. Fruits: Pappus bristles straw-coloured, minutely barbed to some-what feathery. Where Found:** Open forests, ravines and meadows; montane to alpine zones; frequent inland in the southern ½ of the region, rare northward; cordilleran.

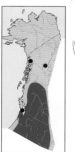

Notes: Polyploidy (multiple chromosome copies), apomixis (reproduction by seed but without sex) and hybridization all contribute to the morphological complexity in *Arnica*. This has perplexed taxonomists since people began naming arnicas. In 1927, Per Axel Rydberg recognized more than 100 species in this circumboreal genus; *FNA* in 2006 indicates 29 species, 26 in North America, 1 in Europe and 2 in Asia.

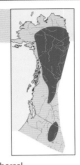

Narrowleaf Arnica
Arnica angustifolia ssp. *angustifolia*

General: Stems 10–40 cm tall, **moderately long-hairy.**
Leaves: 1–5 pairs, **mostly along stem, stalked,** linear
to broadly lance-shaped; blades 2–20 cm long, hairless to
moderately long-hairy, margins entire to irregularly toothed.
Flowerheads: 1–3 **(occasionally 5),** erect, 3–4 cm across;
involucral bracts densely white-hairy and sometimes
stalked-glandular at the base. **Fruits:** Achenes very hairy;
pappus bristles white, minutely barbed. Where Found:
Open forests, riverbanks, meadows, rocky slopes and tundra;
lowland (arctic coast) to alpine zones; frequent in the northern ⅓ of the region, sporadic southward; arctic-alpine, circumboreal.

Other Subspecies: Alpine arnica (A. angustifolia ssp. *tomentosa; A. tomentosa,
A. alpina* ssp. *tomentosa*) is **densely white-woolly on the stems, leaves and
involucres,** and is usually **shorter (5–20 cm tall)** than narrowleaf arnica. It grows
on rocky or gravelly slopes, ridges, meadows and stony tundra, in subalpine and alpine zones. A cordilleran subspecies,
it is frequent in much of interior BC, north to southern YT, south through southwestern AB to western MT; disjunct
populations occur in NL.

Notes: Narrowleaf arnica is also known as *Arnica alpina* ssp. *angustifolia* and
ssp. *attenuata*. • European studies suggest that southern outlier populations
of northern species such as narrowleaf arnica could disappear as the climate
rapidly warms. Warmer temperatures produce smaller rosettes that have
reduced survival. More heat also boosts the growth of taller competitors that
shade the arnica rosettes, further reducing their growth and survival. • The
Gwich'in brewed tea from the flowers of narrowleaf arnica to treat stomach
ailments. European *Arnica* species are used extensively for various medicinal
treatments. *FNA* advises: "*Arnica montana* from Europe has been used
medicinally for centuries, and unsubstantiated claims have been made
regarding the medicinal properties of some North American species."

alpine arnica

Broadleaf Arnica, Mountain Arnica • *Arnica latifolia*

General: Stems 15–50 cm tall. **Leaves:** Basal leaves smaller than stem leaves, often
falling off by flowering time but often persistent on sterile shoots; **stem leaves
2–5 pairs,** stalked below, **unstalked from midstem up;** blades egg-shaped to
lance-elliptic, 2–10 cm long, margins coarsely sawtoothed. **Flowerheads:** Usually
1 **(sometimes 3–5 or more),** erect, 3–5 cm across; involucral bracts hairy, often
glandular. **Fruits:** Achenes hairless or sparsely hairy in the upper part; pappus
bristles white, minutely barbed. **Where Found:** Open forests, meadows and
rocky slopes; montane to alpine zones; frequent in the southern ¾ of the region;
cordilleran.

**Similar Species: Heartleaf arnica
(A. cordifolia)** is generally less leafy
and has **broader, heart- to egg-
shaped leaves, stalked from midstem
down,** and **achenes that are short-**

hairy all over. It grows in forests, meadows and clearings, in montane and subalpine zones, and is frequent
throughout the southern ¾ of the region, from
southern YT and southwestern NT through BC
and AB to CA, AZ and NM.

Notes: Intermittent cloud cover is a feature of
many alpine environments. Broadleaf arnica
does just fine in cloudy weather—photosynthesis
chugs along quite well in the diffuse light, and
respiration is greatly reduced. The result is
a much greater net carbon gain. This is doubtless
important for other alpine plants as well.

Smallhead Arnica • *Arnica gracilis*

General: Somewhat **smaller (10–30 cm tall)** than broadleaf arnica (p. 386), with smaller, darker green leaves (2–6 cm long) and **3–15 smaller flowerheads 2–2.5 cm across. Where Found:** Dry, rocky slopes, ridges and meadows; subalpine and alpine zones; scattered but locally frequent in the southern ⅓ of the region; southern cordilleran.

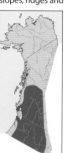

Notes: Smallhead arnica is also known as *Arnica latifolia* var. *gracilis*. • *Arnica* is the genus' classical name and its origin is obscure. In 1625, Jacobus Theodorus Tabernaemontanus used *Ptarmica*, from the Greek *ptaro*, "I sneeze," as a synonym for *Arnica* (plants that cause sneezing). Perhaps *Arnica* is a corruption of *Ptarmica*. Alternatively, it could be from the Greek *arnakis*, "a lamb's skin," referring to the soft texture of the leaves. *Gracilis* means "slender, graceful."

Rydberg's Arnica • *Arnica rydbergii*

General: Similar to but somewhat **smaller (8–35 cm tall)** than broadleaf arnica (p. 386), with unbranched stems, **smaller (2–7 cm long), lance- to spoon-shaped, usually toothless leaves, 1–3 (rarely 5) flowerheads 3–4 cm across** and **achenes short-hairy all over. Where Found:** Dry to mesic, rocky slopes, ridges and meadows; subalpine and alpine zones; frequent mostly in the inland southern ½ of the region; cordilleran.

Similar Species: Sierra arnica (*A. nevadensis*) has **elliptic to egg-shaped leaves, 1** (sometimes 2–3) **flowerheads** and **densely stalked-glandular involucres and achenes.** It occurs in forest openings, meadows and rocky slopes, in montane to alpine zones, and is infrequent in the southwestern corner of the region, in the Cascades (from southern BC) and the Olympics through WA and OR to CA and NV.

Notes: This arnica was named for Per Axel Rydberg (1860–1931), a Swedish-born botanist and a field agent for the U.S. Department of Agriculture, who later became the first curator of the New York Botanical Garden Herbarium.

Sticky-leaf Arnica, Diverse Arnica • *Arnica ovata*

General: Resembles broadleaf arnica (p. 386) but **lacks sterile leafy shoots at base,** with **leaves stalked from midstem down** (like heartleaf arnica , p. 386), minutely hairy and **stalked-glandular,** and **straw-coloured to tawny, somewhat feathery pappus bristles. Where Found:** Moist forests, meadows and streambanks; montane and subalpine zones; infrequent in the southern ⅓ of the region, disjunct in southern AK and YT; cordilleran.

Notes: Sticky-leaf arnica is also known as *Arnica diversifolia* and *A. latifolia* var. *viscidula*. It has long been suspected of having originated as a hybrid between *A. latifolia* or *A. cordifolia* and *A. mollis* or *A. lanceolata*.

Hairy Arnica • *Arnica mollis*

General: Stems 15–60 cm tall, solitary or in clumps, hairy and often glandular. **Leaves:** Basal leaves often falling off by flowering time but often persistent on sterile shoots; **stem leaves 2–4 pairs,** stalked below, **unstalked from midstem up, broadly elliptic to lance-shaped;** blades 4–20 cm long, hairy, often glandular, **margins entire or irregularly toothed. Flowerheads: 1 (sometimes 3–7),** erect, 3–5 cm across; involucral bracts hairy, stalked-glandular. **Fruits:** Achenes greyish brown to black, 4–8 mm long, stalked-glandular, sparsely hairy; **pappus bristles tawny, feathery. Where Found:** Moist to mesic meadows, open forests and streambanks; montane to alpine zones; frequent in the southern ½ of the region, less so northward; cordilleran.

Similar Species: Leafy arnica or meadow arnica (***A. chamissonis***) is **leafier, with 4–10 pairs of lance-oblong, mostly entire stem leaves** and **involucral bracts each with a tuft of long, white hairs at the bluntish tip.** It grows in moist forests, glades, meadows, streambanks and snowbeds, in montane and subalpine zones, and is frequent in the southern ½ of the region, less so northward, from southern AK, southern YT and southwestern NT through BC and AB to CA, AZ and NM. Primarily a cordilleran species, its range extends east to ON and QC.

Clasping Arnica • *Arnica lanceolata* ssp. *prima*

General: Similar to leafy arnica (above) but has **lance-elliptic stem leaves, usually toothed, all unstalked, sometimes clasping or sheathing** at base, and **involucral bracts lacking white-hairy tufts at the pointy tips. Where Found:** Moist meadows, forest openings and streambanks; lowland to alpine zones, reaching high elevations only in the southern part of its range; frequent in the southern ½ of the region, infrequent northward.

Similar Species: Spearleaf arnica or seep-spring arnica (***A. longifolia***) has narrower, **lance-shaped leaves with margins entire or nearly so.** It grows in moist to wet meadows, open forests, streambanks, seepage areas, scree and snowbeds, in subalpine and alpine zones, and is frequent from south-central BC and southwestern AB to CA, NV, UT and CO.

Notes: Clasping arnica is also known as *Arnica amplexicaulis*.

spearleaf arnica

The Genus *Senecio* (Groundsel)

Ours are perennial herbs, the stems usually ascending to erect. The leaves are basal and/or alternate along the stem, lance- to egg- or spoon-shaped, elliptic or triangular, the margins toothed or smooth. The flowerheads are usually several to many in compact to open arrays atop the stems, sometimes solitary, and composed of both ray and disc florets (rarely of disc florets only); both the several to many ray florets and the numerous disc florets are usually yellow. The involucral bracts are narrow, more or less equal in size and arranged in 1–2 series, not overlapping, the margins wax-papery. The receptacles are naked. The cylindric or prismatic achenes are usually 5-angled, hairy or hairless, with a pappus of hair-like bristles.

Senecio remains one of the largest genera of flowering plants, with more than 1000 species. But some species previously in *Senecio* are now in other genera, including, in our region, *Packera*, *Tephroseris* and *Sinosenecio*. • "Groundsel" appears to be derived from the Anglo-Saxon *grundeswelge* or *grondeswyle*, meaning "ground-glutton" or "ground-swallower," because the weedy European common groundsel (*S. vulgaris*) occupies bare ground so rapidly. However, one source claims the original word was actually *gundeswelge*, from *gund*, "pus," and *swelgan*, "to swallow," giving "pus-swallower." Indeed, common groundsel was widely used by ancient physicians to draw pus out of wounds and abscesses and to treat inflammation of the eyes. Whatever the origin, *grundeswelge* was gradually modified in Middle English to *grundswilie*, then to *grundsel* and finally to *groundsel*. Prior (1879) noted that common groundsel was then still referred to as "grundy-swallow" in Scotland. *Senecio* is from the Greek *senex*, "old person," in reference to the white, hair-like pappus bristles.

Key to *Senecio*

1a. Stem leaves well developed, gradually reduced toward top of stem; well-developed tuft of basal leaves usually lacking **2**

    2a. Plants freely branched, sprawling to ascending . . . . *S. fremontii* (p. 390)

    2b. Plants not branched below flower cluster, erect. **3**

        3a. Leaves triangular. . . . . *S. triangularis* (p. 390)

        3b. Leaves tapering to base, not at all triangular **4**

            4a. Leaves narrowly lance-shaped, not clasping at the base; involucral bracts usually green at tip; south of 48° N. . . . . *S. serra* (p. 390)

            4b. Leaves lance-shaped to elliptic, the upper clasping at the base; involucral bracts blackish at tip; north of 57° N . . . . *S. sheldonensis* (p. 390)

1b. Stem leaves strongly and progressively reduced in size toward top of stem; basal and lower stem leaves well developed, often tufted **5**

    5a. Flowerheads 1–2 (to 4). **6**

        6a. Leaves hairless or nearly so at flowering time, blades usually >10 cm long; flowerheads 3–4 cm across . . . . *S. amplectens* var. *holmii* (p. 391)

        6b. Leaves usually cobwebby hairy (at least on lower surface) at flowering time; flowerheads larger, 4–6 cm across **7**

            7a. Leaf blades <10 cm long, margins toothed; flowerheads nodding . . . . *S. neowebsteri* (p. 391)

            7b. Leaf blades >10 cm long, margins entire or wavy, often with dark, leathery toothlets; flowerheads erect. . . . . *S. megacephalus* (p. 391)

    5b. Flowerheads several to many (usually more than 4), occasionally solitary **8**

        8a. Plants hairless, or occasionally thinly woolly when young but soon becoming hairless . . . . *S. crassulus* (p. 392)

        8b. Plants hairy at flowering time. **9**

            9a. Plants from fibrous roots, lacking rhizomes or long stem-bases; leaves mostly entire, sometimes vaguely toothed. . . . . *S. integerrimus* (p. 392)

            9b. Plants from rhizomes or elongate stem-bases; woolly-hairy at least when young; at least some leaves distinctly toothed **10**

                10a. Stems mostly single; leaves lance-shaped to narrowly egg-shaped, nearly entire to toothed, involucral bracts 4–7 mm long; primarily northern and Rocky Mtns . . . . *S. lugens* (p. 392)

                10b. Stems several; leaves egg- to lance-shaped, shallowly toothed; involucral bracts 8–10 mm long; primarily in the Cascades of WA and BC . . . . *S. elmeri* (p. 392)

Dwarf Mountain Groundsel
Senecio fremontii var. *fremontii*

General: Stems several, **branched, sprawling to arching upward,** 10–20 cm tall, **hairless,** often purple-tinged. **Leaves: Along much of stem, somewhat fleshy,** egg- to spoon-shaped; blades 1–3 cm long, **hairless, margins usually coarsely toothed,** sometimes nearly entire; **upper leaves not reduced upward. Flowerheads: Few (1–5)** at branch tips, 2–3 cm across; involucral bracts soft-hairy, green or brownish at tips. **Where Found:** Rocky slopes and ridges, talus, scree, fellfields and snow-beds; subalpine and alpine zones; frequent in the southern ⅓ of the region; cordilleran.

Notes: The species is named for John C. Fremont (1813–90), an army officer, presidential candidate and plant collector in Oregon Territory.

Arrow-leaved Groundsel, Arrow-leaved Ragwort
Senecio triangularis

General: Stems 1 or few, loosely clustered, **erect, 30–150 cm tall,** hairless to thinly soft-hairy when young. **Leaves: Basal and stem leaves triangular to heart-shaped, squared-off at base,** stalked; **blades 3–10 cm long,** hairless except for short hairs on veins beneath, **margins strongly saw-toothed;** stem leaves slightly reduced upward, becoming stalkless. **Flowerheads: 2–3.5 cm across,** several to many **(10–30 or more);** ray florets about 8; involucral bracts usually green or rarely black at tips. **Where Found:** Moist to mesic meadows, glades, open forests, stream-banks, thickets and avalanche tracks; montane to alpine zones; frequent in the southern ⅘ of the region; cordilleran.

Notes: Arrow-leaved groundsel is often a dominant species in moist, high-elevation meadows.

Tall Groundsel, Tall Ragwort • *Senecio serra* var. *serra*

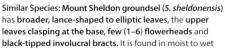

General: Stems 1 or few, loosely clustered, **erect, 40–150 cm tall. Leaves:** Evenly distributed, **lance-shaped, tapering to base; blades 5–15 cm long,** margins toothed to nearly entire; stem leaves gradually reduced upward, **not clasping at base. Flowerheads: 1–2 cm across, numerous (40–90) in long, rounded clusters;** ray florets about 5; involucral bracts usually green, occasionally black at tips. **Where Found:** Moist meadows, glades, open forests, thickets and stream-banks; montane to alpine zones; frequent in the inland southern ¼ of the region; cordilleran.

Similar Species: Mount Sheldon groundsel (*S. sheldonensis*) has **broader, lance-shaped to elliptic leaves,** the **upper leaves clasping at the base, few (1–6) flowerheads** and **black-tipped involucral bracts.** It is found in moist to wet meadows, thickets, forest openings and on streambanks, in subalpine and alpine zones. Mount Sheldon groundsel is an infrequent endemic of northern BC, southern and central YT and southwestern NT.

Notes: The name "ragwort" was originally given to the European *S. jacobea* in reference to its highly divided (ragged) leaves.

Clasping Groundsel
Senecio amplectens var. *holmii*

General: Plants hairless or nearly so at flowering time; stems clustered, arching upward, 10–25 cm tall. **Leaves:** Basal and along stem, egg-shaped to elliptic;

blades 10–20 cm long, on stalks nearly as long as blades, margins toothed; upper leaves much reduced in size. **Flowerheads:** 1–4, nodding, 3–4 cm across; involucres 9–15 mm high, bracts green or pale purplish. **Where Found:** Rocky slopes, meadows and fellfields; subalpine and alpine zones; frequent in the southeastern corner of the region; mostly in the Rocky Mtns.

Notes: Clasping groundsel is also know as *Senecio holmii*.

Olympic Mountain Groundsel
Senecio neowebsteri

General: Plants loosely woolly to thinly cobwebby at flowering time; stems 1 or few loosely clustered, erect to arching, 7–20 cm tall, sometimes purple-tinged.

Leaves: Basal and (mostly) along stem, fleshy, egg-shaped to broadly lance-shaped; blades 4–8 cm long, on stalks as long as blades, margins toothed; upper leaves much reduced, bract-like. **Flower-**

heads: 1 (rarely 2), **nodding, 4–5 cm across;** involucres 10–15 mm high, bracts usually green at tips. **Where Found:** Talus slopes; alpine zone; infrequent endemic of the Olympic Mtns.

Notes: Olympic Mountain groundsel is also known as *Senecio websteri*.

Large-headed Groundsel
Senecio megacephalus

General: Plants loosely woolly to thinly cobwebby, becoming less hairy with age; stems 1 or few, clustered, **15–50 cm tall. Leaves:** Basal and along stem, lance-shaped; blades 10–18 cm long, margins entire or wavy, often with **dark, leathery tooth-**

lets. **Flowerheads: Usually 1, erect, 4–6 cm across,** occasionally flanked by 1–2 smaller heads; involucral bracts not black-tipped. **Where Found:** Rocky slopes, meadows and forest openings; montane to lower alpine zones; infrequent in the southeastern part of the region; endemic.

Western Groundsel, Lamb's-tongue Groundsel
Senecio integerrimus var. *exaltatus*

General: From short, button-like stem-bases with **unbranched fleshy-fibrous roots, woolly-hairy or cobwebby at flowering time,** becoming less so with age; **stem 1, erect, 20–70 cm tall. Leaves:** Basal leaves thick, somewhat fleshy, lance-shaped to elliptic or sometimes nearly round; **blades 6–25 cm long, margins entire or with shallow, irregular teeth;** stem leaves similar, progressively reduced in size upward. **Flowerheads:** Several to many (**6–15 or more**), **about 2 cm across;** in compact arrays; **ray florets usually 5, sometimes lacking; involucral, bracts usually black-tipped. Where Found:** Rocky slopes, open forests, meadows, grasslands and shrublands; steppe to lower alpine zones; frequent in the inland southern ⅓ of the region; cordilleran.

Varieties: The most widespread and variable of the 5 varieties recognized by *FNA*, var. *exaltatus* also is the one most likely to be encountered at high elevations.

Notes: *Integerrimus* means "intact," "undivided" or "whole," in reference to the entire leaves of some forms; *exaltatus* means "lofty."

Black-tipped Groundsel • *Senecio lugens*

General: Similar to western groundsel (above) but arises from **short, thick rhizomes with branching roots; stems usually 1, sometimes several together, 5–40 cm tall. Leaves:** At least **some basal leaves regularly toothed** with thickened toothlets. **Flowerheads:** Generally **fewer (2–12 or more); involucral bracts 4–7 mm long, black-tipped. Where Found:** Rocky slopes, meadows, thickets, open forests, wetlands, streambanks, shores and peaty tundra; montane to alpine zones; frequent in the northern ½ of the region, less frequent southward in the Rockies, disjunct and rare on Haida Gwaii and in the Olympic Mtns.

Notes: Black-tipped groundsel has also been called *Senecio integerrimus* var. *lugens.* • The specific epithet *lugens* means "mourning" or "downcast," presumably referring to the conspicuously black-tipped involucral bracts.

Elmer's Groundsel • *Senecio elmeri*

General: Woolly-hairy at first, then thinning out toward flowering time; **stems several,** clumped, ascending from **rhizomes** and a loose cluster of basal leaves, **10–30 cm tall. Leaves:** Basal and along stem, lance- to egg-shaped or broadly elliptic; blades 4–10 cm long, margins toothed; upper stem leaves progressively reduced in size. **Flowerheads:** Several, 2–3 cm across; **involucral bracts 8–10 mm long,** the **tips long-hairy, purplish black. Where Found:** Rocky slopes, talus and fellfields; subalpine and alpine zones; locally frequent in the Cascade Mtns of southern BC and the Cascade and Wenatchee Mtns of northern WA; endemic.

Similar Species: Thick-leaved groundsel (**S. crassulus**) is **hairless,** tends to be **taller (15–70 cm)** and occurs **singly or in loose clusters.** It grows in open forests, meadows and on rocky slopes, in subalpine and alpine zones. A southern cordilleran species, it is frequent in the southeastern part of the region, from OR, ID and MT to NV, UT and NM.

Notes: Adolph D. E. Elmer (1870–1942) was an American botanist who collected in California and Washington, as well as in the Philippines.

The Genus *Packera* (Packera)

Our *Packera* are perennial herbs, the stems prostrate to ascending or erect. The leaves are basal and alternate along the stem, elliptic to lance-, egg-, spoon- or kidney-shaped or **lyrate** (pinnately lobed, the rounded terminal lobe the largest), with margins entire, toothed or pinnately lobed or cleft. The flowerheads are 1 to few (sometimes several to many) in compact arrays atop the stems, usually composed of both ray and disc florets (occasionally of disc florets only); the 5–13 (sometimes 0) ray florets are usually yellow, sometimes orange-red; the numerous disc florets are yellow to orange-red. The involucral bracts are narrow, more or less equal in size and arranged in 1–2 series, not overlapping, with wax-papery margins, and are themselves often subtended by 1–5 much smaller bractlets. The receptacles are naked. The fruits are cylindric achenes, usually 5–10-ribbed, hairless or stiff-hairy, with a pappus of white, hair-like bristles.

Packera is a relatively small, mostly North American splinter group of 64 species segregated from the much larger (over 1000 species), cosmopolitan *Senecio*. John G. Packer (b. 1929), a taxonomist at the University of Alberta and the author of *Flora of Alberta* (2nd revised edition), is the namesake of this genus.

Key to *Packera*

1a. Plants usually hairless or nearly so, sometimes a bit cobwebby or woolly at base of stem, in axils of leaves and at bases of flowerheads; basal leaves usually entire or coarsely toothed, usually not pinnately lobed or cleft. 2

  2a. Plants mostly 3–20 cm tall; flowerheads usually 1–6. 3

    3a. Flowerheads usually 1–2; ray florets 10–13; involucral bractlets purple-tinged. 4

      4a. Basal leaves more or less kidney-shaped, abruptly contracted to somewhat heart-shaped at the base, margins blunt-toothed or wavy . . . . *P. cymbalaria* (p. 394)

      4b. Basal leaves egg-, lance- or spoon-shaped, usually tapering or wedge-shaped at the base, margins nearly entire to blunt-toothed or shallowly lobed. 5

        5a. Stem leaves gradually or abruptly reduced in size upward, lance-shaped to linear, not clasping at the base, usually weakly pinnately cleft or lobed; disc florets 55–75 or more. 6

          6a. South of 54° N; basal leaves relatively thick and fleshy, egg- or spoon-shaped to oblong, occasionally pinnately lobed; stem leaves gradually reduced upward; involucral bracts white-woolly toward the base . . . . *P. contermina* (p. 395)

          6b. North of 60° N; basal leaves not particularly thick or fleshy, egg- to kidney-shaped or pinnately lobed; stem leaves abruptly reduced upward; involucral bracts hairless
. . . . *P. cymbalaria* (p. 394)

        5b. Stem leaves abruptly reduced in size upward, lance-shaped, weakly clasping at the base, entire or coarsely toothed; disc florets 40–55 or more . . . . *P. subnuda* var. *subnuda* (p. 395)

    3b. Flowerheads usually 4–6; ray florets 8 or 13; involucral bractlets mostly greenish
. . . . *P. dimorphophylla* (p. 396)

  2b. Plants 10–40 cm tall or taller; flowerheads usually 4–20 or more. 7

    7a. Ray florets lacking or rarely 8–13; disc florets orange to reddish; involucral bracts deep red or green with deep red to purple tips . . . . *P. pauciflora* (p. 397)

    7b. Ray florets 5 or 8 or 13; disc florets yellow; involucral bracts greenish. 8

      8a. Basal and lower stem leaves usually not pinnately lobed; stem leaves gradually to abruptly reduced in size upward; disc florets 35–60 . . . . *P. streptanthifolia* (p. 396)

      8b. Basal and lower stem leaves pinnately lobed or sometimes shallowly palmately lobed; stem leaves abruptly reduced upward; disc florets 20–30 . . . . *P. flettii* (p. 396)

P. cymbalaria   *P. contermina*   *P. subnuda* var. *subnuda*   *P. dimorphophylla*   *P. pauciflora*

1b. Plants usually at least somewhat woolly-hairy, sometimes hairless (or nearly so) and/or basal leaves pinnately lobed or cleft. 9

9a. Lower stem and basal leaves usually pinnately lobed or cleft 10

10a. Stems and leaves usually persistently woolly; flowerheads 1 (occasionally 2–3); north of 57° N
. . . . ***P. ogotorukensis*** (p. 395)

10b. Plants hairless except sometimes woolly in leaf axils; flowerheads 4–10 or more; south of 49° N
. . . . ***P. flettii*** (p. 396)

9b. Basal leaves usually entire or coarsely toothed 11

11a. Plants usually hairless, sometimes sparsely woolly toward stem-base and in leaf axils
. . . . ***P. streptanthifolia*** (p. 396)

11b. Plants hairy at flowering time 12

12a. Flowerheads 8–15; stem leaves gradually reduced in size upward, similar in shape to basal leaves
. . . . ***P. cana*** (p. 397)

12b. Flowerheads mostly 1–5; stem leaves abruptly reduced in size upward, the upper ones bract-like
. . . . ***P. werneriifolia*** (p. 397)

P. streptanthifolia   *P. fletti*   *P. ogotorukensis*   *P. cana*   *P. werneriifolia*

Dwarf Arctic Packera
Packera cymbalaria

General: Mat-forming from rhizomes, unbranched, **mostly hairless,** sometimes woolly at stem-bases and in leaf axils; **stem usually 1, prostrate to arching upward, 5–25 cm tall. Leaves:** Basal leaves stalked, **egg- to kidney-shaped or lyrate,** wedge-shaped to abruptly contracted to somewhat heart-shaped at base, **blades 1–3 cm long, margins blunt toothed, wavy or shallowly lobed; stem leaves abruptly reduced** in size. **Flowerheads: 1–2, 1 cm** (if no ray florets) **to 4 cm across; ray florets yellow,** 11–13 (occasionally lacking), 10–14 mm long; **disc florets orange or yellow; involucral bracts reddish purple or green with red tips, hairless. Where Found:** Rocky slopes and ridges, fellfields and tundra; lowland (arctic coast) to alpine zones; frequent in the northern ⅓ of the region; arctic-alpine, amphiberingian plus disjunct in Atlantic Canada.

Notes: Dwarf arctic packera is also known as *Senecio cymbalaria* and *S. resedifolius.*
• The *Packera cymbalaria* complex, which includes *P. contermina, P. cymbalaria, P. ogotorukensis, P. streptanthifolia* and *P. subnuda,* has a complicated taxonomic history.
• *Cymbalaria,* "cymbal," refers to roundish shape of some of the leaves.

Ogotoruk Packera • *Packera ogotorukensis*

General: Similar to dwarf arctic packera (p. 394) but **Ogotoruk packera is hairy** (patchily woolly on stems and leaves), with **frequently branched stems.** **Leaves:** Basal leaves elliptic to egg- or lance-shaped, blades **2–8 cm long,** margins entire, toothed or irregularly pinnately lobed; **involucral bracts green with purple tips,** woolly-hairy toward base. **Where Found:** Gravel bars, terraces, shores and streambanks, rocky slopes, talus, fellfields and tundra; lowland (arctic coast) to alpine zones; arctic-alpine, scattered but locally frequent endemic of the northern ⅓ of the region.

Notes: Ogotoruk packera is also known as *Senecio ogotorukensis.* • Ogotoruk Creek is in far northwestern Alaska, south of Point Hope on the Chukchi Sea. At one time, the U.S. Atomic Energy Commission wanted to detonate an atomic bomb and thus excavate a deep-water harbour from which to ship oil and other resources from the North Slope. In 1958, they selected a site near the mouth of Ogotoruk Creek. After protests, the Strangelovian "Project Chariot," as it was called, was abandoned in 1961.

High-alpine Packera • *Packera contermina*

General: Resembles the preceding 2 northern species but is **4–10 cm tall** and **mostly hairless, with thicker, fleshier basal leaves** that are egg- or spoon-shaped to oblong (rarely lyrate), the **stem leaves gradually reduced in size upward** and **involucral bracts white-woolly** toward the base. **Where Found:** Rocky slopes, meadows, snowbeds and tundra; subalpine and alpine zones; locally frequent in the **southeastern part** of the region.

Notes: High-alpine packera is also known as *Senecio conterminus.* • Some species of *Packera,* including populations of high alpine packera, are believed to have survived the last glaciation in southwestern Alberta, either at low elevations between the Laurentide and Cordilleran ice sheets or on mountaintop refuges above the ice (nunataks). • *Contermina* means "closely related" or "close in habit or appearance," which this species is to a cluster of similar species in the *P. cymbalaria* complex.

Cleftleaf Packera • *Packera subnuda* var. *subnuda*

General: Similar to high-alpine packera (above) but occupies **wetter habitats** and is **5–30 cm tall. Leaves:** Basal leaves egg-shaped to elliptic, **coarsely toothed (not lyrate);** stem leaves **abruptly reduced in size upward,** lance-shaped, weakly clasping at the base and entire to coarsely toothed or pinnately cleft. **Flowerheads: 40–55 (vs. 55–75) disc florets;** involucral bracts hairless. **Where Found:** Wet meadows, fens, shores and streambanks; subalpine and alpine zones; mostly in the southeastern part of the region.

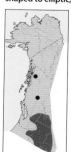

Notes: Cleftleaf packera is also known as *Senecio subnudus* and *S. cymbalarioides* in part. • *Subnuda* means "almost naked," that is, hairless or nearly so.

Splitleaf Packera • *Packera dimorphophylla*

General: Resembles high-alpine packera (p. 395) and cleftleaf packera (p. 395) but tends to have **more flowerheads (usually 4–6),** with **deep yellow to orange ray florets** and **45–60 or more disc florets; stem leaves gradually reduced in size upward,** often **earlobe-clasping at base,** nearly entire to coarsely and irregularly toothed to pinnately lobed; and **hairless involucral bracts. Where Found:** Moist, rocky slopes and wet meadows; subalpine and alpine zones; infrequent in the southeastern corner of the region.

Notes: Splitleaf packera is also known as *Senecio dimorphophyllus.* • *Dimorphophylla* is from *dimorpho,* "having 2 forms," and *phyllos,* "leaves"; i.e., with 2 kinds of leaves, alluding to the 2 extremes of leaf form.

Rocky Mountain Packera
Packera streptanthifolia

General: Tufted from fibrous roots, **usually hairless,** occasionally sparsely woolly at stem-bases and in leaf axils; stems 1 or 2–5 and clustered, erect, **10–40 cm tall. Leaves: Basal leaves relatively thick and firm,** stalked, spoon- to lance- or egg-shaped or round; blades 1–5 cm long, **margins blunt-toothed or entire;** stem leaves gradually to abruptly reduced in size, entire or nearly so. **Flowerheads:** 2–3 cm across, 2–20 in a compact, flat-topped array; ray florets 8 or 13; **disc florets 35–60; involucral bracts green, hairless. Where Found:** Rocky and grassy slopes, meadows and open forests; montane to alpine zones (not at high elevations in the northern part of its range); frequent in the inland southern ¾ of the region; cordilleran.

Similar Species: Flett's packera (*P. flettii; Senecio flettii***)** has **pinnately lobed or sometimes shallowly palmately lobed, basal and lower stem leaves,** stem leaves that are **abruptly reduced in size upward** and **20–30 disc florets.** It is restricted to the Olympic Mtns and the vicinity of Mt. Rainier, WA, plus a few coastal mountains in OR, and grows on open, rocky and gravelly slopes and talus, in montane to alpine zones.

Flett's packera

Notes: Rocky Mountain packera is also known as *Senecio streptanthifolius* and *S. cymbalarioides* in part. • *Streptanthifolia* means "leaves like *Streptanthus,*" a genus in the mustard family (Brassicaceae).

Rayless Alpine Packera, Egg Yolk Packera • *Packera pauciflora*

General: Usually **lacks ray florets** (rarely 8–13) and has **60–80 yellow-orange to reddish disc florets** and **deep red involucral bracts (occasionally green with reddish purple tips). Where Found:** Moist to wet meadows, shores, swamps, thickets and forest openings; montane to alpine zones; frequent mostly inland in the central ½ of the region, disjunct in CA and QC to Labrador; North American.

Notes: Rayless alpine packera is also known as *Senecio pauciflorus.* • It is found in 3 widely disjunct alpine locations: the northwestern cordillera (our region), Québec–Labrador and the Sierra Nevada of California. Though all appear to share a common ancestor, the California plants are genetically distinct from the northern plants. One hypothesis is that the northern plants survived glaciation in a northern refugium, perhaps toughing it out somewhere in eastern Beringia (unglaciated Alaska and Yukon), while the southern plants played golf south of the ice.

Woolly Packera • *Packera cana*

General: Tufted, **white woolly-hairy; stem 1 per leaf rosette** (rosettes often clumped), erect, **10–30 cm tall. Leaves: Basal leaves in a rosette,** stalked, lance-shaped to elliptic or egg-shaped, blades 2–5 cm long, **margins entire to irregularly wavy or weakly toothed; stem leaves gradually reduced in size upward,** entire or toothed. **Flowerheads:** 2–3 cm across, **8–15** in compact arrays; **involucral bracts densely woolly. Where Found:** Dry grasslands, shrublands, rocky slopes, outcrops, scree and fell-fields; steppe to alpine zones; frequent in the southern inland ⅓ of the region; Great Plains–southern cordilleran.

Similar Species: Hoary packera (*P. werneriifolia; Senecio werneriifolius***)** is sometimes also very hairy but is usually **smaller (7–15 cm tall),** with **stem leaves abruptly reduced to bracts** and usually **1–5 flowerheads.** It occupies rocky slopes, sandy forest openings, talus and scree, in subalpine and alpine zones. Hoary packera is infrequent from ID and WY to CA, AZ and NM.

Notes: Woolly packera is also known as *Senecio canus.* • *Cana* is from *cano*, meaning "hairy"; *werneriifolia* means "leaves like *Werneria*," an aster-family genus of the high Andes, named for Abraham Gottlob Werner (1749–1817), a German geologist. Werner championed "Neptunism," a theory of stratification of the earth's crust via differential precipitation of sediments from a primordial, all-encompassing Ocean.

hoary packera

The Genus *Tephroseris* (Arctic-groundsel)

Tephroseris is a relatively small, largely northern Eurasian group of about 50 species, segregated from the much larger, cosmopolitan *Senecio*. Ours are perennial herbs, usually cobwebby, woolly or long-soft-hairy, often in patches as the stems and leaves become unevenly hairless ("patterned baldness"). The stems are sturdy and erect. The leaves are basal and alternate along the stem, the basal and lower stem leaves stalked, lance- to egg-shaped or somewhat diamond-shaped, the margins entire to wavy or toothed. The solitary (or sometimes few to several) flowerheads are usually composed of both ray and disc florets (rarely of disc florets only). The ray florets number 8, 13 or 21 and are yellow, orange or orange-yellow; the numerous disc florets are yellow, orange or orange-yellow, sometimes yellowish white. The involucral bracts are narrow, more or less equal in size, arranged in 1 to 2 series and usually at least partly densely hairy, the margins wax-papery. The receptacles are naked. The cylindric achenes are 10-ribbed or -nerved, hairless or short-curly-hairy, with a pappus of whitish or sometimes brownish, hair-like bristles.

Key to *Tephroseris*

1a. Basal and lower stem leaves irregularly toothed; involucral bracts and upper ⅓ of stems woolly with brown hairs
.... ***T. kjellmanii* (below)**

1b. Basal and lower stem leaves nearly entire or minutely toothed; involucral bracts long-hairy or woolly with yellow, white or purplish hairs, sometimes nearly hairless **2**

    2a. Involucral bracts and upper part of stems tufted-woolly with yellow hairs........... ***T. yukonensis* (p. 399)**

    2b. Involucral bracts long-hairy or woolly with purplish or whitish hairs, sometimes nearly hairless........... **3**

        3a. Involucres tapering to flowerhead stalks; involucral bracts and upper part of stems long-hairy, at least some hairs purple or with purplish crosswalls; florets yellow....................... ***T. frigida* (below)**

        3b. Involucres abruptly contracted to flowerhead stalks; involucral bracts patchily whitish-woolly, becoming unevenly hairless; florets orange or orange-yellow .... ***T. lindstroemii* (p. 399)**

Brown-haired Arctic-groundsel • *Tephroseris kjellmanii*

General: Stems 7–15 cm tall, brown-woolly in upper part. **Leaves:** Basal leaves egg-shaped to roughly diamond-shaped, tapering to stalks; blades 1–3 cm long, **margins usually irregularly toothed;** upper stem leaves smaller, bract-like, unstalked, clasping at base. **Flowerheads: Usually 1** (rarely 2), 1.5–3 cm across; **ray florets pale yellow,** 13 (occasionally lacking); **involucral bracts greenish, densely brown-woolly-hairy. Where Found:** Moist to wet meadows, fens, scree and peaty tundra; montane to alpine zones; frequent inland in the northern ⅓ of the region; arctic-alpine, amphiberingian.

Notes: Brown-haired arctic-groundsel is also known as *Senecio kjellmanii, S. atropurpureus* ssp. *tomentosus* and *S. frigidus* var. *tomentosus*. • Franz R. Kjellman (1846–1907) was a professor of botany in Uppsala, Sweden.

Purple-haired Arctic-groundsel • *Tephroseris frigida*

General: Similar to brown-haired arctic-groundsel (above) but has **long-hairy upper stems and involucral bracts** with at least some **hairs purplish or having purple crosswalls. Leaves:** Basal and lower stem leaves **nearly entire to wavy-toothed. Flowerheads: Ray florets yellow,** usually 13 or 21, rarely vestigial or lacking; **involucres tapering to flowerhead stalks. Where Found:** Meadows, thickets and tundra; lowland (arctic coast) to alpine zones; frequent in the northern ⅓ of the region; arctic-alpine, amphiberingian.

Notes: Purple-haired arctic-groundsel is also known as *Senecio atropurpureus* ssp. *frigidus* and *S. frigida*. • It is common on frost boils or mud boils, small (to 3 m in diameter) patches of sparsely vegetated soil that occur in tundra landscapes. These "boils" are caused by frost heaving in areas underlain with permafrost. Frost boils in the high arctic are largely unvegetated, but those farther south have more plant cover, which insulates the boils and reduces thaw layer thickness in the soils.

Orange Arctic-groundsel
Tephroseris lindstroemii

General: Resembles the preceding 2 species but has **narrower (lance-to egg-shaped) leaves; involucres abruptly contracted** to the flowerhead stalks, the **bracts purplish and nearly hairless to whitish-woolly,** and usually **1–4 larger, orange to orange-yellow flowerheads, 3–5 cm across.** **Where Found:** Meadows, rocky slopes and ridges, scree, fellfields and tundra; lowland (arctic coast) to alpine zones; frequent in the northern ⅓ of the region; disjunct, scattered but locally frequent in MT and WY; arctic-alpine, amphiberingian.

Notes: Orange arctic-groundsel is also known as *Senecio integrifolius* var. *lindstroemii*, *S. tundricola* ssp. *lindstroemii* and *S. fuscatus* (misapplied). • *Tephroseris* is from the Greek *tephros*, "ash-coloured," in reference to the colour of the woolly hairs. • Who was Lindstroem? Perhaps A.H. Lindström, a steward with Roald Amundsen's first Northwest Passage expedition (1903–06).

Yukon Arctic-groundsel
Tephroseris yukonensis

General: Stems 1 or several, loosely clustered, erect, **10–40 cm tall, patchily yellow-woolly in upper part. Leaves:** Basal and lower stem leaves lance-oblong to elliptic, tapering to stalks; blades 2–5 cm long, margins nearly entire to wavy or vaguely blunt-toothed; upper stem leaves smaller, bract-like, unstalked, clasping at base. **Flowerheads:** 2–3 cm across, **1–4 (to 6) in a compact cluster; ray florets pale yellow,** 13–21 (rarely lacking), to 10 mm long; disc florets yellowish white; **involucral bracts purplish, yellow-woolly. Where Found:** Moist meadows, heathlands and turfy tundra; lowland (arctic coast) to alpine zones; sporadic but locally frequent in the northern ⅓ of the region; arctic-alpine, endemic.

Notes: Yukon arctic-groundsel is also known as *Senecio yukonensis* and *S. alaskanus*. • Genetic studies suggest that *Tephroseris* is not monophyletic—that is, the various species currently contained in the genus are not derived from a common ancestor and are not all closely related to each other. Additionally, Haida-groundsel (p. 400) is closely related to some *Tephroseris* species and could eventually end up in this genus. Stay tuned.

Haida-groundsel • *Sinosenecio newcombei*

General: Perennial from short, fibrous-rooted rhizomes; stems solitary or several in loose clusters, erect, unbranched, **10–30 cm tall, hairless or sparsely white-hairy.**

Leaves: Basal and alternate along stem; **basal leaves egg- to kidney-shaped to nearly round,** on stalks 2–3 times as long as blades, which are 1–2 cm long, **palmately veined, hairless** or nearly so, the **margins 5–7-lobed or -toothed;** stem leaves often white-woolly-hairy in axils.

Flowerheads: Solitary, of both ray and disc florets, **3–4 cm across; ray florets yellow; involucral bracts roughly equal in size, green,** margins translucent, tips hairy.

Fruits: Achenes oblong, ribbed, hairless; **pappus bristles white.**

Where Found: Open forests and krummholz, rocky slopes, gullies and ridges, bogs, meadows, heathlands and talus; lowland to alpine zones; frequent on Haida Gwaii; endemic.

Notes: Haida-groundsel is also known as *Senecio newcombei.* • Placed in a genus segregated from *Senecio* primarily on the basis of microscopic characteristics (including chromosome number), Haida-groundsel also has a unique "look," distribution and ecology. Except for Haida-groundsel, the genus *Sinosenecio* occurs in montane regions of the Orient, especially China and Korea. • The species is named for Charles F. Newcombe (1851–1924), an English physician, botanical collector and ethnographer on Vancouver Island and Haida Gwaii.

HAIDA GWAII, GLACIAL REFUGIA AND ENDEMISM

Ice sheets covered much of our region during the Pleistocene, reaching their greatest recent extent between 20,000 and 14,000 years ago. Regionally, the 2 major glacial refugia (ice-free areas) occurred in the far northwest (Beringia, which included much of central and northern Alaska and adjacent Yukon) and south of the ice, which extended to northern Washington, Idaho and Montana. On the Pacific coast, smaller refugia probably existed on parts of the Alexander Archipelago, Haida Gwaii, northwestern Vancouver Island (Brooks Peninsula) and at middle elevations in the Olympic Mountains. Late Wisconsin (about 14,500 years ago) refugia are also suspected on Kodiak Island and along the Gulf of Alaska (Lituya Bay, parts of the Kenai Peninsula and Prince William Sound). Evidence from contemporary species distributions and from fossils is strongest for refugia on Haida Gwaii and the Alexander Archipelago. Some parts of these archipelagos apparently remained ice free throughout the glacial advances, allowing some species to persist, albeit in harsh periglacial environments. Haida-groundsel is one of these species, the most distinctive and abundant of our Pacific maritime endemics and the only one still known only from Haida Gwaii. Four other species (Queen Charlotte avens, Calder's mountain-lovage, Haida false rue-anemone and Taylor's saxifrage) and several varieties or subspecies (including var. *flava* of the alp-lily and Queen Charlotte twinflower violet, *Viola biflora* ssp. *carlottae*), originally thought to be endemic to Haida Gwaii, were subsequently found elsewhere on the north Pacific coast—most notably on northwestern Vancouver Island and/or in southeast Alaska. All of these taxa belong to our high-elevation flora.

Biological evidence supports the geological hints that unglaciated areas persisted in these archipelagos throughout the Pleistocene. The thinking is that island refugia should exhibit some endemism in their biota because evolution has had more time to work; moreover, divergence—and ultimately speciation—has been enhanced by isolation and the interruption of gene flow between island populations and their kin elsewhere. Some taxa of plants (including those mentioned above), insects, birds and mammals on the islands are sufficiently different from their mainland relatives that they are classified as distinct subspecies or species—and some species occurrences represent significant disjunctions. In the Gwaiian bryoflora, for example, 2 of the 136 species of liverworts and 5 of the over 300 species of mosses are known in the Western Hemisphere only from Haida Gwaii. Most of the endemic plants and many of the disjunctions occur in steep, rocky, often high-elevation habitats, where these plants could have persisted in unglaciated terrain.

Although a few species in many taxa of vascular plants, bryophytes and animals apparently survived Pleistocene glaciation in alpine or coastal plain refugia, most of the species that live on these islands today colonized them within the last 10,000 to 12,000 years. Natural selection and genetic drift have nonetheless been strong enough to cause the rapid evolution of significant population differentiation in many species, for example, in stickleback fish.

Thus the story of contemporary species distributions and recent evolutionary processes in northwestern North America is uniquely complex. It includes roles for physiography (especially the 2 parallel north-south mountain systems), widespread Pleistocene glaciation, 2 major, bookend glacial refugia plus several smaller "cryptic" refugia (both coastal and interior, see box essay on p. 112) and island biogeography.

Mountain Mare's-tail
Hippuris montana

General: Small, semi-aquatic to terrestrial perennial from a slender, creeping rhizome; **stems delicate,** erect or ascending, unbranched, **2–10 cm tall,** hairless.

Leaves: In several **whorls of 5–8** along stem, **linear,** unstalked, 2–7 mm long, hairless, pointy-tipped, stiff above water but lax underwater.

Flowers: Tiny, **in whorls** in the axils of some of the leaf whorls, **mostly unisexual** (occasionally bisexual), the female whorls above the male; **petals lacking; stamen 1; ovary 1.**

Fruits: Nutlets single, **1-seeded,** about 1 mm long.

Where Found: Edges of shallow streams and ponds, mossy streambanks, seepage areas and wet to moist heathlands and meadows; upper montane to alpine zones; infrequent (though often overlooked) in the coastal mountains from the Aleutians to northwestern WA, rare inland in YT and NT, more frequently inland in the snowy mountains of central and southern BC; cordilleran–Pacific maritime.

Notes: At first glance, the diminutive mountain mare's-tail looks remarkably like a moss, especially when it is embedded or entangled with them in mossy habitats. • We can't think of any true aquatic species in our alpine flora. However, some species of water-starwort (*Callitriche verna,* *C. hermaphroditicum*), pondweed (*Potamogeton gramineus, P. natans*), bur-reed (*Sparganium* spp.) and quillwort (*Isoetes bolanderi*) can occasionally be found in lakes and ponds at high elevations.

FOUR AQUATIC SPECIES THAT SOMETIMES OCCUR AT HIGH ELEVATIONS

vernal water-starwort (*Callitriche verna*)

Bolander's quillwort (*Isoetes bolanderi*)

narrowleaf bur-reed (*Sparganium angustifolium*)

northern bur-reed (*Sparganium hyperboreum*)

OUR TOP 10 FAVOURITE ALPINE FLOWERS

Which are your favourite alpines? It's tough to narrow it down—there are so many beauties. Our criteria: flower size relative to the entire plant; appearance and colour; impact factor; plant chutzpah or élan.

1. mountain sapphire (*Eritrichium nanum*), p. 331

2. purple mountain saxifrage (*Saxifraga oppositifolia*), p. 142

3. moss campion
(*Silene acaulis*), p. 135

4. Lapland rosebay
(*Rhododendron lapponicum*), p. 88

5. Parry's Easter daisy
(*Townsendia parryi*), p. 362

6. inky-blue gentian
(*Gentiana glauca*), p. 320

7. nodding campion
(*Silene uralensis*), p. 136

8. dwarf alpine hawksbeard
(*Crepis nana*), p. 340

9. spreading phlox (*Phlox diffusa*), p. 313

10. golden fleabane (*Erigeron aureus*), p. 379

Honourable Mention

alpine-azalea (*Kalmia procumbens*), p. 78

spiderplant (*Saxifraga flagellaris*), p. 145

Yukon dwarf-primrose
(*Douglasia gormanii*), p. 304

Indian hellebore (*Veratrum viride*
ssp. *eschscholtzii*), p. 407

river beauty
(*Epilobium latifolium*), p. 239

purple bittercress
(*Cardamine purpurea*), p. 209

mountain monkshood
(*Aconitum delphiniifolium*), p. 197

old-man-of-the-mountains
(*Hymenoxys grandiflora*), p. 383

pixie-eyes (*Primula cuneifolia*
ssp. *saxifragifolia*), p. 306

blue columbine
(*Aquilegia coerulea*), p. 196

net-veined willow
(*Salix reticulata*), p. 59

Lily Family (Liliaceae)

Members of the lily family in our region are perennial herbs from scaly bulbs or rhizomes, with mostly alternate but sometimes whorled, entire, linear to egg-shaped leaves. The flowers are solitary or several to many in open to compact clusters. They are radially symmetric, with 6 similar, petal-like segments called **tepals** or with 3 petals and 3 sepals, the segments distinct to partially fused. There are 6 stamens, a single 3-chambered, superior ovary and 1 or 3 styles, the stigma entire to 3-lobed. The fruits are 3-chambered capsules.

Modern research on this traditionally large and diverse family (about 300 genera, 5000 species) indicates that several genera in our high-elevation flora should be placed in derivative families: Alliaceae or Amaryllidaceae (*Allium*), Tofieldiaceae (*Triantha, Tofieldia*) and Melanthiaceae (*Stenanthium, Veratrum, Xerophyllum, Zigadenus*).

Key to the Genera of Liliaceae

1a. Leaves lance-shaped, elliptic or egg-shaped, less than 8 times as long as wide 2

    2a. Plants to 30 cm tall; leaves basal; flowers mostly 1–3 per stem . . . . **Erythronium** (p. 405)

    2b. Plants more than 40 cm tall; leaves along stem; flowers several to many per stem 3

        3a. Leaves lance-shaped, mostly whorled; tepals orange, 4–6 cm long . . . . **Lilium columbianum** (p. 406)

        3b. Leaves egg-shaped to oblong-elliptic, alternate; tepals green to whitish, <1.5 cm long. . . . **Veratrum** (p. 407)

1b. Leaves linear, grass-like, more than 8 times as long as wide 4

    4a. Petals and sepals different, brightly coloured petals much wider than dull green sepals . . . . **Calochortus** (p. 406)

    4b. Petals and sepals similar, petal-like (i.e., tepals) 5

        5a. Flowers in umbels; plants with odour of onions . . . . **Allium** (pp. 408–409)

        5b. Flowers in loose to tight clusters (not umbels); no onion odour 6

            6a. Tepals 1.5–6 mm long; leaves folded lengthwise (iris-like) 7

                7a. Stems glandular-hairy, at least in flower cluster . . . . **Triantha** (p. 411)

                7b. Stems hairless throughout . . . . **Tofieldia** (p. 411)

            6b. Tepals >5 mm long; leaves not folded lengthwise (not iris-like) 8

                8a. Basal leaves wiry, persistent, numerous, forming large tussocks . . . **Xerophyllum tenax** (p. 412)

                8b. Basal leaves few, not forming tussocks. 9

                      9a. Flowers 1–2, style 1; plants 5–15 (to 20) cm tall . . . . **Lloydia serotina** (p. 410)

                      9b. Flowers usually at least 5, styles 3; plants >15 cm tall 10

                          10a. Tepals greenish white to cream, with gland near base; flowers saucer-shaped to shallowly bell-shaped. . . . . **Zigadenus elegans** (p. 411)

                          10b. Tepals greenish yellow to brownish purple, lacking glands; flowers tubular-bell-shaped . . . . **Stenanthium occidentale** (p. 410)

Erythronium grandiflorum   *Lilium columbianum*   *Veratrum viride*   *Calochortus apiculatus*   *Allium crenulatum*

Tofieldia coccinea   *Xerophyllum tenax*   *Lloydia serotina*   *Zigadenus elegans*   *Stenanthium occidentale*

Yellow Glacier-lily, Yellow Avalanche-lily
Erythronium grandiflorum

General: Hairless plants, from a **slender bulb** 3–5 cm long and a long (but seldom seen), **segmented rhizome;** flowering stems erect, **10–30 cm tall. Leaves: 2 at base,** shiny, green, **lance-oblong to elliptic, 10–20 cm long,** gradually narrowed to broad, **slightly winged stalk. Flowers:** Usually 1 (sometimes 2–5), **nodding atop stem, golden yellow to cream;** tepals similar, distinct, lance-shaped, 2–4 cm long, **strongly curved back;** anthers cream, yellow or dark red. **Fruits:** Capsules cylindric-club-shaped, erect, 3–5 cm long; seeds many (typically 20–50), brown, angular-egg-shaped, papery. **Where Found:** Moist to mesic meadows, shrublands and forest openings; montane to lower alpine zones; frequent throughout most of the southern ⅓ of the region; cordilleran.

Notes: Yellow glacier-lily bulbs are a very good source of starch (770 g per kg) and dietary fibre (57 g per kg), and were a staple food for some First Nations groups. The bulbs were sweetest after long, slow cooking; drying also made them taste better. They were roasted, steamed or boiled and then dried for winter use. The leaves were sometimes eaten, and the seedpods were said to taste like string beans when cooked. • Grizzly bears "cultivate" yellow glacier-lily meadows above treeline. The bears dig up the nutritious bulbs for food. Soil in the grizzly "digs" has higher levels of ammonium and nitrate nitrogen than surrounding meadow soil, and glacier-lilies establish and grow better, as well as produce more seeds on these diggings. • In the Colorado Rockies between 1975 and 2008, the date of snowmelt advanced at a rate of about 4 days per decade and the last flowering dates of yellow glacier-lilies about 3 days per decade. This has important implications not only for this early flowering species, but also for others around it, including its bumblebee pollinators.

White Glacier-lily, White Avalanche-lily
Erythronium montanum

General: Similar to yellow glacier-lily (above). **Leaves: Abruptly narrowed to an almost wingless stalk** 2–7 cm long. **Flowers:** 1–3 (sometimes more), **white to cream with yellow centre,** sometimes turning pinkish with age; tepals egg-shaped to broadly lance-shaped, somewhat curved back; anthers yellow. **Where Found:** Moist meadows, open coniferous forests and recently logged areas; upper montane to lower alpine zones; locally frequent in the southwestern part of the region, infrequent on Vancouver I. and the adjacent mainland (Mt. Waddington area), more common southward, especially in the Olympic Mtns and Cascades from Mt. Rainier to Mt. Hood; Pacific Northwest endemic.

Notes: Both white and yellow glacier-lilies can sprout and even flower under late-lying snowbanks. They bloom during or soon after snowmelt, often in spectacular, large patches.

Tiger Lily, Columbia Lily • *Lilium columbianum*

General: Hairless plants, from a **fleshy-scaled bulb** 3–7 cm long; **flowering stems 40–120 cm tall,** unbranched, slender but sturdy.

Leaves: In 2–9, mostly **several-leaved whorls** along stem, upper and lowermost leaves often scattered and alternate; **blades lance-shaped, 4–10 cm long,** shiny, bright green.

Flowers: Several to many, large, showy, broadly bell-shaped, nodding, in an open cluster atop stem, **bright yellow-orange to reddish orange** with maroon or purple spots near centre; tepals similar, distinct, broadly lance-shaped, **4–6 cm long, strongly bent back.**

Fruits: Capsules erect, barrel-shaped, 6-angled, 3–5 cm long; seeds numerous, flattened.

Where Found: Mesic, open forests, clearings, thickets and meadows; lowland to alpine zones; frequent in the southwestern part of the region; cordilleran.

Notes: The flowers are pollinated primarily by rufous hummingbirds and large butterflies. • The bulbs are strong tasting, rather bitter and peppery, but were eaten by most First Nations groups where the plants grew. The bulbs were generally cooked and eaten with other foods or used as a flavouring, as well as a thickener, in soups and stews and in puddings mixed with fruits and fish eggs. They may also have been dried for winter use by some groups.

Subalpine Mariposa Lily • *Calochortus subalpinus*

General: Perennial herb from a **deep bulb;** flowering stems upright, 5–30 cm tall, unbranched.

Leaves: Usually **1 flat, grass-like basal leaf,** about as long as stem.

Flowers: Large, showy, **broadly tulip-shaped,** erect to spreading, 1–5 in a bracted cluster atop stem; petals 3, distinct, **creamy white,** often with **purple, crescent-shaped gland** near the inside base, **2–3 cm long, long-hairy on inner face;** sepals 3, greenish, shorter, narrower than petals, each sepal with purple spot near base.

Fruits: Capsules nodding, ellipsoid, 3-angled; seeds numerous, net-veined.

Where Found: Open forests, glades and dry meadows, on loose volcanic soils; montane to alpine zones; infrequent in the southwestern corner of the region.

Similar Species: Pointed mariposa lily or three-spot mariposa lily (**C. apiculatus**) has a **roundish, purplish black gland** on the inside base of the **cream petals, broader leaves** and **long-pointy-tipped anthers.** It occurs in dry meadows, glades, open forests and on grassy slopes, in montane to subalpine zones, and is locally frequent from southeastern BC and southwestern AB to WA, ID and MT. • **Wide-fruited mariposa lily** or big-pod mariposa lily (**C. eurycarpus**) has **white, lavender or pinkish petals** with a large, **central, reddish purple splotch.** It grows on grassy slopes, in meadows and shrublands and at forest edges, in montane to subalpine zones, and is locally frequent from southeastern WA, central ID and southwestern MT to northern OR and western WY.

Notes: *Calochortus* is a genus of about 70 species in the western Americas, from BC to Guatemala, with most species having limited distributions. The flowers are diverse and wonderful, described in one paper as "mariposas with large, brightly colored, tulip-like blossoms with conspicuous spots of contrasting hue; cat's ears with smaller, spreading petals densely covered with trichomes; star tulips with spreading, glabrous petals; and fairy lanterns with bell- or globe-shaped, often nodding flowers" (Patterson and Givnish, 2004). • *Calochortus* is from the Greek *kalo*, "beautiful," and *chortus*, "grass." *Mariposa* is Spanish for "butterfly" and is also a California name for pearly white butterflies; the flowers of some *Calochortus* species were thought to resemble butterflies dancing on the ends of long stems.

pointed mariposa lily

Indian Hellebore, Green False Hellebore, Green Corn-lily • *Veratrum viride* var. *eschscholtzii*

General: From a **short, thick rhizome;** flowering stems robust, erect, often clustered, **50–200 cm tall,** unbranched.

Leaves: Alternate and numerous along the stem, broadly egg-shaped to oblong-elliptic, 10–35 cm long, 5–15 cm wide, **prominently ribbed and often accordion-pleated,** clasping at the base, **densely hairy on lower surface,** hairless above, margins smooth; basal leaves lacking.

Flowers: Numerous, stalked, in an open, branched cluster atop stem; branches long, narrow, densely hairy and at least the **lower drooping and tassel-like;** flowers star-shaped, **pale green or yellow-green with dark green centre;** tepals similar, distinct, **6–13 mm long,** margins minutely toothed to fringed.

Fruits: Capsules erect, barrel-shaped, 1.5–3 cm long; seeds numerous, flattened, **broadly winged,** 8–10 mm long.

Where Found: Moist to wet meadows, streambanks, swamps, thickets, snowbeds, glades and open coniferous forests; lowland to alpine zones; frequent throughout the southern ¾ of the region; cordilleran.

Similar Species: California false hellebore or white corn-lily **(V. californicum var. *californicum*)** has **spreading to ascending (not drooping) flowering branches** and white to greenish white flowers. It grows on streambanks and in wet meadows and forest openings, in montane to alpine zones, and is frequent in the southern ¼ of the region, from WA and ID to NM, AZ and CA.

Notes: Indian hellebore is also known as *V. eschscholtzii*. • **All parts of these plants are poisonous.** *Veratrum* species contain a variety of steroid alkaloids that cause nerve cells to fire continuously by increasing the permeability of their sodium channels. Symptoms in humans begin with a sore stomach, frothing at the mouth, vomiting and diarrhea, and progress to blurred vision, abnormal heartbeat and difficulty breathing. Untreated, ingestion sometimes results in death. People drinking water near where this plant grows have reported stomach cramps, and eating even a small amount can result in loss of consciousness followed by death. Some First Nations groups considered salmon-head soup and salmon oil to be the only antidotes. • All indigenous groups regarded this plant as a powerful medicine that could cure almost any disease, but it had to be treated with respect, harvested according to strict rules and used very carefully to avoid poisoning. Medicines made for internal use would be extremely diluted but are too dangerous to recommend. It has been, and still is, used as a treatment for colds, toothache, kidney and bladder problems, acute fevers, gonorrhea, constipation, stomach pains, chest pains and heart trouble, as well as to abort pregnancies and to treat serious diseases such as tuberculosis and cancer. Poultices were made for sprains, bruises, rashes, sores and rheumatism, and the plant was also used to make a general liniment. Dried or powdered roots might be burned in the house to cleanse rooms or added to wash water to drive out evil spirits and disease. Native Alaskans say it will rid dogs of worms. • True hellebores are in the genus *Helleborus* of the buttercup family (Ranunculaceae). Flowers of *Helleborus* don't look much like those of *Veratrum*, but their showy sepals do turn greenish white with age.

California false hellebore

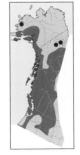

The Genus *Allium* (Onion)

Allium species are perennial herbs with a strong onion odour and taste, from bulbs concentrically covered with sheathing leaf bases, the flowering stems leafless or nearly so. The linear leaves are chiefly basal, flat or rounded in cross-section and sometimes hollow. The relatively small flowers (usually less than 1.5 cm long) grow in showy umbels atop the stems, the umbels subtended by 1–3 papery bracts. Each flower has 6 similar, distinct, white, pink or purplish tepals, becoming dry and persisting. The fruits are egg-shaped capsules with 6 or fewer black seeds in each chamber.

Wild onions usually grow in rocky, exposed sites, mainly at low to moderate elevations, but some species make it up into subalpine and lower alpine zones.

Key to *Allium*

1a. Leaves hollow, cylindric; umbels very compact, head-like, flowering from the centre outward
.... ***A. schoenoprasum*** (p. 409)

1b. Leaves solid, flat or channelled; flower clusters more or less hemispheric umbels, flowering from the outside inward
.... **2**

  2a. Bulbs egg-shaped; rhizomes lacking; leaves longer than flowering stem **3**

   3a. Flowering stem flattened; flowers pink to white .... ***A. crenulatum*** (below)

   3b. Flowering stem round in cross-section or nearly so; flowers mostly white **4**

    4a. Flowering stem 10–20 cm tall, usually as long as leaves; larger bulbs with cluster of bulblets at the base
    .... ***A. madidum*** (p. 409)

    4b. Flowering stem to 10 cm tall, much shorter than leaves... **5**

     5a. Flowering stem 1–5 cm tall, ½–⅓ as long as leaves; ovary with 3 crests; tepal margins finely
     toothed .... ***A. simillimum*** (p. 409)

     5b. Flowering stem 3–10 cm tall, about ½ as long as leaves; ovary not crested; tepal margins smooth
     .... ***A. brandegeei*** (p. 409)

  2b. Bulbs elongate; rhizomes present or not; leaves much shorter than flowering stem **6**

   6a. Bulbs clustered from a very short rhizome or rhizome lacking; flower cluster nodding; tepals blunt-tipped;
   stamens protruding from flowers... ***A. cernuum*** (p. 409)

   6b. Bulbs clustered along a stout, distinct rhizome; flower cluster erect; tepals pointy-tipped; stamens shorter
   or longer than tepals.. **7**

    7a. Stamens and style about ½ as long as tepals, stigma 3-lobed; capsules broader than long
    .... ***A. brevistylum*** (p. 409)

    7b. Stamens and style protruding beyond tepals, stigma head-like; capsules longer than broad
    .... ***A. validum*** (p. 409)

Olympic Onion
Allium crenulatum

General: From a lopsided-egg-shaped, scaly bulb; flowering stems ascending to erect, 5–8 cm tall, **flattened,** 2-angled or 2-winged, edges obscurely scalloped, at least toward tip. **Leaves: Usually 2,** spreading from the base, **flattened,** downcurved and hooked at tip, distinctly longer than flowering stem. **Flowers: Bell-shaped,** several to many, **on stalks about as long as flowers,** in compact, nodding to ascending umbels cradled by 2 membranous bracts; **tepals pink to white, 7–12 mm long,** with deeper pink midveins; **stamens ½–⅔ as long as tepals. Fruits:** Capsules more or less egg-shaped, 3-lobed. **Where Found:** Rock outcrops, rock slides and gravelly ridges; montane to alpine zones; infrequent in the southwestern part of the region; Pacific Northwest endemic.

Brandegee's Onion • *Allium brandegeei*

General: From an egg-shaped to spheric bulb, outer bulb-coat with **net-like pattern** of hexagonal cells; stems ascending-erect, **3–10 cm tall. Leaves:** 2, linear, channelled, longer than flowering stem, 1–3 mm wide. **Flowers:** Bell-shaped, several to many, on stalks a bit shorter than flowers, in compact, hemispheric, erect umbels; tepals 5–8 mm long, **white to occasionally pinkish with green to purplish midveins,**

margins smooth; ovaries and capsules usually not crested. **Where Found:** Gravelly and sandy meadows, rocky slopes and fellfields; montane to alpine zones; locally frequent (often in large numbers) in the southeastern part of the region.

Similar Species: Swamp onion (*A. madidum*) is taller (10–20 cm), with **clusters of bulblets** at the base of its larger bulbs and tepals 6–10 mm long. It is found in seasonally wet meadows, in montane to alpine zones, and is locally frequent in southwestern ID and northeastern OR. • **Idaho dwarf onion (*A. simillimum*) is shorter (1–5 cm),** with **leaves more than 2 times as long as stem,** white (occasionally pinkish), **minutely toothed tepals, no obvious net-like pattern** on the outer bulb-coat and **crested ovaries and capsules.** It grows in coarse, sandy and gravelly soils in open sites, in montane to alpine zones, in central and southwestern ID and southwestern MT.

Short-styled Onion • *Allium brevistylum*

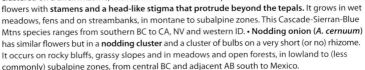

General: From 2–4 egg-shaped bulbs, **at the end of a thick rhizome;** stems erect, 20–60 cm tall, flattened and narrowly winged toward tip. **Leaves:** 2–5, linear, flat, 10–40 cm long, shorter than flowering stem. **Flowers: Pink, narrowly urn-shaped,** 7–20, on stalks about as long as flowers but becoming elongate and curved in fruit,

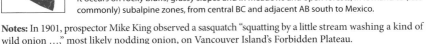

in a loose, erect umbel; **tepals 10–13 mm long; stamens and style about ½ as long as tepals, stigma 3-lobed;** ovaries and capsules not crested, squatly heart-shaped. **Where Found:** Wet meadows and streambanks; subalpine and alpine zones; frequent in the southeastern part of the region, mostly in the Rockies.

Similar Species: Tall swamp onion (*A. validum*) also has bulbs clustered on a thick rhizome, with stems 30–70 cm tall and pink flowers with **stamens and a head-like stigma that protrude beyond the tepals.** It grows in wet meadows, fens and on streambanks, in montane to subalpine zones. This Cascade-Sierran-Blue Mtns species ranges from southern BC to CA, NV and western ID. • **Nodding onion (*A. cernuum*)** has similar flowers but in a **nodding cluster** and a cluster of bulbs on a very short (or no) rhizome. It occurs on rocky bluffs, grassy slopes and in meadows and open forests, in lowland to (less commonly) subalpine zones, from central BC and adjacent AB south to Mexico.

Notes: In 1901, prospector Mike King observed a sasquatch "squatting by a little stream washing a kind of wild onion …," most likely nodding onion, on Vancouver Island's Forbidden Plateau.

Wild Chives • *Allium schoenoprasum*

General: From a cluster of bulbs; stems erect, **20–60 cm tall,** cylindric. **Leaves:** Usually 2, linear, **cylindric, hollow,** usually shorter than flowering stem. **Flowers: Pale pink**

to purplish, vase-shaped, usually numerous, on stalks shorter than flowers, in head-like clusters; **tepals 7–12 mm long;** stamens and style shorter than tepals. **Where Found:**

Wet to moist meadows, floodplains, streambanks and lake margins; montane to alpine zones; scattered but locally frequent in the mostly inland part of the region; circumboreal.

Notes: Although wild chives is a native species in our region, it is also widely cultivated and often escapes. • *Allium* is a fairly large genus with about 750 species worldwide, including about 100 species in North America. The species are distributed around the Northern Hemisphere, mostly in seasonally dry regions.

Alp-lily • *Lloydia serotina*

General: Small, hairless perennial from an oblong, greyish, fibrous-coated, **bulb-like rhizome;** flowering stems ascending to erect, **5–15 (to 20) cm tall,** unbranched.

Leaves: Basal leaves 2, linear, grass-like, somewhat fleshy, 2–10 (to 15) cm long, about 1 mm wide; stem leaves 2–4, alternate, progressively smaller upward.

Flowers: 1 (sometimes 2), cup-shaped, erect to nodding (in poor weather) atop stem, **white or cream** with purplish or yellowish green veins; tepals distinct, 8–13 mm long, each with a gland at the base; stamens about ⅔ as long as tepals.

Fruits: Capsules erect, egg-shaped; seeds numerous, 3-angled.

Where Found: Rocky slopes and ridges, cliff crevices, gravelly meadows, heathlands and tundra; montane to alpine zones; widespread but scattered throughout, locally frequent in the northern ½ of the region, less so southward; arctic-alpine, circumpolar with Eurasian centre of distribution.

Varieties: Plants on Haida Gwaii and northwestern Vancouver I. are recognized as the **endemic var. *flava*** and are typically larger plants, with basal leaves often longer (vs. often shorter in var. *serotina*) than the flowering stems and with yellow or green veins on cream tepals (vs. green to purple veins on white tepals in var. *serotina*).

Notes: This arctic-alpine species is widely distributed in the Northern Hemisphere, with many small, outlier populations. Reproduction is primarily asexual (by rhizomes), but sex is also important. Smaller, more isolated populations have lower genetic diversity, a conservation concern in areas such as Wales. Any individual alp-lily plant can produce male flowers, hermaphroditic (bisexual) flowers or, rarely, both, and the type of flower produced often changes from year to year. A sesquipedalian word for this is "andromonoecious." • The genus is named after Welsh naturalist Edward Lloyd (1660–1709); *serotinus* means "late flowering," but *Lloydia* is one of the earliest alpine flowers to bloom. Lewis Clark (1973) suggests that *serotinus* comes from the verb *sero*, "to weave together," in reference to the network of underground rhizomes.

Western Mountain-bells, Bronze-bells *Stenanthium occidentale*

General: Hairless, from a scaly, **narrowly egg-shaped bulb;** flowering stems ascending-erect, **15–40 cm tall,** unbranched.

Leaves: Basal leaves 2–4, narrowly lance-shaped, **grass-like,** 10–30 cm long, sheathing at the base, arching downward; stem leaves reduced to 2–3 bracts.

Flowers: Few to many (3–25) in narrow clusters atop stems, **tubular bell-shaped,** usually **nodding, greenish yellow to bronze to brownish purple;** tepals 6, similar, weakly joined at the base, narrowly lance-shaped, 8–20 mm long, the tips curled back.

Fruits: Capsules erect, lance-oblong, 1–2 cm long; seeds several, oblong, flattened, winged at both ends.

Where Found: Moist to wet, open forests, thickets, meadows, fens, streambanks, cliffs, mossy scree and rocky slopes; lowland (occasionally) to lower alpine zones; locally frequent in the southern ⅓ of the region; cordilleran.

Notes: The flowers have a tangy perfume. • *Stenanthium* is from the Greek *stenos*, "narrow," and *anthos*, "flower."

Northern False Asphodel • *Tofieldia coccinea*

General: **Hairless,** from a short **rhizome;** flowering stems erect, **5–15 cm tall,** unbranched, **upper part often purplish.**

Leaves: Basal leaves in **fan-like tufts, broadly linear,** mainly 5-veined, 2–6 cm long, **folded like iris leaves;** stem leaves 1, well-developed, often with 1–2 additional bract-like leaves at or above midstem.

Flowers: Several to many, in a head-like or sometimes spike-like cluster, cup-shaped, **greenish white tinged with red or purple;** tepals 6, distinct, spreading, 1.5–3 mm long; anthers often purple.

Fruits: Capsules bent down when mature, **dark reddish to purplish brown;** seeds numerous, with spongy coat, **lacking appendages.**

Where Found: Dry to mesic, usually calcium-rich meadows, rocky slopes, heathlands and tundra; lowland (arctic coast) to alpine zones; locally frequent in the northern ¼ of the region; arctic-alpine, nearly circumpolar.

Similar Species: Common false asphodel (*T. pusilla*) differs in having **pale green stems without leaves** or with 1 small bract, 3-veined basal leaves, **greenish white flowers** and **green capsules.** It is found in moist to wet, turfy, calcium-rich habitats such as fens, marshy meadows, thickets, shorelines and streambanks, gravelly flushes and tundra, in lowland (arctic coast) to alpine zones. An arctic-alpine, circumpolar species, it is locally frequent in the northern ⅓ of the region, south in the Rockies to MT. • **Sticky false asphodel** or **bog-lily** (*Triantha glutinosa*) and **western false asphodel** (*Triantha occidentalis*)—both formerly known as part of *Tofieldia glutinosa* broadly defined—are plants primarily of low-elevation bogs, fens, wet meadows and streambanks, but occasionally occur at high elevations in the southern part of their range (from southern BC and southwestern AB to OR, ID and WY). They have **sticky-hairy stems,** especially toward the flower cluster, longer (3–6 mm) tepals, **red or yellowish capsules** and **seeds with appendages.**

common false asphodel

Notes: The name "asphodel" is obscure but ancient. Asphodel is the flower of the Elysian Fields, as in Homer's "meadows of asphodels" that were inhabited by the souls of the dead. This would fit with an origin from Greek: *a*, "without," and *spodos*, "ashes."

Mountain Death-camas, Elegant Death-camas *Zigadenus elegans*

General: Hairless, from a scaly, **narrowly egg-shaped bulb;** flowering stems erect, 15–50 cm tall, unbranched.

Leaves: Mostly near the base, grass-like, 8–25 cm long, keeled, **glaucous;** stem leaves few, becoming bract-like upward.

Flowers: Several to many, stalked, in a loose, cylindric cluster, **bowl- to saucer-shaped, greenish white to cream;** tepals distinct, spreading, **6–12 mm long,** each with a large, bi-lobed, **green gland** near the base.

Fruits: Capsules narrowly egg-shaped, 3-lobed, 1.5–2 cm long; seeds numerous.

Where Found: Meadows, rocky or grassy slopes, open forests, sandy-gravelly river terraces and tundra; montane to alpine zones; frequent in the northern ⅓ of the region, south mostly inland of the Coast-Cascade Mtns to OR, AZ and NM.

Notes: All parts of this plant are poisonous. • The Okanagan people used the mashed bulb as arrow tip poison. • *Zigadenus* is from the Greek *xugeo*, "to be joined," and *aden*, "a gland," alluding to the deeply notched gland on each tepal. • The genus *Zigadenus* is polyphyletic—that is, the species are not derived from a common ancestor. Accordingly, some taxonomists have split the 22 or so *Zigadenus* species into 5 genera, with this species called *Anticlea elegans*.

Bear-grass, Basket-grass • *Xerophyllum tenax*

General: From a **short, thick rhizome**; offshoots do not flower for several years, then die after flowering and fruiting; **stems erect**, stately, **50–120 cm tall,** unbranched.

Leaves: Basal leaves numerous, in a **large clump or tussock**, persistent, **wiry, grass-like,** arching, 15–60 cm long, **margins harsh** with tiny teeth or bristles; stem leaves several to many, progressively shorter upward, becoming bract-like.

Flowers: Numerous, stalked, atop stem in a dense, showy, **cone-shaped cluster,** at first hemispheric and nippled, later elongating, **10–50 cm long;** individual flowers small, saucer-shaped, **creamy white;** tepals similar, distinct, oblong, **5–9 mm long; stamens equalling or longer than tepals.**

Fruits: Capsules broadly egg-shaped, 3-lobed, 5–7 mm long; seeds 2–5 per chamber.

Where Found: Open coniferous forests, glades, rocky slopes, ridges and meadows; lowland to upper subalpine zones; frequent in the southern ¼ of the region.

Notes: Bear-grass is fundamentally a forest plant, but it is often a conspicuous element of timberline meadows, especially where wildfire has opened up the forest. • Some First Nations used the leaf fibres to make hats and capes and still use them in basketry. Some ate the thick, somewhat bulbous rhizomes after roasting them for several days. • Bear-grass plants flower en masse, with anthers liberally sprinkling their own stigmas with pollen. But wait—pollen grains from one's own anthers germinate on the stigmas, but rarely produce pollen tubes, which almost never reach the ovary. At the same time, however, pollen-eating flies, beetles and bees visit these nectarless flowers and carry pollen from one plant to another. These cross-pollinated grains then germinate, produce pollen tubes and fertilize ovules. • One source claims that bear-grass gets its name from the flowers, which have an unpleasant, bearish odour, but bears do eat the soft, white leaf bases in spring.

Orchid Family (Orchidaceae)

The orchids are either the largest or second-largest family of flowering plants, with 22,000 to 35,000 species, mostly in tropical forests; there are very few orchids at high elevations in North America. The strikingly bilaterally symmetric flowers are complex, with 3 sepals (1 usually modified) and 3 petals; the lower petal is usually modified into a lip, which is often inflated into a pouch or prolonged as a hollow spur. The 1 or 2 stamens are united with the style in a **column**, and pollen is clumped in waxy masses called **pollinia**. The inferior ovary has its stalk typically twisted through a semicircle (180°). The fruit is usually a 1-chambered capsule that opens by slits and has very numerous, tiny seeds.

Fragrant White Bog Orchid, White Rein Orchid, Scent Candle • *Platanthera dilatata*

General: Hairless, rather fleshy, perennial herb from a loose bundle of fleshy roots; flowering stems erect, 15–60 cm tall, unbranched, leafy.

Leaves: Oblong to lance-shaped, 5–20 cm long, sheathing at the base, progressively smaller upward.

Flowers: Several to many (5–30), in a fragrant **spike** atop stem, **waxy, white;** 2 lateral sepals spreading to curved back, upper sepal egg-shaped, erect, **converging with 2 upper petals and forming a hood;** lower petal modified as a **pendent, lance-shaped lip,** 5–10 mm long, round-dilated at the base, prolonged in a **narrowly tubular, sabretooth-shaped spur,** the spur shorter than to about twice as long as lip.

Fruits: Capsules ellipsoid, ascending to erect.

Where Found: Wet meadows, seepage slopes, fens, streambanks, lakeshores and swampy forests; lowland to lower alpine zones; frequent throughout all but the northernmost parts of the region; also in eastern North America.

Similar Species: Northern green bog orchid (*P. aquilonis*) and **eastern green bog orchid** (*P. huronensis*) are 2 similar, greenish-flowered species that can be found in similar habitats as and often co-occur with white bog orchid. Northern green bog orchid is usually scentless and has shorter spurs (generally less than 5 mm long) than the fragrant eastern green bog orchid. Both green-flowered species previously were identified as and lumped in *P. hyperborea* (*Habenaria hyperborea*), which, according to *FNA*, is restricted to Greenland and Iceland. • **Small bog orchid** (*P. chorisiana*) is only 7–15 cm tall, with 2 egg-shaped basal leaves and a bracted cluster of few to several, yellowish green flowers. It occurs from low-elevation bogs to alpine peaty turf habitats and is an amphiberingian species infrequent along the outer coast from southern AK to Vancouver I. and northwestern WA. • **Frog orchid** (*Coeloglossum viride*; *H. viridis*) is 15–40 cm tall, with amply leafy stems and **green to yellowish green flowers** with an **oblong to wedge-shaped lip, 3-lobed at the tip,** and a **scrotiform spur.** An amphiberingian species of open forests, grassy slopes, meadows and shores, in lowland to subalpine zones, it is infrequent throughout the mostly inland portion of the region except the far north, from central AK, central YT and southwestern NT to WA, AZ and NM.

fragrant white and northern green bog orchids

Notes: Fragrant white bog orchid is also known as *Habenaria dilatata*. • The flowers have a strong perfume, described as a mix of cloves, vanilla and mock-orange. • There's a lot of variation in the 75 or so species of *Platanthera*, but all have a single fertile anther with 2 pollinia (pollen masses) on either side of the column. "Viscidia"—sticky organs—are located just above the spur's opening, at the base of the pollinia. Pollinators (beetles, butterflies, moths, bumblebees, flies and mosquitoes) seeking nectar in the spur get the viscidia stuck to their proboscis or eyes and fly off with the pollinia glued to them.

frog orchid (both photos)

OUR FAVOURITE MOUNTAINS

I am a huge fan of the Richardson Mountains, arctic mountains of northern Yukon and its border with the Northwest Territories. Not least because, although way up there, mostly north of the Arctic Circle, they are crossed by a good road from which you can walk right out onto the flower-spangled tundra. Surprisingly, things happen earlier the farther north you go in Yukon. Thus June, with wall-to-wall daylight, is the best time for wildflowers and birds along the Dempster Highway, which connects Dawson City, Yukon, with Inuvik, Northwest Territories. And if you time it right, you can escape the biting bugs, which can be ferocious if you wait until July and the wind drops.

Richardson Mountains, YT–NT

The Richardsons are old mountains, largely unaffected by Pleistocene glaciation. Erosion has had a long time to work on the mostly sedimentary rocks, thus much of the range has subdued terrain with gently sloping pediments in the broader valleys, combined with deeper, steeper valleys in the higher ranges. Much of the bedrock is calcium rich and has weathered to scree and talus ideal for natural rock gardens. For the naturalist, highlights include the refugial Beringian flora; megafauna such as caribou and grizzly bears; birds including gyrfalcons, long-tailed jaegers and red-throated loons; and outstanding periglacial landforms such as cryoplanation terraces and solifluction lobes. Plus the endless ridges, sweeping views and splendid silence.

–Jim Pojar

One of my favourite alpine areas is Waterton Lakes National Park in Alberta. This is one of the few places where the Rocky Mountains arise directly from the prairies below—no foothills to ease the transition. Spectacular! And about a quarter of the park is alpine (here above 2500 metres). Now, a lot of this alpine area is non-vegetated—the climate is fairly severe, and much of the topography is steep. If you're fond of scree slopes, you'll enjoy Waterton. Moreover, here prairie plants meet alpine plants, and species from both sides of the Continental Divide mingle. Thus amplified, the flora of this rather small park includes more than 900 species of vascular plants, a remarkable total. And in the right spots—on more gentle terrain, sheltered from the insistent wind and with deeper soils—many of our favourite alpine species flourish. Fans of moss-campion and saxifrages, Waterton is for you.

Many alpine species transcend international boundaries, so it's appropriate that Waterton Lakes National Park and adjoining Glacier National Park in Montana were together designated as Waterton-Glacier International Peace Park in 1932 and as a World Heritage Site in 1995.

–Andy MacKinnon

Carthew Lakes, Waterton Lakes National Park, AB

It is hard for me to pick a favourite alpine area, because I love them all. The gorgeous scenery, brilliantly coloured flower meadows, the chance of seeing wildlife, the clean air and peaceful quiet are all so spiritually renewing. I am, however, very sentimentally attached to the mountains of Gladys Lake Ecological Reserve nestled within northern BC's Spatsizi Park. I have fond memories of sitting in the subalpine meadows by a small tarn after supper, listening to the gurgling, crystal-clear creek and scanning the surrounding slopes for wildlife. Suddenly caribou and moose appear, rising up from the scrub birch and willow where they have been resting. Up on the grassy slopes below Nation Peak, Stone's sheep and an occasional mountain goat come out to graze. Close by is the ethereal evening song of the hermit thrush, and a hoary marmot whistles out a warning—perhaps it saw the movement of a bear or wolf somewhere.

The excitement of finding the unusual flowers of blue corydalis and seeing meadows splashed with the blues of larkspurs, monkshoods, lupines, bluebells and Jacob's-ladder, the yellows of groundsels and arnicas, the whites of valerian and grass-of-Parnassus, and the reds and oranges of paintbrushes and columbines against a background of emerald green are among my first memories of the wild northern mountains. I was totally hooked!

–Rosamund Pojar

What is my favorite alpine area? Well, looking at a relief map of the northwestern parts of North America, I'm amazed by the vast region of mountains stretching wide (from coast to prairies) and far (from the Arctic to the Great Basin and beyond); in fact, all the way beyond through the cordillera to Tierra del Fuego in South America. There are literally hundreds of named ranges in this region. How to choose a favourite among all these, even if I'm limited to the Northwest?

As many people would do, I'd have to choose my original stomping grounds—the mountains I knew first when, as a teenager, I was finally free with a driver's licence and a faithful old station wagon. That freedom was the ticket to explore the Coeur d'Alene Mountains of northern Idaho. They may not be the highest or the most dazzling of the mountain ranges covered by this book, but they remain a favourite for me. They were the mountains where I first started to learn wild plants, where I first developed my hiking legs and where I learned to feel at home in the wilds. They were the first mountains I came to know, you could say, on a personal level. Each peak climbed became like a friend I was eager to visit again. I'll always be ready at a jump to revisit those peaks. And their flora, some of it found nowhere else on earth, will always be one of the treasures in my life.

–Curtis Björk

Residents of Victoria, BC, think they own the view of them, even if they are located in a different country. Their silhouette tantalizes many of us, but we need a ferry ride to get there. The Olympic Mountains have everything: easy access to a small part of them, great trail routes to their untouched parts, record precipitation on their west slopes and strong rainshadow on the other side. And, of course, their alpine plant treasures.

From a northern and island perspective, and in contrast with Vancouver Island's glacially impoverished flora, the Olympics harbour many more species, alpine and otherwise, for they were only touched, not engulfed, by the last ice age. Plants that we regard as rarities in mountains to the north, including cliff dwarf-primrose, mountain owl-clover and Olympic Mountain aster, are commonplace. To find them there in great abundance is a treat, but discovering some of the exquisite endemics, such as the cushion-forming Olympic harebell, the Olympic Mountain rockmat or the scree-dwelling Olympic Mountain groundsel, is a real thrill for the alpine botanist. It doesn't end there; many species absent from coastal areas to the north, but present in more continental areas farther inland, also make a showing in the Olympics.

Olympic Mountains, WA, as seen from Victoria, BC

As a favourite alpine area, the Olympic Mountains are indeed hard to beat!

–Hans Roemer

Graminoids

squirreltail grass (*Elymus elymoides*), Chilcotin, BC

Graminoids (Grass-like Families)

Rushes (family Juncaceae), sedges (family Cyperaceae) and grasses (family Poaceae) are somewhat similar and can be grouped as graminoids—grass-like plants. They are common and often abundant plants at high elevations throughout the region. In several alpine and subalpine ecosystems, especially at dry and wet extremes, they dominate the plant cover. Graminoids all have long, narrow, parallel-veined leaves and inconspicuous flowers with several scale-like bracts (reduced **tepals**). You can most easily distinguish them by examining their stems: those of rushes are mostly round and also solid (pithy, not hollow), with leaves only or mostly at the base; those of sedges are generally triangular in cross-section and solid, with leaves in 3 rows; those of grasses are round, jointed and often hollow, with leaves in 2 rows. But in the beginning, it isn't going to be easy. This is a large, diverse group of plants, and it takes some time getting used to the keys and specialized terminology. First, try using the key and illustrations below to reach the appropriate family. Then there are keys to the different genera within each family. Once you have the genus, you could be halfway there for some rushes and grasses, but just starting if it's a species of *Carex* (sedge) or *Poa* (bluegrass). We have tried to include all graminoid species you are *likely* to encounter at high elevations in our region. Nonetheless, you should consult regional floras for more detail and to confirm identifications.

Key to the Graminoid (Grass-like) Families

1a. Stems usually cylindric and solid; flowers with sepals and petals reduced to 6 similar tepals or scales, in 2 rows of 3; fruits 3-chambered capsules with 3 or many seeds per chamber . . . . **Rushes (Juncaceae, pp. 418–425)**

1b. Stems usually 3-angled and solid, or cylindric and hollow; flowers lacking apparent petals and sepals; stamens and ovaries enclosed by 1 or 2 bracts, scales or sacs; fruits 1-seeded achenes or grains. 2

    2a. Stems mostly 3-angled and solid; each flower subtended by 1 (rarely 2) scale-like bract; leaves usually in 3 vertical rows . . . . **Sedges (Cyperaceae, pp. 426–452)**

    2b. Stems cylindric, usually hollow, jointed, swollen at leaf nodes; each flower (floret) enclosed by 2 specialized bracts (lemma and palea), forming small clusters (spikelets) of 1 to several florets subtended by 2 bracts (glumes); leaves generally in 2 rows . . . . **Grasses (Poaceae, pp. 453–482)**

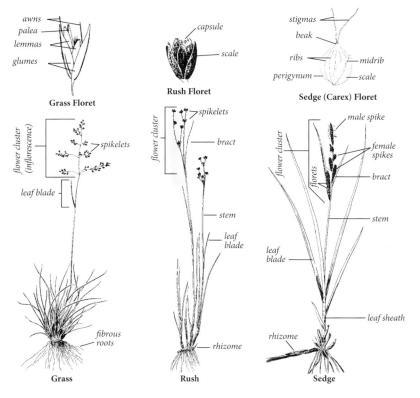

Grass Floret

Rush Floret

Sedge (Carex) Floret

Grass

Rush

Sedge

Rush Family (Juncaceae)

At high elevations, the rush family is represented by perennial, usually tufted herbs from rhizomes or fibrous roots, the stems typically rounded in cross-section and solid (pithy). The leaves are primarily basal, often also alternate and reduced along the stem, flat or rounded, linear or thread-like, with sheathing bases. The small flowers, 1 to several or many, grow in open to more often compact clusters; they look like tiny, brownish lilies, radially symmetric with 6 distinct segments or scales (2 series of 3, equivalent to sepals and petals) that are brown, black or greenish. There are 3 or 6 stamens, a single 1- or 3-chambered superior ovary (attached above the other flower parts), 1 style and 3 stigmas. The fruits are capsules with 3 or many seeds.

Juncus means "binder," referring to the use of some species in weaving and basketry. "Rush" is from the Old English *risc*, meaning "to bind or plait." *Luzula* may be from the Italian *lucciola*, "to shine or sparkle," or the Latin *gramen luzulae/ luxulae*, meaning "grain of light," because the plants are often bedecked with shining dewdrops on the leaf hairs.

Key to the Genera of Juncaceae

1a. Plants hairless; leaves stiff, sheaths open; capsule with 1 or 3 chambers and numerous, very
small seeds
. . . . **Juncus (pp. 419–420)**

1b. Plants hairy, at least on margins of leaves and on sheaths; leaves flexible, sheaths closed; capsule
with 1 chamber and 3 seeds. . . . . **Luzula (pp. 421–425)**

Key to *Juncus* (Rush)

1a. Flower cluster appearing as if on side of stem, subtending (involucral) bract erect and cylindric, resembling
a short continuation of stem. 2

   2a. Leaf blades almost lacking or reduced to bristles 2–10 mm long; capsules retuse (blunt and notched with "inny"
at the top). . . . . **J. drummondii (p. 419)**

   2b. Leaf blades well developed, 2–7 cm long; capsules acute (with pointed "outy" at the top) . . . . **J. parryi (p. 419)**

1b. Flower cluster obviously terminal atop stem, subtending (involucral) bract flattened or channelled, not resembling
an extension or continuation of stem 3

   3a. Leaves all at base of stem; plants mostly <20 cm tall, tufted from fibrous roots 4

      4a. Capsules notched at tip; flowers usually 2 . . . . **J. biglumis (p. 419)**

      4b. Capsules pointy-tipped; flowers 2–5 per cluster . . . . **J. triglumis (p. 419)**

   3b. Leaves basal and along stem; plants often >20 cm tall, from rhizomes or stolons 5

      5a. Flowerheads several to numerous, mostly 3–12; anthers 1.5–2.5 (to 3) mm long. . . . . **J. orthophyllus (p. 420)**

      5b. Flowerheads 1–3 (to 5); anthers 0.6–1.3 mm long 6

         6a. Capsules 6–9 mm long, about 1.5 times longer than flower scales, acute; flower clusters 1 to several,
in egg-shaped heads . . . . **J. castaneus (p. 420)**

         6b. Capsules 2–3.5 mm long, nearly as long as flower scales, blunt or rounded at tip; flower cluster
1 hemispheric head (rarely 2) . . . . **J. mertensianus (p. 420)**

Drummond's rush

Drummond's Rush • *Juncus drummondii*

General: Strongly tufted from short, matted rhizomes; flowering stems numerous, slender, wiry, round in cross-section, **5–30 cm tall. Leaves: Several from the base,** reduced to mere sheaths or sheaths with hair-like bristle-tips shorter than 1 cm; stem leaf blades lacking. **Flowers:** Few (1–5), in compact, **apparently lateral clusters,** lowermost (primary involucral) bract nearly equalling to exceeding flower cluster; flower scales brown with green midstripe, lance-shaped, **5–8 mm long. Fruits:** Capsules about as long as flower scales, oblong-ellipsoid with **rounded, indented tip;** seeds numerous, small, **with membranous tails at both ends. Where Found:** Gravelly slopes, rocky ridges, scree,

heathlands, meadows, snowbeds and streambanks; subalpine and alpine zones; frequent in all but the northernmost part of the region; cordilleran.

Similar Species: Parry's rush (*J. parryi***;** *J. drummondii* var. *parryi*) has leaves with definite **blades 2–7 cm long** and **pointy-tipped capsules.** It is found in similar but somewhat drier habitats, and is frequent from southern BC and southwestern AB to CA, NV, UT and CO.

Notes: Rushes are important early successional species in some areas. As the Lyman Glacier in the Washington Cascades retreats, the first plants to become established on the glacier foreland are Drummond's and Mertens' rushes, Piper's wood-rush and a couple of saxifrage species—a typical "rawmark" community. "Rawmark" is a term for immature soils of alpine and polar environments.

Three-flowered Rush • *Juncus triglumis*

General: Small tufts from fibrous roots; stems erect, slender, stiff, **5–20 cm tall. Leaves:** Several, all from the base. **Flowers:** Few (2–5), in head-like clusters atop stems, **primary bract spreading, about as long as head,** flower scales pale brown or darker, **3–5 mm long. Fruits:** Capsules oblong-ellipsoid with blunt to conic, **short-pointed tip;** seeds with **membranous tails at both ends. Where found:** Wet, mossy sites, snowbeds, lakeshores and streambanks; montane to alpine zones; frequent in the northern ⅓ of the region, infrequent southward mostly in the Rockies; arctic-alpine, circumpolar.

Varieties: Var. *triglumis*, the variety most likely to be encountered at high elevations, has **involucral bracts mostly shorter than the flowerhead** and **capsules 4.5–7 mm long, longer** than the flower scales. • **Var.** *albescens* (*J. albescens*) has **involucral bracts longer** than the flowerhead and **capsules 3–5 mm long, shorter than** or about equal to the scales.

Similar Species: Two-flowered rush (*J. biglumis***)** has an erect primary bract, much longer than the usually 2-flowered head, and **capsules that are indented at the tip.** It occurs in wet seeps, on mossy ledges, gravelly shores, snowbeds, streambanks and wet tundra, in montane to alpine zones. Two-flowered rush is frequent in AK, YT, NT and northern BC, and infrequent south through eastern BC and adjacent AB to MT, WY and CO.

two-flowered rush

Notes: Protists are tiny, usually single-celled, often motile organisms, including protozoa, some (former) algae and water moulds. The roots of some rush species (including three-flowered rush) are parasitized by plasmodiophorids, enigmatic protists with swimming spores, found in freshwater, marine and periodically wet terrestrial habitats. These parasitic protists could be important in rush ecology, but we don't know for sure.

Mertens' Rush • *Juncus mertensianus*

General: Single or in clusters from **rhizomes;** stems 5–30 cm tall. **Leaves:** Basal leaves 1–3; stem leaves 1–2, **half-rounded in cross-section,** with **crosswalls. Flowers:** Several to many (10–60) in a **solitary, blackish brown, hemispheric head** atop stem; flower scales dark brown, lance-shaped, **2.5–4.5 mm long.**

Fruits: Capsules oblong-egg-shaped, a bit **shorter than scales,** abruptly **rounded at tip;** seeds minutely pointed but **not tailed at both ends. Where Found:** Wet meadows, streambanks, rocky runnels, snowbeds, pond edges, bogs and heathlands; montane to alpine zones; frequent in the southern ¾ of the region; cordilleran.

Similar Species: The more robust **chestnut rush (*J. castaneus*) has long, creeping rhizomes or stolons; stem leaves flattened but rolled inward and channelled, without crosswalls;**

chestnut rush

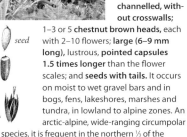
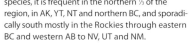
seed

1–3 or 5 **chestnut brown heads,** each with 2–10 flowers; **large (6–9 mm long), lustrous, pointed capsules 1.5 times longer** than the flower scales; and **seeds with tails.** It occurs on moist to wet gravel bars and in bogs, fens, lakeshores, marshes and tundra, in lowland to alpine zones. An arctic-alpine, wide-ranging circumpolar species, it is frequent in the northern ⅓ of the region, in AK, YT, NT and northern BC, and sporadically south mostly in the Rockies through eastern BC and western AB to NV, UT and NM.

Straight-leaf Rush • *Juncus orthophyllus*

General: Scattered or in clusters from **rhizomes;** stems 20–40 cm tall. **Leaves:** Basal leaves several; stem leaves 0–3, **blades flat,** 2–5 mm wide. **Flowers:** 5–10, in **3–12 greenish brown heads** in an **open array;** flower scales brown, lance-shaped, **5–6 mm long. Fruits:** Capsules egg-shaped, **shorter than scales,** abruptly **rounded at tip;** seeds not tailed. **Where Found:** Moist meadows and streambanks; montane to alpine zones; locally frequent in the southern ¼ of the region; southern cordilleran.

Notes: The larvae of at least 14 species of moths in the genus *Coleophora* feed only on *Juncus* species. They munch on the leaves, seeds and flowers of the rushes before constructing their distinctive silken cocoons.

Key to *Luzula* (Wood-rush)

1a. Flowers 1–2, or in small clusters of 3–4, at tips of branches in open arrays, not forming small heads. **2**

    2a. Flower scales with long-pointed, bent-back tips; flowering branches stiff, spreading widely to 90°
. . . . **L. divaricata** (p. 422)

    2b. Flower scales with short-pointed tips (not bent back); flowering branches lax, spreading <90°. **3**

        3a. Flower scales 2.5–3.5 mm long; capsules about as long as scales, egg-shaped, with distinct beak to 1 mm long; anthers 1.2–1.5 mm long . . . . **L. hitchcockii** (p. 422)

        3b. Flower scales usually shorter than 2.5 mm; capsules shorter than scales, ellipsoid or spheric (not egg-shaped), indistinctly beaked; anthers <1 mm long **4**

            4a. Stems usually >30 cm tall; margins of bracts and bractlets (subtending branches of inflorescence and individual flowers, respectively) entire to jaggedly cut . . . . **L. parviflora** (p. 422)

            4b. Stems <30 cm tall; margins of bracts and bractlets fringed **5**

                5a. Lowest involucral bract to 1 cm long; stem leaves 2; stigmas 2 times as long as style; seeds dark reddish brown. . . . . **L. wahlenbergii** (p. 423)

                5b. Lowest involucral bract 0.8–1.5 cm long; stem leaves 2–3; stigmas 5 times as long as style; seeds pale yellowish brown. . . . . **L. piperi** (p. 423)

1b. Flowers in dense heads, spikes or small clusters, mostly of more than 4 flowers **6**

    6a. Flower clusters in single, dense, nodding aggregation, spike-like but often interrupted . . . . **L. spicata** (p. 424)

    6b. Flowers in 1 or several small, head-like clusters (not spike-like), sometimes lax, spreading or arching (not nodding) **7**

        7a. Lowest involucral bract poorly developed, inconspicuous; flower bractlets toothed or strongly fringed, usually more than ½ scale length **8**

            8a. Flower scales usually a bit shorter than capsule, bractlets coarsely toothed; leaf tips often blunt and callous-tipped; plants densely tufted . . . . **L. arctica** (p. 425)

            8b. Flower scales equalling or longer than capsule, bractlets strongly fringed; leaves pointy-tipped; plants creeping or loosely tufted **9**

                9a. Basal leaf sheaths dull brownish grey to greenish; stem leaves equalling or larger than basal leaves; flower clusters pale brown to straw brown. . . . . **L. kjellmaniana** (p. 425)

                9b. Basal leaf sheaths shiny, reddish brown to brown or purple; stem leaves usually smaller than basal leaves; flower clusters dark to blackish brown. **10**

                    10a. Leaves not reaching flower clusters; outer cluster of flowers on spreading or arching stalks; basal leaf sheaths brownish purple, hairy . . . . **L. arcuata** ssp. **unalaschkensis** (p. 425)

                    10b. Some leaves (especially stem leaves) often reaching or exceeding flower clusters; outer flower clusters on erect stalks or almost unstalked; basal leaf sheaths reddish, hairless . . . . **L. confusa** (p. 424)

        7b. Lowest involucral bract well developed, leaf-like, usually exceeding flower cluster; flower bractlets scarcely fringed with few hairs, less than ½ as long as scales. **11**

            11a. Styles much shorter than ovaries; capsules dark reddish, egg-shaped . . . . **L. groenlandica** (p. 425)

            11b. Styles slightly shorter to longer than ovaries; capsules dark brown to blackish, globe-shaped . . . . **L. multiflora** ssp. **frigida** (p. 425)

L. hitchcockii

L. spicata

L. arctica

L. groenlandica

Small-flowered Wood-rush
Luzula parviflora

General: Loosely tufted from **long rhizomes;** stems leafy, **20–50 cm tall.**

Leaves: Basal leaves few to several; **stem leaves 3–6, 3–5 (to 8) mm wide,** sparsely fringed with fine hairs only around sheaths.

Flowers: Single or in pairs at ends of lax, **arching stalks** in a loose, open, nodding array, primary (lowest involucral) bract to 5 cm long; flower scales brown with distinct midribs, **1.8–2.5 mm long;** stamens 6, **anthers 0.4–0.6 mm long; bracts and bract-lets entire to jaggedly cut.**

Fruits: Capsules ellipsoid, pointed but not beaked at tip, dark brown, **slightly longer than scales;** seeds 1–1.5 mm long, lacking appendages.

Where Found: Moist, open forests, meadows, glades, streambanks, thickets and heathlands; lowland to alpine zones; frequent throughout the region except northernmost AK and the southern Cascades; amphiberingian.

Similar Species: Hitchcock's wood-rush (*L. hitchcockii*; *L. glabrata* of some authors) has **longer (2.5–3.5 mm) flower scales; longer (1–1.5 mm) anthers; stigmas 2 times the style length; egg-shaped, **distinctly beaked capsules about as long as the scales; and seeds 1.2–1.8 mm long.** It is recognizable by its broad, flat leaves that are conspicuously red-green bicoloured, often becoming honey-coloured in autumn and forms large, continuous patches, often where snow lies late. Occurring in meadows, heathlands, open forests and on exposed, rocky slopes and ridges, in montane to alpine zones, it is frequent in the Coast-Cascade and Rocky Mtns from southern BC (about 52° N) and southwestern AB to WA, OR (Crater L.), ID and western MT. • **Spreading wood-rush (*L. divaricata*)** has flower clusters with **stiff branches, widely spreading** to 90° or more, and **flower scales with long-pointed, bent-back tips.** It grows in open forests and on rocky slopes, in subalpine and alpine zones, from southern WA and OR to NV and CA, where it is more frequent.

Notes: The "seed bank" (seeds contained in the soil) of small-flowered wood-rush lasts a long time in cold environments. Seeds buried in Alaskan arctic soil reportedly germinated after at least 200 (and perhaps as long as 300) years underground.

Hitchcock's wood-rush

Piper's Wood-rush
Luzula piperi

General: Tufted from short rhizomes; stems leafy, **10–20 (to 30) cm tall.**

Leaves: Basal leaves few to several; **stem leaves 2–3,** mostly **2–3 mm wide.**

Flowers: Single or 2–3 at ends of lax, arching stalks in a loose, open, nodding array, primary bract 0.8–1.5 cm long; flower scales dark brown, lance-shaped, **1–2.5 mm long; anthers 0.4–0.6 mm long;** stigmas 5 times length of style; **bracts and bractlets frilly-fringed.**

Fruits: Capsules ellipsoid, pointed but not beaked at tip, dark brown, longer than scales; **seeds light yellowish brown, 1–1.2 mm long.**

Where Found: Moist meadows, glades, streambanks, thickets, snowbeds, heathlands and tundra; montane to alpine zones; frequent in most of the southern ⅔ of the region; amphiberingian.

Similar Species: Wahlenberg's wood-rush (*L. wahlenbergii*) has **mostly 2 stem leaves** and relatively few-flowered branches, the **primary bract 1 cm long or shorter,** stigmas 2 times as long as the style and **reddish brown seeds 1.2–1.6 mm long.** It grows in wet, mossy tundra, hummocky meadows and on streambanks and shores, in lowland to alpine zones. In the strict sense, Wahlenberg's wood-rush is a circumpolar, mostly low-arctic species, sporadic in the northern part of our region, mostly on the North Slope of AK, YT and adjacent NT.

Notes: Piper's wood-rush is also known as *L. wahlenbergii* ssp. *piperi*. • This species is named for Charles Vancouver Piper (1867–1926), a botanist and agronomist for the U.S. Department of Agriculture. He was the author of *Flora of Washington* and was responsible for introducing the soybean into U.S. agriculture. A grass man, he was chair of the U.S. Golf Association's Green Section from 1920 to 1926.

Wahlenberg's wood-rush (above)

Spiked Wood-rush • *Luzula spicata*

General: Small tufts from fibrous roots; stems erect, slender, reddish, 5–30 cm tall. **Leaves:** Basal leaves erect, linear-lance-shaped, channelled, 2–15 cm long, 1–3 mm wide; stem leaves 2–3, sheath throats densely hairy. **Flowers:** In 5–10 clusters of 3–6 flowers each, clusters aggregated in a **single, dense, nodding spike;** primary bract leaf-like, mostly shorter than spike; flower scales brown with clear margins or pale throughout, **2–2.5 mm long;** bractlets frilly-margined. **Fruits:** Capsules **broadly egg-shaped,** usually **shorter than scales;** seeds brown, egg-shaped, about 1 mm long, with short, rounded appendage at end. **Where Found:** Dry, rocky ridges, scree, fellfields, meadows, heathlands and tundra; subalpine and alpine zones; frequent in the southern mostly inland ¾ of the region; low arctic-alpine, circumpolar with several large gaps.

Notes: Wood-rushes are often among the handful of vascular plants at the highest altitudes and latitudes, especially in rubbly areas with much bare soil (see also Drummond's rush, p. 419).

Northern Wood-rush • *Luzula confusa*

General: Small, **loose tufts** from short rhizomes; flowering stems erect, 5–25 cm tall. **Leaves:** Basal leaves narrow, **folded or channelled,** often curled, gradually tapering to sharp tip, 5–15 cm long, 1.5–3 mm wide, **sheaths reddish brown, shiny, persisting for several years;** stem leaves 2–3, reddish. **Flowers:** In **1–4 head-like clusters,** central cluster unstalked with 8–15 flowers, lateral clusters on **often arching branches** with 1–5 flowers, primary bract scale-like to awn-like, **shorter than flower array;** flower scales dark brown with clear tips, 1.5–2.5 mm long; **bractlets strongly fringed or raggedly frilly. Fruits:** Capsules **broadly egg-shaped,** dark brown, **equalling or shorter than scales;** seeds dark brown, about 1 mm long, without appendages but with **tuft of fine, tangled hairs. Where Found:** Cliffs, rocky slopes, heathlands and turfy and lichen tundra; lowland (arctic coast) to alpine zones; frequent in the northern, mostly inland ⅓ of the region; arctic-alpine, circumpolar.

Notes: Young plants of many species (including northern wood-rush) have higher nitrogen concentrations than older, larger plants. So, younger plants present smaller amounts of higher-quality forage. Given the choice, reindeer on Norway's Svalbard archipelago graze older plants, suggesting that in arctic environments, quantity could be more important than quality in meeting nitrogen and energy needs. Selecting high volumes of low-quality food seems to be a common strategy among many humans as well.

Arctic Wood-rush • *Luzula arctica*

General: Densely tufted, 5–20 cm tall. **Leaves:** Narrow (2–4 mm), flat, ending in swollen, callous-like tips; basal sheaths brown to straw-coloured. **Flowers:** In heads of 1–3 mostly unstalked clusters, each cluster with 8–15 flowers; **primary bract equalling or shorter than flowerhead;** scales dark brown with narrow, clear margins and tips; **bracts and bractlets coarsely toothed,** not frilly. **Fruits:** Capsules spheric, dark reddish to blackish, usually **longer than scales;** seeds translucent brown, with few entangled hairs. **Where Found:** Moist meadows, stony slopes, snowbeds and heathlands; lowland (arctic coast) to alpine zones; frequent in the northern ⅓ of the region; arctic-alpine, circumpolar.

Similar Species: Greenland wood-rush (*L. groenlandica*) has a prominent, **leaf-like primary bract,** usually **exceeding the flower array,** and **scarcely fringed bractlets** around the flowers. It is found on sandy and gravelly shores, peaty pond margins, streambanks, snowbeds and turfy tundra, in lowland (arctic coast) to alpine zones. A subarctic-alpine, North American species, it is infrequent in AK, YT, NT and northern BC.

Notes: Arctic wood-rush is also known as *Luzula nivalis.* • In Yukon alpine meadows, seed capsules of arctic and curved wood-rushes were among the most common plant materials found in the cheek pouches of male arctic ground squirrels (though the seeds and rhizomes of alpine bistort, p. 109, are their absolute favourite). The males cache food for the following spring, when they stagger from hibernation. Then they need all the energy they can muster for producing sperm and for fighting other males for the company of females. Many of the same plant species found in cheek pouches today are present in Pleistocene fossil caches.

Curved Wood-rush
Luzula arcuata ssp. *unalaschkensis*

General: Loose tufts from short rhizomes or stolons; stems slender, ascending to arching, 10–30 cm tall. **Leaves:** Basal leaves flat or channelled, gradually tapering to sharp tips, 2–5 mm wide, **not reaching flower array, sheaths glossy brownish purple;** stem leaves 1–3. **Flowers:** In **8–15 tight clusters** of mostly 3–5 flowers each, on **thin stalks spreading or arching** mostly in same direction, **primary bract scalelike, much shorter than flower array;** scales light brown, awned at tip, 2–3 mm long; **bracts and bractlets strongly fringed.** **Fruits:** Capsules ellipsoid, brown, **shorter than scales;** seeds brown, about 1 mm long, with a few short hairs at the base. **Where Found:** Rocky slopes, snow patches, meadows, gravelly and sandy shores, moraines, bare soil in heathlands and turfy tundra; montane to alpine zones; frequent in most of the region; arctic-alpine, amphiberingian.

Similar Species: Kjellman's wood-rush (*L. kjellmaniana; L. beringiana, L. multiflora* ssp. *kjellmaniana, L. arctica* ssp. *latifolia, L. nivalis* var. *latifolia, L. tundricola*) has **dull, brownish grey to greenish basal leaf sheaths** and **stem leaves equalling or larger than the basal leaves.** It is found in meadows, snowbeds, heathlands and tundra, in lowland (arctic coast) to alpine zones, and is an arctic-alpine, amphiberin-

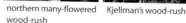

northern many-flowered wood-rush   Kjellman's wood-rush

gian species, frequent in eastern and northern AK, western YT and northwestern NT, south rarely to northern BC. • **Northern many-flowered wood-rush** (*L. multiflora* ssp. *frigida; L. campestris* var. *frigida*) resembles the preceding 2 species but has a **longer primary bract, equalling or exceeding the flower cluster,** and **straight (not curved or arching), branches** in the cluster. It occurs in heathlands and on peaty shores and turfy tundra, in lowland (arctic coast) to alpine zones. A low arctic-alpine, circumpolar species, it is frequent in AK, YT, NT and rare in northern BC.

Notes: Curved wood-rush is also known as *L. unalaschkensis* and *L. beringensis.*

Sedge Family (Cyperaceae)

The sedge family has several genera. *Carex* is the largest; indeed, with over 50 northwestern high-elevation species, it is one of the 3 largest genera in this book (*Draba* and *Saxifraga/Micranthes* are the other 2, both with about 40 species that qualify). Sedges usually occupy open habitats. Many sedge-family species prefer to have wet feet and are very important in wetlands and riparian habitats; others favour well-drained and dry sites such as rocky and grassy slopes, exposed ridges and windswept tundra. *Carex* is distinctive with its ovary and seed-like fruit (**achene**) enclosed in a membranous sac (the **perigynium**) in the axil of a single, scale-like bract. Cotton-grasses (*Eriophorum*), which have achene clusters immersed in showy tufts of long, thin bristles, are also a common and conspicuous element of arctic-alpine peatlands and wet tundra.

Although widespread and often abundant, the family does not have much economic importance. Pith from the stems of *Cyperus papyrus* was used by early Egyptians in papermaking. Sedges provide important forage and habitat for a variety of wildlife, especially waterfowl. Some grassland and tundra sedges are important forage species for domestic and wild ungulates, as well as for hungry bears and geese in spring. A few species of *Carex* and *Cyperus* can be grown as wetland ornamentals. Others are used locally in basketry, matting, hats and chair seats, and the pith has been used for candlewicks. It is likely that several sedges were used by First Nations people in the same manner as were grasses, that is, for food preparation, bedding and on floors.

Key to the Genera of Cyperaceae

1a. Flowers bisexual (with both male and female parts); tepals (flower bracts) represented by bristles; achenes not enclosed in a sac **2**

    2a. Flower bristles 10 or more, silky, much elongated and conspicuous in fruit; stems relatively stout, with at least 1 leaf (often reduced to a sheath) positioned well above the base . . . . ***Eriophorum* (pp. 428–430)**

    2b. Flower bristles 6 or fewer, short, mostly inconspicuous; stems wiry, leaves all basal. **3**

        3a. Style enlarged toward the base like a nose cone, forming a somewhat pinched-off tubercle atop the achene; spike longer than its lowest scale . . . . ***Eleocharis quinqueflora* (p. 427)**

        3b. Style not enlarged at the base, continuous with the achene; spike about the same length as its lowest scale. . . . . ***Trichophorum* (p. 427)**

1b. Flowers unisexual (either male or female only); tepals absent; achenes wrapped or enclosed in a sac (perigynium) **4**

    4a. Perigynium open on 1 side, merely wrapped around achene like a slit skirt (this may not be obvious at first, so try several florets), at least some containing 1–3 male flowers as well as 1 female flower or achene; stems wiry; spikelets much longer than wide and solitary on stem or crowded into a composite spike. . . . . . **Kobresia (p. 431)**

    4b. Perigynium closed (except for a pore or slit at the tip), flask-like, enclosing only 1 female flower or achene; stems variable, sometimes wiry; spikelets variable in shape but often not much longer than wide, solitary, separated or crowded . . . . ***Carex* (pp. 432–452)**

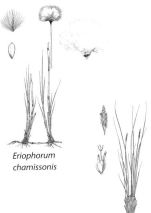

Eriophorum chamissonis

Eleocharis quinqueflora

Trichophorum cespitosum

Kobresia myosuroides

Carex raynoldsii

Tufted Club-rush
Trichophorum cespitosum

General: Densely tufted, often tussock-forming; stems nearly round in cross-section, grooved, smooth, 5–40 cm tall.

Leaves: Several scale-like, brownish, **bladeless leaf sheaths at stem-base,** 1 more leaf a little above base, with slender, short (3–6 mm) blade.

Flowers: Bisexual, 2–5 atop stem in solitary, brownish spike, the lowest scale (**involucral bract) about as long**

(**3–6 mm**) as the spike, with a **prominent, blunt awn;** flower scales 2–3, brownish, egg-shaped; **flower bristles 6,** white to brownish, hair-like, fragile, usually longer than achenes, about as long as scales.

Fruits: Achenes narrowly egg-shaped, 3-angled, brown, 1.5–2 mm long.

Where Found: Bogs, fens, wet meadows, peaty and gravelly shores and turfy tundra; lowland to alpine zones; frequent in most of the region, especially along the coast; circumboreal.

Similar Species: Dwarf club-rush (*T. pumilum*; *Scirpus pumilus, S. rollandii*) grows in **small tufts from long rhizomes,** with **shorter, awnless involucral bracts (less than 2.5 mm long)** and **no flower bristles.** It is found in calcium-rich conifer swamps, fens, wet meadows, bogs and shores, in montane to lower alpine zones. A circumboreal species, it is infrequent east of the coastal mountains from southern YT and NT, south sporadically through BC and AB to CA and MT.

Notes: Tufted club-rush is also known as *Scirpus cespitosus*. • *Trichophorum* comes from the Latin *tricho*, "hair," and *phorum*, "bearer," and refers to the tuft of long bristles surrounding the achenes.

Few-flowered Spike-rush
Eleocharis quinqueflora

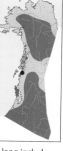

General: **Small tufts** from short rhizomes, often with **tiny, bulb-like resting buds** on rhizomes or around stem-bases; **stems clustered, thread-like,** grooved, 5–30 cm tall. **Leaves: Several but mere sheaths, all basal,** brownish to straw-coloured. **Flowers:** 3–9 in **solitary spikes atop stems,** the spikes 4–8 mm long; flower scales 2–5.5 mm long, blunt, brown with lighter midstripe, the **2 lower scales larger than others but only about ½ as long as spike; flower bristles 3–6,** about length of achenes; stigmas 3. **Fruits:** Achenes 3-angled, 2–2.5 mm long including **nose-cone-like tubercles at tip. Where Found:** Bog edges, fens, peaty wet meadows and calcium-rich seepages along streambanks and lakeshores; lowland to (occasionally) alpine zones; infrequent in most of the region in and east of the coastal mountains, except the far north; interruptedly circumpolar.

Notes: Few-flowered spike-rush is also known as *Eleocharis pauciflora*. • The Chinese water-chestnut (*E. dulcis, E. tuberosa*) has much larger, tuberous or corm-like resting buds that are edible, crispy and flavourful. • Polyploidy (possessing more than 2 copies of chromosomes) is rare in the sedge family but common in *Eleocharis*. Polyploidy could be part of the reason that the spike-rushes are widespread and species-rich, with more than 250 species from sea level to the alpine and on all continents. • *Eleocharis* comes from the Greek *heleios*, "dwelling in a marsh," and *charis*, "grace"—a nice conceit.

The Genus *Eriophorum* (Cotton-grass)

The cotton-grasses are perennial herbs, with stems tufted or single from rhizomes or stolons (runners). The stems are solid, triangular or round in cross-section and covered at the base with persistent, shiny, brown to reddish or purplish, often cross-wrinkled sheaths. The leaves have closed sheaths and long, grass-like blades, or blades lacking on upper stem leaves. There are 1 to several flower spikes per stem, subtended by 1 to several leafy or scale-like involucral bracts, these sometimes resembling flower scales (and then termed sterile scales). The numerous, bisexual flowers are each subtended by a single scale, the scales spirally arranged, wax-papery and unawned. The flower bristles are numerous (10–25 per flower) and much longer than the achenes; in fruit, they are silky and hair-like, white to reddish brown, together forming a cottony tuft. There are usually 3 stamens; the style is 3-lobed. The 3-angled achenes often have a short nib at the tip.

Key to *Eriophorum*

1a. Spikes 2 or more, subtended by 1 or more leaf-like involucral bracts 2

    2a. Leaf-like involucral bracts usually 1 (sometimes 2), shorter than cluster of head-like spikes; anthers 1–2.5 mm long . . . . ***E. gracile*** (below)

    2b. Leaf-like involucral bracts usually 2–3 (sometimes 1), the longest equalling or surpassing the cluster of head-like spikes; anthers 2–5 mm long . . . . ***E. angustifolium*** (below)

1b. Spike 1, involucral bracts scale-like (not leaf-like) 3

    3a. Plants with rhizomes or stolons (runners); stems usually solitary or a few together 4

        4a. Anthers 1–3 mm long; flower bristles reddish brown to white; spikes spheric in fruit . . . ***E. chamissonis*** (p. 429)

        4b. Anthers <1.5 mm long; flower bristles bright white; spikes broadly egg-shaped to spheric in fruit . . . . ***E. scheuchzeri*** (p. 429)

    3b. Plants without rhizomes or stolons (runners); stems densely tufted 5

        5a. Lower scales spreading or bent down in fruit, with whitish margins to 1 mm wide; upper leaf sheaths inflated (gaping) at mouth . . . . ***E. vaginatum*** (p. 430)

        5b. Lower scales appressed to ascending, without conspicuous whitish margins; upper sheaths inflated (gaping) or not 6

            6a. Plants usually <25 cm tall; leaf sheaths confined to lower ½ of stem, inflated upward; flower bristles usually pure white (rarely pale brown) . . . . ***E. callitrix*** (p. 430)

            6b. Plants 20–70 cm tall; leaf sheaths evenly distributed along stem, not inflated; flower bristles cream to yellowish or pale brown . . . . ***E. brachyantherum*** (p. 430)

Narrow-leaved Cotton-grass • *Eriophorum angustifolium*

General: Tufted from creeping rhizomes; stems 20–70 (to 90) cm tall. **Leaves:** Blades 2–6 mm wide, **flat** but becoming narrow and folded toward tips. **Flowers:** Numerous in egg-shaped, head-like spikes, the **spikes 2–10**, ascending to drooping, 1–2 cm long in flower, 2–5 cm long in fruit; involucral bracts several, unequal, **1–3 of them leaf-like, the longest ones equalling or surpassing spikes;** flower scales brownish or blackish green; anthers 2–5 mm long; **flower bristles white or cream to tawny. Fruits:** Achenes blackish, 2–4 mm long. **Where Found:** Bogs, fens, marshes, wet meadows, thickets, shorelines, snowbeds and tundra; lowland to alpine zones; frequent in most of the region; circumpolar.

Similar Species: Slender cotton-grass (*E. gracile*) has linear, **3-angled leaves** and **spikes subtended by usually only 1 leaf-like bract.** It occurs in bogs, fens, wet meadows and peaty shores, in montane to alpine zones. A circumboreal species, it is scattered but locally frequent in the southern mostly inland ⅔ of the region, from BC and AB to CA, NV, UT and CO, rare in southern AK and southeastern YT.

Notes: Narrow-leaved cotton-grass includes *Eriophorum polystachion*. • Inupiat elders of northwestern Alaska pulled out the stems of larger plants and removed and peeled the bottom 4–8 cm, which is whitish, tender and sweet. When snapped in half, the stems look like raw coconut and were eaten raw or boiled, or were preserved in oil. • Narrow-leaved cotton-grass is clonal, with several genetically identical individuals ("ramets") connected to each other. This allows the plant to make use of different resources in different

slender cotton-grass

microhabitats. Ramets photosynthesizing better in sunnier areas transfer sugars to ramets in shadier sites; ramets in nutrient-rich areas send nutrients to ramets in poorer sites.

Rusty Cotton-grass
Eriophorum chamissonis

General: Colonial from extensive creeping rhizomes; **stems solitary or a few together,** 20–70 cm tall. **Leaves:** Stem leaves few, thread-like, 0.5–2 mm wide, channelled; uppermost 1–2 sheaths lacking blades, somewhat inflated at the mouth. **Flowers:** Spike solitary, erect, **globe-shaped in fruit,** 2–4 cm in diameter; involucral bracts absent; sterile scales few, not more than 7; flower scales blackish to grey or purplish brown; **anthers 1–3 mm long; flower bristles rust-coloured, tawny or white.** **Fruits:** Achenes dark, oblong-egg-shaped, 2–3 mm long. **Where Found:** Fens, bogs, marshes, streambanks, lakeshores and wet meadows; lowland to alpine zones; frequent in most of the region; circumpolar.

Notes: Rusty cotton-grass is also known as *Eriophorum russeolum.* • *Eriophorum* is Latin for "wool-bearer," an apt description of these plants in fruit. • The species is named for Adelbert Ludwig von Chamisso de Boncourt (1781–1838), a German poet-naturalist and botanist on board the ship *Rurik,* which visited Alaska in 1816–17.

White Cotton-grass
Eriophorum scheuchzeri

General: Colonial from rhizomes; **stems solitary or a few together,** 10–50 cm tall. **Leaves:** Blades hair-like, 0.5–1.5 mm wide, channelled; upper sheaths black-tipped, usually bladeless, somewhat inflated. **Flowers:** Spike solitary, erect, **broadly egg-shaped to nearly globe-shaped in fruit,** 1–4 cm long; flower scales grey to blackish green; **anthers 0.5–1.5 mm long; flower bristles bright white,** sometimes tinged with red. **Fruits:** Achenes brown or blackish, 0.5–2.5 mm long. **Where Found:** Marshes, wet meadows, peaty banks, lakeshores, shrub thickets and wet tundra; lowland to alpine zones; frequent in the northern ½ of the region, infrequent southward (mostly in the Rockies) to UT and CO; circumpolar.

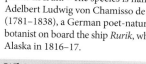

Notes: Eight flavonoid compounds with anti-fungal, antibacterial and antioxidant properties have been isolated from white cotton-grass. • Johann Jakob Scheuchzer (1672–1733) was a Swiss naturalist.

Sipping-straw Cotton-grass
Eriophorum brachyantherum

General: Densely tufted from fibrous roots; **stems 20–70 cm tall. Leaves:** Blades hair-like, about 1 mm or less wide, channelled; **uppermost sheaths above midstem**, bladeless, **not inflated. Flowers: Spikes** solitary, erect, egg- to globe-shaped, 1–2 cm long in flower, 2–4 cm long in fruit; involucral bracts absent; **sterile scales** usually 10–15, **appressed to ascending in fruit;** flower scales blackish green or lead-coloured, **without evident whitish margins;** anthers 0.5–2 mm long; **flower bristles** cream to yellowish or pale brownish. **Fruits: Achenes** brown, about 2 mm long. **Where found:** Bogs, fens, marshes, wet meadows and tundra; lowland to alpine zones; frequent in the northern inland ½ of the region; circumpolar.

Similar Species: Arctic cotton-grass (*E. callitrix*) is **smaller** and stouter, **usually 10–25 cm tall,** with **1 stem leaf (below midstem)** or none, the basal sheaths expanded upward, **anthers to 1 mm long** and **mostly bright white bristles** (rarely pale brown). It is found in wet, often calcium-rich tundra, meadows, thickets, fens and bogs, in lowland to alpine zones. Arctic cotton-grass is an interruptedly circumpolar species, infrequent in the northern ⅓ of the region, from AK, YT, NT and northern BC, south sporadically in the Rockies to southwestern AB, MT and WY.

arctic cotton-grass

Tussock Cotton-grass
Eriophorum vaginatum

General: Large, compact, **densely tufted tussocks;** stems 10–60 cm tall. **Leaves:** Blades hair-like, to 1 mm wide, 3-angled; **uppermost sheaths below midstem**, bladeless, **inflated and gaping toward the top. Flowers: Spike** solitary, erect, egg- to globe-shaped, 1–2 cm long in flower, 2–5 cm in fruit; involucral bracts absent; **sterile scales bent down or spreading in fruit;** flower scales lead-coloured to greenish grey with **whitish-translucent margins** to 1 mm wide; anthers 1–3 mm long; **flower bristles white** (rarely reddish or brown). **Fruits: Achenes** 2–3.5 mm long. **Where Found:** Bogs, fens, marshes, peaty woodlands and tundra; lowland to alpine zones; frequent in the northern ¼ of the region, sporadically southward to about 52° N; circumpolar.

Notes: This is the dominant plant of vast northern areas of wet, peaty tundra and taiga, typically over perma-frost. *E. vaginatum* tussock tundra is circumpolar, said to cover more than 920,000 km² globally. Its hegemony extends to poorly drained alpine tundra in arctic mountains. Tussocks in arctic Alaska were estimated to live an average of 158 years. • Tussock cotton-grass is an important forage species for caribou on their arctic calving grounds. • It was long thought that vascular plants couldn't take nitrogen up from the soil until organic matter was decomposed by soil microorganisms, releasing inorganic nitrogen. In recent decades, it's been found that some heathland plants with mycorrhizae, as well some boreal forest plants, can use organic nitrogen. Moreover, experiments have demonstrated that some non-mycorrhizal tundra plants, including tussock cotton-grass, water sedge (p. 445), curly sedge (p. 437) and two-toned sedge (p. 451), can take up amino acids directly. Thus tundra sedges can obtain both organic (amino acids) and inorganic (nitrate and ammonium) forms of nitrogen, a useful trait in nitrogen-limited tundra.

Mousetail Alpine-sedge
Kobresia myosuroides

General: Densely tufted from **smooth,** fibrous roots; stems slender, **wiry,** 3-round-edged in cross-section, 5–35 cm tall.

Leaves: Numerous; blade-less sheaths at base, **glossy, brown,** persistent, shredding into fibres; **blades hair-like, wiry,** inrolled, usually shorter than stems.

Flowers: Spike solitary, terminal, **linear (2–3 mm thick), erect,** 1–3 cm long, of **several spikelets,** each with usually 1–3 male flowers and 1 female flower, the male above the female; uppermost spikelets with just 1 male flower; all enclosed by a **scale-like bract open on 1 side** (like a slit skirt); **flowers unisexual, lacking sepals, petals or tepals;** male with 3 stamens, female with 1 ovary and 3 stigmas.

Fruits: Achenes 3-angled but somewhat flattened, 1.5–3 mm long, wrapped in a **membranous, brown, scale-like bract 2–3.5 mm long.**

Where Found: Mesic to dry, windswept ridges, rocky slopes, meadows, sandy heathlands and tundra; lowland (arctic coast) to alpine zones; widespread but relatively scattered, locally frequent throughout the mostly inland northern ½ of the region, south through BC and southwestern AB, absent from WA and MT, frequent again in the Rockies from WY to NM, also in OR (Wallowa Mtns), CA, ID and UT; circumpolar.

Similar Species: Simple alpine-sedge (*K. simpliciuscula*) has an oblong-egg-shaped cluster, **3–8 mm thick, of several spikes** and **dull basal sheaths, usually with the remains of blades attached.** It usually occurs in **wet, calcium-rich habitats** such as fens, marshes, wet meadows, gravelly flushes and wet tundra, in lowland to lower alpine zones. A circumpolar species, it is infrequent over a range similar to that of mousetail alpine-sedge, from AK, YT, NT and northern BC, south sporadically in the Rockies to southeastern BC and southwestern AB, disjunct in OR, ID, WY, UT and CO. • **Northern alpine-sedge (*K. sibirica*)** has a **solitary spike** that is oval-oblong and **thicker (4–8 mm)** than that of mousetail alpine-sedge, a **larger (3.5–5.5 mm long) bract** around the achene and **densely greyish-hairy roots.** It is found on mesic to dry, rocky slopes, in heathlands, meadows, fellfields and tundra, in lowland to alpine zones. An amphiberingian species, it is scattered but locally frequent in the north, in AK, YT, NT to northeastern BC and west-central AB, disjunct in WY and CO.

Notes: Mousetail alpine-sedge is also known as *Kobresia bellardii*. • It is one of the dominant species of alpine tundra in the Front Range of Colorado, site of some classic studies of alpine ecosystems (see Bowman and Seastedt, 2001). Mousetail alpine-sedge is very successful in dry meadows with light, ephemeral snowpack, during winter neither exposed to extreme wind and abrasion by snow and sand nor buried under a continuous snowpack. A large part of its success is probably attributable to a very long growing season, 6–7 months annually, combined with some green, overwintering leaves that carry on a low level of metabolic activity during winter months. • Species of *Kobresia* are the only sedge family plants known to form ectomycorrhizae—fungus-root associations in which fungus wraps around roots (see p. 482). With or without mycorrhizae, mousetail alpine-sedge in Colorado can take up organic nitrogen (via amino acids) directly from the soil.

The Genus *Carex* (Sedge)

Sedges are perennial, grass-like herbs, usually **monoecious** (with unisexual flowers, the males and females on the same plant) but sometimes **dioecious** (male and female flowers on different plants), tufted or spreading and sod forming from rhizomes; the stems are solid, triangular (usually) or round in cross-section. The leaves are 3-ranked, with closed sheaths and well-developed blades, the lower leaves sometimes bladeless or nearly so. The flowers are in 1 to several spikes; the spikes are unstalked or stalked atop the stem, occasionally in leaf axils near the base of the stem, and sub-tended by a bract that is longer, equal to or shorter than the inflorescence, or the bract may be lacking. The spikes can be strictly female or male **or** with male flowers above and female flowers below **or** with female flowers above and male flowers below. The tiny, numerous, unisexual flowers are solitary in the axils of the scales, the male flowers with 3 stamens, the female flowers with 2–3 stigmas and an ovary enclosed in a sac-like **perigynium** (interpreted as a scale with fused margins) open only at the tip; petals, sepals and tepals are lacking. The achenes are 3-angled or lens-shaped.

Carex is one of the most species-rich genera of plants, with about 2000 species worldwide, 480 in North America and over 50 at high elevations in our region.

Key to the Groups of Species in *Carex*

1a. Spikes solitary atop stems . . . . Group I (pp. 432–437)

1b. Spikes 2 or more 2

    2a. Spikes unstalked and relatively short, not long-cylindric; each spike bisexual, with both male and female flowers; achenes lens-shaped; stigmas 2 . . . . Group II (pp. 438–442)

    2b. Spikes stalked and often long-cylindric; spikes mostly unisexual, the top spike often all male, less often with female flowers at the base or at the top. 3

        3a. Achenes lens-shaped; stigmas 2 . . . . Group III (pp. 443–446)

        3b. Achenes 3-angled; stigmas 3 . . . . Group IV (pp. 447–452)

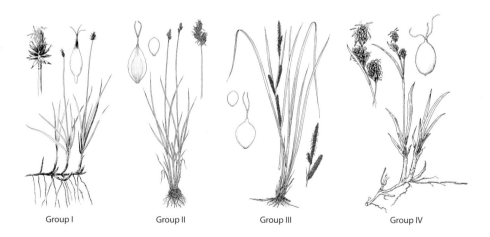

Group I   Group II   Group III   Group IV

Key to Group I: Flower Spike Solitary

1a. Male and female flowers on separate plants (dioecious); spikes either of all male or all female flowers 2

    2a. Mature perigynia hairy, appressed-ascending to slightly spreading; achenes 3-sided with 3 stigmas; leaves flat or somewhat channelled, >1 mm wide . . . . ***C. scirpoidea*** (p. 434)

    2b. Mature perigynia hairless, spreading to bent downward; achenes lens-shaped with 2 stigmas; leaves channelled, <1 mm wide . . . . ***C. gynocrates*** (p. 434)

1b. Male and female flowers on same plant (monoecious); spikes with both male and female flowers 3

    3a. ynia 5–8 mm long, only 1–3 per spike, separate . . . . ***C. geyeri*** (p. 434)

    3b. Perigynia <5 mm long, more than 3 per spike, clustered. 4

4a. Mature perigynia spreading widely or bent downward, the scales dropping off as perigynia mature **5**

5a. Mature perigynia glossy, ribbed, arching from spike axis along length of perigynium; plants usually in calcium-rich habitats. . . . . *C. gynocrates* (p. 434)

5b. Mature perigynia not glossy, not ribbed, spreading from spike axis only by a kink at the base; plants usually in calcium-poor habitats **6**

    6a. Plants densely tufted; leaves slender, 0.3–1.5 mm wide, usually 2–4 per stem
. . . . *C. micropoda* (p. 435)

    6b. Plants with rhizomes, sod-forming; leaves 1.5–4 mm wide, mostly 4–9 per stem
. . . . *C. nigricans* (p. 435)

4b. Mature perigynia ascending to spreading but not bent downward, the mature scales persistent. **7**

7a. Plants with rhizomes, not densely tufted **8**

    8a. Leaves 1–3 mm wide, at least some tapering to long, curly or zigzag tips. . . *C. rupestris* (p. 437)

    8b. Leaves 0.3–1.2 mm wide, tapering to straight tips. **9**

        9a. Perigynia large, 3–7 mm long, 1.5–5 mm wide; spike stout, broadly egg-shaped, 6–12 mm thick; achene much smaller than perigynium **10**

            10a. Female scales 3–5-veined with thick, white median portion, shorter and narrower than perigynia; perigynia broadly elliptic, 5–7 mm long, 3–5 mm wide . . . *C. breweri* (p. 437)

            10b. Female scales 1-veined with narrow, yellow-brown median portion, equalling perigynia; perigynia elliptic, 3–5 mm long, 1.5–2.5 mm wide . . . . *C. engelmannii* (p. 437)

        9b. Perigynia smaller, 2.5–3.5 mm long, 1.5 mm wide; spike slender, cylindric to narrowly elliptic, 4–6 mm thick; achene nearly filling perigynium . . . . *C. subnigricans* (p. 437)

7b. Plants densely tufted; mostly without rhizomes **11**

    11a. Stigmas 2; achenes lens-shaped. **12**

        12a. Spike egg- to globe-shaped, rounded at the base; plants tufted from short rhizomes; perigynia 2–3.5 mm long, unstalked, broadly egg-shaped and rounded at the base
. . . . *C. capitata* (p. 436)

        12b. Spike narrower, cylindric or lance- to egg-shaped or ellipsoid, tapering to the base; plants without rhizomes; perigynia 3–5 mm long, stalked, lance-shaped to narrowly egg-shaped or elliptic, tapering at the base **13**

            13a. Plants densely tufted with persistent bladeless sheaths; spikes 5–13 mm long; perigynia egg-shaped to ellipsoid, finely veined, ascending-erect at maturity . . . *C. nardina* (p. 436)

            13b. Plants tufted but without persistent old sheaths; spikes mostly 10–20 mm long; perigynia lance-shaped to narrowly egg-shaped, unveined, spreading at maturity
. . . . *C. micropoda* (p. 435)

    11b. Stigmas 3; achenes 3-angled. **14**

        14a. Leaves 1–3 mm wide; plants often tufted but also with rhizomes running from the clumps. . . . . *C. rupestris* (p. 437)

        14b. Leaves 0.2–1.3 mm wide, often quill-like; plants densely tufted. **15**

            15a. Male flowers make up about top ½ of spike; perigynia unveined, turgid, lacking thin margins; scales broader than perigynia, with wax-papery margins . . . . . *C. elynoides* (p. 436)

            15b. Male flowers few, inconspicuous at tip of spike; perigynia veined or unveined, flattened to half-convex, with thin margins; scales about as wide as perigynia, without wax-papery margins. **16**

                16a. Plants densely tufted with conspicuous remains of old sheaths; spikes egg-shaped to ellipsoid, mostly ≤1 cm long; perigynia finely veined. . . . . *C. nardina* (p. 436)

                16b. Plants less compactly tufted and without remains of old sheaths; spikes narrowly ellipsoid to cylindric, mostly >1 cm long. **17**

                    17a. Leaves curly at tip; perigynia 4.5–6 mm long, veined; spikes narrowly cylindric, more than 4 times longer than wide . . . . *C. circinata* (p. 437)

                    17b. Leaves not curly at tip; perigynia 3–4.5 mm long, unveined; spikes ellipsoid to lance-shaped, 2–4 times longer than wide . . . . . . *C. micropoda* (p. 435)

Elk Sedge • *Carex geyeri*

General: Loose tufts from long rhizomes; stems 10–50 cm tall. Leaves: Equalling or slightly exceeding stems, borne on lower ⅓ of stems, flat, 1.5–3.5 mm wide. **Flowers:** Spike 1.5–2.5 cm long; male portion on top, linear with a few male flowers, separated slightly from the **1–3 female flowers** below, which are rather remote and spreading; **perigynia beakless** or nearly so, egg-shaped, tapering to **spongy bases, 5–8 mm long;** female scales longer and slightly wider than perigynia. **Fruits:** Achenes 3-angled; stigmas 3. **Where Found:** Dry meadows, grassy slopes, glades, burns and open forests; lower montane to upper subalpine zones; locally frequent from southeastern BC and southwestern AB to OR, CA, NV, UT and CO; cordilleran.

Notes: Elk sedge is reportedly an important forage species in montane grasslands.

Single-spike Sedge • *Carex scirpoidea*

General: Stems solitary or a few together, from stout, scaly, blackish rhizomes, 5–35 cm tall, reddish or purplish at base. **Leaves: Flat or somewhat channelled, 1–3 mm wide,** shorter than to nearly equalling stems, crowded toward base. **Flowers:** Spike unisexual (dioecious), erect, cylindric to narrowly ellipsoid, 1.5–4 cm long; perigynia egg-shaped to elliptic, 2–4 mm long, straw-coloured, **short-hairy,** abruptly beaked; female scales dark brown to blackish with pale centres, about length of perigynia. **Fruits: Achenes 3-angled; stigmas 3. Where Found:** Moist to dry meadows, heathlands, rocky slopes, fellfields and turfy tundra; lowland (arctic coast) to alpine zones; frequent throughout the region; species complex transcontinental in North America with some representation in eastern Asia and Europe (Norway).

Subspecies: Single-spike sedge has 3 subspecies in our region: the widespread **ssp. *scirpoidea*;** the northwestern **ssp. *stenochlaena*;** and the more southerly **ssp. *pseudoscirpoidea*.** See technical manuals for details.

Similar Species: Yellow fen sedge (*C. gynocrates*; *C. dioica* ssp. *gynocrates*) is also **mostly dioecious,** though its spikes can have both female and male flowers. It is a **smaller (usually 5–20 cm tall),** rather delicate plant from **long, slender rhizomes,** with **narrower (about 0.5 mm), channelled leaves,** yellowish to chestnut or brownish black, shiny, **hairless perigynia arching downward** when mature and **lens-shaped achenes with 2 stigmas.** It occurs in swamps, fens, wet meadows and thickets, seepage areas, gravelly flushes and peaty tundra, usually on calcium-rich substrates, in montane to (occasionally) alpine zones. This subarctic-alpine, amphiberingian species is frequent in the northern ⅔ of the region, from AK, YT and NT south through most of interior BC and AB, sporadically to MT, ID, OR, WY, UT and CO, mostly in the Rockies.

male and female spikes

Black Alpine Sedge
Carex nigricans

General: Loosely tufted from stout, creeping rhizomes, **often forming hummocky mats or continuous sod;** flowering stems erect, 5–20 cm tall, clothed with old leaves at base.
Leaves: Numerous, densely packed near base of stems, mostly flat, 1.5–4 mm wide, stiff, shorter than stems; lowest leaves bladeless or nearly so.
Flowers: Spike egg-shaped to cylindric, erect, 8–20 mm long, 6–10 mm wide, with both female and male flowers, the males on top; perigynia initially appressed but **spreading to bending downward at maturity,** lance-shaped to narrowly egg-shaped, 3.5–5 mm long, **blackish brown toward tip,** paler toward base, hairless, not veined, long-stalked, beaked; **female scales dark reddish brown to black** with pale midribs, much shorter than perigynia, **soon dropped. Fruits:** Achenes 3-angled; stigmas 3. **Where Found:** Snowbeds, fens, meadows and heathlands, margins of ponds and rivulets; montane to alpine zones; frequent (especially in coastal and heavy snowfall environments) in the southern ½ of the region, less so northward; cordilleran–Pacific maritime.

Similar Species: Pyrenean sedge (*C. micropoda***;** *C. pyrenaica* ssp. *micropoda,* *C. jacobi-peteri*) also has **ultimately spreading perigynia (3–4.5 mm long)** and early deciduous female scales but is **tufted** from fibrous roots, with **narrow (0.3–1.5 mm), inrolled leaves, spikes 1–2 cm long** and **2 (occasionally 3) stigmas.** It is found in moist to mesic meadows, on rocky slopes and ridges, streambanks, snowbeds, fellfields and grassy tundra, in montane to alpine zones. An arctic-alpine, amphiberingian species, it is frequent in most of the region except the far north, from AK and YT south of about 64° N through BC and southwestern AB to CA, NV, UT and CO. • **Yellow fen sedge** (p. 434) also has ultimately spreading perigynia and early deciduous female scales, but has **thread-like (about 0.5 mm wide), inrolled leaves** and **lens-shaped achenes with 2 stigmas.**

Notes: A doormat species? In experimental studies of the effects of trampling on mountain vegetation, black alpine sedge was the most resistant (with the least change in cover immediately after having been walked on 500 times) and one of the most resilient (with little change a year after trampling) of any species tested. We have noticed that the sedge turf is, perhaps counterintuitively, much tougher than mats of woody mountain-heathers (*Cassiope, Phyllodoce, Harrimanella*). • Black alpine sedge has a phalanx-type growth form, with directional rhizome growth producing small, tufted clumps that migrate slowly along the ground, forming new shoots at the leading edge and dying at the trailing edge, the clumps occupying new ground as they creep along. • Black alpine sedge can survive with a very short growing season and often dominates snowbed areas and pool margins, especially in humid environments.

Pyrenean sedge

Spikenard Sedge • *Carex nardina*

General: Small, dense, firm tufts; **stems 5–15 cm tall,** often somewhat curved. **Leaves: Well developed,** not reduced to sheaths or scales, with **quill-like blades, wiry,** channelled, about 0.5 mm wide, **equalling or slightly shorter than stems; old bladeless sheaths at base conspicuous,** brownish, persistent. **Flowers: Spike 5–13 mm long,** narrowly egg-shaped, erect, with both female and male flowers, the males on top; perigynia erect or ascending at maturity, narrowly egg-shaped to elliptic, 3–5 mm long, hairless, **faintly veined,** tapering at base to a **short stalk** and at tip to a **finely sawtoothed beak; female scales equalling perigynia** and brownish. **Fruits: Achenes lens-shaped; stigmas 2 (occasionally 3-angled, stigmas 3). Where Found:** Dry, exposed ridge crests, outcrops, rocky and grassy slopes, fell-fields, meadows, scree slopes and tundra; montane (in the far north) to alpine zones; frequent in most of the inland part of the region; arctic-alpine, amphi-Atlantic.

Similar Species: Mousetail alpine-sedge (p. 431) grows in the same types of habitat, but its perigynia are open on 1 side, not sealed. • **Kobresia-like sedge** or **blackroot sedge** (*C. elynoides; C. filifolia* var. *miser*) has **3 stigmas, scales broader than the unveined perigynia** and with broad, pale, wax-papery margins and **spikes 8–20 mm long** with prominent male sections. It occurs on dry, rocky slopes, meadows, fellfields and tundra, in montane to alpine zones, and is frequent in the southeastern part of the region, from MT and ID to NV, UT and NM.

Notes: Spikenard sedge is also known as *Carex hepburnii.* Beringia was ice-free during the last glacial period, so what was the upland vegetation of Beringia like back then? A sample was preserved about 20,000 years ago under a metre of tephra (volcanic ejecta) on the northern Seward Peninsula, Alaska. This "fossil ecosystem" was a tundra grassland dominated by mousetail alpine-sedge, *Carex* species (including spikenard sedge) and grasses. Soils were enriched with windblown silt (loess) that probably maintained fairly high productivity in these ecosystems and helped support their incredible Pleistocene megafauna, which included woolly mammoths, steppe bison, wild horses, short-faced bears and scimitar-toothed cats, among others.

Capitate Sedge • *Carex capitata*

General: Tufted from short rhizomes; **stems 10–30 cm tall. Leaves: Usually much shorter than stems,** 2–4 per stem, thread-like, about 1 mm wide; lowest leaves bladeless or nearly so. **Flowers: Spike globe- or egg-shaped with pointed male tips;** perigynia broadly egg-shaped, rounded at base, unstalked. **Fruits: Achenes lens-shaped; stigmas 2. Where Found:** Fens, bogs, rocky slopes, streambanks, seasonally wet meadows, thickets, heathlands and fellfields; lowland to alpine zones; widespread but mostly locally frequent in the inland part of the region; boreal-alpine, circumpolar, also in Mexico and South America.

Notes: Capitate sedge is also known as *Carex arctogena.* • It is fundamentally a species of boreal wetlands and heathlands but extends south at high elevations in the western and eastern cordillera, usually on calcium-rich substrates. • Sedges are almost all wind-pollinated. Their flowers are either male or female, and in most species, each stem has both sexes. Individual spikes can be bisexual (as in capitate sedge) or unisexual. So, how to reduce "selfing" (fertilizing yourself) under such indiscriminate circumstances? In most sedge species, the stigmas of an individual plant are receptive before the male flowers of that plant release their pollen, thus giving outcross pollen priority. But self-pollination will do in a pinch, and selfing is widespread and common in sedges, especially in tufted species with many clumped stems and numerous male and female flowers on the same plant.

Coiled Sedge • *Carex circinata*

General: Tufted from short rhizomes; **stems 5–25 cm tall.**
Leaves: Shorter than stems, crowded toward base, **thread-like (0.5 mm wide)**, with inrolled margins, typically **curved or arched with curly tips. Flowers:** Spike 1.5–2.5 cm long, lance-shaped to elliptic; **perigynia few, lance-shaped, 4.5–6 mm long,** obscurely 3-angled, stalked. **Fruits: Achenes** 3-angled; **stigmas 3. Where Found:** Moist to wet cliffs, rock outcrops, gullies, ridges and talus slopes; montane to alpine zones; locally frequent along the Pacific coast, southern AK and western BC to northwestern WA (Olympic Mtns); Pacific maritime, endemic.

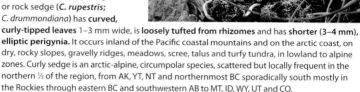

Similar Species: Curly sedge or rock sedge (*C. rupestris*; *C. drummondiana*) has **curved, curly-tipped leaves** 1–3 mm wide, is **loosely tufted from rhizomes and has shorter (3–4 mm), elliptic perigynia.** It occurs inland of the Pacific coastal mountains and on the arctic coast, on dry, rocky slopes, gravelly ridges, meadows, scree, talus and turfy tundra, in lowland to alpine zones. Curly sedge is an arctic-alpine, circumpolar species, scattered but locally frequent in the northern ⅓ of the region, from AK, YT, NT and northernmost BC sporadically south mostly in the Rockies through eastern BC and southwestern AB to MT, ID, WY, UT and CO.

Notes: Coiled sedge is most abundant on acidic igneous bedrock, whereas curly sedge prefers calcium-enriched sites—even on siliceous rocks of the Canadian Shield, where it is frequent—and in our region, it is often associated with another calcium-lover, entire-leaved mountain-avens (p. 70).

Engelmann's Sedge
Carex engelmannii

General: Single or a few together in clumps along **creeping rhizomes; stems 7–15 cm tall. Leaves:** Nearly equalling or shorter than stems, **hair-like (0.3–0.6 mm wide)**, with inrolled margins. **Flowers:** Spike broadly egg-shaped, 7–15 mm long, 6–8 mm wide, of both female and male flowers, the male portion less than 2 mm long; **perigynia elliptic, 3.5–5 mm long, 1.5–2.5 mm wide; female scales 1-veined** with narrow, yellow-brown median portion, **equalling perigynia. Fruits: Achenes** 3-angled, smaller than and loosely enveloped by perigynia; **stigmas 3.**
Where Found: Dry, rocky slopes, gravelly ridges, meadows, talus slopes, fellfields and tundra; upper subalpine and alpine zones; locally frequent in the inland southern ¼ of the region; cordilleran.

Similar Species: Brewer's sedge (*C. breweri*) is larger (15–30 cm tall), with **wider (0.6–1.2 mm) leaves**, a spike with the male portion 2–10 mm long, **larger, broader perigynia (5–7 mm long, 3–5 mm wide)** and **3–5-veined female scales** with a thick, white median portion, the scales **shorter and narrower than the perigynia.** It is found on dry, rocky slopes, scree, talus and fellfields, in upper subalpine and alpine zones, and is scattered but locally frequent in the Cascades of WA and OR from Mt. Hood south to the Sierras of CA and NV. • **Dark alpine sedge** (*C. subnigricans*) has slender, **cylindric to narrowly elliptic spikes, 4–6 mm thick, smaller perigynia (2.5–3.5 mm long, 1.5 mm wide)**, the achenes nearly filling the perigynia, and **1-veined female scales** with a yellow-brown medial portion, the scales as wide as but **shorter than the perigynia.** It occurs on moist, rocky slopes and in meadows, in subalpine and alpine zones, and is scattered but locally frequent in the southeastern part of the region, in central ID, eastern OR, WY, NV and UT.

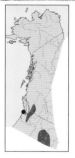

Notes: Engelmann's sedge is also known as *Carex breweri* var. *paddoensis.* • It ranges mostly north and east of Brewer's sedge, but both grow on Mt. Adams, Washington. Engelmann's sedge also occurs usually to the north and east of the range of dark alpine sedge and in drier habitats. • George Engelmann (1809–84) was a St. Louis physician and an eminent botanist.

Key to Group II: Flower Spikes 2 or More, Unstalked, Relatively Short (Not Long-cylindric), Each Bisexual; Achenes Lens-shaped; Stigmas 2

1a. Spikes with male flowers above females; spikes scarcely distinguishable in tight heads 2

2a. Plants densely tufted, without rhizomes . . . . *C. hoodii* (p. 440)

2b. Plants with creeping rhizomes; stems arising singly or a few in loose clusters 3

3a. Stems clustered on short-creeping, compact rhizomes; plants 15–60 cm tall . . . . *C. jonesii* (p. 440)

3b. Stems single or a few together on long-creeping rhizomes; plants 3–30 cm tall. 4

4a. Leaves inrolled, 0.5–1.5 mm wide, about as long as stems; female scales shorter than perigynia . . . . *C. incurviformis* (p. 439)

4b. Leaves flat, 1.5–4 mm wide, shorter than stems; female scales about as long as perigynia . . . . *C. vernacula* (p. 439)

1b. Spikes (at least uppermost one) with female flowers above males, or some lateral spikes wholly female; spikes not so closely aggregated, at least the lower distinguishable (except in *C. illota*) 5

5a. Perigynia not thin-edged or wing-margined 6

6a. Spikes 2–5; female scales about equalling perigynia, which are 2–3.5 mm long . . . *C. lachenalii* (p. 440)

6b. Spikes 3–9; female scales shorter and narrower than perigynia 7

7a. Spikes 3–6, tightly aggregated in a small, dense, egg-shaped to hemispheric head, 8–13 mm long, dark brown or blackish green; perigynium margins smooth to beak tip. . . . . *C. illota* (p. 440)

7b. Spikes 3–10, more loosely aggregated in longer (>1.5 cm) head, green to brownish; perigynium margins often minutely sawtoothed or fringed on beak 8

8a. Spikes 4–10, at least lower ones relatively remote, the intervening space longer than the spikes; perigynia faintly veined, with beaks 0.5–0.7 mm long and a prominent, translucent-margined groove toward the tip. . . . . *C. brunnescens* (p. 441)

8b. Spikes 3–5, all together or female spikes a bit spaced out, the intervening space no longer than the spikes; perigynia distinctly several-veined, with beaks 0.3–0.5 mm long and a short groove at the tip. . . . . *C. praeceptorum* (p. 441)

5b. Perigynia thin-edged or wing-margined 9

9a. Female scales about equalling perigynia, concealing them above or nearly so (best seen in fresh, not pressed, plants; in pressed specimens, compare size of scales with their perigynia only in portions of the spike facing up from the sheet) 10

10a. Perigynia lance- or boat-shaped, 3–4 mm long, 0.8–1.2 mm wide . . . . *C. leporinella* (p. 441)

10b. Perigynia egg-shaped, 4–6 mm long, 1.5–2.5 mm wide 11

11a. Perigynia unveined or lightly 4-veined on back; achenes 1.5–2 mm long, 0.8–1.2 mm wide . . . . *C. phaeocephala* (p. 441)

11b. Perigynia clearly 7–14-veined on back; achenes 1.9–2.4 mm long, 1.2–1.6 mm wide . . . . *C. tahoensis* (p. 441)

9b. Female scales shorter than perigynia and noticeably narrower above, exposing top of perigynia. 12

12a. Perigynia half-convex (like a pear sliced lengthwise in half) to rounded in cross-section; achenes filling more than ½ of perigynial cavity. 13

13a. Perigynia 2.5–3.5 mm long; spikes tightly aggregated in a small, spiky, dark brown or blackish green head . . . . *C. illota* (p. 440)

13b. Perigynia 3.5–6 mm long; spikes loosely aggregated in a green to brown head 14

14a. Perigynia plump, biconvex (like a pine nut); achenes filling about ¾ of perigynial cavity; anthers about 1.5 mm long. . . . . *C. preslii* (p. 442)

14b. Perigynia half-convex (like a pear sliced lengthwise in half); achenes filling ½ to ⅔ of perigynial cavity; anthers 0.7–1 mm long. 15

15a. Female scales with broad (to 0.25 mm), translucent margins; perigynia wings copper-coloured, darker than bodies . . . . *C. macloviana* (p. 442)

15b. Female scales with narrow (<0.15 mm), translucent margins or dark throughout; perigynia wings same colour as bodies . . . . *C. pachystachya* (p. 442)

12b. Perigynia flat in cross-section except distended over achenes; achenes filling <½ of perigynial cavity. **16**

  16a. Spikes closely aggregated **17**

    17a. Perigynia 2–3 times as wide as female scales; leaves 0.5–2 mm wide, often folded or channelled . . . . *C. proposita* (p. 442)

    17b. Perigynia 1–1.5 times as wide as female scales; leaves 2–4 mm wide, flat or nearly so . . . **18**

      18a. Perigynia 4–6.5 mm long, often as dark as scales, the flat margin including wing 0.3–0.7 mm wide; spikes tightly aggregated into a triangular-egg-shaped, blackish green to golden brown head . . . . *C. haydeniana* (p. 442)

      18b. Perigynia 3–5 mm long, usually paler than scales (spike thus bicoloured), the flat margin including wing 0.2–0.5 mm wide; spikes tightly aggregated into a broadly egg-shaped, brown-and-green head . . . . *C. microptera* (p. 442)

  16b. Spikes more loosely aggregated, the individual spikes distinct **19**

    19a. Perigynia egg-shaped, 1.5–2.5 mm wide, no wider than female scales . . . . *C. phaeocephala* (p. 441)

    19b. Perigynia broader, broadly egg-shaped to nearly round, 1.7–3.5 mm wide, much wider than female scales. **20**

      20a. Perigynia broadest at middle, the beak tip cylindric and smooth; leaves often folded or channelled, 0.5–2 mm wide . . . . *C. proposita* (p. 442)

      20b. Perigynia broadest below middle, the beak tip flattened and minutely fringed or sawtoothed; leaves flat, 2–4 mm wide. . . . . *C. straminiformis* (p. 442)

SPIKES SCARCELY DISTINGUISHABLE, HEADS APPARENTLY SINGLE

Incurved Sedge
Carex incurviformis

General: Dwarf colonial; **stems single from a long, creeping rhizome, somewhat curved, 3–12 cm tall. Leaves:** Toward base, **about equalling stems,** flat at base, **inrolled along upper part, 0.5–1.5 mm wide.** Flowers: Spikes 3–7, tightly clumped, **nearly indistin-**guishable in a hemispheric or egg-shaped head 5–12 mm in diameter, with both female and male flowers, the **males on top; perigynia veined, leathery,** few, elliptic, brown, short-stalked, short-beaked; female scales distinctly shorter than perigynia. **Fruits: Achenes** lens-shaped; stigmas 2. **Where Found:** Rocky slopes, meadows, gravelly flushes, fellfields and turfy tundra; alpine zone; infrequent in the north; disjunct in the southeastern part of the region; cordilleran.

Similar Species: Idiomatic sedge (*C. vernacula; C. foetida* var. *vernacula***)** also has several spikes tightly aggregated in a dense head but is taller (8–30 cm), with **flat leaves 1.5–4 mm wide and shorter than the stems** and **female scales about equalling the perigynia.** It is found in moist timberline glades, meadows and tundra, in subalpine and alpine zones, and is locally frequent in the southernmost part of the region, from Mt. Adams, WA, northeastern OR, ID and WY to CA and CO. • Incurved sedge could also be mistaken for **capitate sedge** (p. 436), which is **tufted** (not colonial) and **truly single-spiked.**

Notes: Incurved sedge is also known as *Carex maritima* var. *incurviformis.*
• It is an alpine member of the circumpolar complex around *C. maritima,* which, as strictly defined, is (in North America) apparently a separate, mostly arctic coastal or boreal littoral species of low elevations.

Hedgehog Sedge, Sheep Sedge • *Carex illota*

General: Tufted from fibrous roots; stems slender, stiff, 10–35 cm tall. **Flowers:** Spikes with **female flowers on top**, 3–6, **scarcely distinguishable** in a small, tight, egg-shaped head, 8–13 mm long, dark brown to greenish black; female scales shorter and narrower than perigynia; perigynium margins not winged, **smooth to beak tip.**

Where Found: Wet meadows, fens, bogs, streambanks, peaty shores and willow thickets; montane to alpine zones; frequent in the southern ½ of the region; cordilleran.

Similar Species: Both **Hood's sedge** (*C. hoodii*) and **Jones' sedge** (*C. jonesii*) have **4–10 scarcely distinguishable spikes** in tight, egg-shaped to short-cylindric **heads about 1–2 cm long,** but the **spikes have male flowers on top.** • **Hood's sedge is densely tufted** from fibrous roots and has **scarcely veined perigynia,** glossy and coppery brown with wide, green margins when ripe. It occurs in mesic to dry meadows, forest openings and rocky slopes, in lowland to alpine zones, and is frequent in the southern ½ of the region, from BC and AB from about 56° N to CA, NV, UT and CO. • **Jones' sedge has 1 or a few stems together from short rhizomes** and **several-veined perigynia.** It grows in moist to wet meadows, fens and on streambanks, in montane to alpine zones, and is scattered but locally frequent from eastern WA, eastern OR, central ID and MT to CA, UT, WY and CO.

Notes: Chromosomes have evolved more spectacularly in sedges than in most other flowering plants. These tiny threads carry the genetic instructions (DNA) for assembling organisms. Prior to cell division, chromosomes pair up, usually with a single point of attachment—the centromere. Sedges have unusual "holocentric" chromosomes in which essentially the entire length of the chromosome is centromere. New species can arise quite rapidly as holocentric chromosomes fuse or split, evolutionary improvisation that could partly explain why there are so many kinds of sedges.

SPIKES NOT SO CLOSELY AGGREGATED, AT LEAST THE LOWER DISTINGUISHABLE; PERIGYNIA NOT THIN-EDGED OR WING-MARGINED

Two-parted Sedge, Hare's-foot Sedge *Carex lachenalii*

General: Loosely tufted from very short rhizomes and fibrous roots; stems ascending, 5–30 cm tall. **Leaves:** Shorter than stems, clustered toward base, flat, 1–2 mm wide. **Flowers:** Spikes 2–5, **bisexual with female flowers on top,** erect, **reddish brown,** aggregated into an oblong-egg-shaped **head 6–25 mm long;** perigynia egg-shaped, 2–3.5 mm long, brownish green or brownish yellow at maturity; **female scales about equalling perigynia,** reddish brown with paler centres and margins. **Fruits:** Achenes lens-shaped, filling perigynia; **stigmas 2. Where Found:** Moist to wet meadows, fens, snowbeds, streambanks, heathlands and patterned ground; lowland

(arctic coast) to alpine zones; frequent in the northern ½ of the region, sporadic southward; arctic-alpine, circumpolar, also in New Zealand.

Similar Species: Two-parted sedge could be confused with **hedgehog sedge** (above), which has **tighter, darker heads** and **female scales shorter and narrower than the perigynia.**

Notes: Two-parted sedge is also known as *Carex bipartita* and *C. lagopina.* • Pollen is produced by "pollen mother cells" (PMCs). Each PMC has 4 nuclei, and in almost all plants, each nucleus produces 1 pollen grain, so each PMC produces 4 pollen grains. In the sedge family, however, 3 nuclei in each PMC degenerate, so each PMC produces only 1 pollen grain. This type of pollen development is known only in the sedge family and in the (largely Australian) heath family plants formerly placed in Epacridaceae. • The species is named for Werner de La Chenal (de Lachenal) (1763–1800), a Swiss botanist.

Brownish Sedge
Carex brunnescens ssp. *brunnescens*

General: Tufted from short rhizomes; stems slender, erect or sometimes lax, 15–60 cm tall, usually exceeding leaves. **Leaves:** Numerous, from lower part of stem, flat, 1–2.5 mm wide. **Flowers:** Spikes 4–10 in a narrow, **interrupted cluster 2–5 cm long,** the **lower spikes usually remote,** spikes bisexual with **female flowers on top,** erect, brown; perigynia 5–10 per spike, egg-shaped, 2–3 mm long, dark green or brown, **faintly veined,** with **finely sawtoothed beak 0.5–0.7 mm long** and **prominent, translucent-margined groove toward tip;** female scales about ⅔ the size of perigynia, wax-papery with 3 green midveins. **Fruits:** Achenes lens-shaped, filling perigynia;

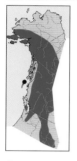

stigmas 2. Where Found: Bogs, fens, wet meadows, glades, seepage areas, thickets, heathlands and turfy tundra; montane to alpine zones; frequent in the northern ⅔ of the region, sporadic southward; species complex circumpolar, ssp. *brunnescens* widespread in North America.

Similar Species: Teacher's sedge or early sedge (**C. praeceptorum;** *C. heleonastes* var. *dubia*) has **3–5 spikes,** all together or female spikes a bit spaced out, in an oblong-egg-shaped **head 1–2 cm long,** the golden brown, **distinctly several-veined perigynia** with a **beak 0.3–0.5 mm long** and a **short groove at the tip.** It is found in bogs, wet meadows, streambanks and pond margins, in upper montane to alpine zones, and is a cordilleran species infrequent in the inland southern ⅓ of the region, from southern BC to CA, NV, UT and CO.

Notes: Brownish sedge includes plants previously known as *Carex brunnescens* ssp. *alaskana* and ssp. *pacifica*.

Spikes Distinct; Perigynia Thin-edged or Wing-margined; Female Scales Equalling and Largely Concealing Perigynia

Dunhead Sedge • *Carex phaeocephala*

General: Densely tufted from fibrous roots; **stems erect, 10–30 cm tall,** exceeding leaves. **Leaves:** Stiff, channelled or folded, 1–3 mm wide. **Flowers:** Spikes 3–7, distinct in a compact head 1.5–4 cm long, spikes bisexual with **female flowers on top,** erect, **golden brown or reddish brown at maturity;** perigynia egg-shaped, **4–5 mm long,** greenish gold or straw-coloured to brown, the margins often greenish, **winged to base, 4-veined** or not on back, the cylindric beaks to 1 mm long, minutely sawtoothed in the lower part; female scales equalling and largely concealing perigynia, brown with white margins, 0.1–0.3 mm wide. **Fruits:** Achenes lens-shaped, 1.5–2 mm long, 0.8–1.2 mm wide; stigmas 2. **Where Found:** Rocky slopes, meadows, talus, scree and fellfields; subalpine and alpine zones; frequent in the southern ⅔ of the region; cordilleran.

Similar Species: Lake Tahoe sedge (**C. tahoensis;** *C. eastwoodiana*) has **larger achenes (1.9–2.4 mm long, 1.2–1.6 mm wide);** more leathery **perigynia that are distinctly veined front and back** and broader (0.2–0.6 mm wide) white margins on the female scales. It can occur at lower elevations and grows in grasslands, shrublands, rocky slopes and meadows, in montane to alpine zones. Lake Tahoe sedge is frequent inland in the southern ⅔ of the region, from southern YT to CA, UT and CO. • **Sierra hare-sedge** (**C. leporinella**) has smaller, narrower, **lance- or boat-shaped perigynia 3–4 mm long and 0.8–1.2 mm wide.** It occurs on rocky slopes and in moist meadows, in montane to alpine zones, and is infrequent and local from southern BC, WA, ID and western MT to northeastern OR, northern CA, NV, UT and western WY.

Notes: According to *FNA*, northern plants identified as dunhead sedge are actually Lake Tahoe sedge; what's more, the range of Lake Tahoe sedge isn't clear because it has been confused with other species.

Lake Tahoe sedge

SPIKES DISTINCT; PERIGYNIA THIN-EDGED OR WING-MARGINED; FEMALE SCALES SHORTER AND NARROWER THAN PERIGYNIA

Falkland Islands Sedge • *Carex macloviana*

General: Tufted from fibrous roots; stems erect, 10–50 cm tall, exceeding leaves. **Leaves:** Flat, **2–4 mm wide,** from lower ⅓ of stem. **Flowers:** Spikes 3–10, aggregated into dense, stiffly erect, **broadly egg-shaped heads 1–2 cm long;** spikes bisexual with **female flowers on top, dark brown at maturity; anthers 0.7–1 mm long;** perigynia egg-shaped, 3.5–4.5 mm long, usually half-convex around the achene, straw-coloured, golden, reddish brown or coppery, several-veined, the **margins winged** (wings 0.2–0.5 mm wide, **darker than the rest of perigynium)** and fringed with tiny teeth to the base; female scales narrower than perigynia, brown with **wax-papery margins to 0.25 mm wide. Fruits:** Achenes lens-shaped, **filling ½–⅔ of perigynium;** stigmas 2. **Where Found:** Moist to mesic meadows, thickets, forest openings, shores, rocky or grassy slopes, fellfields and disturbed areas; lowland to alpine zones; frequent in the northern ⅔ of the region, less frequent along the Rockies to MT, WY and CO; northwestern North American and amphi-Atlantic, also bipolar, occurring in Patagonia and described from the Malvinas (Falkland Is.).

Similar Species: Thick-headed sedge (*C. pachystachya*) has female scales with **narrower (less than 0.15 mm wide), wax-papery margins** and **perigynia wings the same colour as the rest of the perigynium.**

It is found in mesic to wet meadows, on shores, in open forests and thickets and on rocky and grassy slopes, and is frequent throughout the region except the far north, from southern AK and YT to CA, NV, UT and CO. • **Elvis' sedge (*C. preslii*)** has **plump, biconvex perigynia** with **achenes filling about ¾ of the perigynial cavity** and **anthers about 1.5 mm long.** It grows on mesic to dry, rocky and grassy slopes, in montane to alpine zones, and is infrequent from southern AK and YT through BC and AB to CA, ID and MT. • **Hayden's sedge** or cloud sedge (*C. haydeniana*) and **small-winged sedge (*C. microptera; C. festivella*)** both have thin perigynia that are flat except where distended by the achene, which fills less than ½ of the perigynium. • **Hayden's sedge** has **longer (4–6.5 mm) perigynia,** often as dark as the scales, the flat margin including the wing **0.3–0.7 mm wide** and spikes forming a **triangular-egg-shaped, blackish green to golden brown head.** It occurs on rocky slopes, moraines, gravelly meadows and streambanks, in subalpine and alpine zones, and is frequent in the southern ⅓ of the region, from southern BC and southwestern AB to CA, UT and CO. • **Small-winged sedge** has **shorter (3–5 mm) perigynia,** usually paler than the scales, the **spike bicoloured,** the flat margin including the wing 0.2–0.5 mm wide and spikes forming a **broadly egg-shaped, brown-and-green head.** It occupies moist to mesic meadows, wetland margins, streambanks, shores, open forests and disturbed areas, in montane to alpine zones, from southern YT and NT infrequently through inland BC and AB, then frequent to CA, AZ and NM. • **Mount Shasta sedge (*C. straminiformis*)** has **flat leaves 2–4 mm wide** and **perigynia with crinkly wing margins.** It grows on moist, rocky slopes and cirques, often near melting snowbanks, in subalpine and alpine zones, and is sporadic from southern WA and central ID to CA, NV and UT. • **Smoky Mountain sedge (*C. proposita*)** has narrower, **channelled leaves 0.5–2 mm wide** and **perigynia that are broadest at the middle.** It is found on dry, rocky slopes, often on talus, in subalpine and alpine zones, in WA (Wenatchee Mtns), central ID and CA (Sierras).

Elvis' sedge

Notes: These species are all similar, differing mostly in micro-characteristics of perigynia and scales, though some have quite different ecologies. Some taxonomists (not *FNA*) maintain that *C. macloviana, C. pachystachya, C. preslii, C. haydeniana* and *C. microptera* are all varieties of one polymorphic species—*C. macloviana.* • Falkland Islands sedge is one of 6 sedge species with bipolar distributions; two-parted sedge (p. 440) is another. Genetic analysis suggests that most of these distributions result from long-distance dispersal, mostly north to south, despite the lack of any obvious morphological adaptations for long-distance travel. Tell that to a hungry, muddy duck.

Key to Group III: Spikes 2 or More, Stalked, Often Long-cylindric, Mostly Unisexual, Top Spike Often All Male, Less Often with Female Flowers at Base or at Top; Achenes Lens-shaped; Stigmas 2

1a. Lowest bract below cluster of spikes mostly with sheath >4 mm long; spikes few-flowered; perigynia often somewhat fleshy, granular-whitish, orange or golden yellow at maturity **2**

2a. Lowest bracts shorter than or slightly exceeding cluster of spikes, the sheaths 2–4 mm long, with black knobs at mouth; top spike bisexual with female flowers on top and at least ¾ of flowers female; perigynia bluish white. . . . . ***C. bicolor*** (p. 444)

2b. Lowest bracts distinctly exceeding cluster of spikes, the sheaths usually >4 mm long, without black knobs at mouth; top spike male or bisexual with female flowers on top and fewer than ¾ of flowers female; perigynia golden, orange or whitish. **3**

3a. Top spike usually all male flowers; perigynia somewhat fleshy and bright orange (golden or brown if dry) when mature; female scales widely spreading. . . . . ***C. aurea*** (p. 444)

3b. Top spike bisexual with female flowers on top, or sometimes all male; perigynia whitish-granular or golden when mature **4**

4a. Perigynia and female scales crowded; scales reddish brown to purplish, often covering perigynia . . . . ***C. garberi*** (p. 444)

4b. Perigynia and female scales not crowded; scales whitish to pale brown, shorter than perigynia . . . . ***C. hassei*** (p. 444)

1b. Lowest bract below cluster of spikes sheathless; spikes many-flowered; perigynia not fleshy, green to brown at maturity **5**

5a. Perigynia shiny, >3.5 mm long; styles tough, bony, continuous with achenes, persistent . . . . ***C. saxatilis*** (Group IV, p. 452)

5b. Perigynia not shiny, <3.5 mm long; styles rather delicate, jointed with achenes, usually dropped **6**

6a. Perigynia conspicuously veined on both surfaces . . . . ***C. lenticularis*** (p. 445)

6b. Perigynia without veins or indistinctly veined **7**

7a. Lowest bract equalling or overtopping cluster of spikes; female scales with broad, pale midveins . . . **8**

8a. Inflorescence nearly flat-topped, of 3–5 spikes, the top spike bisexual with female flowers above males . . . . ***C. eleusinoides*** (p. 445)

8b. Inflorescence elongate, of 3–10 spikes, the top spike male . . . . ***C. aquatilis*** (p. 445)

7b. Lowest bract shorter than the cluster of spikes; female scales with slender or no midveins **9**

9a. Leaf blades 1.5–3.5 mm wide; female spikes slender, linear-cylindric, 3–4 mm thick, the lowest stalked; perigynia ellipsoid, 1.5–3 mm long, half-convex, ascending . . . . ***C. bigelowii*** (p. 446)

9b. Leaf blades 3–6 mm wide; female spikes oblong-cylindric, 4–5 mm thick, unstalked or nearly so; perigynia broadly egg-shaped to ellipsoid, 1.2–2.3 mm long, soon plump, spreading . . . . ***C. scopulorum*** (p. 446)

C. lenticularis

C. aquatilis

Golden Sedge • *Carex aurea*

General: Loosely tufted; **stems single or a few together** from rhizomes, slender, spreading, 5–40 cm tall, shorter or longer than leaves. **Leaves:** Flat, 1.5–3 mm wide; lowest bracts leaf-like, overtopping cluster of spikes, with sheaths 2–4 (to 10) mm long. **Flowers:** Spikes several (3–6), the lateral spikes stalked, of female flowers only, the **top spike usually all male**, 1–2 mm thick; perigynia 4–20 per spike, **globe-shaped**, 2–3 mm long, ribbed, **somewhat inflated and fleshy, bright orange or golden when mature**, spreading, beakless; **female scales reddish brown** with paler or greenish midvein, spreading, shorter and narrower than perigynia. **Fruits:** Achenes lens-shaped; **stigmas 2. Where Found:** Fens, bog margins, wet meadows, thickets, seepage areas, gravel bars, lakeshores and streambanks, often on calcium-rich substrates; lowland to lower alpine zones; frequent throughout the region except the outer Pacific coast and the far north; widespread North American.

Similar Species: Two-coloured sedge (*C. bicolor*) has lowest bracts shorter than to slightly exceeding the cluster of spikes, the sheaths relatively short (2–4 mm), with black knobs at the mouth; the top spike is bisexual with female flowers on top and at least ¾ of the flowers female; the **crowded perigynia** are somewhat inflated and **granular bluish white**; and the **blackish female scales** are shorter and narrower than the perigynia (thus **2-toned female spikes**). Two-coloured sedge grows in moist to wet meadows and on sandy or silty shores, gravelly seepages and tundra, in lowland to alpine zones. It is a low-arctic, circumpolar species, infrequent in the northern ⅓ of the region, in AK, YT, NT and northern BC.
• **Garber's sedge (*C. garberi*)** has clustered spikes; **crowded, ascending perigynia and female scales;** whitish perigynia; and reddish brown to purplish scales, **often covering the perigynia**. It is found in wet meadows, fens and shores, in lowland to subalpine zones. A cordilleran-boreal, North American species, it is widespread but infrequent in the region, from AK, YT and NT through BC and AB to WA, OR and CA, also in WY.
• **Spotty sedge (*C. hassei*)** has rather distant spikes; ascending and **usually uncrowded perigynia**

and female scales; lightly veined perigynia that are **whitish or golden** when mature and **densely and finely pimply or granular-surfaced;** and light brown female scales that are shorter than the perigynia. It occurs in meadows, on streambanks and gravelly shores, in montane to alpine zones, and is frequent in the southwestern corner of the region, from southern BC through WA and OR to CA, AZ and Mexico.

Notes: The orange, fleshy perigynia of golden sedge are unique among the *Carex* of our region, indeed of North America. The colour doesn't develop until late in the season, when the perigynia are fully mature. • *C. hassei* is named for Herman E. Hass (1836–1915), a German-born army surgeon and lichenologist; he published *The Lichen Flora of Southern California*.

Garber's sedge

Tarn Sedge • *Carex lenticularis* var. *dolia*

General: Densely clumped from short rhizomes; stems 5–35 cm tall, shorter to longer than leaves. **Leaves: Flat, 1.5–2.5 mm wide; brown sheaths at base. Flowers:** Spikes 3–5 in compact clusters, **bicoloured green and brown or black; top spike bisexual with female flowers above** a few male flowers, lower spikes all female, lowest on stalk less than 1 cm long, erect, 1–5 cm long; **lowest bract exceeding cluster of spikes; perigynia egg-shaped,** biconvex, **1.8–2.5 mm long,** bluish green, **distinctly 5–7-veined,** stubby-based, short-beaked at tip; female scales shorter than perigynia, reddish brown or black with paler midstripes and prominent wax-papery margins. **Fruits:** Achenes lens-shaped or oblong-quadrangular; **stigmas 2. Where Found:**

Streambanks, fens, pond margins and gravelly shores; subalpine and alpine zones; infrequent from southern AK and YT through BC in the coastal mountains and sporadically in the Rockies to southeastern BC, southwestern AB and MT; *C. lenticularis* in the broad sense is widespread in North America; var. *dolia* is subalpine-alpine and cordilleran.

Similar Species: Goosegrass sedge (*C. eleusinoides*; *C. kokrinensis*) has **reddish basal leaf sheaths** and **small (about 2 mm long),** ellipsoid, **veinless or indistinctly 3–5-veined perigynia.** It is found on gravel bars, streambanks and floodplain meadows, in montane to alpine zones, and is an arctic-alpine, amphiberingian species infrequent in the north, in AK, YT and northern BC.

Notes: Tarn sedge is also known as *Carex enanderi*. • It is a close relative of water sedge (below). Based on genetic analysis, the *C. lenticularis*–*C. aquatilis* group appears to have originated about 1.9 million years ago. *C. lenticularis* is of New World tropics origin, whence it spread and diverged in western North America to Asia, in eastern North America to Europe and southern South America. The result is 5 North American varieties of *C. lenticularis*, mostly in different geographical areas, and 7 other closely related species in the group.

Water Sedge • *Carex aquatilis*

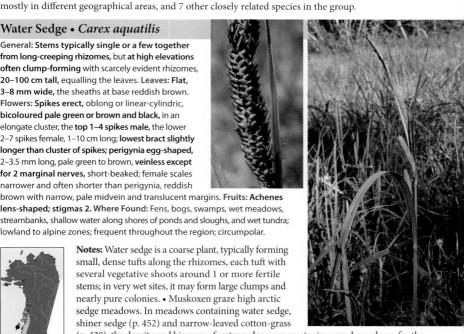

General: Stems typically single or a few together from long-creeping rhizomes, but **at high elevations often clump-forming** with scarcely evident rhizomes, **20–100 cm tall,** equalling the leaves. **Leaves: Flat, 3–8 mm wide,** the sheaths at base reddish brown. **Flowers:** Spikes erect, oblong or linear-cylindric, **bicoloured pale green or brown and black,** in an elongate cluster, the **top 1–4 spikes male,** the lower 2–7 spikes female, 1–10 cm long; **lowest bract slightly longer than cluster of spikes; perigynia egg-shaped,** 2–3.5 mm long, pale green to brown, **veinless except for 2 marginal nerves,** short-beaked; female scales narrower and often shorter than perigynia, reddish brown with narrow, pale midvein and translucent margins. **Fruits:** Achenes lens-shaped; **stigmas 2. Where Found:** Fens, bogs, swamps, wet meadows, streambanks, shallow water along shores of ponds and sloughs, and wet tundra; lowland to alpine zones; frequent throughout the region; circumpolar.

Notes: Water sedge is a coarse plant, typically forming small, dense tufts along the rhizomes, each tuft with several vegetative shoots around 1 or more fertile stems; in very wet sites, it may form large clumps and nearly pure colonies. • Muskoxen graze high arctic sedge meadows. In meadows containing water sedge, shiner sedge (p. 452) and narrow-leaved cotton-grass (p. 428), the density and biomass of water sedge were greater in grazed meadows; for the other 2 species, grazing reduced biomass. Water sedge seems well adapted to grazing. Clipping plants to 1.5 cm height 4 times a year for 4 years did not reduce the overall growth of the plants (compared to unclipped plants), and clipped plants had significantly higher nitrogen levels. It seems that water sedge compensates for grazing by taking up additional nitrogen and growing more quickly. Does that sound like your mowed lawn?

Stiff Sedge, Bigelow's Sedge • *Carex bigelowii* ssp. *lugens*

General: Loosely tufted from rhizomes or densely clumped and forming large tussocks; stems slender, stiff, wiry, **20–50 cm tall,** exceeding leaves. **Leaves: 1.5–3.5 mm wide,** flat with rolled-under margins. **Flowers: Spikes erect,** short-cylindric, **blackish,** in compact clusters, the **top spike male,** the **lower 2–3 spikes female, linear-cylindric,** unstalked or very short-stalked, 1–3 cm long; **lowest bract shorter than cluster of spikes,** leaf- or quill-like; **perigynia ellipsoid, 1.5–3 mm long, 0.9–2 mm wide,** green tipped with purplish black, veinless, very short-beaked; female scales equalling or shorter than perigynia, black; **stigmas 2. Where Found:** Streambanks, peaty margins of ponds and dry to wet tundra; lowland (arctic coast) to alpine zones; frequent and often dominant in the northern ⅓ of the region; subarctic-alpine, the subspecies amphiberingian.

Similar Species: Mountain sedge (below) has **broader leaves, broader perigynia** and a **more southerly distribution.**

Notes: Stiff sedge includes *Carex lugens, C. consimilis* and *C. yukonensis.* • It is widespread, abundant and very variable, with as many as 38 subspecies and varieties described by some overzealous taxonomists. Like most sedges, it is wind-pollinated and self-compatible but mainly outcrossing. Stiff sedge produces seeds that have no obvious adaptation for long-distance dispersal but are transported long distances nonetheless, perhaps by birds. The seeds can persist in the soil for at least 200 years; eventually and rather infrequently, some germinate. Once established, they reproduce primarily vegetatively, by rhizomes, forming extensive clones. The rhizomes spread rapidly and, in what has been termed the guerrilla growth form, can quickly exploit available open ground, the long rhizomes establishing clumps and eventually tussocks. • Some stiff sedge "fairy rings" in Siberia are estimated to be more than 5000 years old.

Mountain Sedge • *Carex scopulorum*

General: Scattered or loosely clustered from rhizomes, often sod-forming; stems stout, stiff, **10–90 cm tall,** exceeding leaves. **Leaves: 3–6 mm wide, firm, flat** with rolled-under margins. **Flowers: Spikes erect,** short-cylindric, **bicoloured green and purplish black,** in compact clusters, the **top 1–2 spikes male,** the **lower 2–4 spikes female, oblong-cylindric,** unstalked, 1–2.5 cm long; **lowest bract shorter than cluster of spikes,** leaf- or quill-like; **perigynia broadly egg-shaped to ellipsoid, 2–4 mm long, 1.2–2.3 mm wide,** green to pale brown, tipped with reddish brown spots, veinless, short-beaked; female scales about equalling perigynia, purplish brown; **stigmas 2. Where Found:** Wet to moist meadows, streambanks and shores; montane to alpine zones; frequent and locally dominant in the southern ⅓ of the region, reportedly rare and disjunct in southern YT; subalpine-alpine, cordilleran.

Similar Species: Mountain sedge has **spikes generally shorter** and **more closely aggregated** than those of the other species in this group and usually **plump (not flattened) perigynia.** It tends to be replaced to west and north by showy sedge (p. 450) and large-awned sedge (p. 450), and farther north by graceful mountain sedge (p. 450) and stiff sedge (above).

Notes: Mountain sedge includes *Carex campylocarpa, C. gymnoclada, C. prionophylla* and *C. tolmiei* in part. • It is a common species of high-elevation, seasonally wet meadows in our southern inland mountains.

Key to Group IV: Spikes 2 or More, Stalked, Often Long-cylindric, Mostly Unisexual, Top Spike Often All Male, Less Often with Female Flowers at Base or at Top; Achenes 3-angled; Stigmas 3

1a. Leaves partitioned by whitish, knot-like crosswalls between veins; styles persistent, tough, bony, continuous with achenes. 2

    2a. Spikes long-stalked, ascending to spreading or drooping; stigmas usually 2 (rarely 3) . . . . . **C. saxatilis** (p. 452)

    2b. Spikes not stalked, erect; stigmas 3 . . . . **C. membranacea** (p. 452)

1b. Leaves not partitioned by whitish, knot-like crosswalls between veins; styles dropping off, not bony, jointed with achenes. 3

    3a. Perigynia hairy over surface or fringed with hairs or bristles along margins, at least in upper portions. 4

        4a. Lowest bract below cluster of spikes sheathless 5

            5a. Loosely tufted; perigynia 2.3–3 mm long, beaks 0.4–0.8 mm long . . . . **C. deflexa** (p. 448)

            5b. Densely tufted; perigynia 3–4.5 mm long, beaks 1–1.7 mm long . . . . **C. rossii** (p. 448)

        4b. Lowest bract below cluster of spikes long-sheathing 6

            6a. Top spike with all male flowers or with male flowers above females; perigynia short-hairy, margins fringed; plants loosely tufted from creeping rhizomes . . . . **C. petricosa** (p. 449)

            6b. Top spike with all male flowers or with female flowers above males; plants densely tufted or with short, ascending runners 7

               7a. Top spike bisexual, female flowers on top; leaves <3.5 mm wide; perigynia narrowly lance-shaped, flattened-triangular, upper ½ of margins strongly fringed with whiskery hairs . . . . **C. fuliginosa** (p. 449)

               7b. Top spike all male; leaves 3–9 mm wide; perigynia lance- to egg-shaped, slightly flattened, upper margins sparingly bristle-fringed. . . . . **C. luzulina** (p. 449)

    3b. Perigynia neither hairy nor distinctly fringed along margins. 8

        8a. Lowest bract beneath cluster of spikes distinctly sheathing. 9

            9a. Female spikes unstalked or short-stalked, short-cylindric with 1–5 perigynia . . . **C. glacialis** (p. 449)

            9b. Female spikes long-stalked, elongate-cylindric with 4–20 perigynia. 10

               10a. Top spike male . . . . **C. capillaris** (p. 449)

               10b. Top spike bisexual, female flowers on top . . . . **C. krausei** (p. 449)

        8b. Lowest bract sheathless or nearly so. 11

            11a. Top spike male 12

               12a. Perigynia plump, rounded or triangular in cross-section; achenes nearly filling body of perigynia 13

                  13a. Leaves about 1.5–4 (mostly 2) mm wide; perigynia 2.5–3.5 mm long, veinless, short-stalked . . . . **C. stylosa** (p. 450)

                  13b. Leaves 3–7 mm wide; perigynia 3.5–4.5 mm long, 2-ribbed and strongly veined, unstalked . . . . **C. raynoldsii** (p. 450)

               12b. Perigynia flattened; achenes filling <½ of body of perigynia. 14

                  14a. Lowest leaves well developed, leaves mostly near base of stem; stems not purplish-tinged, at flowering time clothed with dried-up leaves of previous year. 15

                     15a. Spikes narrowly egg-shaped; perigynia broadly egg-shaped to nearly globe-shaped; southern ½ of the region . . . . **C. paysonis** (p. 450)

                     15b. Spikes cylindric; perigynia narrowly egg-shaped; northern ½ of the region . . . . **C. microchaeta** (p. 450)

                  14b. Lowest leaves reduced to scales, well-developed leaves mostly along central part of stem; stems purplish-tinged at the base, at flowering time not clothed with dried-up leaves of previous year 16

                     16a. Female scales blunt to pointed, not awned; perigynia with 2 marginal ribs, otherwise veinless. . . . . **C. podocarpa** (p. 450)

                     16b. Female scales slender-pointed or awned; perigynia with 2 marginal ribs and several veins. 17

17a. Female scales with midribs extending into slender-pointed tips or awns to 1 mm long; perigynia beaks 0.4–0.5 mm long . . . . *C. spectabilis* (p. 450)

17b. Female scales with slender awns 2–12 mm long; perigynia beaks 0.1–0.3 mm long . . . . *C. macrochaeta* (p. 450)

11b. Top spike with female flowers above male flowers 18

18a. Spikes all unstalked 19

19a. Perigynia >2 times as long as wide, more or less inflated or 3-angled . . . . . *C. nelsonii* (p. 451)

19b. Perigynia <2 times as long as wide, flat. . . . . *C. pelocarpa* (p. 451)

18b. At least the lower spikes on short, stiff stalks 20

20a. Female scales with distinct, whitish, wax-papery margins and usually tips 21

21a. Perigynia 1.5–1.8 mm wide, 3-angled, longer than female scales
. . . . *C. media* (p. 451)

21b. Perigynia 2–2.5 mm wide, flattish, more or less equal to female scales
. . . . *C. albonigra* (p. 451)

20b. Female scales usually without whitish, wax-papery margins and tips 22

22a. Lowest spikes spreading to drooping; perigynia smooth, egg-shaped to circular, 1–1.5 times as long as wide, brown; female scales pointy-tipped
. . . . *C. epapillosa* (p. 452)

22b. Lowest spikes erect, perigynia surface somewhat pimpled or granular, elliptic, 2 times as long as wide, pale green to golden brown, often red-dotted; female scales blunt
. . . . *C. atrosquama* (p. 452)

PERIGYNIA HAIRY OR MARGINALLY FRINGED

Hardscrabble Sedge, Ross' Sedge • *Carex rossii*

General: Densely tufted from short, stout rhizomes; stems ascending, 7–30 cm tall, about equalling leaves, **reddish brown or purplish at base. Leaves:** Flat, 1–2.5 (to 4) mm wide; spikes 3–6, the top spike male, 2–3 few-flowered female spikes clustered below; lowest bract sheathless, well-developed, leaf-like, usually longer than cluster of spikes; **additional spikes on long stalks near stem-base,** widely separated from upper spikes; **perigynia 3–4.5 mm long, short-hairy,** ellipsoid, greenish to straw-coloured, veinless, with **conic beak 1–1.7 mm long;** female scales reddish brown, shorter than perigynia; stigmas 3. **Where Found:** Well-drained, open forests, rocky and grassy slopes, sandy-gravelly flats and meadows; lowland to lower alpine zones; frequent throughout the region except the northern Pacific coast and the far north; cordilleran.

Similar Species: Bent sedge (*C. deflexa* var. *boottii*) is loosely tufted and has **hairy perigynia 2.3–3 mm long,** the beak 0.4–0.8 mm long and often bent. It occurs in well-drained, open forests and gravelly meadows, in montane to alpine zones, and is a cordilleran species, scattered but locally frequent from southern BC and southwestern AB to CA, UT and CO.

Notes: Hardscrabble sedge is also known as *Carex deflexa* var. *rossii*.

Woodrush Sedge • *Carex luzulina*

General: Tufted from short rhizomes; stems erect, 15–90 cm tall, exceeding leaves. **Leaves: 3–9 mm wide, flat,** thick, stiff. **Flowers:** Spikes 3–7, erect, the **top spike male,** the lateral spikes all female or bisexual with males on top, the upper crowded and unstalked, the lower remote and short-stalked; **lowest bract leaf-like, long-sheathing,** shorter than cluster of spikes; **perigynia lance- to egg-shaped,** 3–5.5 mm long, 0.9–1.8 mm wide, green to purplish brown, several-veined including 2 prominent marginal nerves, the surface usually hairless but minutely dimpled, **the margins fringed with bristles toward tip,** with beak 0.5–1.5 mm long; **female scales reddish brown to purple** with paler midvein, shorter than perigynia; stigmas 3. **Where Found:** Wet meadows, fens and bogs; montane to lower alpine zones; frequent in the southern ¼ of the region; cordilleran.

Similar Species: Sooty sedge or **shortleaf sedge** (*C. fuliginosa; C. misandra*) has **bisexual top spikes,** with **female flowers on top; leaves narrower than 3.5 mm** and usually much shorter than the stems; **narrowly lance-shaped perigynia, the upper ½ of the margins strongly fringed** with whiskery hairs; and **perigynia and female scales both dark brown to sooty black.** It is found in meadows and on rocky slopes, scree and turfy tundra, in lowland (arctic coast) to alpine zones. Sooty sedge is an arctic-alpine, circumpolar species, frequent in the northern ⅓ of the region, AK, YT, NT and northern BC, sporadically south to southwestern AB, MT, WY, UT and CO. • **Rock-dwelling sedge** (*C. petricosa* var. *petricosa; C. franklinii*) has a **top spike with all male flowers or sometimes with male flowers above a few females; perigynia that are short-hairy or merely with fringed margins;** the plants with **creeping rhizomes** and often **curved-curly leaves.** It grows on dry, rocky (often calcium-rich) slopes, gravel bars, scree and stony meadows, in montane to alpine zones, and is an arctic-alpine, amphi-beringian species, infrequent from AK, YT and NT south in the Rockies through eastern BC and southwestern AB to MT.

Notes: Woodrush sedge is also known as *Carex ablata*.

PERIGYNIA NOT HAIRY OR MARGINALLY FRINGED; LOWEST BRACT BENEATH CLUSTER OF SPIKES TUBULAR-SHEATHING

Hair Sedge • *Carex capillaris*

General: Tufted from fibrous roots; **stems 5–40 cm tall,** exceeding leaves. **Leaves: Usually flat, 1–4 mm wide. Flowers:** Spikes 2–5, **erect** (especially dwarf alpine or arctic plants) **to spreading or nodding,** the **top spike male,** long-stalked, the **lateral spikes female,** rather distant, with **4–20 perigynia per spike; lowest bract leaf-like, long-sheathing,** shorter to longer than cluster of spikes; perigynia oblong-egg-shaped, green to greenish brown, **veinless except for 2 prominent marginal veins,** often minutely sawtoothed toward tip, with beak 0.5–1 mm long; **female scales pale brown** with green or brown midvein, shorter but often wider than perigynia; **stigmas 3. Where Found:** Swamps, bogs, fens, wet meadows, open forests, thickets, shores, streambanks, seepage sites, wet ledges and tundra, usually on calcium-rich substrates; lowland (arctic coast) to lower alpine zones; frequent in the mostly inland part of the region; circumpolar.

Similar Species: Big-hair sedge or **Krause's sedge** (*C. krausei; C. capillaris* ssp. *krausei* and ssp. *robustior*) has **bisexual top spikes with female flowers on top** and **more (4–10) lateral female spikes,** which are **mostly erect-ascending,** the lowest usually drooping. It grows in calcium-rich meadows, on rocky and grassy slopes, gravel bars, shores and tundra, in lowland (arctic coast) to alpine zones. Big-hair sedge is an arctic-alpine, intermittently circumpolar species, locally frequent in the northern ⅓ of the region, AK, YT, NT (Mackenzie Mtns) and northwestern BC. • **Glacier sedge** (*C. glacialis*) is densely tufted and tends to be **smaller (5–20 cm tall),** with a **male top spike and 1–3, unstalked to short-stalked female spikes (appearing as if 1) in a compact cluster,** with **only 1–5 perigynia per spike** and the **lowest bract short-sheathing and bristle-like.** It is found on dry, calcium-rich, rocky and grassy slopes, sandy-gravelly flats and banks, eskers and talus, in lowland to alpine zones. Glacier sedge is an arctic-alpine, circumpolar species, scattered but locally frequent in the north, from AK, YT, NT and northernmost BC, south sporadically in the Rockies to southeastern BC and southwestern AB. It could be mistaken for **curly sedge** (p. 437), which has rhizomes and solitary spikes.

Notes: Hair sedge is also known as *Carex chlorostachys* and *C. fuscidula*.

LOWEST BRACT SHEATHLESS OR NEARLY SO; TOP SPIKE MALE

Risotto Sedge • *Carex raynoldsii*

General: Loosely tufted from short, stout rhizomes; stems erect, **25–75 cm tall,** exceeding leaves. **Leaves: Flat, 3–7 mm wide,** the lower ones fully developed. **Flowers:** Spikes 3–6, the top spike male, the lateral spikes female, spreading to erect in a crowded cluster, 1–2 cm long, short-stalked, **bicoloured green and purplish black; lowest bract sheathless,** leaf-like; perigynia egg-shaped, **3.5–4.5 mm long, plump,** yellowish green to yellowish brown, **several-veined** including 2 prominent marginal nerves, **unstalked,** short-beaked; **female scales reddish black, shorter** and narrower than perigynia. **Fruits:** Achenes nearly filling body of perigynia; **stigmas 3. Where Found:** Moist to dry meadows, grassy slopes and forest openings; montane to alpine zones; frequent mostly inland in the southern ⅓ of the region; cordilleran.

Similar Species: Long-styled sedge (*C. stylosa*) has **narrower (1.5–4 mm wide) leaves** and **smaller (2.5–3.5 mm long), veinless, short-stalked perigynia,** the **styles prominently protruding** from the tip. It is found in marshes, fens, bogs and wet meadows, and on shores, gravelly ridges and heathlands, in lowland to alpine zones. A maritime/arctic-alpine, marginally amphiberingian species, it is frequent in the western part of the region, especially along the coast, from northern and southern AK and southwestern YT through western BC to northwestern WA.

Notes: Risotto sedge is also known as *Carex lyallii*. • Risotto and other sedges are important grizzly bear food in the Greater Yellowstone ecosystem.

Showy Sedge • *Carex spectabilis*

General: Tufted from short rhizomes; stems erect, **25–50 cm tall,** exceeding leaves. **Leaves: Flat, 2–5 mm wide, lower leaves much reduced. Flowers:** Spikes 3–9, the top spike male, the lateral spikes female, short-stalked and erect except lower spikes often long-stalked and spreading or nodding, **bicoloured green and purplish black; lowest bract sheathless;** perigynia egg-shaped, yellowish green or brown to purplish black, veinless or faintly veined, **beaks 0.4–0.5 mm long;** female scales about equalling perigynia, brown or black with **prominent, pale midveins often prolonged into short awns. Fruits:** Achenes filling less than ½ of perigynia body; **stigmas 3. Where Found:** Meadows and forest openings; montane to alpine zones; frequent in the southern ½ of the region, less so northward; cordilleran.

Similar Species: Like showy sedge, both **graceful mountain sedge (*C. podocarpa*)** and **large-awned sedge (*C. macrochaeta*)** have **basal leaves reduced to bladeless sheaths.** • **Graceful mountain sedge** has **lateral spikes** that are all **long-stalked** and **spreading or drooping, female scales** with inconspicuous midveins and **pointy-tipped but unawned,** and **perigynia beaks 0.3–0.4 mm long.** It is found in meadows, seepage areas, streambanks and tundra, in lowland (arctic coast) to alpine zones. An amphiberingian species, it is frequent in the northern ½ of the region, sporadically south to OR, ID and MT. • **Large-awned sedge** also has **spreading or drooping female spikes,** but its **female scales** have **prominent, green midveins** and **long (2–12 mm) awns;** the **perigynia beaks** are **0.1–0.3 mm long.** It occurs in moist to wet meadows, on beaches, shores, heathlands, streambanks and avalanche tracks, in lowland to alpine zones. An amphiberingian species, it is frequent in the western part of the region, especially in and west of the Pacific coastal mountains, from southern AK and southwestern YT through BC to WA and OR, inland to the Rockies in BC. • Both **Payson's sedge (*C. paysonis*)** and **small-awned sedge (*C. microchaeta*)** have **well-developed lower leaves** and mostly **erect-ascending female spikes.** • **Payson's sedge** has **broadly egg-shaped to nearly spheric, coarsely few-veined perigynia.** It grows on rocky slopes and in meadows, in subalpine and alpine zones, and is frequent in the southeastern part of the region. • **Small-awned sedge** has **narrowly egg-shaped, veinless perigynia** and occurs on rocky slopes, meadows, fellfields and tundra, in montane to alpine zones. It is an amphiberingian species, frequent in the northern ½ of the region, often dominant in windswept alpine tundra.

Notes: Showy sedge is also known as *Carex tolmiei*.

LOWEST BRACT SHEATHLESS OR NEARLY SO; TOP SPIKE BISEXUAL WITH FEMALE FLOWERS ABOVE MALE FLOWERS

Full Nelson Sedge • *Carex nelsonii*

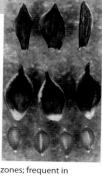

General: Tufted from short, slender rhizomes; stems erect, 15–30 cm tall, exceeding leaves. **Leaves:** Flat with rolled margins, 3–4 mm wide. **Flowers:** Spikes 2–4, unstalked, closely aggregated in a **head-like cluster,** the top spike with female flowers above males, the lateral spikes female, about 1 cm long; lowest bract scale-like, shorter than cluster of spikes; perigynia narrowly elliptic, 3.5–4 mm long, 1.5–1.8 mm wide, plump, granular-surfaced, yellowish green, golden brown, or dark brown with yellow margins,

veinless except for 2 marginal nerves, short-beaked; female scales black, shorter than and about as wide as perigynia; stigmas 3. **Where Found:** Moist, rocky slopes and meadows; subalpine and alpine zones; frequent in the southeastern corner of the region; cordilleran.

Similar Species: Black-tip sedge (*C. pelocarpa*; *C. nova* var. *pelocarpa*) has **wider (2–3.5 mm), flattened, membranous, reddish brown perigynia with black beaks.** It occurs on rocky slopes, ridge crests and rocky shores, in subalpine and alpine zones, and is frequent in the southeastern part of the region, eastern OR, central ID and western MT to NV, UT and CO.

Notes: The species is called "full nelson" sedge because the perigynia are plumply biconvex, not half-convex.

Two-toned Sedge
Carex albonigra

General: Tufted from short rhizomes; stems stiffly erect, **10–30 cm tall,** exceeding leaves. **Leaves:** Firm, flat, 2.5–5 mm wide, greyish green. **Flowers:** Spikes 2–4 (usually 3), unstalked to short-stalked, **erect,** closely aggregated in a **head-like cluster,** the top spike with female flowers above males, the lateral spikes female, 1–2.5 cm long; lowest bract shorter or slightly longer than cluster of spikes; perigynia egg-shaped, 3–3.5 mm long, 2–2.5 mm wide, somewhat flattened, chestnut to reddish black, veinless, short-beaked; **female scales brown to reddish black, with whitish-translucent margins and tips, about equalling perigynia;** stigmas 3. **Where Found:** Rocky slopes, meadows, fellfields and tundra; subalpine and alpine zones; frequent in the mostly inland part of the region except the far north; cordilleran.

Similar Species: Scandinavian sedge (*C. media*; *C. norvegica* ssp. *inferalpina*) has **narrower perigynia (1.5–1.8 mm wide)** that are 3-angled, pale green becoming golden brown and **longer than the female scales.** It is found in moist to wet meadows, thickets, forest openings and on shores and wetland margins, in montane to alpine zones. A circumpolar species, it is frequent throughout the region except along the coast and in the extreme southeast, from AK, YT and NT to WA, OR and MT.

Black-scaled Sedge
Carex atrosquama

General: Tufted from short rhizomes, forming small tussocks; stems slender, erect to arching, 20–50 cm tall, exceeding leaves. **Leaves:** Firm, flat, 3–5 mm wide. **Flowers:** Spikes 3–6, the top spike with female flowers above males, the lateral spikes female, 1–2 cm long, stalked, **ascending to erect;** lowest bract leaf-like, shorter or slightly longer than cluster of spikes; **perigynia elliptic, 2.5–3.5 mm long, 1.5–1.8 mm wide,** half-convex, pale green becoming brown, minutely granular-surfaced, veinless, short-beaked; **female scales dark brown or black to margins,** shorter than and about as wide as perigynia, **blunt;** stigmas 3. **Where Found:** Rocky slopes, gravelly shores, meadows, thickets and fellfields; montane to alpine zones; frequent in much of the inland part of the region except the far north; cordilleran.

Similar Species: Dusky sedge (*C. epapillosa*; *C. heteroneura* ssp. *epapillosa*) has **spreading to drooping lower spikes, brown, smooth, egg-shaped to circular perigynia 1–1.5 times as long as wide** and **sharply pointy-tipped female scales.** It occurs in meadows, forest openings and on streambanks, in subalpine and alpine zones, and is frequent in the inland southern ⅓ of the region, from southern BC and southwestern AB to CA, NV, UT and CO.

Notes: Black-scaled sedge is also known as *Carex atrata* ssp. *atrosquama*.

Lᴇᴀᴠᴇs Pᴀʀᴛɪᴛɪᴏɴᴇᴅ ʙʏ Wʜɪᴛɪsʜ Kɴᴏᴛ-ʟɪᴋᴇ Cʀᴏssᴡᴀʟʟs Bᴇᴛᴡᴇᴇɴ Vᴇɪɴs; Sᴛʏʟᴇs Pᴇʀsɪsᴛᴇɴᴛ, Tᴏᴜɢʜ, Bᴏɴʏ, Cᴏɴᴛɪɴᴜᴏᴜs ᴡɪᴛʜ Aᴄʜᴇɴᴇs

Russet Sedge • *Carex saxatilis*

General: Stems single or in small clumps from short rhizomes, slender, erect, **10–70 cm tall,** exceeding leaves. **Leaves:** Flat with rolled-under margins, **2–5 mm wide,** often partitioned by **whitish, knot-like crosswalls** between veins. **Flowers:** Spikes 4–7, the top 1–2 (to 3) with male flowers, the lateral spikes female, stalked, **ascending to spreading or drooping; lowest bract leaf-like; perigynia ascending,** elliptic to broadly egg-shaped, **somewhat inflated, usually dark brown to reddish black,** smooth, **shiny,** short-beaked; female scales purplish brown, shorter and narrower than perigynia; style bony, persistent; **stigmas usually 2.** **Fruits:** Achenes lens-shaped. **Where Found:** Fens, marshes, bogs, wet meadows, streambanks, shores and wet tundra; lowland (arctic coast) to subalpine zones; frequent throughout the region except in the southwestern corner; circumpolar.

Similar Species: Shiner sedge (*C. membranacea*) has **erect female spikes, 3 spreading to bent-down stigmas, purplish black perigynia** and **long-creeping rhizomes.** It is found in fens, bogs, wet meadows, shorelines and wet or turfy tundra, in lowland to alpine zones, and is an arctic, North American–amphiberingian species, frequent in the northern ⅓ of the region, AK, YT and NT and northernmost BC.

Notes: Russet sedge is also known as *Carex physocarpa*. • Both of these species have a **yellowish green aspect,** which visually sets them apart from some bluish or greyish green, wetland sedges (such as water sedge, p. 445) with which they sometimes occur. • "Russet" and "shiner" both refer to the colour of the lustrous perigynia: reddish brown to black and "bruised" purplish black, respectively.

Grass Family (Poaceae)

Grasses are plants with flowers streamlined to the point of individual obscurity. No doubt some people don't even realize that they have flowers. Grasses are not gaudy, but collectively they dominate large areas of Earth's non-forested landscapes (including croplands and lawns), and the grass family (Poaceae) is indisputably the most useful to humans. Grasses provide us with several times more food than do peas and beans, tubers, fruit, fish, meat, milk and eggs put together. We humans and our civilizations—agrarian or technological—survive and thrive or falter depending on the cultivation of cereals. Grasses include sugar cane and cereals such as wheat, rice, maize (corn), barley, oats, rye, sorghum, the millets and teff. Other grasses are used for pasture, forage and turf, and they provide materials for weaving and thatch, adobe or bamboo structures. Grains such as barley, wheat, rye and corn can be brewed into beers and whiskies, rice into sake and molasses (from sugar cane) into rum. Many species of wildlife, from large grazing mammals to water-fowl, depend on grass and grasslands or grassy wetlands for food, shelter and completion of their life cycles.

Our high-elevation grasses are perennial herbs from rhizomes or fibrous roots, the stems jointed, usually round in cross-section and hollow, but solid at the joints (nodes). The leaves are alternate and 2-ranked, consisting of sheath, ligule and blade; the sheath encircles the stem at the base of the blade; the **ligule** is typically a membranous flap at the junction of sheath and blade; the blade is linear and flat, folded or inrolled. Although grass flowers are tiny and much reduced, they are intricate and complex, and have acquired a peculiar but necessary terminology.

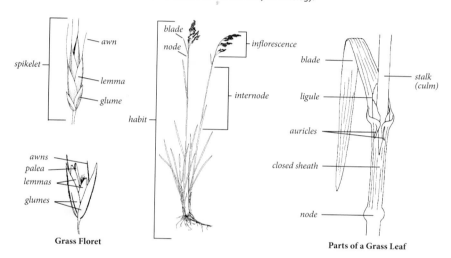

Grass Floret

Parts of a Grass Leaf

The usually bisexual flowers (**florets**) consist of an ovary and stamens, lacking obvious sepals and petals but enveloped by 2 scale-like bracts, the **lemma** and **palea.** There are commonly 3 stamens, 1 superior ovary and 2 feathery stigmas. Below the florets are 2 more bracts, the **glumes.** Florets (1 or more) and glumes together are the **spikelet.** Spikelets are aggregated or arrayed in open or contracted **inflorescences.** The fruit is a single-seeded grain.

Grasses were used by many First Nations, though it is often difficult to tell which species. In the north, the Dena'ina burned fresh grass as a smudge against mosquitoes. Chewed fresh grass was placed on a bee sting to relieve the pain. Five pieces of grass tied around the neck of a person who had eaten too much greasy food would ease an upset stomach. Fish were cleaned and cut up on grass, and in times of starvation, the grass could then be boiled to make a soup. Many groups used dried grass to insulate footwear and clothing; as bedding when camping; for lining steam-cooking pits, storage pits and holes for fermenting salmon; to cover berries and string clams, fish and roots for drying; and to spread on floors and to thatch walls and roofs. Some types of grass were dried and then woven for basketry. Dried grass itself could be fermented in urine to produce a sudsy washing solution. Wicks for grease lamps were made by twisting together soft grasses from vole nests. Other uses included making jump ropes and whistles, covering pitfalls and traps, placing in fish traps to slow down the water, creating alternative nesting sites for gulls (so their eggs were easier to reach) and bunched as scrubbers in steambaths.

Key to the Genera of Poaceae

1a. Inflorescence a true spike, symmetric and solitary atop stem; spikelets attached directly to main stem, unstalked or nearly so 2

    2a. Plants tufted from long rhizomes; leaf blades stiff, harsh; spikelets 2–3 per node of spike; lemmas with awns 2–4 mm long . . . . **Leymus innovatus** (p. 457)

    2b. Plants tufted from fibrous roots, sometimes with short rhizomes; leaf blades relatively soft; spikelets 1–3 per node of spike; lemmas unawned or short-awned (to 3 mm), or with awns >5 mm long 3

        3a. Spikelets closely spaced, overlapping . . . . **Elymus** (pp. 456–458)

        3b. Spikelets spread out along spike axis, not or scarcely overlapping . . . . . **Pseudoroegneria spicata** (p. 457)

1b. Inflorescence a branched, loose or compact cluster or array of stalked spikelets (panicle or raceme), sometimes narrow and spike-like but not a true spike 4

    4a. Each spikelet with 1 flower (floret); glumes usually small 5

        5a. Inflorescence broadly cylindric, tight and spike-like 6

            6a. Glumes awned, with comb-like fringe of bristly hairs on keel; lemmas awnless
. . . . **Phleum alpinum** (p. 458)

            6b. Glumes awnless, hairy all over; lemmas awned from the back below the middle . . . .
. . . . **Alopecurus magellanicus** (p. 459)

        5b. Inflorescence not cylindric and spike-like 7

            7a. Lemmas thickly membranous, toughened in fruit, with a hardened, often sharply pointed base . . . 8

                8a. Inflorescence ≥7 cm long; calluses at lemma base hairy; lemma awns 1–3 cm long, twice kinked
. . . . **Achnatherum** (p. 459)

                8b. Inflorescence 3–7 cm long; calluses at lemma base hairless; lemma awns about 0.5 cm long, once kinked . . . . **Piptatherum exiguum** (p. 459)

            7b. Lemmas wax-papery, not hardened in fruit 9

                9a. Glumes shorter than florets 10

                    10a. Plants small, <15 cm tall; leaves shaped like the prow of a canoe at tip; glumes much shorter than florets . . . . **Phippsia algida** (p. 460)

                    10b. Plants larger, 25–150 cm tall; leaves long-pointed (not prow-shaped) at tip; glumes slightly shorter than florets . . . . **Arctagrostis latifolia** (p. 460)

                9b. Glumes longer than florets 11

                    11a. Base of lemmas evidently bearded (with a tuft of hairs ⅓ or more as long as lemmas); paleas well developed, evident. . . . . **Calamagrostis** (pp. 461–463)

                    11b. Base of lemmas not bearded or with short hairs <⅕ as long as lemmas; paleas lacking, minute or well developed. 12

                        12a. Paleas minute or lacking; lemmas awned or awnless. . . . . **Agrostis** (pp. 463–464)

                      12b. Paleas well developed, more than ½ as long as lemmas; lemmas usually awnless
. . . . **Podagrostis** (pp. 463–464)

    4b. Each spikelet with 2 or more flowers (florets); glumes small or large 13

        13a. Each spikelet with 1 fertile (bisexual) floret above 2 sterile or male ones; plants sweetly aromatic when crushed . . . . **Anthoxanthum** (p. 467)

        13b. Sterile florets lacking or, if present, attached above fertile ones; plants not distinctly aromatic 14

            14a. Glumes shorter than first floret of spikelet; lemmas awnless or awned from tip. 15

                15a. Spikelets ≥15 mm long; lemmas awned from between the teeth of a minutely 2-toothed tip
. . . . **Bromus** (pp. 468–469)

                15b. Spikelets <15 mm long; lemmas awned from the tip or awnless 16

                  16a. Lemmas distinctly rounded on the back 17

                    17a. Lemmas awned or slender-pointed at tip . . . . **Festuca** (pp. 470–474)

                    17b. Lemmas awnless, blunt or irregularly cut at tip . . . . **Poa** (pp. 475–482)

                  16b. Lemmas distinctly keeled on the back 18

                    18a. Leaves tapering to slender point, the sheaths open to the base
. . . . **Leucopoa kingii** (p. 474)

                    18b. Leaves usually prow-shaped at tip, the sheaths closed, at least near the base
. . . . **Poa** (pp. 475–482)

14b. Glumes usually as long as spikelet; lemmas with a bent awn from the back **19**

  19a. Lemmas awned from between 2 teeth at tip . . . . ***Danthonia intermedia* (p. 466)**

  19b. Lemmas awned from the back or awnless **20**

    20a. Lemmas convex on the back, awn attached below the middle **21**

      21a. Glumes <7 mm long . . . . ***Deschampsia* (pp. 465–466)**

      21b. Glumes 9–14 mm long . . . . ***Avenula hookeri* (p. 466)**

    20b. Lemmas keeled on the back, awnless, awn-tipped or awned from the back above the middle **22**

      22a. Lemmas awnless or merely awn-tipped **23**

        23a. Lemmas slightly longer than glumes . . . . ***Koeleria* (p. 467)**

        23b. Lemmas shorter than glumes . . . . ***Trisetum wolfii* (p. 467)**

      22b. Lemmas awned from the back, the awn bent and sticking out from spikelet **24**

        24a. Inflorescence dense, spike-like, the branches short and scarcely evident; lemmas 3–6 mm long; awn attached above the middle, sticking well out from spikelet . . . . ***Trisetum spicatum* (p. 467)**

        24b. Inflorescence diffuse, the branches mostly nodding; lemmas 2–3 mm long; awn attached just below the middle, protruding slightly from spikelet . . . . ***Vahlodea atropurpurea* (p. 466)**

Leymus innovatus

Elymus

Pseudoroegneria spicata

Phleum alpinum

Alopecurus magellanicus

Achnatherum

Piptatherum exiguum

Phippsia algida

Arctagrostis latifolia

Calamagrostis

Agrostis

Podagrostis

Anthoxanthum

Bromus

Festuca

Poa

Leucopa kingii

Danthonia intermedia

Deschampsia

Avenula hookeri

Koeleria

Trisetum spicatum

Vahlodea atropurpurea

The Genus *Elymus* and the In-laws (Wheatgrass, Ryegrass, Wildrye)

Elymus species are tufted from fibrous roots and/or short rhizomes, with stems that are erect, spreading or **decumbent** (prostrate or curved at the base, erect to ascending toward the tip). The inflorescence is a single, symmetric, slender or bottlebrush-like spike. The numerous spikelets are 2- to several-flowered and unstalked, with 1–3 at each node (joint) of the spike axis. The glumes are narrow, mostly lance-shaped to linear, pointy-tipped or awned; awns, if present, are short and straight or long and wavy to spreading. The lemmas are rounded on the back, pointy-tipped or awned from the tip, with 5–7 nerves. The paleas are well developed, shorter than to slightly longer than the lemmas.

The barley tribe is notoriously promiscuous, with frequent hybridization between different species and even genera. All *Elymus* species are allopolyploids—they have multiple (more than 2) paired sets of chromosomes (polyploid), and these chromosomes are derived from different species. *Elymus* is from the Greek *elyo*, "rolled up," and likely refers to the grain, which is tightly enveloped by the lemma and the palea.

Several First Nations groups gathered wheatgrass and wildrye grains for food. As with all grasses, this can be risky if the grains are infected with ergot, a poisonous fungus (*Claviceps* spp.) that can cause severe illness or death in livestock and humans. Infected grains are co-opted by the fungus and transformed into a blackened ergot kernel, a sort of sarcophagus of spores, which you don't want to ingest. Chronic poisoning can cause your nails and eventually your nose, hands and feet to blacken and drop off, and your internal organs to collapse. Hallucinations and convulsions can also result, but migraine headaches could be alleviated, if that's any consolation.

> On either side the river lie
> Long fields of barley and of rye,
> That clothe the wold and meet the sky.
>
> – Alfred, Lord Tennyson, "The Lady of Shalott"

Key to *Elymus* and the In-laws

1a. Plants tufted from long rhizomes; leaf blades stiff, harsh; spikelets 2–3 per node of spike; lemmas with awns 2–4 mm long. . . . . *Leymus innovatus* (p. 457)

1b. Plants tufted from fibrous roots, sometimes with short rhizomes; leaf blades relatively soft or stiff; spikelets 1–3 per node of spike; lemmas unawned, short-awned (<3 mm long) **or** with awns >5 mm long 2

    2a. Spikelets spread out along spike axis, not or scarcely overlapping . . . . . . *Pseudoroegneria spicata* (p. 457)

    2b. Spikelets closely spaced, overlapping (*Elymus* spp.) 3

        3a. Spikelets 1 at all or most nodes of spike; glumes narrowly lance- to egg-shaped, the margins translucent or wax-papery; lemmas awned or awnless 4

        4a. Stems prostrate or decumbent. 5

            5a. Glumes awnless or with awns ≤ 2 mm long; lemma awns 0.5–3 mm long, straight; anthers 0.7–1.3 mm long . . . . *E. violaceus* (p. 457)

            5b. Glume awns 3–30 mm long; lemma awns 15–30 mm long, spreading to curved; anthers 1–3.5 mm long 6

                6a. Spikelets appressed to ascending; internodes ≤5 mm long; anthers <2 mm long . . . . *E. scribneri* (p. 458)

                6b. Spikelets ascending to spreading; internodes >5 mm long; anthers ≥2 mm long . . . . *E. sierrae* (p. 458)

        4b. Stems erect or ascending 7

            7a. Leaves distributed equally along stem, the blades lax; glumes 0.6–1.5 (to 2) mm wide . . . . *E. glaucus* (p. 457)

            7b. Leaves concentrated toward base of stem, the blades often stiff and ascending; glumes 1.8–2.3 mm wide . . . . *E. trachycaulus* (p. 457)

        3b. Spikelets 2–3 at all or most nodes; glumes narrowly lance-shaped to awl- or bristle-like, the margins usually firm; lemmas usually awned. 8

        8a. Axis of spike falling apart at maturity; glume awns 1.5–12 cm long, curved or wavy . . . . *E. elymoides* (p. 458)

        8b. Axis of spike remaining intact at maturity; glume awns ≤1 cm long, straight. 9

            9a. Spikes straight and erect to slightly nodding; lemma awns usually straight. . . . . *E. glaucus* (p. 457)

            9b. Spikes nodding to drooping; lemma awns wavy to curving outward. . . . . *E. hirsutus* (p. 457)

Arctic Wheatgrass • *Elymus violaceus*

General: Tufted; **stems typically decumbent, 20–70 cm long. Leaves: Blades 3–4 mm wide, flat. Flowers:** Spikes dense with overlapping spikelets, **usually tinged greyish purple; 1 spikelet per node of spike; glumes narrowly egg-shaped,** usually

pointy-tipped, **unawned or short-awned (to 2 mm),** the glume margins unequal, the wider margin 0.3–1 mm wide, widest in the upper ⅓; **lemmas usually short-awned (0.5–3 mm),** hairless or hairy especially on the lower part. **Where Found:** Typically in rocky habitats at or above treeline; also gravelly and sandy meadows, shores and river bars, often on calcium-rich materials; lowland (arctic coast) to alpine zones; frequent (but usually not abundant) in the mostly inland northern ¾ of the region, less frequently in the U.S. Rockies to NM; arctic-alpine, North American.

Notes: Arctic wheatgrass is also known as *Elymus alaskanus* ssp. *latiglumis*, *Agropyron latiglume* and *A. violaceum*.

Slender Wheatgrass
Elymus trachycaulus ssp. *trachycaulus*

General: Tufted; **stems ascending to erect, 30–90 cm tall. Leaves:** Concentrated toward stem-base, the blades 2–5 mm wide, **flat to inrolled, relatively stiff. Flowers:** Spikes erect, slender, rather open; **spikelets 1 per node,** at least twice spike internode length; **glumes lance-shaped, 1.8–2.3 mm wide,** pointy-tipped, **unawned or short-awned (to 2 mm),** the **margins about equal,** 0.2–0.5 mm wide, widest at or slightly beyond midlength; **lemmas hairless, unawned or short-awned (to 5 mm),** the **awns straight. Where Found:** Grassy slopes, meadows, riverbanks, forest openings and rocky ridges; lowland to alpine zones; frequent throughout the region except for wet coastal areas; widespread North American.

Similar Species: Bluebunch wheatgrass (*Pseudoroegneria spicata*; *Agropyron spicatum*, *Elymus spicatus*) has **spikelets shorter than or slightly exceeding the length of the spike internodes** and lemmas unawned or with spreading awns to 20 mm long. It grows in dry grasslands, shrublands, forest openings and timberline meadows, in steppe to subalpine zones. Primarily a western North American species, it is frequent in the inland southern ⅓ of the region, from southern BC to northeastern CA, AZ and NM, and rare north to southern YT. • **Blue wildrye** or common western wildrye (*E. glaucus* var. *glaucus*) has **leaves that are evenly distributed along the stem, the blades 4–15 mm wide, flat and lax; erect to slightly nodding spikes, usually with 2 spikelets per node** but sometimes with 1 at most nodes; and **mostly straight-awned glumes and lemmas.** It occurs on open slopes and in meadows, thickets and open forests, in lowland to subalpine zones. This western North American species is frequent in the southern ⅔ of the region, from southeastern AK and southern YT through much of BC and western AB to CA and NM. • **Hairy wildrye** or northwestern wildrye (*E. hirsutus*) resembles blue wildrye but has **nodding to drooping spikes** and **outcurving or wavy (not straight) lemma awns.** It grows in meadows, thickets, beaches, streambanks, gullies, avalanche tracks and open forests, in lowland to subalpine zones. Primarily a Pacific maritime species, it is frequent in and west of the Coast-Cascade Mtns from southern AK to northwestern OR, and infrequent east to southeastern BC. • **Downy ryegrass** or boreal wildrye (*Leymus innovatus*; *E. innovatus*) has **extensive rhizomes, thick (8–20 mm) erect spikes with 2–3 spikelets per node** and **usually conspicuously soft-hairy, short-awned (2–4 mm) lemmas.** It occurs in meadows, on riverbanks, terraces, grassy slopes and open forests, in lowland (arctic coast) to subalpine zones. Downy ryegrass is a widespread North American species, frequent in the inland northern ⅔ of the region, from northern AK, YT and NT south (especially in the Rockies) through eastern BC and western AB to MT.

downy ryegrass

Notes: Slender wheatgrass is also known as *Agropyron caninum* ssp. *majus* and *A. pauciflorum* in part. • All 5 of these grasses are most common at low to middle elevations but ascend fairly frequently to timberline meadows and rocky slopes, especially in the southern part of their ranges—except for downy ryegrass, which extends upward more often in the north, especially on thinhorn (Dall's and Stone's) sheep ranges.

Squirreltail Grass
Elymus elymoides

General: Tufted; **stems mostly ascending to erect,** sometimes decumbent. **Leaves:** Blades 2–4 mm wide, inrolled or folded. **Flowers: Spikes mostly erect, almost as broad (5–15 cm, including awns) as long,** the spike axis falling apart at maturity; spikelets 2–3 per spike node; glumes (linear, bristle-like) and lemmas both with **spreading, curved to wavy awns 1.5–12 cm long. Where Found:** Rocky slopes, thickets, grasslands, open forests, roadsides, fellfields, talus and scree; steppe to alpine zones; frequent in the mostly inland southern ⅓ of the region; widespread western North American.

Similar Species: Scribner's wheatgrass (*E. scribneri*) has **prostrate to decumbent stems; spikes (including awns) 3–6 cm wide,** usually with **1 spikelet per node,** the internodes 2–5 mm long; glumes (linear-lance-shaped) and lemmas with spreading awns; and **anthers 1–1.5 mm long.** It occurs on rocky, open, windswept slopes, meadows, fellfields, ledges and talus, in subalpine and alpine zones. Scribner's wheatgrass is scattered but locally frequent (especially in the Rockies) in the inland southern ⅓ of the region, from southwestern AB to CA, AZ and NM. • **Sierra wheatgrass (*E. sierrae*)** resembles Scribner's wheatgrass but has looser spikes with **longer internodes (5–15 mm)** and **longer anthers (2–3.5 mm).** It grows on rocky slopes and ridges, in subalpine and alpine zones, and is infrequent in the south-central edge of the region, from central WA and eastern OR to CA (especially the Sierras) and NV.

Notes: Squirreltail grass is also known as *Sitanion hystrix.* • Like most *Elymus* species, squirreltail grass is a relatively short-lived grass that's a prolific seed producer with a tendency to fertilize itself. This species is well adapted to dispersal by wind and by furry animals, with widely diverging lemma and glume awns and a spike axis that breaks apart easily.

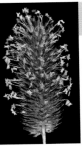

Alpine Timothy
Phleum alpinum

General: Tufted perennial mostly from fibrous roots; stems single or clumped, **erect to decumbent,** 15–50 cm tall.

Leaves: Hairless, the blades flat, 4–7 mm wide; **upper stem leaf with inflated sheath; ligules squared-off and blunt at tip,** 1–4 mm long.

Flowers: Inflorescence broadly short-cylindric to nearly globe-shaped, **spike-like,** 1–6 cm long, 5–12 mm wide; spikelets on very short stalks; glumes 3–4.5 mm long, **often purplish, fringed with long bristle-like hairs on keel,** abruptly **stout-awned; lemmas unawned,** mostly hairless, short-hairy on keels; **paleas almost as long as lemmas;** anthers 1–1.5 mm long.

Where Found: Meadows, grassy slopes, heathlands, streambanks and disturbed soils (e.g., along mining roads); montane to alpine zones; frequent throughout the region except for the far north; interruptedly circumpolar, also in South America.

Notes: Alpine timothy is also known as *Phleum commutatum.* • Alpine timothy has a bipolar distribution. In the Northern Hemisphere, it's a widespread arctic-alpine species extending as far south as 18° N in the Orizaba Mountains of Mexico; in the Southern Hemisphere, it's found in Patagonia and South Georgia.

Alpine Foxtail • *Alopecurus magellanicus*

General: Tufted from short rhizomes; **stems erect or decumbent,** 15–70 cm tall.

Leaves: Blades flat, 3–7 mm wide, rough short-hairy; upper sheaths somewhat inflated; ligules squared-off but finely eroded and **irregularly jagged at tip,** 1–2 mm long.

Flowers: Inflorescence barrel-shaped to egg-shaped, spike-like, 1–5 cm long, 8–14 mm wide; **glumes densely long-hairy or curly-woolly, unawned,** 3–5 mm long, usually purplish-tinged; **lemmas awned from the back** below the middle; **paleas virtually absent;** anthers 2–3 mm long.

Where Found: Wet, often calcium-rich tundra, meadows, thickets, streambanks and shores; lowland (arctic coast) to alpine zones; frequent in the far north (north of about 65° N), less so in southern AK, YT and NT, sporadic south in the Rockies to UT, ID and CO; arctic-alpine, circumpolar.

Similar Species: Alpine foxtail could be mistaken for alpine timothy (opposite), which has awned glumes, unawned lemmas and well-developed paleas.

Notes: Alpine foxtail is also known as *Alopecurus alpinus*. • You have to look closely, but the "spikes" of both alpine foxtail and alpine timothy (p. 458) consist of short-stalked spikelets on short branches, all tightly and tidily clustered in cylindric to barrel-shaped inflorescences. Other high-elevation grasses with less tidy, spike-like inflorescences include spike trisetum (p. 467), purple reedgrass (p. 462), junegrass (p. 467) and even the 2 needlegrasses below. • *Alopex* is Greek for "fox," and *oura* means "tail," referring to the shape of the inflorescence.

Lettermann's Needlegrass
Achnatherum lettermannii

General: Tufted, without rhizomes; stems few to several, erect, 15–60 cm tall.

Leaves: Mostly toward the base; **blades inrolled to hair-like,** 0.5–2 mm wide; ligules squared-off to rounded, 0.2–1.5 mm long.

Flowers: Inflorescence long, narrow, 7–18 cm long, the **branches erect-ascending; spikelets appressed** to branches, **1-flowered;** glumes about equal, 6–9 mm long, longer than lemmas; **lemmas thickly membranous, hardened in fruit,** evenly hairy, with blunt,

little ricegrass

bearded callus at base, awned from tip, the **awns 1.2–2.5 cm long** and twice kinked; **paleas about ¾ as long as lemmas;** anthers 1.5–2 mm long.

Where Found: Rocky slopes, shrublands and meadows; montane to alpine zones; frequent in the inland southernmost part of the region.

Similar Species: Columbia needlegrass (*A. nelsonii* ssp. *dorei; Stipa minor, S. occidentalis* var. *minor, S. nelsonii* var. *dorei, S. columbiana* in part) has **shorter paleas, ⅓ to ⅔ the lemma length,** and **longer awns (2–3 cm).** It occurs on rocky slopes, in open forests and meadows, in lowland to subalpine (especially in the southern part of the range) zones, and is locally frequent in the southern mostly inland ½ of the region, infrequent northward, from southern YT to CA and WY. • **Little ricegrass** (*Piptatherum exiguum; Oryzopsis exigua*) is **smaller (10–30 cm tall),** with a **linear inflorescence 3–7 cm long;** the lemmas awned from the 2-toothed tip, the **awns about 5 mm long,** twisted and once-kinked; and a **hairless callus.** It grows on rocky slopes, ridges, glades and talus, in steppe to subalpine zones, and is locally frequent from inland southern BC and southwestern AB to northern CA, NV, UT and CO.

Notes: Lettermann's needlegrass is also known as *Stipa lettermannii*. • *Achne* is Greek for "scale," *ather* means "awn" and *pipto* means "fall." Both *Achnatherum* and *Piptatherum* have awned lemmas; the awns of *Piptatherum* drop off early. • George Washington Letterman (1841–1913) was a botanist and plant collector from Allenton, Missouri.

Icegrass • *Phippsia algida*

General: **Dwarf, tufted or mat-like,** normally a short-lived perennial but sometimes completes its life cycle in 1 year; stems ascending or sprawling, **3–15 cm tall/long.**

Leaves: Mostly toward the base, hairless; blades flat or folded, 0.5–3 mm wide, **prow-shaped at tip;** ligules membranous, pointed, 0.3–1.5 mm long.

Flowers: **Inflorescence narrow,** usually congested, 1–3 cm long, 3–7 mm wide; **spikelets few, 1-flowered; glumes unequal, much shorter than lemmas,** falling off early; **lemmas often yellow-green with purple highlights,** 1.3–1.8 mm long, broadly egg-shaped, rounded on the back, hairless or sometimes sparsely hairy toward the base, **unawned,** the tips pointed or somewhat rounded; paleas nearly equal to lemmas.

Where Found: Wet tundra, rocky streambanks, mossy seepages and rivulets, shores and snowbeds; lowland (arctic coast) to alpine zones; infrequent in the northern ⅓ of the region, disjunct in the Rockies of southern MT, WY, UT and CO; arctic-alpine, circumpolar.

Notes: This nitrogen lover is concentrated around human habitations in the arctic. One of the first arctic-alpine grasses to flower and set seed, it gets going in a hurry once the snow melts by mobilizing stored carbohydrates. This could contribute to it being an early colonizer of disturbed sites, both those created by human activities and those associated with permanent or lingering snowbeds. • The genus is named for C. J. Phipps, the 2nd Baron Mulgrave (1744–92), a captain in the British Royal Navy and an arctic explorer. *Algida* means "cold."

Reed Polargrass • *Arctagrostis latifolia* ssp. *arundinacea*

General: Stems solitary or clumped from rhizomes, erect, **25–150 cm tall.**

Leaves: Blades flat, **3–15 mm wide, hairless,** the upper sheaths somewhat inflated; **ligules 2–10 mm long,** finely eroded or irregularly jagged at tip.

Flowers: **Inflorescence yellow-green or more often purplish green,** large, open or somewhat contracted, **8–35 cm long,** the branches ascending to spreading; **spikelets numerous, 1-flowered; glumes unequal,** pointy-tipped but awnless, **slightly shorter than or as long as lemmas;** lemmas 2.5–5 mm long, the base (callus) not long-hairy; paleas nearly equal to lemmas.

Where Found: Wet to moist, turfy tundra, meadows, fens, thickets, gravel bars, heathlands and open forests; lowland (arctic coast) to alpine zones; frequent in the northern ⅓ of the region; low arctic–alpine, the species circumpolar, ssp. *arundinacea* amphiberingian.

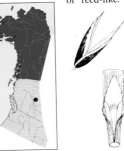

Notes: Cultivars of this subspecies are used for hay production and re-vegetation mixes. • *Arctagrostis* means "northern or polar grass"; *arundinacea* means "*Arundo*-like" or "reed-like."

The Genus *Calamagrostis* (Reedgrass)

Our reedgrasses are tufted perennials with creeping rhizomes and smooth, erect stems. The leaves have flat to inrolled, usually hairless blades. The inflorescence is open, contracted or sometimes spike-like, with numerous, 1-flowered, stalked spikelets. The glumes are about equal in size, narrow, mostly lance-shaped, pointy-tipped but unawned. The lemmas have 3–5 nerves and are awned from the back near the base to near the tip, the base (callus) with long, white hairs. The paleas are well developed, to about as long as lemmas.

Key to *Calamagrostis*

1a. Lemma awns exserted (sticking out) well beyond glume tips, bent and twisted **2**

  2a. Leaf blades usually hairy on upper surface . . . . **C. purpurascens** (p. 462)

  2b. Leaf blades usually hairless **3**

    3a. Awns 3.5–5.5 mm long; leaf blades 0.5–1.7 mm wide; inflorescence usually open . . . **C. breweri** (below)

    3b. Awns 5–13 mm long; leaf blades 2–13 mm wide; inflorescence usually contracted **4**

      4a. Some leaf blades 6–13 mm wide; stems typically 60–120 cm tall . . . . **C. tweedyi** (p. 462)

      4b. All leaf blades 2–7 mm wide **5**

        5a. Leaves 3–7 mm wide; glumes long-tapering to slender, pointed, somewhat twisted tips; glume keels usually roughened their entire length . . . . **C. sesquiflora** (p. 462)

        5b. Leaves 2–3 mm wide; glumes pointy-tipped but tips not so long-tapering and not twisted; glume keels smooth or slightly roughened on upper half . . . . **C. tacomensis** (p. 462)

1b. Lemma awns not reaching glume tips or barely exserted, straight or bent **6**

  6a. Callus hairs usually ≤½ as long as lemmas **7**

    7a. Awns bent, attached near base of lemmas, exserted sideways slightly beyond glumes; ligules mostly 2–4 mm long . . . . **C. koelerioides** (below)

    7b. Awns straight, attached to upper part of lemmas, not exserted; ligules 3–8 mm long . . . . **C. scopulorum** (below)

  6b. Callus hairs usually at least ¾ as long as lemmas **8**

    8a. Inflorescence 4–12 cm long, the longer branches to 4 cm long; ligules blunt and entire at tip; leaf blades often rough above, usually smooth below . . . . **C. lapponica** (p. 463)

    8b. Inflorescence 10–25 cm long, the longer branches 3–8 cm long; ligules jaggedly torn at tip; leaf blades usually rough above and below . . . . **C. canadensis** (p. 463)

Dense-pine Reedgrass • *Calamagrostis koelerioides*

General: Strongly tufted bunchgrass; stems erect, 40–80 cm tall. **Leaves: Blades mostly flat, 2–6 mm wide; ligules mostly 2–4 mm long. Flowers: Inflorescences dense, spike-like,** 7–15 cm long; glumes 5–6 mm long, keeled, the keels somewhat roughened; lemmas 3.5–5 mm long, shorter than glumes, with **bent or twisted awns attached near lemma bases, exserted sideways slightly beyond glumes; callus hairs** ½ as long as lemmas. **Where Found:** Meadows, shrublands, open forests, talus and rocky ridges; montane to subalpine zones; locally frequent in the southern ¼ of the region; southern cordilleran.

Similar Species: Rocky Mountain reedgrass (*C. scopulorum*) has generally **longer (3–8 mm) ligules,** smooth-keeled glumes and **short, straight awns attached to the upper part of lemmas, not exserted.** It occurs in open forests, rocky and sandy slopes, meadows and krummholz margins, in montane to lower alpine zones. Rocky Mountain reedgrass is frequent from southwestern MT and WY to UT, AZ and NM.• **Shorthair reedgrass (*C. breweri*)** is distinguished by its usually **open inflorescence, narrow (0.5–1.7 mm wide), basally concentrated leaves** and **bent, well-exserted awns.** It is found in moist meadows, streambanks and lake margins, in subalpine to alpine zones, and is a Cascade-Sierra endemic, sporadic from Mt. Hood, OR, to northern CA.

Purple Reedgrass • *Calamagrostis purpurascens*

General: Strongly tufted, often from short rhizomes; stems erect, stiff, usually rough to touch, 20–80 cm tall. **Leaves:** Blades stiff, erect, flat or inrolled, **2–5 mm wide, glaucous, usually hairy on upper surface; ligules 2–5 mm long. Flowers:** Inflorescence 4–15 cm long, erect, dense, **contracted, often spike-like, often tinged purple or bronze;** glumes 5–8 mm long, pointy-tipped, unawned, keeled, roughened over the back; lemmas usually shorter than glumes, awned, the awns mostly 6–7 mm long, **stout, twisted, attached near base,** extending well beyond glume tips; **callus hairs of unequal length (1–2 mm), to ⅓ as long as florets. Where Found:** Dry to mesic, well-drained, rocky ridges, gravelly and sandy slopes, grasslands, meadows, shrublands, open forests, scree, talus, fellfields and tundra, on calcium-rich sites; lowland (arctic coast) to alpine zones; frequent throughout the mostly inland portions of the region; amphiberingian.

Similar Species: Cascade reedgrass (*C. tweedyi*) has **broader (4–13 mm wide), flat, mostly hairless leaf blades, ligules 3–8 mm long** and **shorter (to 1 mm) callus hairs.** It grows in moist meadows, glades and open forests, in montane to subalpine zones. Cascade reedgrass is locally frequent in the Cascades of WA and OR, disjunct in northern ID and western MT, and often grows with elk sedge (p. 434).

Notes: *Calamagrostis* is from the Greek *calamos*, "reed," and *agrostis*, "grass."

One-and-a-half-flowered Reedgrass
Calamagrostis sesquiflora

General: Strongly tufted, **usually without rhizomes;** stems erect, 20–50 cm tall. **Leaves:** Blades flat, **3–7 mm wide;** ligules 2–5 mm long. **Flowers:** Inflorescences 4–12 cm long, erect, contracted to somewhat open, usually purple-tinged, the **branches 1.5–4 cm long;** glumes 5–9 mm long, the **tips slenderly long-pointed and twisted,** unawned, keeled, the keels roughened their entire length; lemmas 3.5–5 mm long, awned, the **awns mostly 7–11 mm long, stout, twisted, attached near the base, well-exserted from glume tips; callus hairs 0.1–0.4 times length of lemmas. Where Found:** Moist cliffs, ledges, rocky slopes, heathlands, forest openings, meadows and talus; lowland to lower alpine

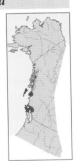

zones; scattered but locally frequent in hypermaritime habitats of the Pacific coast, from the Aleutians to northwestern Vancouver I. (Brooks Peninsula); amphiberingian.

Similar Species: Rainier reedgrass (*C. tacomensis*; *C. purpurascens* in part, *C. sesquiflora* in part) has **narrower (2–3 mm wide) leaves,** slightly longer (2–6 cm) inflorescence branches, **callus hairs longer relative to the lemma (0.3–0.6 times as long)** and **glume tips not twisted.** It grows in dry to moist meadows, seepage areas, talus and cliffs, in montane to alpine zones. Rainier reedgrass is restricted to the Cascades and Olympics of western WA and the Steens Mtns of southeastern OR.

Notes: One-and-a-half-flowered reedgrass is also known as *Calamagrostis purpurascens* ssp. *tasuensis*.

Lapland Reedgrass
Calamagrostis lapponica

General: Loosely tufted from fibrous roots and rhizomes; stems erect, **mostly 30–50 cm tall.** Leaves: Blades flat or inrolled, 2–4 mm wide, often roughened above, smooth below; **ligules 1.5–4 mm long, entire.** Flowers: Inflorescences 4–12 cm long, lax, contracted to somewhat open, the **longer branches to 4 cm long;** glumes 4–5.5 mm **long,** pointy-tipped, unawned, keeled, the keels rough; lemmas shorter than glumes, awned, the **awns slender,** straight to somewhat bent and twisted, attached to lower part of lemmas, **reaching lemma tips but not exserted;** callus hairs of varying length, **mostly nearly as long as lemmas. Where Found:** Moist but usually well-drained tundra,

heathlands, shrublands, streamside meadows and shores; montane to alpine zones;

bluejoint reedgrass

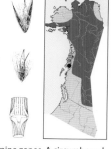

frequent in the northern ⅓ of the region, sporadic southward; arctic-alpine, circumpolar.

Similar Species: Bluejoint reedgrass (*C. canadensis*) has generally **longer (10–25 cm), more open inflorescences** with **longer (3–8 cm) branches; shorter glumes (3–4.5 mm);** ligules **3–8 mm long and jagged at the tip;** and **flat, lax leaves 2–8 mm wide, roughened on both surfaces.** It grows in fens, swamps, marshes, bog edges, riverbanks, mesic to wet meadows, shrublands, clearings and open forests, in lowland to (less frequently) lower alpine zones. A circumboreal species, it is frequent throughout the region, especially inland.

The Genera *Agrostis* and *Podagrostis* (Bentgrass)

Ours are tufted perennials, mostly without rhizomes or stolons. The stems are usually erect and smooth. The leaves have flat, folded or inrolled, usually hairless blades. The inflorescence is open or contracted, with numerous, 1-flowered, stalked spikelets. The glumes are slightly unequal in size, pointy- or awn-tipped. The lemmas are blunt, ½–⅔ as long as the glumes, with 3–5 veins, unawned or awned from the back, the base (**callus**) hairless or hairy. The paleas are absent, rudimentary or well developed but somewhat shorter than the lemmas.

Agrostis is from the Greek *agro*, "pasturage" or "green fodder." "Bent" is from the Old English *beonet*, "grass," where a bentgrass was any grass that grew on a bent or common (unfenced, unbroken ground).

Key to *Agrostis* and *Podagrostis*

1a. Mature inflorescence nearly as wide as long, the hair-like branches diffusely spreading.... ***Agrostis scabra* (p. 464)**
1b. Mature inflorescence not diffusely spreading, contracted to somewhat open, at least twice as long as wide..... 2
  2a. Lemmas awned, the awn bent, 2–4.5 mm long...................................... ***A. mertensii* (p. 464)**
  2b. Lemmas unawned or rarely awned, the awn if present usually <1.5 mm long 3
    3a. Mature inflorescence more or less open, the branches spreading-ascending .... ***A. idahoensis* (p. 464)**
    3b. Mature inflorescence contracted, the branches mainly appressed to the central axis................. 4
      4a. Paleas minute (<0.2 mm long) or absent.................................... ***A. variabilis* (p. 464)**
      4b. Paleas well developed, at least ½ the length of the lemmas 5
        5a. Plants mostly <15 cm tall; leaves 0.5–1.5 mm wide; paleas ⅔–¾ the length of the lemmas; inflorescence contracted, linear-oblong .... ***Podagrostis humilis* (p. 464)**
        5b. Plants 10–30 cm tall; leaves 1–3 mm wide; paleas nearly as long as lemmas; inflorescence somewhat open when young, becoming contracted, oblong-elliptic .... ***P. thurberiana* (p. 464)**

Northern Bentgrass • *Agrostis mertensii*

General: Tufted from fibrous roots; stems erect, 5–35 cm tall. **Leaves: Blades usually flat, 1–3 mm wide. Flowers: Inflorescence usually open,** 3–10 cm long, erect, dark brown or purplish, the branches ascending; glumes 2–4 mm long, pointy-tipped, unawned, keeled; lemmas shorter than glumes, **awned from the back** just below midlength, the **awns 2–4.5 mm long, bent and protruding from spikelet;** callus hairs to 0.4 mm long; **paleas absent or nearly so. Where Found:** Meadows, streambanks, gravel bars, grassy slopes, cliffs, scree, fellfields and tundra; lowland to alpine zones; infrequent but widespread in most of the northern ⅔ of the region, sporadic southward; circumboreal.

Similar Species: Idaho bentgrass or Idaho redtop (*A. idahoensis*) is about the same size as northern bentgrass and also has open inflorescences, but its **lemmas lack awns** and it prefers wetter sites. It occurs in wet meadows,

glades, fens and the edges of bog pools and seepage areas, in montane to alpine zones. A cordilleran species, it is frequent but scattered from southern BC to CA, AZ and NM. • **Ticklegrass** (*A. scabra*) has an ultimately open, **diffuse inflorescence often nearly as wide as long,** with **hair-like, flexible, spreading, roughened branches** and **awnless or awned lemmas,** ½–⅔ as long as the glumes. It grows in meadows, wetlands, on shores, rocky and grassy slopes, ridges, roadsides, trails, outcrops and talus, in montane to alpine zones. An amphiberingian species, in dwarfed, high-elevation form, ticklegrass is locally frequent throughout the region.

Notes: Northern bentgrass is also known as *Agrostis borealis*.

ticklegrass

Alpine Bentgrass • *Podagrostis humilis*

General: Tufted or matted from fibrous roots, sometimes with rhizomes; stems erect to ascending, **5–20 cm tall. Leaves:** Mostly near the base; blades flat or inrolled, **0.5–1.5 mm wide;** ligules 0.5–3 mm long. **Flowers:** Inflorescence usually contracted, narrowly oblong, **1.5–6 cm long,** erect but somewhat lax and sometimes drooping, **often purplish,** the branches ascending to erect; glumes 1.6–2 mm long, pointy-tipped, unawned, keeled, the keels roughened at least toward the tip; **lemmas unawned,** slightly shorter than glumes; **callus hairs absent or sparse,** to 0.5 mm long; **paleas ⅔–¾ as long as lemmas. Where Found:** Mesic to wet meadows, thickets, fens, streambanks, rocky slopes, scree, fellfields and moraines; montane to alpine zones; frequent in most of the southern ⅔ of the region; cordilleran.

Similar Species: Thurber's bentgrass (*P. thurberiana*; *Agrostis thurberiana*) is **taller (10–30 cm)** with **wider (1–3 mm) leaves,** more open inflorescences 5–12 cm **long** and **longer paleas nearly equalling the lemmas.** It grows in meadows, glades, fens and on streambanks and scree, in montane to alpine zones, and is locally frequent in the southern ⅓ of the region, from southern BC, WA, ID and western MT to CA, NV, UT and WY. • **Mountain bentgrass** (*A. variabilis*) resembles both *Podagrostis* species above but has **lemmas without or with very short (to 0.2 mm long) paleas.** It occurs in meadows, open forests and rocky slopes, and is frequent in the southern ⅔ of the region, from BC and southwestern AB south to CA, AZ and NM.

palea

Notes: Alpine bentgrass is also known as *Agrostis humilis*. • *Podagrostis* used to be included in *Agrostis* but has been designated a separate genus because of its long paleas, among other things.

mountain bentgrass

The Genus *Deschampsia* (Hairgrass)

Our hairgrasses are tufted perennials. The inflorescence is open or sometimes contracted, the spikelets with 2 (occasionally 3) somewhat glossy, often purplish florets. The somewhat unequal glumes are longer than the lower floret and sometimes also the upper floret. The lemmas have a slender awn from the back, the awn equalling or exceeding the floret; the calluses are short-hairy.

Key to *Deschampsia*

1a. Glumes mostly green, purple at tip; inflorescence long, narrow, 0.5–2 cm wide, typically greenish when mature
.... ***D. elongata*** (p. 466)

1b. Glumes purplish on lower ½, whitish to golden on upper half; inflorescence usually pyramid- or egg-shaped, sometimes narrower, 1–20 cm wide, bronze to purplish when mature.................................... **2**

   2a. Spikelets arranged like shingles, often clustered toward ends of inflorescence branches; glumes and lemmas dark purple toward the base over more than ½ their surface .... ***D. brevifolia*** (below)

   2b. Spikelets arranged more loosely; glumes and lemmas usually purple over less than ½ their surface, often banded green, purple and tawny from base to tip.. **3**

      3a. Basal leaf blades with 5–11 ribs, usually at least some blades flat and 1.5–3.5 mm wide; lower glumes often minutely roughened along midvein; lower inflorescence branches usually roughened, sometimes smooth.. ***D. cespitosa*** ssp. ***cespitosa*** (below)

      3b. Basal leaf blades with 3–5 ribs, all leaf blades strongly inrolled and hair-like; lower glumes smooth along midvein; lower inflorescence branches usually smooth...................... ***D. sukatschewii*** (below)

Tufted Hairgrass
Deschampsia cespitosa ssp. *cespitosa*

General: Densely tufted; **stems erect, 25–100 cm tall. Leaves:** Mostly basal, blades 5–25 cm long, mostly folded or inrolled and 0.5–1 mm across, **some flat and 1.5–3.5 mm wide, with 5–11 prominent ribs,** mostly hairless; ligules 2–8 mm long. **Flowers: Inflorescence open, often nodding, pyramid-shaped,** 8–30 cm long, 4–20 cm wide, the **branches spreading, usually roughened;** spikelets numerous, 2.5–7 mm long; glumes usually slightly longer than top floret, pointy-tipped but awnless; **lemmas purple and/or green at base,** green to gold toward tip, smooth and shiny, **awned from near the base, the awns 1–8 mm long,** straight or bent, sticking out beyond spikelet or not; **callus hairs about ⅓ length of lemmas. Where Found:** Moist to wet, often calcium-rich meadows, thickets, lakeshores, gravel bars, rocky ridges and talus slopes; montane to alpine zones; frequent throughout the region except the Pacific coast (where other subspecies occur); circumboreal.

Similar Species: Sukatschev's hairgrass (*D. sukatschewii*) has **3–5-ribbed,** hairless leaf blades. It is an arctic-alpine, circumpolar species, frequent but scattered in AK,

south in the Rockies to NV and UT. *FNA* says that "it ranges from short plants that form dense, mossy tufts on the Arctic coast to larger plants in subalpine and alpine habitats of the Rocky Mountains that have frequently been included in *D. cespitosa*." • **Short-leaved hairgrass** (*D. brevifolia*; *D. cespitosa* var. *brevifolia*) is lower growing, **typically 10–30 cm tall,** with **short, narrow leaves** (generally less than 12 cm long and 1 mm wide). The distinctive inflorescence is **dense, dark bronzy-purple, oblong or egg-shaped,** mostly 1–2 cm wide, with **ascending branches** that are spikelet-bearing to near the base. It grows in moist to wet meadows, turfy tundra and solifluction slopes, in lowland (arctic coast) to alpine zones. This arctic-alpine, circumpolar species is frequent in the northern ¼ of the region, from northern and central AK, YT and NT, south reportedly along the Rockies to CO.

Notes: Tufted hairgrass is widespread in western North America and displays much variation. Some of the variation can be ascribed to phenotypic plasticity, whereas some is ecotypic and the result of genetic adaptations for growth, reproduction and phenology specific to different habitats, including high elevations.

short-leaved hairgrass

Slender Hairgrass • *Deschampsia elongata*

General: Densely tufted; stems numerous, slender, 20–80 cm tall. **Leaves:** Mostly basal, **short, thread-like, mostly less than 2 mm wide. Flowers:** Inflorescence narrow, somewhat spike-like, **pale greenish** tinged with purple, 5–20 cm long, 0.5–2 cm wide, the **branches ascending-erect;** lemmas firm, shiny, **often rough short-hairy, awned from the back at about mid-length,** the awns 2–5 mm long, nearly straight; paleas nearly equal to lemmas. **Where Found:** Moist streambanks, shores, clearings, open forests, meadows and rocky slopes; lowland to (occasionally) alpine zones; frequent in the southern ½ of the region, infrequent northward; cordilleran, disjunct in Chile.

Notes: Northern occurrences of this species are in disturbed, low-elevation habitats and could represent introductions.

Mountain Hairgrass • *Vahlodea atropurpurea*

General: Loosely tufted; stems erect, 15–60 cm tall.

Leaves: Mostly along stem; blades flat and 1–8 mm wide, with prow-like tips; ligules rounded to blunt, 0.8–3.5 mm long, margins often jagged and fringed.

Flowers: Inflorescence open, often drooping, pyramid-shaped, relatively few-flowered, 5–20 cm long; spikelets 4–7 mm long, with **2 florets, purple turning bronze;** glumes **nearly equal,** equalling or longer than florets, pointy-tipped but awnless; **lemmas 2–3 mm long, awned from the back near midlength,** the awn 2–4 mm long, usually somewhat bent and protruding from spikelet; **callus hairs about ½ the length of lemmas. Where Found:** Moist to wet, open forests, forest edges, meadows, heathlands, snowbeds, stream-banks and shorelines; montane to alpine zones; frequent throughout the southern ⅘ of the region; interruptedly circumboreal, also in southern South America.

Notes: Mountain hairgrass is also known as *Deschampsia atropurpurea*.

Timber Oatgrass • *Danthonia intermedia*

General: Strongly tufted, with remains of old leaves; stems erect, 10–35 cm tall.

Leaves: Mostly near base; sheaths usually **hairless except long-hairy at throat and collar; blades mostly inrolled,** 1–3.5 mm wide; **ligule a fringe of short hairs.**

Flowers: Relatively few in **narrow, congested, somewhat spike-like cluster, often interrupted and some-**what 1-sided; spikelets 4–10, 1–2 cm long, with **3–8 florets;** glumes usually **longer than florets,** pointy-tipped but awnless, subequal, hairless; lemmas 3–6 mm long, smooth over back, soft-hairy along margins, **awned from between the 2 teeth at tip,** the awns abruptly bent, 6–8 mm long, protruding from spikelet; **callus stiff-hairy along sides;** paleas nearly as long as lemmas.

Where Found: Meadows, grasslands, thickets, open forests, krummholz edges, rocky slopes and fellfields; montane to alpine zones; frequent south of 55° N, infrequent northward; primarily western cordilleran but also on the Great Plains and in eastern Canada and Kamchatka.

Similar Species: Spike oatgrass (*Avenula hookeri; Helictotrichon hookeri, Avenochloa hookeri*) has 2-toothed lemmas that are **awned from the back at about midlength** (not from between the teeth). It occurs on mesic to dry, grassy slopes, in forest openings and timberline meadows, in montane to subalpine zones. Primarily a Great Plains species, it is infrequent, mostly along the Rockies, from southern YT and NT south through western AB and adjacent BC to NM.

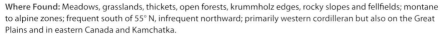

Spike Trisetum, Downy Oatgrass
Trisetum spicatum

General: Tufted; stems hairless or fine-hairy, especially below inflorescence, erect, 10–40 cm tall.

Leaves: Mostly near base; **blades folded to flat, 1–5 mm wide;** ligules squared-off or rounded, finely jagged and fringed, 0.5–4 mm long.

Flowers: Inflorescence **spike-like, greenish, tawny or purplish, usually with silvery sheen,** 5–15 cm long; spikelets with 2–3 florets; glumes usually longer than lower floret and nearly equalling upper florets, pointy-tipped but awnless, upper glume longer and larger than lower; **lemmas 3–6 mm long,** with **2 teeth at tip, awned from slightly below notch** between the teeth, the **awns abruptly bent, 3–8 mm long, protruding from spikelet;** callus short-hairy.

Where Found: Meadows, grasslands, forest openings, rocky and gravelly slopes, ridges, fellfields and tundra; lowland to alpine zones; frequent throughout the region; arctic-alpine, circumpolar, bipolar (also in South America).

Similar Species: Beardless oatgrass or **Wolf's trisetum** (**T. wolfii**) has lemmas that are awnless or with **short awns (less than 2 mm long)** that **do not protrude from the spikelet.** It grows in moist glades, on streambanks and in timberline meadows, in montane and subalpine zones, from inland southern BC and southwestern AB south to WA, CA, NV, UT and NM. It doesn't look much like a *Trisetum* and is placed in a segregate genus—*Graphephorum*—by some. • **Junegrasses** (*Koeleria* spp.) also have tight, spike-like inflorescences and awnless or merely awn-tipped lemmas, but the **lemmas are slightly longer than the glumes.** • **Junegrass** (**K. macrantha**) has **hairless, yellowish lemmas** and mostly grows at low to moderate elevations, occasionally ascending to dry timberline meadows and exposed rocky slopes, especially in the Rockies of the southeastern part of the region. • **Eurasian junegrass** (**K. asiatica**) has **hairy, purplish lemmas** and is an amphiberingian species, infrequent in the far north on gravel bars, scree and tundra, in lowland to alpine zones.

Notes: *Trisetum* is from the Latin *tres*, "three," and *seta*, "bristle," in reference to the 3-awned appearance of the spikelets.

Alpine Sweetgrass
Anthoxanthum monticola ssp. *alpinum*

General: Fragrant, tufted from very short rhizomes; stems hairless, erect, **10–30 cm tall.**

Leaves: Mostly near base; basal sheaths brown to purplish; **blades inrolled or flat, 1–3 mm wide,** sparsely hairy on upper surface; ligules 0.5–1.5 mm long, ½ **basal membrane and** ½ **fringe of short hairs.**

Flowers: **Inflorescence contracted,** relatively **few-flowered** (mostly 5–15), 1–8 cm long; spikelets tawny or bronze, 5–8 mm long, with **3 florets,** 2 lower male or sterile florets and 1 fertile (bisexual) upper floret; glumes about equal, about as long as lemmas, awnless, hairless; **lower 2 lemmas hairy, with 2 deep teeth at tip; awn of lower sterile lemma straight, 1–4 mm long, arising from between the teeth; awn of upper sterile lemma abruptly bent, twisted, 5–10 mm long, arising from the back, protruding from spikelet;** fertile lemma unawned; **callus hairless.**

Where Found: Mesic to dry meadows, rocky slopes, windswept ridges, fellfields and tundra; lowland (arctic coast) to alpine zones; frequent in the northern ½ of the region, infrequent southward; arctic-alpine, circumpolar.

Notes: Alpine sweetgrass was long known as *Hierochloë alpina*. • *Anthoxanthum* is from the Greek *anthos*, "flower," and *xanthos*, "yellow," because of the golden colour of the spikelets. • *Hierochloë* is from the Greek *hieros*, "sacred," and *chloë*, "grass"; "holy grass" is another common name for the former genus. • The pleasant vanilla-like scent comes from coumarin, which is also the active ingredient in an anticoagulant prescription drug.

The Genus *Bromus* (Brome)

Our bromes are perennials from fibrous roots and/or rhizomes, the stems tufted or growing singly, erect or ascending, typically with broad, flat leaves. The inflorescence is an open or contracted array with large, several-flowered, ascending or drooping spikelets on slender branches. The glumes are unequal, narrow, pointy-tipped and shorter than the first lemma. The lemmas are rounded or keeled on the back, 5–9-veined, entire or 2-toothed at the tip, and awned from the tip or from between the 2 teeth. None of the brome grasses in our region are true alpine plants. The following species sometimes occur in timberline meadows and on rocky subalpine slopes, especially in the southern interior parts of their ranges.

Key to *Bromus*

1a. Spikelets strongly compressed; lemmas keeled **2**

    2a. Lower branches of inflorescence 2–4 (to 6) per node, to 20 cm long, spreading to drooping . . . . **B. sitchensis** (below)

    2b. Lower branches of inflorescence 1–2 (to 4) per node, ≤10 cm long, stiffly ascending. **3**

        3a. Earlobe-shaped auricles lacking at base of leaf blades; ligules 3.5–5 mm long; leaves mostly >1 cm wide . . . . **B. aleutensis** (below)

        3b. Earlobe-shaped auricles often present at base of leaf blades; ligules 1–3.5 mm long; leaves mostly <1 cm wide. . . . . **B. carinatus** (below)

1b. Spikelets not strongly compressed; lemmas rounded on the back. **4**

    4a. Plants usually with rhizomes; lemmas usually with awns 1–6 mm long; anthers 3.5–7 mm long . . . . **B. pumpellianus** (p. 469)

    4b. Plants without rhizomes; lemmas with awns 1.5–10 mm long; anthers 2–4 mm long **5**

        5a. Lemmas evenly hairy on the back; glumes usually hairy, the first glume usually with 3 veins . . . . **B. anomalus** (p. 469)

        5b. Lemmas unevenly hairy, hairless at least at tip; glumes smooth or rough short-hairy on veins or keels, the first glume mostly with 1 vein **6**

        6a. Ligules 0.5–2 mm long, lemma awns 2–5 mm long . . . . **B. richardsonii** (p. 469)

        6b. Ligules 2–6 mm long; lemma awns 5–12 mm long. . . . . **B. vulgaris** (p. 469)

Mountain Brome • *Bromus carinatus* var. *marginatus*

General: Stems 35–100 cm tall. **Leaves:** Sheaths usually soft-hairy; earlobe-shaped lobes **(auricles) often present** at base of blade; **blades flat or folded, 3–12 mm wide; ligules 1–3.5 mm long. Flowers:** Inflorescence somewhat contracted, erect, 5–20 cm long, the **branches erect or ascending;** glumes pointy-tipped, unawned; **lemmas 10–15 mm long, laterally flattened, strongly keeled,** hairy on back and/or margins or hairless, 7–9-veined, awned from tip, the **awns 4–7 mm long. Where Found:** Meadows, grassy slopes, thickets and open forests; montane and subalpine zones; frequent in the southern mostly inland ⅔ of the region; cordilleran.

Similar Species: Sitka brome (*B. sitchensis*) **lacks auricles,** has **longer (to 20 cm), spreading to drooping inflorescence branches** and is primarily a coastal species, though the ranges of Sitka, Aleut and mountain brome overlap in the southern interior of the region and it can be tricky to distinguish among them. Sitka brome occurs in moist to mesic meadows, on streambanks, beaches, disturbed areas, open forests, bluffs and rocky slopes, in lowland to subalpine zones. It is a primarily Pacific maritime species, frequent but scattered in and west of the Pacific coastal mountains from southern AK (including the Aleutians) to CA, inland occasionally to central and southeastern BC and northern ID. • **Aleut brome (*B. aleutensis*) has smaller, tighter inflorescences** with **stiffly ascending branches.** It occurs on beaches, gravel bars, shores, disturbed areas, roadsides, avalanche tracks and talus, in lowland to subalpine zones, and is infrequent along the coast from southern AK to northwestern WA, inland occasionally to central and southeastern BC, southwestern AB and northern ID.

Notes: Mountain brome is also known as *Bromus marginatus.*

Sitka brome

Richardson's Brome • *Bromus richardsonii*

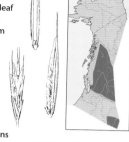

General: Stems 50–100 cm tall, single to a few together, erect or spreading, the **nodes usually hairless. Leaves:** Basal leaf sheaths often soft-hairy; **blades flat, 3–12 mm wide, hairless; ligules 2 mm long or shorter. Flowers:** Inflorescence **open, nodding,** 10–20 cm long, the **branches ascending to spreading or drooping;** glumes usually hairless, pointy-tipped, unawned; **lemmas 9–15 mm long,** blunt and entire at tip, **rounded on the back,** the margins hairy, backs of upper lemmas in spikelet hairy; awns **2–5 mm long,** arising from just below lemma tip. **Where Found:** Meadows, thickets and open forests; montane and subalpine zones; scattered but locally frequent in and east of the Pacific coastal mountains in the southern ¾ of the region; cordilleran.

Similar Species: Columbia brome or common brome (*B. vulgaris*; *B. eximius*) has **longer ligules (2–6 mm)** and **longer lemma awns (5–12 mm).** It grows in moist to mesic meadows, thickets, rocky slopes, streambanks and open forests, in lowland to subalpine zones. Columbia brome is frequent along the coast from northwestern BC to CA, inland less frequently from central and southern BC and southwestern AB, south to UT and WY.

Notes: Richardson's brome is also known as *Bromus ciliatus* in part. • Much of the morphological variation among *Bromus* species results from polyploidy (possessing multiple copies of chromosomes). Richardson's brome, for example, is tetraploid, with 4 sets of chromosomes in each cell. Mountain brome (p. 468) is octoploid (8 sets), and pumpelly brome (below) can be either tetraploid or octoploid.

Pumpelly Brome, Arctic Brome *Bromus pumpellianus*

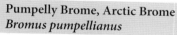

General: Stems usually single or a few from rhizomes, sometimes tufted, 50–100 cm tall, erect or ascending, the nodes and internodes hairy or hairless. **Leaves:** Blades flat, **3–9 mm wide;** ligules to 4 mm long. **Flowers: Inflorescence contracted to somewhat open,** 10–25 cm long, the **branches erect to spreading;** glumes 5–13 mm long; lemmas 9–16 mm long, **rounded on the back,** variously **soft-hairy,** the tips entire or slightly notched;

awns **usually present, 1–6 mm long,** arising from just below lemma tip. **Where Found:** Meadows, sandy-gravelly shores, rocky and grassy slopes, and forest edges; lowland (arctic coast) to subalpine zones; frequent in most of the inland part of the region; broadly amphiberingian.

Similar Species: Nodding brome (*B. anomalus*; *B. porteri*) is tufted, lacks rhizomes, tends to have **narrower (2–6 mm) leaves** and **shorter (1–3 mm) lemma awns** and has **open, nodding, often 1-sided panicles.** It occurs in mesic to dry meadows, grassy slopes, forest edges, open forests and rocky slopes, in montane to subalpine zones. A cordilleran species, it is infrequent in the inland southern ½ of the region, from central BC south to CA, AZ and NM.

Notes: Pumpelly brome is also known as *Bromus inermis* ssp. *pumpellianus*. • *Bromus* is from the Greek *bromos*, "oats," via *broma*, "food." • Pumpelly brome is named for Raphael Pumpelly (1837–1923), a geologist and mining engineer active in Montana, Arizona and the northwestern U.S.

The Genus *Festuca* (Fescue)

Our fescues are perennials, mostly tufted from fibrous roots, with erect or ascending stems that are typically hairless and have inrolled, folded or flat, narrow to thread-like leaves. The inflorescence is contracted and narrow or open, with several-flowered spikelets on slender, erect to spreading branches. The glumes are unequal, narrow, pointy-tipped and shorter than the first lemma. The lemmas are rounded on the back, pointy-tipped, short-awned or awnless, with 5 veins. The paleas are about as long as the lemmas.

Festuca is an ancient word meaning "straw," "stalk" or "stem."

Key to *Festuca*

1a. Most or all spikelets with leaf-like, vegetative proliferations; anthers and ovaries usually absent or abortive... **2**

    2a. Plants with rhizomes; sheaths closed for ¾ or more of their length; stem-leaf blades flat; known only from Haida Gwaii (Queen Charlotte Is.).. ***F. pseudovivipara* (p. 474)**

    2b. Plants lacking rhizomes; sheaths closed for less than ¾ of their length; stem-leaf blades folded; circumboreal, not known from Haida Gwaii.. ***F. viviparoidea* (p. 474)**

1b. Spikelets not vegetatively proliferating... **3**

    3a. Plants usually >40 cm tall **4**

        4a. Inflorescence usually contracted, the lower branches erect to stiffly spreading; leaves grey-green during growing season, wiry, particularly harsh to the touch........................... ***F. campestris* (p. 471)**

        4b. Inflorescence open or somewhat contracted, the lower branches lax, spreading to ascending or bent downward; leaves deep green to yellow-green during growing season **5**

            5a. Mature spikelets usually strongly purplish, glossy; leaves mostly rolled when fresh, yellow-green to dark green during growing season; plants of northern ½ of the region .... ***F. altaica* (p. 471)**

            5b. Mature spikelets not glossy; most leaves flat when fresh, deep green during growing season; plants of southern ⅓ of the region **6**

                6a. Blades of lower stem-leaves shorter and stiffer than those of upper stem-leaves; lemmas hairless, smooth or slightly roughened, unawned or with awns 0.2–1 (rarely to 2) mm long

                .... ***F. viridula* (p. 471)**

                6b. Blades of lower stem-leaves similar in length and stiffness to those of upper stem-leaves; lemmas roughened or short-hairy, usually with awns 1–3.5 mm long .... ***F. washingtonica* (p. 471)**

    3b. Plants mostly <40 cm tall **7**

        7a. Anthers 2–3.5 mm long **8**

            8a. Spikelets 5–7 mm long .... ***F. auriculata* (p. 473)**

            8b. Spikelets 7–9 mm long .... ***F. lenensis* (p. 473)**

        7b. Anthers 0.3–2 mm long **9**

            9a. Upper part of stems with short, upwardly curved hairs...................... ***F. baffinensis* (p. 473)**

            9b. Stems hairless or nearly so... **10**

                10a. Inflorescence mostly >5 cm long; spikelets mostly with 3–5 florets; anthers 1–2 mm long; plants mostly not ascending to the alpine .... ***F. saximontana* (p. 472)**

                10b. Inflorescence usually 1–4 cm long; spikelets mostly with 2–4 florets; anthers 0.5–1.2 mm long; plants mostly of higher elevations **11**

                      11a. Uppermost stem leaf 2–10 mm long; plants 5–15 cm tall; lemmas mostly 4–5.5 mm long; largely Beringian (unglaciated AK and YT) .... ***F. brevissima* (p. 473)**

                      11b. Uppermost stem leaf 7–35 mm long; plants mostly taller; lemmas mostly shorter, 2–4.5 mm long; widespread.. **12**

                          12a. Leaves 0.2–0.5 mm wide (don't flatten them out for measurement); lemma awns 0.5–1.5 mm long .... ***F. minutiflora* (p. 472)**

                          12b. Leaves 0.3–1.2 mm wide; lemma awns 1–3 mm long....... ***F. brachyphylla* (p. 472)**

BIG BUNCHGRASSES

Altai Fescue, Northern Rough Fescue
Festuca altaica

General: Densely tufted **bunchgrass; stems 30–100 cm tall,
the nodes not visible. Leaves:** Old leaf sheaths persistent,
not shredding into fibres; blades mostly folded, sometimes
flat, 1–4 mm wide; ligules 0.2–0.6 mm long. **Flowers:** Inflorescence open, erect, 5–15 cm long, the lower branches lax,
to 10 cm long, often bent down; spikelets purplish bronze,
lustrous, 8–14 mm long, usually with 3–5 florets; **lemmas
7–12 mm long,** hairless but roughened, **5-veined, slenderly
pointy-tipped or short-awned,** the awns 0.2–0.7 mm long.
Where Found: Mesic to dry meadows, grasslands, shrublands, rocky slopes, forest openings and tundra; lowland
(arctic coast) to alpine zones; frequent in the northern
mostly inland ½ of the region, locally frequent southward;
amphiberingian.

Similar Species: Mountain rough fescue (*F. campestris; F. scabrella* var. *major*)
has erect to stiffly spreading inflorescence branches with the **lower branches
2–7 cm long** and **pale green spikelets tinged purple above.** It occupies grasslands, meadows and forest openings, in steppe to subalpine zones. A cordilleran, largely intermontane species, it is frequent from southern interior BC and
southwestern AB to OR, ID and MT. • The southern **green fescue** (*F. viridula*)
has inflorescences like those of Altai fescue but has **stems with visible nodes,
a lush appearance given by the deep green, flat leaves** (the lower blades
shorter and stiffer than the upper) and **spikelets that are not lustrous** , the
lemmas hairless, smooth and short-awned (0.2–2 mm long). It grows in mesic
to dry meadows, open forests, glades and on rocky slopes, in subalpine and
alpine zones, and is locally frequent from inland southern BC through WA,
ID, western MT and OR to CA and NV. • **Washington fescue** (*F. washingtonica*)
is similar to green fescue but has **lower and upper stem-leaf blades similar in
length and stiffness** and **hairy or roughened lemmas with longer awns**
(1–3.5 mm). It occurs in meadows and forest openings, in subalpine and alpine
zones, and is infrequent in the Cascade Mtns of WA and extreme southern BC.

Notes: Altai fescue is also known as *Festuca scabrella* var. *scabrella*.
• In an apparent mutualism, some species of alpine grasses have fungi
growing within their leaves (fungal endophytes). These fungi receive
accommodation and food from the plants, and reciprocate by producing chemicals that deter grazing. In a Yukon study, Altai fescue
heavily grazed by pikas and marmots had *more* (!?) of the endophytes
(*Neotyphodium* spp.) than did ungrazed plants. The researchers

explained their findings this
way: chemical deterrence is an
induced response and hosting
the fungi has a metabolic cost,
therefore the ungrazed (by virtue of
distance from the boulder field homes
of pikas and marmots) grasses have
fewer fungal endophytes because
they don't need them and, indeed,
would be burdened by them. Whereas
the closer to the rock nests, the more
intense the herbivory and the more endophytes the grasses have. Presumably without endophytes, the close-in grasses would
be nibbled into oblivion. There are strange
things done in the midnight sun.

green fescue

TINY TUFTS

The mountains of northwestern North America support a group of very small, arctic, alpine or boreal fescues that all have short, narrow, mostly basal leaves and narrow, contracted panicles. Some are distinctive, others less so. Recent technical treatments rely heavily on micro-characteristics of leaf morphology and anatomy, though some of the key differences could reflect phenotypic plasticity rather than hardwired genetic adaptations.

Rocky Mountain Fescue
Festuca saximontana

General: Largest (to 60 cm tall) species of the group, though high-elevation varieties are about **10–35 cm tall. Flowers:** Inflorescence **4–11 cm long;** spikelets 4.5–9 mm long, with 3–5 florets; lemma awns mostly 1–2 mm long; **anthers 1–2 mm long. Where Found:** Meadows, grasslands, forest openings, rocky slopes and ridges; montane to lower alpine zones; frequent in most of the region except the far north, most common in BC, AB and southern YT, at high elevations mostly inland; broadly amphiberingian but primarily western North American.

Notes: You may need to look microscopically at cross-sections of leaves to be sure it isn't one of the other little species (see *FNA*, vol. 24).

Alpine Fescue • *Festuca brachyphylla*

General: Stems hairless, 8–25 (to 35) cm tall. **Leaves:** 0.3–1.2 mm wide; uppermost leaf sheath not inflated; **blades 1–2.5 cm long. Flowers:** Inflorescence 1.5–4 cm long; spikelets 4.5–7 mm long, usually with 2–4 florets; **lemma awns mostly 1–3 mm long; anthers 0.7–1.2 mm long. Where Found:** Rocky slopes and ridges, scree, talus and fellfields; lowland (arctic coast) to alpine zones; throughout the region; arctic-alpine, the circumpolar ssp. *brachyphylla* in the northern cordillera (south to northern WA), ssp. *coloradensis* in the southern cordillera (WY and UT to AZ and NM).

Notes: Alpine fescue is also known as *Festuca ovina* var. *brachyphylla*. It is closely related to Rocky Mountain fescue (above) and little fescue (below).

Little Fescue • *Festuca minutiflora*

General: Stems hairless, mostly 5–25 cm tall, usually erect, sometimes spreading. **Leaves:** Very narrow, hair-like, 0.2–0.5 mm in diameter. **Flowers:** Inflorescence 1–4 cm long; spikelets 3–5 mm long; lemma awns 0.5–1.5 mm long; anthers 0.5–1.2 mm long. **Where Found:** Stony slopes, ridges and tundra; alpine zone; rare from southeastern AK and southwestern YT to CA, AZ and NM; cordilleran.

Notes: Little fescue has unsurprisingly often been overlooked or included in *F. brachyphylla*.

Baffin Island Fescue
Festuca baffinensis

General: Stems densely hairy near and within inflorescence, mostly 5–25 cm tall. Flowers: Inflorescence 1.5–4 cm **long;** spikelets 5–8 mm long; **lemma awns 0.8–3 mm long; anthers 0.3–0.7 mm long. Where Found:** Scree and talus slopes, gravelly ridges, fellfields and felsenmeer, often on calcium-rich substrates; mostly alpine zone, to low elevations on the arctic coast; frequent in the northern ⅓ of the region, south especially in the Rockies to CO; arctic-alpine, circumpolar.

Notes: As in the bromes, species ploidy level (number of copies of chromosomes) helps explain the patterns of morphological variation in these little fescues. Really short fescue (below) has 2 copies (diploid), little fescue (p. 472) and Baffin Island fescue have 4 copies (tetraploid), and Rocky Mountain fescue (p. 472) and alpine fescue (p. 472) have 6 copies (hexaploid). Just to confuse things, some alpine fescue plants reportedly can be tetraploid.

Lena Fescue • *Festuca lenensis*

General: Stems usually hairless, 10–35 cm tall, densely tufted. **Leaves:** Sheaths closed for about ½ their length; **blades folded, narrow (0.4–1 mm wide). Flowers:** Inflorescence 1–5 cm long; spikelets 7–9 mm long; lemma awns 1–3 mm long; **anthers 2.5–3.5 mm long. Where Found:** Rocky slopes and tundra; alpine and arctic zones; infrequent in the northern ⅓ of the region; amphiberingian.

Similar Species: Really short fescue (**F. brevissima,** F. ovina var. *alaskana*) is another northern amphiberingian species, **shorter (5–15 cm tall)** with **smaller (0.9–1.2 mm long) anthers** than Lena

fescue. It is found on rocky tundra, in montane to alpine zones, and is infrequent in the mountains of AK and YT. • **Lobed fescue (F. auriculata)** has **slightly shorter spikelets** than Lena fescue (about 5–7 mm vs. 7–9 mm). It occurs on dry, rocky slopes and cliffs, in montane to alpine zones. An amphiberingian species, it is rare in AK, northern YT and extreme northwestern NT.

Viviparous Fescue • *Festuca viviparoidea*

General: Tufted, without rhizomes; stems 10–30 cm tall.
Flowers: Inflorescence narrow, spike-like, 1–5 cm long;
spikelets pseudoviviparous, at least upper florets with
vegetative bract-like or leaf-like proliferations; glumes
and often 1–2 lower florets normally developed; **anthers
usually not
developed. Where Found:** Rocky
slopes and tundra; montane
to alpine zones; infrequent in the
northern ½ of the region, south
to southeastern BC and southwestern AB; arctic-alpine, circumpolar with large gaps.

Similar Species: Pseudoviviparous fescue (*F. pseudovivipara*) also
has spikelets with vegetative proliferations, but has **rhizomes** and **open,
lax inflorescences** 5–12 (to 15) cm long. It grows on rocky slopes, cliffs, ledges
and gullies, in montane to alpine zones, and is rare, known only from Haida
Gwaii, BC.

Notes: Noted BC forest ecologist and conservationist V.J. Krajina was also an expert in *Festuca* taxonomy.
In 1980, he proposed the name "*F.* × *viviparoidea*" for what he assumed was the hybrid *F. baffinensis* ×
F. brachyphylla (still listed in *FNA* as likely parents). Leon Pavlick subsequently described the species
(*F. viviparoidea* Krajina *ex* Pavlick).

Spike-fescue • *Leucopoa kingii*

General: Densely tufted, dioecious (male and female
flowers on separate plants); stems few to several, erect,
30–100 cm tall. Leaves: Mostly basal; sheaths open;
blades stiff, glaucous, **flat or somewhat inrolled,
2–7 mm wide;** ligules 0.8–2 mm long. **Flowers:** Inflorescence narrow, contracted, erect, 7–20 cm long, the
branches ascending-erect; spikelets 6–12 mm long,
**usually with 3–5 unisexual florets; glumes shorter
than lemmas,** slightly unequal;
lemmas 4.5–8 mm long, slightly
keeled, roughened, faintly
5-veined, **awnless; anthers of male
florets 3–6 mm long. Where
Found:** Dry to moist meado`ws,
grasslands, rocky slopes and fellfields; montane to lower alpine
zones; frequent in the southeastern part of the region, MT, ID
and southeastern OR to CA and CO;
cordilleran.

Notes: Spike-fescue is also
known as *Festuca kingii, F. watsonii, Hesperochloa
kingii* and *Poa kingii.* • *Leucopoa* is sometimes
included in *Festuca* but differs in its dioecious habit,
among other things. Spike-fesc ue is dioecious, but
the sexual state (male or female) of individual
plants can change in response to poorly understood
environmental cues. • Clarence King (1842–1901)
was a geologist for the California Geological
Survey.

The Genus *Poa* (Bluegrass)

Our bluegrasses are perennials, more or less tufted, with or without rhizomes, and green or bluish green, often variously tinged with purple. The stems are erect or ascending and typically hairless. The leaf blades are mostly rather narrow, flat, folded or inrolled, with upcurved, prow-shaped tips that resemble the front end of a canoe. The inflorescence is contracted or open with 2- to several-flowered spikelets on slender, erect to spreading branches. The florets are mostly bisexual, but sometimes unisexual, and occasionally are replaced by asexual, vegetative buds or bulblets (**bulbils**). The glumes are somewhat unequal, boat-shaped, usually distinctly keeled, pointy-tipped and usually shorter than the first lemma. The lemmas are keeled or, less often, rounded on the back, blunt, unawned and hairless or hairy, with usually 5 veins; some species have a tuft of cobwebby hairs at the toughened lemma base (**callus**). The distinctly 2-keeled paleas are equal to or shorter than the lemmas.

Poa is a large, cosmopolitan genus, with about 500 species worldwide. It seems a "natural" genus—genetic analysis suggests that all species currently in the genus are related, which is reassuring. However, distinguishing species within *Poa* can sometimes be eye-wateringly difficult because of the large number of species, the general lack of useful morphological features, the hybrid origin of polyploid species and the frequency of apomixis (apomixis = asexual reproduction via seeds that contain a false embryo, cloned from the mother plant's tissues, with no pollen or father plant involved) and hybridization. The variability isn't particularly amenable to a dichotomous key, but we'll take a stab at it.

Key to *Poa*

1a. Plants with rhizomes 2

  2a. Spikelets producing leafy bulbils in place of normal florets 3

    3a. Panicles open and diffuse, the branches widely spreading (mostly >45°) away from stem; if some normal florets present, paleas finely hairy between veins . . . . **P. arctica (bulbiferous forms)(p. 477)**

    3b. Panicles contracted, the branches only weakly spreading (mostly <45°) away from stem; if some normal florets present, paleas usually hairless between veins . . . . **P. pratensis ssp. colpodea (p. 477)**

  2b. Spikelets not producing bulbils 4

    4a. Plants effectively unisexual; anthers non-functional (wispy, whitish, containing no pollen) or absent; spikelets 5.5–10 mm long; lemmas not cobwebby at the base; plants of well-drained soil, usually in open, coniferous forests or glades, subalpine zone and lower . . . . **P. wheeleri (p. 477)**

    4b. Plants bisexual, with normal, turgid, yellow anthers containing pollen; spikelets shorter, or if >6 mm long, then growing on wet soil; lemmas cobwebby at the base 5

      5a. Inflorescence open, with branch angles mostly >45° away from stem; paleas finely hairy between veins; lemmas long-hairy on keels and marginal veins and mostly short-hairy between them . . . . **P. arctica (p. 477)**

      5b. Inflorescence narrow, with branches mostly <45° away from stem; paleas usually hairless between veins; lemmas long-hairy on keels and marginal veins, infrequently also on intermediate veins, hairless between them . . . . **P. pratensis ssp. alpigena (p. 477)**

1b. Plants without rhizomes 6

  6a. Lemmas rounded or only vaguely keeled on the back (lemma as seen end-on whale-backed, without distinct ridge line), not cobwebby at the base; plants mostly southern, absent or infrequent north of 55° N 7

    7a. Basal leaves thick and firm, white-margined; ligules 2–5 mm long; Wenatchee Mtns, WA . . . . **P. curtifolia (p. 480)**

    7b. Basal leaves thin, flexible, not white-margined; ligules shorter; widespread species. 8

      8a. Inflorescence open, the branches >45° from stem; basal leaves 0.5–1.5 mm broad, mostly flat or slightly inward folded . . . . **P. gracillima (p. 479)**

      8b. Inflorescences narrow, the branches <45° from stem; basal leaves 1–3 mm broad, mostly incurled or inward folded 9

        9a. Plants green, mostly >30 cm tall; basal leaves >5 cm long, the sheaths minutely roughened (run between thumb and forefinger) . . . . **P. scabrella (p. 479)**

        9b. Plants purplish green, mostly <30 cm tall; basal leaves <5 cm long, the sheaths smooth . . . . **P. incurva (p. 479)**

6b. Lemmas distinctly keeled (as seen end-on) on the back, cobwebby at the base or not **10**

    10a. Leaves firm, broad (2–4.5 mm), trough-like; spikelets broadly rounded at the base, not much longer than wide . . . . *P. alpina* (p. 480)

    10b. Leaves soft or firm, if firm then not broad (0.5–2 mm), not distinctly trough-like; spikelets tapering to the base, mostly much longer than broad **11**

        11a. Lemmas distinctly cobwebby at the base; inflorescence diffuse, the branches spreading at wide angles or even delicately drooping, more than 3 times as long as spikelets **12**

        12a. Lower inflorescence branches reflexed; mostly south of 47° N . . . . *P. reflexa* (p. 478)

        12b. Lower inflorescence branches ascending or spreading, not reflexed **13**

            13a. Plants 10–30 cm tall; leaf sheaths smooth; inflorescence usually 3–8 cm long; mostly north of 47° N . . . . *P. paucispicula* (p. 478)

            13b. Plants 15–50 cm tall; leaf sheaths minutely roughened (run between thumb and fore-finger); inflorescence usually 7–15 cm long; widespread . . . . *P. leptocoma* (p. 478)

    11b. Lemmas not cobwebby at the base, or if so (some forms of *P. glauca* and *P. abbreviata*), then inflorescence compact with ascending to spreading branches. **14**

        14a. Lemmas entirely smooth (except somewhat cobwebby at the base in *P. abbreviata* ssp. *marshii*); plants mostly dwarf, generally <15 cm tall **15**

        15a. Anthers 0.2–0.8 mm long; plants 1–12 cm tall; widespread. . . . . *P. lettermannii* (p. 481)

        15b. Anthers 0.6–1.2 mm long; plants 5–25 cm tall; almost entirely south of 49° N **16**

            16a. Lemmas broadest near the middle, the base minutely cobwebby; U.S. Rocky Mtns . . . . *P. abbreviata* ssp. *marshii* (p. 481)

            16b. Lemmas broadest near the base, the base hairless; Cascades, Olympics and Blue Mtns . . . . *P. suksdorfii* (p. 481)

        14b. Lemmas scabrous (with minute, whiskery stubble, visible under a good hand lens) and/or hairy, at least in the lower portions; mostly taller plants **17**

        17a. Lemmas scabrous, sometimes hairy on veins near the base, but not consistently so; stem relatively long up to base of inflorescence, mostly 4–7 times length of inflorescence **18**

        18a. Inflorescence dense, with little space between most spikelets; occasionally with hairs on veins; widespread south of 62° N . . . . *P. cusickii* (p. 480)

        18b. Inflorescence relatively diffuse, with much space between most spikelets; almost always without hairs on veins; known only from north of 60° N . . *P. porsildii* (p. 480)

        17b. Lemmas not scabrous, always hairy on veins, sometimes also hairy between veins; stem shorter up to base of inflorescence, mostly 2–4 times length of inflorescence (up to 5 times in *P. glauca* ssp. *rupicola*). **19**

        19a. Inflorescence diffuse, most spikelets not overlapping. **20**

            20a. Plants 25–60 cm tall; inflorescence branches bearing mostly more than 3 spike-lets; temperate and coastal-boreal mountains . . . . *P. stenantha* (p. 481)

            20b. Plants 4–20 cm tall; inflorescence branches bearing mostly 1–3 spikelets; arctic and boreal mountains . . . . *P. pseudoabbreviata* (p. 482)

        19b. Inflorescence dense, most spikelets overlapping **21**

            21a. Plants usually glaucous (with waxy, blue-grey appearance to leaves and stems); anthers 1.2–2.5 mm long . . . . *P. glauca* (p. 478)

            21b. Plants not glaucous; anthers 0.2–1.2 mm long. **22**

                22a. Stem leaves with sheath sealed for ⅓–¾ of length (run a toothpick along sheath: the unsealed portion slides apart, the sealed portion tears; use magnification); stems 8–35 cm tall; plants rare; Banff area (AB), Glacier National Park (MT) and northeastern OR . . . . . *P. laxa* ssp. *banffiana* (p. 482)

                22b. Stem leaves with sheath sealed for only ½–¼ of length; stems 5–15 cm tall; widespread . . . *P. abbreviata* ssp. *abbreviata* and ssp. *pattersonii* (p. 481)

PLANTS WITH RHIZOMES

Arctic Bluegrass • *Poa arctica*

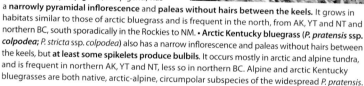

General: Rhizomes usually well developed; stems 10–50 cm tall, erect to ascending, **solitary or a few together. Leaves:** Blades flat, folded or somewhat inrolled, 1–6 mm wide; ligules 2–7 mm long. **Flowers: Inflorescence usually open, egg- to pyramid-shaped,** sometimes somewhat contracted and narrower, **4–15 cm long,** rather sparse, with 10–50 spikelets; **spikelets purplish, 4.5–8 mm long,** usually with 2–6 florets, occasionally with bulbils; **lemmas 3–7 mm long, distinctly keeled, 5-veined, long-hairy on keels and marginal and lateral veins, short-hairy between veins** at least toward base, cobwebby or not at base; **paleas usually fine-hairy on and between keels. Where Found:** Mesic to wet meadows, streambanks, rocky slopes, fellfields and tundra; lowland (arctic coast) to alpine zones; frequent in most of the region except the southwestern portion; arctic-alpine, species complex circumpolar.

Similar Species: Alpine Kentucky bluegrass (*P. pratensis* ssp. *alpigena*; *P. alpigena*) has a **narrowly pyramidal inflorescence** and **paleas without hairs between the keels.** It grows in habitats similar to those of arctic bluegrass and is frequent in the north, from AK, YT and NT and northern BC, south sporadically in the Rockies to NM. • **Arctic Kentucky bluegrass (*P. pratensis* ssp. *colpodea*; *P. stricta* ssp. *colpodea*)** also has a narrow inflorescence and paleas without hairs between the keels, but **at least some spikelets produce bulbils.** It occurs mostly in arctic and alpine tundra, and is frequent in northern AK, YT and NT, less so in northern BC. Alpine and arctic Kentucky bluegrasses are both native, arctic-alpine, circumpolar subspecies of the widespread *P. pratensis*.

Notes: Arctic bluegrass includes *Poa aperta, P. grayana, P. lanata, P. longiculmis, P. longipila, P. malacantha* and *P. williamsii*. • It is a common, highly variable, arctic-alpine species with 3 or 4 subspecies in our region. Bulbil-producing plants occasionally occur, more frequently in the north.

Wheeler's Bluegrass • *Poa wheeleri*

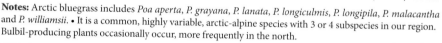

General: Short rhizomes; stems 35–80 cm tall, tufted or solitary. **Leaves:** Sheaths mostly minutely hairy; stem-leaf blades flat or folded, 2–3.5 mm wide. **Flowers: Inflorescence loosely contracted to open, 5–18 cm long;** spikelets 5.5–10 mm long, usually with 2–7 florets; glumes distinctly shorter than lemmas; **lemmas 3–6 mm long, hairless or sparsely short-hairy on keels, marginal veins and between veins but not cobwebby at base; florets usually female;** anthers usually non-functional. **Where Found:** Mesic to dry, open forests, glades and meadows; montane to subalpine and occasionally lower alpine zones; locally frequent inland in the southern ½ of the region; cordilleran.

Notes: Wheeler's bluegrass is also known as *Poa nervosa* var. *wheeleri*. • The species is named for Louis Cutter Wheeler (1910–80), a professor of botany at the University of Southern California, who was a student of *Euphorbia* and the author of *Notes on California Pteridophytes*.

PLANTS WITHOUT RHIZOMES; LEMMAS COBWEBBY AT BASE (EXCEPT *P. GLAUCA* SSP. *RUPICOLA*)

Western Bog Bluegrass • *Poa leptocoma*

General: Loosely tufted, rarely with short rhizomes; stems 15–50 cm tall. **Leaves:** Blades flat, thin, 1–4 mm wide. **Flowers:** Inflorescence open, lax, sparse, 5–15 cm long, the branches rough on angles; glumes unequal, awl- to lance-shaped; lemmas narrowly lance-shaped, 3–4 mm long, **bronze or purplish**, sparsely hairy on keels and marginal veins, hairless between veins; **calluses cobwebby. Where Found:** Moist to wet meadows, thickets, snowbeds, streambanks, shores and bogs; montane to alpine zones; frequent in most of the region but less so in the north; arctic-alpine, amphiberingian.

Similar Species: Few-flowered bluegrass (*P. paucispicula*; *P. leptocoma* ssp. *paucispicula, P. merrilliana, P. glacialis*) is a rather delicate plant that differs in its generally **smaller (3–8 cm long) inflorescence** with **smoother branches,** fewer spikelets, **broadly lance-shaped**

glumes and lemmas, and less-hairy lemmas and calluses. It occurs in snowbeds, meadows, rocky slopes and fellfields, in lowland (arctic coast) to alpine zones. An arctic-alpine, amphiberingian species, it is frequent in most of the northern ¾ of the region, from AK, YT and NT south through BC and southwestern AB to northern WA, ID and WY. • **Nodding bluegrass (*P. reflexa*)** has **smooth inflorescence branches**, the **lower branches bent down**, and **glumes nearly equal in length.** It is a cordilleran species, frequent in mesic to dry, open forests, thickets, meadows and on rocky slopes, in subalpine and alpine zones, and is found primarily in the U.S. Rockies, from MT and ID south to AZ and NM.

Notes: *Lepto* means "slender, weak, thin" and *coma* is "hairy-tufted" or "hair-like," probably in reference to the wispy cobwebs on the calluses.

Glaucous Bluegrass • *Poa glauca* ssp. *glauca*

General: Densely tufted, usually glaucous; stems 10–40 cm tall, wiry. **Leaves:** Blades flat or folded, 1–2.5 mm wide. **Flowers:** Inflorescence lance-shaped, contracted to somewhat open, erect, 4–10 cm long; glumes nearly equal; **lemmas glaucous, bronze at tip,** lance-shaped, 2.5–4 mm long, hairy on keels and veins, **hairless or sparsely hairy between veins, usually weakly cobwebby at base,** sometimes hairless; anthers 1.2–2.5 mm long. **Where Found:** Dry, rocky slopes, sandy-gravelly benches, grasslands, stony meadows and fellfields; montane to alpine zones; frequent throughout except the southwestern part of the region; boreal/arctic-alpine, circumpolar.

Subspecies: Timberline bluegrass (*P. glauca* ssp. *rupicola*; *P. rupicola*) is generally **smaller (5–15 cm tall)** with a **smaller (1–5 cm long), narrower inflorescence, lemmas hairy between the veins** but **not cobwebby at the base** and anthers 1–1.6 mm long. It occupies dry, rocky and grassy slopes, often on limestone and often on mountain sheep and mountain goat ranges, in subalpine and alpine zones. This cordilleran subspecies is scattered but sometimes locally frequent from southern YT south (especially in the Rockies) through interior BC and southwestern AB to CA, AZ and NM.

Notes: *Poa* is Greek for "grass" or "pasturage," and is also a Greek name for a fodder grass. Both the species name *glauca* (Latin for "bluish grey") and the common name "bluegrass" refer to the bluish white bloom (as on a ripe plum) on the leaves, stems and spikelets of *P. glauca*.

timberline bluegrass

PLANTS WITHOUT RHIZOMES; LEMMAS NOT COBWEBBY AT BASE

Roughened Bluegrass
Poa scabrella

General: Densely tufted; stems erect, 30–60 cm tall. **Leaves:** Mostly toward base; blades folded or occasionally flat, **1–3 mm wide,** 5–15 cm long, roughened at least along margins; **ligules 3–7 mm long. Flowers: Inflorescence erect, narrow, usually contracted at maturity, lance-shaped,** 5–15 cm long, the **branches ascending-erect;** spikelets 7–10 mm long, with mostly 3–5 florets, **not strongly flattened;** glumes unequal; lemmas 4.5–5 mm long, **rounded on back,** short-hairy below, roughened above, **not cobwebby at base;** anthers 2–3 mm long. **Where Found:** Dry to mesic grasslands, shrublands, meadows and rocky slopes; steppe to lower alpine zones; frequent in the southern ½ of the region, infrequent northward; cordilleran.

Similar Species: Pacific bluegrass or slender bluegrass (**P. gracillima**) has an **open inflorescence** with typically **spreading lower branches** and **flat, lax basal leaves, 0.5–1.5 mm wide.** It occurs in moist meadows, on rocky slopes and streambanks, and along cascades and waterfalls, in montane to alpine zones. Pacific bluegrass is locally frequent in the southern ¼ of the region, from southern BC and southwestern AB to CA, UT and CO. • **Curly bluegrass (P. incurva)** resembles roughened bluegrass but is **smaller (15–30 cm tall),** with **often flat basal leaves, 1–1.5 mm wide,** and **purplish spikelets.** It grows on rocky slopes, ridges and talus, in montane to alpine zones, and is locally frequent in southern BC, WA, ID, MT, WY, OR, CA and NV.

Notes: Roughened bluegrass is also known as *Poa canbyi* and *P. secunda* ssp. *secunda*. • *FNA* considers *P. scabrella, P. gracillima* and *P. incurva* to be part of *P. secunda* ssp. *secunda*. Lumping these 3, plus 3 or 4 other taxa (from ssp. *juncifolia*), into 1 über-species is the contemporary approach and has some experimental support, but it is unsatisfactory for field-savvy naturalists and botanists. • Summertime drought isn't a problem over much of the range of these species. But in Mediterranean-type climates with a pronounced summer drought (as in California), roughened bluegrass will become dormant, awaiting autumn rains. Even watering the plants over summer won't break dormancy.

Cusick's Bluegrass • *Poa cusickii*

General: Densely tufted; stems 10–50 cm tall, erect or reclining at base. **Leaves:** Blades folded to inrolled, 0.5–3 mm wide; ligules 1–3 mm long. **Flowers: Plants mostly dioecious and alpine plants mostly female; inflorescence erect, congested, lance- to egg-shaped, 2–10 cm long;** spikelets 4–10 mm long, with 2–6 florets; **lemmas 4–7 mm long, hairless or minutely hairy on keel and marginal veins toward base, not or only sparsely cobwebby at base;** anthers (if present) vestigial, abortive or 2–3.5 mm long. **Where found:** Meadows and rocky slopes; montane to lower alpine zones; frequent in the southern ½ of the region, infrequent north to southern YT; cordilleran.

Similar Species: Porsild's bluegrass (*P. porsildii*; *P. vaseyochloa*) is also

dioecious but has a **more open inflorescence with laxer branches, usually hairless lemmas** and **male plants often present.** It occurs on turfy, often calcium-rich alpine tundra and heath-lands, and is infrequent in the northern ¼ of the region, endemic to the unglaciated mountains of east-central AK, central YT and the east slopes of the Mackenzie and Richardson mountains in NT.

Notes: Cusick's bluegrass is also known as *Poa epilis, P. purpurascens, P. subaristata* and *P. alpina* var. *purpurascens.* • These 2 species are named for William Conklin Cusick (1842–1922), a peerless plant collector and explorer of the Blue Mountains, and Alf Erling Porsild (1901–77), curator of the National Herbarium of Canada and a prominent student of Canadian flora who collected some 6000 Alaskan specimens in 1926 with his brother Robert.

Alpine Bluegrass • *Poa alpina*

General: Densely tufted; stems 10–40 cm tall, erect or reclining at base. **Leaves:** Mostly near base, the blades flat, thick, short, 2–4.5 mm wide; ligules 1–4 mm long. **Flowers:** Inflorescence erect, congested, open to rather compact, **egg- to pyramid-shaped, 2–6 cm long; spikelets plump, broadly rounded at base in side view, 4–6 mm long,** with 3–7 florets; **lemmas broadly lance-shaped, silky-hairy on keel, marginal veins and between veins, not cobwebby at base,** 3–5 mm long. **Where Found:** Meadows, gravel bars, shores, rocky slopes, fell-fields and tundra, often on disturbed ground; lowland (arctic coast) to alpine zones; frequent throughout all but the south-western corner of the region; low arctic-alpine, circumpolar.

Subspecies: *P. alpina* ssp. *vivipara* has bulbils but has been reported only from AK in our region; it is common in Europe.

Similar Species: Wenatchee bluegrass (*P. curtifolia*) has leaves similar to those of alpine bluegrass, but has a **narrow inflorescence, prominent ligules 2–5 mm long** and **1–3-flowered, lance-shaped spikelets 7–9 mm long.** It occurs on open, rocky (serpentine) slopes in subalpine and alpine zones, and is endemic to the Wenatchee Mtns, WA.

Notes: Alpine bluegrass is one of the easier bluegrasses to identify, especially by the trough-like leaves, which look like something you could use to play jai alai. • There's a lot going on under-ground in alpine environments. In an Austrian study, the microbial community in the soil around the roots (rhizosphere) of alpine bluegrass in recently deglaciated

areas is similar to the community in soils without the grass. However, as alpine bluegrass communities aged, they altered soil properties and also soil microbial communities. Microbial growth and diversity increased, primarily because of decreases in soil pH and carbon-nitrogen ratios. Soil communities shifted from fungal-dominated to bacteria-dominated, and organic matter decomposition rates increased, making additional nutrients available.

Narrow-flowered Bluegrass • *Poa stenantha*

General: Tufted, 25–60 cm tall. **Leaves:** Mostly toward base, inrolled to flat but **soft and lax,** 1–4 mm wide. **Flowers:** Inflorescence open, lower branches typically **spreading to drooping; spikelets compressed, lance-shaped; lemmas distinctly keeled, usually hairless between**

hairy veins, usually with some whiskery hairs at base but **not cobwebby.** **Where Found:** Moist to mesic meadows, cliffs, ravines, waterfall spray zones, glades and rocky slopes; lowland to lower alpine (southern latitudes) zones; frequent along the Pacific coast, less frequent inland to the Rockies; Pacific maritime with interior incursions, disjunct in Patagonia.

Variety: *P. stenantha* var. *vivipara* (pictured above) has bulbil-forming florets and is frequent in the Aleutians.

Lettermann's Bluegrass • *Poa lettermannii*

General: Densely tufted; stems 3–15 cm tall. **Leaves:** Flat or folded, rather thin, 0.5–2 mm wide. **Flowers:** Inflorescence contracted, dense, roughly cylindric, 1–3 cm long, the branches erect-ascending; **spikelets 3–4 mm long,** green or purplish, with 2–3 florets; glumes equalling or exceeding 2 lowest florets;

lemmas lance-shaped, 2.5–3 mm long, usually **hairless, not cobwebby at base; anthers 0.2–0.8 mm long. Where Found:** Rocky slopes, meadows, solifluction lobes and fellfields; subalpine and alpine zones; infrequent in and east of the coastal mountains in the southern ⅔ of the region; cordilleran.

Similar Species: Suksdorf's bluegrass (*P. suksdorfii*) also has narrow, contracted inflorescences, but with **longer (4–6 mm) lemmas and anthers (0.8–1.2 mm).** It is infrequent with a more restricted distribution, occurring on rocky alpine slopes in south-central BC, WA and OR. • **Dwarf bluegrass** (below) also has tight narrow inflorescences, but its **leaves are inrolled and rather thick,** and its **lemmas are longer and hairy.**

Dwarf Bluegrass • *Poa abbreviata*

General: Densely tufted; stems 5–15 cm tall. **Leaves:** Blades inrolled, rather thick, 0.8–1.5 mm wide; upper stem-leaf sheaths sealed less than ¼ of their length. **Flowers:** Inflorescence contracted, dense, lance- to egg-shaped, erect, 1.5–5 cm long, the branches appressed; **spikelets 4–6.5 mm long,** often purplish, with 2–5 florets (rarely bulblet-forming); **glumes**

about equal; lemmas broadly lance-shaped, 3–4.5 mm long, hairy on keels and marginal veins, hairless or minutely hairy between veins, mostly not cobwebby at base (ssp. *marshii* somewhat cobwebby); anthers 0.2–1.2 mm long. **Where Found:** Mesic to moist, rocky slopes, fellfields and turfy tundra, often on limestone; montane to alpine zones; infrequent in the north and along the Rockies; species complex arctic-alpine, interruptedly circumpolar; the mostly arctic ssp. *abbreviata* circumpolar, the alpine ssp. *pattersonii* amphiberingian, the alpine ssp. *marshii* scattered in the Rockies of MT, ID, WY and in northern CA and NV.

Notes: Dwarf bluegrass is also known in part as *Poa jordalii* and *P. pattersonii*.

Short-flowered Bluegrass, Polar Bluegrass
Poa pseudoabbreviata

General: Densely tufted, rather delicate, glaucous; stems 4–20 cm tall. **Leaves:** Upper stem-leaf sheaths closed less than ¼ of their length; blades thin, soft, 0.5–1.5 mm wide, flat or folded. **Flowers:** Inflorescence open, sparse, erect, 2–7 cm long, the branches thin and spreading; spikelets 3–5 mm long, usually purplish, with 2–4 florets (rarely bulblet-forming); **glumes unequal;** lemmas lance-shaped, 2–3 mm long, hairy on keels and marginal veins, **hairless between veins, not cobwebby at base;** anthers 0.2–0.7 mm long. **Where Found:** Dry, rocky slopes and ridges, and frost boils; montane to alpine zones; infrequent in the northern ¼ of the region; arctic-alpine, amphiberingian.

Similar Species: Banff bluegrass (*P. laxa* ssp. *banffiana*) is a more southern plant with **upper stem-leaf sheaths closed more than ¼ of their length, the inflorescence with ascending branches** and **anthers 0.8–1.1 mm long.** It occurs in moist meadows and ridges in the alpine zone and is rare in the Rockies from southeastern BC and southwestern AB south to OR, UT and CO. The species is arctic-alpine and broadly amphi-Atlantic; ssp. *banffiana* is cordilleran.

Notes: Short-flowered bluegrass is also known as *Poa brachyanthera.* • *Poa* is notable not only for its large number of species, but also because most species are polyploids—possessing multiple copies of chromosomes. Only about 30 of the approximately 500 *Poa* species are known to be diploid, with the "usual" number of chromosomes (2 copies of each), and most of these species are European or Asian. Only 3 native species in North America are diploid, including 2 of ours: Lettermann's bluegrass (p. 481) and short-flowered bluegrass. Many of the polyploid species probably arose from crosses among diploid species, a process sometimes called "reticulate evolution."

MYCORRHIZAE

The roots of most vascular plants are intimately associated with fungi, an association called a mycorrhiza ("fungus-root"). The fungal filaments spread through the soil, gathering water and nutrients for the plant, and the plant produces sugars through photosynthesis and shares these with the fungus. These mycorrhizal associations are believed to be most important in harsh environments, such as the alpine. Most plants have many different fungi associated with their roots, and most fungi are likely associated with the roots of numerous plants. This means that most plants in an alpine plant community are connected to most other plants by their underground fungi, and the plants exchange materials through this network.

There are different sorts of associations, different sorts of mycorrhizae. Ericoid mycorrhizae—the only associations with ascomycete fungi—occur in the heather family (Ericaceae, pp. 74–89, 298), in genera such as *Phyllodoce, Kalmia* and *Vaccinium.* A few heather family plants (in the alpine, *Arctostaphylos, Arctous* and *Pyrola*) form arbutoid mycorrhizae with basidiomycete fungi, where the fungus grows around, and into, the plant's roots. Woody shrubs such as birches and willows, as well as *Dryas* and *Polygonum,* form ectomycorrhizae with basidiomycete fungi, where the fungus grows around, but not into, the plant's roots. The fungi in arbutoid mycorrhizae and ectomycorrhizae are sometimes also attached to the roots of nearby coniferous trees, and alpine mushrooms are often the fruiting bodies of these fungi. Most other plant families (including the grasses, Poaceae) form arbuscular mycorrhizae with glomeromycete fungi. As far as we know, members of the families Brassicaceae, Caryophyllaceae, Crassulaceae, Cyperaceae (except *Kobresia*), Gentianaceae and Juncaceae do not form mycorrhizae in the alpine. Some species, for example, willows and conifers, are never found without their mycorrhizal fungi and may require them for survival and growth. Other species can grow with or without mycorrhizae.

Mycorrhizae are important in determining plant succession following glaciation and in structuring plant communities in the alpine (and elsewhere). What's happening aboveground is greatly affected by what's happening belowground.

Ferns & Allies

mountain holly fern (*Polystichum lonchitis*), Babine Mountains, BC

Ferns & Allies

Ferns and their "allies" (horsetails, clubmosses, spikemosses) are vascular plants; that is, they have internal tubes for conducting fluids, in common with all the other plants in this guide. However, they reproduce not by seeds, but by spores (as do bryophytes and fungi). The spores grow in little sacs, usually clumped as **sori** in ferns or grouped in cone-like structures called **strobili** in horsetails, most clubmosses and spikemosses. Spore-bearing vascular plants (also known as **pteridophytes**) tend to be most abundant in moist habitats, though some species—including several of our alpine representatives—have adapted to dry sites.

This heterogeneous group of mostly perennial herbs represents several ancient lineages rooted deep in the mists of time, back to the Carboniferous age when ferns, horsetails and lycopods were dominant trees and humans weren't even a gleam in Gaia's eyes.

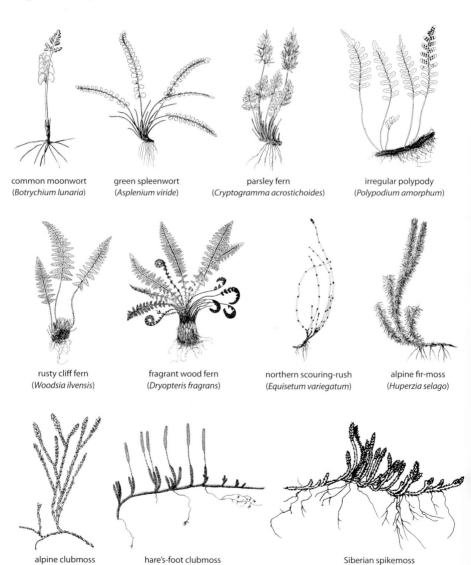

common moonwort
(*Botrychium lunaria*)

green spleenwort
(*Asplenium viride*)

parsley fern
(*Cryptogramma acrostichoides*)

irregular polypody
(*Polypodium amorphum*)

rusty cliff fern
(*Woodsia ilvensis*)

fragrant wood fern
(*Dryopteris fragrans*)

northern scouring-rush
(*Equisetum variegatum*)

alpine fir-moss
(*Huperzia selago*)

alpine clubmoss
(*Diphasiastrum alpinum*)

hare's-foot clubmoss
(*Lycopodium lagopus*)

Siberian spikemoss
(*Selaginella sibirica*)

Key to the Genera of Spore-bearing Herbs (Pteridophytes)

1a. Leaves divided or cleft into many leaflets or lobes on opposite sides of a main axis, feather-like, triangular or fan-shaped (**ferns**)... **2**

2a. Spore sacs spheric, yellowish, in branched clusters on a naked stalk; leaf consists of a green, sterile blade and a spore-bearing branch, both of which arise from a common stem .... ***Botrychium*** (pp. 486–487)

2b. Spore sacs on underside of leaves or on separate, modified, fertile leaves (**true ferns**) **3**

3a. Leaves of 2 very different types, with spore sacs on specialized, fertile leaves; sterile leaves parsley-like .... ***Cryptogramma*** (p. 489)

3b. Leaves all alike, fertile and sterile leaves similar.. **4**

4a. Spore sacs near margins of leaflet, covered (at least when young) by down-rolled edges of leaflet; leaves evergreen **5**

5a. Leaves hairless or sparsely hairy but not woolly; ultimate leaf segments >5 mm long .... ***Pellaea*** (p. 488)

5b. Leaves woolly-hairy on undersurface; ultimate leaf segments <3 mm long, bead-like .... ***Cheilanthes*** (p. 490)

4b. Spore sacs not within rolled leaf margins, either naked or at least partially covered by protective membranes (indusia); leaves withering or evergreen **6**

6a. Clusters of spore sacs (sori) naked, indusia absent or reduced to slender filaments **7**

7a. Leaves usually once pinnately lobed, not cleft or divided all the way to the midrib, evergreen .... ***Polypodium*** (p. 490)

7b. Leaves 1–3 times pinnately divided into leaflets, withering **8**

8a. Leaves small, mostly 5–25 cm long; leaf stalks slender, much narrower than 3 mm; indusia of soon-shrivelling, thread- or ribbon-like segments .... ***Woodsia*** (p. 491)

8b. Leaves larger, to 60 cm long; leaf stalks flattened, >3 mm wide; indusia lacking .... ***Athyrium alpestre*** (p. 493)

6b. Clusters of spore sacs (sori) covered by indusia, at least when young **9**

9a. Indusia elongated, flap-like, attached along 1 side; leaves small, mostly 5–15 cm long .... ***Asplenium*** (p. 488)

9b. Indusia attached at 1 point; leaves often >15 cm long **10**

10a. Indusia circular, attached at centre; leaves evergreen, with spiny-toothed leaflets .... ***Polystichum*** (p. 492)

10b. Indusia attached at side; leaves deciduous or evergreen........................... **11**

11a. Fronds mostly <25 cm long.. **12**

12a. Leaf stalks sparsely scaly, rounded in cross-section; indusia hood-like, delicate, soon shrivelling .... ***Cystopteris*** (p. 492)

12b. Leaf stalks brown-scaly, flattened; indusia kidney-shaped, persistent .... ***Drypoteris fragrans*** (p. 493)

11b. At least some fronds >25 cm tall/long.................................... **13**

13a. Indusia kidney-shaped .... ***Dryopteris*** (p. 493)

13b. Indusia oblong or crescent-shaped .... ***Athyrium filix-femina*** (p. 493)

1b. Leaves narrow, undivided, scale-like or bristle-like (**fern allies**) **14**

14a. Leaves and branches (if present) whorled; stems ribbed and jointed............ ***Equisetum*** (pp. 494–495)

14b. Leaves alternate or opposite; stems not ribbed **15**

15a. Spore clusters in axils of ordinary leaves .... ***Huperzia*** (p. 495)

15b. Spore clusters in axils of specialized leaves in cone-like heads (strobili) **16**

16a. Plants 1–3 cm tall; stems <2 mm thick.................................... ***Selaginella*** (p. 497)

16b. Plants usually >5 cm tall; stems at least 2 mm thick................................... **17**

17a. Leaves <4 mm long, in 4–5 ranks.................... ***Diphasiastrum*** (p. 496)

17b. Leaves usually >4 mm long, in 6–10 ranks .... ***Lycopodium*** (p. 496)

Ferns

The moonworts or grape ferns (*Botrychium* spp.) are small, with fleshy roots and short, vertical, subterranean stems (rhizomes) bearing a single leaf divided into a sterile expanded blade and a fertile, spike- or panicle-like portion. The spore sacs are free (not aggregated in clusters) and short-stalked, stalkless or sunken in the leaf tissue.

The "true" ferns have creeping or erect rhizomes (often very scaly) and stalked, erect or spreading, often large leaves (**fronds**). The leaf blades are curled in bud ("fiddleheads") and are usually lobed, divided or variously compound. Fertile and sterile leaves are most often alike, though they are dissimilar in some genera. The spore sacs are aggregated in **sori**, which are sometimes covered by a membrane called the **indusium.**

| common moonwort (below) | green spleenwort (p. 488) | lace fern (p. 490) | fragile fern (p. 492) | alpine lady fern (p. 493) |

Common Moonwort
Botrychium lunaria

General: Small, hairless, somewhat fleshy herb, from short, erect rhizomes and clustered, fleshy roots; **yellowish green or bluish green,** (2 to) 5–20 cm tall.

Green Leaf Blades: Single, near midstem, **oblong,** 1–10 cm long, **once pinnately divided** into 3–9 pairs of **semicircular to broadly fan-shaped leaflets,** leaflets stalkless or nearly so, usually overlapping.

Spore Clusters: Yellowish, stalkless, **1 mm balls (sporangia)** clustered on branches of long-stalked, **modified (fertile) leaf portion** that is pinnnately divided 1–2 times and arises from **above green, sterile blade,** 0.8–2 times as long as sterile blade.

Where Found: Open forests, meadows, clearings, grassy or turfy slopes, shores and heathlands; montane to alpine zones; widespread but infrequent throughout the region, rare on the coast and in the far north; circumpolar, also in Australia, New Zealand and Patagonia.

Similar Species: Mingan moonwort (B. minganense; *B. lunaria* var. *minganense*) has **narrowly oblong leaf blades,** the leaflets semicircular, fan- or egg-shaped and **not overlapping.** It is found in meadows, clearings and on shores and open slopes, in montane to alpine zones, and is scattered throughout the region, rare on the coast and in the far north.

Notes: Common moonwort is the most widespread of the moonworts, which are odd plants, with lots of lore and allure. English folklore bestowed supernatural powers on common moonwort. It was said to loosen the shoes of horses ridden through it, and supposedly it could be inserted into locks to unlock doors. The spores of moonwort reportedly can even make you invisible. • *Botrychium* is from the Greek *botryose*, "like a bunch of grapes," in reference to the clustered sporangia; these plants are also called "grape ferns." These 2 related species are named *lunaria* for the crescent- or moon-shaped leaflets, and *minganense* for the Mingan Archipelago in the Gulf of St. Lawrence, Québec.

Mingan moonwort

Triangle Moonwort • *Botrychium lanceolatum*

General: Hairless, somewhat fleshy, **dull to shiny, yellowish green to dark green**, 5–25 cm tall. Green Leaf Blades: Single, attached near top of stem, **broadly triangular**, 1–6 cm long, 2–7 cm wide, 1–2 times **pinnately divided** into 2–5 pairs of **linear to lance-shaped, non-overlapping segments**; segments pinnately lobed, **lobes pointy-tipped**. Spore Clusters: **On the several branches of the short-stalked (1–3 cm)**, modified (fertile) leaf portion that is 1–2.5 times as long as the green, sterile blade. Where Found: Rocky slopes, meadows, grassy swales, open forests and heathlands; montane to alpine zones; widespread but infrequent throughout the southern ¾ of the region; circumpolar.

Similar Species: **Pinnate moonwort** (below) has **egg-shaped to triangular leaf blades, the leaflets often overlapping**.

Notes: The gametophytes (see box essay, p. 498) of triangle moonwort live underground and, perhaps unsurprisingly, are not green. So, how do they obtain nutrition? Their rhizoids are attached to filaments of fungi in the genus *Glomus*. These fungal filaments are also attached to the roots of nearby green (photosynthesizing) vascular plants,

and carbon is transferred from the green plants to the moonwort's ghostly gametophytes. The sporophyte produced from the gametophyte also grows underground initially and is similarly colourless. Its rhizoids are attached to the same *Glomus* species. This underground phase can last for up to a decade, during which time the sporophyte is entirely dependent on surrounding green plants for nutrition. Even when the green moonwort sporophytes emerge aboveground, they're often in shady spots and partly mulch-covered, and could still be partially dependent on their underground fungal networks for food. • In the movies, the alabaster-skinned Uma Thurman survived being buried alive (in *Kill Bill 2*) *and* portrayed a green sporophyte, Poison Ivy (in *Batman and Robin*).

Pinnate Moonwort
Botrychium pinnatum

General: Hairless, somewhat fleshy, **shiny, green**, 5–20 cm tall. Green Leaf Blades: Single, attached above midstem, **egg-shaped to triangular**, to 8 cm long and 5 cm wide, 1–2 times **pinnately divided** into up to 8 pairs of **oblong, often overlapping segments**; segments pinnately lobed, **lobes blunt-tipped**. Spore Clusters: On branches of **long-stalked**, modified (fertile) leaf portion. Where Found: Rocky and grassy slopes, meadows, streambanks, open forests and heathlands; montane to alpine zones; widespread but infrequent in the southern ¾ of the region; amphiberingian.

Notes: Pinnate moonwort is also known as *Botrychium boreale* ssp. *obtusilobum*. • *Botrychium* displays the greatest species diversity in the interior north temperate portions of western North America, at moderately high elevations and often in disturbed, open habitats. The moonworts are troublesome taxonomically; they seem to have shape-shifting tendencies, like Raven and Coyote of First Nations legends. Intraspecific variation is large; existing treatments will no doubt change.

Green Spleenwort • *Asplenium viride*

General: Small tufts from short, scaly rhizomes, 5–15 cm tall; some previous year's leaf stalks may persist.

Leaves: Bright green, **soft, not evergreen,** nearly hairless, linear-oblong, **once pinnately divided** into 6–21 opposite or offset **pairs of leaflets, leaflets oval to rhombic,** coarsely round-toothed, **3–8 mm long,** sometimes slightly overlapping; **leaf stalk green,** darkened at base; **leaf axis green.**

Spore Clusters: Several, elongated, **1–2 mm long, taco-like, in arrays along veins** on underside of leaflets, covered by delicate membrane (indusium) attached along 1 edge but shriveling as spore clusters mature.

Where Found: Moist, sheltered, often shady crevices on cliffs, outcrops or talus slopes, on limestone or other calcium-rich bedrock; lowland to alpine zones; widespread but scattered and infrequent in our region; circumpolar with large gaps.

Similar Species: Sinful spleenwort or scarlet-letter spleenwort (**A. adulterinum**) has **brown or purplish brown leaf stalks** and the **leaf axis is brown on the lower part, pale green on the upper ⅓.** It occurs in limestone fissures and on other rocks in the immediate vicinity of limestone, in montane to alpine zones. Sinful spleenwort is rare on Vancouver I. and in the lower Fraser Valley in BC, but is not known elsewhere in North America; it occurs mostly in Europe.

Notes: Green spleenwort is also known as *Asplenium trichomanes-ramosum.* • *Asplenium* is from the Greek *asplenon,* "without spleen," alluding to use of maidenhair spleenwort (*A. trichomanes*) in Europe as a treatment for diseases of the spleen; *viride* means "green."

sinful spleenwort

Brewer's Cliff-brake • *Pellaea breweri*

General: Small, brittle tufts from short, branching rhizomes densely covered with narrow, brown scales, 3–20 cm tall.

Leaves: Firm, **evergreen,** hairless, bluish green, linear-oblong, **pinnately divided** into several to many **pairs of segments or leaflets, lower leaflets deeply 2-lobed (mitten-shaped);** leaf stalks slender, wiry, **brown,** shiny, breaking off well above the ground, leaving **persistent bases marked with a series of prominent, transverse grooves; leaf axis brown in lower part, green above.**

Spore Clusters: At vein ends **along edges of fertile leaflets;** leaflet margins rolled to form **continuous membrane (false indusium)** covering young spore balls.

Where Found: Crevices and niches in dry cliffs and talus slopes, on a variety of rock types including limestone and granite; montane to alpine zones; scattered but locally frequent inland in the southern ¼ of the region.

Similar Species: Smooth cliff-brake (*P. glabella*) has **lower leaflets deeply divided into 3–7 lobes, leaf stalks usually lacking transverse grooves** and the **leaf axis is brown its entire length.** It occurs on calcium-rich (usually limestone) cliffs, crevices and ledges, in steppe to alpine zones. A North American species, it is scattered but locally frequent inland in the southern ½ of the region, in central BC and western AB from about 56° N to WA, ID and MT, and to WY, UT, CO, AZ and NM, disjunct (as ssp. *occidentalis*) in southwestern NT. • **Sierra cliff-brake** (*P. bridgesii*) has once pinnately divided leaves with **unlobed leaflets** and **fertile leaflets with scarcely rolled margins,** the spore clusters thus exposed. It grows on granitic rocks mostly in Sierran CA and adjacent NV, and is disjunct in the Wallowa Mtns of northeastern OR and adjacent central ID.

smooth cliff-brake

Parsley Fern • *Cryptogramma acrostichoides*

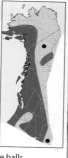

General: Yellowish green, **densely tufted,** from short, scaly rhizomes covered with persistent bases of leaf stalks and with dried leaves of previous year, 5–25 cm tall; **sterile and fertile leaves markedly different.**

Leaves: Sterile leaves **firm, green over winter,** spreading, **2–3 times pinnately divided** into 3–10 pairs of oblong or egg-shaped segments, **ultimate segments lance-shaped, finely toothed; leaf stalks straw-coloured;** fertile leaves erect, exceeding sterile leaves, ultimate segments linear.

Spore Clusters: Eventually covering lower surface of fertile segments, which are rolled so that **margins nearly meet beneath,** forming a **protective pod** (false indusium) covering the young spore balls.

Where Found: Relatively dry, open, rocky sites—cliffs, ledges, crevices, talus slopes—**mostly on acidic rocks;** lowland to alpine zones; widespread in the southern ¾ of the region, frequent on the coast, infrequent inland; amphiberingian.

Similar Species: Sitka parsley fern (*C. sitchensis*; *C. acrostichoides* var. *sitchensis*, *C. crispa* var. *sitchensis*) has **sterile leaves 2–4 times finely pinnately divided,** with egg-shaped, **deeply lobed ultimate segments.** It grows on cliffs, crevices, ledges and talus slopes, in lowland to alpine zones. An endemic species, it is scattered but locally frequent from southern AK, southern YT and southwestern NT to northwestern BC. • **Cascade parsley fern** (*C. cascadensis*) has **thin, withering, sterile leaves, not persisting dried** on the plant. It occurs on dry to mesic cliffs, crevices and talus slopes, often on acidic igneous rocks, in montane to alpine zones, and is infrequent from southern BC to CA, ID and MT, in and east of the Cascade Mtns.

Sitka parsley fern

Cascade parsley fern

Notes: Parsley fern is also known as *Cryptogramma crispa* var. *acrostichoides*. • The Stl'atl'imc ate the raw roots of parsley fern to cure colds. • *Cryptogramma* is Greek for "hidden line," referring to the covered marginal sporangia.

Slender Rock-brake • *Cryptogramma stelleri*

General: Scattered or a few together along a slender, long-creeping rhizome; 5–20 cm tall; **sterile and fertile leaves different but not markedly so. Leaves:** Sterile leaves **thin, membranous, withering by late summer,** erect, **1–2 times coarsely pinnately divided** into egg- to fan-shaped segments; **leaf stalks dark brown on lower half, greenish above;** fertile leaves erect, **exceeding sterile leaves, ultimate segments lance-shaped,** rolled under rather like the leaves of Labrador tea (p. 89). **Spore Clusters: On lower surface of fertile segments,** which are rolled to form continuous **marginal covering. Where Found:** Sheltered, at least seasonally moist, rocky sites often within coniferous forests—cliff crevices, ledges, talus, canyons, cave mouths, waterfall spray zones—**on calcium-rich rocks;** lowland to alpine zones; widespread but infrequent in the northern ¾ of the region; interruptedly circumpolar.

Notes: This plant is called "rock-brake" because it was believed to "brake" up its rocky habitat. • The species name honours Georg Wilhelm Steller (1709–46), a German naturalist who travelled to Siberia and Alaska as a member of Bering's expedition and was the first European to collect Alaskan plants.

Lace Fern • *Cheilanthes gracillima*

General: Small clusters 5–25 cm tall, from short rhizomes; **sterile and fertile leaves alike.**

Leaves: Linear-oblong in outline, **evergreen,** somewhat leathery, **2–3 times pinnately cleft into many ultimate segments or leaflets,** leaflets oblong, **bead-like, 0.5–3 mm long, cinnamon-felted and scaly on underside; leaf stalks dark brown.**

Spore Clusters: **Continuous along margins of lower surface of leaflet,** partly covered by rolled margins (false indusium).

Where Found: Dry cliffs, crevices, outcrops and talus slopes, usually on acidic igneous rocks; lowland to subalpine zones; scattered but locally frequent in the southern ¼ of the region; southern cordilleran.

Similar Species: Lace fern perhaps could be mistaken for a cliff-brake (*Pellaea*) or a parsley fern or rock-brake (*Cryptogramma*), but their leaflets aren't so small (lace fern's are less than 3 mm long) and aren't woolly-hairy beneath.

Notes: Ferns and allies have the highest chromosome numbers of any living organisms. A chromosome count from an adder's-tongue fern (*Ophioglossum*) is reported to have been over 1000. For all plants, the average number of chromosomes is 16. Homosporous ferns average about 57, clubmosses average about 86, and for all the horsetails surveyed so far, the average chromosome number is 108. It's not clear if these high numbers represent ancient polyploidy (multiple copies of chromosomes), or if these plants simply started out with lots of chromosomes. • *Cheilanthes* means "lip-flower," from the Greek *cheilos*, "margin," and *anthos*, "flower," because of the marginal spore clusters; *gracillima* means "very slender" or "most graceful."

Irregular Polypody • *Polypodium amorphum*

General: Scattered or a few together on scaly, bitter-tasting, often glaucous rhizome.

Leaves: Firm, **evergreen,** hairless, 5–20 cm tall, oblong, **pinnately cleft into several to many oblong segments with smooth, parallel edges and blunt or rounded tips;** leaf stalks slender, straw-coloured.

Spore Clusters: **Circular when immature,** in 2 rows on both sides of midrib, at vein tips **toward margins of leaf segments,** lacking protective membrane (indusium); fertile spore balls (sporangia) mixed with **numerous (more than 12) dark, glandular, sterile sporangia.**

Where Found: Crevices and ledges on cliffs and outcrops, usually on igneous rock; lowland to alpine zones; infrequent in the southwestern part of the region; primarily Cascadian.

Similar Species: **Western polypody** (*P. hesperium*) has **oval spore clusters when immature,** located **midway between the margins and the midrib of the leaf segments,** which are oblong to linear-lance-shaped and **blunt to pointy-tipped; sterile sporangia are few or lacking** from spore clusters. It occurs on cliffs, crevices and talus slopes, usually not calcium-rich, in montane to upper subalpine zones. A cordilleran species, it is infrequent in the southern ½ of the region, in central BC from about 56° N and southwestern AB to CA, AZ and NM.

Notes: Irregular polypody is also known as *Polypodium montense*. • Western polypody evidently originated from hybridization between irregular polypody and licorice fern (*P. glycyrrhiza*), followed by chromosome doubling (i.e., allotetraploidy). • *Polypodium* means "many feet," in reference to the numerous knobby bumps or stubby branches on the rhizome.

western polypody

Alpine Cliff Fern • *Woodsia alpina*

General: **Small tufts** from a slender, short rhizome covered with scales and a cluster of **old leaf stalks**; 3–20 cm tall; **sterile and fertile leaves alike.**

Leaves: Narrowly lance-shaped, **2 times pinnately cleft into oval to fan-shaped, entire or blunt-toothed segments,** sparsely hairy below; leaf stalks brittle, **jointed above base at swollen nodes, reddish brown to dark purple when mature, persistent;** leaf axis sparsely scaly and hairy.

Spore Clusters: Rounded, in rows between midrib and margins of ultimate segments, **scantily covered** by centrally attached, encircling **indusium of narrow, hair-like segments** that soon shrivel.

Where Found: Moist, sheltered cliffs, crevices, ledges and talus slopes; lowland (arctic coast) to alpine zones; infrequent in the northern ⅓ of the region; arctic-alpine, circumpolar.

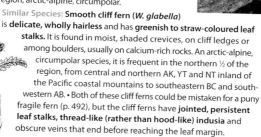

Similar Species: Smooth cliff fern (*W. glabella*) is **delicate, wholly hairless** and has **greenish to straw-coloured leaf stalks.** It is found in moist, shaded crevices, on cliff ledges or among boulders, usually on calcium-rich rocks. An arctic-alpine, circumpolar species, it is frequent in the northern ½ of the region, from central and northern AK, YT and NT inland of the Pacific coastal mountains to southeastern BC and southwestern AB. • Both of these cliff ferns could be mistaken for a puny fragile fern (p. 492), but the cliff ferns have **jointed, persistent leaf stalks, thread-like** (rather than hood-like) **indusia** and obscure veins that end before reaching the leaf margin.

Notes: Pteridomania or "fern fever" broke out in mid-19th-century Britain, when cliff ferns came under attack from Victorian fern collectors. John Sadler, later a curator of the Royal Botanic Garden in Edinburgh, nearly perished while collecting ferns on a cliff. In 1861, William Williams, a botanical guide, was reaching for an alpine cliff fern in Wales when he plunged to his death. Reportedly, the search party found his body beneath the cliff where the species was first collected. Revenge of the ferns!

smooth cliff fern

Rusty Cliff Fern
Woodsia ilvensis

General: **Small tufts** from a short rhizome covered with scales and cluster of **old leaf stalks;** 5–25 cm tall.

Leaves: **Abundantly hairy and scaly,** oblong-lance-shaped, **2 times pinnately cleft into lance-oblong, entire or shallowly lobed segments;** leaf stalks **jointed** above base, **brown to dark purple when mature, persistent.** Spore Clusters:
Rounded, in rows between midrib and margins of ultimate segments, with **indusium of narrow, hair-like segments** that soon shrivel. Where Found: Dry, exposed cliffs, outcrops, crevices, ledges and talus slopes, on a variety of rock types but typically on more acidic rocks; montane to alpine zones; scattered but locally frequent in the northern ½ of the region, infrequent southward; circumpolar.

Notes: A tetraploid hybrid of rusty cliff fern and smooth cliff fern (above) evidently gave rise to alpine cliff fern. • *Woodsia* honours English botanist Joseph Woods (1776–1864).

Fragile Fern • *Cystopteris fragilis*

General: **Delicate tufts** from a slender, short rhizome covered with scales and old, withered leaf stalks, **hairless;** 5–30 cm tall; **sterile and fertile leaves alike.**

Leaves: Lance-shaped, **2–3 times as long as wide,** tapered at both ends, **2–3 times pinnately cleft into many irregularly toothed**

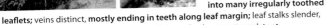

leaflets; veins distinct, **mostly ending in teeth along leaf margin;** leaf stalks slender, brittle, mostly **green to straw-coloured,** darkened at base, **not persistent.**

Spore Clusters: Small, **circular dots on veins on lower leaf surface,** partly covered by delicate, membranous, **hood-like indusium** that soon shrivels.

Where Found: Dry to moist, sheltered to exposed cliffs, crevices and ledges, rock outcrops, talus slopes and rocky forest edges; lowland to alpine zones; frequent throughout the region; cosmopolitan.

Notes: Fragile fern is also known as *Cystopteris dickieana.* • Broadly distributed, very variable and successful over a wide range of elevations, "fragile" fern seems to be remarkably tough when it counts.

Mountain Holly Fern • *Polystichum lonchitis*

General: **Clumped** from a short, stout rhizome covered with scales and old, withered leaf stalks, ascending-erect, **10–50 cm long/tall;** sterile and fertile leaves alike.

Leaves: Evergreen, leathery, once pinnately divided into many asymmetric, pointed, oblong leaflets with spreading, spine-tipped teeth along margins, lowest leaflets triangular; leaflets all in 1 plane; leaf stalks short, densely scaly.

Spore Clusters: Large, circular, in 2 rows halfway between leaflet midvein and margins, mostly covered by **round, centrally attached, membranous umbrella** (indusium).

Where Found: Rocky slopes, open, rocky forests, scree and talus, often on calcium-rich substrates; montane to alpine zones; frequent throughout the southern ⅔ of the region; interruptedly circumpolar.

Notes: Although in our region you may be most familiar with low-elevation species such as sword fern (*P. munitum*), *Polystichum* species worldwide are primarily mountain plants with a fondness for talus.

Kruckeberg's Holly Fern • *Polystichum kruckebergii*

General: **Small clusters** from a short, stout rhizome, ascending-erect, **10–25 cm tall;** sterile and fertile leaves alike. **Leaves:** Evergreen, leathery, once pinnately divided into pointed, egg-shaped leaflets, with coarse, spreading, **spine-tipped teeth along margins; leaflets twisted out of plane of leaf;** leaf stalks short, sparsely scaly. **Spore Clusters:** Large, circular, in 2 rows halfway between midvein and margins of leaflets, mostly covered by **round, centrally attached membrane** (indusium). **Where Found:** Dry to mesic cliffs, rocky slopes, outcrops and talus, **especially ultrabasic (serpentine) rock;** montane to alpine zones; infrequent and scattered in the southern ⅓ of the region, rare northward.

Notes: Kruckeberg's holly fern is thought to be the allotetraploid product of hybridization between mountain holly fern (above) and Shasta holly fern (*P. lemmonii*), which is also restricted to serpentine rock. • This species is named for Arthur R. Kruckeberg (1920–), a geobotanist, naturalist, gardener and bassoonist.

Alpine Lady Fern
Athyrium alpestre var. *americanum*

General: **Medium-sized clumps** from a short rhizome, ascending-erect, **20–60 cm long.**

Leaves: **Numerous,** narrowly elliptic to lance-shaped, **3 times pinnately divided into oblong segments,** margins minutely round-toothed; **leaves somewhat three-dimensional, appearing kind of crinkled,** as if scorched by fire.

Spore Clusters: Large, circular to elliptic, in 2 rows near margins of leaflets; **protective membrane (indusium) lacking** or tiny.

Where Found: Moist cliff bases, talus, boulder fields and rocky meadows; montane to alpine zones; infrequent in the southern ⅓ of the region, rare northward; mostly western cordilleran, also in eastern Canada and Greenland.

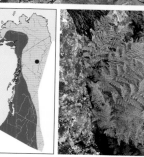

Similar Species: **Lady fern (*A. filix-femina* var. *cyclosorum*)** is **larger** (to 1.5 m tall) with **broader, flatter leaves, less-crowded segments** and **oblong to crescent-shaped indusia.** It grows in moist meadows, thickets, open forests, streambanks and avalanche tracks, in lowland to alpine zones (only occasionally at high elevations), and is frequent throughout the southern ¾ of the region.

Notes: Alpine lady fern is also known as *Athyrium distentifolium* ssp. *americanum.* • *Athyrium* is from the Greek *athyros*, "without a shield" or "doorless," perhaps because the indusium is lacking (as in alpine lady fern) or ultimately forced open by sporangia (as in lady fern).

Fragrant Wood Fern
Dryopteris fragrans

General: **Small, dense cluster** from a short, stout rhizome, erect, **5–30 cm tall;** old fronds form **persistent, curled, shrivelled clump at base.**

Leaves: **Numerous, evergreen, leathery,** narrowly lance-shaped, **2 times pinnately divided into lance-oblong, somewhat overlapping segments,** margins pinnately incised or round-toothed; **glandular, aromatic when handled, densely scaly.**

Spore Clusters: Large, circular, in 2 rows between leaflet midvein and margins; **protective membrane (indusium) large, kidney-shaped,** glandular, often overlapping.

Where Found: Dry, rocky slopes, outcrops, cliff ledges and talus slopes, often on calcium-rich substrates; lowland to lower alpine zones; locally frequent in the northern ⅓ of the region; circumpolar.

Similar Species: **Spiny wood fern** or spreading wood fern (***D. expansa***; *D. assimilis, D. dilatata* in part, *D. austriaca* of some authors) is **larger (to 1 m tall),** with **broadly triangular, 3 times pinnately divided leaves** that are usually **not glandular.** It occurs in moist meadows, thickets, forests, streambanks and avalanche tracks, in lowland to alpine zones (only occasionally at high elevations), and is frequent throughout the southern ¾ of the region.

Horsetail Family (Equisetaceae)

The horsetails are perennial herbs with rhizomes and erect, usually hollow, regularly jointed (like bamboo), ribbed stems impregnated with silica and harsh to the touch. Slender, green branches (which could be mistaken for leaves) and tiny leaves occur at the conspicuous nodes. The scale- or tooth-like leaves are united by a sheath, and they usually lack chlorophyll (though the stems and branches are green and photosynthetic). Spore-bearing cones (**strobili**) are produced atop the stems.

Branched equisetums are called "horsetails" because they resemble a horse's tail, whereas the unbranched species are called "scouring-rushes" because the rough, rush-like stems were used by early Europeans to scour pots and utensils made of wood and pewter.

Common Horsetail, Field Horsetail
Equisetum arvense

General: Perennial from dark, spreading **rhizomes with tubers,** appearing in **2 growth forms: fertile stems brownish, fleshy, unbranched,** 10–30 cm tall; **sterile stems green, bottlebrush-like** with whorls of slender branches, 15–60 cm tall.

Leaves: Reduced to **small scales,** 8–12 **fused into sheaths around stems,** smaller and in whorls of 3 on branches.

Spore Clusters: In **long-stalked, round-tipped cones** 2–4 cm long atop fertile stems.

Where Found: Forests, thickets, meadows, streambanks, floodplains, wetlands, shores, seepage areas and disturbed ground; lowland to alpine zones; frequent throughout the region; widespread, mostly in the Northern Hemisphere.

Notes: The rhizome tubers were collected by northern groups (Dena'ina, Inupiat and others) just after the snow melted and eaten raw and peeled, with or without lard. Sweet and juicy, they were considered a treat because they are too small to make harvesting in quantity worthwhile. • The plants were burned and the ashes placed on sores. The root was heated and placed against aching teeth. Juice from the boiled stems was drunk by the Gitxsan (northern scouring-rush, below) and the Okanagan, Nlaka'pamux and Secwepemc (common horsetail), to treat bladder and kidney problems and as a diuretic.

Northern Scouring-rush
Equisetum variegatum

General: **Evergreen perennial** from branching, blackish rhizomes; **stems 10–50 cm tall, 1–3 mm thick, unbranched, straight or somewhat curved;** central cavity ¼ of stem diameter. Leaves: Reduced to **small scales, fused into sheaths around stems,** the sheaths with **3–14 teeth.** Spore Clusters: In **short-stalked,** 5–10 mm long, **pointy-tipped cones.** Where Found: Wet to moist shores, gravel bars, streambanks, roadsides, ditches, fens, seepage areas and tundra; lowland to alpine zones; frequent in most of the region; circumpolar.

Notes: Horsetails are homosporous—they produce only one type of spore. The gametophyte that germinates from that spore, then, can produce both male and female sex organs. Yet genetic evidence suggests that self-fertilization is uncommon. It turns out that some species initially produce gametophytes with only male or female bits. If cross-fertilization is not forthcoming, they become bisexual and fertilize themselves. • As plants get older, they become tough, and the rough stems were used by coastal and interior peoples as a type of sandpaper to smooth and polish surfaces, especially wooden objects such as canoes, dishes, arrow shafts and gambling sticks.

Dwarf Scouring-rush, Swimmer's Dink
Equisetum scirpoides

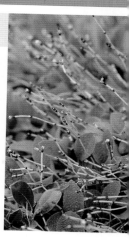

General: Evergreen from short, slender, brownish rhizomes, **stems spreading to ascending, 3–20 cm long/tall, wiry, 1–1.5 mm thick, unbranched, kinked or zig-zag,** lacking central cavity. **Leaves:** Fused into sheaths around stems, the sheaths with **3 teeth.** Spore clusters: In **2–3 mm long, pointy-tipped cones** atop stems. Where Found: Coniferous forests, bogs, fens, swamps, seepage areas and tundra; lowland (arctic coast) to alpine zones; frequent in the northern ¾ of the region; circumpolar.

Notes: The single genus *Equisetum* is all that's left of Class Equisetopsida, which dominated Earth's vegetation for more than 100 million years. Some horsetail relatives, such as the fossil genus *Calamites*, were trees 20–30 m tall. Imagine horsetail trees in the time of dinosaurs!
• "Dink" is slang for penis; "swimmer's dink" because the stems are shrivelled like a brash man's penis in a tarn.

Clubmoss Family (Lycopodiaceae)

The clubmosses are not true mosses, but rather evergreen herbs with creeping or tufted, branched stems covered by rows or spirals of small, narrow, scale-like but green leaves. They have **sporangia** (spore cases) in terminal cones (strobili) or in leaf axils. Clubmosses and spikemosses are lycopods, the oldest living division of vascular plants, with a fossil record dating back 410 million years.

Alpine Fir-moss, Fir Clubmoss • *Huperzia selago*

General: Evergreen perennial from short rhizomes, yellow-green to olive green, stems solitary or more often in clusters of 2–10, often forming **tight, flat-topped tufts,** ascending to erect from a usually curved base, **simple or 2-forked,** 5–20 cm tall.

Leaves: Crowded in 8 ranks, lance- or egg-shaped, broadest at base, 4–6 mm long, appressed to stem or spreading, firm, pointy-tipped.

Spore Clusters: **At base of ordinary-looking leaves, in bands throughout mature portions of shoots,** alternating with bands of sterile leaves (fertile leaves produced early in season, followed by sterile leaves).

Where Found: Forests, rocky glades, bogs, cliffs, talus, boulders, rocky slopes, waterfall spray zones, heathlands and tundra; lowland to alpine zones; widespread but scattered, rarely abundant, throughout the northern ⅘ of the region; circumpolar.

Notes: Alpine fir-moss includes *Huperzia haleakalae, H. miyoshiana, H. chinensis, H. occidentalis* and *Lycopodium selago.* • The western North American representatives of the *H. selago* complex have been variously disposed over the years. *FNA* recognizes 3 species in our region: *H. haleakalae* has ascending leaves and looks more worm-like than pipe-cleaner-like; *H. miyoshiana* has nodding juvenile stems; and *H. occidentalis* has dark green, wide-spreading leaves and is typically a plant of lower elevations. There is probably a fourth entity in the region, *H. selago* in a restricted, North American sense: yellow-green, with gemmae (reproductive buds) in numerous whorls. Until the taxonomy and ecology of these forms is clarified, we use *H. selago* in the broad sense. • Traditional Chinese herbal medicine has long used clubmosses to treat a variety of diseases related to deficiencies in the neurotransmitter acetylcholine (ACTH). Polish doctors reportedly used alpine fir-moss in the 1940s to treat glaucoma, which is also related to ACTH deficiency. Alpine fir-moss contains the alkaloid huperzine, shown to enhance learning and memory in lab animals. Studies continue into using huperzine A, an acetylcholinesterase inhibitor, to treat the symptoms of myasthenia gravis and Alzheimer's disease. Huperzine A has now been produced in culture, which should speed up commercialization and reduce the picking pressure on wild populations of alpine fir-moss.

Alpine Clubmoss • *Diphasiastrum alpinum*

General: Evergreen perennial from horizontal stems creeping on soil or rock surface, or shallowly buried, to 50 cm long, rooting at intervals, sparsely leafy; upright shoots 5–15 cm tall, tufted, forked, with **ultimate branchlets somewhat flatted or 4-angled in cross-section.**

Leaves: Bluish green, in 4 ranks, strongly overlapping, of 3 forms: upper leaves (convex side) lance-shaped; lower (concave side) shorter and trowel-shaped; lateral leaves spreading, with deltoid tips and flange-like bases fused to the branch.

Spore Clusters: Cones stalkless, solitary at branch tips, 1–3 cm long.

Where Found: Dry to moist, timberline tree clumps, glades, rocky slopes, heathlands and tundra; subalpine and alpine zones; frequent throughout the northern ¾ of the region; circumpolar.

Similar Species: Sitka clubmoss (*D. sitchense;*** *Lycopodium sitchense*)** has **ultimate branchlets that are round in cross-section** and

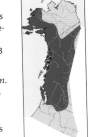

light green, non-overlapping, 5-ranked leaves that are all similar. It occurs in open forests, krummholz, glades, rocky slopes, rocky bogs and heathlands, in montane to alpine zones. This amphiberingian species is frequent in the southern ½ of the region, rare northward, from southern coastal AK and northwestern BC south to OR and west to AB and northwestern MT.

Notes: Alpine clubmoss is also known as *Lycopodium alpinum.* • During the Late Carboniferous Period (315–305 million years ago), areas such as Pennsylvania and Wales were covered by dense, tropical swamp-forests known as the "coal forests." Dominant plants in these forests were giant, tree-sized lycopods to 40 m tall. • Clubmoss spores have been used to stop bleeding,

Sitka clubmoss

as baby powder, to line condoms, as a flammable powder for flash photography and to increase urine flow and treat diarrhea.

Hare's-foot Clubmoss, One-cone Clubmoss
Lycopodium lagopus

General: Evergreen from horizontal stems creeping on the ground, to 1 m long, rooting at intervals, sparsely leafy, branched; **upright shoots 5–20 cm tall,** clustered, irregularly 2–4-branched, with numerous leaves.

Leaves: Medium green, crowded, ascending to appressed, linear-lance-shaped, hair-tipped.

Spore Clusters: Cones short-stalked, solitary at branch tips, 2–6 cm long; cone leaves tapering to hair-like tips.

Where Found: Open forests, roadsides, timberline tree clumps, glades, rocky slopes and heathlands; montane to alpine zones; infrequent mostly in the northern ½ of the region, sporadic southward; circumpolar.

Similar Species: Stiff clubmoss or bristly clubmoss (**L. annotinum**) also has **single spore cones** atop upright shoots, but the **cones are unstalked,** the **shoots unbranched or 1–2-branched** and the **leaves dark green and lacking hairy tips.** It occurs in forests, krummholz, thickets, glades and heathlands, in lowland to subalpine zones, and is an amphiberingian species frequent in most of the region.

Notes: Hare's-foot clubmoss is also known as *Lycopodium clavatum* var. *lagopus* and var. *monostachyon.* • Clubmosses sometimes form well-marked "fairy rings," which are especially noticeable in open, high-elevation heathlands. The rings can be 1 to 4 m wide, grow radially outward, and the clubmosses mostly die within. In upstate New York, researchers found increased nutrient availability and enzymatic activity under the fairy rings, evidently related to endophytic fungi in the clubmosses and the subsequent decomposition of soil organic matter. • *Lycopodium* is from the Greek *lycos,* "wolf," and *podus,* "foot," and *lagopus* means "hare's foot"; both names refer to the fancied resemblance of the branch to a wolf's paw or a rabbit's foot.

Spikemoss Family (Selaginellaceae)

The spikemosses are much like the clubmosses, but spikemosses are usually considerably smaller, with cones that are sharply 4-angled (not round) in cross-section, and they produce 2 kinds of spores—big megaspores and much smaller microspores.

Siberian Spikemoss, Northern Spikemoss
Selaginella sibirica

General: Evergreen perennial forming **intricately branched, long-spreading or occasionally cushion-like mats** 5–20 cm across; stems creeping to reclining, irregularly forked, **1–3 cm tall.**

Leaves: In **tight spirals, linear-lance-shaped, 2–3.5 mm long,** green, **thick, firm,** tippe+d with **whitish bristle less than 1 mm long,** margins fringed.

Spore Clusters: Cones stalkless, solitary and erect at branch tips, 4-sided, 5–25 mm long; spores in axils of triangular, egg-shaped bracts with fringed margins and bristly tips.

Where Found: Dry, rocky and grassy slopes, boulders, outcrops and crevices, rocky meadows, gravelly ridges and tundra; montane to alpine zones; frequent in the northern ⅓ of the region, mostly inland; amphiberingian.

Similar Species: The *S. densa* complex is the southern analogue of *S. sibirica.* The 3 taxa involved are **Rocky Mountain spikemoss (S. densa),** with spore cone bracts hairy from base to tip; **cliff spikemoss (S. scopulorum;** *S. densa* var. *scopulorum*), with spore cone bracts lance-shaped and fringed only at the base; and **Standley's spikemoss (S. standleyi;** *S. densa* var. *standleyi*), with spore cone bracts oval to triangular and fringed only at the base. They all are mat-forming but discretely branched, and have leaves tending to be **longer (2.5–5 mm) than those of Siberian spikemoss,** with bristle tips longer than 1 mm. They occur in habitats similar to those of Siberian spikemoss, in steppe to alpine zones, and are frequent mostly in the southern and southeastern parts of our region, from southern BC and AB to CA, UT and NM.

Notes: All plants in this Ferns & Allies section, except spikemosses (*Selaginella* species), produce spores of one size and type—they are homosporous. Spikemosses produce spores of 2 sizes and types—they are heterosporous. *Selaginella* species produce 4 larger megaspores in each megasporangium and numerous microspores in each microsporangium. Look closely at your spikemoss cone: the lower sporangia are lumpy and yellowish (megasporangia), whereas the upper sporangia are smoother and orange (microsporangia). Unlike ferns, horsetails and clubmosses, spikemosses have no free-living gametophyte stage; eggs and sperm are produced *inside* the megaspores and microspores. The microspore wall cracks, and the sperm swim out to find cracks in the megaspore wall (and the eggs within).

cliff spikemoss

LIFE CYCLES OF VASCULAR PLANTS

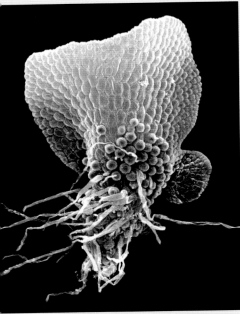

fern gametophyte showing antheridia and rhizoids

All vascular plants have 2 life stages. One is a conspicuous stage—the **sporophyte**. These are the plants described in this book. The other stage is less conspicuous—the **gametophyte**.

Sporophytes are diploid—that is, they have 2 sets of chromosomes like you, our readers. The gametophytes are haploid, with only a single set of chromosomes—like your eggs or sperm. The sporophytes produce spores by meiosis, a process in which the 2 sets of chromosomes are reduced to one. These haploid spores produce the gametophytes.

In seed-producing plants—all the plants in this book except for this section—the gametophyte generation is greatly reduced, short-lived and entirely contained within the sporophyte. For these plants, the gametophyte is part of the life cycle of pollen grains and ovules. Here, the pollen grains germinate on a stigma and produce a pollen tube that grows down the style to the ovule, following which the sperm nuclei migrate from the pollen grain down the tube to the ovule. (Interestingly, spikemosses, along with quillworts and some aquatic ferns, also lack a free-living gametophyte stage, and in this they resemble seed plants.)

But for ferns and allies, except spikemosses, the gametophyte (sometimes called a prothallus) is a separate, free-living stage. Some are green and produce their own food, whereas others are colourless and acquire nutrients by other means. Gametophytes are small—typically 2 to 5 mm wide—and usually heart-shaped, with rhizoids (root-like hairs) beneath and sex organs above. Some live aboveground and some underground. The sex organs are called archegonia (female) and antheridia (male), and produce eggs and sperm. Haploid sperm swim to the haploid eggs and fertilize them, producing a diploid zygote. (The requirement of water for sperm to swim in may explain why these plants often grow in wet places.) This diploid zygote grows into a sporophyte, and the cycle is complete.

Sitka clubmoss

GLOSSARY

Page numbers refer to diagrams in which the word is illustrated.

achene: a small, dry, one-seeded, nut-like fruit

allelopathic: producing biochemicals that inhibit the growth of other plants

allotetraploid: a tetraploid organism in which the polyploid condition is produced by chromosome doubling following hybridization

alluvial: composed of deposits laid down by flowing water

alternate: situated singly at each node (p. 503); compare **opposite**

amphiberingian: found on both sides of the Bering Strait

amphibious: living both on land and in water; especially referring to plants that begin growing underwater and continue on land after the water has receded or evaporated

annual: living for only one year; compare **biennial, perennial**

anther: the pollen-bearing part of a stamen

apex: the tip (e.g., of a leaf) (p. 503)

apical: at the apex or tip

apomixis: a general term for various kinds of asexual, vegetative reproduction in plants, including rhizomes, stolons, bulbils or plantlets, and the production of seeds without sex (i.e., asexual reproduction via seeds that contain a false embryo, cloned from the mother plant's tissues, with no pollen or father plant involved)

appressed: closely pressed against something, as leaves against a stem

arctic slope: northernmost Alaska and Yukon, sloping down from arctic mountains (Brooks Range, Richardson Mountains) to the Beaufort Sea; also known as the **North Slope**

arcuate: curved like a bow, arched; typically refers to veins

armed: having spines, prickles or thorns

ascending: growing obliquely upward

auricle: a small, earlobe-shaped appendage, often at the base of an organ (pp. 453, 503)

awn: a slender, bristle-shaped appendage (p. 453)

axil: the angle between a leaf and the stem (p. 503)

axillary: arising from an axil

axis: the central longitudinal line about which the parts of a plant are arranged

Leaf Shapes

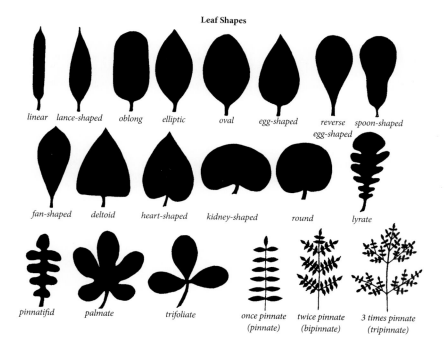

linear lance-shaped oblong elliptic oval egg-shaped reverse egg-shaped spoon-shaped

fan-shaped deltoid heart-shaped kidney-shaped round lyrate

pinnatifid palmate trifoliate once pinnate (pinnate) twice pinnate (bipinnate) 3 times pinnate (tripinnate)

banner: the upper, usually enlarged petal of a flower, as found in the pea family (Fabaceae); also called a **standard** (p. 243)

basal: at the base

beak: a firm, prolonged, slender tip on a thicker organ such as a fruit or seed

beard: a clump of hairs

berry: a pulpy fruit, fleshy throughout, with immersed seeds

biennial: living for 2 years, usually flowering and producing fruit in the second year; compare **annual, perennial**

bilaterally symmetric: divisible vertically into equal halves (typically referring to flowers); compare **radially symmetric**

biodiversity: the full range of life in all its forms—including genes, species and ecosystems—and the ecological processes that link them

biomass: the total weight of living organisms in an area

bipinnate: twice pinnate, with leaflets again pinnate (p. 499)

bisexual: having both male and female sex organs; perfect

blade: the broad, flat part of a leaf or petal (below, p. 453)

bloom: a whitish, often waxy powder on the surface of a plant

bog: an acidic, peat-covered wetland

bract: a reduced or specialized leaf subtending a flower or associated with a flower cluster; in conifers, an appendage of the central stalk of a cone

bracteole, bractlet: a small bract

bryophyte: a plant of the group Bryophyta; a liverwort, moss or hornwort

bulb: a short, vertical, thickened underground shoot with thickened leaves or leaf-bases (e.g., an onion)

bulbil: a small, bulb-like reproductive structure, often located in a leaf axil or replacing a flower

buzz-pollination: a technique employed by bumblebees and some solitary bees in which the rapid movement of flight muscles dislodges pollen by sonicating the anthers

calcareous: calcium-rich; soil rich in lime

callus: the firm, thickened base of the lemma in some grasses

calyx (*pl.* calyces): all the sepals of a flower, collectively

cambium: vascular cambium is the tissue that produces the conducting tubes (xylem and phloem) in plants

canopy: the upper branches of the trees in a forest; a closed canopy conceals the ground when viewed from above

capsule: a dry fruit that splits open at maturity and is composed of more than one carpel

carpel: regarded as a fertile leaf bearing undeveloped seed(s); one or more carpels join to form a pistil

catkin: a cylindric cluster of numerous small flowers, usually of a single sex, that lack petals but usually have subtending bracts (as in willows, alders, birches) (p. 56)

caudex: stem-base; the persistent, thickened base of an otherwise herbaceous stem of a perennial plant

cauline: on the stem

chaffy: thin, dry, scaly, bran-like

channelled: marked with at least one deep, lengthwise groove

chloroplast: a flattened body containing chlorophyll

cilium (*pl.* cilia): a tiny, hair-like outgrowth

circumboreal: occurring in the boreal zone around the Northern Hemisphere

circumpolar: occurring in the polar region around the Northern Hemisphere

clambering: trailing over the ground

clasping: embracing or surrounding, usually refers to a leaf-base around a stem

claw: the stalk-like base of some petals (below)

cleft: cut about halfway to the midrib or base, or a little deeper; deeply lobed

climax: a relatively stable community of plants and animals, dominant in a given locality as long as conditions remain stable

clone: a group of plants that has originated by vegetative reproduction from a single individual

cold-air ponding: the accumulation of cold air in lower, often depressional, topographic areas

Section of a Fireweed Flower
(a regular flower with an inferior ovary)

column: the prominent central structure of an orchid flower, comprised of the fused stamens, style and stigma

compound: divided into smaller, separate parts (e.g., leaves divided into leaflets or flower clusters divided into smaller clusters)

coniferous: bearing its reproductive organs in cones

cordilleran: here used to indicate occurrence in the mountains of western North America

corm: a short, vertical, thickened, underground stem without thickened leaves

corolla: all the petals of a flower, collectively

cortex: the tissue in a root or stem between the epidermis and vascular tissue

creeping: growing along (or beneath) the surface of the ground and emitting roots at intervals, usually at nodes

crenate: scalloped, edged with rounded teeth

crisped: irregularly curled or rippled along the edges

culm: the stem of a graminoid (grass-like plant) (p. 453)

cyanobacteria: photosynthetic bacteria (sometimes incorrectly called "blue-green algae")

cylindric: shaped like a cylinder

deciduous: falling after the completion of its normal function, often at the approach of a dormant season (typically referring to leaves or petals); compare **persistent**

decoction: a solution prepared by boiling an animal or plant substance in water

decumbent: reclining or lying flat on the ground, but having ascending tips

dehiscence: the act or method of opening, as in fruits, anthers or spore capsules

dehiscent: opening by definite pore(s) or along regular line(s) to discharge seeds or spores

dichotomous: branching into 2 equal parts, like a "Y"

dicotyledon, dicot: a seed plant in which the seedling has 2 cotyledons or seed leaves (includes most families of flowering plants); most have leaves with net veins; compare **monocotyledon, monocot**

dimorphic: occurring in 2 forms, as in ferns with both sterile and fertile leaves

dioecious: producing male and female flowers (or other reproductive structures) on separate plants; compare **monoecious**

diploid: having 2 sets of chromosomes in each cell

disc floret: a flower with a tubular corolla found in plants of the aster family (Asteraceae) (p. 339); compare **ray floret**

disjunct: separated, referring to plant populations that are separated (distant) from all other populations of that species

dissected: deeply cut into segments or lobes

distylous: having 2 flower forms: one with short styles and long stamens, and another with short stamens and long styles; compare **homostylous**

"doghair" stand: a very dense stand of spindly coniferous trees, often lodgepole pine

drupe: a fleshy or pulpy, one-seeded fruit in which the seed has a stony covering (e.g., a cherry)

drupelet: a small drupe, usually many in a cluster (e.g., a raspberry)

ecotone: a transitional area between 2 different ecosystems

elfinwood: dwarf forests or clumps of stunted trees near treeline

elliptic: shaped like an ellipse; widest in the middle with rounded ends (p. 499)

emergent: coming out from; often referring to plants that are partly submerged in water

endemic: growing only in a particular geographic area

endophyte: a fungus or bacterium that lives between the cells of living plants

entire: without indentation or division

exserted: protruding; projecting beyond an envelope

fascicle: a small bundle or cluster

fellfield: rocky habitat on exposed summits, plateaus and ridges, with patchy (less than 50%) cover of low-growing plants and abundant surface rocks

felsenmeer: a level or gently sloping expanse of moderate to large blocks of broken rock, shattered by intensive frost action

fen: a mineral-rich wetland with slow-moving, often alkaline water with sedge and mostly brown moss (not *Sphagnum*) peat

fibrous roots: slender, fibre-like roots, usually numerous and clumped

fiddlehead: the young, coiled leaf of certain ferns

filament: the stalk of a stamen; supports the anther

fleshy: plump, firm and pulpy; succulent

floret: a tiny flower, usually part of a cluster; usually applied to single, specialized flowers in the grass (Poaceae) or aster (Asteraceae) family (p. 339)

flowerhead: a dense cluster of tiny flowers (florets), often appearing as a single flower; found in plants of the aster family (Asteraceae) (p. 339)

follicle: a dry, single-carpel fruit that splits at maturity along one side only

forb: a broad-leaved, non-woody plant that dies back to the ground after each growing season

frond: a fern leaf

fruit: the seed-bearing product of a plant; a mature ovary, together with any other structures that ripen with it as a unit

galea: part of the corolla or calyx shaped like a hood or helmet

gametophyte: a plant that produces sexual reproductive structures: in ferns and allies, separate and free-living (p. 498), in other vascular plants contained within the sporophyte; compare **sporophyte**

geophyte: a perennial plant that reproduces by buried bulbs

gland: a bump, appendage or depression on a plant's surface that secretes a sticky or greasy, viscous fluid

glandular-hairy: having gland-tipped hairs

glaucous: covered with a white, waxy powder (bloom) that can be rubbed off

globose: shaped like a sphere

glume: one of 2 empty bracts at the base of a grass spikelet (p. 453)

glycoside: a chemical compound in which a sugar is bound to a non-carbohydrate compound, often an alcohol or phenol

graminoid: an herbaceous plant with narrow, parallel-veined leaves and inconspicuous flowers with scale-like bracts; includes grasses (Poaceae), rushes (Juncaceae) and sedges (Cyperaceae)

gynobasic: flowers in which the style arises directly from the receptacle between the lobes of the ovary

haploid: having a single set of chromosomes in each cell

haustorium (*pl.* haustoria): the portion of a parasitic plant or fungus that penetrates the host's tissue and derives nutrients from it

helicoid: spirally coiled, unrolling with maturity

hemiparasite: a green plant that obtains nutrients via parasitism but also manufactures its own food through photosynthesis

herb: a plant without woody aboveground parts, the stems dying back to the ground each year

herbaceous: herb-like

homostylous: having styles all of approximately the same length; compare **distylous**

horizon: a soil layer parallel to the surface with characteristics different from those of the layers above and beneath

humus: the organic constituent of soil; all dead organic material on and in the soil that undergoes decomposition, change and synthesis

hybrid: an individual that is the offspring of parents of different kinds (usually different species); a cross-breed of 2 different species

hybridization: the process of creating a hybrid

hydathode: a tissue in leaves that secretes water through pores, often leaving a crystallized residue of salts, sugars or other compounds

hypanthium: a ring or cup around the ovary, formed by the union of the lower parts of the sepals, petals and stamens

hypermaritime: cool, very humid climates and vegetation immediately adjacent to and strongly influenced by the ocean

hypha (*pl.* hyphae): tiny, multicellular fungal threads that make up the main body of a fungus or lichen

igneous rock: rock that has solidified from lava or magma

incurved: curved upward and inward

indusium (*pl.* indusia): in ferns, an outgrowth covering and protecting a spore cluster (p. 506)

inferior ovary: an ovary located below the point of attachment of the petals, sepals and stamens

inflated: swollen, puffed out or bladdery

inflorescence: a flower cluster

insectivorous: feeding on insects

internode: the portion of a stem between 2 nodes (p. 453)

introduced: a new element in the flora of a region, brought in from elsewhere

involucre: a set of bracts beneath an inflorescence (as in Asteraceae and Apiaceae)

irregular flower: a flower with petals, or less often sepals, dissimilar in form or orientation (e.g., orchids); compare **regular flower**

keel: a sharp or conspicuous longitudinal ridge, like the keel of a boat; the 2 partly united lower petals of many species of the pea family (Fabaceae) (p. 243)

krummholz: dwarf, bushy trees at treeline, stunted and twisted by exposure to winter cold, desiccation and abrasion by windblown snow, often layering at the base

lanceolate: lance-shaped, much longer than wide, widest below the middle and tapering to both ends (p. 499)

lateral: on the side of

latex: the milky juice of some plants, containing rubber-like compounds

layering: vegetative reproduction in which branches droop to the ground and root

leader: the terminal shoot of a tree

leaflet: a single segment of a compound leaf

legume: the fruit of a pea family (Fabaceae) plant, composed of a single carpel, typically dry and splitting down both seams; a plant of the pea family

lemma: the lower of the 2 bracts immediately enclosing an individual grass flower (p. 453); compare **palea**

lenticel: a slightly raised pore on root or stem bark

ligule: the flat, usually membranous projection from the top of the sheath of a grass (p. 453); the strap-shaped corolla of a ray flower in the aster family (Asteraceae) (p. 339)

linear: very long and narrow with essentially parallel sides (p. 499)

lip: a projection or expansion of something, such as the lower petal of an orchid or violet flower

loam: a loose-textured soil consisting of a mixture of sand, silt, clay and organic matter

lobe: a rounded division of a leaf (p. 503)

loment: a jointed legume that is usually narrowed between seeds

lycopod: a plant in the Division Lycopodiophyta (clubmosses, spikemosses and quillworts)

lyrate: pinnatifid with the terminal lobe largest and rounded (p. 499)

marsh: a nutrient-rich wetland periodically inundated by slow-moving or standing water, characterized by emergent vegetation on mineral soils

mesic: characterized by medium moisture supplies, neither very wet nor very dry

Leaf Characteristics

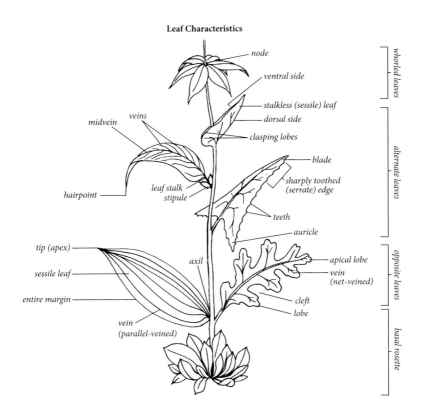

midrib: the central rib of a leaf

midvein: the central vein of a leaf (p. 503)

monocotyledon, monocot: a seed plant in which the seedlings have one cotyledon or seed leaf (includes orchids, lilies, grasses, rushes and sedges); most have leaves with parallel veins; compare **dicotyledon, dicot**

monoculture: a single species comprising the vegetation of a tract of land

monoecious: producing male and female flowers (or other reproductive structures) in separate flowers or cones on the same plant; compare **dioecious**

montane: on or of the mountains

moraine: a mass of rocks and earth (till) deposited beneath and along the edges of a glacier

mucilaginous: sticky; producing gummy or gelatinous substances

mycorrhiza (*pl.* mycorrhizae): the symbiotic association of fungi with the roots of plants

mycotrophic: plants that obtain all or part of their nutrients from fungi

naked: lacking hairs

naturalized: an introduced species that has adapted to the environment of a region

nectary: a gland that secretes nectar, usually associated with a flower

nerve: a prominent longitudinal line or vein in a leaf or other organ

net-veined: with a network of veins; compare **parallel-veined**

nivation: the removal by meltwater of sediments around a snowfield or snowbank, resulting in a depression or shallow basin

node: the place where a leaf or branch is attached; a joint (pp. 453, 503)

nunatak: a mountaintop protruding from an icefield

nut: a hard, dry, usually one-seeded fruit that does not open at maturity; larger and thicker-walled than an achene

nutlet: a small nut; a very thick-walled achene

oblique: an angle of leaf attachment between 0° and 90° to the stem

oblong: shaped more or less like a rectangle with rounded corners (p. 499)

offset: a short shoot arising near the base of a plant; usually propagative in function

opposite: situated across from each other, not alternate or whorled (p. 503); situated directly in front of organs of another kind

outcross: cross-fertilize; to introduce new genetic material into a breeding line

outwash: the stratified drift deposited by streams of meltwater flowing away from a glacier

oval: broadly elliptic (p. 499)

ovary: the expanded basal part of a pistil containing the young, undeveloped seeds (p. 500)

palea: the upper of the 2 bracts immediately enclosing an individual grass flower (p. 417); compare **lemma**

palmate: typically referring to leaves; divided into 3 or more lobes or leaflets diverging from a common point, like the fingers of a hand (p. 499); compare **pinnate**

panicle: a branched flower cluster blooming from the bottom up (below)

papilla (*pl.* papillae): a tiny, wart-like or nipple-shaped projection

papillose: having papillae

pappus: the hairs or bristles on the tip of an achene, especially in the aster family (Asteraceae) (p. 339)

parallel-veined: with veins running parallel to one another, not branching to form a network; compare **net-veined**

perennial: growing for 3 or more years, usually flowering and producing fruit each year; compare **annual, biennial**

Types of Flower Clusters (Inflorescences)

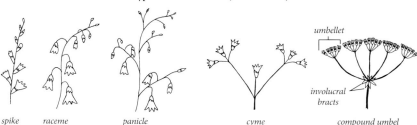

spike   raceme   panicle   cyme   compound umbel

perfect flower: a flower with both male and female functional reproductive organs; bisexual

perfoliate: with a leaf or bract that clasps the stem and is apparently pierced by it

perianth: the sepals and petals of a flower, collectively

periglacial: close to, or recently exposed by, retreating glaciers

perigynium (*pl.* perigynia): the inflated sac enclosing the achene of a sedge (p. 417)

persistent: remaining attached after normal function has been completed; compare **deciduous**

petal: a member of the inside ring of modified flower leaves, usually white or brightly coloured (p. 500)

petiole: a leaf stalk

photosynthesis: the process by which green plants produce their food (carbohydrates) from water, carbon dioxide and minerals, using the sun's energy

phytogeography: the study of the geographic distribution and relationships of plants

pinna (*pl.* pinnae): the primary division of a pinnate leaf or frond

pinnate: a compound leaf with leaflets on each side of a common axis (p. 499); compare **palmate**

pinnatifid: pinnately cleft halfway to the middle (p. 499)

pinnule: the secondary or ultimate leaflet or division of a pinnately compound leaf or frond (p. 506)

pistil: the female organ of a flower, usually consisting of an ovary, style and stigma (p. 500)

plane: flat

pod: a dry fruit that opens to release its seeds

pollinium (*pl.* pollinia): a waxy mass of many pollen grains transported as a unit during pollination (e.g., orchids)

polyploid: having more than 2 sets of chromosomes in each cell

pome: a fruit with a core (e.g., an apple)

poultice: a moist mass of plant material applied to a sore or inflamed part of the body

prostrate: growing flat along the ground

raceme: an unbranched cluster of stalked flowers on a common, elongated central stalk, blooming from the bottom up (p. 504)

radially symmetric: developing uniformly on all sides, like spokes on a wheel; compare **bilaterally symmetric**

rank: a row (e.g., a vertical row of leaves on a stem)

ray floret: a flower with a flattened, strap-like corolla, found in flower clusters of the aster family (Asteraceae), often radiating from the edge of the flowerhead (p. 339); compare **disc floret**

receptacle: the end of a stem to which the flower parts are attached

recurved: curved downward or backward (usually referring to leaf margins)

reflexed: abruptly bent or turned back or down

refugium (*pl.* refugia): a localized ice-free area where plants survived a period of continental glaciation isolated from other plant populations by ice

regular flower: a flower in which the members of each circle of parts (or at least the sepals and petals) are similar in size, shape and orientation; a radially symmetric flower; compare **irregular flower**

rhizomatous: having rhizomes

rhizome: an underground, creeping stem that is distinguished from a root by the presence of nodes and buds or scale-like leaves

riparian: of or pertaining to a river

rosette: a cluster of organs (usually leaves) arranged in a circle or disc, often at the base of a plant

runner: a slender, horizontally spreading stem on the ground, usually rooting at nodes or tips; see also **stolon**

samara: a dry, usually one-seeded, winged fruit (e.g., a maple or ash fruit)

saprophyte: a plant that obtains its nutrition by processing dead organic matter

scree: rock debris mantling a mountain slope, with pieces potato- to pea-sized; includes loose material lying on slopes without cliffs; compare **talus**

scurvy: a disease caused by the lack of vitamin C in the diet, characterized by swollen and bleeding gums

senescent: aging or growing old

sepal: a member of the outermost ring of modified flower leaves, usually green and somewhat leafy in texture (p. 500)

septum: a membrane separating 2 cavities; in an ovary, separating the walls of adjacent carpels (chambers)

serotinous: appearing, blooming or producing leaves late in the season; often applied to the cones of evergreens that remain unopened until high temperatures (e.g., wildfires) melt their resins, opening the scales

serrate: sawtoothed; having sharp, forward-pointing teeth (p. 503)

sheath: an organ that partly or completely surrounds another organ, as the sheath of a grass leaf surrounds the stem (p. 453)

shrub-carr: a shrub-dominated wetland with mineral soils

silicle: a short silique, not much longer than wide

silique: a pod-like, 2-chambered capsule of certain members of the mustard family (Brassicaceae), much longer than wide

simple: not divided or subdivided

solifluction: the slow creep downslope of waterlogged or saturated soils and rocks over an impermeable surface such as permafrost or bedrock

solifluction lobe: a tongue-shaped feature formed by more rapid solifluction on certain sections of a slope; typically having a steep front and a gentle upper surface

sorus (*pl.* sori): a cluster of small spore cases (sporangia) on the underside of a fern leaf

spatulate: shaped like a spatula or like a long section through a pear; rounded at the tip and rounded but narrower at the base (p. 499)

spike: a somewhat elongated inflorescence with unstalked flowers on a common axis (p. 417)

spikelet: a small or secondary spike; the floral unit, or ultimate cluster, especially of a grass or sedge inflorescence (pp. 417, 453)

sporangium (*pl.* sporangia): a spore case

spore: a reproductive body with one to several cells produced in a capsule (mosses) or sporangium (ferns and allies), and capable of giving rise to a new plant

sporophyll: a spore-bearing leaf

sporophyte: the spore-bearing part or phase of a plant (p. 498); in vascular plants, the conspicuous leafy plant; compare **gametophyte**

spreading: diverging widely from the vertical, becoming almost horizontal

spur: a hollow, sac-like or tubular appendage on a petal or sepal, usually functioning as a nectary

stamen: the pollen-bearing (male) organ of a flower, consisting of an anther and a filament (p. 500)

staminodium (*pl.* staminodia): a modified, sterile stamen

stand: a group of growing plants (especially trees) of the same type

standard: the upper, usually enlarged petal of a flower, as found in the pea family (Fabaceae); also called a **banner** (p. 243)

stigma: in plants, the receptive tip of the female organ (pistil) where the pollen lands (p. 500)

stipule: a leaf-like appendage at the base of a leaf stalk (p. 503)

Pinnate Fern Leaf (Frond)

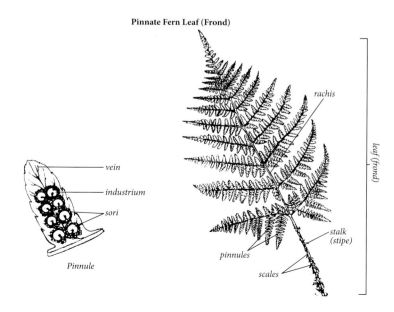

vein

industrium

sori

Pinnule

rachis

leaf (frond)

stalk (stipe)

pinnules

scales

stolon: a horizontally spreading stem or runner on the ground surface, usually rooting at nodes or tips; see also **runner**

stoloniferous: having stolons

stoma, stomate (*pl.* stomata): a tiny opening in the epidermis of a plant, bounded by a pair of guard cells that can close off the opening by changing shape

striate: marked with fine, parallel ridges

strobilus (*pl.* strobili): in ferns, a cone-like cluster of leaves bearing sporangia (sporophylls)

style: the neck, or middle part, of a plant's female organ, connecting the stigma and ovary (p. 500)

substrate: a surface on which something grows

subtend: to be directly below and close to

succession: the process of change in an ecosystem's composition and structure over time

succulent: fleshy and juicy; a plant that stores water in fleshy stems or leaves

superior ovary: an ovary located above the point of attachment of the petals, sepals and stamens of a flower

suture: a seam or line of fusion; usually applied to the vertical lines along which a fruit splits open

swale: a low, moist tract of land

swamp: a wetland with a permanently waterlogged subsurface, periodically inundated by standing or gently moving water, and nutritionally intermediate between a bog and a fen

talus: coarse, often loose, rocky debris at the foot of a cliff or rock wall, with pieces fist-sized and larger; compare **scree**

tannin: a brownish white, astringent polyphenolic compound extracted from plants and used in the manufacture of leather

taproot: a primary, descending root

tepal: a sepal or petal, when these structures cannot be differentiated (e.g., in lilies)

tephra: fragmental material produced by the eruption of a volcano

terminal: located at the end or tip

terrane: a once-mobile fragment of the earth's crust, broken off from a tectonic plate

tetraploid: having 4 sets of chromosomes in each cell

throat: the opening of a corolla or calyx of fused petals or petal-like sepals; in grasses, the upper part of a leaf sheath

till: unstratified, non-sorted glacial drift; a deposit of gravel, boulders, sand, silt and clay, transported and laid down by glaciers with little or no transportation or sorting by water

tomentum: a matted covering of woolly hairs

torulose: cylindric or ellipsoid and constricted at intervals

trailing: lying flat on the ground, but not rooting

trifoliate: having 3 leaves

tripinnate: 3 times pinnate (usually referring to leaves), with leaflets twice divided (p. 499)

tuber: an underground thickening, usually at the end of a rhizome, which serves in food storage and often also in reproduction; sometimes loosely applied to tuberous roots

tubercle: a small swelling or stubby projection on an organ

tuberous: thickened like a tuber

tussock: a compact tuft of grasses or sedges

umbel: an often flat-topped flower cluster in which the flower stalks arise from a common point, much like the stays of a reversed umbrella (p. 504)

umbellet: one of the clusters in a branched (compound) umbel (p. 504)

unarmed: without spines, prickles or thorns

understorey: the vegetation growing below the main canopy of a forest

utricle: a small, thin-walled, one-seeded, bladdery fruit

vegetative reproduction: producing new plants from asexual parts (e.g., rhizomes, leaves, bulbils); the offspring are genetically identical to the parent plant

vermifuge: a remedy that destroys intestinal worms

viviparous: able to reproduce asexually by producing vegetative plantlets or bulbils

whorl: a ring of 3 or more similar structures (e.g., leaves around a node on a stem) (p. 503)

wing: a thin, flat extension or projection from the side or tip; one of the 2 side petals in a flower of the pea family (Fabaceae) (p. 243)

wintergreen: having leaves that remain green through winter but die the following summer; also, some species of *Gaultheria* and *Pyrola*

withe: a slender, flexible branch or twig

REFERENCES

Field Guides and Semi-technical References

Buckingham, N.M., E.G. Schreiner, T.N. Kaye, J.E. Burger and E.L. Tisch. 1995. *Flora of the Olympic Peninsula*. Northwest Interpretive Association and Washington Native Plant Society, Seattle, WA.

Bush, C.D. 1990. *The Compact Guide to Wildflowers of the Rockies*. Lone Pine Publishing, Edmonton, AB.

Clark, L.J. 1973. *Wildflowers of British Columbia*. Gray's Publishing, Sidney, BC.

Clark, L.J., and J.G.S. Trelawney. 1975. *Wild Flowers of the Mountains in the Pacific Northwest*. Gray's Publishing, Sidney, BC.

Collet, D.M. 2002. *Willows of Southcentral Alaska*. U.S. Fish & Wildlife Service and Kenai Watershed Forum, Soldotna, AK.

Craighead, J.J., F.C. Craighead Jr. and R.J. Davis. 1963. *A Field Guide to Rocky Mountain Wildflowers*. Houghton Mifflin, Boston, MA.

Dorward, D.M., and S.R. Swanson. 1993. *Along Mountain Trails (and in Boggy Meadows): A Guide to Northern Rocky Mountain Wildflowers*. Boggy Meadows Press, Ketchum, ID.

Duft, J.F., and R. Moseley. 1989. *Alpine Wildflowers of the Rocky Mountains*. Mountain Press Publishing, Missoula, MT.

Earle, S., and J. Lundin. 2008. *Idaho Mountain Wildflowers: A Photographic Compendium*. 2nd ed. Edited by J.L. Reveal. Larkspur Press, Boise, ID.

Ells, J., and M. Borneman. 2012. *Rocky Mountain Wildflowers*. Colorado Mountain Club Press, Golden, CO.

Flygare, H. 2012. *A Field Guide to Alpine Wildflowers of the Rocky Mountains*. Harbour Publishing, Madeira Park, BC.

Fries, M.A. 1970. *Wildflowers of Mount Rainier and the Cascades*. Mount Rainier Natural History Association and the Mountaineers, Seattle, WA.

Gadd, B. 2009. *Handbook of the Canadian Rockies*. Corax Press, Jasper, AB.

Jennings, N.L. 2007. *Alpine Beauty: Alpine and Subalpine Wildflowers of the Canadian Rockies and Columbia Mountains*. Rocky Mountain Books, Surrey, BC.

Kershaw, L., A. MacKinnon and J. Pojar. 1998. *Plants of the Rocky Mountains*. Lone Pine Publishing, Edmonton, AB.

Manning, H., B. Spring and I. Spring. 1979. *Mountain Flowers*. The Mountaineers, Seattle, WA.

Mathews, D. 1988. *Cascade-Olympic Natural History: A Trailside Reference*. Raven Editors and Portland Audubon Society, Portland, OR.

Nelson, R.A. 1992. *Handbook of Rocky Mountain Plants*. 4th ed. Revised by R.L. Williams. Roberts Rinehart Publishers, Niwot, CO.

Nicholls, G. 2002. *Alpine Plants of North America: An Encyclopedia of Mountain Flowers from the Rockies to Alaska*. Timber Press, Portland, OR.

Phillips, H.W. 2012. *Central Rocky Mountain Wildflowers*. Falcon Guides, Helena, MT.

Phillips, H.W. 2012. *Northern Rocky Mountain Wildflowers*. Falcon Guides, Helena, MT.

Porsild, A.E., and D.T. Lid. 1974. *Rocky Mountain Wild Flowers*. National Museums of Canada and Parks Canada, Ottawa, ON.

Pratt, V.E., and F.G. Pratt. 1993. *Wildflowers of Denali National Park*. Alaskakrafts, Anchorage, AK.

Pyle, R.M. 1995. *Where Bigfoot Walks: Crossing the Dark Divide*. Houghton Mifflin, New York, NY.

Roemer, H. 2010. *Alpine Flowers of Vancouver Island*. Distributed through islandalpineflowers.ca.

Schreier, C. 1996. *A Field Guide to Wildflowers of the Rocky Mountains*. Homestead Publishing, Moose, WY.

Scotter, G.W., and H. Flygare. 1986. *Wildflowers of the Canadian Rockies*. Hurtig Publishers, Edmonton, AB.

Soper, J.H., and A.F. Szczawinski. 1976. *Mount Revelstoke National Park Wildflowers*. National Museums of Canada, Ottawa, ON.

Stewart, C. 1994. *Wildflowers of the Olympics and Cascades*. Nature Education Enterprises, Port Angeles, WA.

Strickler, D. 1990. *Alpine Wildflowers: Showy Wildflowers of the Alpine and Subalpine Areas of the Northern Rocky Mountain States*. The Flower Press, Columbia Falls, MT.

Taylor, R.J., and G.W. Douglas. 1995. *Mountain Plants of the Pacific Northwest: A Field Guide to Washington, Western British Columbia, and Southeastern Alaska*. Mountain Press Publishing, Missoula, MT.

Tracy, D., and D. Giblin. 2011. *Alpine Flowers of Mount Rainier*. Distributed through www.flowersofrainier.com.

Trelawny, J.G. 2003. *Wild Flowers of the Yukon, Alaska and Northwestern Canada*. 2nd ed. Harbour Publishing, Madeira Park, BC.

Turner, M., and P. Gustafson. 2006. *Wildflowers of the Pacific Northwest*. Timber Press, Portland, OR.

Visalli, D., D. Ditchburn and W. Lockwood. 2004. *Northwest Mountain Wildflowers*. Hancock House Publishers, Surrey, BC.

Weber, W.A. 1976. *Rocky Mountain Flora*. Colorado Associated University Press, Boulder, CO.

Willard, B.E., and M.T. Smithson. 1989. *Alpine Wildflowers of the Rocky Mountains*. Rocky Mountain Nature Association, Estes Park, CO.

Wingate, J.L., and L. Yeatts. 1995. *Alpine Flower Finder: The Key to Wildflowers Found Above Treeline in the Rocky Mountains*. Roberts Rinehart Publishers, Boulder, CO.

Technical References

Arno, S.F. 1984. *Timberline: Mountain and Arctic Forest Frontiers*. The Mountaineers, Seattle, WA.

Billings, W.D. 2000. "Alpine Vegetation of North America." In *North American Terrestrial Vegetation* (2nd ed.), eds. M.G. Barbour and W.D. Billings, 537–72. Cambridge University Press, Cambridge, UK.

Bostock, H.S. 1948. *Physiography of the Canadian Cordillera, with Special Reference to the Area North of the Fifty-fifth Parallel*. Geological Survey of Canada, Memoir 247. Department of Mines and Resources, Ottawa, ON.

Bowman, W.D., and T.R. Seastedt, eds. 2001. *Structure and Function of an Alpine Ecosystem: Niwot Ridge, Colorado*. Oxford University Press, New York, NY.

Buckingham, N.M., E.G. Schreiner, T.N. Kaye, J.E. Burger and E.L. Tisch. 1995. *Flora of the Olympic Peninsula.* Northwest Interpretive Association and Washington Native Plant Society, Seattle, WA.

Calder, J.A., and R.L. Taylor. 1968. "Systematics of the Vascular Plants." *Flora of the Queen Charlotte Islands, Part 1.* Monograph No. 4. Department of Agriculture Research Branch, Ottawa, ON.

Cannings, S., J. Nelson and R. Cannings. 2011. *Geology of British Columbia.* Greystone Books, Vancouver, BC.

Chadwick, D.H. 1983. *A Beast the Color of Winter: The Mountain Goat Observed.* Sierra Club Books, San Francisco, CA.

Chapin, F.S. III, and C. Körner, eds. 1995. *Arctic and Alpine Biodiversity: Patterns, Causes and Ecosystem Consequences.* Ecological Studies 113. Springer, Berlin.

Clausen, J., D.D. Keck and W. Hiesey. 1940. "Experimental studies on the nature of species. I. Effects of varied envionments on western North American plants." Publ. Carnegie Institute of Washington 520: 1–452.

Cody, W.J. 2000. *Flora of the Yukon Territory.* 2nd ed. NRC Research Press, Ottawa, ON.

Cronquist, A., A.H. Holmgren, N.H. Holmgren, J.L. Reveal, P.K. Holmgren and R.C. Barneby. 1984–1994. *Intermountain Flora.* 6 vols. New York Botanical Garden Press, Bronx, NY.

Daubenmire, R. 1969. "Ecologic plant geography of the Pacific Northwest." *Madroño* 20: 111–28.

Davis, R.J. 1952. *Flora of Idaho.* Wm. C. Brown, Dubuque, IA.

Dorn, R.D. 2001. *Vascular Plants of Wyoming.* 3rd ed. Mountain West Publishing, Cheyenne, WY.

Douglas, G.W., G.B. Straley, D.V. Meidinger and J. Pojar, eds. 1998–2002. *Illustrated Flora of British Columbia.* 8 vols. BC Ministry of Environment, Lands and Parks and BC Ministry of Forests. Crown Publications, Victoria, BC. PDF format available at www.for.gov.bc.ca/hfd/pubs/docs/Mr/MR_IllustratedFlora.htm.

Flora of North America Editorial Committee, eds. 1993–. *Flora of North America North of Mexico.* 30 vols. Oxford University Press, New York and Oxford. Online at floranorthamerica.org.

Franklin, J.F., and C.T. Dyrness. 1973. *Natural Vegetation of Oregon and Washington.* Gen. Tech. Rep. PNW-GTR-008. U.S. Department of Agriculture, Forest Service, Pacific Northwest Research Station, Portland, OR.

Hansen, L.J., and J.R. Hoffman. 2011. *Climate Savvy: Adapting Conservation and Resource Management to a Changing World.* Island Press, Washington, DC.

Hitchcock, C.L., and A. Cronquist. 1973. *Flora of the Pacific Northwest.* University of Washington Press, Seattle, WA.

Hitchcock, C.L., A. Cronquist, M. Ownbey and J.W. Thompson. 1955–1969. *Vascular Plants of the Pacific Northwest.* Vols. 1–5. University of Washington Press, Seattle, WA.

Holland, S.S. 1964. *Landforms of British Columbia: A Physiographic Outline.* Bulletin No. 48. British Columbia Department of Mines and Petroleum Resources, Victoria, BC.

Howe, G.F. 1968. "Seed germination, sea water, and plant survival in the Great Flood." *Creation Research Society Quarterly* XX: 105–12.

Hultén, E. 1968. *Flora of Alaska and Neighbouring Territories.* Stanford University Press, Stanford, CA.

Körner, C. 1999. *Alpine Plant Life: Functional Plant Ecology of High Mountain Ecosystems.* Springer, Berlin.

Körner, C., and E.M Spehn. 2002. *Mountain Biodiversity: A Global Assessment.* The Parthenon Publishing Group, New York, NY.

Kozloff, E.N. 2005. *Plants of Western Oregon, Washington and British Columbia.* Timber Press, Portland, OR.

Kuijt, J. 1982. *A Flora of Waterton Lakes National Park.* University of Alberta Press, Edmonton, AB.

Lackschewitz, K. 1991. *Vascular Plants of West-central Montana: Identification Guide Book.* Gen. Tech. Rep. INT-277. U.S. Department of Agriculture, Forest Service, Intermountain Research Station, Ogden, UT.

Lesica, P. 2002. *Flora of Glacier National Park.* Oregon State University Press, Corvallis, OR.

McKee, B. 1972. *Cascadia: The Geologic Evolution of the Pacific Northwest.* McGraw-Hill, New York, NY.

Moss, E.H. 1983. *Flora of Alberta.* 2nd ed. Edited by J.G. Packer. University of Toronto Press, Toronto, ON.

Parmesan, C. 2006. "Ecological and evolutionary responses to recent climate change." *Annual Review of Ecology, Evolution, and Systematics* 37: 637–69.

Patterson, T.B., and T.J. Givnish. 2004. "Geographic cohesion, chromosomal evolution, parallel adaptive radiations, and consequent floral adaptations in *Calochortus* (Calochortaceae): evidence from a cpDNA phylogeny." *New Phytologist* 161: 253–64.

Pielou, E.C. 1991. *After the Ice Age: the Return of Life to Glaciated North America.* University of Chicago Press, Chicago, IL.

Porsild, A.E., and W.J. Cody. 1980. *Vascular Plants of the Continental Northwest Territories, Canada.* National Museums of Canada, Ottawa, ON.

Savile, D.B.O. 1972. *Arctic Adaptations in Plants.* Monograph No. 6, Department of Agriculture Research Branch, Ottawa, ON.

Schofield, W.B. 1969. "Phytogeography of northwestern North America: bryophytes and vascular plants." *Madroño* 20: 155–207.

Scott, R.W. 1995. *The Alpine Flora of the Rocky Mountains. Vol. 1: The Middle Rockies.* University of Utah Press, Salt Lake City, UT.

Scudder, G.G.E., and N. Gessler (eds.) 1989. *The Outer Shores.* Queen Charlotte Islands Museum Press, Skidegate, BC.

Shafer, A.B.A., C.I. Cullingham, S.D. Côté and D.W. Coltman. 2010. "Of glaciers and refugia: a decade of study sheds new light on the phylogeography of northwestern North America." *Molecular Ecology* 19: 4589–621.

Viereck, L.A., C.T. Dyrness, A.R. Batten and K.J. Wenzlick. 1992. *The Alaska Vegetation Classification.* Gen. Tech. Rep. PNW-GTR-286. U.S. Department of Agriculture, Forest Service, Pacific Northwest Research Station, Portland, OR.

Welsh, S.L. 1974. *Anderson's Flora of Alaska and Adjacent Parts of Canada.* Brigham Young University Press, Provo, UT.

Zwinger, A.H., and B.E. Willard. 1972. *Land Above the Trees: A Guide to American Alpine Tundra.* Harper and Row, New York, NY.

Resources for Plant Names

Avis, W.S., C. Crate, P. Drysdale, D. Leechman, M.H. Scargill and C. J. Lovell (eds.). 1967 and 1991. *A Dictionary of Canadianisms on Historical Principles*. Gage Educational Publishing, Toronto, ON.

Charters, M.L. 2003–2008. *California Plant Names*. www.calflora.net (last updated 2009).

Clark, L.J. 1973. *Wildflowers of British Columbia*. Gray's Publishing, Sidney, BC.

Coffey, T. 1993. *The History and Folklore of North American Wildflowers*. Facts on File, New York, NY.

Gledhill, D. 2002. *The Names of Plants*. 3rd ed. Cambridge University Press, Cambridge, UK.

Grigson, G. 1958. *The Englishman's Flora*. Reprinted in 1987 with introductions by Jane Grigson and W.T. Stearn. Phoenix House, J.M. Dent and Sons, London, UK.

Grigson, G. 1973. *A Dictionary of English Plant Names*. Allen Lane (Penguin Books), London, UK.

Prior, R.C.A. 1879. *On the Popular Names of British Plants: Being an explanation of the origin and meaning of the names of our indigenous and most commonly cultivated plants*. 3rd ed. Frederic Norgate, London, UK.

Shosteck, R. 1974. *Flowers and Plants: An International Lexicon with Biographical Notes*. Quadrangle/The New York Times Book Co., New York, NY.

Stearns, R.P. 2002. *Stearn's Dictionary of Plant Names for Gardeners*. Reprinted and revised version of *A Gardener's Dictionary of Plant Names* (1972). Timber Press, Portland, OR.

Watts, D.C. 2000. *Elsevier's Dictionary of Plant Names and Their Origin*. Elsevier, Amsterdam, Netherlands.

Ethnobotanical References

Andre, A., and A. Fehr. 2002. *Gwich'in Ethnobotany: Plants used by the Gwich'in for Food, Medicine, Shelter and Tools*. Gwich'in Social and Cultural Institute and Aurora Research Institute, Tsiigehtchic and Inuvik, NWT.

Carrier Linguistic Committee. 1973. *Hanuyeh Ghun Utni-i: Plants of Carrier Country*. Summer Institute of Linguistics, Fort St. James, BC.

Gottesfeld, L.M.J. 1991. *Plants That We Use: Traditional Plant Uses of the Wet'suwet'en People*. Kyah Wiget Education Society, Moricetown, BC.

Gottesfeld, L.M.J., and B. Anderson, 1988. "Gitksan traditional medicine: herbs and healing." *Journal of Ethnobiology* 8: 13–33.

Jones, A. 2010. *Nauriat Nigiñaqtuat: Plants That We Eat: From the Traditional Wisdom of the Inupiat Elders of Northwest Alaska*. 2nd rev. ed. University of Alaska Press, Fairbanks, AK.

Kari, P.R. 1991. *Tanaina Plantlore, Dena'ina K'et'una: An Ethnobotany of the Den'ina Indians of Southcentral Alaska*. Alaska Native Language Centre with Alaska Natural History Association and National Park Service, AK.

Marles, R.J., C. Clavelle, L. Monteleone, N. Tays and D. Burns. 2000. *Aboriginal Plant Use in Canada's Northwest Boreal Forest*. Natural Resources Canada and Canadian Forest Service, UBC Press, Vancouver, BC.

People of 'Ksan. 1980. *Gathering What the Great Nature Provided: Food Traditions of the Gitksan*. Douglas and McIntyre, Vancouver, BC, and University of Washington Press, Seattle, WA.

Porsild, A.E. 1953. "Edible Plants of the Arctic." Reprinted from *Arctic: Journal of the Arctic Institute of North America* 6:1.

Schofield, J.J. 1993. *Alaska Wild Plants: A Guide to Alaska's Edible Harvest*. Alaska Northwest Books, Anchorage, AK, and Seattle, WA.

Smith, H.I. 1994–95 (1925–27). *Ethnobotany of the Gitksan Indians of British Columbia*. Unpublished manuscripts prepared for the National Museum of Canada. Revised by B.D. Compton, B. Rigsby and M-L. Tarpent. On file at the Canadian Museum of Civilization, Ottawa, ON.

Turner, N.J. 1995. *Food Plants of Coastal First Peoples*. UBC Press, Vancouver, BC.

Turner, N.J. 1997. *Food Plants of Interior First Peoples*. UBC Press, Vancouver, BC.

Turner, N.J. 1998. *Plant Technology of First Peoples of British Columbia: Including Neighbouring Groups in Washington, Alberta and Alaska*. UBC Press, Vancouver, BC.

Turner, N.J. 2004. *Plants of Haida Gwaii = Xaadaa Gwaay gud gina k'aws (Skidegate) = Xaadaa Gwaayee guu giin k'aws (Masset)*. Sono Nis Press, Winlaw, BC.

Viereck, E.G. 1987. *Alaska's Wilderness Medicines: Healthful Plants of the Far North*. Alaska Northwest Books, Anchorage, AK, and Seattle, WA.

PHOTOGRAPHY CREDITS

All photographs are printed by permission. The numbers refer to pages; the letters indicate the photograph's relative position on the page.

Cherry Alexander: 17b, 20a, 157b, 162e, 403b. **Inger Greve Alsos:** 425a. **Associated Press / François Mori:** 12a. **Allen Banner:** 271f, 471a. **Ryan Batten:** 45a, 193b, 450a, 487b. **Brian Bell:** 211c. **Bruce Bennett:** 129b, 482. **Curtis Björk:** 42b, 59c, 71bd, 76c, 109a, 113c, 115c, 143e, 144a, 159b, 174b, 177c, 189c, 194c, 199c, 206c, 208b, 213d, 217cd, 223abc, 241c, 259c, 268c, 269b, 270c, 271e, 279b, 285a, 287abc, 296c, 297c, 302b, 303, 311c, 315c, 316d, 334b, 342b, 343b, 346c, 350a, 351c, 352b, 354cd, 357d, 362a, 363cd, 367b, 376a, 377b, 381a, 388a, 397d, 401d, 406c, 409d, 422b, 434c, 441ad, 442b, 443a, 446c, 459d, 464d, 468b, 471d, 486b, 488c, 489cd, 493b, 494b. **Frank Boas:** 443b. **Alan Bradshaw:** 206a, 281d, 285c, 305c, 334c, 375c. **Eileen Brown:** 205b, 444b. **Syd Cannings:** 120e. **Gerald D. Carr:** 116c, 127d, 271d, 293a, 458d. **Robert L. Carr:** 422a. **Central Yukon Species Inventory Project (CYSIP):** 54a, 61b. **Adolf Ceska:** 248b, 434a, 439, 452ac, 460c, 466ac. **Alfred Cook:** 68c, 79bc, 81b, 129a, 137a, 172c, 208a, 209d, 228c, 256a, 264c, 276a, 280a, 311a, 379b, 386a, 398a, 399c, 411a, 493d. **Alfred Cook / Laurel Tyrrell:** 110cd, 120d. **Pat Costello / Accent Alaska.com:** 5. **Ian Cumming:** 203a, 256c, 267d, 269d, 274c. **Jerry DeSanto:** 363a. **Joe Duft:** 375a. **Ryan Durand:** 55b. **Jamie Fenneman:** 40b, 176b, 222d, 224d, 228a, 242b, 288b, 419e, 427c, 435c, 449b, 464c, 466e, 472c, 481c, 491d. **Robert Flogaus-Faust:** 322c. **Bob Frisch:** 60c, 73b, 147b, 168b, 202a, 229a, 239b, 304b, 331c, 399b, 402f, 403e. **Andy Fyon:** 70b, 121c, 125a, 356a, 379c. **Ian Gardiner:** 319b, 326a. **Jeremy Gatten:** 284a. **Val George:** 110b. **Rod Gilbert:** 117b, 151b, 226a, 259a, 278a, 305b, 310c, 335b, 338ab, 382a. **Matt Goff:** 481a. **Sherel Goodrich:** 224c. **Tim Hagan:** 148d, 158b, 402j, 410c. **Sheri Hagwood:** 307b. **Kristen Harrison:** 171, 185b. **Harvard University Portrait Collection:** 316c. **R.T. Hawke:** 294b, 346d. **Mike Hays:** 39b, 44c, 45c, 77b, 177a, 212a, 268a, 284c, 285b, 287de, 292c, 337b, 391c, 420d, 480d. **Ivar Heggelund:** 224a, 425b. **Judith Holm:** 250b, 411c, 490c. **Emerenciana Hurd:** 451ab. **David Ingram:** 124a, 405a. **Norm Jensen:** 143b, 197a, 206b, 214c, 280b, 297a, 310b, 323bc, 336, 362c, 409a, 422c, 489a. **Linda Kershaw:** 41a, 46a, 89a, 131, 133b, 146c, 148a, 165a, 195b, 213b, 225a, 257b, 348b, 366ac, 401c, 419d, 429b, 430ac, 436c, 442a, 446b, 459a, 464a, 467b, 473a, 497a. **Martin Kretschmer:** 473b. **Matt Lavin:** 474c. **Franck Le Driant:** 491a. **Chris Lee:** 363b. **Ben Legler:** 43b, 61a, 88a, 111b, 112a, 117d, 176a, 192a, 214b, 254a, 291d, 298a, 316a, 321b, 347b, 401ab, 440a, 486a, 490a, 494c, 496c. **Jouko Lehmuskallio:** 82d, 109c, 128c, 150a, 195d, 260b, 277a, 288a, 311e. **Peter Lesica:** 460a, 474a, 481b. **Robert Lichvar:** 221h. **Ron Long:** 9, 11a, 82c, 115b, 116b, 122b, 144b, 147c, 155b, 158c, 164ab, 174c, 192c, 196ab, 198b, 199b, 216b, 217b, 254c, 256e, 273, 274a, 284b, 302c, 311d, 317d, 319a, 323a, 340, 347d, 356b, 358b, 378bc, 386b, 396b, 403j, 407c, 412a, 413d. **Stein Erik Lunde:** 109b, 222b, 449c, 491c. **Will MacKenzie:** 20b, 41c, 44a, 74b, 76a, 78c, 89b, 108a, 112b, 120ab, 125b, 142a, 143c, 146b, 150c, 151c, 167a, 169a, 182, 185c, 239c, 243, 251a, 301a, 320a, 329c, 332ab, 333a, 357e, 372c, 381b, 385a, 388c, 411b, 418, 425c, 435d, 436ab, 451d, 467c, 478c, 498b. **Andy MacKinnon:** 244c, 329b, 405d, 450c. **Ernie Marx:** 121b, 189a, 245c, 246ab, 254d, 302a, 307a, 314b, 351a, 359b, 390b. **Steve Matson:** 478a. **Gisela Mendel:** 59a, 86gi, 127b, 173b, 403k, 494a. **Scott Mincemoyer:** 69d, 212c, 383a. **James Miskelly:** 297b. **Gary Monroe:** 286c. **Daniel Mosquin:** 286b, 360b. **Gerald Mulligan:** 221abcdefg. **Timm Nawrocki:** 214a. **Robert Norton:** 87b. **Federico Osorio:** 49. **Juri Peepre:** 48e. **Jim Pojar:** 12b, 13, 14ab, 15abc, 16, 18abc, 19, 26, 27, 32, 33a, 34ab, 35a, 37, 40c, 41de, 42a, 43a, 45b, 46b, 47ac, 48abdf, 53ab, 54bc, 55a, 56ab, 58ac, 61c, 62abc, 63abc, 64ab, 65abc, 67bc, 68ad, 71a, 72b, 77a, 80bc, 82ab, 86adh, 113ab, 116d, 119, 126a, 132a, 142b, 145ac, 146d, 147a, 148c, 149ab, 150bd, 153b, 154ab, 155c, 156d, 157a, 158a, 161cde, 162c, 163ab, 165b, 166a, 167c, 168c, 169b, 173c, 175ab, 176c, 186b, 187cd, 191, 192b, 193ac, 194a, 195a, 197b, 198ad, 203b, 207, 211d, 213a, 216de, 225b, 227d, 228b, 237, 240b, 241bd, 247ab, 248a, 252abc, 254b, 255ac, 256bd, 257a, 258, 259b, 260c, 263a, 269ce, 274b, 276bc, 277bc, 278b, 290ab, 291b, 292b, 293b, 299a, 300, 304c, 307c, 311f, 313a, 314d, 321a, 322ab, 324a, 328b, 329d, 337c, 338c, 341b, 343a, 347c, 348a, 350c, 351b, 352a, 353bcd, 357f, 358ac, 364bc, 365c, 367d, 372a, 373b, 374a, 376b, 377a, 379a, 385b, 386c, 392b, 394, 395a, 396c, 399a, 401ef, 402bhi, 403chi, 407b, 410a, 413ce, 414a, 419c, 420c, 423bc, 424c, 425c, 427ab, 428ab, 429a, 431, 435a, 437c, 445a, 446a, 451c, 452b, 457abd, 460b, 462a, 463b, 464b, 465b, 466b, 468a, 469ac, 471bc, 472b, 477a, 478b, 480b, 483, 488d, 489b, 490d, 492e, 493c, 495abc, 496b, 497b. **Igor Pospelov:** 365b, 459b, 463a, 469b. **Dan Post:** 472d. **Richard Ramsden:** 66, 260a, 263b, 283e, 305a, 308, 312, 315b, 378a. **Neil A. Rawlyk:** 414b. **Jim Riley:** 117ae, 118, 156c, 188a, 198c, 344b, 407a. **Anna Roberts:** 40d, 127a, 227a, 236, 346b, 358e, 413b, 416, 419b, 420a, 424a, 457c, 458b, 465a, 466d, 472a, 477bc, 480ac. **Hans Roemer:** 11b, 33b, 39c, 42c, 44b, 47b, 58b, 59b, 60ab, 67d, 69a, 70ac, 74a, 78b, 80a, 86ce, 87a, 115a, 120c, 123a, 124b, 126b, 130b, 13c, 134, 136a, 137c, 141, 144c, 145b, 149cd, 153a, 168e, 173a, 174a, 175c, 183, 184, 189b, 194b, 197d, 199a, 202c, 211a, 213c, 226b, 227b, 239a, 240a, 242a, 244ad, 261ab, 265, 267c, 269a, 271a, 277d, 283ad, 292a, 296a, 298b, 313c, 314c, 317b, 320b, 324b, 325b, 326cd, 327, 328a, 339, 342c, 345, 347a, 353a, 357b, 360c, 364a, 365a, 367ae, 368a, 373ac, 375b, 380, 382c, 388b, 391b, 392c, 396d, 400, 402cdg, 403a, 405c, 406a, 408, 415, 424b, 430b, 437a, 448a, 479b, 487a, 488a, 491b, 492a, 493a. **R.E. Rosiere:** 459c. **Jeffery M. Saarela, Canadian Museum of Nature:** 462b. **Bjørn Erik Sandbakk:** 148b, 440c, 474b. **Al Schneider:** 40a, 69bc, 136cd, 151a, 167b, 209ab, 211b, 222a, 224b, 229b, 248c, 268b, 270bd, 275b, 310a, 319c, 326b, 335a, 372b, 374c, 377c, 387b, 391a, 396a, 410b, 492bd. **J.C. Schou:** 440d. **David Sellars:** 7, 35b, 90, 117c, 121a, 271b, 315a. **Bruce Selyem:** 1, 69e, 73a, 78a, 122a, 145d, 159a, 160, 161a, 202b, 209c, 240c, 246c, 250a, 264b, 281c, 299b, 306, 313bd, 314a, 359c, 362b, 373d, 383b, 402e, 403f, 409b. **Stan Shebs:** 154c. **Virginia Skilton:** 10, 23, 39ad, 48c, 67a, 75b, 78d, 79a, 81d, 83b, 86f, 128b, 137b, 143a, 144e, 146a, 155a, 156ab, 158d, 161b, 168a, 185a, 186a, 187a, 188b, 197c, 205a, 229cd, 245b, 251bcd, 267ab, 270a, 275a, 279a, 281b, 283b, 284d, 301b, 305d, 309, 311b, 317ac, 331a, 332c, 342ad, 346ae, 360d, 361, 368b, 379d, 402a, 403dg, 409c, 412b. **Lori Skulski:** 43c, 216c, 227c, 256f, 390a, 395b. **Paul Slichter:** 22, 41b, 68b, 72ad, 75a, 76b, 81ac, 83a, 86b, 88b, 110a, 111a, 116a, 128a, 130ac, 132b, 133a, 142c, 143d, 153c, 162a, 166bc, 172ab, 177b, 186c, 201, 205c, 210ab, 212b, 215, 216a, 217a, 222c, 225c, 245a, 255b, 264a, 274d, 279d, 283c, 291ac, 294a, 296b, 304a, 319d, 325a, 333b, 337a, 341a, 344a, 350b, 354ab, 357ac, 358df, 359a, 366b, 367c, 372d, 382b, 385c, 386d, 387ac, 387c, 390c, 392a, 395cd, 397c, 398b, 406b, 412c, 413a, 419a, 420b, 423a, 425d, 434bde, 435b, 437b, 440b, 441bc, 444a, 445bc, 446d, 448b, 449a, 450b, 458ac, 467a, 479a, 490b, 496a. **Hedwig Storch:** 334a. **Jason Straka:** 17a, 21ab, 136b, 144d, 168d, 187d, 188c, 195c, 244b, 331b, 405b. **Dean William Taylor:** 127c, 461. **J. William Thompson:** 374b. **Donovan Tracy:** 71c, 72c, 123b, 135, 241a, 271c, 279c, 281a, 286a, 316b, 360a. **Visuals Unlimited / Masterfile:** 498a. **Steve Wirt:** 162bd. **Ken Wong:** 167d, 488b, 492c.

ILLUSTRATION CREDITS

All previously published drawings are reprinted with the permission of their respective publishers. The individual illustrators have been identified where possible. The numbers refer to the pages on which the illustrations appear; letters indicate the relative position of the drawing on the page.

Lynne Bartosch: From *Vascular Plants of the Continental Northwest Territories*, Canada, by A.E. Porsild and W.J. Cody. 1980. National Museums of Canada, Ottawa, ON: 132, 133a

Mary Bryant: From *The Ferns and Fern-allies of British Columbia*, by T.M.C. Taylor. 1973. Handbook No. 12, Royal British Columbia Museum, Victoria, BC: 484i

Oldriska Ceska: From *Illustrated Flora of British Columbia. Volume 5: Dicotyledons (Salicaceae through Zygophyllaceae) and Pteridophytes*, by G.W. Douglas, D. Meidinger and J. Pojar. 2000. BC Ministry of Environment, Lands and Parks and BC Ministry of Forests. Crown Publications, Victoria, BC: 484dfj

Valerie Fulford: From *Ferns and Fern Allies of Canada*, by W.J. Cody and D.M. Britton. 1989. Research Branch, Agriculture Canada, Ottawa, ON: 484eg, 491, 497

Evan Gillespie: From *Taxonomy of Flowering Plants* (2nd ed.), by C.L. Porter. 1967. W.H. Freeman, San Francisco, CA: 243, 289

Donald Gunn: From *Illustrated Flora of British Columbia. Volume 1: Gymnosperms and Dicotyledons (Aceraceae through Asteraceae)*, by G.W. Douglas, G.B. Straley, D. Meidinger and J. Pojar. 1998. BC Ministry of Environment, Lands and Parks and BC Ministry of Forests. Crown Publications, Victoria, BC: 290d

From *Illustrated Flora of British Columbia. Volume 3: Dicotyledons (Diapensiaceae through Onagraceae)*, by G.W. Douglas, D. Meidinger and J. Pojar. 1999. BC Ministry of Environment, Lands and Parks and BC Ministry of Forests. Crown Publications, Victoria, BC: 73

From *Illustrated Flora of British Columbia. Volume 5: Dicotyledons (Salicaceae through Zygophyllaceae) and Pteridophytes*, by G.W. Douglas, D. Meidinger and J. Pojar. 2000. BC Ministry of Environment, Lands and Parks and BC Ministry of Forests. Crown Publications, Victoria, BC: 153b

From *Illustrated Flora of British Columbia. Volume 6: Monocotyledons (Acoraceae through Najadaceae)*, by G.W. Douglas, D. Meidinger and J. Pojar. 2001. BC Ministry of Environment, Lands and Parks and BC Ministry of Forests. Crown Publications, Victoria, BC: 421d

Gail F. Harcombe: From *Illustrated Flora of British Columbia. Volume 1: Gymnosperms and Dicotyledons (Aceraceae through Asteraceae)*, by G.W. Douglas, G.B. Straley, D. Meidinger and J. Pojar. 1998. BC Ministry of Environment, Lands and Parks and BC Ministry of Forests. Crown Publications, Victoria, BC: 39a, 40b, 41b, 42b, 43, 44a, 45, 46b, 53

From *Illustrated Flora of British Columbia. Volume 2: Dicotyledons (Balsaminaceae through Cuscutaceae)*, by G.W. Douglas, G.B. Straley, D. Meidinger and J. Pojar. 1998. BC Ministry of Environment, Lands and Parks and BC Ministry of Forests. Crown Publications, Victoria, BC: 129b, 133b

From *Illustrated Flora of British Columbia. Volume 4: Dicotyledons (Orobanchaceae through Rubiaceae)*, by G.W. Douglas, D. Meidinger and J. Pojar. 1999. BC Ministry of Environment, Lands and Parks and BC Ministry of Forests. Crown Publications, Victoria, BC: 92d, 118d

From *Illustrated Flora of British Columbia. Volume 5: Dicotyledons (Salicaceae through Zygophyllaceae) and Pteridophytes*, by G.W. Douglas, D. Meidinger and J. Pojar. 2000. BC Ministry of Environment, Lands and Parks and BC Ministry of Forests. Crown Publications, Victoria, BC: 274b

Linny Heagy: From *Flora of North America North of Mexico. Volume 5: Magnoliophyta: Caryophyllidae, Part 2*, by Flora of North America Editorial Committee (eds.). 2005. Oxford University Press, New York and Oxford: 393d

Jeanne R. Janish: From *Vascular Plants of the Pacific Northwest, Part 1: Vascular Cryptogams, Gymnosperms, and Monocotyledons*, by C.L. Hitchcock, A. Cronquist and M. Ownbey. 1969. University of Washington Press, Seattle, WA: 47a, 92i, 404abcdeghij, 417abcdef, 418ab, 420, 421ab, 422, 423, 426d, 432a, 434, 444, 448, 455abcdegjklmnpqrstuvw, 462ab, 464ab, 465, 469ab, 473, 478a, 479, 480, 481, 484abchk, 487ab, 488, 489, 492

From *Vascular Plants of the Pacific Northwest, Part 2: Salicaceae to Saxifragaceae*, by C.L. Hitchcock and A. Cronquist. 1964. University of Washington Press, Seattle, WA: 54, 55, 59b, 61a, 63, 64b, 65b, 91ad, 110, 112, 114abcdef, 118abc, 121a, 122, 123, 124, 125, 128, 137, 188, 206, 207, 222b

From *Vascular Plants of the Pacific Northwest, Part 3: Saxifragaceae to Ericaceae*, by C.L. Hitchcock and A. Cronquist. 1961. University of Washington Press, Seattle, WA: 67, 91bcf, 92ac, 143ab, 145, 151, 153a, 154, 159, 166, 174ab, 175b, 177ab, 259, 290abcefghi, 296, 298

From *Vascular Plants of the Pacific Northwest, Part 4: Ericaceae through Campanulaceae*, by C.L. Hitchcock, A. Cronquist and M. Ownbey. 1959. University of Washington Press, Seattle, WA: 75, 76ab, 78b, 80, 82, 83, 88, 92efgi, 261, 265ac, 266abcdflqr, 276b, 299, 301, 318abcefg, 321, 323, 324, 327, 330ab, 337

Katherine Jones: From *Pacific Northwest Ferns and Their Allies*, by T.M.C. Taylor. 1970. University of Toronto Press, Toronto, ON: 490

Linda Kershaw: Original line drawings: 56, 339, 453c

Jane Lee Ling: From *Illustrated Flora of British Columbia. Volume 1: Gymnosperms and Dicotyledons (Aceraceae through Asteraceae)*, by G.W. Douglas, G.B. Straley, D. Meidinger and J. Pojar. 1998. BC Ministry of Environment, Lands and Parks and BC Ministry of Forests. Crown Publications, Victoria, BC: 393a

From *Illustrated Flora of British Columbia. Volume 2: Dicotyledons (Balsaminaceae through Cuscutaceae)*, by G.W. Douglas, G.B. Straley, D. Meidinger and J. Pojar. 1998. BC Ministry of Environment, Lands and Parks and BC Ministry of Forests. Crown Publications, Victoria, BC: 288

From *Illustrated Flora of British Columbia. Volume 3: Dicotyledons (Diapensiaceae through Onagraceae)*, by G.W. Douglas, D. Meidinger and J. Pojar. 1999. BC Ministry of Environment, Lands and Parks and BC Ministry of Forests. Crown Publications, Victoria, BC: 199

From *Illustrated Flora of British Columbia. Volume 4: Dicotyledons (Orobanchaceae through Rubiaceae)*, by G.W. Douglas, D. Meidinger and J. Pojar. 1999. BC Ministry of Environment, Lands and Parks and BC Ministry of Forests. Crown Publications, Victoria, BC: 189

From *Illustrated Flora of British Columbia. Volume 5: Dicotyledons (Salicaceae through Zygophyllaceae) and Pteridophytes*, by G.W. Douglas, D. Meidinger and J. Pojar. 2000. BC Ministry of Environment, Lands and Parks and BC Ministry of Forests. Crown Publications, Victoria, BC: 60b

From *Illustrated Flora of British Columbia. Volume 6: Monocotyledons (Acoraceae through Najadaceae)*, by G.W. Douglas, D. Meidinger and J. Pojar. 2001. BC Ministry of Environment, Lands and Parks and BC Ministry of Forests. Crown Publications, Victoria, BC: 404f, 424, 426a

From *Illustrated Flora of British Columbia. Volume 7: Monocotyledons (Orchidaceae through Zosteraceae)*, by G.W. Douglas, D. Meidinger and J. Pojar. 2001. BC Ministry of Environment, Lands and Parks and BC Ministry of Forests. Crown Publications, Victoria, BC: 455i, 455o, 460, 463, 471, 474, 477

Sherry Mitchell: From *Illustrated Flora of British Columbia. Volume 3: Dicotyledons (Diapensiaceae through Onagraceae)*, by G.W. Douglas, D. Meidinger and J. Pojar. 1999. BC Ministry of Environment, Lands and Parks and BC Ministry of Forests. Crown Publications, Victoria, BC: 78a, 89, 242a, 318d

From *Illustrated Flora of British Columbia. Volume 4: Dicotyledons (Orobanchaceae through Rubiaceae)*, by G.W. Douglas, D. Meidinger and J. Pojar. 1999. BC Ministry of Environment, Lands and Parks and BC Ministry of Forests. Crown Publications, Victoria, BC: 193

From *Illustrated Flora of British Columbia. Volume 5: Dicotyledons (Salicaceae through Zygophyllaceae) and Pteridophytes*, by G.W. Douglas, D. Meidinger and J. Pojar. 2000. BC Ministry of Environment, Lands and Parks and BC Ministry of Forests. Crown Publications, Victoria, BC: 59a, 61b, 64a, 146

From *Illustrated Flora of British Columbia. Volume 6: Monocotyledons (Acoraceae through Najadaceae)*, by G.W. Douglas, D. Meidinger and J. Pojar. 2001. BC Ministry of Environment, Lands and Parks and BC Ministry of Forests. Crown Publications, Victoria, BC: 421c

John Myers: From *Flora of North America North of Mexico. Volume 7: Magnoliophyta: Salicaceae to Brassicaceae*, by Flora of North America Editorial Committee (eds.). 2010. Oxford University Press, New York and Oxford: 65a

Lora May Richards: From *Illustrated Flora of British Columbia. Volume 4: Dicotyledons (Orobanchaceae through Rubiaceae)*, by G.W. Douglas, D. Meidinger and J. Pojar. 1999. BC Ministry of Environment, Lands and Parks and BC Ministry of Forests. Crown Publications, Victoria, BC: 121b, 161

John H. Rumely: From *Vascular Plants of the Pacific Northwest, Part 5: Compositae*, by A. Cronquist. 1955. University of Washington Press, Seattle, WA: 394be

Shirley D. Salkeld: Original line drawings: 453ab

Elizabeth J. Stephen: From *The Figwort Family (Scrophulariaceae) of British Columbia*, by T.M.C. Taylor. 1974. Handbook No. 33, Royal British Columbia Museum, Victoria, BC: 92b, 265bde, 266eghijkmnops, 273, 274a, 275ab, 276a, 282, 286

From *Illustrated Flora of British Columbia. Volume 1: Gymnosperms and Dicotyledons (Aceraceae through Asteraceae)*, by G.W. Douglas, G.B. Straley, D. Meidinger and J. Pojar. 1998. BC Ministry of Environment, Lands and Parks and BC Ministry of Forests. Crown Publications, Victoria, BC: 92h, 340, 362, 364, 371, 373ab, 381, 385, 393bce, 394acd

From *Illustrated Flora of British Columbia. Volume 2: Dicotyledons (Balsaminaceae through Cuscutaceae)*, by G.W. Douglas, G.B. Straley, D. Meidinger and J. Pojar. 1998. BC Ministry of Environment, Lands and Parks and BC Ministry of Forests. Crown Publications, Victoria, BC: 91e, 204ab, 209, 210, 212, 222ac, 226

From *Illustrated Flora of British Columbia. Volume 7: Monocotyledons (Orchidaceae through Zosteraceae)*, by G.W. Douglas, D. Meidinger and J. Pojar. 2001. BC Ministry of Environment, Lands and Parks and BC Ministry of Forests. Crown Publications, Victoria, BC: 455f, 478b

Dagny Tande-Lid: From *Flora of Alaska and Neighbouring Territories*, E. Hultén. 1968. Stanford University Press, Stanford, CA: 242b, 455h

Karen Uldall-Ekman: From *Illustrated Flora of British Columbia. Volume 6: Monocotyledons (Acoraceae through Najadaceae)*, by G.W. Douglas, D. Meidinger and J. Pojar. 2001. BC Ministry of Environment, Lands and Parks and BC Ministry of Forests. Crown Publications, Victoria, BC: 432d

Stanley L. Welsh: From *Revision of North American Species of Oxytropis de Candolle (Leguminosae)*, by S.L. Welsh. 2001. E.P.S. Inc., Orem, UT: 253abc, 255, 257ab

Yevonn Wilson-Ramsey: From *Flora of North America North of Mexico. Volume 3: Magnoliophyta: Magnoliidae and Hamamelidae*, by Flora of North America Editorial Committee (eds.). 1997. Oxford University Press, New York and Oxford: 160

R.A. With: From *The Rose Family (Rosaceae) of British Columbia*, by T.M.C. Taylor. 1973. Handbook No. 30, Royal British Columbia Museum, Victoria, BC: 68ab, 70, 164, 165, 168, 172, 173, 175a

From *The Pea Family (Leguminosae) of British Columbia*, by T.M.C. Taylor. 1974. Handbook No. 32, Royal British Columbia Museum, Victoria, BC: 250

From *The Sedge Family (Cyperaceae) of British Columbia*, by T.M.C. Taylor. 1983. Handbook No. 43, Royal British Columbia Museum, Victoria, BC: 426bce, 431, 432bc, 439, 440, 441ab, 442, 452ab

Miscellaneous: Original line drawings. Courtesy of the BC Ministry of Forests, Research Branch: 39b, 40a, 41a, 42a, 44b, 46a, 47b

From *Flora of the Queen Charlotte Islands: Part 1*, by J.A. Calder and R.L. Taylor. 1968. Monograph No. 4. Research Branch, Department of Agriculture, Ottawa, ON: 195

INDEX

AUTHORS & CONTRIBUTORS

Andy MacKinnon   Jim Pojar   Rosamund Pojar

Curtis Björk

Hans Roemer